W9-CHD-534

A COMPLETE GUIDE TO PREPARING A CORPORATE ANNUAL REPORT

A COMPLETE GUIDE TO PREPARING A CORPORATE ANNUAL REPORT

Elmer L. Winter

VNR VAN NOSTRAND REINHOLD COMPANY
New York

Library of Congress Catalog Card Number: 84-23433
ISBN: 0-442-29233-3

Manufactured in the United States of America

Published by Van Nostrand Reinhold Company Inc.
135 West 50th Street
New York, New York 10020

Van Nostrand Reinhold Company Limited
Molly Millars Lane
Wokingham, Berkshire RG11 2PY, England

Van Nostrand Reinhold
480 Latrobe Street
Melbourne, Victoria 3000, Australia

Macmillan of Canada
Division of Gage Publishing Limited
164 Commander Boulevard
Agincourt, Ontario M1S 3C7, Canada

15 14 13 12 11 10 9 8 7 6 5 4 3 2 1

Library of Congress Cataloging in Publication Data
Winter, Elmer L.
A complete guide to preparing a corporate annual report.

Includes index.
1. Corporation reports. 2. Financial statements.
3. Business report writing. I. Title.
HF5681.B2W54 1985 648.1'512 84-23433
ISBN 0-442-29233-3

CONTENTS

A COMPLETE GUIDE TO PREPARING A CORPORATE ANNUAL REPORT

I
INTRODUCTION

We are in the age of advanced communications. The electronic media have changed many of our habits of the past. Reading has oftentimes given way to viewing. Others select what we want to hear and see according to their timetable. We are given information in short doses—"spoon fed," so as to speak, punctuated by light—action—camera.

How does the corporate annual report fit into the information explosion? What are the chances that the reader, sophisticated as he or she may be, will spend the time reading through your annual report? The answer in many cases may well be "zero." These are the corporate reports that do not have the ability to stop the reader—to pull the reader into the report and to become absorbed in its content.

The name of the game in the preparation of an annual report is: *"Get the reader involved."* That's the only way your report can be considered to be cost effective. You want the reader involved to the point where he or she, if a stockholder, will look favorably upon your company, and will continue to hold your stock, and hopefully buy more. If the reader is a security analyst, the involvement in your report should lead to a "buy or hold" recommendation. You want your report to say to the employee who leafs through it, "I'm glad to be on the team—I like the recognition given to me—I'd like to help my company grow and succeed."

Wanting and getting this type of involvement are two different things. Grinding out a standard report won't do the job for your company. You need to be innovative—find new ways to present your corporate story. Oftentimes this can be done with exciting color, but there's a limit to that. The manner in which your CEO talks about your company—the way you answer the questions relating to the future—a change of pace into a magazine style—the informality of the report—and yes, the clarity of the report, all lead to getting readership and involvement.

That's the challenge that faces you as you pull out your yellow legal pad and start to pour out your creative ideas for next year's annual report. Remember always—you are fighting for your readers' time. Be sure you tell your corporate story in a dynamic way, beamed more to the future than the past.

FACING THE NEW REALITIES

Tax changes at the federal level were designed to alter business and investment practices so that there would be a massive infusion of capital into the private business sector. The changes were:

1. A reduction in the personal income tax rates.
2. A reduction of long-term capital gains tax to a maximum of 20 percent.
3. The elimination of the estate tax for many individuals, and the steep reduction in its rate over a period of years.
4. The more liberal and expanded use of individual retirement accounts (IRAs).
5. The liberalization of incentive stock options for corporate employees.
6. The reduction of the income tax rate on dividends received.
7. The provisions for accelerated cost recovery.
8. The allowance of a 25 percent investment tax credit on research expenditures made in the United States.

Each of these changes will encourage savings which will be directed towards investment in common stock and preferred stocks, bonds, and debentures of corporations.

Many individuals will turn to corporations to invest their new found funds. The competition for these dollars amongst publicly held corporations will be severe and ongoing. As a result, the way in which a corporation presents itself to stockholders, both existing and potential, will become increasingly important.

It is the purpose of this book to do the following:

1. To analyze what it is that stockholders, security analysts, employees, etc., are interested in finding in your corporate annual report.
2. To suggest ways in which there can be a better presentation of this type of information.

I have reviewed several thousand corporate annual reports in an effort to find the answers to the question "*What makes an effective annual report?*" I have tried to separate the puffery, the clichés, and the overoptimistic statements from the hard facts that need to be presented in an annual report. I have found that there are many companies that face up to reality and present the bad news as well as the good news in a fair and objective way. I have found that many companies are telling it like it is, but more important, are telling it like they think it will be. I have presented a number of ways in which companies are presenting their views of the future . . . how they are projecting their sales and profits and goals in clear and concise terms. This is what stockholders want to hear from corporate management.

Why have I written this book? I served as president of a New York Stock Exchange listed company, Manpower, Inc., for over 30 years. For 11 years of that time, Manpower was publicly held, and its stock sold first in the over-the-counter market, and then later was sold on the New York Stock Exchange. I spent a considerable amount of my time working with our executives on the preparation of our corporate annual report. I tried each year to challenge our group to come up with a report that clearly answered the questions of our stockholders and security analysts, employees, franchisees, etc. The design and artwork that we used were important in presenting our company. However, of greatest importance was the effect that our report would have on those who picked up a copy and tried to understand our company: its past, its present, and its future.

American corporations can do a great deal to maintain the confidence of our citizens in the free enterprise system. Annual reports play an important role in maintaining and building this confidence which is so very important to the well-being and prosperity of America. This book is intended to help those who are engaged in the preparation of corporate annual reports to maximize their efforts and to give their readers the true facts as well as a portrayal of what lies ahead for the corporation. Good luck.

UNDERSTANDING THE IMPORTANCE OF YOUR CORPORATE ANNUAL REPORT

Let's agree: "*Your corporate annual report is the most important tool in your company's financial public relations program.*" It is the showcase of your company. It tells your various publics a great deal about your company, its management, its products, its operations, its future, etc. An investment decision—to buy or sell your company's stock—is often based upon a review of the annual report.

Your annual report must deliver a message to many different audiences. It is more than just a financial report to your stockholders. It affords you the opportunity to portray the breadth and scope of your corporation to its many publics. Your annual report is your "once a year" vehicle to talk it over with your stockholders who have made an investment in your company—an investment that can turn into a sell order if your report turns a stockholder off.

It is important that you answer the question "What is the major purpose in getting out an annual report?" I would suggest the following answers:

1. To influence your present stockholders to continue to maintain their investment in your company. The annual report has to speak to them in a language that is readily understandable and persuasive. The stockholder, after spending the necessary amount of time with your annual report, must say, "This is a company where I have confidence, where I want to put my money and watch it grow." This requires a type of communication that is persuasive, credible, and honest.

   Your stockholders must sense that your company is on the move; that it has strong management currently and will have it in the future; and that the value of the stock will increase.

Your annual report is your best device to "talk it over with your stockholders," and persuade them that their future and yours are closely tied together. Think in terms of sitting across the table in a restaurant, having a cup of coffee with your stockholder—and explaining why the relationship between your company and the stockholder is to the stockholder's benefit—not only now, but why it will be in the future.

2. Your annual report must persuade others to become stockholders in your company. Your report will be circulated in the investment community. Hopefully, it will be read by many security analysts who will include yours as a company that they will feel confident to recommend to their clients. Your annual report is the vehicle to add to your existing number of shareholders and to replace those who sell their stock.

   To recommend or not recommend your company, will depend upon how effectively your message comes across in your annual report to the security analysts.

Your corporate annual report has other publics as well that are described on the following pages.

It's important to keep in mind that the annual report that you will be preparing has to carry a major load in your communications efforts with present and future stockholders. If you fall short of pressing the appropriate hot buttons, your annual report will be just another document that is dropped rather quickly into the wastebasket.

In this book, we will try, together, to maximize your presentation so that when the final annual report is dropped in the mail to your stockholders, you can sit back and say, "We've produced an annual report that will do the job intended for it."

NOTE: Examples from actual reports have been used extensively throughout this book. Consequently you will find different type styles. An effort has been made to reprint full pages for certain of the reports and as a result there are some pages which have less than a full page of copy to lead you into the subject.

FACE UP TO THE FACTS OF LIFE

Stanley Lanzet, first vice-president research of Drexel Burnham Lambert, points out that there are 15,000 publicly held companies in the United States that distribute a combined total of 50 million annual reports to their shareholders. He has stated:

> "Unfortunately, much of the approximately $120 million cost of production and mailing plus the efforts and energies of top level corporate executives is for naught, since all too often the annual report goes unread, or is just merely glanced at. However, the market value of a security is often greatly influenced by the information contained in the annual report. Important data is sometimes spelled out up front in the chief executive's letter, or it can be hidden in an obscure footnote."

II
MEETING THE LEGAL AND ACCOUNTING REQUIREMENTS IN THE PREPARATION OF YOUR CORPORATE ANNUAL REPORT

It is not my intention to take you into the legal and accounting requirements which are an integral part of the preparation of a corporate annual report. There are many good legal/accounting books that go into these requirements in depth. However, from time to time, it is important to discuss the basics (legal and accounting) to put the text into proper perspective.

Your annual report should contain certain basic financial information relating to the following:

Financial Highlights
Sales and Earnings by Product Lines
Financial Statistics for 10 years
R & D Expenditures
Foreign Sales and Earnings
Quarterly Sales and Earnings

This information will be supplied to you by your CPA after the annual audit is completed.

You are required to make the following disclosures:

1. Certified financial statements for the issuer's last two fiscal years.
2. A summary and management's analysis of the issuer's operations for the last five fiscal years.
3. Description of the nature and scope of the issuer's business and that of its subsidiaries.
4. Information on lines of business.
5. Information about the management of the company, including identification of the issuer's executive officers and directors.
6. Market and dividend information.

Discuss with your professionals the timetable they will require to get their information to you on time. Have this understanding very early in the process to avoid errors, overtime, and ulcers. Try to reach an understanding as to how they will present their information. You will want to have it in an understandable format—yes, in a format that can be read easily.

THE REPORTING REQUIREMENTS OF THE SEC

As a publicly held company, you will of course be required to comply with the requirements of the SEC in the preparation and publication of your annual report—I will not go into the details of the SEC reporting requirements. Your attorney will advise you as to the manner in which you are required to comply.

Basically, you must keep in mind the following SEC requirements in the preparation of your annual report:

1. A description of the business of the corporation together with information about the company's lines of business for the last five fiscal years.
2. A "Summary of Operations" similar to that required in the SEC Form 10-K, and a management analysis.
3. Certified financial statements for the company's last two fiscal years.
4. Identification of the directors and executive officers of the company, and the disclosure of each such person's principal occupation or

employment and identification of the names and principal businesses of any organizations by which such persons are so employed.

5. The identity of principal market(s) where shares are traded.
6. High and low sales prices or range of bid and ask quotations for securities for each quarterly period within the most recent two years.
7. Dividends paid on securities for those two years.

You are dealing with some very specific legal requirements. You need to rely on competent advisors to ensure that your final draft of the annual report complies in every respect with the SEC requirements. Be sure you allow sufficient time for your advisors to review the final draft of the report before you turn it over to the printer.

SHOULD YOU INCLUDE A FORM 10-K IN YOUR ANNUAL REPORT?

Many companies have included the form 10-K—which is prepared for the Securities and Exchange Commission—as part of their annual report. There are certain advantages in doing this. While much of the material in the 10-K duplicates that in the annual report, there is a section in the 10-K that will be of particular interest to the readers of your annual report: that is the section that refers to the directors and executive officers of your corporation.

The 10-K provides a considerable amount of detail relating to the executive officers and their tenure, age, background, etc. In addition, the 10-K describes the current remuneration of the officers and directors, including their proposed remuneration, transactions with management, security ownership by the officers and directors, etc. The 10-K provides greater in-depth information concerning your management and directors than is customarily provided in the annual report.

The disadvantage of including the 10-K in the annual report is that the 10-K duplicates many of the financial statements and footnotes that you will include in the annual report. If you are having a problem in getting strong readership from your stockholders, you might find that by including the 10-K, the annual report becomes a rather foreboding document which your stockholders may be tempted to put aside and read another day or just toss into the circular file.

COMPLIANCE WITH THE REPORTING REQUIREMENTS OF VARIOUS STOCK EXCHANGES

If the stock of your company is listed on one or more stock exchanges, you will, of course, be required to comply with their regulations (your attorney will advise you). Keep in mind that if your company is listed on the New York Stock Exchange, you will be required to:

1. Publish at least once a year and submit to stockholders at least 15 days prior to annual stockholders' meeting and not later than three months after the close of the preceding fiscal year:
   a. A consolidated balance sheet.
   b. A consolidated retained earnings statement.
   c. A consolidated income statement.
   d. Appropriate footnotes.
2. Have published annual financial statements audited by independent public accountants.

The New York Stock Exchange paper entitled "Recommendations and Comments on Financial Reporting to Shareholders and Related Matters," has suggested that companies expand their annual report disclosure in the following areas:

1. Quarterly sales and earnings data for each of the quarters compared with prior year's data.
2. Form 10-K (annual report to SEC) data that is material to the financial status of the company.
3. Annual debt maturities for the succeeding five years, if debt structure is complicated.
4. Line-of-business data similar to that disclosed in the SEC 10-K report.
5. Computation of federal income tax, if reported tax percentage to income is materially different from the statutory rate.
6. Clarification of the computation of earnings per share.
7. Nature and volume of transactions between the company and affiliated and related parties (in financial statement footnotes).
8. Material deferred charges and provisions for unusual items.
9. Common stock price ranges, price/earnings ratio ranges, dividends, and rate of payout and return, along with book value.

10. Current year versus prior year detailed analysis of increase or decrease in earnings, in tabular form, supplemented by descriptive text.
11. An offer to make the 10-K available to stockholders.

COMPLIANCE WITH THE ACCOUNTING PRINCIPLES OF THE FINANCIAL ACCOUNTING STANDARDS BOARD (FASB)

It is important that you review with your CPA, the accounting principles of the FASB to determine the impact on your corporate annual report.

By way of history, the Financial Accounting Standards Board was established in 1973. This is a nongovernmental board and is financed by contributions from businesses as well as from accounting firms. The FASB has adopted certain accounting principles which serve as authoritative statements of accepted accounting principles and practices.

The SEC considers pronouncements of the FASB to constitute substantial authoritative support for accounting and reporting procedures and practices used in the preparation of financial statements that are filed with the SEC.

Meet with your accountant and lawyer in advance of the preparation of your corporate annual report. Decide on what they will provide to you; the limits placed on your narrative; and the review they will make before the final copy goes on the printing press.

Submit the final draft of the annual report to your CPA before sending the report to the printer. Have the CPA initial each page of the draft as assurance that the necessary review has been made.

III
THE INGREDIENTS OF A UNIQUE, INFORMATIVE, EXCITING, WELL-DESIGNED ANNUAL REPORT

As you start out on the road to develop your corporate annual report, in all likelihood, you will be saying to yourself, "This year I'm going to turn out a super report—a report that the reader will be pulled into quickly and will not want to put down until he or she has read the complete report." That ought to be your goal. It is one that can be accomplished if you set your mind to it.

Let me share with you what I consider to be the ingredients of a super corporate annual report. This is based upon my having reviewed thousands of annual reports of companies—large, middle-sized, and small—over the years. You don't have to be a corporate giant to have a super report. It is how you tell the story of your company—the style—the photography, that counts. Let me give you the following guidelines that I consider to be important in the preparation of that super corporate annual report.

1. *The look and feel of the report itself.* When I pick up an Annual Report, I look at it from a presentation standpoint. Is it presented on good paper stock? Does it feel good to hold in my hand? Is the photography relevant? Does it tell the story of the company in an exciting manner? The report simply must feel good and look good from an initial approach.
2. *The cover.* I like to see a cover that fits the theme of the report. All of the sections of the report should tie into the theme. The theme should be exciting. It should show how the company will grow and be out there ahead of the pack.
3. *The inside of the cover.* As a stockholder, I would like you to provide information about my stockholder relationship with you. I don't want to have to search around in the back of the report for information about stock prices, dividends, transfer agents, etc.
4. *The first page.* I want you to give me comparative information about the sales of the company; its income; backlog; etc. Give me percentages of increase or decrease. Put some charts alongside the financial highlights. Make the charts easy for me to read. Don't let the designers get carried away with charts that are beautifully prepared but impossible to read.
5. *The president's letter.* I want to read a letter from the president of the company that gives me assurance that, as with Allstate Insurance Company, "I am in good hands." Provide a good informal photograph of the chief executive officer who, in effect, is saying, "I'm glad you're a stockholder. Let me tell you how I am running your company to your advantage." After reading the president's letter let me end up by saying to myself, "I'd like to meet the president of the company. I'd like to tell the president, 'I like your style. I like your goals. I like what you have accomplished. I have confidence in your company. I intend to continue as a stockholder.' "
6. *Questions and answers.* I like the question and answer concept. I would like for the president to anticipate my questions about the company and answer them head-on. *U.S. News and World Report* effectively uses questions and answers in their reporting of interviews with certain experts. This same technique makes

for more informed readership and forces the president to "tell it like it is."

7. *Divisional reports.* I like to, in effect, meet the executives of your company through the divisional reports. I want to see photographs of them at work. I'd like to hear from them about the results of the past year compared to prior years. I want to know how they see the future and the role that they will play in increasing the sales and profits of their division. I'd like to see the products at work—particularly in customers' offices or factories. I would like to hear the customers' comments on how the products save them time, trouble, money, etc.
8. *Future Product Lines.* With the rapid changes that are taking place in technology, no company can stand still. I'd like to know a lot about how your company is developing new products, what they are, and what share of the market they will capture. Tell me all about your R & D. I'd like to be sure that you are spending enough money to meet your R & D requirements.
9. *Projections.* I like to see projections, not in generalities, but in specific terms. I realize that this is risky business, but many companies are now willing to lay it on the line and project what they see for the future. If they have made projections in the past, I'd like to see a report of how well they performed against the projections.
10. *Financial information.* I realize that financial information and footnotes are provided by accountants and that there are certain rules of the game that they must follow. I'd like them to simplify the terminology, using the pattern of the insurance companies, which are providing easily understood language for their policyholders.
11. *Management.* Frankly, I'd like the discussion of the management of the company to be up front, but that does not seem to be the accepted place for a discussion of management succession, photographs of managers, etc. I would like the annual report to leave me with a very strong impression that there is good management at the top—that the company is not a one-man show—that there is plenty of quality management to run the company for a good number of years ahead. I'd like to get as much information as I possibly can about top management from the annual report.
12. *Directors.* I not only want the names of the directors and the committees that they serve on, but I would like to know their background in relationship to other companies with which they have been or are presently associated. I want to end up with an impression that the directors have a breadth of experience working for other companies that qualifies them to serve as your directors.

Can your annual report be considered an advertising piece for your company? All too often, corporate annual reports end up being primarily advertising pieces plus some financial reports and footnotes. There is too little attention paid to providing substance in terms of what the company does, its management, its future, etc. Sometimes one gets the impression that the photography that is taken from advertising brochures is meant to cover up the failures or lack of performance on the part of the company.

Certainly, there is room for good product photography in the annual report—especially where the company manufactures consumer products. The Chrysler Corporation, for example, will have photographs of their new cars in their annual report. But more important, there are strong messages, predictions, etc., that come on strong and clear through the chairman and his top management.

It's important that you have a good mix of advertising material and an explanation of where the company has been, where it's going, how it's getting there, etc. I would urge you to go light on advertising and more heavily on the written communication from the president and other members of the management group. This will prevent the reader from concluding, "This report is nothing more than an advertising piece, covering up some of the problems of the company."

WHAT TURNS ME OFF WHEN I READ AN ANNUAL REPORT

Having read many annual reports over the years, I have developed certain, "They turn me off," objections. It might be well for you to know my list. I'm sure that if you talk to security analysts, you will find an additional number from their experience that you ought to consider when you prepare your coporate annual report. Here's my list:

1. I don't like to read that everything is going well for the company when the facts and figures don't bear out the general statements.

2. I don't want to read an outlook statement from the president that stresses that the future looks rosy without the report telling me how the president intends to turn around a bad profit situation within the company.
3. I don't like to have the president choke and cover up when there is a bad result that has to be reported. Stockholders and security analysts can draw their own conclusions as to whether all goes well, or the company has a problem. It is not a crime to run into a difficult period. The president ought to own up to the problem and spell out what steps they have taken to get back on the profit direction once again.
4. I don't like to see the president monopolize the report to the point where one gets the impression that it's a one-person show. I like to read about other management people. I like to hear from them, and, in effect, meet them through the annual report.
5. I don't like small type. I refuse to read type that is less than 8 point. When I see type under this size, I sometimes get the impression that the company doesn't want me to read the information that they report in small type.
6. I get turned off by design work in charts, particularly where I am expected to analyze a bar with three different colors for three different segments of the business. I don't want to have to translate, which the designer has asked me, in effect, to do.
7. I don't like overprint on photographs where the designer may think it is a good design, but I can't read the type because it is fighting the background. Oftentimes, the company approves the annual report without realizing that the artwork, which contains an overlay of printing, makes it almost impossible for the reader to get through the script. My preference is black ink on white paper.
8. I object to the use of a great amount of silver paper. It seems to be finding its way into corporate annual reports. Silver paper as a divider of sections is okay; but oftentimes, it is impossible to read black, white, or blue printing that is printed on silver paper stock.
9. I object to footnotes that can only be interpreted and understood by accountants. The purpose of a footnote is to give the reader further information beyond the figures in the statements. Oftentimes, footnotes are set out in legalese or accounting terms to the point where a stockholder simply cannot dig out the meaning intended to be provided.
10. Certain types of photography turn me off. I don't like to see artificially posed photographs of executives. I'd rather see them in their natural habitat. If they operate with a desk that has a lot of papers on it, let the photograph show the papers rather than a shiny desk top that looks unused. I can spot professional models in the photographs. I'd rather have employees shown at work to describe the products. I'd like to see real-life customers using the products in their places of business.

WHAT MAKES ONE ANNUAL REPORT STAND OUT ABOVE THE OTHERS?

There are a number of elements that go into creating an annual report that will make your corporate report get a rating of "super."

The *Financial World* magazine annually reviews a large number of corporate annual reports and issues awards. *Financial World* appoints an independent Board of Judges and a Screening Committee of Security Analysts. Awards are based upon:

Broad Essentials:

- President's letter
- Highlights (2 years); % change a plus factor
- Narrative section
- Per share earnings, dividends
- Balance sheet and income statement with prior year's data
- Source and application of funds
- Adequate and easy-to-read notes to the financial statement
- Auditor's statement
- Statistical summary, minimum of five years

Desirable information:

- Construction and financing data
- Late information
- Territory development
- Outlook
- Stockholder data
- Sales and earnings breakdown by products and/or divisions, quarterly sales, earnings
- Research and development
- Foreign business
- Labor relations
- Advertising/marketing data
- Management

Additional and useful information:

- New Products
- Advertising policies
- Affiliations of directors
- Length of service; officers and directors
- Basic data such as address of executive office, transfer agent, registrant, etc.
- Special feature on industry or related subject
- Table of contents
- Map of territory
- Public relations activities
- Profile of company
- Social/economic problems

Appearance and understandability:

- Design and typography
  - Cover
  - Inside pages
- Useful charts
- Appropriate photos and/or illustrations
- Material organized logically
- Useful subject area headings
- Text clear, interesting, easy to read

MASCO CORPORATION—AN ANNUAL REPORT THAT TELLS IT ALL

It is difficult to single out any report that "tells it all." I find that each year Masco Corporation comes closest to meeting this standard. Take a look at Masco's 1983 Annual Report. (Their address is 21001 Van Buren Road, Taylor, Michigan 48180.) You will find some key ingredients for an annual report that tells it like it is and what management expects it to be.

Examples from Masco Report 1983

MASCO...A UNIQUE GROWTH COMPANY

Masco Corporation, a diversified manufacturing company with leadership market positions, has reported 27 consecutive years of earnings growth.

Masco manufactures faucets, plumbing fittings, builders' hardware, steel measuring tapes, venting and ventilating equipment, insulation products, water pumps, and other building and home improvement products, scanning monitors, recreational accessories, metal office products, and other products for the home and family; and oil-field equipment, specialty valves and closures, and a broad range of other products for industry.

CONTENTS

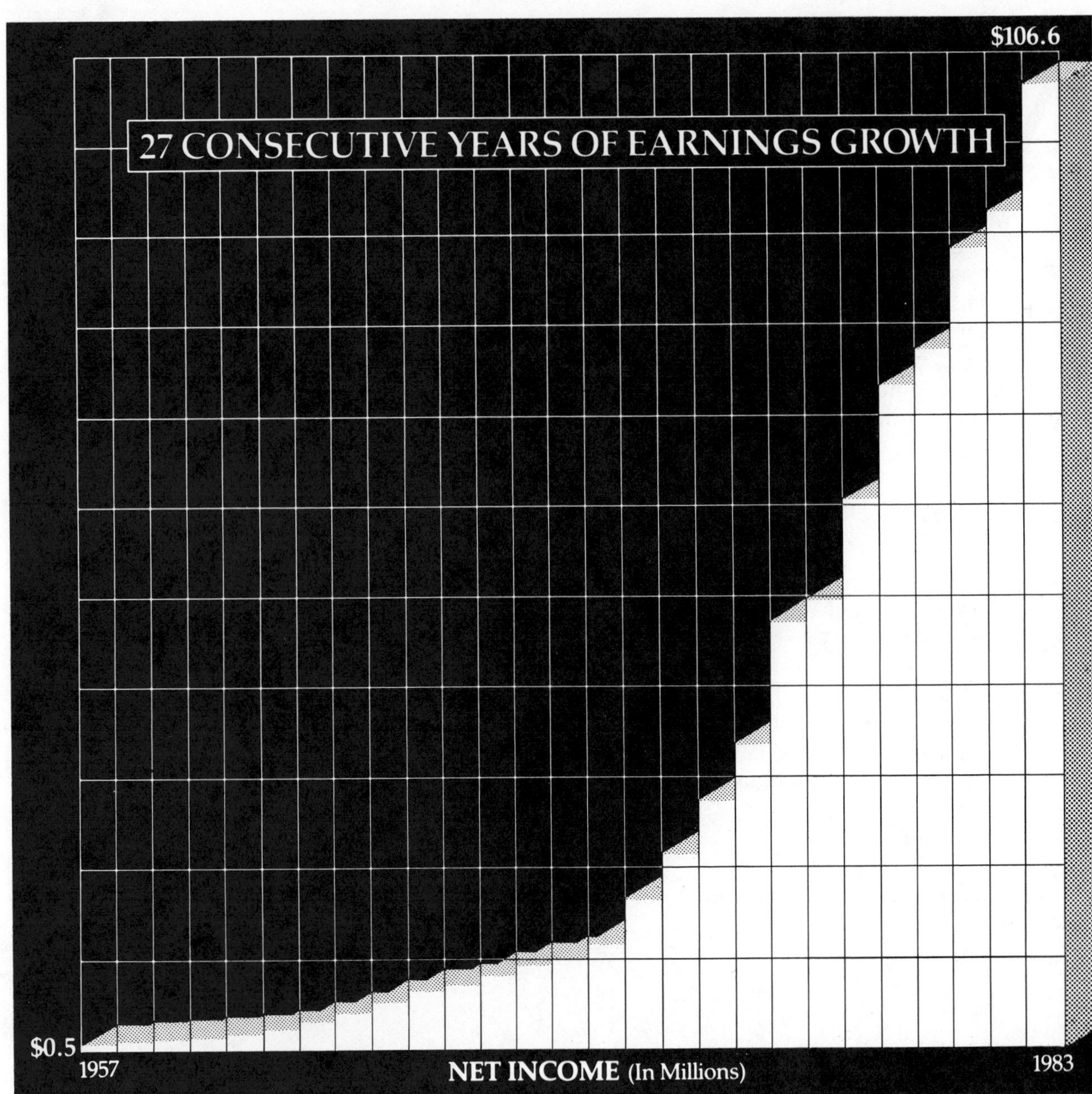

FINANCIAL HIGHLIGHTS

	1983 vs. 1982	1983	1982	27-Year Growth Rate	1956
Net Sales	+24%	$1,059,450,000	$855,740,000	19%	$9,960,000
Net Income	+16%	$ 106,560,000	$ 92,150,000	22%	$ 450,000
Net Income as a % of:					
Net Sales		10.1%	10.8%		4.5%
Shareholders' Equity		18.1%	18.7%		9.0%
Shareholders' Equity	+24%	$ 728,800,000	$589,390,000	20%	$5,420,000
Per Share Data:					
Net Income	+ 8%	$1.93	$1.78	21%	$ .01¼
Dividends Paid	+10%	$ .44	$ .40	21%	$ .00¼

To our shareholders

March 26, 1984

Richard A. Manoogian, *President*

Alex Manoogian, *Chairman of the Board*

A CORPORATE MILESTONE

Masco sales in 1983 reached a new plateau by exceeding $1 billion, increasing 24 percent over the previous year. To many in the business of management, this level of sales represents a significant achievement. We are even more proud of the fact that we have reported 27 consecutive years of increased earnings; this accomplishment is shared by only a few companies in all of American industry.

Net income in 1983 was $106.6 million or $1.93 per share, representing increases from the previous year of 16 percent and 8 percent, respectively. Excluding extraordinary income in 1982 from the retirement of debentures, net income in 1983 increased 37 percent.

OPERATING HIGHLIGHTS

Sales of our Products for the Home and Family increased by 49 percent. Sales of building and home improvement products, aided by acquisitions, were particularly strong as increased housing starts, new products, increased market penetration and the expanding Do-It-Yourself market all contributed to the record sales and earnings performance.

Sales of our Products for Industry approximated the previous year as an increase of over 20 percent in specialty industrial products sales were offset by the decline in sales of oil-field and related products.

FINANCIAL RETURNS

After-tax profit margin on sales was 10.1 percent, the 23rd consecutive year that our profit margin on sales was in excess of 10 percent. After-tax profit return on shareholders' equity was 18.1 percent.

CAPITAL INVESTMENT AND EXPANSION

Capital expenditures were $47 million, compared with $59 million in 1982.

Expenditures declined in each of the last two years reflecting, in great measure, the completion of several significant investment programs.

DIVIDENDS

Our quarterly dividend, which is currently $.11 per share, was again increased in 1983 representing the 25th consecutive year of dividend increases.

CORPORATE DEVELOPMENT

Although we continue to have a very active program of seeking business partners who meet our acquisition criteria, no major acquisitions were made during 1983. We did benefit, however, from the over $165 million we invested in acquiring several companies in 1982. Their full-year contribution to Masco in 1983 was a positive factor in our year's performance.

RESTRUCTURING PLAN

Our experience in recent years has reinforced our belief that applying our business strategies to products whose markets or market share opportunities exhibit above-average growth potential, yields greater and more predictable growth than the same effort and investment in relatively static or declining markets, particularly those that may also be subject to a high degree of cyclicality.

As a consequence, we are evaluating a plan that would transfer all of our Products for Industry operations to a new company, half of whose shares would be distributed to Masco shareholders in the form of a dividend. This new company could then set its own criteria for future growth in industrial markets while Masco would concentrate on products for the home and family. By retaining a major shareholding in this new company, Masco would also benefit from the future growth of the new company.

FINANCIAL STRENGTH

Record year-end cash of $209 million should enable us to finance our projected growth and capital requirements during 1984. Our high degree of liquidity is reflected in the fact that our year-end cash exceeded our total current liabilities.

To maintain our strong financial position, Masco sold two million shares of common stock during 1983 for approximately $64 million.

CURRENT OUTLOOK

Our major markets continued to improve as 1983 progressed and we have entered 1984 on a strong note. With inflation at a lower rate, unemployment declining and consumer confidence increasing, 1984 should present Masco with a positive economic environment within which to grow.

Virtually all of our major markets should be stronger in 1984 than last year. This economic background, combined with new products and anticipated increased market penetration, we believe will enable Masco to achieve significant growth in 1984.

FIVE-YEAR FORECAST

Masco's ability during recent years to maintain its growth record while the economy was experiencing the worst post-war recession, is a tribute to our very special employees whose talent, enthusiasm and dedication guided us through that difficult period. Now our challenge will be to demonstrate what we can accomplish during the more positive economy that we foresee for the next several years.

We remain convinced that we have the human and other resources, effective business strategies and the commitment necessary to achieve well-above-average growth during the balance of the 1980's.

More specifically, as summarized in the following table and explained in greater detail elsewhere in this annual report, we expect Masco's sales from internal growth alone will double over the next five years.

Alex Manoogian, *Chairman of the Board*

Richard A. Manoogian, *President*

SALES GROWTH—FIVE-YEAR FORECAST

(In Thousands)

	Sales Forecast		Actual Sales		
	Growth Rate 84-88	1988	Growth Rate 79-83	1983	1978
PRODUCTS FOR THE HOME AND FAMILY					
Building and Home Improvement Products:					
Faucets	15%	$ 490,000	9%	$ 243,000	$155,000
Other Building Products	14%	510,000	30%	261,000	71,000
	15%	1,000,000	17%	504,000	226,000
Other Products for the Home and Family:					
Personal Communications	1%	60,000	4%	56,000	46,000
Recreational Accessories	12%	50,000	1%	28,000	26,000
Other Specialty Products	18%	115,000	38%	50,000	10,000
	11%	225,000	10%	134,000	82,000
Total Products for the Home and Family	14%	$1,225,000	16%	$ 638,000	$308,000
PRODUCTS FOR INDUSTRY					
Oil-Field and Related Products	23%	$ 290,000	21%	$ 104,000	$ 40,000
Specialty Industrial Products:					
Cold Extrusions	14%	170,000	5%	88,000	70,000
Specialty Valves and Closures	12%	150,000	21%	85,000	33,000
Other Industrial Products	13%	265,000	1%	144,000	135,000
	13%	585,000	6%	317,000	238,000
Total Products for Industry	16%	$ 875,000	9%	$ 421,000	$278,000
Total Masco Sales	15%	$2,100,000	13%	$1,059,000	$586,000

MASCO...A UNIQUE GROWTH COMPANY

	27-Year Growth Rate	1983	1956
			(In Thousands)
Net Sales	19%	$1,059,450	$9,960
Net Income	22%	$ 106,560	$ 450
Net Income as a % of:			
Net Sales		10.1%	4.5%
Shareholders' Equity		18.1%	9.0%

Over the last quarter century, Masco has grown from a relatively small company to an organization whose sales exceeded $1 billion in 1983. Even more gratifying have been the consistency and rate of growth of our earnings: 27 consecutive years of increased earnings with earnings growing at an average annual rate in excess of 20 percent.

Although it is important for a company to continually be alert to changing economic conditions which may require modification of its basic business strategies, at Masco we believe the following objectives and strategies pursued to achieve these objectives, which have proven successful for us in the past, will enable us to maintain our record of growth in the future.

MASCO . . . DEDICATION

A key to our basic goal of building a unique growth company has been the leadership, purpose and resolve of our people and their ability to successfully achieve our goals for growth while adhering to our business strategies. Masco employees, while diverse in skills, are alike in their commitment to excellence and their desire to achieve our goals. In our opinion, this dedication has been instrumental in accomplishing our unique record of growth.

OBJECTIVES

FINANCIAL

- Increase earnings per share, on average, 15-20 percent or more annually through internal growth and carefully selected acquisitions.
- Earn 10 percent after-tax profit margin on sales and 20 percent after-tax return on shareholders' equity.

These financial objectives, while admittedly ambitious, have been attained by Masco in nearly every year in the past quarter century.

OPERATING

- Achieve consistent and predictable growth.

With a great measure of pride, we point to our record of 27 consecutive years of increased annual earnings. This record of earnings growth consistency has been achieved even though there have been frequent recessions during this period.

Success in the business of management should be judged in terms of measurable performance. This forms a basis for investor

credibility. A well-managed growth company is one that consistently performs well over an extended period of time. It is evident from the table below that Masco's sales and earnings performance have outperformed an objective standard, the all-U.S. manufacturing corporation average, even during periods of recession.

MASCO IN PERIODS OF RECESSION

	1982 vs. 1981	1975 vs. 1974	1970 vs. 1969	1967 vs. 1966
Sales:				
Masco*	− 2.4%	+21.5%	+16.7%	+19.1%
All U.S. Mfg.**	− 5.0%	+ .6%	+ 2.0%	+ 3.8%
Earnings:				
Masco*	+ 4.3%	+25.4%	+15.8%	+ 3.5%
All U.S. Mfg.**	−25.1%	−16.6%	−14.1%	− 6.2%

*As reported in annual report. **Dept. of Comm., Bureau of Census.

■ Maintain the financial strength to support our growth objectives.

An analysis of our cash flow reflects the financial capacity to support our growth objectives. High profit margins contribute importantly to our cash flow. The average manufacturing company earns approximately 5 percent after-tax margin on sales which must provide for working capital, debt repayment, capital expenditures and dividend requirements. Masco has consistently achieved a 10 percent after-tax margin on sales which has given us an "extra" 5 percent cash flow to finance our above-average growth.

Also, we have a record of consistently maintaining above-average liquidity. This gives us the flexibility to take timely advantage of investment opportunities without having to readjust our plans during periods of economic contraction or "tight money" conditions.

■ Organize, structure and operate the Company so that it remains manageable.

Complementing our value-added product and market specialization and positions of leadership strategies is a "proprietary company strategy." Masco is organized into decentralized, highly autonomous divisional profit centers which are complete functional business units. Our experience has proven that those operations which successfully implement our business strategies in pursuit of Masco objectives and which are entrepreneurially managed will successfully develop their own unique "proprietary" quality.

Masco has over 40 such operating units. We have found them to be quite manageable and that when problems occur they can be addressed and immediate action taken, secure in the knowledge that our other businesses are running smoothly.

We find our time spent making good companies even better is more rewarding than attempting to effect turnarounds of problem companies.

Furthermore, our operating companies have many fundamental elements in common, making them easier to manage. For example, we have five separate cold extrusion divisions each with its own particular metalworking expertise. We specialize, at different plant locations, in short-run jobs, long-run high-volume production, relatively small parts, and large parts as well as components utilizing different metalworking techniques; even though these divisions operate independently, they have functional similarities and collectively provide the position of leadership we enjoy in the cold extrusion industry.

BUSINESS STRATEGIES

MARKETS

- Invest our resources in selected market "niches" where we can achieve and maintain positions of leadership.

We seek specialized market "niches" where our product development, manufacturing and marketing skills can contribute to achieving proprietary positions and ultimately positions of market leadership.

By concentrating on "niches," we have become product leaders in a number of areas rather than diluting our strengths by becoming a broad-line manufacturer within one industry as have many of our competitors; e.g., we make high-performance front-wheel drive products for autos but not commodity-type parts such as common stampings. By focusing on these special segments (markets within a market), our performance is not solely determined by the overall industry cycle; e.g., we have achieved consistent growth in the faucet market even though the plumbing or building materials markets experience cyclical patterns.

We sell nothing under the Masco name but take pride in the leadership positions that our operations have established over the years under their own names. The majority of their products have become the recognized leaders within their fields. Masco's optimistic appraisal of its future opportunities is derived, to a very great extent, from these positions of leadership.

MASCO LEADERSHIP PRODUCTS–1983 SALES

	(In Thousands)	% of Total
Faucets	$ 243,000	23%
Other Plumbing Products	129,000	12
Oil-Field and Related Products	104,000	10
Cold Extruded Products	88,000	8
Specialty Valves and Closures	85,000	8
Other Specialty Transportation Products	58,000	6
Personal Communications Products	56,000	5
Recreational Accessories	28,000	3
Insulation Products	28,000	3
Ventilating Equipment	24,000	2
Builders' Hardware	22,000	2
Other	23,000	2
Leadership Products Sales	$ 888,000	84%
Total Masco Sales	$1,059,000	100%

HUMAN RESOURCES

- Recognize and develop our most important resource–our people.

Business strategies directed to the fulfillment of ambitious financial objectives will be successful only if the people responsible for implementing them are highly capable and properly motivated. Thus, we seek people with superior potential and work closely with them to encourage their development.

We work very hard to maintain an atmosphere that is intellectually challenging, yet also personally oriented. In our judgment, a company cannot grow at an above-average rate, as we have, through competent people alone; they must also have the proper environment. At Masco, we pride ourselves on having created a work environment that encourages and rewards innovation and above-average performance.

We believe that one of the most important factors of our success has been our ability to attract, motivate and promote a very special and talented group of men and women–the Masco team.

- Encourage an entrepreneurial management style.

We welcome flexibility, encouraging our employees to use their business judgment with a minimum of corporate operating constraints. Individual initiative was the entrepreneurial base upon which Masco was founded and upon which it has flourished. Important, too, has been our ability to blend this entrepreneurship with the professional managerial strengths and other resources available in a larger organization. While it is necessary to have the management and financial controls with which to plan and monitor the running of the business, it is

even more important that these controls not inhibit the entrepreneurial style which has contributed so significantly to our success.

DIVERSIFICATION

- Control our own destiny, and not have our growth dependent on any single market or product.

Attaining a significant measure of control over a company's destiny is a formidable challenge in the complex, competitive and highly regulated business environment that exists in this country. We have been successful by doing a number of things: 1) maintaining a diversified product base (characterized by positions of leadership) so that we are not dependent on any one product or market to sustain our growth; 2) building on existing strengths by concentrating our resources on those products and businesses which are compatible with our proven skills in product development, manufacturing and marketing, and not just diversifying into any business; and 3) avoiding markets subject to significant external influences beyond our control, such as excessive government regulations.

- Concentrate on businesses which are neither labor nor capital intensive and which are not subject to rapid technological change.

By avoiding businesses that are labor or capital intensive, we not only achieve consistently higher profit margins but also keep the Company more manageable. We therefore require less labor and capital for future expansion, and we have more flexible manufacturing operations. Also, we avoid disproportionately large investments (such as in single-purpose, high-cost manufacturing facilities) where a mistake in judgment can have a significant adverse effect on our overall performance.

High technology, while often exciting, has another side–namely, exposure to rapid obsolescence. Where there is a market characterized by a high rate of technological change, there is usually greater attendant risk. For the most part, Masco's markets are mundane and change within them is usually slow and evolutionary. Thus, we concentrate our efforts on product improvement, marketing programs, manufacturing efficiencies and expansion with less concern that a revolutionary new product will unexpectedly obsolete or impair our investment. This is particularly important in successfully managing a decentralized multi-divisional company such as Masco.

ACQUISITIONS

Internal growth has historically accounted for the major part of our growth in earnings per share; this emphasis continues and will be the primary basis for future growth. There are sound reasons, however, supporting an active program to locate and acquire selected new business partners. Our acquisition program has contributed to increasing our total growth, and has proven to be an attractive investment opportunity for a portion of the cash flow generated by our high-margin businesses.

Acquisitions can be an efficient means of entering attractive new market segments or obtaining particular product, market or technical capabilities. These often can be more expeditiously and economically accomplished through acquisitions than by pursuing the same goals through internal product development or by starting a new operation. An acquired company generally has been successful in its particular business for many years with an established management team enjoying a reputation for product and/or service superiority which would be costly and unnecessarily time-consuming to duplicate.

Certainly there are risks inherent in any acquisition. We attempt to minimize these risks by focusing our search on companies that:

1) are at the forefront of their particular market and technology–an industry leader;

2) offer growth in a compatible new field or complement or accelerate growth of an existing business;

3) are entrepreneurially oriented;

4) have a proven record of sales and earnings growth and the prospect for above-average profitability over an extended period of time; and

5) bring people to Masco who can contribute to the continued success not only of their own business, but also to our overall performance.

Generally, companies that have joined the Masco family have subsequently accelerated their growth. We believe the major reasons for this increased rate of internal growth have been: the Masco operating environment which fosters freedom of action and a high standard of performance; Masco's added resources, whether in terms of capital, people or know-how; the frequent benefits from close interaction with other Masco operations; and our corporate staff services which relieve entrepreneurs of many of the details and non-productive aspects of running a business, giving them more time to do those things they enjoy and do best such as manufacturing, marketing or product development.

We also realize that simply to acquire is not to grow. Growth which is not a logical and consistent extension of proven capabilities is diversification at risk. A conglomerate generally pursues an investment philosophy designed to broaden financial opportunities but with no homogeneous or sustainable market or product denominator; to such a company, financial services, entertainment or other widely diverse fields are looked upon as investment opportunities. At Masco, on the other hand, while we have diversified and broadened our horizons, we have built on proven capabilities. While the products we produce and number of markets we serve have expanded in recent years, our common denominator is our metalworking expertise.

RESEARCH AND DEVELOPMENT

An integral part of our goal of building a unique growth company is in the planning and development of new products.

Our financial new-product objective is to develop quality value-added products with the potential to realize a 10 percent after-tax profit on sales and a 20 percent after-tax return on investment. Strategies employed in pursuit of this objective include the following:

1) establish the long-range growth potential of appropriate market opportunities;
2) work closely with customers to ensure that we are responsive to their needs;
3) evaluate new-product uniqueness as compared with present products to determine if a premium value will be accorded by the user; and
4) avoid products where frequent incidence of obsolescence adds inordinately to the risk.

Masco is not a broad-based research company by traditional definition. We are primarily product development, engineering and applications oriented.

Our corporate product development staff has new, expanded facilities. Their technical expertise includes: product design and evaluation, process improvement, specialized machine development, new technology assessment, plant layout and construction as well as environmental, metallurgical, chemical, elastomeric and analytical engineering skills.

These Corporate Research and Development Center specialists contribute to new product and process idea generation and development, and serve as an integral support function for our operating divisions

where our primary product development activities take place.

Historically, Masco has spent the equivalent of approximately 10 percent of its pre-tax income on product development.

INTERNATIONAL EXPANSION

International expansion adds a further dimension to our growth opportunities. Masco acquired its first European operation eleven years ago. Today, we believe there are many opportunities to further expand into international markets with products and know-how currently being developed within our Company.

While economic conditions and the strength of the U.S. dollar have adversely affected our international growth in recent years, we believe this trend will be reversed with our business opportunities expanding significantly in the future.

International sales have grown at an average annual rate of 31 percent and have been as follows (in thousands):

1983	1982	1981	1980	1979	1978
$135,000	$120,000	$115,000	$128,000	$82,000	$72,000

1977	1976	1975	1974	1973
$59,000	$36,000	$32,000	$19,000	$9,000

FUTURE GROWTH

The preceding restatement and reaffirmation of our objectives and strategies should provide a greater insight and perspective for understanding Masco's operating disciplines.

A few additional observations perhaps will also shed light on our competitive posture and prospects for growth in the years ahead.

Just over a decade ago, corporate revenues were slightly over $100 million. Today, with sales larger by ten-fold, many investors ask, "Will your increasing size impede your future rate of growth and manageability?"

We have found that size alone is not the key to the growth prospects of a company; there are a number of large companies which have grown rapidly while many smaller companies have not grown at all. We are now more optimistic about Masco's growth prospects than we were ten years ago because we are a much more resourceful company and our current financial, product and people resources give us a much broader base upon which to build.

Furthermore, Masco consists of a number of businesses with several million to over $100 million in sales; most of these businesses have considerable opportunity for growth through increased market share, new product development, international expansion, increased exports and the entry into other related markets. By way of contrast, if our sales of over $1 billion last year were entirely in faucets, given the absolute size of the world market, our growth objectives would be unrealistic. Thus, there is considerable aggregate potential in our operations which should enable Masco to achieve its long-term growth objectives.

We must continually evaluate each of our businesses to insure that they have inherent in them the potential to contribute to Masco's growth; we must continually review our objectives and strategies to see if we are adhering to them and if they should be modified to meet changing circumstances, and we must continually monitor our efforts to build and develop the resources we will need to grow.

Based upon our 27-year record of earnings growth, our management and operating decisions have usually proven to be sound. Our mistakes, such as developing or acquiring products that were not truly proprietary or acquiring a company that did not enjoy a position of leadership, have taught us the importance of diligently adhering to the disciplines inherent in our objectives and strategies.

Our management experience–translated into knowing where and how to achieve profitable growth–has built what we believe to be a unique growth company and gives us confidence that we will meet the challenges of the future.

TEN IMPORTANT SUBJECTS YOU WILL WANT TO DISCUSS IN DEPTH IN YOUR CORPORATE ANNUAL REPORT

In addition to the financial information, you will want to present to your readers a well-thought out and carefully documented narrative of the activities of your company—past, present, and future (with heavy emphasis on the future). Photographs depicting your company at work will round out the portrayal of your company to your stockholders, present and potential, security analysts, employees, suppliers, etc.

Place yourself in the position of your stockholders. What would be of greatest interest to you as you read through (hopefully) your company's annual report. I suggest the following questions for your consideration.

1. What is the financial strength of your company?
2. How profitable has your company been—last year versus prior years?
3. What is the future profit potential of your company?
4. How strong is the management of your company—now and for the years ahead?
5. Does your company have a strong R&D program?
6. Has your company developed new technologies and new products to assure a strong position in the marketplace?
7. Is your company sufficiently diversified to withstand future recessions?
8. Does your company have a well-designed export program?
9. If you are an international company, how has your company structured its operations to maximize foreign sales?
10. What are the financial and operational goals your company has set for the next five years? How successful has your company been in meeting its stated goals over the past five years?

BUZZ WORDS AND PHRASES TO INCLUDE IN YOUR ANNUAL REPORT

There are a number of key words and phrases that you will want to consider in developing your corporate annual report. These are words and phrases that are in vogue—words and phrases that your readers will want to have discussed in detail. Consider including a description of how your company relates to the following buzz words and phrases:

1. Asset Redeployment

Crown Zellerbach

Asset Redeployment. The key elements of our plan are to focus the company's resources—human, physical, and financial—on the most promising markets available to us, and to develop cost-effective production and marketing systems to supply them. This involves shifting resources from operations that cannot meet those criteria to others that do meet them.

In 1982, we agreed to sell our interests in Crown Zellerbach Canada Limited and Norsk Pacific Steamship Company, and we sold interests in a northern California pulp mill, a Chilean paper operation and some smaller, non-economic facilities. When completed, these sales will have produced a total cash flow of about $200 million to reinvest in key domestic operations and strengthen our financial position.

1982's results reinforce the validity of that strategy. Although unusual charges and continuing losses by Crown Canada produced a net loss for the corporation as a whole, the domestic operations on which we are focusing our resources produced pretax profits of $29 million in the worst year of the current recession.

McGraw-Edison

The company's asset redeployment program, initiated five years ago, was completed in 1982. This effort resulted in a substantial expansion of the company's revenue base since 1978 and significantly improved the quality and earnings potential of its businesses.

The recession that persisted throughout 1982 did not deter McGraw-Edison from taking steps to further improve its 10 divisions. Investments in new products, research and development, and more efficient manufacturing plants and equipment continued during the year. As the marketplace became more competitive, all divisions reassessed the profitability and potential of their product lines. Significant steps were taken company-wide to insure that McGraw-Edison can continue to serve the growing segments of its markets with cost-effective products.

Among the efficiency measures instituted during the year was a program to reduce working capital requirements. This resulted in a reduction of inventories and receivables by a total of more that $80 million. Significant efficiencies were also achieved through cost reduction programs instituted company-wide.

Facility utilization was analyzed, and in some cases, plants were combined to maximize manufacturing efficiency.

In summary, these actions benefited the company's results during 1982 and, more importantly, positioned all 10 McGraw-Edison divisions to effectively participate in the anticipated economic recovery.

Redeployment Adds Strength and Diversity. The redeployment program has resulted in a stronger company with greater geographic and market diversity. Where previously McGraw-Edison had little participation in international markets, the company and its consolidated subsidiaries now have 45 international manufacturing locations in 14 countries, and during 1982 had international sales of more than $640 million. Since the beginning of 1979, McGraw-Edison has spent more than $300 million strengthening the company, which represents an annual capital spending rate of more than three times the level spent in the three years preceding the redeployment. This investment was made during a period when the company also reduced debt by more than $400 million.

While the company was faced with a difficult economic environment that persisted throughout the period of the company's restructuring efforts, this did not impair its ability to compete in a number of additional growing markets, and improve its overall market share.

McGraw-Edison now competes in 25 major domestic markets, a third of which grew faster than the GNP prior to the 1982 recession.

In 1978 one-third of the company's businesses held a 15 percent market share or greater; currently two-thirds of its businesses have at least a 15 percent share. Moreover, during the same period, the businesses in which McGraw-Edison holds a market share of 24 percent or greater has increased fourfold to more than 40 percent.

The narrative that follows portrays the technological strengths and market positions of the 10 divisions that now comprise McGraw-Edison. This discussion is intended to focus on the role that these businesses play within the overall corporate strategy for growth through the 1980's and beyond.

2. Capital Restructuring

In addition to cash proceeds and debt reductions resulting from the sale of non-strategic facilities, the balance sheet was materially strengthed by replacing $150 million of variable-rate debt through intermediate-term borrowings at competitive rates, and by a new issue of cumulative preferred stock.

3. Cash Conservation and Cost Reduction

To sustain a prudent level of capital investment and continue the modernization of our large pulp and paper mill at Camas, Washington, in the face of the recession, non-strategic expenditures were deferred or eliminated from the capital spending budget, reducing it from a projected $330 million to $305 million. Costs were substantially reduced by streamlining the salaried and hourly workforces, and by instituting productivity improvement programs, increasing energy efficiency through the use of alternative fuels, cogeneration and conservation, and controlling sales and administrative expenses. Finally, to conserve cash the annual common stock dividend was reduced to $1.00 from $2.30 per share.

4. Focus for the 80s

Our focus for the 1980s is to capitalize on the attractive opportunities presented by our three basic businesses: power, building systems, and electronics. These markets are expected to record long-term steady growth in the future. Most of our divisions are leaders in their markets, and we have the technology and product development to maintain or increase our market share.

5. Management Team

Crown Zellerbach

A reorganized management team was developed with more direct reporting lines, closer coordination, and wider participation in corporate decision making.

These examples of the coordinated, creative management of resources that Crown is achieving are described in more detail in the remainder of this report. Through this process, a new Crown Zellerbach is evolving with fully competitive mills and plants and a more productive work force serving our most profitable markets from a sound financial base.

Looking ahead, the economic indicators for our industry point to recovery beginning in the second quarter of 1983 and gathering momentum as we move into 1984. Crown enters this recovery period stronger, better equipped, and more determined than ever before to build the value of our company for shareholders, employees, and customers.

6. New Businesses

CBS, Inc.

Beyond the base of our four operating groups, we also entered into two exciting new business ventures during the year. The first was The CBS/FOX Company, a joint venture created in July 1982 with Twentieth Century-Fox Video, Inc. CBS/FOX is the nation's largest marketer of videocassette and videodisc home entertainment. It also operates the former CBS Studio Center film production facility. Our second new venture, announced in late 1982, is a major, new motion picture company being formed in conjunction with Columbia Pictures (a subsidiary of The Coca-Cola Company) and Home Box Office (a subsidiary of Time Incorporated). The establishment of this new enterprise underscores the commitment of CBS and our new partners to film production and distribution, while providing the opportunity for the joint development of emerging areas of video programming such as pay-per-view.

In addition to these two new business ventures, we undertook a major market test of an entertainment/information product with striking market potential for the future—videotex. Utilizing computer technology and the home television set, videotex can provide a wide array of information services, interactive banking and shopping services, and entertainment for the consumer at home. In the fall of 1982, in conjunction with AT&T, CBS began testing a state-of-the-art videotex system to gather information vital to understanding its full potential and to developing a long-range business plan.

7. Operations Restructuring

Key management decisions were made to restructure operations over the next two or three years, which resulted in writing down certain assets and making provision for their disposal. An early retirement program was offered certain employees as part of streamlining our operations. We elected to recognize these obligations during 1982.

8. Positioned for Success

Wang

Wang Laboratories is, obviously, an organization made up of several major and hundreds of minor components. Success, however, is fleeting if each area is not managed effectively. At Wang, a solid and successful corporate structure is in place. The result: Wang stands at the head of the office automation industry. The office automation industry traditionally respects Wang for superior products and solid service and support. It can now respect the corporation as a whole.

Wang Laboratories is a pioneer; we take the latest technology and develop meaningful applications to fill needs in the office. A pioneer relies on intelligence, entrepreneurial skill, adaptability, and courage. This mixture, for Wang, translates into a record of sustained growth, despite the hardships that strike at every business.

A complementary trait, though, is Wang's strong, traditional theme of marketing—customer satisfaction. Wang aims at this sometimes elusive commodity in three ways: by satisfying the real needs of today's user; by recognizing future trends and anticipating their opportunities; and by preparing for the next generation of technology—technology that may not yet be defined.

In terms of present-day requirements, Wang relies on its package of products, services, support, and people. And, naturally, the Company continuously refines its day-to-day operations.

In the near term, Wang will continue to take advantage of the opportunities of emerging technology through solid management and controls.

And Wang, in the long term, intends to remain at the forefront of the office automation industry. Just as Wang word processing in 1972 and WangNet in 1981 opened new doors, future innovation will develop into sensible, usable products and services.

Wang Laboratories believes this is a comprehensive approach to office automation. Now, Wang must continue to build aggressively on our services, products, and the philosophy behind them to attain new levels of achievement.

The Company, in summary, belives we are very good at what we do. The challenge now is to get even better.

9. Transition

Scott

Scott is a company in transition. Change is not an option for us but a necessity. With this in mind, during 1982 we tightened up the criteria we expect our businesses to meet and now are rigorously examining each of our businesses against these criteria. Our goal is to become a low-cost producer, focusing only on those products and market segments in which Scott has unique competitive advantages and can achieve substantially higher returns on investment. We have placed more emphasis on management excellence and creating a climate which encourages our employees to realize their full potential. Our goal is to provide a challenging and rewarding work environment which will enable the Company to realize significant growth in earnings, cash flow, and most importantly, return on equity. All of our dedicated employees and the key management group are jointly committed to achieving this end.

10. Revitalization Program

Most companies that were hit hard by the recession of 1981–82 have developed a "Revitalization Program." Clark Equipment Company designed such a plan which it described on the cover of its 1982 annual report as being "Revitalization: The Foundation for a Stronger Clark."

The president of Clark described their revitalization program in the 1982 corporate annual report as follows:

Clark Equipment Company launched a comprehensive revitalization program in 1982 which, upon completion, will result in a significantly stronger Clark well positioned for growth in a changing, more competitive, and geographically integrated marketplace. The program involves evaluation and restructuring of every facet of the Company's operations, including its philosophy of management and its approaches to manufacturing, manpower, inventory, products, marketing, and financial controls.

A special section concerning the revitalization program is included in the annual report, beginning on page 5. Briefly, the program has three basic objectives:

First, it is designed to ensure the Company's survival in each of its primary business lines.

Second, it will maintain and reinforce Clark's current leadership position in the industrial truck market, and enable the Company to take full advantage of the most profitable segments of the construction machinery, components, and credit markets.

Third, it has established an efficient management framework through which the Company can generate profit and growth in both traditional and new markets.

The costs of the program are considerable but necessary. In the third quarter of 1982 Clark established a pre-tax provision of $214.5 million to cover costs related to the plan. The Company believes this is a sound investment in its future, and is confident that it will result in a stable, growth-oriented Clark that will benefit our stockholders, employees, dealers, customers, and suppliers.

Clark described its revitalization program as follows:

Revitalization: Overview. Clark's revitalization program is directed at three fundamental objectives: survival, viability, and growth. At its most basic level, each of the Company's primary businesses must survive the immediate difficulties it faces, caused largely by the adverse economic conditions. If the word survival seems to strong, one need only look at the growing list of prestigious companies that did not discipline themselves to a survival strategy until after they were in serious trouble.

On a second level, Clark must be viable. It must achieve and maintain a quality and cost competitive advantage to assure product acceptance and strong market position.

The third level—the ability to achieve real planned growth—is the true test of management, and the ultimate goal to which the revitalization plan is directed.

The program is governed by four parameters established to protect the shareholder investment and allow for planned progress.

First, the plan is based on a realistic projection of continued depressed conditions in global industrial markets. It does not anticipate a near-term improvement in business levels.

The second requirement is that sufficient cash flow be available to cover Clark's operating requirements, investment needs, and debt service.

The third parameter is the restoration of operating profit at current depressed business levels. Lower fixed cost will achieve upside leverage through improved profit margins as manufacturing levels increase.

The fourth parameter concerns Clark's ability to

pay for the revitalization program, and the requirement that the company not exceed a 35 percent debt-to-capitalization ratio at any time during implementation of the plan. It also requires the ability to liquidate all debt incurred from implementation within three years.

Within these parameters, the program reaches to all levels and operations of the Company. It redirects resources, prunes excesses, and implants a management philosophy that emphasizes teamwork, organizational effectiveness, and growth objectives. Moreover, the revitalization program speaks to Clark's need as an international company, implanting a worldwide, integrated philosophy that governs all operations.

Finance in the Financial Area. Clark took several important steps to ensure short-term survival throughout the current slow economic period as well as during the ongoing revitalization program.

First, a pre-tax reserve of $214.5 million ($139 million after tax) was established in the third quarter of 1982 to cover all revitalization costs. These include costs for four U.S. plant shutdowns (which are expected to be completed by year-end 1983); operating losses anticipated during the phase down period; relocation and integration of production at retained plants; certain hourly and salaried employee costs; and certain international revitalization expenses.

Second, as part of the aggressive inventory reduction program that took place through 1982, controls were put into place requiring all capital expenditures be funded through inventory reductions. This has helped to further improve Clark's cash position.

Third, the Company established a growth strategy for its finance operations which involves a new emphasis for the Clark Equipment Credit Corporation. This business will now be actively soliciting business outside Clark Equipment Company and will be doing both financing and leveraged leases.

As part of this growth strategy, Clark Credit recently acquired The White Motor Credit Corporation and entered into an agreement with Volvo White Truck Corporation to finance Volvo White's U.S. truck dealers and retail customers. The White Motor Credit acquisition increased Clark Credit's receivables by $220 million, and paved the way for further implementation of its aggressive growth strategy.

The acquisition, along with the Volvo White financing agreement, brought non-Clark receivables in the Clark Credit portfolio to about $380 million, or approximately 29 percent of the total portfolio. Growth in non-Clark business is expected to continue to increase outside receivables to one-half of Clark Credit's total portfolio by the mid-1980's. The objective is to provide a source of fast growing earnings for Clark, and to allow Clark Credit to become a distinct, independent entity capable of expanding its operations into new, growth-potential businesses.

Manufacturing During 1982. The utilization of Clark manufacturing capacity was at record lows: below 35 percent at some plants. To reduce overhead costs and increase the utilization of plant capacity, Clark reorganized its manufacturing activities and announced plans to consolidate its operations into its newest, most productive facilities. This requires the phase out of the Clark domestic manufacturing plants in Benton Harbor, Jackson and Buchanan, Michigan. In addition, the industrial truck assembly operation in Battle Creek will be consolidated into other Clark operations, although domestic production of uprights will remain at the Michigan plant. Overseas, the industrial truck operations at Aumenau, West Germany, will be consolidated into the Mulheim operation.

The most significant impact of this manufacturing consolidation will be the reduction of Clark's manufacturing break-even point in 1984 by about 35 percent, from a sales level of $1,425 million to a sales level of $925 million. When consolidation is complete, the Company will still have retained sufficient capacity to exceed the historic peak in demand experienced in 1979.

To achieve continued viability in Clark manufacturing plants, the remaining operations have been scrutinized for opportunities to improve quality and reduce manufacturing costs. Emphasis will be placed on increased equipment technology and utilization, expanded worldwide sourcing, and improved manpower effectiveness.

To provide for future efficiencies, Clark will make the investments necessary to ensure its facilities are utilizing state-of-the-art processes for production, inventory control, and manpower utilization. Intracompany sourcing will also be closely evaluated to ensure the use of the highest quality, most economical components in our product lines.

Additional progress in revitalizing Clark manufacturing operations is expected during 1983 and, when complete, will position the Company to respond quickly, more efficiently, and more profitably to market opportunities with a competitively priced quality product.

Marketing. Clark's marketing efforts are marked by two significant trends in 1982: the Industrial Truck Division increased its market share during the year, and the dealer organizations supporting industrial trucks and construction machinery remained healthy despite the difficult economy.

Clark's dealer organization is one of the Company's most valuable marketing assets. Clark has the largest distributor network for industrial trucks in the world, and one of the largest in the construction machinery business. This extensive dealer network not only establishes Clark's market presence and position, but also serves to increase sales through parts and service.

Clark and its dealers worked in concert during the year to reduce inventory both at the manufacturer and dealer level. These efforts helped to increase dealer cash flow and thereby reduced financing costs during the depressed economy. In addition, Clark's strong parts operations helped dealers pursue sales in this area.

Clark Credit has also helped some Industrial Truck and Melroe dealers establish equipment leasing programs which provide revenues in periods of extremely low business activity. The success of these programs is evidenced by the strong market position of these Clark product lines.

Clark believes these marketing programs will position the Company for growth when the economy rebounds. Significant cost reductions will give Clark an advantage over many manufacturers that have approached the market less aggressively. Clark is also positioning itself for additional growth in the parts and service areas with its Construction Machinery dealers, and further expansion in the leasing area with Industrial Truck and Melroe dealers. New products and marketing efforts are also being developed for components sold to original equipment manufacturers.

Products. Clark's product development efforts are currently directed at becoming more competitive by meeting changing market demands. Based on the experiences of the current prolonged recession, product price is becoming increasingly important in customer decisions. Recognizing this, Clark's first priority in the product development area is to ensure its products are both quality- and cost-competitive throughout the world. A number of programs were launched in 1982 to accomplish this objective.

The manufacturing consolidation program detailed in this report is central to Clark's cost reduction efforts. The plants that will be building Clark's products are the Company's most cost-efficient. Further installation of new, more productive equipment will continue to increase manufacturing cost-effectiveness.

Clark is also looking closely at the design of each of its products to identify areas where cost savings can be achieved without sacrificing quality. Rationalization of parts, elimination of non-competitive and expensive product features and product design changes that will result in manufacturing efficiencies are all under consideration.

A third area important to reducing costs is materials management, particularly sourcing. Clark is examining worldwide sources for both raw materials and components to ensure product cost is at a minimum.

Each of Clark's operating divisions is embracing these product strategies designed to reduce manufactured costs. In addition, Industrial Truck is focusing its efforts on high volume markets which offer the greatest growth potential. Material Handling Systems is capitalizing on warehousing trends with products aimed at increasing space utilization and productivity. Construction Machinery is targeting products to meet the needs of coal, pipe handling, and forestry markets. Components is introducing products to meet the specific needs of the off-highway vehicle market, as well as of large truck manufacturers.

Human Resources. Clark recognized the need to reduce the manpower levels of both its salary and hourly workforces as an important part of revitalizing Clark's operations. In the hourly workforce, most of the planned reductions will result from plant consolidations and improved manufacturing productivity.

A program was also developed to reduce the number of management levels within the organization to make it leaner and more effective over the long-term. As a result, between January 1, 1982, and year end 1983, the North American salaried workforce will be reduced by approximately 1,500, or one-third. Similar man-power reductions will also be made in Clark's international operations in the near future.

This manpower reduction program, although

considered necessary for the survival and future stability of the Company, takes into consideration the human impact both on those who are leaving the Company and those who will remain. To minimize the adverse human impact, a plan was structured that permitted maximum self-selection.

First, a worldwide hiring freeze was instituted on January 1, 1982. This assured that natural attrition would be fully translated into manpower reductions. This freeze will continue, with few exceptions, through 1983.

Second, an early retirement incentive program was offered to 514 eligible employees. On September 15, 1982, when the program was completed, 412 employees (or 80 percent of those eligible) had elected to retire early. Of that number, more than 70 percent came from the management or supervisory ranks.

Finally, Clark incorporated a voluntary separation option in its reduction plan. Altogether, the Company expects nearly 50 percent of its total reduction goal to come through these three self-selection options. The balance of reductions will come from manufacturing consolidations and a performance-based reduction-in-force.

For remaining employees, ongoing human effectiveness programs are being developed and implemented to encourage more active participation among all levels of the organization and to give employees a stronger feeling of ownership in the Company's goals and strategies. These ongoing programs are based on the recognition of the individual dignity of employees. They are designed to increase employee involvement and organizational effectiveness through teamwork and to maximize the employee contibutions that are necessary to Clark's success.

Clark's management is committed to improving growth opportunities for its employees and to introducing development and training programs to allow them to take advantage of new opportunities as they arise.

Management Synergism. A major step in creating a positive, participatory environment throughout the Company has been the establishment of the Management Committee. The Committee, formed in early 1982 to increase the effectiveness of individual managers by introducing a teamwork approach, is expected to set the management style of the entire Company. Through this approach, Clark is assured full, open communication and close coordination for genuine progress toward corporate goals.

Through its eight members, the Clark Management Committee oversees every operating entity and staff function within the corporation.

The Chairman has also encouraged each of the members of the Clark Board of Directors to take a more active role as advisors and consultants to the Company. The number of Board meetings has been increased from the traditional four to six annually, and two new committees governing objectives and Board member selection were formed in 1982 to bring Board members into a closer relationship with the long-term strategic planning of the company.

The Clark Board of Directors, the Management Committee, and Clark employees around the world have worked diligently over the past year to develop meaningful, achievable strategies to maintain the Company's strength and to make it even stronger and more viable.

The Company has been extremely proactive in its planning and has taken a realistic, but conservative view of the business outlook for the near future.

The people of Clark are united in their commitment to the hard work and fiscal prudence necessary to revitalize the Company to assure it a strong, healthy future.

HOW TO DESCRIBE THE STRENGTHS OF YOUR COMPANY

Accentuate the positive in describing your company by outlining its strengths. The following are some suggested statements to include in describing your corporation (to be backed up with facts and figures).

1. Growth program delivers the highest sales, earning, and dividends in our history.
2. A strong contributor to our continuing records is our 1976–1986 growth program. It has been supported by the most vigorous level of capital investment in our history.
3. Westvaco gets things done as planned. Our standards are high. We have a restless determination to be the best. Our leadership is bold and aggressive, and you can sense Westvaco esprit de corps.
4. We are innovative leaders in the fields we serve—in paper, packaging, and specialty chemicals, and in the aggressive management of resources and technology required to manufacture and market our products.
5. Our research momentum and technology enable us to produce and market products others find hard to make. We are never satis-

fied. We press continuously for the highest standards of quality and service.

6. Westvaco has a long tradition of remembering its shareholders. We work hard to maximize our financial strength.
7. Our substantial investment in new equipment and processes has paid off in increased productivity and outstanding product quality.
8. We have a new game plan for attacking and penetrating international markets in 19__.
9. We consistently have gained ground on our competitors in recessions. Example: in 19__ our market share increased by 20 percent.
10. While many motor manufacturers slashed their advertising investments in 19__, ours was at a record high. Result: increased customer awareness and preference for Baldor products.
11. Through our position in therapeutic and diagnostic medicine and biomedical research, we have the business and technological resources to become one of the very few companies that will shape the future of world health care markets.
12. New business control system will help manage company's growth.

THE MESSAGE TO YOUR STOCKHOLDERS

Your stockholders may spend a total of 10 to 15 minutes reading your corporate annual report. Basically, they are very interested in what you have to report. They will not review the detailed financial sections or the footnotes. They want to know—particularly from the president's report, that the company is making progress; that the future looks good; that there will be a continuous flow of dividends; and that, in all likelihood, the price of the stock will rise in the OTC market or on the Exchange if the company's stock is listed.

Photos and graphics are important to the stockholders who get a "feel"—a quick impression of the product lines, customer usage of the products, the management, etc., through visual presentation. That is why so many companies will devote 40 to 50 percent of the space in the report to photos to which stockholders can relate.

Stockholders want to have the annual report submitted to them in very clear and easily understood language. It is important that you give the stockholders as much information as possible in the early part of the report—information that is of importance to them and that they can readily understand.

Basically, a stockholder reads your corporate annual report to determine whether to hold or sell the stock. As an owner of your company, he or she wants to get a quick overview of the company to help in an investment decision.

Here are five guidelines that will help you in addressing your stockholders:

1. Keep in mind that most stockholders are not interested in detailed facts and figures. Telegraph the important data in easily understood language.
2. Let your pictures tell part of your story—employees at work—how your products are used—work being done in your research laboratories, etc.
3. Let the president's letter carry the major message to your stockholders. There is a good chance that this section of your report will have the greatest readership.
4. Test out the first draft of your annual report with ten employees (non-financial) of your company (include secretaries, plant foremen, and assembly line workers). Ask them specific questions as to what they glean from your annual report. You might be surprised by the answers.
5. Conduct a stockholder survey to get feedback that will help you in the preparation of your next year's annual report.

EIGHT SUBJECTS THAT YOUR STOCKHOLDERS WANT YOU TO DISCUSS IN YOUR CORPORATE ANNUAL REPORT

Oftentimes the complaint is made, "Our stockholders don't read our annual report." Rather than being critical of your stockholders, if you are of this opinion, you would be better advised to ask yourself the question, "Why should our stockholders read our annual report?"

It is up to you to present your company in a manner that will attract and hold the interest of your stockholders in your annual report. It is possible that the way you have presented the company in your past annual reports has been too formal and too legalistic. You may have been talking down to your stockholders rather than assuming a "sitting at the kitchen table" manner with them and explaining your company. Let's review the areas of interest to your stockholders.

1. *Your stockholders want to own stock in a company that is successful.*

   Does your corporate annual report portray your company as successful? Even though the earnings may be off, a mark of success should still come through your annual report. Stockholders recognize that profits can be off temporarily. They want to be sure that your company will make the appropriate comeback to warrant their confidence in keeping an investment in your company.

2. *Your stockholders want to own stock in a company that is on the move.*

   Your annual report has to portray your company as having the ability, the energy, and the drive to stay out front—to be a winner. You have to show the ingredients that exist within your company to qualify it as a "company on the move."

3. *Your stockholders want to be assured that you have top-flight management.*

   They want to be assured that your company has depth of management—that it is not a one-person show.

   Put in plenty of pictures of your management. Show them in a working environment. Let them talk about their jobs and the future. Describe the experience and background of your top management people. Give an impression—using the old slogan "You are in good hands—in our company."

4. *Your stockholders want to know about your future plans.*

   All too often too much of what appears in the annual report can be classified as ancient history. A certain amount of discussion of the past is valid, but your stockholders want to know your thinking and plans for the future. Yes, they would like to have projections if you are willing to make them. They want to know about new products that you are developing and have developed to replace some of those that have become obsolete. They want to think in terms of your company being "future oriented."

5. *Your stockholders want to know about your management style.*

   They read a lot about quality circles, management task forces, etc. In your annual report, tell your stockholders about your programs to increase the productivity of your work force.

6. *Your stockholders want to know about the response of your corporation to the social needs of the United States.*

   Many companies are expanding the amount of information on their social involvement in their corporate annual reports. Talk about your company's involvement with its employees in the cultural life of your community; your participation in assisting the disadvantaged, etc. Your stockholders want to know in detail what you are doing to merit the statement, "We are good corporate citizens."

7. *Your stockholders want to know how well your company's stock will perform in future markets.*

   Your stockholders will constantly ask the brokers, "Is this company a winner?" "Should I hold on to this investment or would I get a greater capital appreciation if I were to sell this stock and invest in another company?" Provide answers in your annual report that will convince your stockholders to continue their investment in your company.

8. *Your stockholders want to know what dividends they can expect.*

   They are interested in knowing the answers to, "Will the company increase the dividends paid to stockholders?" "Can I count on a certain percentage of the profits going into the payment of dividends?"

These are the types of questions that your stockholders will want your annual report to answer. You have the opportunity to address these questions openly, frankly, and in detail.

WHAT DOES A SECURITY ANALYST LOOK FOR IN YOUR ANNUAL REPORT?

You will want to provide widespread distribution of your annual report to security analysts of financial houses—national, regional, and local. Your annual report will go a long way towards assisting the analyst in making a buy, hold, or sell decision on your company's stock.

Security analysts live on information—the more the better. They want the facts. They do not want you to gloss over the essentials—particularly if they are adverse. They do not want to be manipulated. It is important that you do not insult their intelligence. Analysts are not swayed by sales techniques, the presentation of pictures, or unsubstantiated statements. They want a balanced presentation. Approach the analyst as a person who will question everything. That's the analyst's job.

Security analysts will review your corporation's 10-K report, which is factual and subject to close regulation. Your annual report supplements the 10-K report, and is of interest to the security analysts because it will contain the CEO's analysis of operations, projections, new product ideas, competitive position, marketing strategies, R & D expenditures, etc.

Here are some guidelines for you to follow in presenting your information to satisfy the requirements of the financial community:

1. The truth—the whole truth and nothing but the truth. Analysts want to know exactly what happened in the year covered by the report. If it shows a down year, they want to know exactly what happened and what steps you have taken to correct the situations. Honesty is the best policy in dealing with the analysts.
2. Make it easy on the analysts. Keep in mind that yours is just one of hundreds of reports that the analysts will read. They want to get the information in concise format; easy to follow; with appropriate detailed information.
3. If you set out projections in your prior reports, you would be well advised to report on how the projections matched up to reality. Analysts have a way of keeping reports and bringing out old projections to check against your current year.
4. Security analysts are future oriented. Most of what you have in your annual report on the financial side they already know. They are experienced at digging through your annual report to find out how your management plans for the future. They can see through the rhetoric. They would like to know about your management back up, your projections and its views of the future with facts, figures, market studies, expansion plans, etc.
5. Analysts carefully review the president's letter. They want to know about important management changes; who the new management is; background; etc. They are interested in the president's comments about future acquisitions; sale of subsidiaries; diversifications; etc. If there is any new financing contemplated, they would like to know the details.

HOW CREDIBLE IS YOUR ANNUAL REPORT?

There is oftentimes a perception among some security analysts that annual reports are not much more than advertising pieces—that they gloss over the trouble spots within the company and are not credible. There is some validity to this perception. As you read through annual reports, you will often find that the negatives are buried, that problems are not addressed, and that the optimism expressed is whistling in the dark.

It is up to you in the preparation of your corporate annual report to present the facts and figures as well as the projections for the future in a manner that is believable. Security analysts don't expect your management to have a 100% batting average in all the decisions that have been made. They recognize that oftentimes conditions and events change and bring about failures in any business. They expect you to face up to adversity and to tell them not only what you have learned but how you have corrected the situation so as to get back on track again. They appreciate management that "tells it like it is."

ELEVEN AREAS OF IMMEDIATE CONCERN TO SECURITY ANALYSTS

Security analysts will examine your annual report to answer such questions as:

1. *How competent is the management of the company?*

   In many companies, the management was able to cope and turn in reasonable profits in the 70s. They were not faced with foreign competition, new technologies, robotics, etc. The security analysts will be examining your report to help form an opinion as to the competence of the present management to emerge as a winner in the years that lie ahead.

2. *What is the depth of management?*

   Security analysts will look beyond the chief executive officer and try to determine whether there is a strong layer of management that can step in—particularly where the CEO is approaching retirement age. Are there people in the top echelon of management with a strong background of experience and talent that could move in to replace the CEO? Who are these potential top management candidates? It would be well to let them make some of the statements about their work in the annual report.

3. *How credible is the management of your company?*

   This is a subjective test to which your top management is put. The way the CEO faces up to problems in the annual report oftentimes can give either high marks or low marks to a Chief Executive Officer. Telling it like it is helps build credibility. If the security analyst, in putting down your annual report, says "I have confidence in the management of this company. I believe in what they say and their integrity," you have made a good booster for your company.

4. *Are the profits of the company pumped up?*

   The security analysts will go to the heart of the annual report—the profits earned by the company. They have been trained to sort out fact from fiction. They are familiar with how some companies have juggled earnings to soften the blow. They will examine your profits to see whether the profits are inflated through the use of debt buybacks, accounting changes, pension plan modifications, and other legal maneuvers that have increased the profits of the company. They look for nonrecurring charges which have an impact on comparing profits of one year to the next.

   Security analysts will examine your annual report carefully to determine whether your company repurchased low coupon debt at a steep discount from face value in return for stock. They will want to determine whether you have included in your earnings statement the differences between the low buyback price and the par value at maturity.

   Security analysts are familiar with one of the favorite ways to prop up earnings—namely, to raise the assumption about how much the company can earn on its pension plan for its employees. By doing this the company lowers the contributions to the pension plan that can increase the bottom line profits.

   If your company conducts international operations, the security analysts will carefully examine the way in which your company has translated balance sheet items for foreign currency gains or losses. The new accounting methods for translation of foreign profits will be carefully reviewed by the security analysts. There will be close scrutiny by the security analysts of bottom line increases due to gains from the sale of divisions, plants, or physical equipment, as well as from court judgments, insurance adjustments, lower effective tax rates, etc.

5. *How liquid is the company?*

   Many companies have had an erosion of capital due to loss years. Analysts will carefully review your balance sheet to determine the capacity of your company to expand with existing capital plus borrowed funds. On the other hand, many companies were able to reduce their debt during the recession years (1981–83) and emerged stronger as a result. The security analysts want to take all of this into consideration as they prepare a report on your company.

6. *Is your company able to stay lean?*

   Most companies had to go through a serious cost cutting process during the 1981–83 recession as a result of reduced revenues. Cuts were made not only in the factory and warehouse, but in the office as well. The question that the analysts will want to ask is, "Will the company continue to operate on a lean basis or will the overhead creep up again to offset increased profits that will come from increased revenues?" The security analysts will look to the increased revenues to produce substantially higher profits—provided the company continues to operate on a lean basis.

7. *Is the company tuned in to new technologies?*

   We hear a lot about the new technologies of the future. "Hi tech" seems to be the buzz word that is popular in the business community. Is your company moving into the hi tech areas? If so, have you spelled this out in considerable detail? The security analysts will be looking for this type of information.

8. *Is your company increasing productivity through the use of computers, advanced automation, robotics, etc.?*

   If your company faces foreign competition, the security analysts will want to know how you can be competitive. They know about the rapid advances being made abroad through the use of robots, computers, etc. They will want to know whether your company is keeping pace, or better yet, staying ahead of foreign competition through the introduction of advanced automation in your company. They want to be sure that you are not falling behind and that your costs are such that you will be able to compete with foreign companies.

9. *Is your company spending a sufficient amount for R & D?*

   A number of companies cut back on R & D during the recent recession. As a result, they do not have a sufficient number of new products on stream to be ahead of the competition. Describe in detail your R & D programs and expenditures. After studying your report, security analysts will form an opinion of R & D as to whether your company has what it needs to meet the future challenges of the marketplace. They want to be sure that you are leading and not following the pack.

10. *Has your company depth in marketing?*

    Many companies lost customers as a result of the recession of 1981–83. Has your company geared up to recapture these customers and expand into new markets? It would be well to describe in some detail your marketing strategies and strengths to satisfy security analysts as to your ability to expand revenues, not only in the U.S. markets, but in overseas markets as well.

11. *Is the bloom off the rose of your company?*

    Many companies suffered severe losses during the past recession. Stock values plummeted. Many stockholders lost interest in these companies and turned to other places to invest. If your company is in this situation, the security analysts will want to determine whether the bloom is off your company's rose. Will stockholders want to invest in your company again? Do they see a bright future and an increased interest by those who have funds to invest? Will your company get back on the "purchase" list of a number of investment advisors? These are the questions that security analysts will struggle with as they write their report on your company. Be sure that you have answered these questions in as much detail as possible.

TWENTY AREAS WHERE SECURITY ANALYSTS WILL ZERO IN ON YOUR ANNUAL REPORT

Security analysts are skilled in going for the jugular. They have the ability to go behind the written word. They look for nonanswers. They are trained to read between the lines. They need information to prepare financial reports on your company for their principals. They need to gather information from your annual report that will help them answer these questions:

1. How well has the company done in the past year compared to prior years?
2. How competent is the management to run a profitable company in the future?
3. Are there plans that will produce an orderly transfer of management to responsible and experienced individuals in the future?
4. How well has the stock of the company performed in the over-the-counter market or exchanges, if listed on an exchange?
5. What are the company's future plans in terms of expansion, new products, plant facilities, etc.?
6. How much money does the company spend on research and development? Is this adequate to do the job?
7. What new products are being researched and developed at this time?
8. How liquid is the company?
9. Will the company have enough capital to meet its expansion needs?
10. What share of the market does the company have?
11. How does the company stack up in relation to its competitors?

12. Does the company have and carry out a strong commitment to social involvement?
13. What are the employment policies that the company has put into effect that will guarantee a productive work force in the future?
14. How will the company expand marketing of its products?
15. What are the sales and profits of each division compared to the prior year and what return on investment does each division provide to the company?
16. Does the company have plans for acquisitions? If yes, what are the criteria that the company uses for acquisitions?
17. Does the company plan to divest itself of any unprofitable operations?
18. What is the company's policy relative to the payment of future dividends?
19. Does the company have a well-designed five-year plan with sales and profit goals?
20. Is the company willing to "bite the bullet" and state its financial goals in its annual report?

We will discuss these questions in subsequent chapters. The presentation of your responses can materially affect the attitudes of your stockholders, analysts, etc., as they review your corporate annual report.

NINE AREAS OF INTEREST TO YOUR EMPLOYEES

In preparing your annual report, keep in mind that this is an important vehicle of communication for your employees. It may well be that many of your employees have become stockholders in your company—with more to come. You will want to address yourself to the numerous subjects of interest to your employees, such as:

1. *Your employees want to feel that the management of the company can be trusted.*

   Unfortunately, during the recession period of 1981–83, many companies had to cut back and terminate a number of employees. Oftentimes this came as a bolt out of the blue. Employees who had been with the company for a long period of time did not expect that their employment would be terminated. They felt the company was unfair in the way it treated them.

   This will require a building up of confidence in the company and the management. Your company's employees need to have the security that in the future they can trust the management of the company. This does not mean a guarantee of a job, but a guarantee of fairness in future relationships. The annual report has to portray the management of your company as people who can be trusted.

2. *Your employees want to feel that they are needed by the company.*

   All too often the sole mention of the employees of the company is at the end of the chief executive officer's letter, where there is an expression of the company's thanks for the employees' efforts during the past year. Many companies are recognizing that this is an inadequate way to express their appreciation for the work that has been done by their employees. Reference is made to this in several places in this book.

   Chrysler Corporation is a good example of how they gave credit to their employees in their 1982 Annual Report when they stated:

   > **PEOPLE**—Chrysler employees are a team of experienced, dedicated, success-oriented people. They are entering 1983 confident that their teamwork is making Chrysler successful in one of the most competitive industries in the world.
   >
   > **Turnaround**—In 1982, nearly 80,000 Chrysler people, working in more than 125 plants, offices and parts depots in the United States, Canada and Mexico, continued one of the most dramatic turnarounds in the history of American industry. Despite the worst automotive sales year in two decades, Chrysler improved its earnings position by more than $645 million over the previous year.
   >
   > Chrysler people did it through hard work, personal sacrifice, good management, and the careful use of resources. They worked more closely and effectively with suppliers. And they increased the efficiency of such internal operations as dealer ordering policies.
   >
   > • Chrysler people in the plants turned out cars and trucks that plant audits showed were 30 percent improved in quality over 1981.

• Chrysler people in the zone sales offices helped capture 10 percent of the U.S. car market and raise the Corporation's share of the U.S. truck market to 9.5 percent. In Canada, Chrysler's car market share was 15.4 percent and the truck market share was 12.1 percent.

• Chrysler manufacturing and engineering people launched the 1983 models with one of the best, most efficient, highest quality kick-offs in Chrysler history.

• Chrysler financial people developed innovative strategies to gain the maximum impact from limited dollars.

Close Cooperation—Teamwork is the foundation on which Chrysler is growing. At our Detroit Trim Plant, for example, union and management people cooperated to create a plan that will keep the plant competitive and operating, despite initial predictions that it would close this year.

Another example of teamwork between the company and the union is the Chrysler–UAW Joint Quality Improvement Program. Quality Action Teams, established in the plants as cooperative efforts, were expanded in 1982 to all major U.S. manufacturing locations. Hundreds of individual workers have become involved in the quality improvement process, either formally or informally. Building and delivering quality to the customer is our employees' goal.

The Team is Ready for More—Chrysler people are a highly skilled, thoroughly trained, professional force of designers, product planners, engineers, manufacturing people, marketers, salespeople, financial planners, and managers. They approach 1984 more united, more confident, and even more determined than ever before."

3. *Your employees want to feel that they are working for a company that has a future.*

   There may be some scars as a result of plant shutdowns and moving out of a particular community. This raises questions in the minds of many employees as to whether they are working for a company that has a future. Your annual report gives you an excellent opportunity to show that your company is future oriented and that it has the drive, determination, the product lines, etc., to be in the forefront for many years to come.

4. *Your employees want to have a feeling that there are opportunities for upward mobility within the company.*

   You can show through pictures and statements of the management people in your annual report how many of them came up through the ranks to hold high positions within the company.

5. *Your employees want to know that there is good management coming along at the top.*

   They want to see a backup of management to replace top executives when they retire or in the event of death. They want to see an orderly transition where that is required.

6. *Your employees want to be associated with a leader.*

   Everyone likes to be on the winning team. Portray in your annual report the way in which your company has been regarded particularly by outside souces, as the leader in your field. Talk about awards and honors that have been given to the company and to management people.

7. *Your employees want to be part of the team.*

   Describe in your annual report how your company has developed quality circles, management teams, etc., to help the company improve productivity.

8. *Your employees want to see employees and not models portrayed in your annual report.*

   Your report will come through with much more sincerity and integrity if it contains photos of actual employees at work. Show them in the plant operating equipment, or out in the field doing service work in customer's places of business. When you use a picture of an employee in your annual report, give the employee's name and job as further recognition of the value of this employee to the company.

9. *Your employees want information about the future dividends that they will earn on their stock held in the company.*

Are the dividends being increased? Are dividends being restored if they were eliminated during the 1981–83 recession? Many of your employees rely upon dividends from your company. Share with them as much information as you can about the future of the dividends that they will receive from your company.

HOW TO DEVELOP A THEME FOR YOUR ANNUAL REPORT

It is well to give serious thought to a theme for your annual report. The report holds together better if each section relates to the theme that has been set for the report. The theme is the vehicle that carries or projects the objective of the report, and it provides a cohesiveness that you will want to have.

Some companies, in an effort to establish a progressive image, use research and development themes in their reports. Others, for example, will use a 50th or 100th anniversary theme, where appropriate. You will be trying, through the development of a theme, to give to your readers a feeling of your company's leadership, its resourcefulness, and its dedication to excellence.

I have found that very few companies have a theme that they play throughout the annual report. Some companies will carry out the 100th anniversary theme—what progress the company has made over the years—what's ahead, etc. Others use a "We are a company on the move" scenario—backed up by statements and photos. Some reports portray a theme of diversification of product lines—others use a new technology thrust.

The readers of your annual report will stay with your report if it is held together by a well-thought out theme.

STOP A MOMENT: GET A FIX ON THE COSTS OF YOUR PROPOSED ANNUAL REPORT

There are many cost items that go into the preparation and distribution of your annual report. Before developing your "blockbuster" for the coming year, you'd better sit down with top management and go over the cost involved. Be sure to include every item of cost and put in a good extra margin for delays, errors, corrections, etc.

Get a budget approved before you do a lot of creative work which may later be axed by a highly cost-conscious chief executive officer.

Refer to the section on "Preparation of Annual Report" for detailed discussions on how to arrive at your cost. Your management may say, "This is the year, since profits are down, that we will go black and white"—or—"Let's have a brief narrative and include the 10-K in the annual report."

One of the best kept secrets in most corporations is the answer to the question, "How cost effective is our annual report?" It is my observation that many corporate presidents are not knowledgeable as to the cost of preparing the annual report or the effectiveness of what the corporate annual report is designed to accomplish. All too often the cost of the annual report is limited to the charges made for typesetting, printing, mailing, etc. The high cost of time expended by executives is generally not included in the cost of preparation of the annual report. The charges for the expenditure of time for the executives should, of course, be considered one of the major costs of preparing the corporate annual report.

The president of the corporation might well ask, "How effective has our annual report been in terms of doing the job assigned to it?" In my book, the corporate annual report has two main functions: (1) to influence stockholders to continue to hold their stock in the company, and (2) to attract others to become stockholders. If the annual report is not accomplishing these two goals, the cost effectiveness is minimal.

SHOULD YOU USE BLACK-AND-WHITE INSTEAD OF FOUR-COLOR PHOTOGRAPHY IN YOUR CORPORATE ANNUAL REPORT?

I have examined a number of very effective corporate annual reports that have been printed in black and white. Some of them have a color on the cover, but the narrative, photos, and the financial data are in one color. This might represent a good change of pace for you.

Generally, companies that have had a decline in earnings, or are showing a loss, are looking for ways to show their stockholders that they are aware of the need for cost controls, which includes the cost of preparing and printing an annual report. Good black-and-white photography can effectively present the activities of your company.

Stockholders are sometimes critical of high cost

four-color annual reports when the dividends have been cut or eliminated.

WHAT ROLE SHOULD YOUR PRESIDENT PLAY IN PREPARING THE ANNUAL REPORT?

Your president should be involved in the preparation and approval of your company's annual report. This is particularly true in the preparation of the Letter to Shareholders. The president will want to present his thoughts, problems, accomplishments, and projections in his own way—yes, in his own language.

You will want to discuss with the president the length of the message, the directness of approach, clarity, brevity, etc. Arrange with the president for a new photograph. A picture of the president in the plant or cafeteria talking to an employee might be preferable to a stilted bust shot showing a smiling face.

The president should approve in advance the theme of the report after having been given several choices.

There is no question—the greater the degree of involvement you can get on the part of your president in the annual report process—the better your chances are for a successful report. You will need to be in close contact with your president from the start of the process through the final draft. Your president will undoubtedly realize the important role that he or she can and should play in the development of a theme, the content of the report, the photographic presentation, the discussion of the future of the company, etc.

Here are some thought-starters for use in your discussions with your president:

1. Determine exactly what the role of the president will be through a discussion at the very earliest moment. Present in your initial meeting your ideas of a theme, content, format, photos, etc. Present your ideas for discussion. Don't expect the president to do the creative planning for you. That's your job. Let the president add to, modify, or subtract from the ideas that you present.
2. Get an agreement from the president as to who will write the president's letter. It would be preferable to have the president write the letter in draft form using certain guidelines that you will present.
3. Review with the president the ideas that you recommend be covered in the president's letter.
4. Discuss the possibility of having the president make projections as to future revenues, profits, return on investment, etc. If you have done this in the past, then determine whether the president wants to have you include a section that compares past projections to last year's results.
5. If the corporation has had a down year in terms of profits, or has shown a loss, discuss with your president how these results are to be handled in the annual report. This is a sensitive subject. There are many ways of accentuating the positive and minimizing the negative.
6. Review with your president the good news of the past year so that you will be able to present this information in an upbeat manner in the annual report.
7. Review with your president the sections of this book relating to "Eight Subjects that Your Stockholders Will Want You to Discuss in Your Corporate Annual Report" and "Eleven Areas of Immediate Concern to Security Analysts."
8. Reach a decision as to what information you will provide as to the future payment of dividends to your stockholders.
9. Discuss whether the president wants to include information concerning any acquisitions or divestitures.
10. Review in detail the top management changes, as well as changes in the members of the Board of Directors to be referred to in the annual report.
11. Discuss the photo that you will use of the president. Try to incorporate in the annual report an informal shot of the president at work. Talk about other photos of products, management, personnel, etc.
12. Discuss in what form the president would like to see the next copy of the annual report—semi-finished or finished.
13. Agree with the president that you can stop by from time to time to discuss parts of the annual report requiring the president's approval.

You will be calling upon various people in your organization to assist in the development of an effective annual report. It genuinely must be a team effort. A letter from the CEO to those who will be involved in the preparation of the report—asking for their fullest cooperation—will ease the way for a smooth operation.

Keep in mind that the work that you are asking others to do in the preparation and review of the annual report will be time consuming, and oftentimes will have to be handled over and above the regular responsibilities of the executive. You will want to make sure that you lessen the burden by providing all the help that you can in presenting a workable format for them to use.

IV HOW TO DESIGN A UNIQUE FRONT COVER FOR YOUR ANNUAL REPORT

Considerable thought should be given to the design of the cover of your annual report. A potential reader of your report can get a positive or a negative feeling about your company merely by taking a quick glance at the cover of your annual report.

Industry Week reported, "The purpose of the cover of a magazine is to get someone to pick it off the newsstand or to dramatize articles so that a reader will open the magazine. An annual report cover is different. Recipients get the report free. They are holding it in their hands when they see the cover. In fact, the cover is the one page shareholders are almost certain to see for a few seconds. Use that time and space to tell a brief story about the company—a story that affects the shareholder's pocketbook."

Some annual reports have been designed to tell a quick and hard hitting message that the company wants to get across. Some examples are:

Man is still the most extraordinary computer of all.

Apple Computer, Inc.

Annual Report

XEROX

Xerox Annual Report 1982

We exist to earn profits.

We use technology to develop product leadership.

We require satisfied customers for success.

We value our employees.

We behave responsibly as a corporate citizen.

Barnes Group Inc.

Strategies for Growth:

Develop or maintain leading positions in markets we serve or plan to enter.

Maximize internal growth by providing sufficient resources to our three operating groups.

Improve long-term return on investment by allocating greater resources to high-growth segments of our business and by improving productivity in all groups.

Accelerate our diversification program into new worldwide markets.

Stay flexible enough to respond to new growth opportunities and pursue these opportunities aggressively.

Beatrice Foods Co.

Five Year Corporate Objectives:

Return on equity to 18%.
Market Leadership.
Net earnings growth to 16%.
Diversification.
Real growth to 5%.
Community Responsibility.

ConAgra

Nothing fancy, just grow and earn.
This report tells how we increased sales over sixty percent this year to $1.37 billion, returned 26% on common equity and strengthened our hold on the future.

Hathaway Corporation

The major aim at Hathaway is to make money for shareholders through profitable growth.

To this end, fiscal 19__ net income more than doubled to $1,423,000 from $522,000.

H. J. Heinz Company

This H. J. Heinz Company Annual Report for 19__ contains more than the usual corporate accounting of a 12-month fiscal period. The year speaks for itself, and a good year it was, for the company and for its shareholders. The proof has been detailed between these covers. It need not be repeated here.

Let us talk instead about some remarkable people. First ten Heinz employees, who responded notably well when challenged to express themselves by way of poetry.

Then, ten of the world's leading illustrators, who applied skill and imagination to enhance what those employees had written.

Their story is inside.

Holiday Inns, Inc.

We make the world feel welcome . . .

Lear Siegler, Inc.

Objectives

Select and develop quality people

Achieve productivity improvement in all operations

Stimulate development of new products and markets

Maximize profitability and return on investment

Deploy assets according to changing economic conditions

Pursue acquisitions in complementary growth markets

Results

Six consecutive years of record sales and earnings

Six consecutive years of increased common share dividends

Ten consecutive years of increased earnings per share

Compound annual earnings growth of 25% since 19__

Levi Strauss & Co.

Quality never goes out of style

Merrill Lynch &Co., Inc.

Whatever direction the financial services industry may take, Merrill Lynch will be in front.

We will anticipate and guide this change, not just react to it. We will shape our own destiny.

Merrill Lynch & Co., Inc.

Our philosophy has always been: The customer comes first.

This has never been more important. We must constantly refine our organization to satisfy our customers' needs efficiently and creatively every working day.

Merrill Lynch & Co., Inc.

Our shareholders, clients and employees often judge us solely on the numbers. Certainly, the numbers are a legitimate measure of leadership.

But they're the rewards of leadership, not the reason.

PHH Group

What we do best is manage and control costs of company vehicles on the road and personnel on the move. And we do it efficiently in good times, and in bad. Last year, our 29% earnings growth exceeded our 22% growth rate for 20 years.

Standex

Standex ended fiscal 19__ with the best quarter and the best six-month period in its history. And the Company today enjoys the strongest Balance Sheet ever.

As a result of the implementation of cost-saving contingency plans, the upgrading of product mix and profit margins, and generally better business conditions, Standex is operating at improving levels of profit.

Westinghouse

We at Westinghouse are making productivity a way of life . . . and quality a matter of pride.

Many companies use the front cover of their annual report to portray their various product lines.

Examples:

Ford Motor Company—Portrayed photos of all of their cars and trucks.

Esmark, Inc.—Designed a montage of their various consumer products found on retailer shelves.

Hueblein, Inc.—Portrayed photographs of their wines, whiskies, Kentucky Fried Chicken, Grey Poupon Mustard, A-1 Steak Sauce, etc.

These covers become an advertising piece . . . an easy association of corporate products with consumer knowledge.

If your company is in the high technology field, you might want to show new and exciting products.

Example:

NCR

The Cover of this year's Annual Report shows a silicon wafer etched with over 100 miniature integrated circuits. Each circuit (shown about twice actual size) is a central processor for the revolutionary NCR/32 microprocessor chip set, introduced in 1982, and contains more than 70,000 components. Photo on facing pages shows wafers being prepared for plasma etching at NCR's new Colorado Springs facility which opened during the year.

For a change of pace, you might want to include a full-page photograph of the executives of your various divisions on the cover of your annual report. Amerace Corporation showed the executives of their seven divisions on the cover of their report. They are not only paying tribute to these executives, but as they stated on the inside of the cover, "They and thousands of other employees like them are the principal reason Amerace has long held a position of leadership in its various businesses."

Some reminders for the cover of your annual report.

Be sure that the name of your company is clearly displayed and in easily readable form at the top—preferably the right hand corner of the cover. It would be well to indicate the fiscal year of the report. This helps in the filing of annual reports by security analysts.

Make certain that the year is clearly indicated.

V
THE INSIDE FRONT COVER

Most readers of your annual report will look at the inside of the front cover. This is a place to provide information that will be of particular use to your stockholders. I recommend that you consider placing some of the following information on the inside cover:

1. *Explanation of the Cover*—Often the cover message is strengthened by a short paragraph of explanation, usually placed on the inside cover.
2. *Corporate Profile*—Since many companies have diversified, or made acquisitions, or have entered entirely new markets, their former profile has become obsolete. A brief description of the corporation should be provided on the inside cover.
3. *Stockholder Information*—Notice of annual meeting, corporate address, names of transfer agents, registrars, stock exchange, etc., might well be placed on the inside front cover.
4. *Outline of Key Management Policies*
5. *Table of Contents*—Most reports include a table of contents for reader convenience.
6. *Note*—This is a good place to include the address, phone number, and TWX of the corporate headquarters. All too often this is neglected, and the reader has to turn to the back pages to get this important information.

EXPLANATION OF THE COVER

It is helpful to your readers to explain the artwork that is on the front cover of your annual report.

Examples:

AMP Inc.—This photovoltaic solar energy panel module—which generates electricity directly from sunlight—exemplifies the exciting new uses of electronics arising as we enter the 1980s. AMP provides this special rugged environmentally sealed connector to link solar modules and is also developing new interconnection devices to more effectively join the generator cells within the module. As the leader in connection technology, AMP is deeply involved in meeting the challenge of the increasingly complex, varied requirements of electronic equipment being designed for the 1980s.

Robertshaw Controls Co.—Flashing on the NYSE big board and in brokers' offices across the country, Robertshaw's stock ticker symbol is a graphic reminder to investors of our total corporate capabilities.

Federated Department Stores, Inc.—The cover photograph of the main floor of Burdine's new store in West Palm Beach, Florida, is a vivid illustration of the visual excitement constantly sought by the interior designers of Federated stores.

Dun & Bradstreet—The computer terminal screen on the cover of this year's annual report graphically displays the progress of Dun & Bradstreet's earnings and dividends per share during the past 40 years. For a closer look at the chart, please see page 49. Earnings growth in recent years resulted, in part, from investments in the development of new products and from widespread application of computer technology. For a special report on the Company's recently launched products, services and businesses, please turn to page 7.

YOUR CORPORATE PROFILE

All too often, those who plan the corporate annual report overlook the importance of the corporate profile. In many cases, the profile is placed in an inconspicuous corner of the report.

I suggest that considerable care and thought be given to the manner in which the company's profile is described. This is your opportunity to provide an overall look at the company. It is particularly important to stockholders who oftentimes have not had a full grasp of the size and scope of the company's operations. The corporate profile in effect gives an opportunity to say to your stockholders, "Here is what your company is all about."

CHECKLIST OF FACTS TO BE INCLUDED IN YOUR CORPORATE PROFILE

As you prepare your company's "Corporate Profile," determine if you want to make reference to the following:

Amount of Assets
Brand Names
Growth Pattern
Environmental Problems
Finding the Niche
Competitive Position
Date Company Started Operation
Number of People Employed
Listing on Exchanges
Marketing Patterns
Overseas Operations
Principal Products
Product Lines
Representation
Restructuring of Company
Sales and Earnings Increase over the Years
Worldwide Operations

The following are examples of corporate profiles:

AMERICAN HOME PRODUCTS

American Home Products Corporation is a leading manufacturer and marketer of prescription drugs and medical supplies, packaged medicines, food products, and household products and housewares. Our sales and earnings have increased for 30 consecutive years.

We have accomplished these records with products that receive the highest recognition from health care professionals and consumers. Many of our brands are the largest selling in their respective categories.

Prescription drugs and medical supplies represent an increasing portion of our business, accounting for 47% of total sales and 62% of earnings in 1982. Leading products include *Inderal, Lo/Ovral, Isordil* and *Monoject.*

Packaged medicines are a growing market with familiar, trusted names like *Anacin, Dristan* and *Preparation H.* 1982 sales were $595 million.

From *Chef Boy-Ar-Dee* pasta products to *Brach's* chocolates, our food products have solid shares of their market categories. Total sales in 1982 were $817 million.

Our many household products and housewares brands such as *Woolite, Easy-Off* Oven Cleaner, and *Ekco* pots, pans and packaging, generated total sales of $1,027 million.

The Corporation employs over 54,000 people in facilities around the world.

American Agronomics Corporation

American Agronomics Corporation is a vertically integrated citrus company, involved in every phase of growing, processing and marketing citrus. The Company owns groves, and through its division, Gold Grove Management Corporation, maintains groves for other owners. The Company plants trees, maintains them, harvests the fruit and supplies it to a number of processing plants including the Company's own processing subsidiary, American Orange Corporation, producers of orange concentrate and other citrus products and related by-products.

Con Agra

ConAgra is a diversified family of basic food businesses growing in partnership with the land.

We operate across the food chain in three basic food industries: Agriculture, Grain, and Food.

ConAgra's segments include major businesses in agricultural chemicals, feed and fertilizer, specialty retailing, grain processing, grain merchandising, poultry products, frozen prepared foods, and seafood. Our businesses have over 500 operating locations in 40 states, Puerto Rico, Canada, Spain and Portugal.

Many of our businesses lead their industries. ConAgra holds the number one position in the United States in crop protection chemicals distribution, flour milling, poultry processing, frozen prepared foods brand, and shrimp processing. And we are the largest publicly-held merchandiser of grain.

We are committed to demanding financial objectives and measuring our results against them as portrayed on pages four and five of this report. We achieve premium results through professional management, careful planning, and by doing many little things very well.

ConAgra's overall objective is to be the best earning food company in the United States as measured by return on common stockholders' equity.

"We build on Basics" summarizes our strength, success, and strategy for continued growth.

Digital

Digital first earned its reputation in the technical and scientific marketplace by building systems for computer users who needed powerful, well-engineered and inexpensive products to do their jobs. After 26 years of business, Digital continues to serve users who consider quality the key to their success.

Digital has carried that quality to a broad range of products and services now sold to a diversity of markets. The company sells equipment to laboratories, government, factories, schools and universities, small businesses, large offices, hospitals and farms. From the corner grocery store to Federal agencies, from the one-person law office to the largest industrial corporations, Digital provides products and services that meet the growing and changing needs of customers around the world.

As the price of computers has come down and as computers have become easier to use, markets have expanded rapidly. Digital's product range has expanded as well, and flexibility has allowed the company to become an important force in responsibly shaping the face of the computer age.

Digital is the world's second largest manufacturer of computers, associated peripheral equipment and related software and supplies. During Fiscal 19__ the company grew to 73,000 employees, with 30,000 sales and support specialists in 43 countries. In 19__ Digital ranked 95th on the Fortune 500 list of the largest industrial corporations in the United States.

Growth is the natural result of high demand for products, but it is not Digital's major goal. The company's primary goal is, and always has been, quality—in products, services, people, values and relationships with customers.

Holiday Inns, Inc.

Holiday Inns, Inc., is in the business of making people feel welcome—all over the world. In 19__, more than 220 million people enjoyed Holiday Inns' hospitality at its hotels, casinos and restaurants.

In 53 countries on five continents, Holiday Inn hotels offer comfortable accomodations to both the business and leisure traveler. Our hotel system is the world's largest with 312,302 rooms in 1,744 hotels, and has a 30-year history of providing guests quality and value for their lodging dollar.

The company's gaming operations are under the direction of Harrah's, which many consider the industry's premier hotel/casino operator. Our gaming facilities are located in all four U.S. gaming markets, and collectively have more table games, slot machines and square feet of casino space than any competitor. Harrah's hotel/casinos are rated among the finest in the world and are recognized for their superior service to customers.

Perkins Restaurants, Inc., is Holiday Inn's restaurant subsidiary, with 311 restaurants in 26 states and an established reputation as a quality family-restaurant chain.

Hospitality is the common denominator of our three principal businesses. Each was founded on the concept of providing excellence in quality and service at reasonable prices. In 19__, Holiday Inns, Inc., entered its fourth decade with renewed commitment to that ideal.

Honeywell

Honeywell is an international company dedicated to advanced technology and offering high quality products and services in the fields of information processing, automation and controls. Our products and services are used by Honeywell customers to improve the productivity of their employees, processes and businesses, and to assist in the management of energy resources and the environment.

Rockwell International

We are a $7.4 billion, multi-industry company that manufactures a wide range of high-technology products in four major business areas—Aerospace, Electronics, Automotive and General Industries.

Of the 100,000 Rockwell International employees, more than 16,000 are engineers and scientists, the source of our technological strength.

In profiles beginning on page 14, we recognize a few of the tens of thousands of people who help make us the company "where science gets down to business."

Rockwell's continuing progress is a tribute to the talent and hard work of all our employees in 26 countries throughout the world. This report is dedicated to them.

SCM Corporation

SCM Corporation is a diversified manufacturer of consumer and industrial products with most of its operations in five industries: chemicals, coatings, pulp and paper, foods and consumer products.

About half of SCM's products are well known to consumers: Smith-Corona typewriters, Glidden paints, Durkee foods and Proctor-Silex appliances. SCM's major businesses are divided into operating groups competing in over 100 product lines.

SCM's 9.5 million common shares are owned by 29,300 shareholders. The Company employs approximately 25,500 people and has over 70 major manufacturing locations in the U.S. and around the world.

Spectra-Physics

Throughout our 22-year history, a basic tenet of Spectra-Physics' business strategy has been to explore the enormous potential of laser energy; to support the work of others in this field through our research and applications engineering and expertise; to keep abreast of emerging laser technologies, and to invest aggressively in those appearing to have outstanding market potential. Our successful ventures into advanced gas and solid-state laser instruments, laser alignment and machine control systems, optical scanning, high-power industrial lasers, and more recently, free electron laser research and miniaturized diode laser chips are examples of our commitment to that original strategy.

We estimate the current world market for laser technology to be about $3.2 billion, and growing at roughly 23% a year. Spectra-Physics enjoys a special position in this market as the largest and best known of some 75 companies specializing in the manufacture of laser devices and components. It is also the most broadly diversified of these companies, participating in each of the seven largest commercial markets for lasers, as well as the large government-funded sector.

Spectra-Physics is also a major manufacturer and marketer of chromatographs and specialized computers for automating analytical chemistry.

Our stock is traded on the New York Stock Exchange under the symbol SPY.

The Travelers Insurance Co.

The Travelers Insurance Co. is the basic business of The Travelers, which is one of the largest investor-owned insurance and financial service institutions in the world. Our purpose is to provide security for individuals, families, businesses and other organizations. The Company writes every principal form of life, accident and health and casualty-property insurance. We also offer a broad array of pension and other investment management services.

There are 30,000 people at work in The Travelers organization, many of whom are stationed at some 375 field offices that together serve all the company's geographic markets. Throughout the world, The Travelers makes insurance and related services available through subsidiaries or arrangements with foreign-based carriers.

At the end of the year, The Travelers had assets of $24 billion, more than $119 billion of life insurance in force, and shareholders' equity of $2.8 billion.

Varo, Inc.

Varo, Inc. is a major manufacturer of high technology products, such as night vision equipment and image intensification tubes, weapons delivery systems, power conversion products, metal optics and semiconductor products. Most of the Company's products have applications in the defense industry. In fiscal 19__, approximately 53 percent of revenues came from the U.S. government, 29 percent came from other domestic customers, and 18 percent came from foreign customers.

Varo, Inc. was established in 1946 and is based in Garland, Texas, near Dallas. The Company employs approximately 1,490 people. Varo's common stock is traded on the New York Stock Exchange with symbol: VRO.

Western Digital Corporation

Western Digital Corporation has established a unique position in the fast-moving microelectronics industry. We've played an important role in extending the limits of electronic technology. More importantly, we've succeeded in making the leading edge work for our customers. By listening to their needs, and by applying our technological expertise to specific, well-defined opportunities, we have developed a selection of proprietary LSI devices and intelligent subsystems that are particularly responsive to the needs of the marketplace. Today, we manufacture and market over 150 such products serving the personal computer, office automation and industrial automation markets with innovative approaches to the storage and communication of digital information.

Shareholders—The Owners of Ball Corporation

Who owns Ball Corporation? At the end of 1983, there were 5,830 individuals, trusts and other shareholders of record who can be identified as owners of Ball Corporation common stock. In addition, there were another 1,988 shareholders who were Ball employees enrolled in the company's stock purchase plan. Most of their stock is held by a trustee. Finally, countless more are represented in the stock held by financial institutions or owned by banks, mutual funds and pension funds. On the following pages, you will meet three of these owners of Ball—a farmer-homemaker, a stockbroker and a participant in the Ball employee stock purchase plan. They will share their thoughts on the company, what prompted them to buy Ball stock and what they expect to receive on their investments.

CPT Is Committed

CPT believes its success is a direct result of serving its customers—not by selling hardware and software, but by providing solutions. We have supported this precept since our founding and will continue to uphold it in the future. As stated in the company's Corporate Philosophy Statement, CPT has made the following commitments:

CPT is committed to excellence.

We are committed to excellence. Our products and services will be of the highest quality and highest value. We will develop some products internally; but, where others excel, we will work with them to obtain products that will best meet the needs of our customers. In short, we will offer the best that can be found—anywhere.

CPT is committed to its customers.

We at CPT are committed to developing, with each of our customers, a permanent relationship. To achieve this we will continue to develop mutual confidence, treat each customer honestly and individually, and provide practical solutions for enhancing office productivity. We value each of our customers and will convey that attitude in all of our dealings with them.

CPT is committed to its distribution network.

CPT will continue to maintain its extensive distribution network to ensure we are able to address the worldwide needs of our customers. We will continue to be selective in our choice of dealers and distributors and will provide them with the products, training, and support they need to achieve success.

CPT is committed to its employees.

Our employees are our primary asset. We will provide for them a working environment where everyone can contribute, where challenge and opportunity abound, and where talent is recognized and hard work rewarded.

CPT is committed to the community.

We will be a responsible citizen in every community and nation we serve. It is our intention to see that each environment in which we operate will be enhanced by our presence.

STOCKHOLDER INFORMATION

I would suggest that you provide shareholder information on the inside front cover. There is no reason why your shareholders should have to search through your annual report to find information about the annual meeting, stock listings, transfer agents, etc. A good example of shareholder information that should be included on the inside front cover is as follows:

Arvin:

Annual Meeting:

The annual meeting of Arvin shareholders will be held at 10:30 a.m. (E.S.T.) on Thursday, April 16, 19__ at Lincoln Center in Columbus, Indiana. All shareholders are cordially invited.

Stock Listings:

The common shares and preferred shares of the Company are listed on the New York and Midwest Stock Exchanges. Common stock symbol: ARV.

Transfer Agent and Registrar:

Harris Trust and Savings Bank, Chicago.

Form 10-K:

A copy of Arvin's Form 10-K, as filed with the Securities and Exchange Commission, is available to shareholders upon written request to The Secretary, Arvin Industries, Inc., 1531 Thirteenth Street, Columbus, Indiana 47201. The Form 10-K will be printed and ready for distribution on April 15, 19__

Company Headquarters:

Arvin Industries, Inc., 1531 Thirteenth Street, Columbus, Indiana 47201 Telephone: (812) 372-7271.

Arvin Industries, Inc. is an equal opportunity employer.

Johnson:

Shareholder Dividends

Johnson Controls has paid consecutive quarterly cash dividends since 1901. The cash dividend on common shares was increased for the seventh successive year in 1982.

Shareholders are able to conveniently acquire common shares of Johnson Controls, Inc. by participating in our Automatic Dividend Reinvestment Plan. Purchases through supplemental cash payments are also permitted under the plan, which eliminates broker fees and commissions. Participation authorization cards are available from the First Wisconsin Trust Company, P.O. Box 2054, Milwaukee, WI 53201.

Research reports on Johnson Controls are available by writing:

Robert W. Baird & Co., Inc.
777 East Wisconsin Avenue
Milwaukee, WI 53202
Martin A. McDevitt, Jr.

Drexel Burnham Lambert, Inc.
60 Broad Street
New York, NY 10004
Terence M. York

Kidder Peabody & Co., Inc.
10 Hanover Square
New York, NY 10005
Stephen J. Albert

The Milwaukee Company
250 East Wisconsin Avenue
Milwaukee, WI 53202
William R. Walker

Paine Webber Mitchell Hutchins Inc.
140 Broadway—25th Floor
New York, NY 10005
Robert T. Cornell

Stock Market Information

Hospital Corporation of America

The Company's common stock is listed on the New York Stock Exchange and is traded under the symbol HCA. On December 31, 1983, HCA had 21,298 shareholders of record.

Quarterly stock and dividend information for the last two years is shown below. The stock prices and the dividend per share data have been adjusted to reflect the 4-for-3 stock split effective in January 1983.

	Common Stock				*Dividends Declared Per Share*	
	1983		*1982*		*1983*	*1982*
	High	*Low*	*High*	*Low*		
1st Qtr.	$52.63	$35.38	$26.38	$18.50	$.10	$.0825
2nd Qtr.	56.63	47.38	25.50	20.00	.10	.0825
3rd Qtr.	55.38	42.00	33.50	21.00	.10	.0825
4th Qtr.	47.88	35.38	44.75	31.63	.10	.0825
Full Year	$56.63	$35.38	$44.75	$18.50	$.40	$ .33

Quarterly Stock Prices
(high and low dollars, adjusted for splits)

$60

45

30

15

0

79 80 81 82 83

Dividends Declared
(dollars in millions)

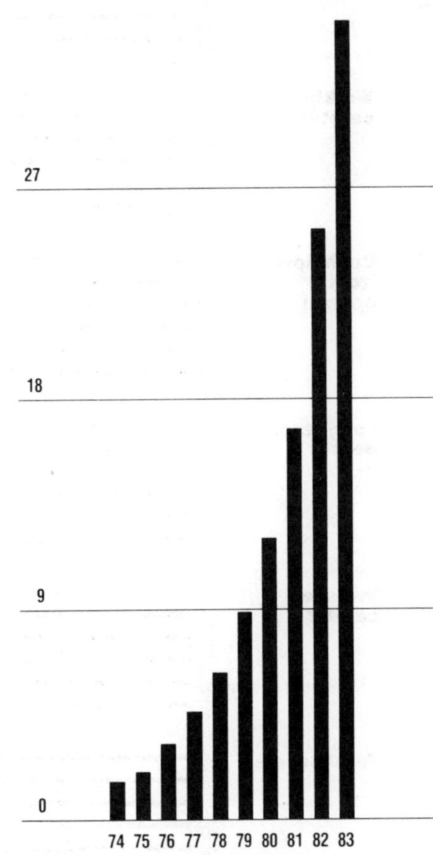

Selected Financial Data

Corcom, Inc. and Subsidiaries

Net sales *(In thousands of dollars)*

Year	Value
83	$26,120
82	20,986
81	19,385
80	19,030
79	15,449
78	11,713

Earnings before income taxes *(In thousands of dollars)*

Year	Value
83	$2,205
82	1,580
81	2,002
80	1,917
79	1,796
78	1,933

Net earnings *(In thousands of dollars)*

Year	Value
83	$1,808
82	1,304
81	1,542
80	1,392
79	1,092
78	1,005

Net earnings per common and common equivalent share *(In thousands of dollars)*

Year	Value
83	$ .61
82	.47
81	.56
80	.55
79	.52
78	.49

Stockholders' equity *(In thousands of dollars)*

Year	Value
83	$22,983
82	12,224
81	10,904
80	9,362
79	4,073
78	2,878

Stockholders' equity per share *(In thousands of dollars)*

Year	Value
83	$7.69
82	4.42
81	3.99
80	3.73
79	1.93
78	1.39

Working capital *(In thousands of dollars)*

Year	Value
83	$17,509
82	7,069
81	6,715
80	6,040
79	3,414
78	3,027

Cash flow from operations *(In thousands of dollars)*

Year	Value
83	$3,414
82	2,409
81	2,265
80	1,957
79	1,447
78	1,236

Long term debt *(In thousands of dollars)*

Year	Value
83	$1,235
82	1,247
81	1,258
80	1,234
79	3,243
78	1,000

Invested capital *(In thousands of dollars)*

Year	Value
83	$24,218
82	13,471
81	12,162
80	10,596
79	7,316
78	3,878

Total assets *(In thousands of dollars)*

Year	Value
83	$27,519
82	16,785
81	13,677
80	12,519
79	10,442
78	5,431

KEY MANAGEMENT

Most companies list the names and titles of their key executives at the end of their annual report. It's difficult to get a good sense of who—beyond the president—is running the show if the reader has to read through 40 pages of an annual report. Oftentimes the reader has cast aside the report before getting to the key management review.

In view of the importance of the management of the company, I suggest you include a "Key Management" section in the early pages of the report. Set out the names of the major personnel, job titles, ages, length of service with the company, etc. Use good-sized pictures—preferably in work situations.

HOW TO OUTLINE YOUR KEY MANAGEMENT POLICIES

Some companies use the inside of their front cover to outline their key management policies, purpose, or strategies:

Examples:

Ryan Homes, Inc.

1. Our objective is to show yearly growth of at least 15% in the number of customers we supply with our products and services; growth in the opportunity for individual self-development in order to fulfill our professional responsibilities; and growth in the value of our shareholders' investment.
2. Our primary marketing effort is directed toward moderate income families with the aim of providing new housing for an increasingly larger share of the population.
3. We intend that our product planning and pricing strategy will result in houses which provide "an easily observable better value" while at the same time being responsive to customer product preferences.
4. We expect to develop important changes in product design, manufacturing techniques, and organizational structure through evolution rather than revolution.
5. Our allocation of financial, physical, and personnel resources will be creative and aggressive but nevertheless conservative in terms of risk.
6. We are committed to a program of fair, courteous treatment of our customers from the moment of their first contact as prospects through the sale, construction and occupancy of their homes.
7. We encourage our people to develop their maximum potential and believe in sharing the benefits that accrue to the company with those who helped to create them.
8. Our theory of management is reflected in a "consultative" style of decision-making whereby we arrive at decisions after consulting with those who are expected to execute the decisions.
9. Our organization is structured to achieve the delicate balance between centralization and decentralization which should blend the specialized experience and judgment of the central staff with the market knowledge of the local manager.

Simmonds:

Simmonds Precision—A Profile

Simmonds Precision designs and produces advanced electronic systems and components for aerospace and industrial applications. We employ approximately 3,000 men and women at manufacturing, assembly, repair, sales and support facilities in the United States, Canada, Europe and the Far East. Our stock is traded on the New York Stock Exchange. (Symbol: SP)

Purpose:

It is our purpose to be an outstanding company which provides essential, high quality products and services and earns significant profits and a high return on invested capital. To fulfill this purpose, we will:

Encourage participative management at all levels of the company.

Strive for excellence and not efficient mediocrity.

Encourage individual development and promote dignity and respect for each employee.

Accept the social responsibilities of doing business.

Reject unethical business practices.

Regard the quality of the process as important as the results.

Strategy:

Our strategy is to build Simmonds Precision into an international electronics company and be a leader in providing systems, hardware and service to defined aerospace and industrial markets. We will:

Apply our resources to produce extraordinary results, recognizing that establishing priorities for critical new investments and abandonment of old investments are essential management disciplines.

Make strategic investments to insure long-term competitiveness.

Achieve the corporate goals on a medium-risk basis.

Develop an active marketing and engineering capability to achieve and maintain leadership in our chosen markets.

Establish an effective business development process to generate new products, use new technologies and enter new markets through internal development and acquisition.

Develop our human resources as our most valuable asset.

VI
HOW TO PRESENT THE TABLE OF CONTENTS IN AN INTERESTING WAY

There are various ways to present the "Table of Contents."

Examples:

CONTENTS

Contents

ELECTRO-NEUCLEONICS, INC.

Contents

Table of Contents

Damon Corporation Annual Report 1983

Table of Contents

VII
FINANCIAL HIGHLIGHTS

Many readers of your report won't go much beyond analyzing the highlights of your operations. For many stockholders, this is the most important part of your annual report. This is the place to present your figures in clear and concise terms.

SHOWING PERCENTAGES OF INCREASES IS VERY HELPFUL TO THE READER

Examples:

Financial Highlights

For the years ended August 31, 1983, 1982 and 1981 (Dollars in thousands, except per share amounts)

	1983	**% Change**	1982	% Change	1981
Net sales	**$564,497**	**+ 15.1**	$490,567	+ 18.0	$415,747
Income before taxes	**49,972**	**+ 14.7**	43,584	+ 74.9	24,925
Provision for taxes	**19,240**	**+ 12.8**	17,052	+ 39.9	12,188
Net income	**30,732**	**+ 15.8**	26,532	+ 108.3	12,737
Per share data:					
Earnings	**$1.50**	**+ 15.4**	$1.30	+ 85.7	$0.70
Cash dividends paid	**0.60**	**+ 11.1**	0.54	+ 3.8	0.52
Shareholders' equity	**11.26**	**+ 8.7**	10.36	+ 6.6	9.72
Average shares outstanding	**20,536**	**+ 0.3**	20,466	+ 11.8	18,300

Financial Highlights

FISCAL YEAR ENDED JUNE 30

	1983	1982	% Increase
Total Revenues	**$178,455,000**	$145,027,000	23
Net Income	**$ 17,721,000**	$ 15,863,000	12
Primary Earnings Per Share	**$ 1.07**	$ .97	10
Number of Common Shares Outstanding	**16,551,587**	16,282,068	2
Long-Term Debt (exclusive of debentures)	**$ 5,327,000**	$ 4,712,000	13
Shareholders' Equity	**$111,651,000**	$ 89,421,000	25
Number of Employees	**1,581**	1,368	16
Net Income as Percent of Revenues	**9.9%**	10.9%	
Return on Average Shareholders' Equity	**17.6%**	22.3%	
Current Ratio	**4.4-1**	3.9-1	

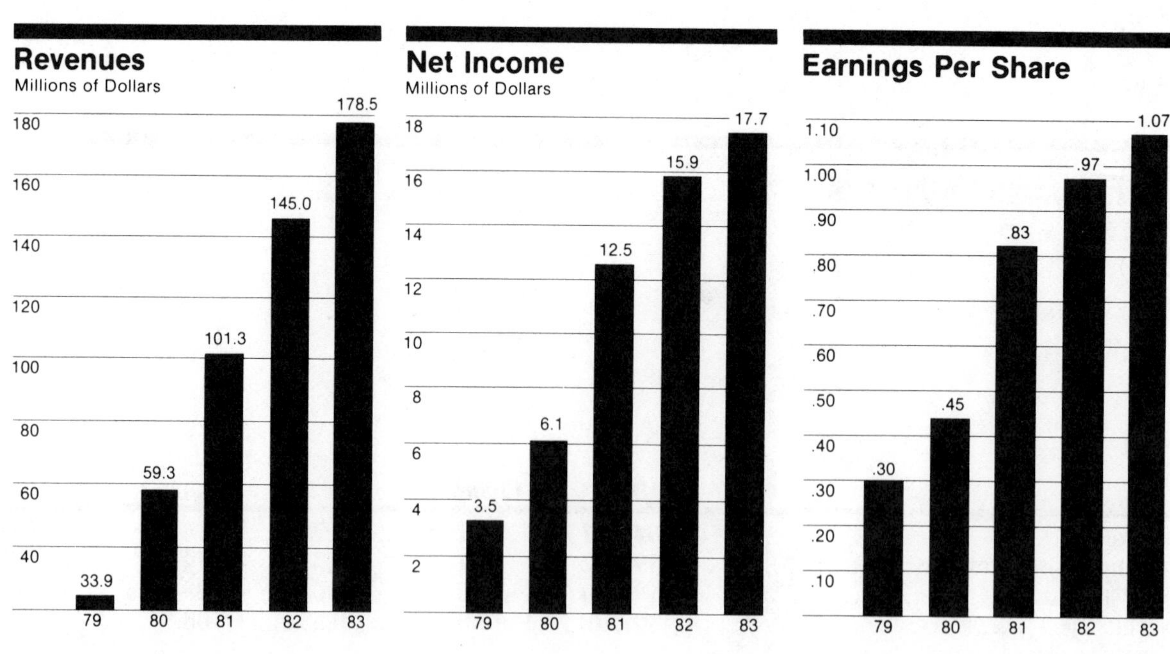

Financial Highlights About This Report

DESCRIPTION	1983	1982
Net sales	**$ 17,561,888**	$ 16,040,999
Income before provision for income taxes	**$ 1,749,462**	$ 2,260,969
Net income	**$ 1,844,469**	$ 1,726,093
Net income per share (Primary)	**$ .35**	$ .32
Stockholders' Equity	**$ 12,947,926**	$ 12,068,318
Net worth per share	**$ 2.44**	$ 2.28
Order backlog	**$ 9,400,000**	$ 7,600,000
Working capital ratio	**1.72 to 1.00**	2.77 to 1.00
Working capital in dollars	**$ 4,061,002**	$ 4,337,160
Investments	**$ 7,211,761**	$ 4,696,110
Cash dividend per share	**5¢**	5¢

The Last Five Years

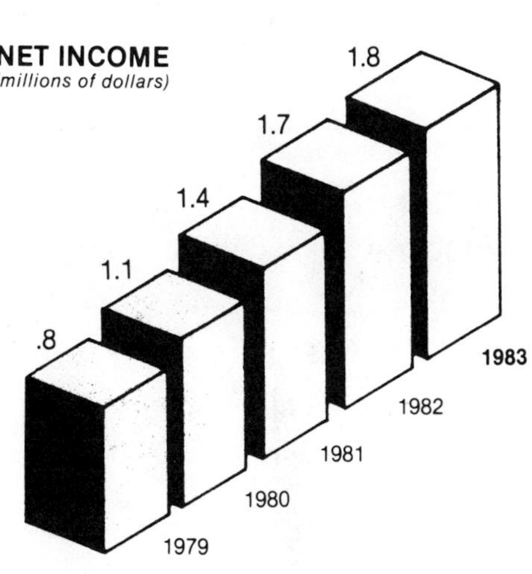

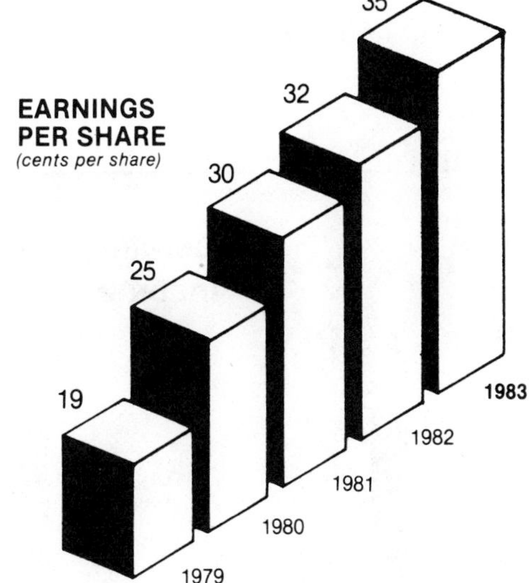

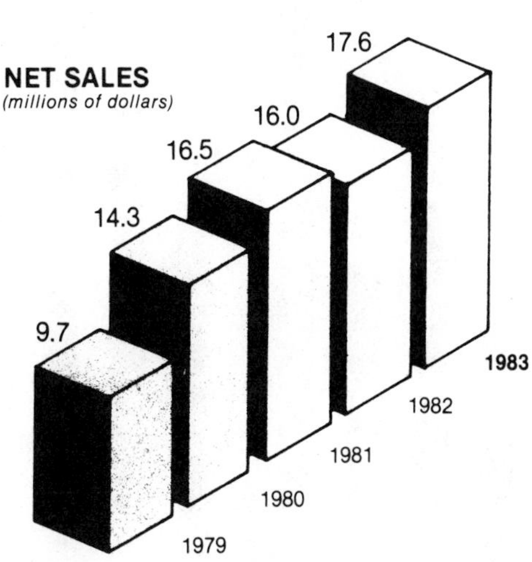

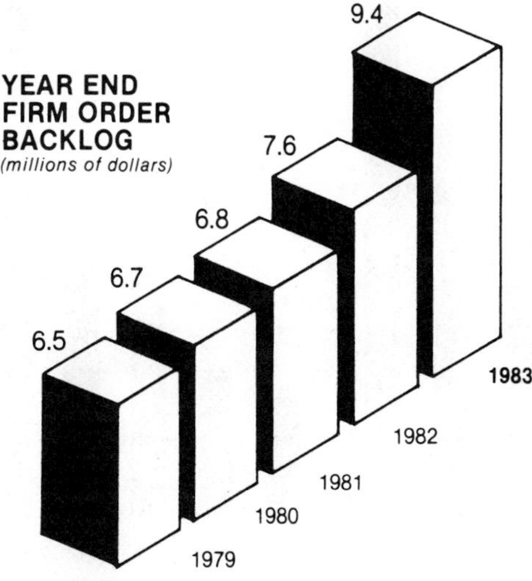

Financial Highlights – Consolidated

	Fiscal Years		Percent
	1983	1982	Increase (Decrease)
Net Sales	**$24,422,000**	$13,174,000	85%
Operating Income	**$ 2,747,000**	$ 959,000	186%
Federal and State Income Taxes	**$ 696,000**	$ 100,000	596%
Net Income	**$ 1,111,000**	$ 356,000	212%
Average Common and Common Equivalent Shares Outstanding	**5,483,515**	4,486,626	22%
Primary Earnings Per Common Share	**$ .22**	$ .09	144%
Backlog of Unfilled Orders	**$ 9,294,000**	$ 6,507,000	43%
Working Capital	**$ 7,574,000**	$ 8,848,000	(14%)
Current Ratio	**2.2**	3.2	(31%)
Long-term Debt to Equity	**86%**	174%	
Stockholders' Equity	**$ 4,682,000**	$ 3,507,000	34%
Equity Per Share	**$ .85**	$ .78	9%

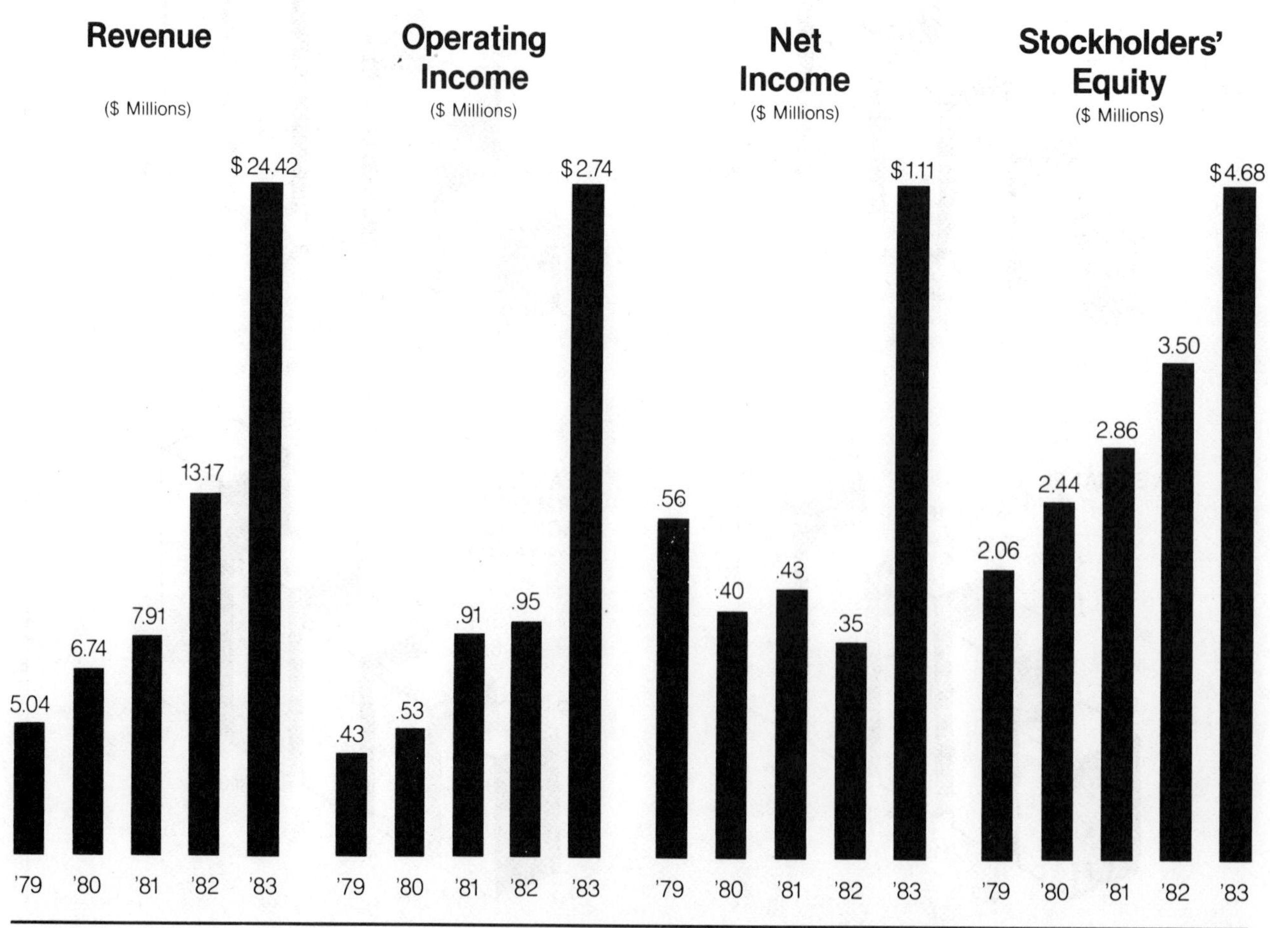

Tektronix 1983 Income Highlights in thousands

52 Weeks to May 29, 1982		52 Weeks to May 28, 1983		Increase (Decrease)		
$1,221,000	**100%**	**$1,124,000**	**100%**	**$(97,000)**	**−8%**	**CUSTOMER ORDERS,** some of which were
321,000	26%	253,000	23%	(68,000)	−21%	UNFILLED ORDERS at year-end.
$1,195,748	**100%**	**$1,191,380**	**100%**	**$ (4,368)**		**SALES REVENUE comprised of**
567,994	47%	526,681	44%	(41,313)	−7%	INSTRUMENT products,
441,420	37%	455,336	38%	13,916	3%	DESIGN AND DISPLAY products, and
186,334	16%	209,363	18%	23,029	12%	COMMUNICATIONS products—sold to
729,369	61%	734,223	62%	4,854	1%	UNITED STATES customers, and
466,379	39%	457,157	38%	(9,222)	−2%	INTERNATIONAL customers.
14,470	2%	12,601	1%	(1,869)	−13%	OTHER REVENUE from non-operating sources.
$1,130,765	**95%**	**$1,155,267**	**97%**	**$ 24,502**	**2%**	**LESS COSTS AND EXPENSES** to be paid
581,269	49%	613,637	51%	32,368	6%	TO EMPLOYEES who design, produce, sell and service products or who support their efforts;
436,726	36%	448,807	38%	12,081	3%	TO SUPPLIERS for materials, components, supplies, services and the use of their property and funds;
56,297	5%	26,113	2%	(30,184)	−54%	TO GOVERNMENTS as taxes in the United States and abroad—and to provide
56,473	5%	66,710	6%	10,237	18%	FOR FACILITIES depreciation which allows for the use, wear and aging of buildings and equipment.
$ 79,453	**7%**	**$ 48,714**	**4%**	**$(30,739)**	**−39%**	**RESULTING IN EARNINGS** to be reinvested in the business and for dividends to shareowners.
$4.25	**100%**	**$2.57**	**100%**	**$(1.68)**	**−40%**	**EARNINGS PER SHARE** based on average shares.
.98	23%	1.00	39%	.02	2%	DIVIDENDS PER SHARE paid to shareowners.

Vital Statistics of SGL Industries, Inc.

- 1,931,000 shares outstanding
- 2,400 shareholders
- Cash dividends of $.25 per share adjusted (have increased each year since 1972)
- Stock dividends, generally 6% since 1962
- Sales from continuing operations of $45,218,000
- Net income of $1,620,000
- Adjusted earnings per share of $.69
- Gross margin = 29%
- Return on sales = 4%
- Capital expenditures = $1,322,000
- Depreciation = $1,225,000
- Working capital = $8,777,000
- Current ratio = 2.4:1
- Total assets = $26,246,000
- Debt-equity ratio = 16%
- Shareholders' equity = $17,799,000
- Stock price = 10¾ (7/29/83)
- Employees = 850
- Backlog = $7,579,000

Financial Highlights

Years ended July 31,	**1983**	1982	1981
Net sales	**$45,218,000**	$48,520,000	$45,942,000
Net income	**$1,620,000**	$2,783,000	$2,686,000
Per share(1)	**$.69**	$1.16	$1.13
Cash dividends declared	**$576,000**	$514,000	$455,000
Per share(2)	**$.25**	$.23	$.22
Stock dividend	**6%**	6%	6%
Stock split	**3 for 2**	—	—
Repurchased shares	**470,000**	—	—
Backlog	**$7,579,000**	$6,768,000	$7,840,000

(1) Based on weighted average number of shares outstanding adjusted for subsequent stock dividends and the 3 for 2 stock split in June 1983.

(2) Restated to reflect June 1983 stock split.

Three for Two Stock Split and Repurchase at a Glance

During June 1983, SGL Industries split its stock 3 for 2 and repurchased approximately 470,000 shares of stock from the Lax trusts and family. Here's the effect at a glance.

As of July 31, 1983	Before Stock Split	After Stock Split	After Stock Repurchase**
Total shares outstanding	1,601,000	2,401,000	1,931,000
A shareholder owning 1,000 shares (1,000 × 3/2)	1,000	1,500	1,500
Shareholder proportional increase in ownership of the Company	N/A	None	24.3%
Adjusted earnings per share*	$1.02	$.67	$.69
Current ratio	4.1:1	4.1:1	2.4:1
Debt-equity ratio	7.6%	7.6%	15.6%

*Based on weighted average number of shares outstanding.

**As reported in accompanying financial statements.

Highlights of 1982

Allied Corporation

In 1982 Allied...

- **made the third highest profit in its history**
- **agreed to acquire The Bendix Corporation and acquired a large minority interest in the Martin Marietta Corporation**
- **increased domestic oil and gas reserves by 38 percent through an acquisition**
- **established two new operating companies to expand its electrical/electronic businesses**
- **continued to increase R&D spending and funding of oil and gas exploration**
- **improved productivity, reduced costs and cut working capital needs to position itself for faster growth when the economy recovers**

UTL ACTIVE CONTRACTS AT JUNE 30, 1983

Contract Type	Customer	Product	Contract Value	Backlog
Fixed Price	Foreign Government	Shipborne C^3I System	$ 6,776,000	$ 342,000
Fixed Price	U.S. Government	Sub-system improvement for AN/ALQ-133	4,901,000	2,082,000
Fixed Price	U.S. Government	Advanced Quick Look	22,085,000	18,675,000
Fixed Price	40 contracts for U.S. Government	Spares and support for AN/ALQ-133	1,764,000	1,020,000
Cost-plus	U.S. Government	Ground ESM system	400,000	221,000
Various	12 contracts for various customers	Airborne ESM systems	31,339,000	15,460,000
			$67,265,000	$37,800,000

Employee Data	
Research and Engineering	100
Manufacturing	39
Other Technical	49
Administrative, Sales and Clerical	68
	256

1973-1983: TEN YEARS IN REVIEW

A review of Emerson's performance over the past ten years puts into perspective the basic elements of the Company's growth and operations strategy. During the ten-year period, 1973-1983, the size and scope of the Company's operations has changed. Sales have grown to approximately three times their former size and net earnings are now approximately three and one-half times those of 1973.

The corporate strategic planning framework consists of a growth strategy that can be broken down into Emerson's fundamental sources of growth;

Domestic Core Business,
New Products,
International,
Government and Defense,
New Partners

and an operations strategy based on being the low-cost producer in the major markets served by the Company.

The plans and programs required to meet the Company's growth and profit targets are developed in detail at annual division planning conferences. During the past ten years, the plans and programs identified and implemented in support of the growth and profit targets required a gross investment of $1.6 billion and provided an incremental rate of return on total operating capital of 18.6 per cent.

Emerson Performance

(Dollars in Thousands Except Per Share Amounts)	1973	1983	10-Year Growth Rate
Net sales	**$1,192,790**	**$3,475,709**	**11.3 %**
Net earnings	**88,137**	**302,927**	**13.1 %**
Earnings per share	**1.32**	**4.42**	**12.8 %**
Dividends per share	**0.625**	**2.10**	**12.9 %**
Stockholders' equity	**536,600**	**1,701,745**	**12.2 %**
Return on average stockholders' equity	**17.4 %**	**18.6 %**	
Return on average total operating capital	**15.8 %**	**17.7 %**	
Long-term debt/total capitalization	**13.7 %**	**7.9 %**	

The performance of Emerson Electric against its strategic objectives over the past ten years can be summarized as follows:

- Achieved consistent, above-average sales and earnings growth.
- Repostured Emerson's core businesses for stronger market leadership, faster growth and better diversification through acquisitions and divestitures.
- Successfully blended short-term performance with a commitment to sustained new product and technology development.
- Managed a period of profitable international growth.
- Built a major defense supplier.
- Improved the profitability of the Company.
- Financed above-average growth and maintained a AAA balance sheet.

▪ *Achieved consistent, above-average sales and earnings growth in a volatile economic environment.*

Fiscal 1983 was the 26th consecutive year of increased earnings and earnings per share. This record of consistency was achieved in the volatile economic environment of the past ten years, ending with a two-year-long recession in 1982 and 1983 that dampened end-point growth comparisons. The ten-year period included three recessions, large swings in interest rates, both a weak and a strong dollar, double-digit and low inflation and fluctuating energy prices.

Results in Periods of Recession and Special Challenge

	1958 vs 1957	1961 vs 1960	1967 vs 1966	1970 vs 1969	1975 vs 1974	1980 vs 1979	1982 vs 1981	1983 vs 1982
Earnings								
Emerson(1)	**+0.8%**	**+15.3%**	**+13.3%**	**+9.7%**	**+0.8%**	**+13.1%**	**+5.5%**	**+1.9%**
All Mfgrs.(2)	−28.8%	−12.9%	−4.9%	−10.0%	−17.3%	−4.3%	−22.9%	−4.3%(3)
Sales								
Emerson(1)	**+6.5%**	**+32.7%**	**+13.2%**	**+3.9%**	**−2.2%**	**+9.9%**	**−3.2%**	**−2.4%**
All Mfgrs.(2)	−5.8%	+1.1%	+5.3%	+4.7%	+4.1%	+10.4%	−3.0%	+1.1%(3)

(1) Excluding acquisitions for each two-year period.
(2) Based on U.S. Commerce Department figures and years ending September 30.
(3) Projection by Merrill Lynch Economics based on three quarters of actual data.

During this period, Emerson continued its record of above-average growth. Earnings for the ten-year period grew at an annualized rate of 13.1 per cent while those of all manufacturers gained only 5.4 per cent. Emerson's sales grew at 11.3 per cent for the ten years, compared to all manufacturers at 8.0 per cent. Emerson's average earnings growth for the six five-year periods during the decade was 15.3 per cent while all manufacturers averaged 8.2 per cent. The Company's sales growth for the five-year periods averaged 13.6 per cent compared to 9.9 per cent for all manufacturers.

▪ *Repostured Emerson's core businesses for stronger market leadership, faster growth and better diversification through acquisitions and divestitures.*

During the last ten years,Emerson has improved its position in the markets it serves. In 1973, 66 per cent of Emerson's product lines held the number one or two position in their market. By 1983, 80 per cent of Emerson's product lines held the number one or two position, with 46 per cent in market leadership positions. This strong market position has contributed to the Company's programs to maintain its low-cost producer position, improve profitability and further increase market penetration. This has been key to the growth of the Company's core businesses during the past decade.

Market Leadership

Per Cent of Product Lines	Market Position 1	2	3	4	Other
1973	33%	33%	18%	11%	5%
1983	46%	34%	13%	4%	3%

In keeping with Emerson's goal of continually repositioning itself into faster growing market niches, the Company has successfully altered its mix of businesses through acquisitions, divestitures and internal growth. Between 1973 and 1983, the Company's mix of businesses changed significantly. While Emerson's basic businesses, appliance components and industrial motors and drives, have declined as a percentage of the total mix, the Company's higher technology process control and government and defense areas have increased. Most of the process control companies were acquired during the period and subsequently experienced rapid growth. The government and defense business grew to its present size primarily from internal development.

The Company's successful acquisition program has been based on a policy of limiting acquisitions to well-managed companies in markets Emerson knows and serves. Less publicized, but important to the process of repositioning the Company, are divestitures. Although Emerson has on occasion sold complete divisions, a more usual form of divestiture is product line pruning. Over the ten-year period, the Company has made 33 product line divestitures with combined annual sales of approximately $171 million in the year of divestiture. The result of Emerson's program to reposture the Company has been to increase the capital goods related portion of Emerson's commercial business from 44 per cent to 51 per cent during the past ten years.

- ***Successfully blended short-term performance with a commitment to sustained new product and technology development.***

An ever-increasing emphasis on the development of new products and technology within the Company has been one of the important achievements of the past ten years. In 1975 an aggressive new products program was introduced to formalize and focus the Company's development efforts, providing a key element of Emerson's internal growth plan. The objective of the new products program was to have new products represent ten per cent of total sales by 1985. The program has exceeded expectations and targets and is an important source of both past and future growth. 1983 new product sales represented $402 million, or 11.6 per cent, of the Company's total sales.

New Product Sales
(Dollars in Millions)

	1975	1976	1977	1978	1979	1980	1981	1982	1983
Sales Amount	$16	$33	$62	$103	$160	$256	$312	$356	$402
Per Cent of Total Sales	1.3%	2.2%	3.4%	4.7%	6.1%	8.3%	9.1%	10.2%	11.6%

In support of the new products and technology programs, the Company has increased its engineering and development expenditures every year since 1973. Total expenditures have grown from $16 million, or 1.71 per cent of sales, in 1973 to $93 million, or 2.68 per cent of sales, in 1983. This represents a growth rate of approximately 20 per cent over the ten-year period.

Research and Development Spending
(Dollars in Millions)

	1973	1974	1975	1976	1977	1978	1979	1980	1981	1982	1983
Expenses	$16	$21	$24	$30	$37	$45	$53	$68	$78	$90	$93
Per Cent of Sales	1.71%	1.85%	1.92%	1.99%	2.05%	2.07%	2.03%	2.22%	2.27%	2.57%	2.68%

The objective of Emerson's technology program is to develop within the divisions the technologies required to support both core and new product development. Emerson's divisions carry on their own development work, focused at the markets they serve. In addition, the divisions share the resources of three Advanced Development Centers working in areas of strategic importance to the Company. Advanced Development Centers are dedicated to motor technology, solid state sensors and microprocessor-based appliance controls. The Company also encourages research and development by funding projects beyond an individual division's resources with a Strategic Investment Program.

The Company has expanded its technology base through its venture capital company, InnoVen, which invests in emerging businesses with technologies of interest to Emerson. The Company also funds projects at major universities and employs a Technical Advisory Committee of distinguished engineering faculty members to keep it current with the latest technologies.

▪ *Managed a period of profitable international growth.*

In 1983 international sales totaled $832 million or 23.9 per cent of total sales, a dramatic increase from $149 million or 12.5 per cent of total sales in 1973. International sales' compound annual growth for the ten-year period was 18.8 per cent. This rapid growth was consistently accompanied by returns on total capital that approximated those of the Company as a whole.

International Sales
(Dollars in Millions)

	1973	1974	1975	1976	1977	1978	1979	1980	1981	1982	1983
International Sales	$149	$223	$280	$345	$410	$499	$610	$791	$807	$819	$832

Emerson's international growth has originated at the division level, with each autonomous unit developing its own foreign markets both through exports and foreign-based manufacturing. The Company's strategy has been to establish assembly operations overseas, sourcing component parts from our low-cost domestic plants.

International sales have leveled out over the past three years as the result of the strong dollar making export-led strategies less competitive and lowering the translated sales of our subsidiaries. International sales have, in addition, been impacted by the worldwide recession.

The result of Emerson's international expansion over the last ten years has been to position the Company in terms of products, markets and organization, to aggressively compete in global markets in future years.

▪ *Built a major defense supplier.*

In 1973 Emerson's government and defense business represented only three per cent of the Company's total sales, with $34 million in annual revenues. Emerson's defense-related business grew at 28.7 per cent during the past ten years to $423 million, or 12 per cent of Emerson's total sales.

Government and Defense Sales
(Dollars in Millions)

	1973	1974	1975	1976	1977	1978	1979	1980	1981	1982	1983
Gov't and Defense Sales	$34	$71	$103	$125	$146	$176	$199	$239	$288	$368	$423

Emerson's government and defense business today is broadly diversified over a relatively large number of programs which have increased in technological complexity. As the government and defense business has grown, it has segmented its activities into four areas of strategic importance: Electronics, Automatic Test Equipment, Electronic Warfare and Armaments.

Emerson's government and defense business finished fiscal 1983 with a record backlog of $715 million. Both the magnitude and the composition of the backlog point to continued strength in the government and defense business in the coming years.

▪ *Improved the profitability of the Company.*

By any measure, Emerson's profitability improved significantly between 1973 and 1983. Margins and returns on both equity and capital have shown marked increases. The key to this objective of increasing profitability is the Company's commitment to being the low-cost producer in each of the markets it serves.

Profitability

	1973	1974	1975	1976	1977	1978	1979	1980	1981	1982	1983
Return on Average Stockholders' Equity	17.4%	17.6%	17.1%	18.1%	19.7%	20.6%	20.6%	20.4%	21.1%	20.1%	18.6%
Return on Average Total Operating Capital	15.8%	15.4%	15.1%	16.4%	18.2%	18.5%	17.7%	17.4%	18.7%	18.2%	17.7%

Emerson's cost reduction program is one of the key elements of its low-cost producer strategy. Cost reduction has long been a way of life at Emerson. The momentum of this long-standing program helps to make it increasingly effective each year.

Individual projects are identified and implemented by cost reduction teams in each of Emerson's plants. These teams ensure the involvement of personnel at all levels. In 1983 cost reductions totaled $176 million, marking the 29th consecutive record year of the program. At 7.7 per cent, 1983 cost reductions were the highest as a percentage of cost of sales in the Company's history. An important part of the cost reduction effort is the Company's productivity improvement programs. In 1983 productivity improvement in our domestic plants reached 6.5 per cent.

The Company has the opportunity to continue to improve its relative low-cost position by capitalizing on the major strategic advantages it has established over the past decade. Emerson's strong market positions provide the Company with the economies of scale to justify major capital expenditures on manufacturing technology and systems aimed at improving process automation and our operating capital turnover. An increasing portion of the Company's capital budget is being allocated to cost reduction and productivity improvement programs, reaching a record level of $53 million, or 41 per cent of total capital expenditures in 1983.

▪ *Financed above-average growth and maintained a AAA balance sheet.*

During the past ten years Emerson has invested $1.6 billion in the Company, maintained sales and earnings growth at double-digit rates, and improved both the levels of profitability and the strength of the balance sheet. Emerson's financial position has never been stronger than at the close of 1983. The following chart details Emerson's financial position during the past ten years.

Financial Position

	1973	1974	1975	1976	1977	1978	1979	1980	1981	1982	1983
Current Ratio	3.5:1	2.9:1	3.2:1	2.9:1	2.7:1	2.6:1	2.5:1	2.6:1	2.5:1	2.6:1	2.7:1
Interest Coverage	26.8X	19.1X	17.2X	22.2X	23.0X	28.2X	16.2X	15.7X	18.8X	27.6X	33.8X
Long-Term Debt To Total Capital	13.7%	13.5%	13.5%	13.5%	10.9%	9.9%	14.9%	13.0%	10.8%	8.2%	7.9%

END

Note:

In preparing your corporate highlights, be sure that the type is bold. You are trying to deliver an important message to your readers—a message that will be retained.

OUR MOST RECENT 15 YEARS

	Number of Stores in Operation at Year-End	Average Size of Stores (Sq. Ft. of Selling Area) in Thousands	Average Sales Per Store in Millions	Total Sales in Millions	Net Income in Thousands	Earnings* Per Share
1983	147	30	$5.4	$784.7	$19,375	$2.14
1982	143	30	5.3	758.5	16,649	1.85
1981	144	30	5.0	750.9	14,317	1.61
1980	89	29	4.5	380.5	12,400	1.41
1979	80	27	4.5	345.6	9,853	1.13
1978	77	27	4.4	298.3	8,252	.95
1977	80	27	4.0	247.3	7,142	.83
1976	50	29	3.8	193.4	5,750	.68
1975	48	30	3.5	172.9	4,544	.55
1974	47	30	3.1	150.3	4,048	.49
1973	44	29	2.9	128.7	3,518	.42
1972	42	27	2.6	110.3	2,944	.35
1971	39	27	2.5	101.4	2,289	.28
1970	38	27	2.3	91.3	2,204	.27
1969	33	23	2.2	76.5	2,335	.28

FIVE YEAR COMPARISON

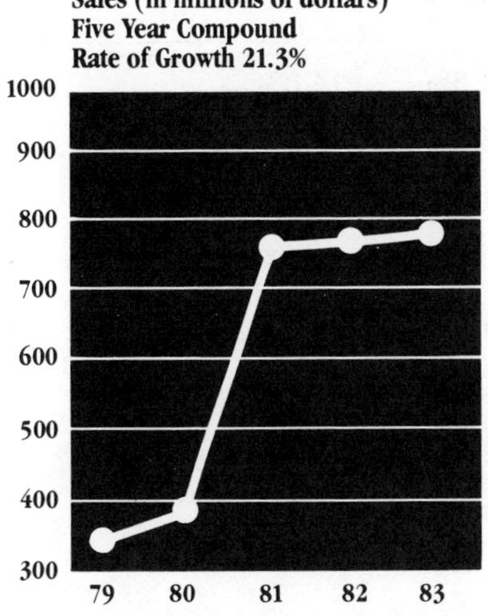

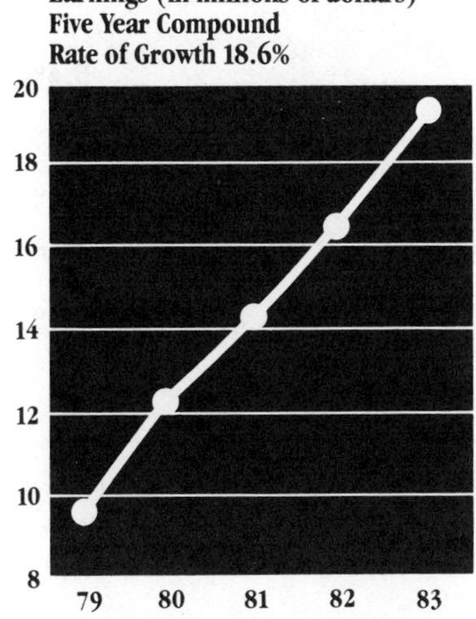

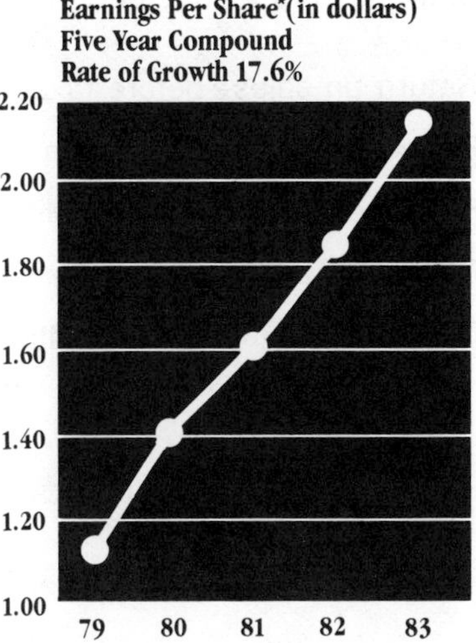

*Adjusted to reflect the one hundred percent common stock dividend declared in May, 1981 and the twenty-five percent common stock dividends declared in June 1977 and March 1978.

Note: Place the Current Figures Adjacent to the Headings

The readers of your annual report will appreciate your placing the current year's figures adjacent to the various headings. To further accommodate the readers, it would be helpful if you were to use a bolder type for the current year's figures in comparison to prior years' figures.

Financial Highlights

Dollar amounts in thousands, except per share data.

THREE YEARS' PERFORMANCE AT A GLANCE:

Fiscal Years Ended June 30	**1983**	1982	1981	% Change 83/82	% Change 82/81
Net sales	**$397,451**	$487,964	$570,693	−19	−14
Net income	**$ 16,042**	$ 33,162	$ 44,731	−52	−26
Net income per share	**$ 1.86**	$ 3.85	$ 5.20	−52	−26
Dividends per share	**$ 2.10**	$ 2.10	$ 2.00	—	+ 5
Shareholders' equity per share	**$ 33.30**	$ 33.48	$ 32.29	−1	+ 4
Return on sales—before taxes	**5.4%**	11.5%	14.8%		
Return on sales—after taxes	**4.0%**	6.8%	7.8%		
Return on average shareholders' equity	**5.7%**	11.9%	17.6%		
Return on average capital employed	**4.5%**	10.4%	15.8%		
Debt to capital employed ratio	**16.4%**	14.6%	1.8%		

If you wish to emphasize "Corporate Highlights" you might want to include a fly leaf.

Example:

19___ *Highlights*

New records again established for both sales and earnings

Acquisition of The McLain Grocery Company completed

Dividend rate increased to $1.24 per share

Warehousing productivity increased 4.9% marking the seventh consecutive year of improvement

Capital expenditures totaling $51.3 million were an all-time high

New foodservice center completed in Austin

Major enlargement of Houston distribution center enters final stage

New IGA group formed in Northern California

Highlights of the Year

- Delivered significant additions to the OASys product family, including the OASys 4000 series of ergonomic workstations, the OASys Laser Printer, 20- and 30-megabyte models of the OASys 64 clustered product and 3270 communications capability

- Demonstrated major new OASys products for managers and professionals: the OASys 2000 personal computing workstation and the OASys Interface for personal computers

- Introduced an entirely new product architecture for professionals and knowledge workers: SYSTEM ONE, which includes the Integrated Workstation and the Integrated System Server

- Introduced NBI NET, a local area network which ties the OASys and SYSTEM ONE product families together

- Hired 497 new NBI direct employees for a total of 1,846 and developed major new employee training and benefits programs to maintain a high quality work force

- Strengthened research and development substantially, increasing staff in the engineering department by more than 40 percent

- Continued to strengthen the sales organization, expanding the direct sales force by nearly 30 percent

- Opened four new domestic branch offices for a total of 33 and added 15 new dealer locations for a total of 76

- Took control of key international markets by purchasing distribution rights and operations for NBI products in Canada, West Germany and the United Kingdom and building direct sales organizations in those countries

- Developed a strong organizational relationship between manufacturing and engineering which shortened product development cycles and allowed the timely development and delivery of a broad range of new products

- Completed construction of and occupied a new 250,000-square-foot headquarters facility in Boulder, Colorado

- Obtained $40 million of new financing through the issuance of convertible debentures bearing 8.25 percent interest and listed the debentures on the New York Stock Exchange

SIMMONDS PRECISION

What We Did In 1982

Achieved record sales and earnings

Secured record new orders

Reported record year-end backlog

Increased dividend for 8th consecutive year

Achieved record productivity gain

Important "new wins" increased our market share

Installed our first robot

Made record capital expenditures

What We Didn't Do In 1982

Operate our industrial business profitably

Substantially increase our aerospace overhaul and repair business

What We Plan To Do In 1983

Again increase sales and earnings to record levels

Reduce our industrial business losses

Evaluate and modify our strategy to address the challenge and opportunities of the late 80's and early 90's

Widen our strategic productivity improvement program

Increase our investment in advanced manufacturing technology

Expand our internal management development capability

CONSIDER PLACING THE CHART UNDER THE HIGHLIGHTS OF THE YEAR

Charts are of great interest to your stockholders and to the security analyst. They give a quick overview of the results of the corporation's operation for at least a five-year period. Include charts showing:

1. Income from continuing operations.
2. Return on sales.
3. Return on equity.
4. Return on invested capital.
5. Dividends paid on common shares.

UNITED ENERGY

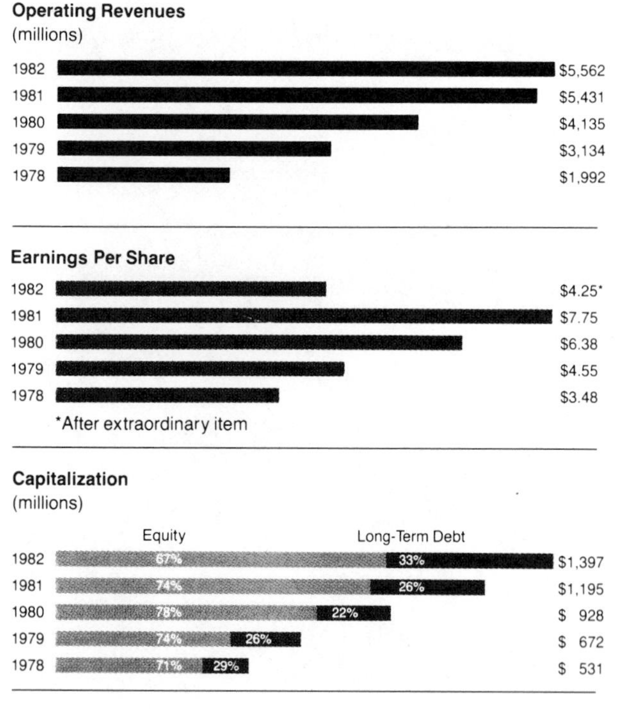

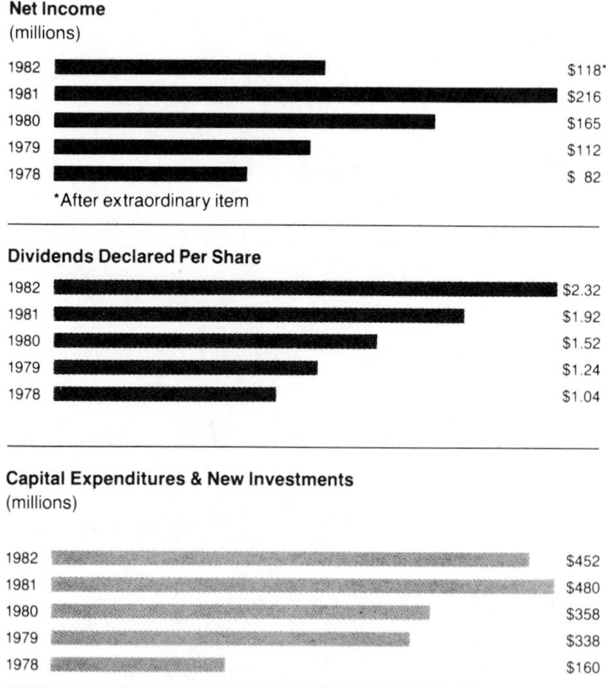

25 Consecutive Years of Earnings Growth

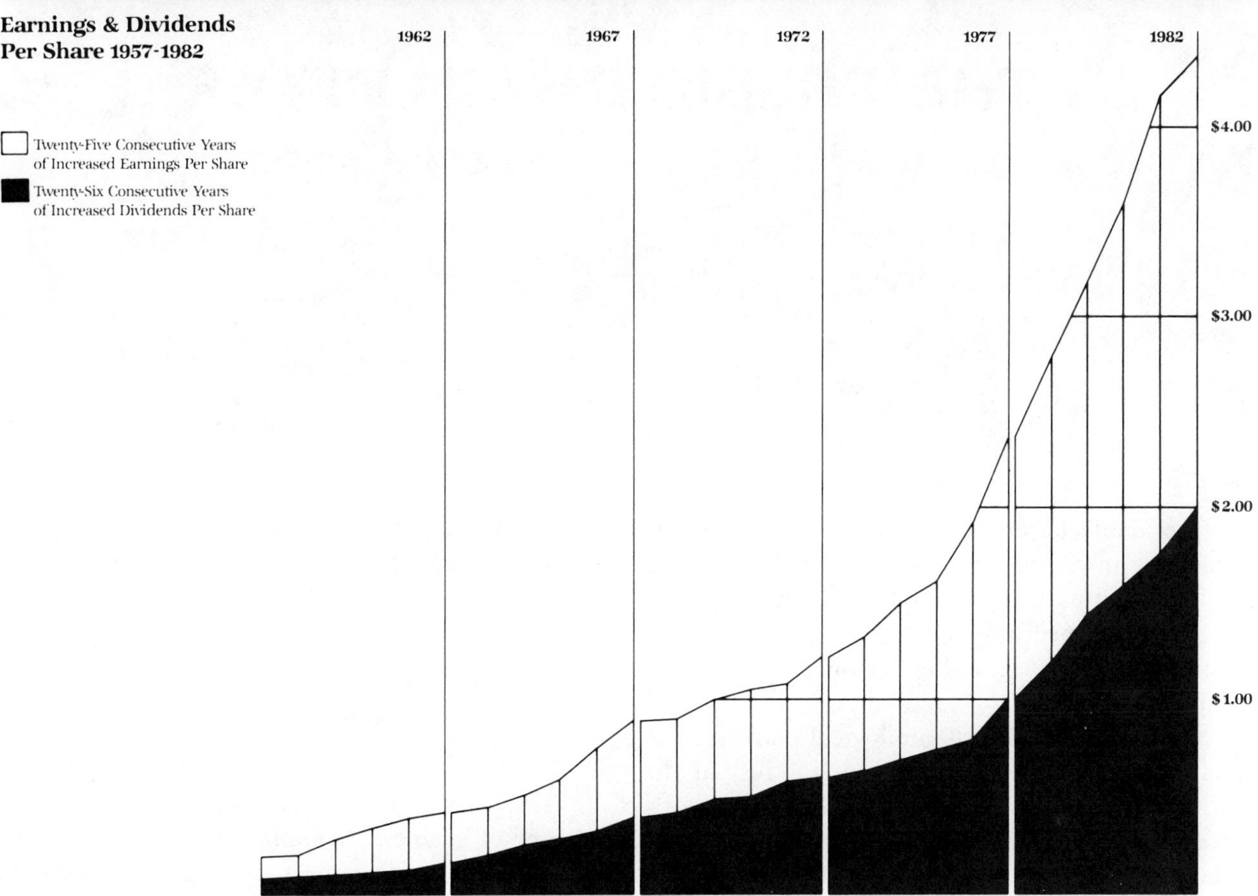

VIII
THE PRESIDENT'S LETTER

The president's letter is generally the best read portion of the annual report. The major purpose of the president's letter is to provide the stockholders with information concerning the past operations . . . but even more important, a view of the future for the company.

The president's letter is the logical place for the chief executive to set the stage for the rest of the report. The letter should interpret the entire year's performance. The president, in all candor, should review the company's accomplishments, plans, future directions, goals, etc. This is the place for the president not only to give the reasons for disappointments and failures to meet previously set goals, but to describe the actions taken to get the company back on track. Your stockholders will welcome an admission by your president that all did not go well, and what steps were taken to correct the situation.

"Stereotyped" language and clichés in the president's letter will turn off the reader of your report. The use of short paragraphs and subheads invites greater readership.

Jane Bryant Quinn, author and business commentator, advises:

> "Now turn to the letter from the chairman. Usually addressed "to our stockholders," it's up front, and should be in more ways than one. The chairman's tone reflects the personality, the well-being of his company.
>
> In his letter he should tell you how his company fared this year. But more important, he should tell you why. Keep an eye out for sentences that start with "Except for . . ." and "Despite the . . ." They're clues to problems.
>
> On the positive side, a chairman's letter should give you insights into the company's future and its stance on economic or political trends that may affect it.
>
> While you're up front, look for what's new in each line of business. Is management getting the company in good shape to weather the tough and competitive 1980's?
>
> Now—and no sooner—should you dig into the numbers!"

HOW TO GET THE PRESIDENT'S PERSONALITY TO COME THROUGH IN HIS LETTER

Corporate executives have different styles—different ways of communicating their ideas. Try to capture your chief executive officer's style so that it is included not only in his or her letter, but throughout the annual report. Your chief executive must come through as a human being who has the interest of the stockholders very much at heart—is a forward-thinking individual—has a social conscience and knows how to get things done.

Lee Iacocca, chairman of the board of Chrysler Corporation, provides a good example of a personality coming through effectively in an annual report.

TO OUR SHAREHOLDERS

Chrysler won its long battle for independence in 1983.

As the economy revived, our sales picked up dramatically. We were able to repay our U.S.-guaranteed loans and maintain substantial progress on building new financial and market strength. We began 1984 on a crest of record profits.

Chrysler has moved firmly into a new era of profitability and financial strength, producing industry leading vehicles with superior quality, backed by superior warranties.

In 1983, net income was $700.9 million, 312 percent better than in 1982. This produced earnings of $5.79 per common share in 1983, compared with $1.84 per common share in 1982. Our 1983 earnings were 66 percent better than our previous profit record, set in 1976, when Chrysler was a larger company.

The operational restructuring undertaken over the last few years produced results extraordinary for any company, especially an automobile company.

Our financial position improved dramatically during the year. At the end of 1982, total debt was 69.8 percent of the total of debt plus equity. At the end of 1983, it had fallen to 52.7 percent. Further improvement is anticipated.

In the last quarter of 1983 we executed the most complex and expensive product launch in the company's history, introducing the brand-new Laser/Daytona sports cars and the Voyager/Caravan garageable mini-wagons. Strong buyer response across our entire product line indicates 1984 may be another record year for Chrysler.

We expect the industry to sell 10.5 million cars and 3.7 million trucks in the United States in 1984, for a 15 percent increase in U.S. car sales and an 18 percent increase in truck sales over 1983.

In this larger market, Chrysler is planning to sell more than a million cars, or 10.6 percent of the domestic market. And, with sales of the Voyager/Caravan, which are classified as multi-purpose vehicles/trucks, we expect to sell more than 500,000 trucks, boosting our share of the truck market from 9 percent to 14 percent.

The 1983 results included four dramatic financial actions that position us well for 1984:

- *We repaid the $1.2 billion in loans guaranteed by the Federal Government. This action was taken seven years early, saving $392 million in interest and government fees. It strengthened our balance sheet and helped facilitate our access to traditional credit markets.*
- *We cleaned up our balance sheet by reclassifying $1.1 billion of preferred stock into common stock, and by exchanging common stock for lender warrants. We also accelerated the expiration date on 5 million warrants held by the public. These actions increased the number of shares outstanding, from 79,475,287 to 121,811,855. The market value of our stock rose during the year, with the aggregate market value of our outstanding common stock increasing from $1,410.7 million to $3,365.1 million.*
- *We placed the winning bid of $311 million for the 14.4 million Chrysler warrants held by the U.S. Government. We've retired those warrants–and with them the uncertainty about their potential dilution and stock-price effect.*
- *In December, we resumed preferred dividend payments, and paid all arrearages, on the 10 million shares of preferred stock held by the public.*

In April 1984, we will resume dividend payments on our common stock, with a quarterly payment of 15 cents per share payable to stockholders of record as of March 15, 1984.

The results of 1983 and prospects for 1984 underscore the success of our strategy for rebuilding Chrysler's profitability. During our turnaround we cut the company's size, closing some 20 plants and modernizing remaining facilities, trimming white collar personnel from over 40,000 in 1978 to 21,000 in 1983, and reducing our breakeven point from 2.4 million in 1979 to 1.1 million units in 1983. We cut fixed costs, in constant dollars, from $4.7 billion in 1979 to $3.54 billion in 1983.

But we didn't trim budgets for future products. When the long-overdue upturn arrived, Chrysler was ready with a full line of high-value vehicles.

We emerged from the crisis as planned–not as a shaky recuperant but as a vigorous, lean, and tough competitor with technologically advanced cars and trucks carrying the best warranties in the business.

All of Chrysler's constituents made sacrifices to help Chrysler survive and prosper. One such sacrifice came from the United Automobile Workers, which agreed to pay cuts in the darker days. In August, we signed a new 25-month union agreement which restored $2.42 an hour and enables us to plan on two years of labor stability.

This new pact, however, did not avert a strike over local issues in November at our stamping plant in Twinsburg, Ohio. Because Twinsburg serves most of our assembly plants, the strike cost the company $89 million in earnings and cut our production by 30,000 vehicles. Workers in other Chrysler plants lost a total of $11.2 million in wages as a result.

In 1983, Chrysler's management was strengthened by creation of an Office of the Chairman. I'm joined in it by Gerald Greenwald, Vice Chairman; Harold K. Sperlich, President; and Bennett E. Bidwell, Executive Vice President.

Late in the year, I made a decision to stay with Chrysler. I accepted a generous stock grant and a stock option offer from our Board of Directors in return for three and possibly four more years of service as Chairman and Chief Executive Officer. I had considered retiring, but I'm eager to lead our excellent Chrysler team in a good economy and to help meet the strategic challenges that face our company.

Looking at the long-range prospects for our industry and our entire economy, I see a continued need for major changes:

- *The U.S. automobile industry will continue to need restraint on Japanese imports until our government counter-balances the subsidies Japan's tax and currency policies give to cars shipped here from Japan. I'm not advocating a protectionist policy for our country. But it is essential for our government to provide a level playing field in international trade.*
- *The proposed joint venture between GM and Toyota is a clear violation of the antitrust laws. It could lead to the end of the subcompact business for U.S. car builders because it would permit two of the world's largest car manufacturers to stop competing against each other. In January, Chrysler filed suit in Federal court to stop the joint venture.*
- *The prospects of a $100 billion trade deficit in 1984, and the likelihood of an additional trillion dollars in U.S. debt by 1988, are bad news for everyone—but especially for interest-sensitive industries such as automobiles. Inflation has subsided but interest rates remain high because of the deficits and other negative economic factors. I'll continue to encourage our political leaders to set political differences aside and respond to these threats to the national interest.*

The Chrysler turnaround demonstrated one important fact. It showed that a private corporation, together with its employees, dealers, stockholders, bankers, suppliers, and Federal, State and Canadian Provincial Governments, can save jobs and restore competitive basic industry. This was done without impairing private enterprise or using the taxpayers' money.

We will move ahead in 1984 and beyond because our employees are dedicated to producing best-in-class products with state-of-the-art technologies. We will dramatize this for the public at Chrysler's major exhibition at the Louisiana World Exposition in New Orleans this summer. We hope you will visit us there.

Lee A. Iacocca

LEE A. IACOCCA
Chairman of the Board, Chief Executive Officer
February 21, 1984

THE USE OF A "CONVERSATIONAL STYLE"

For a change in format, you might wish to consider a more personal type of message from the president. Your stockholders will get the feeling that they are sitting in the office of the president—in a relaxed atmosphere, listening to the president "tell it like it is."

Annual reports typically carry a statement from the chairman.
I started to write one but didn't feel comfortable with it.
I know *my* way of looking at this company, but what about *yours* as a stockholder?

I began to imagine the questions you might ask. I made a list of those I would ask if I were in your place. Then I tried to answer them as straight-forwardly as I know how. Though the list is not all-encompassing, it deals with the major issues of 1983.

After all, if we ask you to invest here, we owe you candor.
That's a moral commitment I believe in.

Our story needs no frills. Of course, it's not perfect.
But it is a story of strengths far outnumbering weaknesses.

Here it is, through "your" questions and my answers:

How do you assess the financial results for 1983, your first year as chairman and CEO?

I am clearly not satisfied with the absolute level of performance, but feel that we made progress in our program to restore the long-term profitability of the company.

Consolidated sales were essentially unchanged. However, this includes the effects of the worldwide restructuring program initiated in 1982 under which certain mature or less-profitable businesses were sold or closed. In addition, falling exchange rates reduced our reported sales outside the U.S. by a significant amount. Excluding these two factors, sales would have increased 11 percent, which I consider a respectable showing. Further, the end-result of restructuring will be a more growth-oriented, more cycle-resistant mix of businesses.

Despite the flat overall sales, operating income increased 134 percent over 1982. This improvement reflected the positive results of restructuring, excellent control of fixed costs, and the best manufacturing efficiency levels in several years. Net income, as a result, improved to $92.2 million, a 24 percent increase over 1982's $74.5 million.

Among the businesses that performed strongly in 1983 were automotive headlamp glass and pollution-control substrates, color-television bulbs, electronic products, and optical waveguides—all reflecting strong segments of the economy.

Those which were disappointing included some which serve depressed-market heavy industries, like refractories, most of the businesses serving weak economies in Latin America, and our consumer businesses, which recovered somewhat in the second half but have not yet shared fully in the economic recovery. In all cases, we expect improved results in 1984.

In sum, we improved over 1982, but held no celebration. There's still much ground to be regained as we recover from the recent recession.

Could you expand on the executive and organization changes made last year?

The changes, in planning for two years, were made for several reasons.

First, as I've mentioned on previous occasions, Amo Houghton and Tom MacAvoy had jointly decided some time ago to pass on the top management of this company to a new team. I'll have more to say about them later.

Secondly, ever-increasing competition, an explosion of new technologies, shorter product life-cycles, mercurial marketplaces—all of these meant we needed to become a more market-driven, faster-response, decentralized company.

Our major businesses had to be re-grouped to gain autonomy—to be, in effect, entrepreneurial companies of their own, close to their markets.

We established three major operating groups in 1983, each led by a president. Two vice chairmen of the corporation were named: for technology, and for finance and administration. The pages that follow contain details about each area.

A corporate Management Committee was formed, made up of these five executives and myself, to operate as the company's chief decision-making unit. Intimate knowledge of individual businesses and a broad corporate perspective are thus fused in one group, a formula for the prompt, balanced and thoroughly-informed decision-making required in today's marketplace.

Does this market emphasis mean less commitment to technology?

Absolutely not. Technology is the major source of our competitive edge in most markets. The goal is simply to focus these technologies.

In the past, we could develop a promising technology with confidence it would in time find or create its market. Those days are gone. Opportunities must be pinpointed and technology harnessed to seize those opportunities quickly, or they vanish. So it's not an either-or situation, technical skills or marketing skills. It's both interacting.

Two related points should be made here.

First, our "traditional" technologies are in reality a dynamic and evolving force. 1983 offered an historic contrast that underscores the point.

On one hand, we continued disengaging from incandescent bulbs, one of yesterday's technological landmarks but no longer a profitable growth opportunity.

On the other hand, we perfected new, higher-performance optical fibers, an improved auto-pollution ceramic substrate and superior LED and LCD display glasses.

Thus we may note with nostalgia the fading of an historic business, while noting with satisfaction the continual advance to new technical frontiers for the uses of glass and ceramics.

The second related point: where the use of nonglass materials and technologies can provide logical market growth, we apply those materials and technologies. For a few examples, we make tissue-culture vessels of plastic, microminiature capacitors of tantalum, and consumer products by Corning Designs using wood and metals.

Further, our medical diagnostics business, while stemming from our decades of experience with laboratory ware, competes in a business area with no direct connection to customary Corning markets or technology. The manufacturing techniques are unique and so are the selling and distribution methods. But it's become one of the fastest-growing businesses in Corning history.

I believe it all adds up to this: we'll remain the world's leading specialty glass and ceramic company, growing in the areas of historic Corning expertise, and growing at the same time in new directions where the elements come together—the right market with the right products and the right expertise at the right time—and we will develop whatever technology is necessary to support these new thrusts.

Despite the recovery in 1983, income from operations is well below historic levels. How will you restore it to levels that will provide for satisfactory stockholder return and company growth?

The ways to achieve strong operating income are clear. We're aggressively pursuing every one of them:

- Restructuring—the disengagement from selected mature, normally cyclical businesses into high-growth, more cycle-resistant businesses.
- Reorganization—the new grouping of businesses to spur faster, surer market decisions leading to more volume.
- A program of continued emphasis on research and new-product development geared to proven market needs.

–A total-quality effort—in products and employee performance—involving every employee.

–Continual improvement of manufacturing efficiencies with upgraded facilities, precision scheduling, inventory management and thorough training for operating personnel.

–Planned annual productivity and cost-reduction goals for both plant and administrative units, supported by comprehensive programs and training.

–Expansion into service businesses. We've begun by acquiring MetPath Inc., a medical diagnostic laboratory, and by establishing Corning Engineering, a company to market our technical expertise.

In short, as much as we can be masters of our own ship, we are. External forces will affect us, as they will everybody else. There's the durability of the recovery, federal deficits, interest rates, international debt problems—the potential shoals are familiar enough. Our object is to steer powerfully around them, to keep the generating of operating income in our own grasp by every possible method.

You mentioned quality. How does Corning intend to improve upon it?

Quality has definitely not fallen here. In fact, it's improved steadily. But foreign competition has assaulted us in several areas. We're not alone: it's a common problem for U.S. industry.

We've already started to reverse the trend. In fact, quality-passionate Japanese companies are leading customers for many Corning products.

The quality spirit runs deep here. It's a matter of great satisfaction to me that employees, on their own, have formed Quality Circles throughout the company.

What we're doing is to channel that spirit with a permanent, total-quality effort. We appointed a corporate Director of Quality and established a Quality Council in 1983 with wide-ranging authority to set goals and see that they're met.

We founded a Quality Institute that all employees will attend over time. Other, individual training programs are operating for specific job areas.

Corning has a "nice guy" image. Can you afford to be "nice guys" in these times?

It's easy to be cynical. It's tempting to reach for the passing short-term gain of a patent infringement, a callous treatment of employees, an indifference to the community where you're located, an exploitive deal with a customer in urgent need of your product.

Long term, it's a net loss.

It results in the creative executive who goes elsewhere, the lathe operator who works listlessly, the customer whose door is closed the next time you visit.

The values embedded in the Corning name and history do bring a return. Nobody can assign actual numbers, but our balance sheet simply has to reflect a gain from 133 years without serious labor-management trouble, and from the fact that major customers have stayed with us for decades.

None of which says we live in an ivory tower. We recognize it's a world that demands heightened performance standards when it comes to judging and rewarding employees. It's a world that demands aggressive sales and marketing and pricing. It's a world that demands a head-on, bruising competitive spirit.

We're no strangers to all of this—but we operate within boundaries of integrity we've always set. Will this "nice guy" corporation of ours thus finish last?

We've been a leader in major markets for more than a century—and we will be in the future. I can't find a better answer than that.

I hope you've found these questions and answers useful. I've tried to paint a true picture of a company committed to a new direction while preserving the best of the past.

In the short time that I've been chairman, I've found the sense of responsibility to be as great as I expected. Even greater is a sense of confidence. For that, I credit Corning employees—two in particular: Amo Houghton, who was chairman of this company for 19 years, and Tom MacAvoy, who was president for 12.

In any historical context, the period of their leadership will be looked upon as a period of major achievement. Their vision and commitment led to many of the strong positions we now have. Fortunately for us, Amo continues in an active role, as chairman of the Executive Committee. His management skills and counsel will continue to benefit this company in the years ahead. Tom, of course, is part of the management team as vice chairman.

After 21 years with the company, I feel I know our employees well and I believe they're unmatched for dedication and ability. No annual report can be complete without recognition of these men and women. More than any other factor, they assure us of a bright future.

James R. Houghton

James R. Houghton
Chairman of the Board

February 24, 1984

Financial Executive, in referring to the president's letter, commented, "The letter should be a personalized document to shareholders in which the president is speaking on behalf of management. It should be understandable to the average shareholder, while having enough meat in it to satisfy the professional investor. There is one cardinal rule for a president's letter: "Avoid propaganda." This means hyperbole, platitudes, clichés of any kind. Nothing will turn a reader off more quickly than subjection to vague, abstract 'horn blowing.'"

The president's letter should be prepared by the firm's chief executive. Letters with the broadest appeal are those presenting an intimate, personal, reflective discussion of the company's current and future operations.

SUBTITLES IN THE PRESIDENT'S LETTER TO THE SHAREHOLDERS

Subtitles make the president's letter more readable. All too often, the president's message is deadly in that the reader doesn't get a stopping-off point—a place to pause—a place to reflect. Subtitles make a difference, and should be used in the president's letter.

There are two types of subtitles:

1. **Simple Headings:**

   Financial Highlights
   Redeployment of Assets
   Capital Expenditures
   Research and Development
   Management Outlook
   Return on Shareholders Investment

2. **Use Subtitles in the President's Letter to the Shareholders**

   R & D Investment Rises to New Record
   UTC Climbs in Rank in R & D Spending
   Returns Reaped in New Programs
   Capital Investments Grow
   Earnings and Sales Set Records
   Sales Up in All Major Business Lines
   Business Balance Enhances Stability
   International Sales Strong
   Return on Assets Reaches 15.5 percent
   Cash Dividend Increased
   Potential Partners Must Fit Criteria
   People at Work Doing a Good Job
   Equal Opportunity Practiced
   Portfolio Has Been Strengthened
   R & D and Capital Spending Up
   Dividends Increased
   Policy Dialogue Continues
   Optimistic About Future

Additional Examples of Subtitles

- Our 19__ results continued the trend which, over the past five years, has seen consolidated sales and net earnings grow at annual compound rates of 15 percent and 17 percent, respectively.
- In 19__, R. J. Reynolds Industries extended its already significant global business presence and enhanced its status as an international consumer goods company.
- In 19__, Reynolds Tobacco achieved a 33.1 percent share of the domestic market, our highest share in recent years, and established an industry record for annual cigarette unit volume in the United States for the second consecutive year.
- The More brand family led all major cigarette brands in growth for the year, increasing almost 32 percent to a share of market in excess of 1.5 percent, and moving from 20th to 15th position among the best-selling brand families.
- No other domestic tobacco company can match Reynolds Tobacco's broad strength in the domestic cigarette market. The company is the only manufacturer with leading brands in every market segment.
- In 19__, R. J. Reynolds Tobacco International grew faster than the industry as the 7.4 per cent unit sales growth was more than three times the growth rate of the world cigarette market and exceeded the average of 5 percent annual unit growth achieved by the company during the past five years.
- Operating income before interest improved 85 percent, as the figures above indicate.
- Debt was cut from an anticipated peak of $279 million to $187 million.
- The initial steps of corporate reorganization were accomplished.

STAY AWAY FROM CORPORATE DOUBLESPEAK

William Lutz, Professor at Rutgers University, in an interesting article published in *Business and Society*

Review (1982) discussed his theory that as profits go down, business doublespeak goes up. He pointed out:

Sweetening the Annual Report

"During a recession the doublespeak flows thick in corporate reports to the stockholders. Instead of being active, dynamic, aggressive forces acting on behalf of their shareholders, corporations become helpless and hapless victims of economic forces beyond their or anyone's control. With this reasonable loss of control goes any responsibility for the bad news in the annual report. Companies are "impacted" by the recession because of the "climate of high interest rates" that produces a "cloudy future." Management, however, remains "cautiously optimistic" and performance (or profits) for the year, given the "atmosphere of recession," was "reasonable," "acceptable," or "satisfactory." But then it was a Wall Street analyst who praised the GAF Corporation for its "enterprise restructuring" when GAF announced it would sell nearly half of its subsidiaries.

Mirro Corporation had a "milestone year" in 1981. Indeed it did. Mirro lost $1.2 million and plans to sell more than half the company. Ceco Corporation "enjoyed another good year" in 1981 with net income "second only to the record achieved in (1980)." This is one way of saying that earnings fell 13 percent. RCA Corporation noted "abnormally high interest rates" as one of several outside forces that "constrained" earnings, but it failed to note that it increased its short-term borrowing by 60 percent. Pacific Power noted that although the operations of NERCO, its subsidiary, "fell short of budget" they were "satisfactory." Fairchild Industries noted that "despite the chilling effect of the recessionary climate on many American businesses, Fairchild has succeeded in maintaining and, in many cases, improving its position for future growth."

Public Service Electric and Gas Company of New Jersey had a bad year, but not for any fault of management as "weaknesses in the economy, accompanied by high inflation and interest rates, continued to exact a toll on the utility industry," a toll which, for some reason, was not exerted on many other utilities. PSE&G, however, saw earnings decline "as a consequence of the bleak economic climate and erosion of the rate relief received in 1980." PSE&G will, however, attempt to cope with the "continuing unfavorable economic atmosphere" even though "high inflation and money costs continue to plague the utility industry." The message seems to be that when business makes money it's because of the skill of management, but when business loses money it's because of outside forces beyond the control of management. Heads management wins, tails the shareholders lose.

What is achieved by the use of doublespeak in business? Are the public or shareholders fooled by such language? Probably not. However, language that attempts to avoid responsibility for action, that attempts to make the bad seem good, the negative appear positive, something unpleasant appear attractive, and that seems to communicate but doesn't is language that violates the very purpose of language: communication between people. Such language breeds suspicion, cynicism, distrust, and, ultimately, hostility. Executives do themselves and the business community a great disservice by using such language and they mislead themselves if they believe that they are really fooling anyone. Clarity in language is not difficult to achieve, if executives want to achieve it. But if they want to mislead, conceal, evade, deflect, or avoid the truth through language, that too is not difficult. The price for the latter, however, is far greater. Perhaps some day business executives will learn this lesson."

Check your report to make certain you are not falling into the "doublespeak" syndrome.

TEN CLICHÉS TO AVOID IN THE PRESIDENT'S LETTER

Don't underestimate the sophistication of your stockholders and security analysts. They want facts, not clichés. Avoid the following generalizations without backup information.

1. "We have depth in management."—without describing the competence and experience of management.
2. "People are our most important asset."—Why?
3. "Our corporation has a great many things going for it."—without any elaboration.
4. "We have come out of the recession, a stronger company."—without supporting data.
5. "We are on the move."—without giving the necessary backup.
6. "We have substantially reduced our overhead."—without supporting information.

7. "We will diversify."—without describing the new fields to be entered.
8. "We have the financial muscle to withstand future downturns in the economy."—without financial data.
9. "We are future oriented."—Why?
10. "We face the future with confidence."—without giving the reasons why.

Be sure you back up your claims with the necessary evidence. It's easy to make sweeping generalizations. The reader of your report wants to know how you justify your claims.

USE SUFFICIENTLY LARGE TYPE IN THE "LETTER FROM THE PRESIDENT"

Type that is too small will turn off the reader. An example of a "too small to read" type size is the following:

President's Report

Acklands Limited is in a period of substantial expansion and much improved efficiency. However, costs associated with expansion and divestiture, combined with a sluggish economy and higher interest rates, reduced our 19__ earnings performance.

Revenues

The Company recorded 19__ consolidation sales of $349,973,000, which is 4.2 percent above the level of the previous year Sales of discontinued operations, including home entertainment products, were $12,494,000 compared with $27,242,000 in 19__. Adjusting for these divestitures, sales increased by $28,938,000, or 94 percent.

Costs

Operating costs increased by 12.2 percent, or $12,456,000. As a percentage of sales, total expenses were up by 2.3 percent.

Payroll costs accelerated by $5,737,000 or 11.0 percent over 19__ despite a reduction in the number of employees because of divestitures. Increased rates of interest, combined with a higher level of borrowing, escalated the cost of financing the Company's business by $2, 289,000, or 17.5 percent, in 19__.

As a result of these and other expense factors, operating and financial costs increased disproportionately to the gross profits achieved on sales volume.

PHOTOGRAPH IDEAS TO ACCOMPANY THE PRESIDENT'S LETTER

We come now to what can be a very delicate subject—the way in which you present the photograph of your president in the annual report. There are a number of ways of doing this. You might want to consider the following:

1. A bust shot of the president. Generally, the president has a smile, and is, in effect, saying, "I'm your president. You can trust me."
2. A posed photograph of the president standing next to a globe, or standing in the entrance of the new administration building.
3. The president seated at a directors' table with ten other smiling directors.
4. A posed picture of the president with a hard hat standing next to one of the employees in the factory.

These photos will suffice. I prefer a good candid shot showing the president in the plant or office of one of the customers of the company, or on the run. I like candid shots of the president reviewing the computer printout with one of the employees. A candid shot showing the president visiting with the management of a subsidiary either in this country or abroad, also puts some life into the photograph. If the president of your company works in shirt-sleeves, why not portray him in that manner. At a very early stage, you will want to clear how your president wishes to be photographed.

If you have an "Office of the President," you might want to show a photograph of the group in an informal setting, again using the candid photo technique.

SUBJECTS GENERALLY DISCUSSED IN THE PRESIDENT'S LETTER

There is a wide variety of subjects to be reviewed in the president's letter. Your readers will look to the president's letter for a review of the past year's operations, management and broad changes, acquisitions, divestitures, future outlook, etc. The following offers you a checklist of items you may wish to cover in the president's report.

Acquisitions and Divestitures
Board Changes
Broadening the Business
Business Mix for the 80s
Business Operations
Business Overview
Capital Expenditures
Capital Improvements
Capital Investment

Concerns for the Future
Corporate Responsibility
Decentralization
Diversification
Dividends
Executive Appointments
Expansion Program
Financial Goals
Financial Results
Financial Strength
Five-Year Forecast
Global Perspective
Government Action
Health and Safety
Imports/Exports
Management
Management Elections
Operating Highlights
Outlook
Productivity
Professional and Business Policies
Professional Development
Realignment of Management Organization
Reorganization
Research and Development
Strengthening Existing Product Lines
Technology

MODEL LETTERS TO SHAREHOLDERS

The following letters are unique and contain the type of information that will be of interest to your stockholders.

To Our Stockholders:

We are pleased to report that the year ended January 30, 1983, was another year of record sales and earnings. As you can see from the financial highlights page, our sales exceeded the one billion dollar mark, our net earnings rose 31% and we continued to strengthen our already solid financial base. We now have 144 toy stores operating in 21 states.

What cannot be gleaned from the financial statements is exactly *how* we achieved these results or *what* we did in terms of assuring for ourselves a future that can be as exciting as our past.

Our performance gains are attributable to several important factors.

—First, we were more productive in our stores; comparable toy store sales rose 19.5% during the year.

—Second, we strengthened our position as a leading retailer of video games and home computers. This product category accounted for 18% of our sales in fiscal 1983 compared to 11% during the previous year.

—Third, and perhaps most important, we further enhanced our position as the nation's largest toy specialty retailer. Excluding video games and home computers, we estimate that Toys "R" Us now commands an 11% share of the total United States toy retailing market, up from about 9½% last year.

With the advent of the electronics age, the merchandise categories we sell are undergoing continuous changes. We have been able to successfully introduce more sophisticated merchandise into our stores. As a result, we expanded the toy market from the more traditional age groups to include teenagers and adults. This expansion of our consumer and merchandise base is especially significant as it by and large represents *new* add-on sales for us.

Along these lines, we further strengthened our position as a leading seller of video games and home computers. The evolution of this business has required that we improve our display of this merchandise category. Our new layout, designed to make the electronics area of the store easier to shop, will be completed shortly in all of our stores throughout the country. The new design will allow our customer to examine the merchandise through plexi-glass containers positioned at eye level.

As an integral part of our long-range growth plans, we have been increasing our toy store square footage by about 18% per year by expanding our penetration in existing markets and by entering a new geographic region each year. During fiscal 1983, we opened 24 new stores including five stores in a new market: southeastern Florida. During this coming year, we intend to open approximately 25 new toy stores including entry into a new market centered in Atlanta. This new region includes Georgia, Alabama and part of Tennessee. Our store plans for fiscal 1985 are well underway; we plan to open a new market centered in Cincinnati, Ohio covering southern Ohio and parts of Kentucky and Indiana.

We also intend to move into toy retailing in the international market. Our first group of stores in Canada is scheduled to open in Toronto in the fall of 1984, and through an agreement with Alghanim Industries, we will provide technical assistance and buying services to this major Kuwait-based corporation in its efforts to launch toy stores throughout the Middle East. The first store will open in Kuwait in September, 1983. We believe major opportunities exist in international markets in coming years. W. John Devine was named Executive Vice President—Director of International Operations and will head our international efforts.

During the past year we have made some important management promotions that will strengthen our merchandising and operating organization. Seymore L. Ziv was named to the new position of Executive Vice President—Product Development. In his new role, Mr. Ziv will devote more time to developing merchandise strategies and product categories for our toy stores and expanding customer base. Howard W. Moore was appointed Executive Vice President—General Merchandise Manager and assumes responsibility for buying, merchandising and marketing for all Toys "R" Us stores in the United States. Brian K. Devine was named Senior Vice President—Director of U.S. Toy Stores and Robert J. Weinberg was appointed Vice President—Divisional Merchandise Manager.

We recently formed a new division to engage in selling brand name, off-price, first quality children's clothing. We will apply the same operating and specialty retailing concepts that we pioneered over thirty years ago to this business. Two pilot stores will open in the New York area prior to the back-to-school season this Fall. It is our intent that these stores will contain the widest selection of children's apparel found anywhere. Judy Stewart has been named President of this new division. Prior to joining our company, she was the President of August Max, a retail division of U.S. Shoe Company.

On March 1, 1983, the Board of Directors declared a 3-for-2 stock split to be issued July 26, 1983 to stockholders of record June 27, 1983. The measure is subject to stockholder approval, at the June 1, 1983 annual meeting, of a resolution to increase the number of authorized shares from 40 million to 200 million. If the measure is approved, it will mark the fourth consecutive year in which Toys "R" Us has issued a 3-for-2 stock split.

Last, but certainly not least, we would like to thank our talented and devoted employees for their contribution to our record performance this past year. Their commitment is one of the keys to our successful expansion and the best guarantee of our continued success. Together we share a view of optimism regarding this coming year and the years beyond.

Sincerely,

Norman Ricken President and Chief Operating Officer	Charles Lazarus Chairman and Chief Executive Officer

March 31, 1983

To Our Stockholders:

I am pleased to report that 1983 was a year of solid worldwide unit volume gains and higher sales and earnings for 3M.

Our net income rose 5.6 percent to $667 million, or $5.67 per share, despite continuing adverse currency effects and substantial investments in future growth. On a before-tax basis, earnings showed an even better performance, increasing 9.6 percent.

Worldwide sales surpassed the 7-billion-dollar mark for the first time, totaling $7.039 billion, an increase of 6.6 percent from 1982.

Stockholder dividends also grew. During the year, stockholders received a record $388 million in dividends. On February 13, 1984, the Board of Directors approved another increase in the quarterly dividend rate, to 85 cents a share from 82½ cents a share, effective with the March dividend payment. This marks the 26th consecutive year in which the dividend has been increased.

3M outperforms economies

The past year was one of mixed conditions in world economies. After three years of virtually no growth, the United States economy advanced at a healthy rate. However, economic output in major overseas economies remained sluggish. Once again, our businesses grew considerably faster than the markets they serve.

In the United States, our unit volume rose about 12 percent, nearly double the increase in industrial production and the strongest 3M volume gain since 1978. Outside the U.S., unit volume increased about 6 percent in economies which, on balance, showed minimal growth. Favorable acceptance of new and improved products again was a major factor in our results worldwide and contributed to an increased share of major markets.

Earnings reach higher levels

As a ratio to sales, our net income equaled 9.5 percent, considerably above the average for other industrial companies. In the United States, healthy unit volume gains, combined with benefits from cost control efforts, resulted in a substantial increase in earnings and profit margins. Earnings gains were particularly strong in our Industrial and Consumer Sector and our Life Sciences Sector.

Outside the U.S., earnings declined moderately, due largely to the effects of currency rate changes. We estimate that our net income was reduced by about $48 million, or 41 cents a share, due to the strength of the dollar compared with last year. This estimate includes the higher costs in local currencies of importing goods from 3M in the United States, the impact of translating profits from local currencies into dollars and net transaction losses in countries not considered to be highly inflationary.

Our growth in earnings was impacted not only by the strength of the dollar, but by large investments and strategic actions to enhance the future growth of the Company. Expenditures for research and development, for example, increased 10 percent to $384 million, equal to 5.4 cents of each sales dollar. Investments also were sharply increased in several fast-growing product areas, including videocassettes and computer data storage media. During the year, we made large investments in new-generation technologies, state-of-the-art manufacturing processes and aggressive promotional programs. These investments are enhancing our already favorable position in the memory media business and will help us take full advantage of future market opportunities.

While we were accelerating spending in high-growth market areas during the year, we also withdrew from a number of smaller businesses which no longer were compatible with our objectives. These investments and actions should significantly enhance our prospects for the future.

3M firsts in space research and China

In February of 1984, 3M took a pioneering step when we announced the first major cooperative program of basic materials research in space. Our program, in association with NASA, is designed to explore the potential for commercializing technologies and products developed in space.

Long-term in nature, the program is being instituted not only to enhance our already strong technology base, but in recognition that technological progress in space can make important contributions to living standards for people worldwide.

1983 marked the beginning of what we hope will become an important 3M presence in the People's Republic of China, a country with approximately one-quarter of the world's population. After three years of discussions, we reached an agreement in principle with Chinese authorities under which 3M would become the first major foreign company to establish a wholly owned subsidiary in China. Initially, we will manufacture products to help meet the country's telecommunications and electrical needs.

Jacobson joins Board

Allen F. Jacobson, executive vice president of our Industrial and Consumer Sector, was elected to the Board of Directors in May.

Lewis W. Lehr

During the year, three new corporate officers were elected. Donn R. Osmon became vice president, Marketing, succeeding Charles W. Higgins, who retired. Roger W. Roberts was elected vice president and controller. And Christopher J. Wheeler became vice president, Human Resources, following the retirement of Gordon W. Engdahl.

Outlook for 1984

As we enter 1984, we are optimistic about our prospects. In both U.S. and International markets, our operating leverage remains good, and we expect continued benefits from higher utilization of manufacturing capacity. We are assuming that the U.S. economy will continue to show good growth and that inflation will be moderate. This should result in another solid increase in unit volume and further improvement in U.S. profit margins.

Outside the U.S., we expect our results to benefit from gradual improvement in economic activity. Nonetheless, the magnitude of any improvement will be affected by the performance of the dollar.

Our costs and assets remain under good control. Higher 1983 sales were achieved with approximately 1,700 fewer employees worldwide, which means we significantly improved productivity. Close attention to asset management also continues to yield favorable results. During the past year, our inventories and accounts receivable grew at a slower rate than sales, which had a favorable impact on our cash position.

While the performance of the dollar remains an imponderable, we expect, at this juncture, that 1984 will be a year of good unit volume gains, higher earnings and improved profit margins for 3M.

Longer-term outlook

Our goals remain the same.

We look for unit volume growth of approximately 10 percent a year, on average. We look for profit margins before taxes of 20 percent or better. And we look for a return on stockholders' equity of between 20 and 25 percent.

As always, the achievement of these objectives will depend in large measure on creative and efficient ways of doing things in our laboratories, manufacturing plants and offices. Innovation is a trait that has become synonymous with 3M. Today, we are working to weave innovation even more strongly into the fabric of the 3M organization.

In the section that follows, we have highlighted how 3M people are continuing to find better ways of doing things. Innovation clearly has been a hallmark of 3M's past success, and we want to insure that it is just as much a part of the 3M tradition in the years ahead.

On behalf of the Board of Directors, I would like to thank the 85,700 3M men and women around the world for their hard work and dedication in 1983. With their help, combined with the continued support of our customers and suppliers, I am confident the years ahead will be good ones for 3M and its stockholders.

L. W. Lehr
Chairman of the Board
and Chief Executive Officer

February 13, 1984

To Our Shareholders:

November 18, 1983

Records are made to be surpassed and we are pleased to again report a record-breaking year in fiscal 1983, despite the many economic headwinds during the past twelve months.

On a 10% sales increase from $14.5 million to $15.9 million, net income rose 16% to $1.1 million up from $949,000 in fiscal 1982. Per share earnings calculated on the basis of a larger number of shares outstanding that resulted from a public offering and adjusted for a 3-for-2 stock split in January 1983, and 10% stock dividend declared September 2, 1983, were $.53 for fiscal 1983, an increase of 6% over $.50 for fiscal 1982.

Our shares were listed on the American Stock Exchange under the symbol DSG in August, 1983 and on the Pacific Stock Exchange in November, 1983. A successful public offering of 400,000 shares resulted in a reduction of long-term debt by $1,660,000, a substantial increase in working capital to $6.7 million in fiscal 1983 compared to $4.3 million in our prior year for a current ratio of 5.3 to 1 compared to 3.8 to 1 in fiscal 1982, and we nearly doubled stockholders' equity in 1983 to $8.2 million from $4.2 million as a result of the increase in retained earnings and the net proceeds of the offering.

Our backlog of $4.6 million at August 31, 1983 increased slightly compared to the previous year. It includes an initial order of $500,000 received in the final quarter of 1983 as a part of the five-year blanket purchase agreement from a major military prime contractor for the purchase of precision components. Subsequent releases of orders under this agreement will have a significant impact on the future sales volume and earnings of your Company.

Your attention is directed to our plans and capital investments reported in your fiscal 1982 statement. We expanded our manufacturing capabilities with additions of computerized numerical controlled equipment, significantly expanded our computer capacity for storage and retrieval of information, and we embarked upon a plan to penetrate the robotics industry in a specifically-targeted area.

During fiscal 1983, our plans were implemented by the creation of the Techno Division of United Products Co. to conduct research and development in microcomputer-controlled automation and robotics under an exclusive agreement with two principals of Technovation Inc. We participated in the funding of a robotics laboratory at Columbia University with an opportunity to consult with faculty as we develop our robotics product line. Management concluded our fiscal year with an agreement for a joint research project in robotics with an engineering company in Israel. The first phase of this joint research project is funded by a conditional grant of $300,000 from the Binational Industrial Research & Development Foundation and matching funds from your Company and our Israeli co-venturer.

Your management is firmly convinced that the above combination of technical knowledge and talents, and our commitment and resources will succeed in the development and marketing of a group of robotic devices.

Our growth-oriented future years will be supported by the introduction of new products and an expanding base of our existing product lines.

Our successful fiscal 1983 is due, in a great measure, to the loyal support of our customers, the superb efforts of our talented employees in all divisions and subsidiaries, and our loyal shareholders.

Respectfully,

Sol Schwartz
President

Chairman's Report to Our Shareholders

Wow, what a wild year! Avnet's fiscal 1983 monthly sales chart looked like a roller coaster. The year began with a steep business slide from June into November, followed by a moderate pickup over the winter, which gained momentum during the spring and was roaring upward as summer began and our fiscal year ended. I've never seen a faster turnaround. The late fourth quarter surge enabled us to finish the year with a slight sales increase and an earnings decrease from continuing operations of only 10% after being down almost 20% at the third quarter mark. During fiscal 1983 many of our new investments in businesses such as computer products, microcircuitry, and home satellite earth stations began to pay off. This encouraged us to make further investments in computer businesses, in the new gate array technology and in additional inventory and terminals within customers' plants while at the same time we reduced debt, increased net worth, and upped short-term investments by some $60 million.

Semiconductors, our major product line, experienced the strongest rebound, setting new booking and shipping records each month of the final quarter. By June, with the recovery far exceeding earlier expectations, our semiconductor orders were surging and have continued at a similar rate into the new fiscal year. Semiconductor suppliers could not react swiftly enough and their deliveries substantially trailed the increased demand resulting in extended lead times. A fear of product shortages grew in the marketplace causing some disarray. The market pendulum swung almost overnight from a buyer's market to a seller's market with only a short period of normal conditions.

In the vanguard of increased semiconductor purchasing from vendors were the electronic distributors...some of us were quick to perceive the turnaround. Distributors ordered a record 31% of suppliers' U.S. semiconductor output in May, up from a low of 20% last October. The Semiconductor Industry Association's supply/demand imbalance for semiconductors reached a 1.5:1 book-to-bill ratio by June. Semiconductor suppliers were forced to allocate many parts for the rest of calendar 1983 both to distributors and direct customers and were reporting the imminence of further allocations and extended lead times as their customers' orders ballooned...a far cry from year-ago inventory surplusses.

Sales of other product lines also began to swing upwards, although less dramatically. Some of our passive component manufacturers announced a supply crunch including some modest allocations. Connectors, which do not generally react as quickly to economic fluctuations as other components, also showed improvement from December onward despite continued weakness in two major market segments, airframes and airlines. Our combined computer products businesses ended the year at almost a $1 million daily sales rate, up over 50% from the beginning of the year. Video products business, especially home satellite earth station volume, was thriving by June...and although our Electrical and Engineering and Automotive Groups' business remained relatively flat at year-end, signs of their recovery were also at hand. What a finish for a year which showed such poor promise at its outset! So far in the first quarter of fiscal 1984 this momentum continues.

Almost three-quarters of the Company's 1983 sales came from the Electronic Marketing Group. At Electronic Marketing's current rate of growth, my early vision of it as the first billion dollar Group within Avnet may be realized this fiscal year.

1983 Results — Despite the difficult first half and the effects of charging off $2.4 million after-tax or $.07 per share in the third quarter from Hamilton/Avnet's Japanese operation, the Company's earnings for the year were $50.4 million or $1.43 per share compared with $56.1 million or $1.61 per share from continuing operations last year; and its sales were $1.165 billion compared with $1.112 billion last year. To compare this performance with our competitors, a July 29th Media General study covering the 9 largest publicly reporting electronics distribution companies, including Avnet, revealed that Avnet accounted for about one-third of the combined sales and about one-half of the combined profits in the four most recent quarters reported by these 9 companies.

Our year-end balance sheet ratios were improved. Total debt was reduced to $24 million, about 4% of total capital. Our short-term marketable securities, which were $40 million at the beginning of the year, were $100 million at its end. We finished the year with especially strong fourth quarter performances by both our Electronic Marketing and Video Communications Groups. Fourth quarter sales were up $52.9 million at $326.1 million compared with $273.1 million last year. Earnings were $15.9 million and $.45 per share compared with $13.4 million and $.38 per share last year.

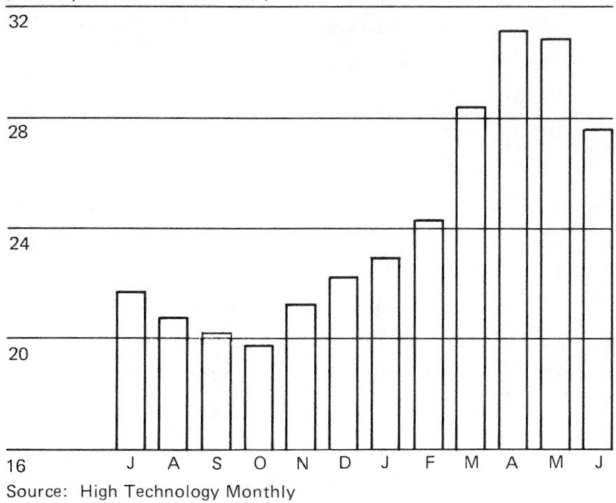

Summary — As the protracted recession finally wound down and the recovery began to gain momentum, we looked back at the fiscal year 1983 as one of major accomplishment in the face of adversity. Avnet's executive team enhanced our Company's position of industry leadership by managing its business skillfully. Their efforts were not overlooked. Financial World Magazine recognized our Company and the team by presenting me with their Electronics Industry CEO of the Year Award. Wall Street also noted our accomplishments; the market price of our common shares doubled in value by the end of fiscal 1983.

We continued to invest in dynamic new businesses. We continued to be dedicated to a program of growth both from within and from without. We continued to improve our cash position and our borrowing capability which will help us implement these plans.

Outlook — The prospects for our Electronic Marketing and Video Communications Groups continue to brighten as the protracted recession recedes. They operate in two of America's most dynamic growth industries, electronic distribution and television equipment. (Since about 85% of Avnet's total business now comes from these two business sectors, I thought our shareholders would be interested in the "History of Distribution" and "History of Television" which are to be found on pages 6-9 and 18-21 of this Report.)

In my opinion, we have now reached the final phase of the typical five phase recovery pattern the electronics industry goes through...(1) increased bookings, (2) increased sales, (3) delivery stretchout, (4) price stability, (5) improved margins. We should now start to enjoy the improved profitability which better margins bring.

Avnet is fortunate to be entering this period of recovery with great financial strength, substantial borrowing ability, an excellent balance sheet, and lean, streamlined operations. We continue on the course we set of pruning sluggish companies and product lines and replacing them with technology-related companies and products with high growth potential. Our electronic components shipments, the mainstay of our business, are reaching record levels, our microcircuitry and customized chips businesses are exhibiting good growth, as is our TV earth station business; and our Micro-Beam relay devices show great promise. Our Electrical and Engineering business may be just turning the corner along with our Automotive business. Fiscal 1984 will be a strong year for our Company if it finishes as positively as it began.

I am gratified by our recent accomplishments and extend thanks to our suppliers, our customers and our dedicated employees for their outstanding support as we rode the roller coaster together in wild, wild fiscal 1983.

Respectfully submitted,

Anthony R. Hamilton
Chairman and
Chief Executive Officer

August 19, 1983

To the Owners of Beatrice Foods Co.

Fiscal 1983 was a turning point for Beatrice. During the year, your company embarked on a new strategic course built around a total commitment to marketing.

This new plan calls for transforming Beatrice into a unified, directed marketing company, with real power in the markets we serve, and with the skills needed to enter new markets successfully.

Marketing will be the decisive element in our future program of internal growth, while acquisitions will play a smaller role.

We have begun to group our domestic businesses together to increase marketing effectiveness. By combining similar businesses into larger cohesive units we also can achieve additional efficiencies in cost, productivity and distribution.

This program is already under way in our grocery, confections, agri-products, dairy, building products, graphic arts, warehousing and chemical operations.

We have established a new corporate marketing department to coordinate our efforts and to provide research and other marketing services.

To enhance the marketing presence our realignment will bring, we've initiated a corporate-wide identity study to recommend ways to increase the marketing equity of the Beatrice name. The Beatrice name will become a more recognized identity with our customers and consumers.

The shift toward internal growth generated by a total commitment to marketing is a major new direction for Beatrice, but it is a course we must follow. We already have begun to recognize progress from our new marketing focus, and many marketing successes are detailed throughout this year's annual report.

Your company performed well last year given the circumstances of recession, the strong dollar and continued softness in consumer demand. Both sales and earnings before special actions were slightly ahead of last year's record operating results.

Each of our five operating segments responded differently to these economic circumstances, and their performance is highlighted in separate sections of this year's annual report. Earnings excluding special charges were $321 million, or $3.06 primary earnings per share, compared with fiscal 1982 earnings of $313 million before special items, or $3.02 primary earnings per share. Fiscal 1983 sales were $9.2 billion, up 2 percent from last year's $9.0 billion. Fully diluted earnings per share, before special actions in both years, reached $2.91 in fiscal 1983 compared with $2.87 the previous year.

As I discussed with you in a recent letter, the company's board of directors decided to take several special charges against fourth quarter earnings. These special charges reduced fiscal year reported earnings to $43 million, or 27 cents for earnings per share. Net earnings in fiscal 1982 were $390 million, or $3.80 primary and $3.58 fully diluted earnings per share.

This year-to-year comparison is notable because it pairs special items that increased reported results in fiscal 1982 with special charges that reduced net earnings in fiscal 1983.

Fiscal 1982 results included gains from the sale of Dannon and gains from adopting the flow-through method of accounting for investment tax credit.

Special charges taken this year include:

First: an increase of $75 million after-tax in our divestiture reserve to accommodate continuing plans to position Beatrice in the most promising industries and businesses.

The increased divestiture reserve will allow Beatrice to move out of cyclical, capital-intensive industrial operations as well as food and non-food businesses in which our market position is not meaningful. Within two years we plan to sell approximately 50 domestic and international companies, which reported $872 million in sales and $36 million in segment earnings during fiscal 1983.

Second: a write-down of $188 million after-tax in goodwill largely associated with our acquisition of Tropicana. Tropicana and the citrus juice industry remain promising, but repeated weather abnormalities reduced Tropicana's performance and diminished the value of its goodwill. We're now carrying our investment in Tropicana at a more realistic valuation.

Third: a $15 million after-tax charge to initiate a voluntary early retirement program for employees who meet certain age and service requirements. This program is part of a continuing effort to improve productivity. We have undertaken it in a manner which best benefits Beatrice and the employees who volunteer for the program.

These three charges are part of our long-term plan to situate Beatrice for strong internal growth. We are convinced that these actions best serve the long-term interests of Beatrice and its owners.

FINANCIAL HIGHLIGHTS

Dividends: In March 1983 the board of directors voted a 6.7 percent increase in the quarterly common stock dividend, raising it to 40 cents per share from 37½ cents, or to an annualized rate of $1.60 per share. This increase reflects our expectations for improved earnings in fiscal 1984.

Return on Stockholders' Equity: In fiscal 1983, return on average stockholders' equity was 13.1 percent before the special charges, compared with 13.6 percent in fiscal 1982, before special items. Including special actions in both years, the return on average stockholders' equity was 1.9 percent in fiscal 1983 and 16.9 percent in fiscal 1982. Although charges against earnings depressed return on average stockholders' equity in fiscal 1983, the long-term effect will be positive, due to increased earnings levels.

Net Capital Expenditures: As a result of the recession, we reduced our capital expenditures to $211 million in fiscal 1983, compared with $216 million last year. For fiscal 1984, Beatrice expects to invest over $250 million in plant and equipment to maintain facilities, expand production and improve efficiency.

Indebtedness: The ratio of long-term debt to stockholders' equity was 35 percent this year compared with 31 percent in fiscal 1982.

Currency Translation: In fiscal 1983, Beatrice adopted the provisions of FASB 52 for foreign currency translation. This change reduced net foreign currency translation losses and other expenses included in fiscal 1983 net earnings by $11 million, or an effect of 11 cents on earnings per share. Under this rule, fiscal 1983 foreign currency translation losses were $13 million. In fiscal 1982, this amount was $2 million under FASB 8.

Advertising: In fiscal 1983, advertising and promotion expenditures increased to $271 million from $200 million in fiscal 1982. The large increase resulted from the advertising and promotion expense associated with the beverage operations acquired in fiscal 1982.

SALES
(In Millions of Dollars)

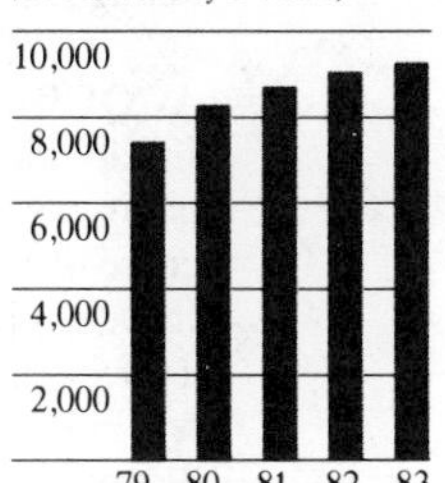

SEGMENT EARNINGS
(In Millions of Dollars)

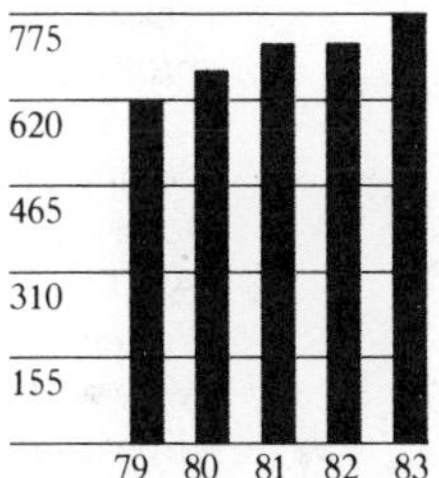

MANAGEMENT

As part of my personal commitment to Beatrice operations, I assumed the additional position of president following the resignation of Donald P. Eckrich last year. William W. Granger, Jr., former executive vice president of the International Division and one of the company's most experienced managers, now assists me with operations in his new role as vice chairman. Also, retiring during fiscal 1983 was James Weiss, executive vice president, Consumer, Industrial & Chemical, and a director of the company.

Everyone throughout Beatrice was saddened by the death in December of Theodore R. Ruwitch, vice president and assistant to the chairman. Ted headed our China group, and in 1981 helped negotiate the first joint venture agreement with China by any major U.S. company. He was a wise business associate, a good friend, and a fine man.

With the increased focus on marketing, John J. McRobbie, formerly president of LaChoy, has assumed the position of senior vice president, director of corporate marketing. William E. Reidy was appointed senior vice president, director of strategy and will coordinate the combining of our domestic businesses.

During the year several other managers were promoted to positions of greater responsibility.

Anthony Luiso, president of the International Division, was promoted from vice president to senior vice president.

William L. DeHaven, president of Specialty Meats, was elected a corporate vice president.

Thomas P. Kemp, president of Soft Drinks and Bottled Water operations, was named a corporate vice president.

Mary D. Allen, previously assistant vice president in the legal department, became vice president and assistant general counsel.

Barbara M. Knuckles, formerly manager of community and consumer relations, was named vice president and director of corporate marketing research.

ACQUISITIONS AND DIVESTITURES

In addition to finding familiar faces in new positions, many new faces appeared around the company because of acquisitions completed during fiscal 1983. In December we acquired Termicold Corporation, a refrigerated warehouse company with headquarters in Portland, Oregon. Beatrice now operates 41 warehouses nationally.

In June we completed acquisitions of Coca-Cola Bottling Company of San Diego and Coca-Cola Bottling Company of San Bernardino. These acquisitions, along with a few smaller Coca-Cola franchise territories acquired this year, complement our profitable and promising beverage operations.

During the year Beatrice sold a number of companies, including Amarillo By-Products and John J. Riley from the agri-products operations; A-1 Tool, Acme Die Casting, and Accurate Threaded Fasteners from industrial operations; and Brookside Vineyard. Financial details of acquisitions and divestitures are found in note 2 of Notes to Consolidated Financial Statements.

COMMUNITY RESPONSIBILITY

Your company continues to invest time and resources to enhance the quality of life in the communities in which its employees live and work.

During fiscal 1983, the company contributed $3 million in direct financial support to a variety of educational, cultural, civic and medical institutions. In addition, Beatrice maintained its leadership position in the national food bank program, providing nearly 2 million pounds of surplus food to the needy, and continued its financial support for Second Harvest, the national food bank network.

The company's gift-matching program received wide support from employees who contribute to many educational, cultural and health-related organizations.

PRODUCTIVITY/EXPORTS

Much of the credit for Beatrice's ability to grow during this difficult year must go to our employees. Through unselfish dedication and commitment to a strong work ethic, Beatrice showed a substantial increase in worker productivity even though there were fewer employees. For all operations, sales per employee increased nearly 7 percent, while the work force was down almost 5 percent.

Productivity improvements during fiscal 1983 resulted in a savings of $40 million, up about 60 percent from the $25 million saved last year.

Beatrice continues to promote export activity throughout the company through its program "Expro." Overall, exports declined moderately in fiscal 1983 as a result of the world-wide recession and the strong U.S. dollar. We are positioned well to take advantage of world-wide export opportunities as conditions improve.

OUTLOOK FOR FISCAL 1984

Given our new marketing direction, the appointments of capable people to key positions, and the promising upturn many of our businesses experienced at the close of the fiscal year, we are optimistic about prospects for each of our five operating segments and for the company as a whole in fiscal 1984.

Beatrice is a company that plans not for a single year but for the long-term. Even though we are optimistic about next year, we are more concerned with providing a stable base of profitability for years to come.

The steps we've taken should enable Beatrice to make substantial progress toward meeting our long-term objectives of 5 percent real annual growth and 18 percent return on equity.

We wish to acknowledge the loyalty and support of our employees, as well as that of Beatrice stockholders, customers and suppliers throughout the world. It is with them that we share the past successes and the promise of the future.

Sincerely yours,

James L. Dutt
Chairman
Chief Executive Officer
President

May 5, 1983

To Our Stockholders:

In 1983 we had another successful year. We achieved financial results consistent with our stated goals. We also made progress in building our management capability and in strengthening our market positions to enable us to continue this success.

Our financial performance is highlighted on the opposite page and discussed in detail beginning on page 20. Several accomplishments are noteworthy, including:

—The achievement well ahead of schedule of our goal of 18% return on stockholders' equity
—An 8.8% increase in sales to a record $6.6 billion
—A gain of 9.3% in net income, which reached $171 million
—A 9.7% advance in fully diluted earnings per share, which were $5.66, compared with $5.16 in the previous year.

The mission of Consolidated Foods, our financial goals and policies, and our business strategies are discussed on the pages following this letter. The businesses of Consolidated Foods and the fiscal 1983 results of our operating units are described in the Review of Operations on pages 8 through 18.

You will find on page 7 a statement of our serious commitment to being socially responsible in all that we do. The management of Consolidated Foods has the clear objective of being a leading and responsible corporate citizen in all communities where we do business and with all constituents we serve.

Dividends and Stock. In October 1982 the board of directors increased the dividend on our common stock 20 cents per share to an annual rate of $2.32. This was the 21st dividend increase in the last 23 years; the corporation has paid its stockholders dividends on common stock for 38 consecutive years.

In January 1983 the corporation redeemed all the outstanding shares of its $4.50 cumulative convertible preferred stock at a price of $101 per share.

Acquisitions and Divestments. During 1983 we acquired Standard Meat Company, a processor of meat products with major customers in the foodservice industry; Flexnit, a manufacturer and marketer of intimate apparel; and the foodservice distribution business of Malone & Hyde. After the end of the fiscal year, we acquired Fleming Foodservice, a foodservice distributor. Also, we sold Oxford Services and L'erin Cosmetics, and reached an agreement in principle to sell Oxford Chemicals.

Management. There were several management changes of significance during the year. In December, John J. Cardwell resigned as president. We value highly the contributions he made to the corporation during his six years as president and a director of Consolidated Foods. Following his departure, the duties of chief operating officer were shared by Robert E. Elberson, as vice chairman, and Robert Jaunich II, as president. In January, Mr. Jaunich resigned as an officer and director, and Mr. Elberson was elected president and chief operating officer.

During the year four new senior vice presidents were named; all had previously held key management positions within the operating units of the corporation. George W. Bryan, John B. McKinnon, C. Steven McMillan and Andrew E. Weidener joined Paul Fulton and P. Frederick Kahn as senior vice presidents with responsibility for groups of businesses; all report to the president and chief operating officer. David E. Harrold, already a senior vice president, assumed responsibility for corporate strategic planning, reporting to the chairman.

Six new corporate vice presidents were elected during 1983: Cornelis Boonstra, Philip R. Currier, James W. Fidler, Patty Delony Kester, Joseph F. Neely and Leslie W. Riley, Jr.

Charles A. McKee, who had served as chief executive of Electrolux since 1969 and as an officer and director of Consolidated Foods since 1971, retired as executive vice president on June 30; he will retire from the board of directors in October. Charlie McKee has had an extraordinary career. He was a dynamic and highly effective leader of Electrolux during a period that spanned 42 years. He was a major contributor to the development of Consolidated Foods. We greatly appreciate his service to the corporation.

Outlook. We are pleased with the progress of the corporation in recent years, and we believe we have good prospects for achieving another year of increased earnings in 1984.

John H. Bryan, Jr.
Chairman of the Board and
Chief Executive Officer

Robert E. Elberson
President and
Chief Operating Officer

August 25, 1983

HOW TO OPENLY DISCUSS YOUR COMPANY'S PROBLEMS

Your president must be candid in describing corporate results in the president's letter. The president should discuss internal problems that were created by management, and external problems brought on by government, social, or economic influence. Credibility is very important. If there are problems, the president should own up to them. They should not be swept under the rug. If your president doesn't face the facts, your company's credibility will be adversely affected. The president should not only discuss the problem, but equally important, should describe in detail what steps have been taken to correct the problem.

HOW TO REPORT DECREASED EARNINGS

How does the president describe the reasons for the company's decline in profits? Many start their letters by stressing the positives and then going, on to describe the decreased earnings.

The *Wall Street Journal,* in an article headlined, "Double Talk Grips Business Reports as Firms Try to Sugarcoat Bad News," reported:

"Along with layoffs and losses, recessions breed gobbledygook.

Even in the best of times, corporate America is prone to murky prose. But when the economy turns lousy, the traditional "letter to shareholders" in annual reports can get more baffling than usual.

The executive double talk springs from a special vocabulary. It favors the passive voice, allowing troubled firms to depict themselves as victims of sinister forces beyond their control. Corporate wordsmiths indulge at these times in various forms of understatement, overstatement and nonstatement.

The latest buzzwords prove useful. Thus DeSota Inc. and Santa Fe Industries Inc. claim this year to be "impacted" by the recession. Impacted is a word normally associated with wisdom teeth and overcrowded cities.

Some companies are fetching up such vague words as "reasonable," "acceptable," and "satisfactory" to characterize 1981 or comment on 1982. "It's as if they're saying, 'At least we didn't go bankrupt,'" says William Lutz, head of the English department at Rutgers University and chairman of a group called the Committee on Public Doublespeak. "It's like the first line of a song I heard,'' he adds. ''I had a good meal/I didn't throw up.''

No wonder, then, that professional investors skip past the shareholders' letter. "They dazzle you with rhetoric," says the head of research at one of Wall Street's biggest brokerage houses. "Any good analyst goes right to the numbers."

Abraham Krasnoff, president of Poll Corporation, in an article "How to Present Bad News and Good News Constructively" advised:

"If it's bad news you have to tell—get it over with and if possible couple it with the good that will come from what you have learned. End on a positive note. Again remember—your outlook is what is being depicted.

Let me give you an example—again from our forthcoming report—of getting the bad news over with and coupling it with the good to come:

'After many years of uninterrupted growth, largely in the aerospace market, we have for some time been in a period of earnings fluctuation, although sales have been maintained in an upward trend. For the last three years we have suffered low profits but no losses, during a growing depression in what was our basic market—aerospace.'

'Major new product and new market development takes from three to five years and we believe we have used the period of this earnings hiatus to accomplish just such developments. This, we believe, will lead to a new period of extended growth.'

These two paragraphs told the undeniable fact that a period of low earnings had been suffered—but led from that to the positive statement that we believe ourselves to be in a new period of growth. This set the tone for a positive report and the pages that follow are used to show the future benefits accrued during a period of low profitability."

Dear Fellow Shareholder:

March 1, 1984

Harry Holiday, Jr. and Robert E. Boni

The numbers in this annual report summarize 1983, repeating what you already know. Our 1983 results were dreadful. But now we think we've cleared the way for a better future.

As we go to press with this letter — the part of Armco's annual report we do last — we want to share a twofold message with you:

- *First,* Armco is once more becoming profitable from continuing operations.
- *Second,* Armco and the best of basic industry have a bright future.

We think it is time to stand up and shout: "Don't sell industry short!"

That's a brave boast these days. But we aren't Pollyannas. Who could be, after these past two awful years? Besides the *Year in Brief* summary which begins this annual report, you can read details of Armco's results in management's discussion and analysis of our full financial statements.

Armco owners, reading our quarterly shareholder reports, have followed our efforts as we carried out dramatic cost-cutting measures and radically restructured Armco's operations. You know about our bold quality improvement program. You've seen our writeoffs and consolidations in carbon steel. You're aware of our decision to sell our insurance businesses. You've read about our retargeted strategic plan to achieve our goals for Armco's future.

The quick list of highlights on the facing page summarizes major accomplishments. You'll see more about each of Armco's lines of business following this letter. As a result, your company enters 1984 far stronger operationally. We're a smaller company, but healthier now.

Now that we've gone through the fire, we can see that even as the past two years brought us scars, they also taught us much. We'd like to share a few of the lessons we've relearned.

- We *can* produce consistently high-quality products.
- We *can* lower our break-even points and reduce our costs.
- We *can* create innovative new products and services.
- We *can* serve our customers with greater marketing strength.
- No matter what the problem is, we *can* cope with it. Since we can, then we are confident others can, too. Don't sell industry short.

We've all seen gloomy discussions of the so-called structural crisis in our nation's greatest industries. This talk is the latest chorus in a long dirge claiming America has entered a post-industrial society. Obviously, many great basic companies have been going through terrible times. But the doomsayers miss the main point: there is no such thing as a post-industrial economy. People will always need products as well as services. The only important question is: who will make and sell these products?

Our answer is clear. Armco will — efficiently and profitably. We will produce goods and services with increasing productivity and quality, responding swiftly to our customers' needs. We will continue to do this around the world — most emphatically including the United States.

The key to industry's survival is simple: love your customers as you love yourself. It takes more than lip-service to a marketing orientation. You've got to live it, every day. At Armco, we've rededicated ourselves to this axiom. All those lessons we learned were already engraved in our hearts — the past two years merely gave us an acid test.

This won't be Armco's final test, to be sure. We still have much to do to improve our performance. This makes a good time, after this dark year, to repeat our five basic financial goals:

- Bond rating of A or better
- 12% Return on Net Assets
- 15% Return on Shareholders' Equity
- Higher dividends whenever prudent
- Improved stock price

That list should keep us humble until we achieve it.

To reach those goals, we have major strategic moves to make as we continue shifting Armco's assets into profitable businesses along our strategic path. You can see in the pie charts where we stood by the end of 1983 and where we currently intend to go.

One more point was demonstrated dramatically over the past two years. Armco's inherent philosophy — the moral code we espoused more than 60 years ago in Armco Policies — continues to be the strongest weapon we can bring to bear to solve problems. Armco Policies and Armco Spirit give us the strength and enthusiasm to overcome our troubles. They are the binding force knitting us all together in a team.

Some people seem reluctant these days to mention morality and spirit in a business report. We think that's too bad. As we move along in 1984, expecting better times in nearly every one of Armco's markets, we are more convinced than ever that Armco Policies pay.

Let us end our letter by thanking you for sticking with Armco through this trying time. We're very grateful for your faith and support.

Sincerely,

Harry Holiday, Jr.
Chairman & Chief Executive Officer

Dr. Robert E. Boni
President & Chief Operating Officer

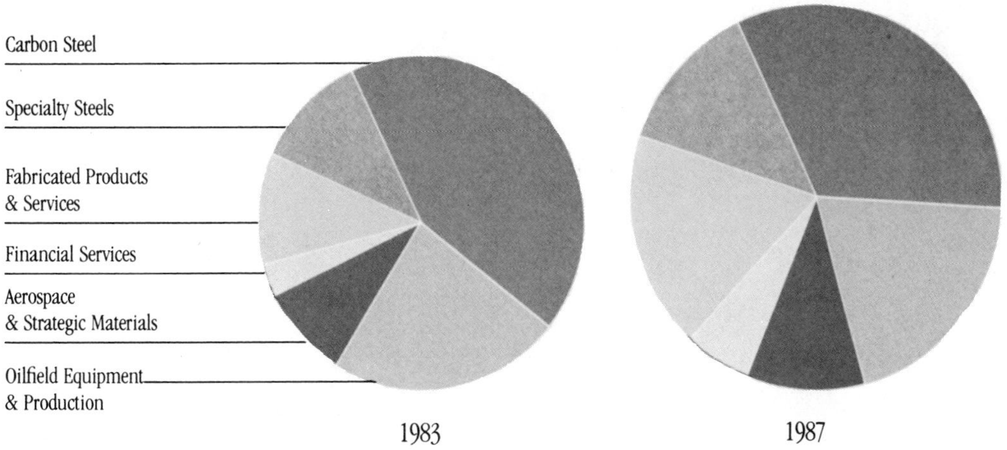

Carbon Steel
Specialty Steels
Fabricated Products & Services
Financial Services
Aerospace & Strategic Materials
Oilfield Equipment & Production

1983

1987

The following are examples of how some companies described the results of a "down" year.

To our shareholders:

Revenues for the year ended March 27, 1982 were $268,956,000, compared to $270,125,000 last year. Net income was $6,572,000, compared to $17,207,000 last year.

Earnings per share were $.74, compared to $2.21 a year ago.

Revenues in the fourth quarter were the best of the four—$73,862,000 compared to $74,908,000.

Net income in the final quarter was $834,000 or $.09 per share, compared to $4,579,000 or $.57 per share last year.

The primary cause behind these decreases was the recession, which until this year had not seriously hurt the computer industry.

There were, however, contributing causes that were within the company's control.

We did not act quickly enough to reduce costs and capacity to levels that could have produced a substantial improvement in earnings. We underestimated the severity of the recession, and in the interest of increasing our market share, we elected not to reduce our product development and marketing efforts.

In addition, the costs of matrix printer production were higher than expected in the last six months, a period of rapidly expanding production.

The downside of this year's performance is disappointing, of course. But an analysis of the company's products, its marketing accomplishments and its balance sheet reveals a strong position.

TEKTRONIX

Interrupting the Growth Habit

So as not to hem and haw about it: Yes, this has been a poor year.

Details are on pages 3 through 12, with further elaboration elsewhere in the appropriately muted gray text pages.

We did convert the preceding year's roughly billion-dollar order total into roughly a billion dollars of sales; but that seemed a hollow achievement in light of our drop in earnings. For a company habituated to strong earnings growth (we've had nine straight years of it), it's traumatic to have to pause. We're not used to that.

We'd be ducking responsibility to lay it all at the feet of the US economy, or the wild terpsichore of currencies, or stultifying interest rates. Those things did happen – but that's life. The job of managing is to take the world the way it's dealt out and make the most of it; somewhere it says that.

Tek, as past annual reports have divulged to you, tends to be run in a participative fashion; most decisions are consensual. Regarding the past year, our management's consensus isn't just that we didn't do very well (shucks, this year a ***lot*** *of companies could say that) but, worse:* ***That we should have done better.***

Some of the bad things we'd blame if we could are summarized on pages 7 through 9.

If at one time the handwriting was on the wall, today the alphanumerics are on the terminal screen. What they say is that the '80s are going to be an increasingly competitive time.

Tektronix, in a significant organizational change, is at work forming the kind of company the new decade demands. The main building blocks have been set in place: Product-oriented divisions, designed to move with sureness and alacrity through the uncharted '80s.

Divisionalizing means different things to different folks. What ***we*** *mean by it is explained on page 17 and beyond.*

An outrush of innovative products – our strongest in many years – has begun. They represent advances in major product areas, and have a real excitement about them: Not only in analog instrumentation, where we made our fame and early fortune; but also in the newer area of digital, or logic, products, where a good share of our future rests.

What the products are and what they do are discussed in some detail beginning on page 23.

A Bittersweet Billion-Dollar Year

It was a tough, tough 12 months. And Tektronix didn't do at all well.

To start things off, the order rate nosedived; then orders staggered barely upward, in a fitful, unreassuring manner. They ended just below those of the year before. Earnings — after nine years of continued increases—fell off by 6 per cent.

Sales were up a bit — in dollars. But those dollar figures don't give the whole picture. Sift from them the effect of our product price increases, and it's possible we actually sold **fewer** products than the year before.

Part of the problem was the economic recession. But only part. Another part was us, and our failure to live up to our own set of performance standards. It's ironic, and most disappointing, that Tektronix' first billion-dollar sales year should be a downer.

Sales were up by 9 per cent from those of a year earlier. They moved to $1,061,834,000 from $971,306,000. Of those, the *US portion* increased by 6 per cent; the *international segment* by 15 per cent. Figures were: US sales, $625,335,000, up from $591,760,000; international sales, $436,499,000, up from $379,546,000.

Sales of *Test and Measurement products* increased, to $757,973,000 from $722,060,000, or up 5 per cent; those of *Information Display products* increased 22 per cent, going to $303,861,000 from $249,246,000.

Earnings declined for the first time in 10 years. They were off by 6 per cent, totaling $80,167,000, compared to $85,072,000 last year. Similarly, *earnings per share* dropped, to $4.34 from $4.66. Of the earnings, about 28 cents per share resulted from the sale to Squibb Corporation of our portable-patient-monitor business unit.

Incoming orders were about flat, down 1 per cent from those of the year before, at $1,040,000,000. *Unfilled orders* decreased to $295 million from $317 million.

We had 24,028 employees when the year ended. We had started out with 23,890. Normal attrition wore away that original total; so did the sale of our patient-monitor business

THE TOUGHEST JOB OF ALL: HOW TO REPORT A LOSS YEAR

One of the most difficult tasks confronting a corporate president is to report on a loss year. At best, the president can attempt to soften the blow through a candid explanation and a discussion of steps taken to bring the corporation back into a profitable position.

Letter to Shareholders:

In fiscal 1983 CRAIG CORPORATION experienced a loss of $6,895,000 after having earned $1,393,000 in the prior fiscal year. Sales fell from $83,485,000 in 1982 to this year's $58,371,000. The combination of a difficult economic environment and reductions in the company's consumer electronic program were important factors in bringing about the fiscal year loss. Additional accounts receivable revaluations, inventory mark-downs, and operating losses in the ordinary course of business all contributed to the losses sustained during the fiscal year. An additional contributing factor to the fiscal year loss was CRAIG'S divestiture of the major assets of Hastings & Richardson Communications, Inc., a manufacturer of Satellite Earth Station equipment. A non-recurring loss of approximately $1,500,000 was experienced in this transaction.

A major development was the purchase, by CRAIG, on February 16 1983, of the 40.6% interest in the company's common stock held by Monogram Industries, at a price of $10.25 per share. The 1,219,401 shares repurchased constituted the total holdings of Monogram in CRAIG. In spite of the large cash outlay for the repurchase of stock and the year's operating losses, CRAIG continues to be well positioned with respect to balance sheet strength:

Current Ratio	3:1
Debt to Equity Ratio	.35:1
Book Value per Share	$10.58

CRAIG ELECTRONICS has continued to pursue the strategy of concentrating its asset deployment, sales effort and marketing capability in a much narrower product range, primarily automotive sound equipment. A new range of more than twenty models of car stereos and car speakers was introduced to the trade toward the close of the fiscal year. In this connection, a marketing program was devised which relies heavily on distributors, thereby reducing CRAIG'S customer base and the related selling expenses . The new products and the new sales approach have been enthusiastically received.

The contraction of product lines and the introduction of new products required extra start up expenses. However, in positioning ourselves for the new fiscal year, we have significantly lowered expense levels and the CRAIG Electronic business has been restructured with much lower inventory and accounts receivable levels. We feel that the CRAIG Electronics division is now very compact, flexible and better able to meet the rapid changes and frequent opportunities inherent in that business.

MAGNASYNC/MOVIOLA, the CRAIG subsidiary producing Magnasync Communications products and Videola Editing products, continued to reflect steady sales and earning results. A major effort to develop new state of the art communications equipment has been the prime focus of Magnasync's engineering group.

DYNATECH, our subsidiary engaged in the manufacture of components for the computer and telecommunications field, was adversely affected by the recent recession. However, the beginnings of the recovery are bringing about gradual sales improvements. Substantial investments have been made to expand Dynatech into other service-related activities connected with its industry. Dynatech now manufactures printed circuit boards, has facilities for stuffing and wire-wrapping boards and panels, and has developed in-house capability for building test fixtures for electronic testing of boards and panels. These capabilities will dramatically improve Dynatech's ability to perform a full range of services for its customers.

DIMENSION SPECIALTY COMPANY is a CRAIG subsidiary active in the importing of custom photographic accessories for major retailers. "DSC" had a good year and continued to make a positive contribution to sales and earnings.

In the following pages we will describe in greater detail some of our current plans, especially with respect to CRAIG Electronics and Dynatech, where major repositioning is taking place. We feel that these plans, coupled with our conservative management of the company's assets during recent, difficult times, places us in a position to capitalize on an improving business environment.

Sincerely

ROBERT CRAIG
Chairman of the Board
Chief Executive Officer

PETER M. BEHRENDT
President

THE PRESIDENT SHOULD SPELL OUT STOCKHOLDER'S RETURN ON INVESTMENT AND DIVIDENDS

All too often, the president of a company, in writing his letter, neglects to stress two important subjects:

1. Return on investment
2. Dividends

Certainly these subjects are of great interest to your stockholders.

Examples:

Return on Shareholders' Investment

The rate of return on shareholders' investment improved for the tenth consecutive year, increasing to 22.7 percent from 22.2 percent in 19__.

Dividends

Our company has paid 232 consecutive quarterly dividends since 1924. In March 19__, the board of directors increased the quarterly dividend to 18 cents per share—double the rate of just three years earlier. A total of seven increases in the dividend rate since March of 1976 has resulted in a compound annual growth of 27 percent. After adjusting for inflation, dividends in constant dollars have more than doubled during this period.

Dividends

Fiscal 19__ represented the 16th consecutive year of increase in the annual dividend payment. The total dividend payment in 19__ was 96 cents compared with 90 cents in 19__. The quarterly dividend paid in December was the 167th consecutive dividend on the Company's common stock. Our stated policy continues to be to distribute 30% of the earnings in dividends and reinvest 70% in the business. During this period of depressed earnings the payout ratio will be higher than 30 percent but we intend to return to our targeted payout ratio as earnings recover.

Dividend Rate Reduced

In response to current adverse conditions, the board of directors in October reduced the common stock dividend by 50 percent. This was not an easy decision because in addition to paying consistent dividends it is our goal to provide shareholders with a real return on their investment by increasing dividends at a rate that exceeds inflation.

The difficult decision to reduce the dividend temporarily reflects the need to conserve our financial strength under the present difficult conditions. The conservation of shareholders' equity will provide the greatest degree of financial flexibility to take advantage of opportunities that could develop in the future. Our dividend objective has not been altered, and the highest priority has been assigned to the restoration and continued increase of cash dividends.

New Dividend Policy

Traditionally, the Company has maintained an exceptionally generous dividend policy. Since 1977, we have paid out an average of 75 percent of earnings as dividends. However, an increased level of earnings reinvestment in our growth opportunities will better serve our shareholders' long-term interests. At its August 1982 meeting, the Board of Directors therefore approved an annual dividend rate reduction to $2.00 as part of a new dividend policy under which we expect eventually to pay out approximately 50 percent of earnings as dividends. This will bring our pay-out ratio into line with other comparable, financially sound corporations. The Company remains committed to maintaining its strong balance sheet—a most valuable asset in today's difficult economic climate.

Dividend Up For Ninth Straight Year

Increase Again Outpaces Inflation

For the ninth year in a row Grace increased its dividend, raising the quarterly cash payment from 65 to 70 cents per share, or an indicated $2.80 annually—20 cents, or eight percent, above last year's rate.

The dividend increase was in line with the Company's goal of matching or exceeding the rate of inflation, which was 3.9 percent in 1982 as measured by the Consumer Price Index.

BITING THE BULLET—SPELLING OUT YOUR COMPANY'S FINANCIAL OBJECTIVES

Most companies refrain from setting out financial objectives in their annual reports. Stockholders and security analysts, of course, are interested in knowing your corporation's financial objectives.

The following are examples of companies that outline financial objectives in their annual report.

ConAgra's Objectives and Results

ConAgra is committed to major objectives which guide us in fulfilling our responsibility to our stockholders.

OBJECTIVES

Return on Common Equity

ConAgra's most important objective is to average in excess of a 20 percent after-tax return on year-beginning common stockholders' equity, and to earn in excess of a 15 percent return in any given year.

In the results shown at right, the fiscal 1983 return is based on year-beginning common equity which includes a pro rata share (10 months) of the common equity associated with the merger of Peavey Company and ConAgra.

Growth in Primary Earnings Per Share

ConAgra's objective is to increase trend line earnings per share, on average, in excess of 14 percent per year from the fiscal 1973 base — the record year prior to restructuring of the company.

The cyclical nature of some of our basic food businesses does not always permit quarter-to-quarter, or sometimes year-to-year, increases in reported earnings. However, ConAgra expects to increase its trend line earnings in excess of 14 percent per year.

Compound annual growth rates since fiscal 1973 are represented by the trend line objective and the actual ten-year rate through fiscal 1983.

Financing

ConAgra's primary financing objective is to maintain a conservative balance sheet.

Long-Term Debt

Will not exceed 40 percent of total capitalization.

Short-Term Debt

Each of ConAgra's businesses will normally eliminate net short-term debt at the end of its natural fiscal year.

Natural year end occurs when inventories and receivables are at their annual low points — for example, the end of February in our agricultural chemicals business and the end of May in many other businesses.

We are improving our financing objective in fiscal 1984 as discussed in the "Corporation" section of this report.

Dividend Rate at Year End

ConAgra's objective is to increase dividends consistent with growth in basic trend line earning power.

Over a period of time we expect dividend payments to average in the range of 30-35 percent of earnings.

The result shown is the five-year compound annual growth rate of the year-end dividend rate from 1978 to 1983.

P E R F O R M A N C E A G A I N S T

The following describes the progress we have made toward achieving the corporate objectives outlined in last year's Annual Report.

FINANCIAL DIRECTION

Our overriding concern in 1983 was to operate profitably, despite the continuing recession at the beginning of the year that was adversely affecting our sales level. At the same time, we were determined to support those internal programs that would have a significant impact on our future growth. We believe that these overall objectives were accomplished. Beginning in the second quarter, we reported strong earnings with dramatic improvement in almost all segments of our business. Our product development programs, such as those for our aftermarket test equipment business, moved forward and are now yielding excellent returns.

Objective 1: Managing our overhead structure to achieve profitability even at recession levels.

Performance: Overhead was tightly controlled. Spending levels, adjusted for inflation, are down from pre-recessionary periods in proportion to changes in sales volume.

Objective 2: Continuing an aggressive margin improvement program.

Performance: Our margin improvement program was a success. On a direct operating cost basis, our margins were at record levels by the end of 1983. From a low point of 38.5% in 1977, we reached 42.3% in 1983. At present sales levels, this has the potential to improve pre-tax earnings by approximately $16 million.

Objective 3: Achieving additional gains in working capital efficiency.

Performance: Improvement in working capital efficiency exceeded our 5% target. This was a considerable accomplishment in view of the rapid sales growth during the second half of the year and the additional working capital required for new product programs.

Objective 4: Redeploying assets from weak product areas of low potential to ones with high returns.

Performance: We continued to redeploy assets from marginal commitments. Our Cal Chrome Division, a maker of customized wheel rims, was sold, parts of our international service operations were restructured, and programs were launched to eliminate low-return products in several areas of our business.

Objective 5: Continuing a strong emphasis on cash management to permit sales growth and to take advantage of external opportunities.

Performance: Cash management continued to be one of the important strengths of the Company. In addition to increasing the efficiency of our working capital, we continued to closely monitor capital expenditures and used the proceeds from asset sales to invest in more promising and profitable programs. Our financial posture was greatly strengthened through a successful equity offering. At the end of 1983, Allen's balance sheet had no short-term debt, and the Company's debt-to-equity ratio was its best in twenty years.

PRODUCT AND TECHNOLOGY DIRECTION

Uniqueness remained the focus of our product and technology development. Through the successful implementation of this strategy, we have gained market share in most key areas of the Company.

1983 OBJECTIVES

Objective 6: Ensure the availability of resources for our aftermarket test equipment business.

Performance: Our aftermarket test equipment business received a substantial portion of the Company's resources during 1983. Both manpower and financial resources were directed to the following: the Firestone program; our selection as the supplier of engine diagnostic equipment to General Motors Dealer Equipment; our entry into the California market with an emissions analyzer; large increases in Smart Scope sales; and continued new product development. We believe we are the technology leader in this industry as well as the domestic sales leader.

Objective 7: Continue to actively pursue new technologies with a high degree of sophistication and profit potential.

Performance: Our pursuit of new technology was directed primarily to our aftermarket test equipment business. Our new product offerings in this area are being recognized for their uniqueness and state-of-the-art technology. We also achieved gains in the area of production-line test equipment and material-handling systems. Our Translift® technology is an integral part of a major system for General Motors' Harrison Radiator Division. In the area of mobile communications, we enjoy a leading share of the cellular radio antenna market.

Objective 8: Continue to invest in our electronics expertise, including product development capability; continue support of the growth of our electronics manufacturing capability in Puerto Rico.

Performance: Our electronics expertise was strengthened by organizational improvements in both our Puerto Rico and Kalamazoo, Michigan plants. At both locations, we supported improvements in our electronics manufacturing capability. We made considerable progress in the transfer of high technology to our Puerto Rico plant.

Objective 9: Lessen our dependence on cyclical markets by applying our unique technologies to other industries.

Performance: The greatest progress made in this area was achieved in our production-line test equipment and material-handling systems business. We have successfully broadened our customer base to include a large number of non-automotive industrial companies. Our traditional automotive customers now account for less than half of new orders for this business. Customer diversification programs have been successfully implemented in other parts of the Company, including our rubber manufacturing business and our original equipment radiator business, in order to reduce the cyclical aspects of the automotive market. However, certain parts of Allen that we support continue to be subject to cyclical market influences. Nevertheless, we believe that these markets have the potential for attractive long-term growth.

Avon

Our primary financial objective is to generate consistent long-term earnings growth that will provide a high rate of return on shareholders' investment. Given relatively stable economic and political conditions throughout the world, the Company's specific goals are to generate average annual sales and earnings growth of at least 12 percent and return on shareholders' equity of 20 percent or more.

Corporate Philosophy

The principles on which Avon was founded remain the core of our corporate philosophy. These principles affirm our respect for people and belief in their initiative. Our success as a Company derives from a corporate environment that encourages and rewards creativity and excellence. In this setting, talented and motivated people thrive—and the Company prospers.

FMC

Reaching this goal calls for substantial changes in FMC's portfolio of businesses. FMC is making these changes through the selective redirection of major resources to its higher-return businesses and through divestitures and acquisitions. FMC's return-on-equity goal is ambitious and long term; progress toward its attainment may not always be smooth. In 1981, significant momentum was gained by raising return on equity to 13.9 percent from 11.7 percent in the prior year. The recession of 1982 depressed performance, with return on equity falling to 11.5 percent, but FMC's resolve to attain the 18-percent goal during the 1980s has not diminished.

Campbell

The Company is moving toward its long-term financial goals: a 15% annual increase in earnings . . . a 5% increase in volume . . . a 5% increase in sales, plus inflation . . . and an 18% return on equity.

Molex

"The corporate objectives of Molex are to grow at 20%–25% per year and generate a net, after-tax profit of 10%.

Medtronics

Compound annual revenue and earnings-per-share growth from our present business should be approximately 20 percent.
Compound revenue growth has been 17.7 percent for the last five years. Earnings-per-share growth averaged 25.3 percent during the same period. Last year sales were up 7 percent, with earnings per share increasing 13 percent.

The return on average shareholders' equity is targeted to exceed 20 percent.
The return on shareholders' equity for fiscal 1982 was 21.1 percent. Return on equity for the past five years has averaged 20.7 percent. (Return on equity is calculated by dividing net earnings by average equity.)

Growth in investment should approximate 20 percent annually, exclusive of acquisitions.
Investment grew to $279 million from $237 million during the year, an increase of 18.1 percent. Over the past five years compound growth in investment was 17.8 percent. (Investment is defined as year-end total assets less non-interest bearing liabilities and is not expected to increase at the same rate each year.)

The capital structure will consist primarily of equity, with interest-bearing debt as an alternative which, over a period of years, should not exceed 20 percent of total investment.
Total interest-bearing debt at year end was $34 million, up from $32 million last year. Debt was 12.2 percent of investment compared to 13.5 percent a year ago.

Dividends will be equal to approximately 20 percent of the previous year's net earnings.
Four quarterly dividends of 14 cents each were paid during the year. In June, Medtronic's board of directors raised the quarterly dividend to 16 cents per share.

Carpenter Technology Corp.

- Maintain a stong financial structure and limit debt to 25 percent of total capital employed.
- Continue the cash dividend policy which calls for a 40 percent average payout over an extended period of time.
- Insure adequate inventories of raw materials as dictated by our assessment of changing economic and political conditions.
- Continue our strong commitment to advanced technology.

- Continue to strengthen the organization through employee development programs.

Honeywell

Financial Objectives—Having achieved the long-range financial objectives set in 19__, we have now established new higher targets:

- 18 percent return on shareholders' equity
- 14 percent return on total capital employed
- debt ratio remaining under 30 percent
- regular dividend increases as earnings increase with a payout of a quarter to a third of prior year's earnings.

These higher return targets are necessary in a period of high inflation, and, if achieved, would allow us to fund much of our growth internally.

Kimberly-Clark

External Financial Goals. Our external financial objectives are:

1. In 19__, attain a level of earnings per share which, compared to 19__, will reflect an annual compound growth rate of 11 to 14 percent with earnings in each intervening year being not less than the preceding year.
2. Annually increase dividends by the amount necessary to insulate the 19__ quarterly rate of 65 cents per share against the effects of future inflation and, subject to capital needs, by such further amount as will provide a measure of real growth.
3. Long-term debt as a percentage of capital will be no higher than 28 percent and lower if consistent with capital needs.

I emphasize that we do not intend this statement of objectives to be a forecast. Naturally, we will strive every year to achieve the high side of the objective range for earnings growth. But if the past is any guide, we might expect at some time or another to produce annual earnings lower than the low side of the range.

McCormick

Objectives. This momentum and our ability to move quickly and efficiently to develop strategies attuned to the changing marketplace make us confident that we can achieve the aggressive financial objectives we have set for ourselves in the 1980's:

1. Annual net sales growth of 15%;
2. Annual growth in net ncome of 15%;
3. After-tax return on assets of 12.5%;
4. Target capital structure of 35 to 40%;
5. Target current ratio of 2 to 1;
6. Dividend payout ratio of 27 to 30% of net income.

By 19__ we plan to be a billion-dollar company with profits and dividends nearly two and one-half times their 19__ levels.

Zero Company

Corporate Objectives. Our overall financial objectives are:

- Achieve a 15 to 20 percent compound growth rate in earnings per share.
- Produce a return on average shareholders' equity of 18 to 20 percent a year.
- Pay dividends equal to 25 to 30 percent of the preceeding year's earnings.

During the past ten years we have more than achieved these objectives:

- Earnings before extraordinary items have grown at a compound growth rate of 33 percent.

REPORTING ACTUAL RESULTS vs. PAST FORECASTS CONSOLIDATED FOODS

Financial Goals and Policies. Last year, Consolidated Foods announced new goals for the two financial measures we consider most important: return on stockholders' equity and growth in earnings per share. The announced goals were:

–To reach a return on equity of 18% no later than 1986.

–To achieve and maintain a growth rate of 5% in real terms.

It is the corporation's policy to maintain a long-term debt to invested capital ratio of less than 35% and to increase the dividend on the common stock annually in a continual and dependable manner.

We believe that achieving these goals will give our corporation a ranking among the best of the diversified consumer products companies.

Results versus Goals and Policies. In 1982, Consolidated Foods achieved a record 17.3% return on average stockholders' equity. The corporation's return on equity has improved in each of the last seven years, and the present level is somewhat ahead of the progression planned to reach 18% no later than 1986.

Earnings per share increased by 17.0% in 1982, the seventh consecutive year of earnings improvement. Fully diluted earnings per share have increased at a compound annual rate of 13.2% since 1977.

In 1982, our annual dividend rate was increased to $2.12; 40.0% of earnings per share for the year was paid to common stockholders as dividends.

The ratio of long-term debt to invested capital at the end of 1982 was 23.1%, well below our maximum of 35%. The long-term debt to invested capital ratio has been reduced in each of the last three years; our strong capital structure allows us considerable financial flexibility.

Strategies. Specific strategies for meeting our goals have been developed and refined in recent years. As a first priority, the corporation will manage its businesses with a strong emphasis on improvement of return on investment and return on equity. In so doing, we will allocate capital to those businesses that meet our criterion for return on investment, or can be brought to that level in a reasonable period of time. We will divest companies that we conclude cannot reach and maintain our targeted performance levels.

We will continue to consolidate sales and earnings around our several large businesses which occupy leadership positions in attractive markets. The main sources of growth will be building market share of existing brands, developing new products internally and making integrating acquisitions which add to the earnings potential of existing businesses.

We will consider acquisitions that would not integrate into an existing business, but would be consistent with our strategic commitment to consumer goods and services. Such acquisitions must be capable of achieving steady growth and, except in unusual circumstances, will not dilute our stockholders' stake in the corporation.

There will be increasing efforts to refine and improve the process of decentralized management at Consolidated Foods. We will maintain a high degree of operating autonomy at the individual business units, with final responsibility for strategies and policies at the corporate level. We will provide overall direction and review through a planning system that focuses management attention on the most significant issues, using long-range strategic plans and detailed annual operating plans and budgets. Perhaps most importantly, we will continue to develop our human resources at all levels throughout the corporation.

THE ELECTION OF A NEW PRESIDENT

The readers of your annual report would like to have detailed information about the background of a newly elected president and chief operating officer of the corporation. All too often there is not sufficient information provided in the annual report.

An example of information that is helpful is as follows:

DiGiorgio Corporation

A New President

On June 16, the directors elected Peter F. Scott president and chief operating officer of the corporation. Formerly vice president and chief financial officer, Mr. Scott, 53, joined Di Giorgio Corporation in 1963. He was elected a vice president in 1969 and a director and member of the executive and member of the executive committee in 1974.

Mr. Scott brings strong qualifications to his duties as president. In addition to his responsibilities for the corporation's financial development, he has gained wide operating experience and close familiarity with the broad range of our activities as corporate liaison to our food processing and international operations and most recently as group vice president for our building materials group.

SEVEN SUBJECTS FOR THE PRESIDENT TO DISCUSS IN HIS OUTLOOK FOR THE YEAR

Your shareholders want your president to present the corporation's outlook for the future. This means spelling out what tomorrow looks like—based upon the best information available. All too often, clichés are used expressing confidence in the future. Remember—next year your shareholders will check back to see what your president said a year ago.

All too often, presidents end their letters with a blend, "take it from me . . . things look good for the future." These leave me cold.

Your stockholders want to know the factors that give the president confidence in the future. Here are seven suggestions to help your president put some meat into his outlook statement:

1. Show the outlook for the industry and its continuing growth.
2. Describe the capital investments the company will make.
3. Outline the investments that will be made in computerization of certain functions.
4. Describe the amounts to be expended on research and development.
5. Describe how the company will add marketing units.
6. Describe how the company will emphasize the improvement in profit margins, and controlling expenses.
7. Set out the rate at which your company sales have grown over the past ten years and your expected rate of growth anticipated for the coming year or years.

Some examples of the president's "Outlook" are as follows:

Long-Term Outlook

We feel confident that the North American automotive companies will be successful in overcoming the challenges facing the automobile industry. The primary challenge of producing a more efficient, high-quality vehicle presents a great opportunity for Magna to increase its penetration into the automotive marketplace. Given the advantages of our unique operating structure, we are certain Magna will be able to significantly increase its relatively small share of this enormous market.

In order to accomplish this growth, your Company is already laying the groundwork to become even more competitive in terms of cost and quality. During fiscal 1983 Magna opened an in-house centre for robotics and process automation. This centre is responsible for developing automated applications for various Magna production processes, including the use of internally designed and manufactured industrial robots.

Your Company has also taken the initial steps to establish a CAD/CAM (computer aided design/computer aided manufacturing) centre. This state-of-the-art division will have two purposes. First, it will form an integral part in Magna's component design studies. Second, it will be of great assistance in determining the most efficient manufacturing application(s) for various products.

The use of robotics, process automation and CAD/CAM will not only increase the efficiency of Magna's operations, but will also enhance your Company's product reliability and overall quality.

With regards to quality, your Company has effectively implemented Statistical Process Control (SPC) techniques where applicable. Simply stated, SPC is the application of statistics to quality control procedures. At the conclusion of fiscal 1983, more than 350 Magna employees, including machine operators as well as quality inspectors, had been thoroughly trained in the use of SPC. This program will continue to receive emphasis in the coming years.

Adding to Magna's technical base will remain a high priority in the coming years as we continue to offer more services to our customers, and strive to remain current and competitive. This diversification within our area of expertise will continue to be achieved via internal development and joint ventures.

Finally, a major advance in the development of your Company occurred in fiscal 1983 with the completion of Magna's Research and Development Centre, located in Markham, Ontario. The Centre was established to bring new product development capability to Magna as we position ourselves to meet the automotive industry's rapid advances in technology. Automobile companies expect suppliers to have product development capabilities and this Centre, with its design and development resources, will enable Magna to better service its customers' needs and thereby achieve greater market penetration.

With the growing trend towards single-sourcing, (the practice of sourcing 100% of a component's requirements with one supplier), the original equipment manufacturers (OEMs) are seeking longer-term contracts with key suppliers. In selecting these vendors, OEMs are focusing on price competitiveness and superior quality. We are confident Magna's expanded technical base, as outlined previously, will permit Magna to take advantage of this new relationship between customer and supplier.

Black and Decker

Future Outlook

We expect to be solidly profitable in 1983 despite the strong dollar which reduces the translation of our overseas results, generally weak worldwide economic conditions and continued competitive pressures in the professional power tool business. As the year unfolds, any significant economic improvement would result in substantial increases in our earnings. With generally low inventories in the distribution channels increased sales will lead to increased factory capacity utilization and provide better return for our shareholders.

We are concentrating on strategies that will lead us through the decade: Worldwide leadership in the growing professional power tool and consumer do-it-yourself markets and new business opportunities flowing from our strengths in manufacturing, marketing and distribution. During 1982 we have worked hard to build on these strengths to maintain focus on our long term objectives and to assure improved profitability in the future.

3M

Outlook for 1983

Over the last three years, the output of goods and services in major world economies has shown essentially no growth, in large part because of high interest rates. At this point, we have seen little evidence of significant economic improvement in our own business, but there are signs that the long-awaited economic upturn may begin this year.

We are generally positive about 1983. We expect gradual improvement in world economies as the year progresses, improvement that will lead to a higher level of unit volume growth. We also anticipate that the dollar will stabilize or decline somewhat in relation to other currencies.

We are in good position to capitalize on economic recovery when it arrives. For example, we enter the year in lean condition, a result of close control of operating expenses, including employment. Our worldwide employment was reduced significantly in the past year, falling approximately 4,000 to about 87,400 at year-end. A major portion of the decline occurred in the United States and was due to attrition and to a voluntary early retirement program.

HOW TO EXPRESS APPRECIATION TO YOUR EMPLOYEES

It's been my general feeling that too little thought and space are devoted to expressing appreciation to the company's employees in the annual report. We talk about our employees being our greatest asset—we know how important a role employees play in improving productivity.

Many of your employees may be stockholders in your company.

Most companies give their employees a quick pat on the back. Frank B. Hall goes further:

A NOTE OF APPRECIATION

We have had many positive improvements in your Company's operations this past year. Thousands have been working together for that improvement. It has been gratifying for me to see the effort that has been given by so many dedicated people. It has been a particular pleasure working with those persons with whom I have direct daily contact.

There are more effective ways to express appreciation; for example, Frank B. Hall uses the Letter from the President to speak to its employees as follows:

Your diligent and intelligent performance of your duties is evidenced in the fine financial results you achieved for your company this year as in those of the past. Nevertheless, I want to add my personal thoughts to this public record of your success.

Ours is one of the few businesses in which the entire inventory leaves the premises every evening. We don't make tangible products and we don't have warehouses of goods to sell. You are the complete inventory of Frank B. Hall. Your ideas are our products: your minds, our storage facilities. Hall's success depends on your dedication, direction, knowledge, experience and creativity. Without you, there would be no Frank B. Hall. So it is with all due respect that we shall continue our strong human resources development programs, our equitable compensation programs and our excellent benefits programs on your behalf.

These are trying times in our industry. But your hard work has brought us to new heights even in the present market. Your talent is truly appreciated. And, for your fine efforts, I promise you a professional environment, free of encumbrances, in which you may strive for even greater personal and professional success in the year ahead.

SIGNATURES TO THE LETTER

There is no uniformity amongst corporations as to who signs the letter to stockholders.

Examples:

Philip Morris Inc.
Chairman of the Board
Vice-Chairman of the Board
President

VAL Inc
Chairman
President—Chief Executive Officer

Wheelabrator-Frye Inc.
Chairman & Chief Executive Officer

Gould Inc.
Chairman of the Board & Chief Executive Officer

McDonald's Corp.
Founder & Senior Chairman of the Board
Chairman of the Board
President
Senior Executive Vice-President

Digital Equipment Corporation
President

A CONVERSATION WITH THE PRESIDENT OF YOUR COMPANY

For a change of pace, you might want to consider a reporting technique where your president answers questions that might be on the minds of your stockholders. Some questions that your president might answer are:

1. To what extent did your company expand any of its operations during the past year?
2. Do you plan additional internal expansion of operations in the coming year?
3. If another company that had a compatible type of business mix were offered for sale to your company, would your company aggressively seek such an acquisition, assuming the price was reasonable?
4. What is your acquisition program?
5. What size company would you buy if you had your choice?
6. Are you presently negotiating for any acquisition?
7. Does the board plan to increase dividends?
8. You declared a 20% stock dividend last year. Do you plan another in the coming year?
9. In the light of the present economic climate, what performance do you anticipate for your company next year?
10. What are the company's growth objectives over the next three years?
11. For the coming five-year period, does your company expect its sales and earnings growth rate to exceed, be the same as, or be less than the sales and earnings growth during the past five-year period, and why?
12. Your company has a good record of meeting its publicly announced sales and earnings forecasts. What specific means does the company use to control its day-to-day operations and to guard against unpleasant surprises? How does the company do its long-range planning.
13. Would you comment on your company's dividend policy? How do you determine what you will pay from earnings in the form of dividends?
14. How can you effectively offset the effects of what must be large increases in your cost of materials?
15. Explain the strategy behind the acquisitions by your company?
16. Your balance sheet is highly leveraged at this time. What is management's strategy to improve its quality?
17. What is the current outlook for your company's industry?
18. What are your company's plans for capital expenditures to replace older machinery in some of its plants?
19. Some economists are predicting a recession for your industry. Is you company financially capable of surviving a recession?
20. What are your company's plans for continuing or even expanding its corporate advertising program in an effort to familiarize more people with the company?
21. During the past three years, your company has invested about $700 million in a new plant and equipment. When are we likely to see the resulting improvement in profitability and cash flow?
22. What is the company's long-term strategy for the geographic distribution of operations and investments?

23. If interest rates remain at the present level, what effect will they have on your company's fundamental earning capacity?
24. Last year your company spent $9.6 million on research and development. What are your research and development department's principal areas of activity?
25. How can you ensure that the company's expenditure program will provide adequate returns for shareholders?
26. What are your company's policies concerning diversification?
27. What are your company's major strengths?
28. What is being done to improve the work environment?
29. What programs do you have to upgrade employee skills?
30. What are the major environmental challenges over the next decade and what will it cost the company to meet more stringent environmental regulations?

QUESTIONS AND ANSWERS FOR YOU TO CONSIDER

Comtech

What kind of acquisition is Comtech looking for?

Mr. Kornberg: "In order to meet our growth objectives for the next five years, we are seeking situations which will provide allied technology to contribute to both our sales and profit growth."

Could you be more specific as to the type of company and product and size of company you are looking for?

Mr. Kornberg: "We are looking for companies in the $5 and $10 million volume range in such areas as microwave components, communication test equipment, time division multiplexing, and similar related products which will fit in with our overall product mix and provide entry into additional market areas and possibly also give us some vertical integration. In this respect, we would also be interested in companies with products in the high frequency communications area, in the anti-submarine warfare area, and companies with technology and product in the Time Division Multiple Access (TDMA) Systems area."

How do you fit into the AntiSubmarine Warfare Defense Market?

Mr. Reed: "A fast growing segment of the Federal Defense Budget for the next five years is probably going to cover expenditures for research as well as production funds for equipment pertaining to underwater accoustics. The objective in Anti-submarine Warfare is first of all to locate a target submarine and then to destroy it. Obviously therefore, our government is interested in developing improved search and communications systems in the area of underwater accoustics. The propagation and processing of data transmitted in the waters of our oceans is very similar to Comtech's technology in the tropospheric scatter communications area and has similar characteristcs of signal fading. Therefore, we believe that we can."

What steps have you taken to intensify your marketing activities?

Mr Reed: "We have been adding marketing staff in all divisions. A Washington, D.C. office, and a European marketing office in West Germany have been opened recently. They will serve all our divisions."

How do you feel about Comtech Data Corporation's growth potential?

Mr Reed: "Frankly, we feel that Comtech Data is presently only beginning to reach its potential. The domestic demand for Comtech Data's satellite communication products should really begin a rapid growth curve when satellite earth stations at corporate facilities begin delivering telephony, facsimile and digital data business information to thousands of offices throughout the country. We also see the continuation of the cable TV and broadcast markets bringing entertainment to an even greater extent to hotels, condominiums and private houses."

What about Comtech's technological capabilities?

Mr. Kornberg: "We operate in various technologies within our corporate structure.

Comtech has been and continues to be the clear leader in cryogenic low noise parametric amplifier technology. However, cryogenic solutions for the attainment of low noise parametric amplification, because of greater satellite power, are now only being used in those sophisticated communications systems requiring the ultimate in low noise amplification. This has substantially curtailed the market for our original leading technology which represents only about 10% of our annual revenues.

We are at the forefront in a number of technology areas. Among others, these include one of the finest lines of communications modems for application in satellite, microwave, troposcatter, cable, and wire systems. These modems include very powerful coding fast becoming a standard in the industry, and a data-over-voice bridge between digital computer and analog radio technologies.

Brunswick

Q Brunswick has been following a policy of diversification in the last 10 years in order to obtain better balance for its businesses. Do you feel you have achieved this balance?

A Not yet, but we're clearly making progress. Ten years ago, Brunswick was principally a recreation company with a promising line of medical products and some involvement in technical areas. Since then, we've made a number of acquisitions, developed a broad range of technically-oriented products, improved our market share in many key non-recreational product lines, and shown continued growth in our medical and technical businesses. Our Technical and Medical Groups combined accounted for 46% of total Company sales and 80% of group operating earnings in 19 up from 27% of sales and 29% of operating earnings in 1973, the year the four Groups were formed.

Q Brunswick has divested some 16 businesses in the last decade Do you anticipate there will be add tional divestitures?

A In a diversified company such as ours, the portfolio of businesses is constantly being examined to assure that they meet with corporate objectives. We will not hesitate to divest a business or product line that, for a period of years, consistently fails to meet established goals for growth or returns, or that cannot be a significant factor in the market it serves. In 1980, we sold our Ozite carpeting operation and discontinued the manufacture of medical gloves for these reasons.

Q Is the Marine Power Group a possible candidate for divestiture?

A We don't turn negative about a business on the basis of one year's performance. We haven't lost sight of the fact that Mercury Marine's sales have grown considerably since it was acquired in 1961, and that when the economy is healthy, it can be highly profitable.

Q On the other side of the equation, you have acquired a number of businesses since 1970. What is your acquisition strategy for the 1980's?

A Our strategy is to continue acquiring businesses, as we have in the past, which are logical extensions of existing Brunswick businesses, and which tie into areas where we have unique product, technological, manufacturing and marketing strengths. We seek companies with quality proprietary products that command strong market share or exhibit potential for greater market penetration. We look for a level of return exceeding that of Brunswick's current businesses.

Q Which of the Company's businesses will realize the greatest growth in the immediate future?

A Our medical and technical businesses have very strong growth characteristics. We've been expanding in both of these areas as quickly as possible, and have been committing most of our resources here in an effort to maximize growth and profitability.

From a financial point-of-view, we're using our recreation business as a source of cash flow to fund the growth of our medical and technical operations. Our marine business grows rapidly in a normal environment, but it has the cyclicality and volatility of a capital goods business. We are attempting to soften that with investments in businesses that have higher rates of return.

Q What are Brunswick's greatest strengths as it enters a new decade?

A We are in generally good and growing businesses in which we have market and technological leadership positions. We have made substantial investment in facilities and in new product development which will benefit the Company in the future. We have the necessary human resources in place. And we are entering an age that is

Brunswick (*Continued*)

going to expect more from technology, a better quality of life, more time for recreation and better health care, all of which should benefit the sales of Brunswick products and services.

Q What are your prospects for continued growth in international markets, and what is your strategy in this area?

A The prospects are excellent. Brunswick has long felt that geographic diversification is as important as product line diversification, and that international markets offer unusual growth opportunities for new and existing products previously sold mainly in the United States. In the past, our growth abroad has occurred at a much faster rate than the growth of our domestic business. Since 1970, Brunswick's sales in the United States have grown by 125%, while international sales, including exports, increased by 460% and accounted for more than 26% of total 19 sales. They should account for an even larger percentage of Company sales in the future.

We are aggressively pursuing new marketing opportunities outside the United States for all our businesses, since virtually all of our products have global appeal. We believe we are well positioned for growth internationally in the coming decade, with 12 plants and more than 50 other facilities, such as sales offices and bowling centers, located outside the United States. superior value to our customers. In addition, we have spent a portion of our resources acquiring companies with a strong technical base. In a way, we have purchased significant research and development, adding to our own internal spending.

To put things in perspective, Brunswick has spent more than a quarter of a billion dollars in product development since 1970, including federally-funded defense development work.

Q Where have you been allocating your capital in recent years, and where do you anticipate the largest share of capital spending in the future?

A Since 1970, Brunswick has invested approximately $570 million in new facilities and other capital additions, with particular focus on our technical and medical businesses. Since 1976, the Company has invested over $170 million in its technical and medical areas, more than four times the net of approximately $40 million we invested in the marine business. Outlays for acquisitions alone for the Medical and Technical Groups exceeded $135 million in the last five years—a period in which 12 acquisitions were made, including 10 in the technical and medical areas.

It's fair to assume we'll be following a similar pattern in the future.

Q Research and development expenditures have averaged 2-3% of Brunswick's net sales, below the level for many technologically-oriented companies. Why hasn't Brunswick spent more in this area?

A We have been careful to concentrate our research and development resources in areas where there was a need for new or better products, and where we had the expertise to find the best solutions to specific problems and to provide a

United Telecom

Q: A question on the minds of a number of investors relates to the sale of Calma and the acquisition of Megatek. What is the strategy behind the sale of one and the purchase of the other?
A: Calma obviously was in a dynamic industry, the CAD CAM business, and had a good market position. We bought Calma on the basis that it would have a synergistic effect on our remote computing services business. Their product line had inherent computer capability in the terminals themselves, and was not reliant on a host computer. We think we will have more of a creative load demand on our basic remote computing services with Megatek than we would have had with Calma.

Despite all the uncertainties with telecommunications legislation, you have to make some plans. What businesses are you going to be in five years from now that you are not in now?
We can't just stop and wait for a clear cut national telecommunications policy. We are trying to move from a regional telephone company to a national telecommunications company. This will take us into some markets we have not served previously and way from the regional aura we have had. Five years from now, we will be more in the basic computing business than we are today, and we will be more in enhanced voice and data than today. Our Uninet data communications service is a good example of what we are trying to do—offer a very competitive value-added service in a rapidly growing market. Voice mail, with store and forward capabilities will lead some day, to voice actuated devices and recognition systems, and to services we can scarcely imagine today.

Will the change in the nature of United's business over the next several years result in a change in the company's objectives with respect to capital structure, payout ratio and so forth?
Yes, it will. Many of the things we have in place right now, such as dividend reinvestment, employee stock plans and increased earnings, along with lessened external capital needs, will drive the company to a capital ratio with a higher percentage of equity. Those forces are in place and will reposition the capital structure appropriately as the nature of the company changes. We will continue in our effort to reduce our payout ratio gradually, even as we continue to increase our dividend.

Three of the five major telephone companies recently had equity issues during periods when their prices were at or below book value. Where does United fit within that equity financing philosophy?
We have no plans for an equity offering even though our common stock is trading comfortably above book value. We are generating a significant amount of internal equity with the plans we just discussed. In addition, the sale of Calma produced $100 million with an expectation of more in 1985. If we make acquisitions for stock, such as we are doing with Megatek, we are increasing our equity base. If we were to make sizable acquisitions for cash, we would have to re-examine our position.

Can we discuss United's acquisition strategy? What do you look for when you consider a merger?
Our recent past experience is probably the best delineation of what our present policy is. We are driving the growth of our competitive services. We have concentrated in the computer services area. Our emphasis on strategic planning has more sharply focused our future plan, enabling us to look at opportunities and eliminate those which don't fit our strategic plans. Our acquisitions are going to have to fit in very well with the businesses that we have or we won't even consider them. We are trying to increase the proportion of our business which does not have a fixed regulatory ceiling on the earnings capability.

What do you think of the challenges and opportunities facing United over the next five to ten year span?
We have more opportunities than we have ever had in our corporate life. As new technology and market demand make new services possible, United is postured as well as anybody in the industry to escape the constraints of the kind of rate regulation that have characterized the major portion of our business in the past. We have some unique combination of talent. The so-called computed communications interface is where a lot of growth opportunities are going to occur. We have a good position there, we have a service orientation, we have a flexible management and we have a strong financial structure. We're in a number of strong and growing markets. We're confident we can leverage our present telecommunications, distribution and computer services businesses to enhance our growth and enhance our profitability.

Questions From Stockholders and Analysts

Following are some of the questions recently asked about Standex International . . . and our answers to those questions:

■ *What would you say has been the most important recent development at Standex?*

■ The demonstrated ability of Standex to withstand the worst recession since the Great Depression of the 1930's . . . and its ability to bounce back with such speed and vigor. This further validates everything we have said about the soundness of our business philosophies and about our principles of organization and management. Diversity works – and the success and resilience of Standex proves it.

■ *Many books are written about effective management styles and techniques. Can you briefly sum up some of the techniques which have enabled Standex to achieve such consistent, long-term growth?*

■ Our acquisition criteria, as well as the standards used in allocating capital for internal expansion, have served us well in maximizing the return from our available cash flow and credit sources.

Our management style is based primarily on the following elements: (1) Install the best operating/management teams and keep them motivated. (2) Give them substantial operating autonomy, so that they can operate in an innovative and entrepreneurial manner. (3) Control and carefully allocate capital expenditures to areas where the long-term payout prospects are best. (4) Provide a complete array of corporate staff services, such as industrial engineering, legal, auditing, computer, labor relations, marketing and communications, etc. (5) Encourage new product development at the divisional levels. (6) Install strong financial and cost systems. (7) Work out reasonable budget prospects for each unit and monitor them carefully.

■ *You have mentioned that Standex has excellent management throughout its organization. How do you keep them motivated?*

■ We believe our divisional managements are highly motivated. To begin with, they are skilled and dedicated "professionals."

We track "peer" companies and we believe that our managers are as well – or better – compensated than most. We have an excellent bonus system related to the success of both the Corporation and the Division. At the divisional level, we place emphasis on the continuing *degree of improvement* in the Return on Net Assets Employed. We have an excellent Pension Plan . . . fine insurance, medical plans, etc. Of special importance is our ESOT (Employee Stock Ownership Trust).

We have an Incentive Stock Option Plan as well as a PIPS Plan (Profit Improvement Performance Shares). This latter program is geared to the *increase* in corporate earnings per share over a running five-year period. In this type of plan, the rewards are dependent on the increase in the per share earnings of the Corporation – and not on the vagaries of the stock market.

All in all, we believe we have an excellent and well-balanced program to motivate a group of highly talented managers. And their performance reflects it.

■ *What was the purpose of your two spin-offs to Standex stockholders?*

■ A prime responsibility of responsible management is to enhance shareholder values. It was felt that the specialized nature and more-than-usual growth prospects for Dresher and Bingo King – standing alone – would command substantial premiums in the stock market as compared with Standex itself.

■ *Have the spin-offs worked as well as you expected?*

■ Even better than expected! Bingo King initially traded at $3.25 a share and Dresher at $3.50. Bingo King recently traded at $7.50, 18 months after distribution; and Dresher at $19.00, 7 months after distribution. This has been very rewarding to our stockholders.

■ *Standex has made many acquisitions in the past. What is its present acquisition policy?*

■ Since its founding 28 years ago, Standex has made over 100 acquisitions – and most have worked out very successfully. Initially, the quality of the company to be acquired and its earnings record were the prime considerations, not the specific markets in which it operated.

About four or five years ago, however, we decided to concentrate our efforts and resources in our five "core" groups that could be built upon by utilizing internal cash flow and by complementary acquisitions. Since that time, we have confined our acquisiton searches to companies that *directly* complement existing operations.

We actively continue to seek companies which can make a contribution to our existing divisions. Since the "fit" is already there, this type of acquisition is relatively "low risk".

■ *Liquidity and financial strength have become increasingly important as a measure of corporate success and strength. Has Standex any liquidity problems?*

■ Standex has *never* had a liquidity problem – today it is more liquid than ever, and stronger financially. In the past three years, while spending $33 million for capital expenditures, we have reduced total debt by over $34 million. Our debt-to-capital ratio is now a very comfortable 23%, which is a very conservative figure for a manufacturing company.

With our very strong balance sheet, we probably have the capability of comfortably borrowing $50-75 million if needed for acquisitions or other purposes. Our annual amortization of the present relatively low-cost debt averages about a modest $5 million through 1987. Then, $3 million in '88 and '89, and thereafter, nominal amounts.

In addition, our very excellent relationships with our leading banks and our four institutional long-term lenders go back many, many years. They stand ready to supply additional capital if or when we can productively put it to work. Since our overall operations are not capital intensive, absent large acquisitions, foreseeable capital needs for future growth can be comfortably furnished by internally-generated cash flow.

■ *Everyone is talking about the need for greater productivity in order to thrive – and to survive – in the future. What are Standex's plans along these lines?*

■ We have attacked the productivity problem on a number of fronts.

We have instituted a program for the formation of "Quality Circles" throughout the Corporation. When employees leave or retire, we have tried not to replace them. We have attempted to reduce redundancy wherever possible . . . eliminated various functions that were not absolutely necessary . . . invested capital in new and improved plants and machinery . . . begun to introduce "robotics" where such applications seemed promising.

Increasing productivity cannot be accomplished by a stroke of genius or some magical formula. Results come from a myriad of small improvements and advances. Throughout the Corporation, work in these areas represents a daily on-going effort on the part of our management and employees.

■ *Someone once said that "nothing happens until someone sells something." What have been Standex's major strengths in its various market-places?*

■ In all of our acquisitions, one of the main considerations has been the position of the company in its market: every operating unit of Standex has a proprietary line of products plus a strong and/or dominant position in its major markets. In other words, we are the "big fish" in many relatively small ponds. This is one of the major strengths of Standex.

Our units have attained their leadership positions through their superiority in technology, through their marketing skills, and through their quality and/or uniqueness of product. While many of their markets may be modest in size, our Divisions produce and market products which are basic and essential to the American economy.

As the "big fish", our Divisions are in a unique position to achieve consistent earnings growth and profitability.

■ *Do you feel that Wall Street and the investment community have had a proper appreciation of Standex's accomplishments?*

■ No, we really don't. Our diversity – which has been one of our major strengths – has also been a major problem for the investment community since our Company is fairly complex and difficult for "outsiders" to effectively understand. So, in the past, too few analysts and brokers – as well as investors – have been willing to take the time to study our Company and its accomplishments and prospects. As a result, we have rarely had a P/E ratio which we felt was appropriate.

Since the first of this year, Wall Street has finally bestowed on Standex a modest degree of recognition. It has been gratifying to have had quite a number of leading Wall Street analysts publishing favorable reports on Standex and its prospects, and recommending that their clients consider the purchase of our stock.

■ *What about the future – where do you expect Standex's major growth to come from?*

■ We do not have any very "hi-tech" or "bio-genetic" operations that are currently fashionable – and selling at astronomical prices per share. A few years from now, there will probably be a few strong survivors in these highly-competitive fields, and many casualties will result.

On the other hand, most of the areas in which we are now engaged offer us excellent opportunities for low-risk and steady – if not spectacular – growth.

While our operations are not "sexy" or potentially explosive as such, they provide useful and necessary products and services in a number of interesting and growing industries. They will be around for a long – and profitable – time. Some perhaps have a greater growth potential than others, but with few exceptions, we like the prospects of all of them.

IX
AN INSIDE LOOK AT YOUR COMPANY

THE READERS OF YOUR ANNUAL REPORT WILL WANT TO READ ABOUT THE FOLLOWING

Acquisition
Advertising
Asset Management and Liquidity
Backlog
Business Conduct
Business Integrity
Business Strategies
Capital Resources
Commitment to Fundamental Values
Company Profile
Competition
Continuing Concerns
Corporate Environment
Corporate Responsibility
Cost Reduction
Critical Issues
Customers
Customer Service
Decentralization
Distribution
Dividends
Energy
Environmental, Occupational Health and Safety Regulations
Expansion Program
Facilities
Factory of the Future
Field Service Organization
Future Thrust of Your Company
Growth
Government Contracts
Health and Safety
Human Resources
Industry Affairs
International Operations
Labor Contracts
Liquidity and Capital Resources
Management
Management Changes
Management Style
Maps
Markets
Marketing Highlights
Minority and Female Employment
Minority Dealer Program
Minority Entrepreneurs
Mission
New Products
Operating Objectives
Operating Practices
Principles That Guide Us
Product Review
Productivity
Public Offering
Public Service
Quality
Reindustrialization
Research and Development
Robots
Strategies
Strengths of Your Corporation
Technology

Acquisition

"Effective October 1, 19__ the company acquired all of the outstanding stock of Filac Corporation (Filac), a domestic manufacturer specializing in electronic technology as applied to hospital products, for a purchase price of $3,986,000, including expenses of the acquisition. This acquisition has been accounted for as a purchase and, accordingly, the results of Filac's operations have been included in the accompanying financial statements since the acquisition date. The excess of the purchase price over the fair value of the net assets acquired of $3,792,000 is being amortized on a straight-line basis over 40 years."

Advertising

Perry Drug Stores, Inc.

Our advertising themes . . . "Everything You Want A Drug Store For And More" and "Ask Your Perry Red Coat—Get Your Answer Now!" . . . have already demonstrated their meaningfulness. We expect them to continue to better reflect our broadening merchandise mix, to further strengthen our customer appeal and to help produce larger per store sales.

All Perry advertising is internally conceived, developed and produced in conjunction with our advertising agency.

Asset Management and Liquidity

Most of ConAgra's businesses are current asset intensive. At the end of fiscal 1983, cash, accounts receivable, and inventory accounted for approximately 63 percent of asset investment. These are highly liquid investments. Wheat, flour, and major feed ingredients are hedged to protect grain inventory value against major price fluctuations. Finished products and grain represented over 90 percent of year-end inventory investment.

For fiscal 1983, total sales invoiced to customers were approximately $5.7 billion. This is above net sales reported in ConAgra's financial statements because grain and ingredient merchandising transactions include only gross margins in reported sales. At the end of fiscal 1983, net accounts receivable represented 13 days of annualized total sales (including Peavey on a full-year basis) invoiced to customers, compared to 16 days at the end of 1982.

During fiscal 1983, ConAgra's current assets increased 72 percent, while current liabilities increased 75 percent. Working capital increased 65 percent to $203.3 million. These increases were due principally to the Peavey merger.

ConAgra's current ratio (current assets divided by current liabilities) at the end of fiscal 1983 was 1.52 to 1, compared to 1.55 to 1 at the end of fiscal 1982. Related to ConAgra's financing objective discussed above, when evaluating liquidity the company intends to look at its current ratio two ways—with and without hedged commodity inventories and associated short-term financing.

Backlog

The following summary presents the backlog for each of the past five years:

	(In Millions)				
	19__	19__	19__	19__	19__
F-14	**$ 946**	$ 871	$ 844	$ 764	$ 782
Other Government	**2,067**	2,041	1,347	1,106	973
Total Government	**3,013**	2,912	2,191	1,870	1,755
Commercial	**506**	522	567	626	211
Total Backlog	**$3,519**	$3,434	$2,758	$2,496	$1,966

Government backlog totals are limited to amounts obligated to contracts by the procuring agencies through December 31 of each year.

Business Conduct

Ford Motor Company

Ford has policies against illegal or improper behavior by any employee and a formal system for monitoring adherence to these policies.

International Codes of Conduct

Ford endorses the voluntary "Guidelines for Multinational Enterprises," established by the Organization for Economic Cooperation and Development (OECD) in 1976, to promulgate standards of behavior for multinational firms doing business in host countries. Ford also supports the "Rules of Conduct" contained in the 1977 International Chamber of Commerce Report on Extortion and Bribery in Business Transactions and the voluntary "Guidelines Governing the Protection of Privacy and Transborder Flows of Personal Data" approved by the OECD in 1981.

Ford is one of more than 135 U.S. companies endorsing the "Sullivan Principles" for corporate conduct in South Africa. An independent evaluation ranked Ford of South Africa in the highest category of companies making progress toward fulfilling those principles.

Business Integrity

One paragraph in the preamble to HP's statement of corporate objectives states, "The organization should conduct its affairs with uncompromising honesty and integrity. People at every level should be expected to adhere to the highest standards of business ethics, and to understand that anything less is totally unacceptable. As a practical matter, ethical conduct cannot be assured by written policies or codes; it must be an integral part of the organization, a deeply ingrained tradition that is passed from one generation of employees to another."

On occasion, however, policy memos have been issued as added assurance that as the company grows and decentralizes, the traditional HP values are fully understood and followed by employees everywhere. In 19__ HP's business conduct policies (written and unwritten) were consolidated into two documents.

One of these, dealing specifically with the Foreign Corrupt Practices Act, was distributed primarily to HP people who deal with international trade. The second, "Standards of Business Conduct," was given wide distribution and intended for reading by all employees. This document discusses conflicts of interest, the handling of company information, restrictions on payments and contributions, trade regulations and the consequences of violating them, and conduct with respect to competitors, customers, and suppliers.

Business Strategies:

Masco

BUSINESS STRATEGIES:

- Recognize and develop our most important resource—our people.

Corporate strategies directed to the fulfillment of ambitious goals will be successful only if those responsible for implementing them are capable and properly motivated.

- Concentrate on businesses which are neither labor nor capital intensive and which are not subject to rapid technological change or other obsolescence.

By avoiding businesses that are labor and/or capital intensive, we not only achieve higher profit margins but also keep the Company more manageable. We require less labor and capital for future expansion, and we have more flexible manufacturing operations. Also, we avoid disproportionately large investments (such as in special-purpose, high-cost manufacturing facilities) where a mistake in judgment can have an adverse effect on the overall Company performance.

High technology, while seemingly exciting, can have another side—namely, exposure to rapid obsolescence. Where there is a market characterized by a high rate of technological change, there is usually greater risk. For the most part, Masco's markets are prosaic. Change within them is usually slow and evolutionary, and competition tends to be less aggressive. Thus, we can concentrate our efforts on product improvement, marketing programs, and expansion with less concern that a revolutionary new product will abruptly and unexpectedly obsolete our investment. This is particularly important in successfully managing a multi-purpose product company such as Masco.

- Control our destiny by not having our growth dependent on any single market or product.

Attaining a significant measure of control over a Company's destiny is a formidable challenge in a complex and highly regulated business environment. We have had success by: 1) maintaining a diversified product base (characterized by positions of leadership) so that we are not dependent on any one product or market to sustain our growth; 2) diversifying our business by building on existing strengths and concentrating our resources on those products compatible with our proven skills in product development, manufacturing and marketing; and 3) avoiding markets subject to significant external influences beyond our control, such as government regulation.

- Recognize that errors in judgment may occur and when this happens, acknowledge and correct them.

Based upon our record of accomplishment in sales and earnings growth, our management and operating decisions have usually been sound. Our mistakes, in our judgment, such as developing or acquiring products that truly were not proprietary or acquiring a company that did not enjoy a position of leadership, were generally made when we were not diligently adhering to the disciplines inherent in our corporate objectives and strategies.

ACQUISITION STRATEGY:

- Complement internal growth with selected acquisitions.

Internal growth has accounted for over 60 percent of our growth in earnings per share. This emphasis continues and will be the primary basis for our future growth. There are reasons, however, that we support an active program to locate and acquire selected business partners. For example, we have an opportunity to supplement internal growth through the utilization of the excess cash flow generated from our high-margin businesses; also we can complement internal growth by entering selected markets or by obtaining particular products or capabilities. This strategy can often be better accomplished through an acquisition than pursuing the same goal through internal product development or starting up a new operation.

Capital Resources

CONAGRA'S capital investment consists of working capital (current assets less current liabilities) plus noncurrent assets. This capital investment is financed principally with stockholders' equity and long-term debt.

During fiscal 1983, capital investment increased by $245.5 million to $511.5 million. The 1983 increase was 92 percent compared to 19 percent in 1982. The 1983 increase in capital investment went 67 percent to noncurrent assets and 33 percent to working capital. The 1982 increase of $41.6 million went 33 percent to noncurrent assets and 67 percent to working capital. The capital investment increases are after depreciation and amortization of $24.6 million in 1983 and $14.3 million in 1982.

The merger of Peavey Company with ConAgra effective August 1, 1982 accounted for 88 percent of the increase in capital investment in 1983. Excluding post-merger operations, Peavey added $118.2 million of noncurrent assets and $98.3 million of working capital.

In fiscal 1984, ConAgra plans to further increase investment in its existing businesses approximately $52 million, after depreciation and amortization of about $33 million. The net increase in capital investment is expected to go roughly 40 percent to noncurrent assets and 60 percent to working capital.

ConAgra financed its capital investment at the end of fiscal years 1983 and 1982 as shown in the Capitalization table.

Common stockholders' equity increased $116.8 million in fiscal 1983. Common stock issued for the Peavey merger accounted for $85 million. The balance of the increase came primarily from earnings. Preferred stockholders' equity increased $18.3 million due mainly to preferred stock issued for the Peavey merger. Long-term debt increased $106.6 million. The major portion of the increase was associated with the Peavey merger.

ConAgra relies primarily on the sale of commercial paper to finance short-term, seasonal requirements, although the company also borrows from commercial banks. Commercial paper borrowings are always backed by unused bank credit lines and were at interest rates below prime. During fiscal 1983, short-term borrowings averaged $236 million compared to $97 million in 1982. Higher borrowing levels resulted principally from the addition of Peavey's businesses.

ConAgra uses operating leases primarily for multi-purpose transportation equipment and selected facilities. In fiscal 1983, the company's noncancellable operating lease rentals were $36.7 million compared to $20.3 million in fiscal 1982.

ConAgra's financing objective is to maintain a conservative balance sheet.

Equity and long-term debt are used to finance noncurrent assets and the permanent working capital of the corporation. The company's objective has been to have long-term debt finance not more than 40 percent of total invested capital. Long-term debt was 40 percent of invested capital for fiscal 1983, and 40 percent or less for the last eight years.

It also has been ConAgra's objective to use short-term debt to finance only seasonal requirements and to eliminate year-end net short-term debt. For the last eight years, including fiscal 1983, ConAgra has had no year-end short-term debt.

Capitalization

In millions	1983		1982	
Short-term debt	**$ -0-**	**0%**	$ -0-	0%
Long-term debt	**203.4**	**40**	96.8	36
Deferred income taxes	**8.3**	**2**	4.5	2
Preferred stockholders' equity	**26.5**	**5**	8.2	3
Common stockholders' equity	**273.3**	**53**	156.5	59
Total capitalization	**$511.5**	**100%**	$266.0	100%

Commitment to Fundamental Values

"Quality must be standard equipment. We cannot view it as an option for which customers must pay extra. Rather, it must be the reason why customers buy from Brunswick."

In its 139 year history, Brunswick has developed a culture which is deepseated in the tradition of caring for our customers, our people and the quality of our goods and services. This tradition, which continues today, is based upon value—to provide the very best of the very best in every market we serve. It likewise is the way through which we can provide lasting values to our shareholders.

This commitment started with John Brunswick in 1845 and has passed from generation to generation, from chief executive to chief executive, and lives today as our heritage. It can be expressed as simply as the statement on the cover of this report which expresses the philosophy of our founder: "Quality must be standard equipment. We cannot view it as an option for which customers must pay extra. Rather, it must be the reason why customers buy from Brunswick." Or, in more recent times, a statement attributed to the late founder of our Mercury Marine operation, E.C. Kiekhaefer, who often stated, "give the customer a little more value than he paid for."

Recently a lengthier, yet simple, statement of philosophy and purpose has been communicated to all of our people. It is the value system which is driving the Company. It is the very foundation on which we intend to build an excellent Company. We would like to share this statement with you.

- We are committed to becoming an excellent Company. We will conduct our business in an honest, ethical and nondiscriminatory fashion... providing value and service to our customers, fair treatment to our suppliers, equitable compensation and benefits to our people, and above-average return to our shareholders.

- Our highest priority will be our people...to respect their personal dignity and to provide them with a meaningful work experience so they commit themselves to common, worthwhile goals and are proud of what they are doing.
- We are totally committed to providing quality goods and services at all levels of our Company.
- We will be a market-driven Company, recognizing that the customer always comes first.
- We will grow worldwide, with greater expectations than in the past.
- We will be leaders in the markets we serve and act like leaders, perform like leaders and serve like leaders.
- We will operate in a decentralized mode at corporate and division levels, with authority being delegated to the lowest possible level.

To demonstrate to consumers and the business community the Company's commitment to quality and excellence and to position Brunswick as a leader in the markets it serves, a Pre-Christmas corporate advertisement (shown at left) was prepared describing some specially crafted Brunswick products as being the "Very Best of the Very Best." Not only did this advertisement capture the attention of the readers of the leading business and consumer magazines in which it appeared, it also generated numerous stories in newspapers and comments on television and radio around the country, that stressed the quality products offered by Brunswick.

During the past year, the pride of Brunswick people was reinforced through an emphasis on the foundation on which the Company was built. We look to the future with confidence, knowing that our values have stood the test of time.

Company Profile

Levi Strauss

Levi Strauss & Co., founded in 1850, has become the world's largest manufacturer of branded apparel. The corporation markets its products throughout the U.S. and in more than 40 foreign nations, utilizing manufacturing and distribution facilities in North and South America, Europe, Asia and Australia.

The various divisions and their product lines are briefly described below. Major operating entities are Levi Strauss USA and Levi Strauss International. All larger operating units are directed from the company's San Francisco headquarters except the two European divisions that are headquartered in London and the Canadian division, managed from Toronto. (Each major division's contribution to total company sales in 1982 is noted in parentheses below.)

LEVI STRAUSS USA

Jeanswear Division (35 percent of sales): This operating unit is the company's largest and most profitable division, and its products formed the base from which the more diverse lines flowed. Jeanswear's products include basic and fashion jeans in a variety of fabrics for males aged 14 and older, a broad line of western wear, casual slacks for young men aged 14 to 34 as well as knit and woven shirts, and casual jackets for men and young men.

The *Resistol* operating unit, administered under Jeanswear, markets western, dress and casual hats.

Menswear Division (8 percent of sales): Markets men's slacks, sport coats and vests as separates; and Levi's for Men, a line of jeans and casual pants "With a Skosh More Room,"™ for males aged 25 and over. Sportswear products also include the Levi's Action lines and Tailored Classics. The David Hunter line of traditional sport coats and slacks will be stocked at retail in the fall of 1983.

The *Activewear, Accessories* and *Oxxford* operating units are administered under Menswear. *Activewear* markets participant and spectator sportswear such as shorts, tops and warm-up suits as well as lines of skiwear and rugged outerwear. *Accessories* offers a range of accessory products for men, women and children including belts, wallets, handbags and casual hats. *Oxxford* produces men's and women's fine suits.

Womenswear Division (11 percent of sales): Lines of separates include jeans, slacks, skirts and tops. They are marketed to three customer groups: Juniors (ages 15 to 34); Misses (age 25 and above); and Special Sizes, including large, petite, tall and maternity. Sweaters and woven and knit shirts for misses and large sizes also are offered.

Koret of North America Division (5 percent of sales): Markets moderately priced coordinates and related separates in misses, petites and large sizes. Its lines include skirts, pants, jackets, blouses and other tops. The division markets its products in Canada as well as the U.S.

The *Rainfair* operating unit, administered under Koret of North America, produces protective clothing that resists rain and chemicals for industrial and commercial use.

Youthwear Division (9 percent of sales): Markets lines of apparel for boys and girls aged 2 to 14. Youthwear's varied product offerings include basic and fashion jeans, slacks, knit and woven tops, jackets and vests, activewear, Koveralls™ and Shortalls, as well as jumpers and skirts.

LEVI STRAUSS INTERNATIONAL

Unlike Levi Strauss USA, which is organized along product lines, the international business is administered geographically. Though the composition of the line varies by country served, the international lines include a higher percentage of jeans than their domestic counterparts.

Group I

(17 percent of sales)

Northern Europe Division: Markets jeanswear, youthwear, menswear and womenswear in the United Kingdom, Ireland, Sweden, Denmark, Norway and Finland.

Continental Europe Division: Markets jeanswear, youthwear, tops and women's-fit jeans in Germany, France, Italy, the Netherlands, Belgium, Spain and Switzerland.

Fra-For Division: This French operating unit produces quality infants' and children's wear under the Dinou and Babygro labels.

Group II

Canada Division (4 percent of sales): Markets products throughout Canada under the Levi's and GWG brands. Levi's branded lines include bottoms and tops in jeanswear, womenswear and youthwear. The GWG lines include workwear as well as those categories marketed under the Levi's brand.

Latin America Division (6 percent of sales): Major lines are jeanswear, including women's-fit models, youthwear, tops and some activewear. Primary markets are Mexico, Brazil, Argentina and Puerto Rico. There is a joint venture operation in Venezuela and products are marketed through licensees and distributors in 11 Latin American countries.

Asia/Pacific Division (4 percent of sales): Lines include jeanswear, youthwear, women's-fit jeans and tops, which are marketed throughout Australia, New Zealand, Japan, the Philippines, Hong Kong, Malaysia and Singapore. Licensees market the company's products in Thailand and Indonesia.

Competition

It would be well for you to face up to the importance of describing in a forthright manner the nature of your competition. Companies describe their competition in a number of ways.

Example:

Nature of Our Competition
The importance of this new marketing concept cannot be overstated. The nature of our competition is far different from that at any time during our existence. Our competitors are no longer just the regional or local banks for American National, nor are they only other finance companies for our domestic finance units. Rather, they are the largest banks, domestic and foreign, seeking to penetrate the U.S. middle market through the offering of direct commercial banking services or "asset-based lending services," another name for commercial finance.

Northern Telecom

Tough competition
The opening up of the marketplace has put Northern Telecom into direct competition with huge multinationals such as Siemens, Phillips, Nippon, Exxon, Xerox and IBM. All of these companies, in the same way as Northern Telecom, are trying to increase sales in order to cover the high costs of research and development.

Northern Telecom's technological leadership has assured its success in recent years, but technological excellence is no longer enough. While it is true our customers look to Northern Telecom for technologically superior products, they are now demanding much more. They want products which, although competitively priced, are custom tailored to their needs. They want products which are so designed and built that they can be easily modified or expanded when the need arises. They want top quality on-time maintenance and service. They want to deal with dependable, efficiently administered companies.

The Competition*	Sales	Employees
L.M. Ericsson	$ 2.2 billion	60,000
Exxon	84.0	170,000
GTE	6.8	200,000
IBM	22.9	337,000
ITT	22.0	368,000
Nippon	3.4	60,000
Phillips	17.5	380,000
Siemens	16.2	334,000
Western Electric	11.0	168,000
Xerox	7.0	116,000
Northern Telecom	$ 2.1 billion	33,700

*Figures are approximate

Continuing Concerns

Your stockholders will welcome a candid analysis of your company's continuing concerns. They realize that your company and others have to face new circumstances from time to time that can affect the profitability of your company. It is best that your CEO define these concerns.

Examples:

Carpenter
There are external factors beyond your management's direct control which impact on our business. Let's discuss the most important of these—raw materials and energy availability, as well as imports:

Raw material availability of our two most critical alloys—nickel and chromium—does not appear to be a problem in the foreseeable future. We do anticipate market disruptions for some raw materials from time to time, but such disruptions should be temporary. On energy, you are as familiar as we are with the present situation. A clear energy policy in this country, with a strong thrust toward self-sufficiency, is urgently needed. Our judgments are that the Company's energy needs will be met.

Imports of foreign specialty steels have long been a serious problem to the domestic steel industry because of unfair pricing policies of the foreign producers. Such pricing practices are often supported by foreign governments through direct and indirect subsidies. President Carter recently provided for an eight-month phase-out from June 14, 1979, of import restraints that have been in place since June 1976. These restraints have been helpful to Capenter and we supported their extension for an additional three years. We are extremely disappointed in the President's actions and feel that he has not given proper recognition to all the facts of the petition for quota extension and to the many requests for its support by elected officials, employees, shareholders, vendors, customers, and other concerned citizens.

You can be assured that Carpenter will continue as a viable and profitable specialty steel producer. The restraints cover only a portion of our diversified mix of products. Also, our unique combination of basic strengths, which we have described to you in the past, places us in a very strong position to compete effectively against both foreign and domestic producers.

Conserving Human Talents

Conservation usually conjures up carpools or switching off the hallway lights. But a computer program that teaches a programmer to write programs faster can save human and material resources beyond the reach of a million light switches. Not using the computer and its programs can mean a waste of energy greater than all the world's gas guzzlers.

To provide the talented people needed in the "knowledge industry" for the next 10 years will require a major restructuring of the educational system. From secondary schools to graduate universities, insufficient funds, facilities and equipment are available to educate the thousands of people needed by Data General and its customers.

The shortage of engineers and electronic technicians is especially acute. It can cost a college as much as three times more to graduate an electrical engineer than a social scientist, largely because of the cost of laboratories and equipment.

To help relieve the budget constraints on schools planning to expand their engineering and technical programs, Data General has developed a program to donate computers. To date we have donated computers, associated equipment and software to 16 schools to be used exclusively in classrooms and laboratories.

The value of 19__ donations at list price, not including the value of delivery, installation and warranty, was $585,000. This equipment was reserved not just for universities and graduate schools. Community colleges, technical and vocational schools also were recipients. Our people also worked with the schools to develop curricula, documentation and support.

To continue producing and conserving for ourselves and for our customers we made investments in: *Research and Development*, expanding facilities and programs; *Manufacturing*, using more automated processes and improved systems; *Marketing*, broadening distribution channels and developing a more customer-responsive sales force; and *Customer Service*, introducing more effective and efficient service techniques.

Corporate Environment

Unlike much of our competition and quite apart from the stereotype image of the insurance industry at large, Frank B. Hall is a company full of vitality. Many of our professionals are young, aggressive people who devote their extraordinary energies to improving our company's capabilities. And those of us who are not so young in years like to think of ourselves as being young in attitude. Everyone at Hall performs his or her job with emphasis on an individual responsibility to achieve personal and professional results.

We are a fast paced company. It is our desire to act rather than react. So we constantly strive to stay a step or two ahead of client needs. This necessitates a thorough understanding of our business as well as that of our clientele.

Hall is structured in such a way as to eliminate organizational red tape and political barriers. Communication is quick and easy. Our corporate management is only a phone call away from any local manager who might require guidance.

We are a flexible organization. We have to be. The needs of the corporate community are constantly changing. In order to protect their human and financial assets, Hall must be ready to handle any situation that arises, with speed and intelligence.

The environment we have built at Frank B. Hall promotes creative thinking. We encourage and reward original ideas. Perhaps this is why we have the reputation as the "inventor", the "company with the creative character" in our industry. Indeed, we have developed a number of innovative programs that have become industry standards. Innovations are imperative to the future well-being of our clients and we shall continue to provide the proper climate to encourage extraordinary creative accomplishments.

Corporate Responsibility

Many corporations take the position that it is impossible to view the business community and society as separate entities. R. J. Reynolds Company stated in its Annual Report:

> "A corporation doesn't operate in a world unto itself. It is a vital part of the whole of society. Cor-

porations and the diverse communities in which they live and operate are mutually dependent. Society provides business with the skilled people and the franchise to produce goods and services. Businesses, in turn, provide needed goods and services for which society pays.''

''R. J. Reynolds believes that corporate responsibility involves more than monetary contributions to worthwhile causes. It means the commitment, as a corporate citizen, to the broader goals of society as a whole such as educational advancement . . . equal employement . . . support for minority enterprise . . . expansion of and access to the cultural arts . . . support of basic research that will benefit society . . . a meaningful involvement in the mainstream of the communities where we live. It is RJR's philosophy that the 'right' granted by society to operate a business confers upon the corporation an opportunity, even a duty, to direct a portion of its resources to the betterment of society as a whole. A stable, healthy community provides its corporate residents with a well-rounded pool of potential employees.''

In describing your company's activities in meeting its social responsibilities you should consider describing in some detail the following:

1. Your company's philosophy in meeting its social responsibilities, not only in the community in which your headquarters is located, but in the other communities in which your company operates;
2. A description of the dollar amounts expended by your corporation to nonprofit organizations, and a description of the recipients of the funds;
3. The percentage of pretax domestic income given as contributions to nonprofit organizations;
4. The support that your company provides to United Way in various communities;
5. The program that your company has adopted to provide volunteers to community organizations for tutoring, visits to hospitals, JA, etc.;
6. The extent to which your company has provided pro bono business advice to community organizations;
7. The manner in which your Corporate Responsibility Committee operates, if there is a committee designated for this purpose;
8. Programs to encourage your company's employees to become involved in community affairs;
9. The program established to match employee contributions to educational and cultural organizations, hospitals, etc.

Corporate Responsibility—Honeywell's community participation progresses through several levels: from contributions to nonprofit agencies, to the involvement of employee and retiree volunteers, and finally to partnerships with community organizations. We place special emphasis on linking the skills of our volunteers to community projects in order to leverage our resources and achieve maximum benefit for people with unequal or limited opportunities. As a result honeywell was one of only two companies to receive President Reagan's 1983 Volunteer Action Award in recognition of our many volunteer programs.

Last year more than 3,000 employee volunteers in Minneapolis planned and conducted a Special Olympics and Honeywell family day for 1,300 handicapped children and adults. In Philadelphia employees counseled teen-age parents and improved area day-care facilities. Employees of Honeywell's Scottish factories raised over $3,500 to help refurbish a residence for handicapped adults that was gutted by fire.

Financial contributions are closely tied to volunteer efforts. Total contributions to nonprofit organizations in 1983 increased 12 percent to $7.1 million, including in-kind support. Of the total, approximately 10 percent went to the arts, 45 percent to education, and 45 percent to human-service programs, including $1 million to national and local United Ways. Honeywell employees contributed an additional $3 million to United Way campaigns.

Honeywell's community partnerships continued to thrive in 1983. In Wellesley, Massachusetts, Honeywell and the Chinese-American Civic Association use Honeywell computers to teach office skills to Asian refugees. In Minneapolis more than 180 students attend Summatech, a math and science magnet school led by Honeywell's Corporate Technology Center and the Public School District.

Community concerns have also resulted in innovative programs within the company. Honeywell's Handicapped Employees Task Force is studying ways to improve the work environment for disabled employees. The Honeywell Women's Council conducts seminars and studies issues of concern to women.

Borden

The company responded to its social responsibilities through its contribution program and through operational decisions responsive to social concerns. The

Borden Foundation Inc., the company's conduit for charitable contributions, helped to support 69 United Fund drives and more than 40 hospital and health care facilities in communities where Borden has operations. The foundation's Matching Gifts Program for Higher Education was joined by a program to match eligible employee contributions to health care organizations, effective in 1983. In addition, the foundation continued underwriting a demonstration of a unique public nutrition education program conducted by the Center for Human Nutrition of the Columbia University College of Physicians and Surgeons. Nearly 180 radio stations across the country carried the Columbia Nutrition Bulletin, a daily public service program offering basic nutrition advice. The foundation also increased attention to in-kind donations through cooperation with Food Banks around the nation.

The company's minority purchasing program continued to give positive assistance to the development of minority-owned businesses. Despite the recession and the divestiture of several additional operations, purchases from minority-owned businesses increased to $17.7 million. The number of minority suppliers selling products and services to the company increased from 400 to 500. Deposits of tax payments in minority-owned banks jumped 125%, from $8 million to $18 million. In 1981, a security insurance policy for the company was underwritten by an agency owned by women; in 1982, additional security coverage was obtained from an insurance agency owned by blacks.

Employment data gathered in 1982 revealed yet another slight increase in the percentage of minority employees in top job categories. Overall minority employment held steady despite divestitures that reduced the total number of employees. Divestitures of operations with high percentages of female employees caused a small drop in the number and percentage of women employed. With the redeployment program completed, the company is intensifying its efforts to increase the representation of women and minorities in its work force.

FOREMOST-McKESSON

Taking the Initiative in Community Action

Never before has the voice of community concern been raised with such intensity. In the past year, requests for financial and volunteer assistance from Foremost-McKesson more than doubled as local, state and federal governments sought to shift social responsibility to the private sector.

We at Foremost-McKesson recognize that the private sector—including schools, churches, civic groups, unions and foundations, as well as corporations—must intensify its efforts in the social arena. We support recommendations made by the President's Task Force on Private Sector Initiatives established to align the private sector with government in serving the needs of American communities.

The President's Task Force calls for corporate action on four fronts:

- an increase in cash contributions to at least 2% of pretax profits within four years.
- a doubling of community service involvement within four years.
- a reassessment of the direction of corporate philanthropy programs.
- a commitment to an active partnership with American communities.

Foremost-McKesson is well on its way to meeting these challenging goals. In fiscal 1982, we contributed 1.45% of our prior year's pretax profits, or more than $1.5 million, in grants to public service organizations—up from 1% or $1.2 million the previous year. We plan to raise our total contributions to approximately 1.7% of pretax profits in fiscal 1983, and to reach the recommended goal of 2% in two, not four, years.

As a founding member of the San Francisco Bay Area Corporate Two Percent Club, Foremost-McKesson shares the philosophy that the only way to build a strong business is to build a strong community. By investing 2% of corporate pretax dollars in community service, we hope to stimulate other companies to do the same.

The Foremost-McKesson Foundation is our principal philanthropic entity. In fiscal 1982, Foundation contributions reached $645,000—more than twice the amount given three years ago. Direct contributions of funds and merchandise from the corporation totalled $400,000, and our operating groups collectively added more than $500,000 to the community relations program.

Last year, some 70% of Foundation dollars supported programs in special education, criminal justice, minority and disabled assistance, physical and mental health and nutrition awareness. We also backed senior citizens projects, shelters for battered women, job training, youth development and myriad other social programs. Support for cultural development—museums, ballet, opera, art and the sciences—accounted for 14%. Twelve percent was designated for civic and neighborhood improvement, and 5% supplemented international and employee involvement programs.

Increased volunteerism, the President's Task Force's second recommendation, calls for corporations to double their level of community involvement within four years. We established our volunteer network in the late 1960s, and in 1979 added full-time corporate staff to manage and direct expanding community outreach programs. In the San Francisco area, employees have been mobilized into the Foremost-McKesson Community Action Team. The program will soon be duplicated in eight other cities.

In their continuing projects throughout the year, our employees donated blood, shared job-related skills with student interns, adopted a wing of residents at a facility for the aged and chronically ill, collected food and medical supplies for victims of a hotel fire, tutored children, coached the mentally retarded in the Bay Area Special Olympics, manned phone banks at the Easter Seal Telethon, took to the streets in the March of Dimes Superwalk, painted a San Francisco boys' home and supported a receiving center for families of prisoners. Under our newest program, we are the first San Francisco corporation to "adopt" a school.

In the first year of Foremost-McKesson's Board Candidate Program, 35 management employees volunteered their time and business expertise to serve on boards of directors of nonprofit organizations in the Bay Area. From childcare centers to symphonies, Foremost-McKesson employees are working at board level to help organizations manage their resources.

The Foremost-McKesson Community Action Fund was established last year to encourage employees to apply for grants for eligible nonprofit organizations in which they are actively involved. During fiscal year 1982, 13 grants totalling nearly $7,000 were awarded to a wide range of employee interests.

Employees participate in the political process through a nonpartisan federal level Political Action Committee. In calendar 1981, they raised over $10,000 for the Foremost-McKesson Employees Political Fund by soliciting voluntary, confidential contributions from eligible employees. Their goal for 1982 is to raise $20,000 to support some 60 federal candidates at the primary and general election levels. Copies of the fund's report are available through the Public Affairs Department.

For more information on the company's public policy projects or for a copy of the annual report of the Foremost-McKesson Foundation, write to Marcia M. Argyris, president, Foremost-McKesson Foundation, One Post Street, San Francisco, CA 94104, or call (415) 983-8673.

Many corporations provide information in their annual reports as to nonprofit agencies funded and the amounts of the grants, as part of their corporate activities.

W. R. Grace Co.

Corporation, Foundation Donations Grow

Donations and grants from the Company and Grace Foundation, Inc. rose significantly in 19__ , totaling $3.6 million.

Corporate donations were awarded to New York City civic-boosting groups such as the Economic Development Council (a private public coalition of concerned citizens dedicated to revitalizing New York): Avenue of the Americas Association (home of Grace's headquarters); the Urban League, and various trade associations and worldwide chambers of commerce in which Grace maintains corporate memberships.

About 100 charitable, civic and trade groups received Grace corporate gifts in 1980.

Grace Foundation, a tax-exempt organization for which the Company provides annual funding, boosted its contributions by more than 41 percent, including matching gifts for education.

With funds allocated by its board of directors, Grace Foundation concentrates its aid on higher education, health, science and social welfare, urban and minority affairs and culture. More than 40 percent of the Foundation's budget is earmarked for education.

Organizations which received funds from either the Company or the Foundation in 19__ included The Salvation Army, Boy Scouts of America, American Cancer Society, Young Women's Association, Ear Research Institute, Marine Biological Laboratory and Brooklyn Academy of Music, among many others.

Borden

The company channels its charitable contributions through the Borden Foundation Inc. United Way agencies in 125 Borden communities benefited from company donations made through the foundation. The foundation again gave priority to health care and nutrition programs. Health care organizations in the United States received 90 individual grants in support of a wide range of activities, from the purchase of pulmonary function Va., to the operation of a poison control center, in Columbus, Ohio.

The Matching Gifts Program for Higher Education pledged to match gifts by eligible employees to 88 colleges and universities during 19__ . Further support of higher education was given through the United Negro College Fund, Inc. and the Independent College Funds of America, Inc., which together represent more than 600 colleges and universities.

Cost Reduction

The recession of 1981–82 brought about substantial reduction in cost of operations in many companies. Your stockholders and security analysts will be interested in how your company reduced its costs.

Example:

International Paper Co.

Faced with a prolonged recession, we intensified our efforts to reduce costs. Salaries throughout the Company were frozen for five months, and intervals between salary increases were extended. We continued the process of streamlining our organization so it would operate more efficiently with fewer people and we reduced all 1982 expense budgets. As a result of these efforts, selling and administrative expenses declined 4% in 1982, and we expect at least to hold these expenses level in 1983. In addition, we permanently closed a number of inefficient facilities, including a corrugating medium mill in Bastrop, Louisiana, and several packaging plants. We also sold two of our least modern wood products plants.

And finally there is the all-important issue of reducing our cost base. During 1982, we continued to take decisive action in this area. Commitment to cost effectiveness became part of the very fabric of this company. Between mid-1981 and the end of 1982, we eliminated about $300 million from our cost base. The major portion came from manpower reductions. During the 18-month period, we reduced our worldwide employee population by about 12,250 people. Further reductions will be necessary in 1983. This downsizing effort, painful though it has been, is critical to our future success and to the employment stability of the majority of our people.

We have taken other major cost-reduction actions in the past year. Our very large and excellent U.S. field organization has been streamlined to reduce overhead and needless duplication. Similar consolidations have taken place in Rank Xerox.

In the area of manufacturing, we have moved aggressively toward automation. For example, the level of automation in our Memory-writer plant in Dallas has allowed us to price a superior machine very attractively. Throughout our worldwide manufacturing operations we are making greater use of computer technology and robotics to make our copiers and duplicators. Overall, however, our unit manufacturing costs are still too high and we will continue to drive them down this year.

Critical Issues

Many presidents view the annual report as a means to express their concerns over national and international issues. Stockholder support is oftentimes elicited to support the corporation's legislative concerns.

Corporations have long used employees or industry groups to sway legislators. But increasingly, they see their individual shareholders as an untapped, and potentially powerful lobbying resource.

Some companies are asking holders to give money to their political action committees (PACs), which in turn donate to congressional candidates. Others are creating so-called grass roots "action networks" of stockholders who can be enlisted to lobby Washington.

Examples of Efforts to Gain Support for Issues Affecting Corporations:

National Semiconductor

U.S. Industrial Policy

An absolute requirement for the future of this industry, indeed for this country, as we see it, is a firm commitment to, and the adoption of a *national industrial policy*. We must define the terms and conditions under which we as a nation will compete, and we can ill afford to allow foreign powers to compete under different terms and conditions with American industry. Allowing this practice will erode the strengths we have developed in this country, and diminish this nation's long-standing reputation as the premier technology nation. The implications, if we allow this to continue unchecked, clearly point to the debasement of our strength as a national power.

While this nation's leaders have been slow in the past to recognize the importance of the semiconductor industry to our country's future, there is a general ground swell of opinion in Washington now, focusing on legislation which would address the inequities caused by foreign government practices.

In one legislative area, which we fully support, "The High Technology Trade Act," an upcoming bill in Washington, would give the Executive Office legislative powers to review and act quickly where the nation's best interests are threatened by unfair foreign practices. This is clearly the action that other countries take when threatened. We must have the ability to act with the same initiative to protect this country's valued resources from predatory practices.

Further, we must encourage our leaders to create incentives, through legislation, for industry and educational cooperation that will facilitate the development of people resources for this industry's future growth. The total number of graduating scientists, engineers and chemists, for example, is appallingly low in this country and certainly not competitive with other nations.

Urging legislative action of this kind is an area where you can help this industry.

W. R. Grace & Co.

We take this opportunity to offer our views on matters of utmost importance to shareholders and citizens alike. The economic condition of the United States continues to be beset by a tax structure that destroys incentives to work, by low productivity in manufacturing, chronic inflation and an enormous Federal deficit. Recent strength in industrial output, however, suggests that the recession may have bottomed and that gradual improvement can be expected.

This prospect can be enhanced by steps the new Administration is proposing to provide incentives for capital formation and investment through enlightened tax legislation (including the removal of tax disincentives on capital gains), to allow more rapid depreciation on plant and equipment and to narrow the gap between government spending and receipts. Such fiscal measures, if enacted by the Congress, combined with firm monetary policies by the Federal Reserve, will speed growth and lead to a balanced budget and lower inflation.

We firmly support this as a wise program which can restrain inflation, secure economic stability, restore fiscal sanity and create new jobs, together with higher productivity and increased capital investment.

We discern a new and progressive spirit in this country which will help us in the coming test of our ability to accomplish these critical objectives.

Customers

General Data Comm is now the largest independent supplier of equipment to the rapidly expanding data communications market. GDC believes it represents approximately 10% of the total market and has captured 25% of the low speed data transmission business. GDC's business approach was to start with low-priced high-volume items and achieve mass market penetration, which has been achieved. The emphasis now, as evidenced by Company product introductions in 19__ is in the high-speed area.

Digital Equipment Corp.

This past year saw the continued aggressive build-up of Digital's customer support organization, with significant additions to our sales, maintenance, software services and training organizations. In total, Digital now has more than 13,000 customer support personnel deployed in 40 countries on five continents to serve our growing world-wide customer base. Additions to these key groups accounted for most of the increase in our worldwide employee population, which at year end totaled more than 44,000.

Computervision Corporation

Customer Education and Training. Our Education Services Group began 19__ in a new two-classroom facility equipped with dedicated training systems and twelve student terminals. By mid-year, increased demands for customer training required expansion. In July, the Group moved into enlarged quarters in Woburn, Massachusetts. Six classrooms and three CAD/CAM systems with fifteen terminals are now available exclusively for customer training.

The Group's training staff is made up of full-time expert instructors who conduct a variety of comprehensive courses covering every aspect of customer involvement from basic terminal operation through high-level applications and management strategies for increasing productivity.

In the next three to five years, our Education Services Group expects to introduce CAD/CAM techniques to thousands of engineers, designers, draftsmen and managers from customer companies throughout the world.

Customer Service

Carpenter

Customer service is another strength that gives us confidence that Carpenter's rate of growth can exceed the overall demand growth rate in our markets. Customer service strategy includes both direct customer interface by our technical and commercial personnel, as well as our Company-owned warehouses and inventories located in major industrial cities throughout this country.

Carpenter technical people work directly with customers to determine the proper specifications for their applications and to solve individual metallurgical problems. Supporting this personal interface is a nationwide network of regional metallurgists, backed by a highly-trained technical staff located at our manufacturing facilities.

Carpenter works closely with more than 14,000 customers. We inform our customers about Carpenter products and our customers inform us about their special needs or problems. We have the technology and production facilities to produce sophisticated, high performance metals which serve our customers' individual needs.

Our highly-trained sales personnel make in-depth calls on customers. They review our product line of over 450 different specialty grades in billets, bars, rod, wire, narrow strip, and hollow forms with design technology suited to the unique customer application.

Supporting this direct interface is our unique, wholly-owned distribution system of 21 warehouses which inventory and sell only Carpenter products.

Our continuing marketing strategy is to maintain our leadership as a supplier to those specific segments of the end-use markets which can benefit from the high technology, quality, and service we can provide to our customers. The customers we serve represent a broad spectrum of both industrial and consumer applications.

Ramtek

Customer satisfaction means more than having state-of-the-art products. It means the customer can be sure those products won't let him down at critical times.

That's where Ramtek's support and service people come in. Operating out of our Santa Clara headquarters plus 14 service centers in the U.S. and Europe, more than 60 field engineers and technical support staffers can be at customer sites in 24 hours or less. Usually they can provide immediate help by replacing the part that's causing the difficulty—printed circuit board, light pen, monitor, etc.—and taking the original back to the service center for detailed analysis.

Sometimes, a field engineer may solve an elusive problem that has cropped up in more than one customer location. Using Ramtek's dial-up electronic-mail network, which links all our service centers, he can quickly inform all centers of the solution. Thus a field support staffer in Amsterdam—Ramtek's European headquarters—may indirectly provide the answer to a problem in Santa Clara, New York or London.

But providing spare parts and keeping graphics hardware "downtime" at a minimum is only part of the picture. In a world that's becoming more and more software oriented, the importance of software support is growing dramatically.

Ramtek's software analysts often serve customers in the role of consultants. Even before a purchase order is signed, they work closely with our sales personnel, taking an informed look at a prospective customer's long-term needs to ensure that that customer gets a product that will take him beyond his immediate graphics requirements.

This level of support continues long after the sale is made. While they can't claim expertise in every one of the many applications for our equipment, our software analysts can make sure Ramtek software is doing the best job possible for the customer. Ramtek creates and supports software at the *system* level—the software that tells our equipment how to perform basic functions such as graphics and imaging, rather than how to do specific tasks such as routing railroad trains or realigning congressional districts. Supporting such software is a continuing process because software is never really complete. It's constantly evolving and being refined to best meet a specific need.

But certain types of system-level software frequently are written by the customers themselves—for example, those programs that interconnect Ramtek equipment with their own computer systems. Ramtek's software support group members are in constant touch with a large number of such customers. So when one of these customer-generated programs is general-purpose enough to be of use to others, Ramtek can serve as a communication channel between various companies.

We try to promote an ongoing exchange of ideas this way. And on more than one occasion we've been able to prevent a customer from re-inventing the wheel when a good solution to his problem already existed.

Triad—unlike suppliers of only hardware or only software—assumes responsibility for working closely with customers and their employees to enhance success of the customer's total application. Even before Triad installs the system, support begins with a complete installation plan and professional training of customer employees by the Triad Marketing Representative, backed-up by Marketing Applications and Customer Education Representatives. Customers also can get immediate help by calling applications experts at Triad's 800-number Advice Line. During 1982, 85% of Advice Line questions were solved over the telephone.

For the other 15%, a call to the nearest Triad office will dispatch the Triad Field Engineer assigned to the account—an expert with extensive factory training in both hardware and software. Each Field Engineer has a complete system available for loaned replacements, and carries some $10,000 in test equipment and spare parts drawn from an inventory of over $5 million at strategically located depots. Advanced diagnostic aids such as high-speed telecommunications links between the customer's computer and corporate field engineering computers further streamline service.

The efficient techniques of Triad service enables the company to keep its total-system service costs well below the national computer industry average—an average that includes only service on the hardware portion of systems. Yet Triad support goes beyond keeping hardware running: It also includes software maintenance, feature enhancements, documentation and ongoing training. Triad will even train customers' new employees.

A user's ability to get total hardware/software system support from a single source is an extremely important aspect of protecting the system investment. Other systems that require service from more than one company can present the system owner with a confusing dilemma in the event of a system failure because the owner must determine the failure's source, call the appropriate vendor, and possibly arbitrate the mixed vendors' disagreement over the source of the failure.

Triad users do not have such experiences. Over 850 Triad experts in over 150 Triad offices support every customer's total system. Without total system support, Triad would not be able to so freely distribute its complete customer list in evidence of the Triad commitment.

Decentralization

The dramatic growth of your company has prompted a shift toward a decentralized management style. The relocation of corporate headquarters to Dallas, Texas assists in this effort by physically separating the corporate offices from all operating Units.

We are presently completing a program that moves many staff functions into operating Units. This enables operating management to tailor these functions more precisely to support their business objectives. At the same time, decentralization enables corporate staff to focus more fully on strategic and planning matters.

Decentralized Operations

Size equals strength, many business people believe.

But bigness, others insist, is stifling. It drains creativity, creates the kind of bureaucratic inertia that results in missed opportunities.

It doesn't have to be that way. Consolidated Foods' concept of a decentralized operating company encourages—indeed, insists on—the right of individual businesses to determine their own destiny. The corporate structure helps establish overall goals and strategies, and provides the kind of financial and technical support that can make the difference between stagnation and growth.

All along the line, however, there is an emphasis on direct contact, lean management structures, decisions based on facts and logic. It's a system that works.

Ask Mike Dennos, chairman of Chef Pierre. His family has been making pies, mostly for sale to institutional markets, for more than 60 years. In 1978, the company became part of Consolidated Foods.

"We chose Consolidated Foods because they have a reputation for letting you run your own business," Dennos says.

And has it worked out that way? "Absolutely," he says. "We still run Chef Pierre the same way, with an emphasis on quality products and salesmanship. Our people still take great pride in their work. The major difference is, when we have needed capital and other support to expand, we have had it.

"Today, our business is twice as big as it was when we joined Consolidated Foods."

Distribution

Foremost-McKesson

Wholesale distribution is in the midst of a quiet but dramatic revolution. The upheaval is altering the way goods move to the marketplace, the way Americans shop, how retailers manage their businesses and how manufacturers map their marketing strategies.

In the wake of this revolution, the role of the distributor—once characterized by forklifts and freight trucks used for shuttling goods from manufacturers to retailers—is undergoing a radical change.

Nowhere is this change more evident than at Foremost-McKesson, which, says *Business Week* magazine, is "redefining the function of the middleman [and] leading a revolution in the way U.S. wholesaling is practiced."

It is a revolution being staged simultaneously on two fronts: in the way Foremost-McKesson manages and controls its own businesses and in the ways the company is increasing services to its customers far beyond the simple logistics of buying a lot of boxes and selling them off one at a time.

To a degree unmatched in the distribution industry, Foremost-McKesson has adopted modern computer technology and marketing techniques. Propelled by the concept of adding value to services, Foremost-McKesson is moving full-force into marketing and gaining an increasingly key position in the channels of distribution. These value-added services include:

- comprehensive management reports that provide detailed analyses of product movement, enabling retailers to adjust their inventories, margins and pricing.
- service merchandising for retailers, providing a labor force to set up and maintain store shelves and displays and manage inventories.
- repackaging of bulk quantities of chemicals into smaller bags and drums.
- product marketing know-how for identifying new uses for chemicals.
- market audits to help alcoholic beverage suppliers expand their local market penetration.
- a voluntary association for independent pharmacies, offering the private-label pricing, advertising and identification advantages of chain stores.
- machine-vended purified drinking water as an alternative to conventional bottled water for supermarkets.

The company's position as the number one distributor of drugs and health care products, wines and spirits, chemicals and bottled drinking water makes it the largest wholesaler in the U.S. Every working day some 3,000 vehicles fan out across the country from about

200 Foremost-McKesson distribution centers. Each day they move some $15 million worth of merchandise, from table wine to toothpaste, chlorine to clock radios, drugs to disposable diapers.

There is hardly anyone in any of the 50 states who can go for very long without using a product that has been marketed by one of Foremost-McKesson's 2,200 salespeople, passed through one of its distribution centers or tracked by its nationwide computer network.

As both manufacturer and wholesaler, Foremost-McKesson understands the market forces all along the distribution channel. With the aid of advanced computer and materials-handling technology, the company is reducing total distribution costs and simultaneously offering valuable marketing services to both suppliers and retailers.

By transforming the traditional wholesale channel into a finely tuned marketing and information distribution network, Foremost-McKesson is helping its suppliers and customers make sense and profits out of an increasingly complex business environment.

Dividends

Your stockholders are interested in:

1. Your company's past record of the payment of dividends.
2. Your company's dividend action during the past year.
3. Your company's future dividend policy.
4. Your company's dividend reinvestment and common stock purchase plan.

Clarity and ease of understanding are most important.

Examples:

Dividends are important to our shareowners. We know it, and are doing something about it.

Dividends have been raised in each of the last five years. The current annual rate of $2.48 per common share is 84% above the rate in 1975. That's an average annual jump of 13%, compared with an inflation rate of about 9% in the same period.

We hope to continue these annual increases to keep our shareholders ahead of inflation—even in a year when earnings are down.

Our policy is to pay dividends equal to about 40% of the prior year's earnings averaged over the long term. In the last ten years we've accomplished about exactly that.

Dividends alone are only part of the equation. Most investors hope for some combination of dividends and stock appreciation to provide a fair return. The present yield to our owners is nearly 6%—not enough by itself to offset inflation. Fortunately, those who bought our shares in January 1980 and held them through the year, found that appreciation added about 20% to the dividend for a total investment return of 27%.

Dayco's Board of Directors is vitally interested in maintaining a dividend policy appropriate for the long-term capital needs of the Corporation. At the same time, the Board intends to provide current income to our shareholders.

In light of improved operating profits during the last half of 1983 and the Company's expectations for 1984, the Board in December, 1983, increased the quarterly dividend from $.04 per share to $.06 per share. The Board will continually review the dividend policy in light of prevailing events and economic circumstances throughout the year. We do expect, however, that in pursuance of the opportunities available to us, earnings will increase at a faster rate than dividends. It is our belief that this dividend policy is responsive to our stated objectives.

Dividends

Cash dividends paid in 1983 totaled 83 cents per common share compared with 78 cents in 1982. The company's 1983 quarterly dividends per common share were 19.5 cents in the first and second quarters and 22 cents in the third and fourth quarters. Quarterly dividends were 19.5 cents in each quarter of 1982. Cash dividends per share on the Series A and B preferred stocks in both 1983 and 1982 were $4.75 and $1.35, respectively.

Dividends on all classes of stock in 1983 amounted to a record $129.1 million, or 33% of net income for the year, compared with $120.6 million, or 36% of net income for 1982. The company has paid dividends for 36 consecutive years.

Quarterly common stock information

The quarterly market price ranges of the company's common stock during 1983 and 1982 were as follows:

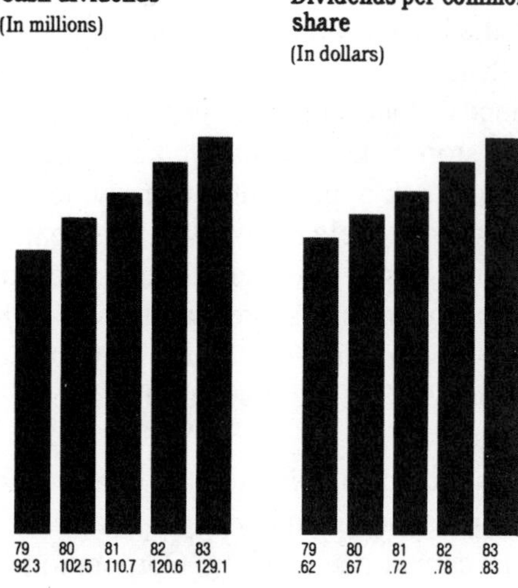

	1983		1982	
Fiscal Quarters	High	Low	High	Low
First	23½	19⅜	16⅝	13¾
Second	26¾	21⅛	16¾	12½
Third	35½	24¾	17	12⅞
Fourth	34½	26½	20½	15⅛

Armco

Armco's objective is to increase the dividend to common stockholders from time to time in order to consistently improve their return on investment. Over time, we believe this will create a sustained appreciation in our shareholders values.

To carry out this policy, Armco's Board follows these general guidelines:

- Dividend rates are established at rates which provide reasonable assurance that they can be maintained during down cycles in the economy.
- Dividend payout will normally range between 30% and 40% of Armco's total net income, depending upon corporate needs and the business outlook.
- The dividend rate is reviewed each quarter.

Some companies are unwilling to make a future dividend commitment.

Examples:

While earnings were substantially improved during 19__ your Board of Directors felt they were not sufficient to warrant the declaration of dividends for the third and fourth quarters. We anticipate resuming dividend payments when profit levels reach the point where they will provide a return that assures the company's internal and external growth, while providing a meaningful distribution to you, the shareholders.

Energy

With the high cost of energy, many companies spell out their energy reduction activities in their annual reports. Subjects that you will want to cover are:

1. Your company's policies on energy conservation.
2. Goals that have been set for the reduction of energy usage, and how these goals were met.
3. Financial savings resulting from energy conservation cogeneration, etc.
4. Use of waste materials for energy purposes.
5. Fuel conservation programs in the operation of your trucks.
6. Energy efficiency as part of the construction of new buildings.
7. Employee involvement in energy conservation.

IU International

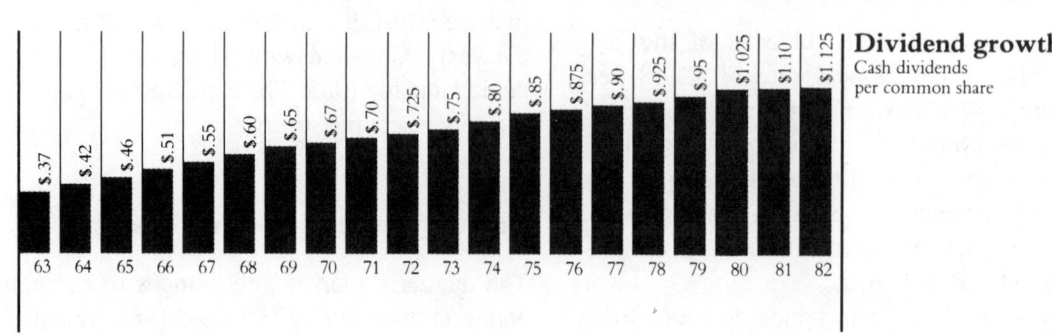

8. The methods used to monitor your energy conservation program.
9. Recycling heat given off by your equipment.
10. Energy savings through application of advances in lighting techniques.

EXAMPLE

"The Forest Products Division provides an excellent example. By 19__, the division had achieved a 40 percent reduction in the amount of fossil fuel used per ton of output, compared with 19__. More important perhaps, by 19__ over 63 percent of the total energy used by the division's mills came from waste fuels either purchased from others or generated by their own production processes."

In addition to developing alternative, nonpurchased fuel sources, some companies describe how they have installed the most modern computerized energy management systems which control multiple power boiler operations and their energy generation and balance. Thus, in areas of the country where purchased electricity is priced depending on the time of day and rate of consumption, computer systems can transfer mill equipment to internally generated power sources at appropriate times or power need levels. Similarly, demand for certain process energy requirements can be fulfilled by switching to the most economical source available.

Energy Costs have risen over the past two years despite a reduction in usage resulting from the lower production levels and our energy conservation programs. All energy forms have been readily available, but at significantly higher costs.

Here is a comparison of energy costs and percentages of total energy costs by source for the past three fiscal years:

	Dollars in Thousands					
	19__		19__		19__	
Energy Source	Cost	%	Cost	%	Cost	%
Electricity	$17,547	58	$13,920	52	$10,386	49
Natural Gas ..	10,988	37	11,846	45	9,557	46
Oil	1,471	5	850	3	1,085	5
Total	$30,006	100	$26,616	100	$21,028	100
% of Sales ...	5.3		4.8		4.5	

Charted below is the steady rise in costs per million Btu (British thermal unit) of the forms of energy we consume:

	Cost per Million Btu		
	19__	19__	19__
Electricity	$16.36	$12.22	$8.77
% Change	+33.9	+39.3	+ 3.2
Natural Gas	$ 3.77	$ 3.33	$2.74
% Change	+13.2	+21.5	+ 6.6
Fuel Oil	$ 5.13	$ 3.48	$3.19
% Change	+47.4	+ 9.1	+15.6

We have reduced the use of energy needed to produce a ton of steel by 18 percent in the past five years through our continuing conservation efforts.

Our Energy Program. During the past several years, we have significantly reduced the energy we use for each unit of production, particularly in the U.S. However, much remains to be done in view of the serious problem facing all of us.

In the U.S., energy per unit of production in 19__ was 4.1 percent less than in 19__ and 17.1 percent less than in 19__. However, the per unit cost of energy has increased over 200 percent since 19__, and the company's energy costs in the U.S. in 19__ were approximately $96.6 million. Over the next five years, our goal is a further reduction of 25 percent in energy consumed per unit of production.

To reach this goal, we are determined to shiver a little more in the winter, sweat a little more in the summer and to undertake any number of projects which will increase our energy efficiency and lessen our dependence on purchased energy. For example, the new manufacturing facility proposed for Augusta, Ga., would use wood wastes, such as bark, sawdust and chips, as its primary source of energy; and some of the wastes collected by the environmental protection system would be used as boiler fuel.

Also, programs have been developed to increase employee awareness of the urgent need for conservation at work and at home; and, at some locations, the company has introduced van pools and encouraged car pools to promote energy-saving transportation for employees.

IBM

IBM further improved its energy efficiency in 19__ with conservation measures that amounted to a 5% saving per sq. ft. at major U.S. locations, compared with 1978. This reduction brought the company's total U.S. saving from the 1973 pre-conservation level to 45%.

In the past six years, IBM has conserved enough electricity in the U.S. to meet the needs of 380,000 homes for a year. Enough oil has been saved to serve 160,000 homes in northern states.

In IBM World Trade countries, where conservation has been practiced for many years, the energy savings per sq. ft. at major IBM locations from 19__ through 19__ came to 40%.

IBM's experience with the use of computers for energy management at its facilities shows typical savings of 10% to 15% through control of electrical, heating and cooling equipment.

Gillette Company

"Since the outset of our program, Gillette has saved some $20 million in energy costs worldwide. In the United States alone, this saving reflects a reduction of more than 30% in energy consumed per unit of production.

"The company's success in curbing energy use, and its continuing commitment to conservation, have been recognized by the Alliance to Save Energy in its recent film, 'The Dynamics of Energy Efficiency.' The film reviews both public and private initiatives in this area and cites Gillette, among several firms, as a leader in energy conservation.

"Energy saving also can be measured in terms of individual Gillette products. For example, the energy required to manufacture a Paper Mate pen has decreased by more than 40% over the past six years.

"Gillette believes conservation will remain a critical concern. Building on the progress achieved thus far, the Company will continue to emphasize efforts to reduce consumption in all of its operations.

"Stockholders interested in showing the energy conservation film should contact Cameron D. Beers, Gillette Energy Conservation Coordinator, Prudential Tower Building, Boston."

Environmental, Occupational Health and Safety Regulations

Koppers

The Company is subject to federal, state and local regulations on the environmental impacts of solid waste disposal, air and water quality impacts of its manufacturing operations, toxic substance control, and occupational health and safety of its employees. About $4 million, or 4.5% of Koppers capital investments for plant and equipment in 19__ went to eliminate pollution or to bring it within satisfactory levels. Environmental improvements are expected to account for a comparable proportion of the total funds investe new facilities in 1982. No estimates are available subsequent years. Operating expenses attributabl pollution control equipment are increasing at a roughly equivalent to the increases in the cumulat capital base of the Company. Although environmen regulations have not yet had a material adverse eff on operations, governmental action has required a may continue to require the Company to modify, su plement, replace or abandon equipment and faciliti and may delay or impede construction and operatic of new facilities. These potential costs cannot be fore casted with precision.

Koppers, in common with many other enterprises is subject to evolving regulations under the federal Occupational Safety and Health Act. Health and safety regulations have not materially affected the Company's operations in the past. If the standards applicable to chemical processors continue to be made more stringent, these regulations could affect certain of Koppers businesses more significantly in the future.

Some aspects of the Company's business will be affected by U.S. Environmental Protection Agency (EPA) regulations requiring premarket disclosure of the potential health and environmental impact of new chemicals and environmental and health testing of some existing chemicals. The promulgation of stringent federal regulations on chemical solid waste disposal under the Resource Conservation and Recovery Act will add substantially to operating costs in a number of Koppers chemically related businesses and may also require some remedial environmental cleanup at existing Company waste disposal sites. In related matters, ground water quality investigations have been or are being conducted at a number of current manufacturing sites as well as inactive plant sites.

Expansion Program

Anheuser-Busch

The major aspects of that capital investment program are expansions of our Williamsburg and Los Angeles breweries, and the purchase of the Jos. Schlitz Brewing Company's Baldwinsville, New York brewery. The expansions in Williamsburg and Los Angeles, which will bring approximately 12 million barrels of additional brewing capacity to the system, are expected to be completed in March 19__ and mid-19__ respectively. The Baldwinsville brewery, which we must extensively modify to meet the requirements of our natural brewing process, will commence production in 1982 and will provide approximately 6 million barrels of capacity annually.

FACILITIES

Rohr is continuing to upgrade facilities and equipment to meet requirements of advancing manufacturing technology. Many of the new and improved equipment items feature computer-controlled or computer-aided devices which produce repeatable parts of higher quality and reduce costs.

At the Riverside operations, work previously performed at the satellite Edgemont plant has been consolidated into the Riverside and Arlington sites, resulting in improved performance levels and reduced overhead costs. The Edgemont facility will be retained as a warehousing center.

A substantial expansion was made in 1983 to the Rohr subsidiary in Toulouse, France, to accommodate increased work associated with the build-up on Airbus A310 assemblies.

Award of the C-5B contract from the Lockheed-Georgia Company early in 1983 has brought about a need for additional assembly space.

It is planned to complete all the relevant fabrication, machining, adhesive bonding and subassembly at the California facilities with the final assembly and engine build-up work on the General Electric TF-39 engines performed in a new facility under construction in Foley, Alabama. Occupancy of this facility is scheduled for Spring 1984 and initial deliveries to Lockheed begin in May 1985.

During fiscal 1983, Rohr installed a new state-of-the-art telephone system for the Chula Vista and Riverside facilities. A similar system will be installed at the Foley plant. The multi-million-dollar expenditure yields an early payback plus protection against rapidly escalating external telephone rates. Its many new features provide a more efficient company-wide communication system. Under consideration is a microwave link between the Chula Vista and Riverside facilities for voice and data transmission. As a part of the new telecommunications system, Rohr is installing an Energy Management Control System. With no relief in sight from electrical rate increases, this is a cost saving measure with a projected payback period that is very attractive.

Several major long-term facility improvements are in process at Rohr. These include the progressive upgrading of all the numerically-controlled bridge mills, a total rework of the Chula Vista processing facility and additional modern machine tools to replace obsolete items. Plans are being developed for the addition of an electrical and steam co-generation system at the Riverside plant to reduce utility costs. Assessments are in process regarding future actions to control electricity cost at the Chula Vista facility which experiences one of the highest rates in the nation.

These additions and upgrades, and the cost reduction measures noted, provide the factory and support areas with the modern facilities needed to remain cost competitive.

Facilities, Product and Market Overview

CTS Corporation Operating Groups

Group	Facilities			Major Products
COMPUTER PERIPHERALS GROUP *President: Ralph Gabai*	**Micro Peripherals, Inc.* Chatsworth, California	*Micro Peripherals Singapore (Private) Limited* Republic of Singapore	*Micro Peripherals Mexico* Tijuana, Mexico	Floppy Disk Drives
ELECTROMECHANICAL GROUP *President: Charles C. Smith*	**Elkhart Division* Elkhart, Indiana *Asheville Division* Skyland, North Carolina	*Bentonville Division* Bentonville, Arkansas *Paso Robles Division* Paso Robles, California	*CTS of Canada, Ltd.* Streetsville, Ontario Canada	Carbon and Wirewound Variable Resistors DIP, Rotary and Specialty Switches Automotive Sensors and Actuators Custom Electromechanical Assemblies
SYSTEMS AND INTERCONNECT GROUP *President: Emmett W. Johnson*	**Systems Division* Eden Prairie, Minnesota	*Circuits Division* Mountain View, California Baldwin, Wisconsin Santa Clara, California *Connector Division* New Hope, Minnesota Cokato, Minnesota	*Fabri-Tek Computer Components* Blantyre, Scotland United Kingdom *Fabri-Tek H.K. Limited* Kowloon, Hong Kong	Printed Circuit Boards Electronic Connectors Backplanes Computer Memory Subsystems
THICK FILM PRODUCTS GROUP *President: Robert G. Early*	**Berne Division* Berne, Indiana	*Bentonville Division* Bentonville, Arkansas	*Tool, Die & Machine Division* Fort Wayne, Indiana	Resistor Networks
ELECTRONIC PRODUCTS GROUP *President: Larry K. Shaum*	**Microelectronics Division* West Lafayette, Indiana	*Knights Division* Sandwich, Illinois	*Halex Division* Irvine, California	Hybrid Microcircuits Frequency Control Devices Modems
INTERNATIONAL GROUP *President: John P. Colglazier*	**CTS Corporation* Elkhart, Indiana *CTS Singapore Pte., Ltd.* Republic of Singapore	*CTS Components Taiwan, Ltd.* Kaohsiung, Taiwan Republic of China	*CTS of Brownsville, Inc.* Brownsville, Texas *CTS de Mexico, S.A.* Matamoros, Mexico	Hybrid Microcircuits Frequency Control Devices Carbon and Cermet Variable Resistors Loudspeakers Switches Resistor Networks
METAL PRODUCTS GROUP *President: Berl J. Grant*	**Middlebury Division* Middlebury, Indiana *Monon Division* Monon, Indiana	*Paso Robles Division* Paso Robles, California	*San Jose Division* San Jose, California	Metal Shelving and Store Fixtures Metal Enclosures

**Headquarters*

Factory of the Future

The challenges facing America's industrial companies are formidable. The task is clear: Produce higher quality, more reliable, competitively-featured products quickly and efficiently, and at lower cost.

High technology is no panacea. Increasingly, though, microelectronics have been expanding the horizons of industrial and process control and, more importantly, are improving the flow of information across the factory floor and into computer assisted manufacturing systems.

Wherever computers and microprocessors can be applied to measure, regulate, control or automate any process, function or manufacturing step, our basic technologies of storage management and communications play a vital role.

Digital communications is helping to create the Factory of the Future, a fully integrated manufacturing environment that spans horizontally across the plant floor and vertically through engineering and management for enhanced planning and decision making.

Intelligent machine-to-machine communications using our WD2840 Token Passing Network controller or systems we have in development based on the new IEEE-802 network standards, are allowing an entire process or manufacturing line to be perceived as a single machine, to be fine-tuned and optimized by management in realtime. This concept can be extended to an entire plant, or even a group of plants over a broad geographic area, relying on an X.25 network using our WD2501/II VLSI controllers.

CAD/CAM, using computers to assist in the design and manufacture of new products, is boosting productivity, shortening new product development schedules, and giving engineers more time to test new products before introducing them. Our customers rank among the leaders in the development of engineering workstations, and our products play an integral role in the continued advancement of this technology.

America's best hope for winning the Productivity Wars, we firmly believe, is in applying the latest advances in technology to control and automate. Western Digital remains firmly committed to working with our customers to bring our technological expertise to bear in support of a strong, revitalized industrial sector.

Field Service Organization

The people of Measurex not only design and engineer the products the Company sells—hardware, software and systems—but they also work with customers to ensure high-level economic results. In the United States alone, there are more than 450 trained field service people with expertise in digital-based hardware, software, communications and control applications. At the end of fiscal 1983, the worldwide field service organization included 1,100 people.

Measurex technical representatives are trained to maintain both the hardware and the software for digital control systems. They are organized with several back-up levels so that customers are assured of 24-hour service, 365 days a year. Service is a vital part of the total package Measurex offers because it helps customers achieve superior financial return from the systems they buy.

From its inception, the Company guaranteed a minimum ''up'' time of 99.0 percent on Measurex serviced systems. The actual percentages have been better than the guarantee. On the average, all Measurex serviced systems, in all industries in the United States, were available to the customer for use 99.6 percent of the time during fiscal 1983.

Future Thrust of Your Company

General Electric, in its annual report, set forth its challenge:

> Today, business faces intensified worldwide competition and more rapid shifts in market structures.
>
> General Electric's aim in this environment is to have an organization more high-spirited, more adaptable and more agile than companies a fraction of its size.

The report covered such subjects as:

1. Going for fast growth in a slow-growth world.
2. Creating high-technology materials.
3. Growing transportation markets.
4. Developing worldwide energy horizons.
5. Packaging new energy solutions.
6. Becoming a world-class competitor.
7. Increasng the emphasis on technology.
8. Insisting on quality better than the best.
9. Discovering natural resources.
10. Serving a discerning consumer.

What About the Future

As we look at the future and evaluate our potential, we realize that if we are to create economic value we must accomplish even more than we have already achieved. Still, we know that it is not in our best interest to maximize short-term returns at the cost of eliminating long-term opportunities. Producing consistently superior returns over the long-term is our goal. We think our plans for achieving that objective will become more clearly understood as we discuss some of our major areas of focus for the time ahead.

Improving Net Margins

The level of net income produced on sales is referred to as net margin. It is our objective to achieve a net margin of at least 5%. While this level of performance is higher than we have achieved previously, we are convinced that this objective is attainable.

In the past we acquired numerous businesses which were either unprofitable or marginally profitable at the time. We succeeded in most of these cases in producing profits from these businesses; and even in those cases where profitability didn't reach levels we considered acceptable, positive cash flows were usually produced through increased financial control. These profits and cash flows have been available to invest in our business and to support our development activities.

Product quality will continue to be a major factor in WCI's long-term strategy as one element in helping to increase our net margin. While quality improvements will require substantial investments in the early stages, they will provide major benefits long-term. Solid product quality will reduce warranty costs and assure continued market acceptance of our products. We are investing heavily in quality now, and we will make additional improvements in the future which we believe will help to increase our returns.

Increasing our sales through an improved marketing effort is another way in which we expect to increase net margins. Delivering the products which are most desired by our customers through the most efficient use of available distribution systems, is part of our plan. Focusing directly on those customer needs which can be satisfied through the product technologies we can effectively provide is an efficient method for us to use.

Our marketing plans include increased spending on advertising and promotional activity. However, we realize that increased spending alone will not guarantee success in this area. It is important for us to communicate directly and meaningfully with those who buy our products and those who influence purchase decisions. We are convinced that more efficient investment of the resources available for advertising and promotion will help us to produce the returns we require.

Productivity improvements beyond those we've already realized will be achieved in the future. Sales-per-employee and output-per-man hour, though commonly used measures of productivity, fail to address the subject fully. Manufacturing productivity is actually the result of the partnership of labor, management, financial capital and a substantial resource base. In line with that point we will increase our capital spending well above current levels in order to improve our productivity and, thereby, reduce costs.

Future investments will improve returns by increasing the volume and quality of units produced while limiting increases in production costs. These productivity-improving investments will not be restricted to the addition of physical capacity since we plan to spend heavily to improve our manufacturing efficiency. However, we may add new plants where well defined, long-term capacity shortages exist and where those shortages threaten our present and planned market positions.

The industries in which WCI now participates are highly competitive. In many of those industries, we encounter strong foreign-source competition as well as aggressive competition from domestic sources. In the marketplace, prices are established by the one or two industry participants having the largest market share and/or the lowest production costs. When market prices are controlled by the competition, we must function more efficiently in order to compete effectively. In the past we have approached this challenge through product design consistent with manufacturing efficiency. In the future, we will expand our research and development programs so that we design and produce innovative products which will even better satisfy the needs of customers while meeting our tougher cost targets. We expect this increased investment in product research and development to produce strong returns and to further enhance our market position.

Controlling costs is one of the most important elements of improving long-term profitability. While we have a record of successfully controlling our costs, we expect to be even more effective in the future. We think it is important to make a distinction between merely cutting costs and strategically controlling costs. Cost cutting alone without a longer view to our future would deny us many benefits by restricting product development, reducing our market position, eroding product quality and reducing long-term manufacturing efficiency. Comprehensive cost/benefit analysis will assure that we will not be guilty of short-sighted actions which could endanger the basic components of our value creation strategy. Strategic control of all of our costs will eliminate non-productive expenses today and will free-up capital for us to invest in assets which will help produce more profitable sales in the future.

Asset Utilization

The amount of annual sales supported by each dollar of assets is known as asset turnover ratio. WCI's asset turnover objective is a ratio of 1.6:1. This means we expect to produce a minimum of $1.60 in sales for every $1.00 of book value of our assets. This compares with our 1983 ratio of 1.57:1. Our 1983 ratio is below our target principally because of the addition of cash assets which did not produce sales during the year. We expect this to be a short-term condition.

We believe the key to efficient utilization of assets is the acquisition and efficient management of those assets which produce the highest level of high-profit sales. In order to acquire assets efficiently it is necessary to have a comprehensive plan which provides for the use of those assets. In the past few years, but more particularly in the past two years, WCI has dedicated substantial management time and resources to providing a framework for sound planning. As a result, our strategic planning has become more comprehensive and more systematic.

The systematic elements of objectives achievement relate to how strategies or policies are developed, evaluated and implemented. This suggests that actions are taken consistent with well defined and well understood strategies and with a view to achieving specific objectives. This systematic approach limits the dilution of management time and talent and provides for more efficient use of all resources. Diverting limited resources from strategies in order to chase "opportunities" is an inefficient allocation of those resources.

To be effective, an organization's formalized objectives and strategies must be developed, communicated, understood and agreed upon as deeply into the organization as possible. It is important that as many employees and managers as practical understand specifically the importance of their individual role in achieving the agreed-upon objectives. When comprehensive strategies are developed systematically and become organizationally formalized, initiating action and managing the organization consistent with achieving those objectives becomes an efficient task.

Adhering to a well-defined strategy does not mean that WCI will no longer seek opportunities in the acquisitions area, since business acquisitions are often a very efficient way of obtaining productive assets. However, we will evaluate and invest in only those assets or businesses which are consistent with our strategies and which provide the most efficient support for high-return sales. By employing a strategically efficient program of resource allocation we will accomplish our goals more effectively in the future, helping to create additional economic value.

Yet another way our performance can be improved is through the consolidation of assets which are inefficiently performing, underutilized or inconsistent with our current strategies and objectives. In certain circumstances we may consolidate through divestiture in one of its many forms. In other situations, where our options are more limited, it might be necessary to consolidate operations through the closing of less-efficient facilities. Consolidation may include moving manufacturing from some of our plants into other of our existing facilities or even into new plants. In some instances we might sell entire groups of businesses within an industry in order to free-up resources to be invested in businesses that are more strategically consistent for us. There are numerous consolidation alternatives available to us and we will evaluate each of them.

There are costs which are associated with any restructuring effort, regardless of its size. That will certainly be true for us in the future. At present, neither the actions which we might take nor their aggregate impact on our operating results nor the timing of either can be identified with any degree of certainty. We fully expect, however, that if significant actions are taken, any short-term negative effects will be offset in a major way by long-term benefits to WCI and its stockholders through increases in manufacturing, product development and marketing-distribution efficiencies.

We believe the traditional wisdom that an efficient company constantly increases the sales produced by its asset base will change in the 80's. Advances in manufacturing technology coupled with the requirement to produce products on a less labor intensive and more cost-efficient basis are increasing the requirement to invest more heavily in assets which increase the productivity of labor. Our near-term asset turnover objective reflects our plans to invest several hundred million dollars in capital equipment during the next few years. Over time, an increase in this ratio is expected to help us to produce even more high-return sales.

Finally, asset control programs which we have used successfully in the past will be improved upon and used even more effectively in the future. Restricting the level of current assets and therefore working capital required to support sales is an important element in our plans to improve profitability. Short-term debt reductions have provided benefits to us in the past and the restrictions on the use of debt will be continued and will add value in the future.

Responsible Capital Structure Management

One of the objectives of investors is to receive the benefits of the maximum amount of high quality assets for the minimum equity investment. This goal is usually achieved when the capital available to acquire assets is increased through the use of debt, a practice known as financial leverage. WCI's financial leverage ratio objective of 2.5:1 means that we expect to receive the benefits of $2.50 of assets for each $1.00 of common stockholders' equity. At year-end 1983 our leverage ratio was 2.21:1, actually lower than we desire. Again, the primary reason for this low ratio in 1983 was the strengthening of our equity through the issuance of common stock earlier in the year.

While leverage enables the investor to acquire additional assets for his or her equity investment, it also increases equity risk because of the requirement that the business repay the debt. Therefore the more debt (leverage) an investor uses, the greater the risk. As risk increases, the return the investor requires in order to compensate for the increased risk also increases.

In the past, our leverage ratio was higher than our objective but it has been steadily decreasing. As a result, WCI now has the strongest equity base in its history. That equity base is larger and represents less investor risk than at any time in our past. As we identify future opportunities which are consistent with our strategies, we will increase our leverage in order to take advantage of those opportunities. However, when leverage is increased, it will be increased prudently, consistent with our objectives and without adding inordinate risk.

In the future, as we add assets we will carefully select those which maximize high-return sales. For example, our present liquidity position enables us to add more than $150 million of high quality assets without incurring additional debt or increasing leverage. By increasing net income through the addition of high sales producing high-quality assets, while sharply restricting the addition of risk, we will successfully satisfy our objective of creating economic value for our stockholders.

Growth

"How is your company preparing for its future growth?" This question is constantly on the minds of your stockholders and the investment community. It will be useful to describe your corporate thinking on this subject in your corporate annual report.

Opportunities For Growth

Economic indicators point to a more favorable business climate for the balance of the 1980's. For example, the fixed investment sector, which represents markets traditionally served by Square D Company, is expected to grow faster than the rest of the economy (Chart A below).

All three components of fixed investment—residential construction, non-residential construction and the production of durable equipment—are predicted to show steady, substantial increases through 1990 (Graphs B, C and D below). Merrill Lynch Economics predicts an average annual growth of 8.9% in residential construction, a 9.9% average annual growth in non-residential construction and a 10.2% average annual increase in the layout for producers of durable equipment. This should provide a solid potential for growth in the markets served by Square D.

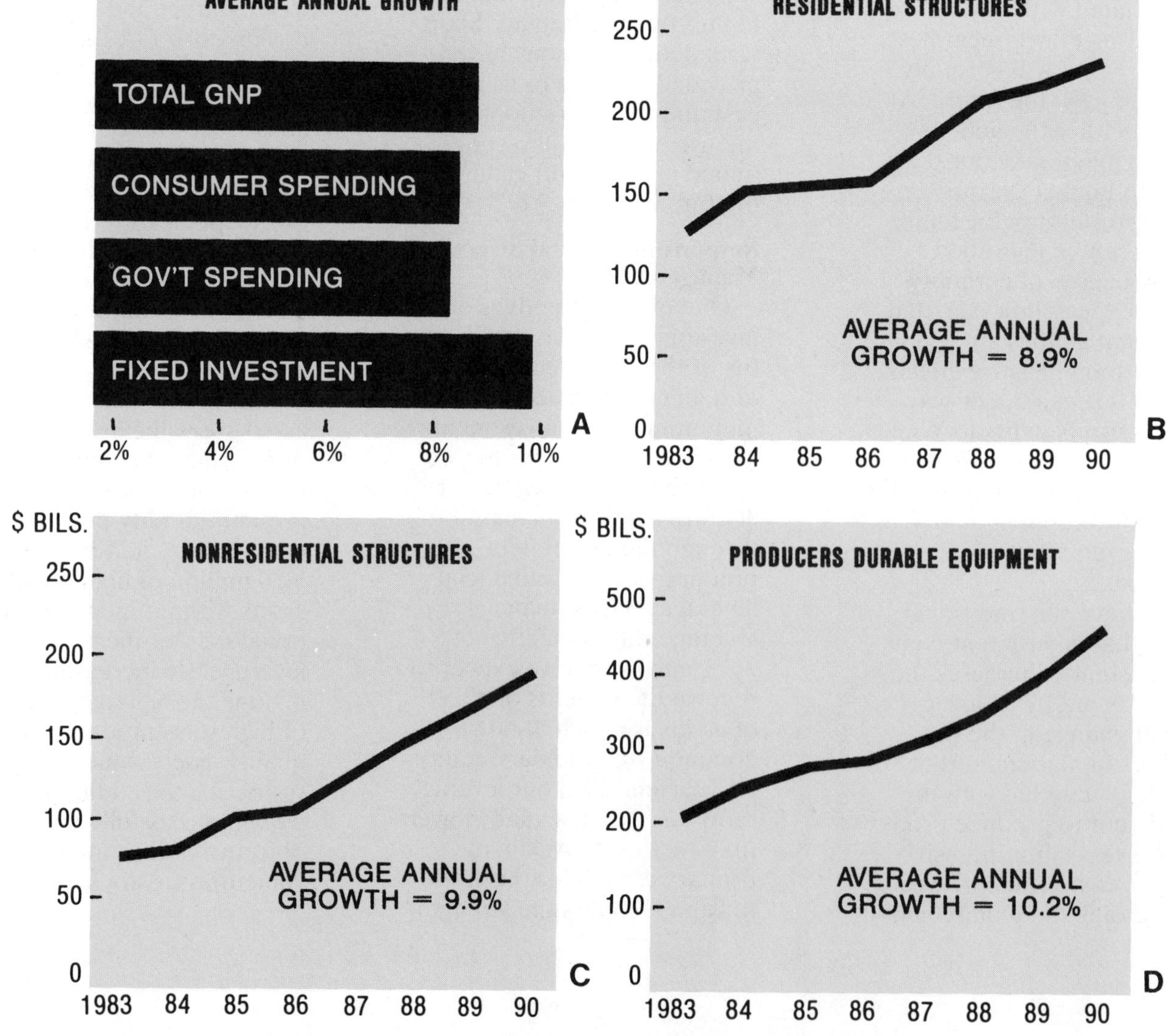

Even greater potential is forecast for the markets involved in the advanced technology area according to several independent research organizations and McGraw-Hill. The anticipated growth through 1987 in the robotics area alone, for example, should average 38.4% per year. Growth potential for the other product lines is also impressive. The various bar graphs below show the growth forecast for some of the advanced technology markets in which Square D is involved. Of the six advanced technology categories shown, Square D developed its own product lines in two of the categories—programmable controllers and adjustable frequency controls. We are involved in the other four product areas as a result of acquisitions.

$ IN MILLIONS

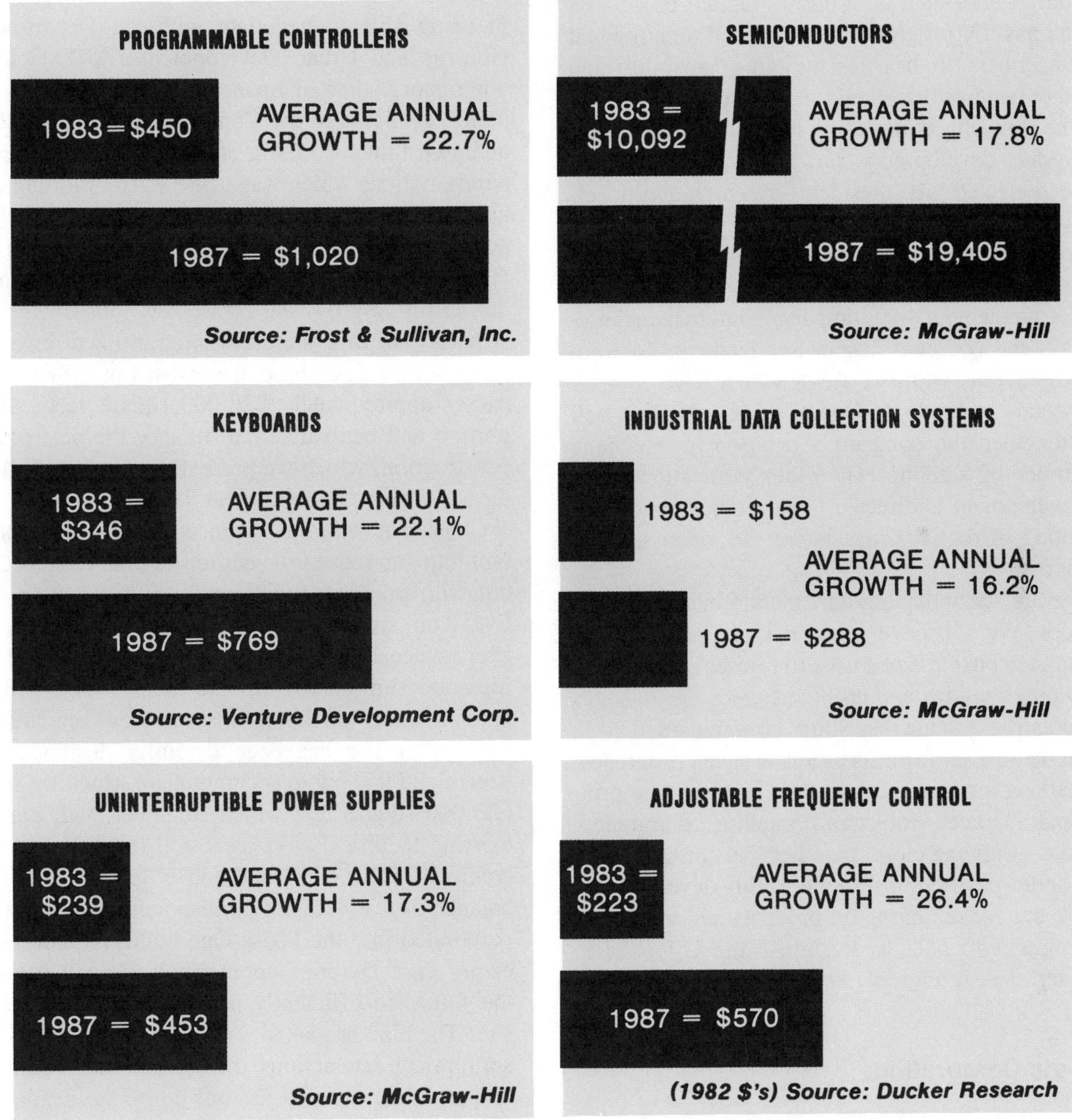

Square D Company's plan for long range growth is to have the advanced technology area represent 50 percent of our total business, with 50 percent devoted to our basic distribution equipment and control products. We feel that this balance has to be achieved through internal development and expansion, as well as continued, selective acquisitions of companies which will take us into new markets which offer greater potential for profit and growth. The following pages discuss our plan for growth in markets involving advanced technology and basic electrical products.

Scientific Atlanta

We are undertaking positive steps that will resume Scientific-Atlanta's growth. Among the more important actions are:

- Scientific-Atlanta has introduced its Model 8500 cable-TV set-top terminal. The new product is addressable—that is, it allows regular broadcasts and pay-TV programs to be directed to individual subscribers. It has descrambling capability and other features that should make it a market leader.
- The company is increasing its commitment to new product development. Dr. Guy W. Beakley has been elected vice president—research and development to provide corporate direction to this essential function. Staff additions have been made to support product development.
- To supplement the company's internal technology, the company began arrangements to form associations with two firms which have complementary technology. One of these initiatives will strengthen the company's position in telephone service by satellite. The other association under development is directed toward design and marketing of digital products for the video satellite market.
- We are strengthening our internal business practices. We will have sound risk analysis and disciplined business practices to foresee and respond to opportunities and problems.
- Scientific-Atlanta has long been regarded as a market-driven firm. Its products have created new markets for its customers. We now see two principal markets—cable and satellite communications—drawing closer together. No company is in a better position to respond to this development. We are concentrating on products and marketing programs to hold leadership in the U.S. and to assert it in foreign markets.

Analogic Corporation

Analogic is committed to continued growth. As tangible evidence of this commitment, we have, during the past year, in Peabody, Massachusetts, been building a major new additional facility designed to accommodate our needs throughout the present decade. First conceived and planned more than a year and a half ago, this facility is being built on an attractive 80-acre site directly abutting Route 128, "America's Technological Highway." With planned construction of a full, major, east-west highway interchange at the boundary of our property, this new location not only provides us with an environment representative of the rock-ledge, wooded beauty of eastern Massachusetts, but extends further our viable sources of skilled workers which are critical to our sophisticated products.

Consistent with our desire to efficiently use our available financial resources, we were very fortunate in being able to negotiate with the Department of Housing and Urban Development a UDAG loan as one major source of financing for this project, which makes available to the Company up to $8,500,000 at an interest rate of 3% for 36 years. This governmental appropriation, which was made after a thorough evaluation by the Department of a number of such proposed projects, was the largest ever made to a small city in the United States and indicates their faith in our ability to grow and create new jobs for this area. A portion of this money is being utilized toward carrying out the first phase of construction which encompasses approximately 220,000 square feet. Another portion will be available to finance the next phase of construction, which we presently anticipate will commence during our fiscal year 1984.

Consistent with our engineering attitudes, the new building and indeed the entire site plan have been laid out with practical functionality as their main objective. Our architects, Sasaki Associates, have, however, succeeded in designing a combination of facilities and surrounding service areas which befits the natural beauty of this northshore New England area. The entire site has been carefully designed, engineered and laid out to accommodate structures totaling 600,000 square feet which, together with our other existing facilities, we expect will be sufficient to accommodate our continued rate of growth through the balance of this decade. Correspondingly, we have incorporated into the Phase-One building plan the necessary core facilities upon which we can expand in the future to efficiently service the fully-developed site. The plan has taken into account the necessity for appropriate interactions throughout the organization so that when we relocate our corporate headquarters to Peabody early next year, we will have instrumented the appropriate means of effecting control and communications between our various locations, all within a few miles of each other in Danvers, Peabody and Wakefield, Massachusetts.

It is helpful to back up the description of your corporate growth program through the use of outside reports.

Example:

National Machine Tool

"The outlook for capital goods producers in the 1980s is optimistic. Rapidly growing demand, coupled with slow growth in the manufacturing labor force, will require large increases in manufacturing productivity if supply is to keep up. That will require substantial investment in productivity-improving machine tools..."

James A. Gray
President,
National Machine Tool Builders' Association

"Healthy growth through the 1980s is the outlook for the $3 billion-a-year U.S. valve manufacturing industry, especially in the areas of oil and gas production and processing, which today account for nearly 35 percent of total valve industry sales..."

Dr. Malcolm O'Hagan
President,
The Valve Manufacturers Association

"What will the machine tool industry be like in 1986? According to the experts, the companies building the most advanced equipment will be very large and heavily capitalized. These builders will manufacture the flexible manufacturing systems and unmanned factories. It is reasonable to believe they will be international in scope so that they can benefit from the specialized abilities and comparative advantages overseas..."

James A. Gray
President,
National Machine Tool Builders' Association

Government Contracts

With the emphasis on large expenditures for defense, the readers of your annual report will be interested in how your company will benefit, if at all, by sales to the U.S. defense agencies.

Examples:

Sanders

Approximately 53 percent of Sanders revenues in fiscal 19__ was derived from work for United States Government agencies under fixed-price, cost-reimbursable, and incentive-type prime contracts and subcontracts. Under fixed-price contracts Sanders realizes any benefit or detriment occasioned by lower or higher costs of performance. Cost-reimbursable contracts provide for reimbursement of costs incurred, to the extent such costs are allowable under Government regulations, plus a fee. Under incentive-type contracts the amount of profit or fee realized may vary with the attainment of incentive goals such as costs incurred, delivery schedule, quality and other criteria.

In common with other companies which derive a substantial portion of their revenues from the United States Government, Sanders is subject to certain basic risks, including rapidly changing technologies and possible cost overruns. Recognition of profits is based upon estimates of final performance which may change as contracts progress. Work may be performed prior to formal authorization or adjustment of contract price for increased work scope, change orders and other funding adjustments. Contract prices and costs incurred are subject to Government Procurement Regulations, particularly Defense Acquisition Regulations, and may be questioned by the Government and are subject to disallowance.

All U.S. Government contracts contain a provision that they may be terminated at any time for the convenience of the Government. In such event the contractor is entitled to recover allowable costs plus any profits earned to the date of termination.

Sanders believes that adequate provision has been made in the financial statements for these and other normal uncertainties incident to its Government business.

Health and Safety

St. Joe Minerals Corp.

St. Joe's Viburnum lead mine in southeast Missouri won the top national award for safety from the Mine Safety and Health Administration (MSHA) of the U.S. Department of Labor and the American Mining Congress. The lead mines were cited at length for excellence in the MSHA's house magazine.

Continued progress was made in reducing blood lead levels among the work force at the Herculaneum smelter. Also, there has been substantial progress in reducing air lead levels in the vicinity of the plant.

Human Resources

There is widespread interest on the part of your stockholders and employees in the relationship of your company to its employees. While some reports merely pay tribute in general terms to the importance of the efforts of the work force in profit production, most reports contain considerable information on such subjects as:

1. Your company's commitment to your people.
2. Your company's management philosophy to help you attract and develop high caliber personnel.
3. The manner in which your employees are trained.
4. Your incentive programs beyond the base salary.
5. Your productivity improvement programs.
6. The sales per employee.
7. The number of employees in the current year compared to preceding years.
8. Compensation as a percentage of sales.
9. Opportunities for your employees to participate in college and university programs.
10. The status of your labor relations with unions.
11. The description of strikes, if any.
12. The extent of collective bargaining agreements with labor organizations.
13. Statistics relating to the employment of minorities and women.
14. Your company's commitment to equal employment opportunities for all employees.
15. Payroll and related costs compared to prior years.
16. Expenditures for salaries and related costs as a percentage of the revenue dollar compared to the prior year.
17. Supplemental unemployment programs provided.
18. Savings and stock investment plans.
19. Retirement plans.
20. University recruiting programs.
21. Hiring the handicapped.
22. Skills needed for the future.

Examples:

Keene People

A key factor in our continuing growth is the above-average performance of highly motivated Keene people.

The company's management philosophy is: attract and develop high-caliber, experienced personnel, delegate responsibility to them and compensate them well for superior performance.

This philosophy has helped create the profit-oriented environment that exists at Keene. Superior performance and individual progress not only are expected but required. This makes great demand on Keene people. It also stimulates their performance and accelerates their development by constantly presenting them with new challenges.

Each manager is measured against a specific set of annual profit-generating goals he or she helps establish. The manager then meets with his or her supervisor three times a year to review and evaluate progress. Those who achieve their goals by the end of the year are well rewarded through incentive compensation—additional payment beyond the individual's base salary.

Management believes that everyone who helps improve Keene's performance should share in the benefits. At nine Keene plants, productivity improvement programs have been established through which hourly employees can earn a part of the additional profit they help generate by increasing productivity. Our goal is to have all plants participate in such a program.

Human Resources—Programs were expanded to increase participative management throughout Honeywell to improve product quality and promote good health.

Employee compensation including benefits was $2.8 billion, 52 percent of total 1983 costs and expenses. Total worldwide employment was 93,500,down about 500 from the previous year. The largest decline was in Information Systems. Honeywell employs about 25,700 people abroad, of whom fewer than 200 are U.S. citizens.

We expanded efforts to improve the quality of worklife. More than 12,000 employees including union, nonunion and supervisory workers from five divisions participated in day-long sessions to define standards of quality.

The company established long-range goals to increase the number of women and minority employees in management, professional and sales positions to equal their representation in Honeywell's total employee population.

A Honeywell task force investigated ways to maintain the quality of medical benefits while holding down costs, which have increased 19 percent annually for the past five years to approximately $125 million in 1983. Divisions instituted programs to reduce costs by promoting good health, making the administration and design of benefits more cost-effective, and creating better relationships between Honeywell and health-care providers. All Honeywell employees are being asked to become active partners in their health care by learning how to prevent illness and make better informed choices for treatment.

The search for people with training and experience in key technologies continued. We launched an annual Futurist Awards Competition, granting cash prizes and internships to college students with the most creative ideas about technological advancements by the year 2000 in computer science, marine systems, communications, aerospace, energy and biomedicine. Ten winners were selected from hundreds who entered.

On- and after-hours courses were expanded. In 1983, over 11,000 employees worldwide attended classes on subjects ranging from basic electronics to intercultural business practices.

CREATIVE EMPLOYEE INVOLVEMENT

Most companies are perceived as extensions of the products they make. For example, the name Kodak immediately brings to mind a camera. Mention Xerox, IBM or General Motors and the association with each of their products is immediate. Undoubtedly, those who are familiar with Allen think of Smart Scope. This tendency is an outgrowth of successful marketing and advertising. However, in reality, a company is not its products but, rather, the people who make those products—the people who design them, move them through the assembly line and then, finally, create the advertising and marketing programs to generate sales.

In 1983, The Allen Group began the formalization of a corporatewide program to encourage greater involvement on the part of each employee in the success of the Company. This seems only logical when we consider that no group has a greater stake in Allen than its employees. Along with the investment of their careers and livelihood, our employees, as a group, form a major stockholder constituency. And finally, there is the psychic and emotional involvement that comes from spending the greater part of one's life in the work environment. It is our objective to recognize this total investment and create an atmosphere that stimulates a genuine sense of accomplishment on the part of each employee in fulfilling his or her job requirements. We are striving for a sense of enrichment and satisfaction in the contribution our employees make to the success of Allen's business.

All our divisions have implemented Creative Employee Involvement Programs. The most common form this has taken has been the formation of employee committees to participate in the planning and thought processes related to on-the-job problem solving, quality control, productivity and efficiency. These are known as "Quality Circles." There already have been tangible results where employees have been permitted to take the lead in tackling problems within their own sphere of responsibility. Not only are the solutions often creative, but since they are stimulated by first-hand knowledge of a problem, they are also more readily accepted by the employees.

We have made commitment to our employees a stated corporate objective and have published it in our Annual Report for many years. Therefore, our efforts in the area of employee involvement are not a new concept at Allen. However, we believe there is a great deal more that we and other companies can do to enhance the working relationship between a company and its employees, and we are confident that everyone will benefit from such an approach. Allen will be a better place in which to work and a more profitable Company.

Talented and dedicated people remain the key Carpenter resource, and are indispensable to the achievements of Company goals and objectives.

Managing Our People Resources

While raw materials, energy, and capital equipment are physical resources required in our business, we fully realize that the key to their effective use is the motivation and ability of our human resources. Talented and dedicated employees at all levels have been responsible for past accomplishments and are indispensable to the achievements of the Company's goals, objectives, and related strategies.

At the same time, we have been greatly concerned about the rapid escalation of employment costs over the past few years, which were driven primarily by the basic steel industry wage settlement patterns. Although most Carpenter employees are nonunion, our hourly pay practices have historically followed the basic steel industry patterns.

Carpenter's employment level at June 30, 1983, was 4,192 employees, down from 4,348 in June 1982, reflecting the lower operating levels. Our total payroll cost for fiscal 1983 was $162.1 million, consisting of $120.2 million in wages and $41.9 million in benefits—an average cost per employee of about $39,141.

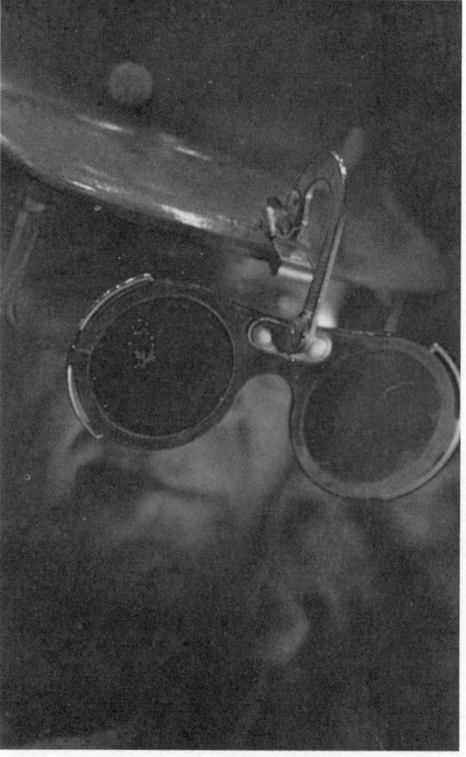

This total cost represented about 41 cents of every sales dollar. The average employment cost for Carpenter hourly workers was $23.42 per hour worked, about the same as for the steel industry. The pattern of employee benefits included in these total costs was typical of most practices in effect today, in that benefits provided the same level of protection for all employees and did not differ among employees to fit individual circumstances.

In March of 1983, the basic steel industry negotiated a new labor agreement to expire in 1986. It became apparent to us much earlier that we needed a different way to deliver compensation and benefits to *our* employees. As a result, we decided on a new, forward-looking, flexible compensation program that represents a significant departure from past compensation practices.

Because of the importance and long-term benefits offered by our new compensation program, both from employer and employee viewpoints, we are highlighting the major objectives, key elements, and benefits of this compensation package.

Our flexible approach to compensation and benefit planning tailors programs to fit circumstances that differ among employees and that can vary over time as a result of changing events in a person's life. From an employee's perspective, the program permits every employee to:

- Select from benefit programs offered which are most meaningful and with coverages truly needed and wanted.
- Increase financial security for both the short term and the long term.
- Save money in a tax-effective manner.

From the Company's viewpoint, flexible compensation presents a workable system for effecting a compromise between rising employment costs on one hand and moti-

1984 is currently estimated at about $50 million. This lower projected spending level in 1984 is a direct result of the stretch-out of the hot mill project. By fiscal 1985, we expect capital spending to return to the former higher levels as work resumes on the hot mill project.

Managing Our Raw Material/Energy Resources

Carpenter is in a strong raw materials position, and we believe that adequate supplies will be available to support our growth plans.

A buyer's market for raw materials continued throughout fiscal 1983. Because of lower raw material consumption worldwide, producers had ample supplies, prices were soft, and there were no supply disruptions. Raw material supplies are currently plentiful and prices are down, but it must be remembered that the United States is import-dependent for most critical raw materials. As such, a long-range potential for supply disruptions and price volatility will remain.

We continue to believe that key raw materials will be available to support our growth plans, and we will be able to manage our way through these potential situations for two reasons. First, we are optimistic that no prolonged disruption in supply will occur, because of the importance of exports of such raw materials to the economies of the mineral-rich foreign countries. Second, we believe that Carpenter's position in the specialty metals industry and our relationship with raw material suppliers should enable us to obtain a fair share of the free market raw material supplies at competitive prices.

We are confident that energy in the form of electricity, natural gas, and oil will continue to be available to meet our growth needs. Electricity prices are expected to rise in excess of the underlying rate of inflation. Accordingly, we will continue our thrusts in energy conservation and efficiency.

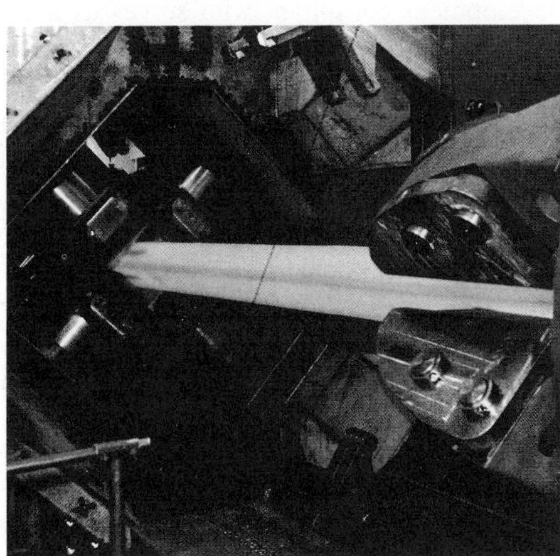

Raw materials are vital to our specialty metals production. We believe that adequate supplies of these important alloying elements will be made available from the producing sources.

Digital Equipment Corporation

Credit for Digital's progress to date must go directly to the 55,000 individuals who comprise the company's employee population world-wide, for it is their hard work and dedication to the pursuit of our goal of quality that make them Digital's most valuable resources.

Digital strives to recognize their contributions by providing programs designed to enhance their effectiveness in the overall organization and to promote their individual development as well.

Making certain that all employees have equal opportunities for hiring and advancement is a serious commitment and Digital continues to actively pursue affirmative action programs to attract and develop minority and female employees at all levels.

A comprehensive in-company program of continuing education offers individual courses, high school equivalency and University level courses leading to degrees. Opportunities are also available for employees to pursue further education through company-sponsored programs at scores of colleges and universities. In both cases, the goal is to encourage employees to increase their job-related knowledge and broaden their personal skills and experiences.

Tuition refunds, student loans (which are also available to dependents of employees) and scholarships are offered to encourage employees to participate in programs of continuing education.

As the use of Digital's products continues to grow around the world, the company will continue to expand its organization. Thus, Digital is committed to ensure that the jobs it creates are useful and challenging and the environment in which our people work is attractive and enjoyable.

By meeting commitments to its employees, Digital strengthens its ability to meet its commitments to customers, investors and the community.

Employee Development Programs

Example:

Abbott

Abbott's employees are its most important resource,'' Robert A. Schoellhorn, chairman and chief executive officer, said recently. ''It is our 31,000 employees who determine how successful the company is. To ensure that we attract and retain the best employees, we must provide the means for their effective development.''

This statement is reinforced by G. Kirk Raab, president and chief operating officer, who says, ''it's essential that we continue to build the organization because no company can be successful unless it has the human resources necessary to execute its plans. One of our goals is to see Abbott promote people from within the company as much as we can.''

These convictions of Abbott's two top officers are put into practice through a company-wide policy regarding development of employees' capabilities.

''Abbott policy states that each employee has primary responsibility for the fulfillment of his or her human potential,'' says Ralph Edwards, divisional vice president, human resources and organization. ''However, the company stands ready to help employees achieve their potential by creating an environment that stimulates growth. The company does this by providing performance standards and performance review; by making coaching, counseling, and training available, as needed; and by providing opportunities for promotions and transfers, when appropriate.''

The manager's review of employees' performance is the first step in Abbott's organization development program. This review results in an annual Organization Inventory for each division. In this document, which is reviewed by Schoellhorn and Raab, the division head summarizes the performance of management employees and describes succession planning for key positions.

Each division has a Personnel and Organization Development consultant who serves as a resource for employee development and succession planning. Along with other responsibilities, these consultants advise managers on training opportunities for employees who show potential for greater management contributions.

Abbott training and development departments are staffed by professionals who present a broad spectrum of courses. These range from voluntary, afterhours basic education programs to three-day seminars on specific management skills (see box at right).

In addition to these in-house educational opportunities, Abbott has a tuition assistance program to reimburse employees for the cost of college courses. Company training programs such as the Finance Training Program and the Engineering Professional Development Program (*Commitment,* Summer 1979) add another dimension to Abbott's training process.

Internal placement systems give employees an opportunity to be considered for job openings for which they are qualified. The resumes of salaried employees who participate in the professional placement program are entered in a computerized system from which those who meet requirements for available positions can be retrieved. Other employees may be considered for promotional opportunities through systems established in local personnel departments.

"These development programs motivate Abbott employees and give them opportunities to move ahead if they want to and are qualified," Edwards says. "This has tremendous advantages for both the employees and Abbott. The more successful we are in training and developing people, the more opportunity we will have to provide future managers from within the company.

"Our record for promotions from within Abbott is very good—over the last five years more than 80 percent of senior management promotions were from within the company—but we are always striving to improve this number," Edwards notes.

"Our goal is to help Abbott employees reach their full potential and in the process to develop a reservoir of talented employees to manage the company in the years ahead," Edwards concludes. "They hold the key to Abbott's future success."

Courses Available at Abbott

Representative courses available through Abbott's training and development departments are listed here. Production employees receive job training and instruction in quality control, productivity improvement, and other skills important to effective job performance.

Basic education
: *General Educational Development, English as a Second Language* (See *Commitment,* Summer 1977 for a detailed description of these two programs.)

For secretaries and clerical employees
: *Interpersonal Skills*

For supervisors
: *Basic Supervisory Skills*
: *Effective Communictions*
: *Job Instruction Training*

For management and professional employees
: *Consulting Skills*
: *Financial Management*
: *Goal-Setting and Performance Review*
: *Presentation Skills*
: *Project Management*

Sterling Institute Seminars
: A series of career-planning and development programs designed to assess supervisory ability and plan the development of supervisory skills.

Employee Relations

Example:

Employee Relations

Employment levels in continuing operations at NL increased from 18,650 persons at the end of 19__ to 23,200 at year end 19__. The 19__ figure is comprised of 16,650 at domestic locations and 6,550 outside of the United States. This increase in the number of employees is primarily attributable to the acquisition of NL Sperry-Sun and to business related growth in the petroleum services divisions.

The company continues to place major emphasis on reducing accidents at the workplace as well as those associated with all types of vehicles. NL's commitment to safe working conditions and a healthy environment is supported by active involvement at all levels of the company to bring about accident reduction, ongoing plant and vehicular safety training and appropriate recognition to plants and divisions which achieve or exceed pre-determined goals. 19__ results clearly justified the company's safety programs with plant lost-time accident frequency 29% lower than in 19__ and preventable vehicular accidents 23% under the prior year.

The company continues to enjoy favorable relations with employees represented by unions. During 19__ all contract negotiations were concluded without a work stoppage.

Equal employment opportunity continues to hold a high priority in NL's conduct of its businesses. During 19__ emphasis was placed upon management and supervisory training to support attainment of equal opportunity goals. Concurrently, efforts continue to recruit and promote minority and female employees for positions in management sales and professional categories.

Industry Affairs

Anheuser-Busch

Industry Affairs. While we believe that the industry will remain generally healthy throughout the 1980s, that is not to say that it will be free of challenges. Perhaps the most significant problem on the horizon will be to deal with the growing dilemma of alcoholism. The pressure to combat this social problem grows more intense each day.

Anheuser-Busch is very much concerned with the problem of alcohol abuse and has taken constructive action on several fronts. We support continuing research efforts designed to develop an understanding of the problem. On an industry level, we continue to support the United States Brewers Association, which has instituted the "Think Twice" program, a two-pronged approach that involves work with beverage retailers as well as direct communication with students. The company's grant to the University of California at Los Angeles financed broad dissemination of the Alcohol Research Center's "Abstracts on Alcohol and Driving."

International Operations

One of America's urgent needs in the 1980s is to compete aggressively in the international markets. If you are operating internationally, you should consider describing the extent of your operations in some detail. Your stockholders will want to know the following:

1. Countries in which you are operating.
2. The sales and profits generated in your operations abroad.
3. The relationship of sales and profits earned abroad to U.S. sales and profits.
4. The investments that you have made in overseas markets.
5. Plant facilities abroad.
6. Modernization of plants abroad.
7. Research.
8. Product adaptation.
9. Price competition.
10. Service facilities.
11. Management of your overseas operations.
12. Necessity to close down operations because of governmental decrees.
13. Plans to enter new markets.
14. Joint ventures entered into abroad.

Some examples of how companies describe their international operations are as follows:

For 3M and other U.S.-based companies serving international markets, 1983 saw a continuation of the challenges of the two previous years.

Economic activity generally remained sluggish, and the U.S. dollar continued to strengthen against other major currencies.

Against this backdrop, our International companies turned in a good performance:

- Our unit volume rose about 6 percent in economies which, on balance, showed little growth, which means we increased market share.
- We continued to see a high level of innovation in the development of new products, businesses and marketing approaches. Our Pathfinder program recognizes innovation of this kind, and suggestions within the last five years generated over $163 million in 1983 revenues.
- In Latin America, where the level of economic activity remained weak and several countries sharply devalued their currencies, we maintained reasonably good profitability, the result of sound operating and financial practices.
- The financial condition of our subsidiary companies remained strong, placing them in good position to take advantage of opportunities as they enter a new year.

As in the prior two years, the strengthening of the dollar had a substantial adverse effect on our reported sales and earnings.

Measured in local currencies, our sales increased about 8 percent. However, because a strong dollar causes sales in British pounds, French francs and other currencies to translate into fewer dollars, our reported sales actually showed a decline of about 3 percent to $2.553 billion.

Our operating income in 1983 declined 12.5 percent to $406 million. However, had currency exchange rates remained unchanged from a year earlier, we believe our operating income would have surpassed 1982 levels.

The strength of the dollar depressed our reported earnings in two principal ways. First, it increased the cost in local currencies of importing goods from the parent company in the United States. Reflecting our desire for optimum long-term geographic balance in our manufacturing capabilities, about two-thirds of the 3M products sold overseas are produced overseas, with the remainder manufactured in the United States. Second, a strong dollar meant that profits in overseas currencies translated into fewer dollars.

Looking to 1984, we expect to report higher sales and earnings.

The economic recovery which began in the U.S. early in 1983 now appears to be spreading to major overseas markets. If sustained, a higher level of economic activity should contribute to unit volume growth significantly higher than the 6 percent we saw in 1983.

New products will continue to be an important factor in our success longer-term. Increasingly, our International people are becoming a good source of such products. In the past year, we established a new Pathfinder Merchant award, which recognizes the transfer of creative product and business ideas from subsidiary to subsidiary.

Offering products of the highest possible quality and producing and distributing them at competitive costs also will continue to be vital. In 1983, the first phase of a systematic quality program, designed to help us consistently meet the highest expectations of our customers, was completed in most of our major overseas companies.

In addition, we continued to install state-of-the-art manufacturing control systems in our larger plants. By better matching output with current product demand, the systems are resulting in lower costs and improved customer service.

Economic conditions over the last three years have presented our International companies with a major challenge. Our people have responded by outperforming the economies they serve and achieving profitability above that of major competitors.

With the resumption of economic growth in overseas markets, a somewhat more favorable currency picture and our many internal strengths, we expect to report substantially better sales and earnings in the years ahead.

The International Marketplace
By David Christopher
Senior Vice President—
Tandy International Electronics

Outside of the United States, Tandy Corporation is represented by almost 2,000 company-owned stores and affiliated dealers. The focal points of our international operations will continue to be directed toward Canada, Australia, Great Britain, West Germany, France, Belgium, Holland and Japan. There are more than 1,800 sales outlets in these countries backed up by full support operations. In addition, our international dealer network provides representation in 67 other countries through 164 dealers. This network not only provides the vehicle to introduce our exclusive product line to many remote areas, it affords valuable insight for potential company development of other foreign markets.

Within each primary international market, emphasis is placed on expansion and market development. Following the formulas and creating the operating structures proven so successful by Radio Shack-U.S. has been the cornerstone in developing each country's operation. Of particular importance in the overall development plan for each country is the recruitment and training of local citizens to fill the majority of the key and top management posts in their countries. U.S. personnel dispatched to our foreign operations serve on temporary assignment, bringing many years of Radio Shack know-how, plus the latest hands-on experience and management techniques necessary in the selling of new sophisticated products.

HEWLETT-PACKARD

In 1959, HP established its first overseas operations: a European marketing office in Switzerland and a manufacturing plant in West Germany. Today, Hewlett-Packard has 19 manufacturing divisions and operations outside the United States. More than half of these include research laboratories where engineers develop products for worldwide distribution. The company also has more than 220 sales and support offices and distributorships in 71 countries.

From this broad base, HP is able to serve its customers around the world. The company's international presence also enables it to draw on the imagination and talent of HP people in many countries—one advantage enjoyed by a high-technology company whose most critical "raw material" is creativity.

During the past year, HP's international operations continued to expand. The company established manufacturing operations in Bristol, England and Toronto, Canada, and expanded its personal-computer manufacturing to Grenoble, France. In Guadalajara, Mexico, where HP has been producing HP 3000 business computers, it established a software center for Latin America. In November 1983, HP increased its equity position in Yokogawa-Hewlett-Packard, its Japanese joint venture, from 40 to 75 percent.

When it manufactures in a country, HP becomes attuned to local markets and is in a better position to compete in the country or region. Having operations in a country enables HP to better serve customers there. This is especially true in the development of computer software, which must reflect differences in language and customs. To meet this need and to provide customers with consulting, training and post-installation services, HP now has in place 20 software application centers worldwide.

While HP continues to expand its worldwide manufacturing operations, it remains among the top 20 exporting companies in the U.S. As with many companies, HP's operating results have been adversely affected by the strength of the U.S. dollar relative to other major currencies.

HP's continuing development of international manufacturing sites is one way the company is working to manage an uncertain economic situation. By making products in the country where they will be sold and by exporting from that country to others, HP can maximize its currency flexibility while effectively serving local markets.

Square D

Square D's plan for growth also includes the continued expansion of its manufacturing and marketing operations in the international area.

Our Saudi Arabian joint venture recently opened a new 54,000 square foot plant in Riyadh, Saudi Arabia, that manufactures and assembles switchboards, panelboards and load centers and can be expanded to produce other related products.

In March, we acquired an existing facility in Little Island, Cork, Irish Republic, for the production of electrodeposited copper foil used in the manufacture of printed circuits for electronic and electrical applications. The Irish Republic facility functions as part of Yates Industries, Inc., our subsidiary headquartered in Bordentown, New Jersey, and serves all world markets, including Western and Eastern Europe, South America, the Middle East and the Far East.

To better serve the international markets, we established an International Marketing Services Group with headquarters in Florence, Kentucky, which is responsible for coordinating and controlling sales and shipments of Square D products worldwide. The Florence facility is ideal for this operation because it functions as a data center as well as a central service point. In addition, a similar operation was established in Swindon, England, to coordinate international activities on products manufactured in the United Kingdom. These operations work closely with offices in major locations around the world and are staffed by personnel well versed in the handling of orders involving a wide range of products from various Square D locations.

In order to further develop our export business with U.S. firms doing business overseas, we also have established international sales offices at key export locations in the United States.

New Products

We also continue to develop new products for the requirements of the international markets. The Domino push button line manufactured by Square D Starkstrom, our West German subsidiary, has been accepted widely in European markets because of its design and performance. This push button line also will be produced in Mexico for Western Hemisphere markets. In 1983, we introduced a number of new electronic devices in our international control products line. These also are manufactured in West Germany and include solid state protective relays, timing relays and contactors.

Square D Limited, our United Kingdom affiliate, is introducing a new consumer circuit breaker panel for the residential construction market; and Square D Starkstrom has introduced a new, improved line of press safety systems designed and rated to meet European standards.

Our medical and construction products are in demand in Third World nations, particularly the Middle East, for large hospital complexes and commercial centers. We are pursuing these markets vigorously.

Recently, we established a separate electronics division in Swindon, England, to give further emphasis to research, development and manufacturing of products in the expanding electronics field. This will increase our capabilities to meet the growing demand by international customers for electronic products.

Molex

The Far East Division is headquartered in Yamato City, Japan which is also the home of Molex Japan, the Company's largest subsidiary. Molex has two manufacturing factories and six sales offices located throughout Japan. Additionally, the Far Eastern Division comprises manufacturing facilities and sales offices in Singapore and Taiwan and sales offices and warehouses in Hong Kong and Korea. No other connector company can match Molex's range of manufacturing facilities and the depth of our support organizations in the Fast East.

The Molex Far Eastern Division services the region's leading manufacturers of home entertainment equipment which includes VTR's, electronic games, home computers, stereos, and televisions. As important are sales made to manufacturers of home appliances, business machines and computer peripheral equipment. Molex has long been a leader in providing multi-national support to American, European and Japanese companies who have located facilities in South East Asia. We have always worked to serve these customers by providing locally made products and services throughout the region. In fact, this emphasis on providing multinational service and coordination is not confined to Asia but is also an integral part of our worldwide service. We feel this is a distinct advantage which Molex can offer its ever increasing number of multinational customers.

During the fiscal year, Molex Japan completed a new automated warehouse; began construction on a new plating facility; and purchased 25 acres of land for a third manufacturing facility to be built in the future. We also introduced a wide range of new interconnecting products including the smallest commercial connector range currently available . . . *Micro Spox.* It was designed for the new generation of VTR's and television cameras. Molex Japan also introduced a range of .050″ ribbon cable connectors and transition sockets, a new series of I.D.T. products and a number of custom products designed to meet the special needs of some of our major customers.

The European Division is headquartered in Aldershot, a suburb of London, and directs all the Company's European operations. During the course of the year, we moved into larger quarters in order to accommodate the expansion of our European engineering, marketing and service groups. In addition to the European Headquarters, we have manufacturing and tooling facilities in Shannon, Ireland, as well as sales offices and warehouses in Stockholm, Sweden; Eindhoven, The Netherlands; Frankfurt, Germany; Paris, France; Milan, Italy; and Aldershot, England. To keep pace with our growth, a second manufacturing facility is now under construction in Ireland.

During the past year, Molex introduced a series of new Insulation Displacement products that were designed to meet European specifications. These products are presently being sold to manufacturers of home entertainment units, business machines, computer peripheral equipment, instrumentation and testing apparatus throughout Europe. Molex also launched a number of new crimp type products and sockets in the European marketplace.

Molex European sales, in local currency, advanced dramatically during the period, but due to the strength of the U.S. dollar, show only modest gains when converted back to U.S. dollars.

We believe that Molex European operations are well situated to share in the growth of the European electronics industry. The Company's combination of well-designed, cost effective products and its emphasis on providing excellent customer service will ensure continual progress in this portion of the world.

The Molex Americas Division includes Molex Canada, where we have a sales office and warehousing facility; Molex Brazil with its manufacturing facility in Campinas and sales office in Sao Paolo; and the Molex Export Operations located at the International Headquarters in Lisle, Illinois.

Brunswick

Brunswick Corporation recognizes that new products are the lifeblood of any business. Substantial amounts are spent each year at the division level to develop and market new products that enhance and expand existing product lines.

To assure a continuing flow of new product development, in 1982 Brunswick established an internal Venture Capital operation to fund development of exciting new technologies which have application to existing core businesses. This Venture Capital operation combines the best of the entrepreneurial spirit with the professional management of a large, decentralized company.

This investment in the future operates under the direction of senior corporate executives. This group allocates corporate funds for development of new technologies which are sponsored by a division. This allows the division general managers the freedom to explore and develop new products and technologies without any financial impact on their core businesses.

Generally the Venture Capital projects have three common threads: 1) the idea, or sponsorship came from the division level; 2) the technology involved has been acquired from an entrepreneur or scientist; and 3) the market potential for the new technology represents large growth opportunities in markets the Company now serves.

The first venture undertaken through this program is a state-of-the-art line of sub-micron membranes designed for use in the pharmaceutical and electronics industries where extremely high levels of filtration are required. Introduced in 1982 by the Technetics Division, this product gained acceptance after extensive testing by potential customers in 1983 and will become a production item in 1984.

The Technetics Division, in late 1982, acquired new technology for the injection molding of powdered metal parts. This venture project has completed its R & D phase. In 1984 the Technetics Division will offer three related product lines: 1) injection molded parts produced to customer specifications; 2) equipment to produce these parts; and 3) supplies of the basic raw materials used in the process.

In 1982, Brunswick purchased an interest in Enhanced Energy Systems, Inc., a New Mexico firm that produces direct contact steam generators for down-hole and surface applications for the recovery of heavy oil. These units produce high pressure steam and emission gases which increase oil recovery. Several units are now being tested by domestic oil companies and performance to date has been encouraging. The Valve & Control Division manages this venture operation.

In 1983, Brunswick purchased a 30 percent interest in Nuvatec, Inc., a Chicago area computer design and software company. This company was involved in the design of the automatic scorer for the Brunswick Division and a solid state, digital/analog locomotive speedometer for the Vapor Division. This purchase affords Brunswick the opportunity to apply Nuvatec's extensive electronics hardware and software know-how to all business areas within Brunswick.

Brunswick management is confident that through

"Real growth for the future requires some entrepreneurial risks that carry with them potentially high future rewards."

this unique Venture Capital operation, it is not only supplementing normal, ongoing research and development, but is achieving an infusion of new technologies into markets it presently serves and where the Company has leadership positions.

Management is aware of the inherent risks of new, unproven technologies and the likelihood that not all ventures will be commercial successes. By the same token, real growth for the future requires some entrepreneurial risks that carry with them potentially high future rewards. The Venture Capital Program is such an investment in the future.

Labor Contracts

The new labor agreement reached in September should give Chrysler two years of labor stability in which to achieve our quality and productivity goals. Chrysler employees realize that the best job security comes from making high quality cars that people will buy. The new labor contract means that Chrysler can count on continued employee cooperation in our drive to improve our products and the way we make them.

Liquidity

Liquidity and Capital Resources

In 1983, the Company sold 810,000 shares of common stock in a public offering generating proceeds of approximately $27,400,000. The proceeds from the stock sale will be used for capital expenditures and working capital requirements. Excluding the proceeds of the stock sale, working capital decreased approximately $5,378,000 from 1982, primarily due to increased capital expenditures and working capital requirements of operations. Capital expenditures in 1983 were approximately $15,402,000, a decrease of approximately $2,674,000 from 1982. The expenditures in 1983 were comprised of modifications and improvements to the 103,000-square-foot building in Goleta, California, purchased in 1982, and expenditures for production equipment required to manufacture the new products developed in 1983, and to increase production capacity to comply with increased sales demand for existing products. In 1982, capital expenditures were significant due primarily to the purchase of a Goleta, California facility for approximately $7,600,000 and the completion of a 40,000-square-foot facility in Ireland at a net cost, after grants from the Irish government, of approximately $1,600,000.

At September 30, 1983, the Company had cash and cash equivalents of $31,584,000 compared to $11,280,000 at September 30, 1982. The current ratio increased to 3.1:1 from 2.5:1 in 1982, primarily a result of the proceeds from the stock sale in June 1983.

Capital expenditures in 1984 are estimated at $25,800,000. Major expenditures relate to the construction of a 40,000-square-foot facility in Singapore, a 60,000-square-foot facility in Korea, and ongoing preparations for large-scale production of thin-film magnetic heads, as well as equipment needed for other new products. The Company is presently leasing a 16,000-square-foot facility in Singapore until the new facility is completed. These expenditures will be funded from existing cash-on-hand and cash provided from operations.

In 1983, the Company sold the assets of Key Electro Sonic Corporation for $3,500,000, resulting in a gain, after loss from operations to the date of sale, of $197,000 (see Note 2 in the accompanying financial statements). The Company received $1,500,000 in cash and a $2,000,000 12% secured note receivable from the sale. The sale will not significantly affect either the operations or the liquidity of the Company.

Liquidity and Capital Resources

The Company substantially improved its financial position during fiscal 1983. Total debt was $10.7 million at the end of fiscal 1983, a reduction of $1.4 million from the end of fiscal 1982. While cash and cash equivalents increased by $17.7 million from $3.4 million at the end of fiscal 1982 to $21.1 million at the end of fiscal 1983, a substantial portion of this increase was attributable to the Company's foreign operations. To the extent that cash is generated outside the United States, the Company's flexibility in using such cash worldwide may be limited. The Company also generated cash from reductions in accounts receivable and inventories.

Total indebtedness was 13% of shareholders' equity at the end of fiscal 1983, compared to 16% at the end of fiscal 1982. See "Foreign Currency Translation" under Notes to Consolidated Financial Statements. The current ratio increased from 2.2 to 2.3 during this same period.

Availability of funds under the Company's long-term loan agreement and short-term bank lines of credit remained relatively unchanged from the end of fiscal 1982. There are no significant commitments for capital additions at this time, other than the Company's intention to construct a customer demonstration and training center during fiscal 1984 for an approximate cost of $3 million. The Company believes that its financial position, future earnings and borrowing capabilities provide adequate flexibility to fund financial requirements for operations.

Liquidity and Capital Resources

The Company's primary sources of liquidity have been cash flow from operations, customer advances and progress payments, and bank borrowings. Due to the periodic-reimbursement feature of most U.S. Government contracts and subcontracts, the Company's capital requirements have been small in relation to the aggregate value of such contracts. For the fiscal years ended June 30, 1983, 1982 and 1981, 74.6 percent, 78.7 percent and 62.8 percent, respectively, of the Company's revenues were generated from U.S. Government fixed price contracts. Most of the revenues generated from these fixed-price orders are under contracts that provide for monthly progress payments of up to 95 percent of the allowable costs. The Company's cost-plus type contracts generally provide for monthly payments equal to 100 percent of allowable costs plus a pro rata portion of the fee.

The Company is expanding its marketing efforts to foreign governments. Foreign contracts are generally negotiated with substantial advance payments and a limited number, if any, of progress payments. The lack of progress payments on any new foreign contracts received by the Company would result in an increase in working capital requirements. As a condition of receiving advance payments, the Company is generally required to furnish the customer an offsetting standby letter of credit, which provides for payments to the customer if the Company does not fulfill the contract terms. The issuance of standby letters of credit could result in a corresponding reduction in the Company's borrowing capability.

In addition to the increased working capital that would be required to support any new foreign contracts, the Company has budgeted approximately $750,000 for the purchase of capital equipment and building improvements in fiscal 1984. In order to meet these anticipated working capital requirements, in April 1983, the Company sold 1,020,000 shares of common stock in a public offering resulting in net proceeds of $16,019,577. Pending their use, the proceeds have been invested in short-term interest bearing securities. The Company believes that its working capital and capital expansion needs for the foreseeable future will be met by its present cash balance, the proceeds from this offering, cash flow from operations and its bank credit agreements. At June 30, 1983 the Company had bank lines of credit totalling $6 million, all of which were unused.

Management

Stockholders have a serious concern as to how your company is managed. They want to know about your present management as well as the continuity of management. A description of your management in depth would be most helpful. Subjects to be covered are as follows:

1. Strengthening of your management committee during the past year.
2. Names, titles and backgrounds of new executives added to your staff during the past year.
3. The creation of various management committees during the past year.
4. A realignment of your executive office, if one took place.
5. Decentralization.
6. Reorganization of staff.

The following are examples of how corporations have referred to their management:

American Can Company

Our management organization was strengthened and expanded during the year. We created a Corporate Operating Committee, consisting of the President and five Senior Vice Presidents appointed as Sector Executives, to provide the best possible coordination of day-to-day decisions with long-term strategies. In September, Alfred G. Goldstein was appointed as Senior Vice President, Consumer Businesses. He previously held a similar position with a major consumer goods retailer. Senior Vice President Theodore Deikel, for the last six years the Chief Operating Officer of Fingerhut, was named the Chief Executive Office of both Fingerhut and Pickwick, which are headquartered in the Minneapolis area.

Analogic Corporation

Management Structure for Growth

During the recent year, as in the past, we have continued to expand our management strength and to modify in an evolutionary manner our corporate structure. Generally, we are moving toward a combined corporate and product group management organization. Within the corporate management group are technical-development, manufacturing-operation, quality control, financial, administrative and legal specialists whose function it is to guide and oversee the various product group activities—acting as planners, leaders, and teachers.

Within each product group, it is our intention to build management capability correlating to the breadth of experience collectively available in the corporate group, thereby maintaining an entrepreneurial spirit and growth rate commensurate with that achieved by the founding members of the company.

Nearly all the senior members of our corporate and product group staffs, about a third of whom joined us during the past year, have had substantial technical background as well as business experience. Our management organization has been deliberately structured to enable us to perceive, conceive, and initiate activities in new product areas expeditiously. Toward this end, we have placed our Advanced Instrumentation Development Engineering Group and the Advanced Physics and Software Group within the corporate structure. These technical groups together with our Manufacturing and Quality Control, Financial, Administrative, and Legal officers interact with the managements of our Advanced Technology Products Group, our Medical Technology Products Group, our Industrial Technology Products Group, and our Test and Measurement Products Group.

Key Management Policies

1. Our objective is to show yearly growth of at least 15% in the number of customers we supply with our products and services; growth in the opportunity for individual self-development in order to fulfill our professional responsibilities; and growth in the value of our shareholders' investment.

2. Our primary marketing effort is directed toward moderate income families with the aim of providing new housing for an increasingly larger share of the population.

3. We intend that our product planning and pricing strategy will result in houses which provide "an easily observable better value" while at the same time being responsive to customer product preferences.

4. We expect to develop important changes in product design, manufacturing techniques, and organizational structure through evolution rather than revolution.

5. Our allocation of financial, physical and personnel resources will be creative and aggressive but nevertheless conservative in terms of risk.

6. We are committed to a program of fair, courteous treatment of our customers from the moment of their first contact as prospects through the sale, construction and occupancy of their homes.

7. We encourage our people to develop their maximum potential and believe in sharing the benefits that accrue to the company with those who helped create them.

8. Our theory of management is reflected in a "consultative" style of decision-making whereby we arrive at decisions after consulting with those who are expected to execute the decisions.

9. Our organization is structured to achieve the delicate balance between centralization and decentralization which should blend the specialized experience and judgment of the central staff with the market knowledge of the local manager.

Applied Digital Data Systems, Inc.

NCR Corporation conducts its business through eleven organizational units responsible for marketing, development and production under the direction of Corporate officers and staff.

The Company markets its products through 1200 offices in more than 120 countries. It operates 88 facilities worldwide for the development and manufacture of products and systems. In addition, NCR operates 52 Data Centers throughout the world, which provide customer processing services.

Data Processing Groups

The marketing force for NCR data processing systems is organized by divisions. These divisions are: Retail Systems, Financial Systems, CI/MEG (Commercial-Industrial/Medical-Education-Government) Systems, Data Pathing Systems, Field Engineering, and Data Centers.

Geographically, NCR is organized into five regions: The United States, Europe, Pacific (comprising Far East/Australasia and Canadian operations), Middle East/Africa, and Latin America.

NCR products and systems are marketed through 781 districts in the United States and, internationally, through 70 Company-owned organizations and 23 authorized distributors.

Systemedia Group

The Systemedia Group consists of four divisions: Business Forms and Supplies, Micrographic Systems, Direct Marketing and Source Document Services. Business forms and supplies are manufactured in 9 United States plants and 49 overseas facilities, and are sold to both NCR and non-NCR equipment users. In the United States, the Business Forms and Supplies Division markets media through a selling force in 11 regions, while the Direct Marketing Division provides catalog sales for smaller users.

The Micrographic Systems Division is headquartered in Mountain View, California, and operates one plant there and a second plant in West Salem, Wisconsin. The Division manufactures and markets a complete line of Computer Output Microfiche recorders, duplicators, and readers and is one of the largest suppliers of COM equipment in the world. Source Document Services markets conventional microfiche and ultrafiche processing systems and related equipment for publishers, printers and libraries. Its headquarters are in Kettering, Ohio.

Office Systems Division

The Office Systems Division, established in 1981, has development and marketing responsibility for NCR's line of WorkSaver office automation workstations and associated peripherals and software. The development organization is located in Columbia, South Carolina, and has direct marketing and support personnel located in major U.S. cities. The division staff is headquartered in Dayton, Ohio.

OEM Marketing Division

The OEM Marketing Division was also established in 1981 to broaden worldwide distribution channels for NCR products by addressing new markets not covered by the traditional direct sales organization.

Development and Production Group

The Development and Production Group consists of five divisions: Retail Systems, General Purpose Systems, CI/MEG Systems, Financial Systems, and Microelectronics. It comprises 24 operating units in 9 countries. These consist of 14 engineering and manufacturing plants, 3 microelectronic design and fabrication facilities, and 7 systems engineering units, each with its own specific product charter. In addition to designing and fabricating semiconductor circuits for NCR's own use, the Microelectronics Division also has responsibility for external sales of selected circuits.

NCR Comten, Inc.

NCR Comten, Inc., a wholly-owned subsidiary, has its own marketing, field support, development, engineering, and manufacturing organizations. Headquartered in St. Paul, Minnesota, NCR Comten operates one plant there and a second in Medford, New Jersey. Its products encompass a complete line of programmable communications processors, proprietary communications software and performance measurement systems for host computers and communications networks.

Applied Digital Data Systems Inc.

Applied Digital Data Systems Inc. (ADDS) is also a wholly-owned subsidiary. ADDS is headquartered in Hauppauge, New York, and has manufacturing facilities there and in Draper, Utah. ADDS manufactures and markets a broad line of general-purpose computer video-display terminals and small business computers.

Management Changes

I think it is a mistake to report on management changes on the inside of the back cover. The management of your company is certainly of great importance, and should be described in an earlier portion of the report. Dow Jones & Company describe their management changes as follows:

Management Changes

Betty A. Daval joined Dow Jones as Vice President/ Staff Development, a new post, and a member of the Dow Jones Management Committee. She had been Director of Personnel Planning and Development for a major foods company. At Dow Jones she will concentrate on further development of the talents that will be needed in the future, on broadening career opportunities within Dow Jones and on continued progress in using the abilities of women and minorities.

In mid-1980. John P. Young, President and Chief Operating Officer of Richard D. Irwin, Inc., Dow Jones' book-publishing subsidiary began taking over some of the duties of Irwin's Chief Executive Officer, Irvin L. Grimes, at Mr. Grimes request. In February 1981, Mr. Young was named Chief Executive of Irwin. Mr. Grimes, who has been with Irwin 35 years, continues as Chairman.

Bernard T. Flanagan, previously Publisher of Barron's Business and Financial Weekly, was named Vice President/Marketing of The Wall Street Journal, with responsibility for the Journal's Advertising Sales and Service Departments. Robert M. Bleiberg, Editor of Barron's, was named to the additional post of Publisher, with overall responsibility for the magazine.

At Ottaway Newspapers, Inc., John S. Goodreds, formerly Senior Vice President, was named Executive Vice president, with responsibility as Ottaway's chief administrative officer, chief financial officer and coordinator of newspaper acquisitions. Richard A. Myers, formerly Publisher of The News-Times, an Ottaway daily at Danbury, Conn., was named a Vice President of the Ottaway group. He was succeeded as Publisher by Forrest C. Palmer, formerly General Manager of the newspaper.

Frank C. Breese, III, Vice President of Dow Jones' Operating Services Group, and Kenneth L. Burenga, Vice President/Circulation of The Wall Street Journal, were named to the company's Management Committee.

Management Style

Some companies describe their management style. A good example is as follows:

How we work. Inseparable from a company's objectives is how it operates to achieve those objectives. We think our operating structure and management style are among our greatest strengths.

We maintain a simple, flexible structure. We are essentially decentralized—ultimately our success depends on the performance of our operating companies, and we believe that the decentralized structure best enables our line managers to be innovative, entrepreneurial and consumer-oriented. Subsidiary managers are responsible for operating decisions and their results. At the parent level, we maintain a small professional staff which focuses on long-range corporate planning and on activities that add value to the individual operations.

We pride ourselves on having an open, nonbureaucratic style. We emphasize decision-making based on communication and analysis of facts. We encourage an unimpeded flow of information between the subsidiaries and the parent and among the subsidiaries as well. Our subsidiary heads sit on each others' boards; they serve on task forces to study common problems and opportunities.

Crown Zellerbach

Along with this physical reorganization, Crown is refreshing and redirecting the spirit of its human resources. Executive Vice President MacDonald S. Denman was appointed chief administrative officer to develop and direct a company-wide program to broaden involvement in the operation of the company and foster a greater sense of personal responsibility for its progress in every employee.

A set of *Corporate Beliefs* has been adopted committing Crown to "unleashing the constructive and creative abilities and energies of each of its employees" in order to achieve:

- Superior value for customers
- Superior returns for shareholders
- Superior rewards for employees

A "collegial" management philosophy has been adopted that involves wider participation in addressing the major issues that confront the company. Organizational effectiveness training has been instituted that eventually will involve all personnel, along with a program to evaluate and direct employee capabilities more effectively. A new compensation policy for salaried employees places primary emphasis on personal performance and less on length of service. And although the recession made it necessary to suspend bonuses and virtually cease hiring, Crown was able to avoid the across-the-board salary cuts and freezes imposed by many other large companies.

Maps

If you operate throughout the U.S. on an international basis, consider the use of maps showing your location. By use of different symbols, you can effectively pinpoint the following:

- Manufacturing
- Research
- Sales and distribution

International Sales

ENI products are represented by direct or dealer sales in the following countries:

Argentina
Australia
Austria
Belgium
Brazil
Brunei
Bulgaria
Canada
Colombia
Chile
Czechoslovakia
Denmark
Finland
France
Germany
Greece
Guam
Guatemala
Indonesia
Iraq
Israel
Italy
Jamaica
Japan
Jordan
Korea
Kuwait
Maylasia
Mexico
The Netherlands
Netherland Antilles –Curacao, Aruba
Nigeria
Norway
New Zealand
Okinawa
Pago Pago
Peru
Philippines
Puerto Rico
Portugal
Roumania
Saudi Arabia
Singapore
Sweden
Switzerland
Spain
Republic of South Africa
Taiwan
United States of America
Union of Soviet Republic
United Kingdom
Uruguay
Venezuela
Yugoslavia
Zimbabwe

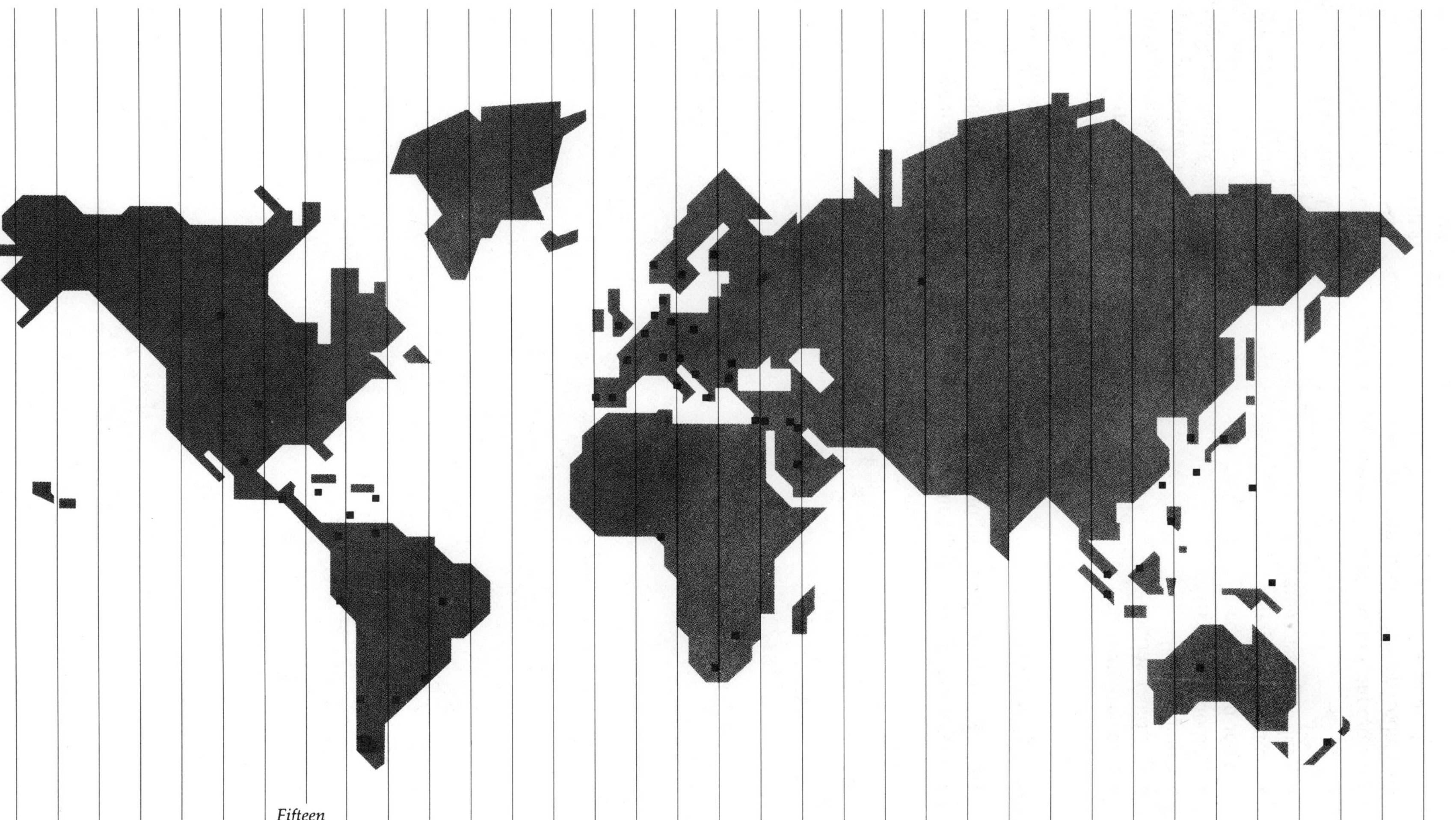

Markets

It is important that you describe in your corporate annual report detailed information about the marketing of your products or services. This should include:

- Range of customers
- Branch operations
- Your market share
- Corporate objectives
- Competitors
- Customer service
- Overseas markets

Keene's Markets

In 19__, Keene's two principal markets—capital goods and commercial & industrial construction—combined accounted for more than 85% of Keene's total sales and virtually all of the company's growth product sales. The inherent annual growth rates of these markets is estimated at 7% to 10%.

The capital goods market influences sales of *bearings, laminates* and *filtration* products. The Conference Board has estimated 19__ appropriations for capital spending were up 16% over 19__ in constant (1972) dollars. Also, the long-term trend appears to remain strong, as shown in the chart below.

The commercial and industrial construction market influences sales of *lighting* and building products, with demand, particularly for lighting fixtures, following contract awards by six months or more.

Contract awards for commercial and industrial construction grew by about 10% on a square-foot-basis during 19__ according to F. W. Dodge. This suggests market demand will continue to help expand Keene's lighting business well into 19__.

Marketing Highlights

Revlon continued to be the largest manufacturer of cosmetics and fragrances sold at retail in the United States and certain foreign countries.

Charlie and *Jontue* sustained leadership among women's fragrances in the United States. In prestige fragrance, *Ciara* outpaced the market.

Flex Shampoo achieved record sales and continued to be America's number one cosmetic shampoo. *Flex* Conditioner continued to be the number one after-shampoo conditioner.

Pure Radiance, a newly introduced special-effects powder for face, eyes and lips, interacts with individual skin chemistry for a radiant and glowing fashion look.

Skin Balancing Makeup was introduced to help women attain, with a single formulation, a flawless balance between oily and dry-skin areas.

Flex Appeal Mascara is our waterproof formulation packaged with a wand that adjusts to different angles to assure perfect application.

We continued to build our skin treatment business in the United States through *European Collagen Complex* at popular price, and introduced the new *CHR Skin Structure* series and *Hydro-Minerali* Skin Revitalizing Extract, both at prestige price.

Chaz, men's cologne, was introduced in Italy, Germany and the United Kingdom. *Revlon Esteem* All-Over Deodorant Cologne for Men was launched overseas.

Barnes-Hind/Hydrocurve introduced a new extended wear soft contact lens to correct astigmatism, and *GP-II,* a second generation semi-soft contact lens of the gas-permeable type. The Barnes-Hind/Hydrocurve 1982 share of new fittings for contact lenses of all kinds was twice that of 1981 and its extended wear lenses were the most prescribed in the United States.

Soft Mate Weekly Cleaning Solution from Barnes-Hind/Hydrocurve was the first Food and Drug Administration-approved intensive cleaning solution for the care and maintenance of all soft contact lenses, particularly those for extended wear. Early in 1983, Barnes-Hind/Hydrocurve received Food and Drug Administration approval to market four new solutions for patients sensitive to currently available products.

Choyce Mark VIII and *Choyce Mark IX* intraocular lenses, which were the first to receive Food and Drug Administration approval to be marketed as "safe and effective," enabled Coburn to broaden its position in the IOL field.

C-Lite is our new eyeglass lens. Developed in 1981, *C-Lite* is a bond of thin, light glass and polyurethane. It is scratch resistant, tintable and comes in photochromic form.

The *Technicon RA-1000,* based on a new and patented hydraulic technology, was introduced successfully both in the United States and abroad.

Technicon was awarded an $11.4 million government contract in December for a medical information system for the William Beaumont Army Medical Center in El Paso.

Plasma fraction sales rose substantially.

A licensing agreement was concluded to market chymopapain outside the United States, Japan, Canada and the Caribbean. The new injectable drug was recently approved by the United States Food and Drug Administration as an alternative to surgery in the treatment of "slipped" discs.

NoSalt, Norcliff Thayer's salt alternative, reached national distribution.

Research and development expenditures reached $114.7 million for both beauty and health care, and advertising costs rose to $223.5 million.

MARKETING

Every market where Heinz sells its products was subject to economic stress during a year in which recession reached the shores of such previously immune areas as Japan and Southeast Asia. In the United States, conditions were easing at year end, but the strength and duration of the economy remained uncertain. Most of Europe saw little relief from high unemployment and stubborn inflation. Mexico and Venezuela experienced the shock of declining oil prices. Australia, which relies heavily on exports of commodities, suffered from weak overseas demand.

Heinz U.S.A.'s marketing environment in fiscal 1983 was one of negligible growth in retail grocery sales, strong resistance to price increases at the trade and consumer levels, and a tendency for hard-pressed consumers to turn to less costly products. To compete effectively, the company upgraded its sales organization, tailored sales and marketing programs to meet the needs of more sophisticated retailers, and sharply increased spending on promotion.

Results of these efforts were outstanding.

Three major promotions produced increased sales. The Burger Giveaway Program was a rousing success in its fourth year, with consumers turning in some two million Heinz labels. A tie-in promotion involving Heinz, Ore-Ida and Crisco products was repeated. New during the year was a Fourth of July hot dog refund program that helped Heinz ketchup sales and market share to reach new records during the holiday period.

Ketchup sales rose to another new high for the entire year, giving Heinz, on a unit basis, a 47% share of the grocery market by year end. Chili sauce also achieved a new high in market share, at 55%. The company's seafood cocktail was introduced and quickly won leading-brand status. HomeStyle gravies also were up.

Heinz peppers, formerly sold only to private-label customers, were introduced on a test basis into military markets, whose consumers represent a wide cross section of the population. Four varieties of strained baby juices in 8-ounce containers entered Southeastern test markets. Distribution of Lite Ketchup, now with fewer calories and less salt, was expanded to a third major metropolitan area.

Marketing of products sold under the Weight Watchers label continued to be notably successful. Frozen Treat bars, with three flavors, moved into national distribution, ranked among the leaders in their category and became one of Heinz U.S.A.'s fastest-growing products. Two varieties of the Weight Watchers sandwich bar, made by placing dietary dessert between chocolate wafers, entered test markets.

THE ALBA LINE OF REDUCED-CALORIE MIXES, THE LEADING brand in its category, was reformulated to enhance its chocolate flavor and extended to include a new mocha variety made with real coffee to attract adult consumers.

Faced with a decline in the market for fast food and vending machine products, Heinz U.S.A. stepped up its promotion and brought out several new products for the foodservice sector. Among these was its popular seafood cocktail sauce, newly packed in #10 tins for high-volume operators. Addressed to the same market was tomato soup in Vol-Pak containers, placed in four test markets. Ketchup in Vol-Pak containers chalked up its eighth consecutive year of record volume as its sales rose by more than one-third.

Star-Kist logged a satisfactory year despite weakness in the tuna business due to recession, raw product oversupply and intensified competition from low-priced imports. Star-Kist Select, three varieties packed with 60% less salt to meet growing consumer demand for low-sodium products, extended the canned tuna line.

Now the leading tuna brand in the U.S., Star-Kist has set its sights on Europe with a new marketing and sales group within the International Business Development Division to investigate opportunities on the Continent, using Ets. Paul Paulet, our new French acquisition, as a base.

The company tackled the strong pet food sector with heavy promotion, including a unique free veterinary checkup program undertaken by 9-Lives in conjunction with the American Animal Hospital Association.

Offering "Western quality at Eastern prices," Ore-Ida deepened its penetration of Eastern foodservice markets. The strategic location of the expanded Wisconsin factory lowered

Marketing

Staying close to the customer long has been a major factor in 3M's success. Today, despite its size and product diversity, 3M is working to carry on that tradition.

For 3M sales people in remote areas of the Philippines, where telephones are few and mail delivery poor, this means using bicycles, boats and buses to reach customers. Sales people not only carry large sample bags, but frequently are required to make product deliveries themselves. There often is no other way to deliver abrasives, X-ray film, overhead projectors and dozens of other goods to customers, which include furniture makers, hospitals and schools.

At 3M Germany, staying close to customers means serving people on a market, rather than on a product-line basis, in the office equipment and automotive industries.

Every sales representative in the country's office markets carries the full range of 3M office products. In the automotive market, a supervisor responsible for several product lines is assigned to each of West Germany's major auto manufacturers.

The result has been increased sales, with 3M now being viewed as a problem-solving resource, rather than just a supplier of hundreds of individual products. In the United States, Canada, Sweden and other countries, a program called Cooperating for Growth is helping 3M people do a better job of satisfying customer needs.

The program is an effort to make customers more aware of 3M's total capabilities, in part by encouraging the exchange of information among 3M sales people and through the establishment of an organized procedure for following up such leads.

3M sales people have responded not only by trading sales leads and other customer information, but by joining together to conduct special trade shows for 3M customers. In the U.S., sales people from as many as 30 divisions demonstrate 3M's diverse capabilities, either for a single major customer or for many customers in a single geographic area.

The benefits of staying close to the customer, of course, are never more satisfying than when the effort results in a solution to an important need.

Such was the case recently with the development of a patent-pending filter for use with a new 3M X-ray film and screen. The system gives doctors an improved image of a patient's chest area.

The filter was the idea of a 3M Twin Cities sales representative, who saw a need for such a device in working with one of his customers, a radiologist. With the help of a team of 3M technical, manufacturing and other people, as well as the radiologist, the product was readied for introduction in 1983 and is enhancing 3M's already strong reputation as a technological innovator.

Triad Marketing: Unique added value of

Industry-Knowledgeable, Professional Marketing

Because professional marketing of industry-specific systems is dependent on individuals with thorough knowledge of the customers' industry as well as of computers, each Triad division markets its products with its own force of highly-qualified, highly-trained Marketing Representatives.

Many of these representatives have earned advanced degrees in business administration or have gained first-hand industry knowledge on the customers' side of the counter. All have undergone intensive training at Triad headquarters and in the field—learning the Triad technology as it applies to their division's customers.

The appropriateness of Triad's marketing motto, *Knowing Your Business is Our Business,* is intended to be apparent to customers from the moment of their first contact with a Triad representative.

Prospects, expecting to hear another computer salesman speaking curiously of bits and bytes and ROMs and RAMs, instead hear Triad talk of inventory turns, pricing strategies and returns on investment. They learn of proven solutions to a myriad of management problems— specific solutions to specific problems for the prospect's specific business.

As a system proposal is developed, the Triad Marketing Representative works with the owner of the business to produce a professional plan—using actual numbers—that details the potential to increase that particular business' profitability, return on investment, customer service and cash flow.

The analysis is designed to establish believable goals that will more than justify the cost of the system.

The prospect is given Triad's complete customer list, and encouraged to talk with as many as possible. Visits to customer sites are arranged to enable the prospect to witness results in the same business as his, and to see how much easier it is to manage and control with a Triad.

Once convinced, the customer is offered complete training, and the system is installed on Triad's 60-Day Evaluation Program. *During this period, the customer has the opportunity to observe progress toward goals established in the pay-back analysis.* (Historically, over 98% have kept their systems after evaluation.)

And then there begins the long relationship between Triad and the customer that will last through the life of the system.

Zero Corp.

Our Market

Approximately 75 percent of Zero's sales are to customers that span the many segments of the electronics industry. Approximately 28 percent of sales are electronic enclosures meeting rigid military specifications which are sold to the Federal government or its major contractors.

We do business with approximately 9,000 customers with none of them accounting for more than 4 percent of sales. An important facet of our marketing strategy is not to become dependent on any single customer.

In six of our twenty product lines we command a significant share of the market.

Each division has its own organization to market its products. Company-wide our marketing organization is comprised of 17 direct salespeople. 64 manufacturers representatives and 70 distributors.

Minority and Female Employment

The concept of equal employment opportunity is consistent with HP's philosophy of treating all its people with fairness, dignity and courtesy. Affirmative action in HP employment and training helps ensure that positive, ongoing activities occur to attract and retain minorities, women and disabled people.

Three areas are important to the success of affirmative action at HP: university recruiting and hiring of minorities and women; guiding company employees to their fullest employment potential; and, at the local level, providing promising minorities and females in high school with knowledge for mathematics-based careers.

When recruiting college students in engineering, computer science, finance and other disciplines, HP emphasizes schools with large minority enrollments. In addition, HP technical employees serve as loaned professors to campuses with high minority populations. To address the U.S. shortage of university professors in electrical engineering and computer science, HP has committed $6 million to 23 selected colleges to develop technical professorships. Minorities and women are part of this important program.

In the precollege area, community programs in Colorado, New Mexico, Washington and California expose students in the seventh through 12th grades to careers in science, finance, computer science and engineering and help them develop the capabilities needed to be successful in a technical university curriculum. This year more than 200 HP people worked with students in these programs.

Ongoing commitment to affirmative action is indicated by the work force figures in the adjacent table. A booklet explaining HP's affirmative action programs is available from the company's corporate offices in Palo Alto, California.

Affirmative Action Review	Total Number	Minority Total	Minority Percent	Female* Total	Female* Percent
Managers & Supervisors					
1978	3,849	302	7.9	640	16.6
1983	7,866	806	10.2	1,863	23.7
Professionals					
1978	7,278	748	10.3	1,132	15.6
1983	15,175	1,832	12.1	3,998	26.3
Technicians					
1978	3,338	448	13.4	367	11.0
1983	5,379	896	16.7	831	15.4
Skilled/Craft					
1978	2,283	366	16.0	292	12.8
1983	2,843	552	19.4	448	15.8
Percent of Total U.S. Work Force**			18.9		41.0

*Includes minority females

**1980 Equal Employment Opportunity Commission all-industry data

Examples

Employment	19__	19__ (Dollars in Thousands)	19__
Average Number of Employees	5,415	6,259	6,395
Total Payrolls	$128,246	$130,354	$118,474
Employee Benefits			
Group Insurance Plans Cost	$ 11,903	$ 10,874	$ 9,377
Unemployment Compensation Taxes and Contributions to Supplemental Unemployment Benefits (S.U.B.) Funds	2,042	1,780	1,691
Pension Plans Contributions	10,555	11,510	8,600
Federal Insurance Contribution Act (F.I.C.A.) Taxes Paid	7,144	7,261	6,092
Total Benefits Cost	$ 31,644	$ 31,425	$ 25,760

Membership in the Quarter Century Club was 1,912 on December 31. Of these 1,282 were active, 49 having served over 40 years. At year end 1,856 retired employees and beneficiaries were drawing benefits under Company pension plans.

Employment of Minority-Group Personnel and Women at Year-End

	19__			19__		
	Company	Minority	Women	Company	Minority	Women
Hourly Employees	135,600	23.2%	8.1%	160,900	24.1%	9.3%
Salaried Employees	72,000	9.7	18.1	82,900	9.7	17.6%
Combined	207,600	18.5%	11.6%	243,800	19.2%	12.1%

*Includes Ford-U.S. and its domestic subsidiaries.

Representation of Minority-Group Members and Women in EEO-1 Job Categories at Year-End

	19__				19__			
Job Categories*	Blacks	Hispanics	Other Minorities	Women	Blacks	Hispanics	Other Minorities	Women
Officials and Managers	6.1%	1.0%	1.0%	2.1%	6.4%	1.1%	0.9%	2.1%
Professionals	5.0	1.3	2.6	11.7	5.3	1.1	2.6	11.6
Technicians	5.1	1.9	2.9	9.9	5.1	1.8	2.5	9.8
Office and Clerical	13.5	2.8	1.1	49.5	13.3	2.7	1.1	49.5
Craft Workers (skilled)	7.1	1.1	0.3	0.5	7.0	1.0	0.3	0.4
Operatives (semiskilled)	24.8	2.5	0.4	10.9	24.9	3.3	0.4	12.3
Laborers (unskilled)	27.5	2.0	0.5	6.1	27.6	2.1	0.4	6.4
Service Workers	24.7	2.4	0.3	11.7	23.7	2.7	0.4	12.0
Percentage of work force	15.7%	1.9%	0.9%	11.6%	16.0%	2.3%	0.9%	12.1%

*Excludes Sales Workers (retail), a category that is not applicable to Ford.

Minority Dealer Program

Goodyear

Goodyear's dealer network expanded into markets dominated by minority groups in 19__ as the company's Minority Dealer Recruitment Program added Blacks, Hispanics, Orientals and females to the roster. The national Urban League, Hispanic organizations and various community groups lent support to the recruitment of these minority business persons as Goodyear dealers.

Minority Entrepreneurs

Many of your stockholders will be interested in how you cooperate with minority entrepreneurs. If you have a policy and a practice of this type, it is important to spell it out.

Example:

MDC

In 19__ MDC awarded 8,281 contracts worth $29.2 million to businesses owned and operated by minorities or women or employing handicapped persons. MDC formalized a longstanding policy when it signed an agreement under which it will seek minority suppliers to participate in the U.S. Small Business Administration's Capital Development Plan.

Mission

Every successful company must have a basic purpose—the understanding that guides the company and its employees in their service to society. HCA's Mission is its statement of purpose, set forth clearly and simply. Since the words of the Mission were framed, through all the change and growth the Company has experienced, they have never lost their meaning and importance.

Today, the Mission is a way of living and working for thousands of HCA employees around the world. It is the underlying measure by which all HCA accomplishments are valued. Beginning and ending with our commitment to the patient, it is the promise HCA makes to every person whose life is in some way touched by the Company:

To attain international leadership in the health care field,
To provide excellence in health care,
To improve the standards of health care in the communities in which we operate,
To provide superior facilities and needed services to enable physicians to best serve the needs of their patients,
To generate measurable benefits for:
The Company,
The Medical Staff,
The Employee,
The Investor,
and, most importantly,
The Patient.

New Products

Your new products represent the lifeblood of your business. Your stockholders and security analysts want to know what new products you have brought to market during the past year.

Example:

IBM

New Products

To aid customer productivity, we brought significant new products and technology to market in 19__ across the full range of our product line. Through technical innovation, we continued to lower the cost of information processing and also offered customers a broader set of price/performance options. Among the new product developments:

- We began shipping the industry's most advanced computer disk file, the IBM 3380, which uses "thin film" technology to read or write data at 3 million characters a second.
- A new model of our most powerful computer, the IBM 3081, has internal speeds up to 40% faster than previous models. The logic and memory packaging in the IBM 3081 is the densest available in the industry.
- The IBM Personal Computer can be used in many productive ways in the office or at home.
- The IBM Datamaster is the company's newest low-priced computer designed specifically for business applications. It is easy to use and can handle text processing as well as data processing.
- Several new models of the IBM 4300 and IBM 8000 processors simplify system use and give customers added flexibility in choosing the computing power and memory size that will best meet their processing needs.
- The IBM Displaywriter, an office system widely installed in many countries, now has greater file processing and communications capabilities, enabling it to handle many more office tasks.
- A new IBM voice message distribution system utilizing the IBM Series/I permits people using telephones to record, play back, change and forward messages to one or several persons, under computer control.

Dynatech

One of the main challenges we face in managing a fast growing and diversified high technology company is balancing the potential explosive growth of our new products with our overall plan to grow consistently, evenly and profitably. Some new products grow so rapidly that, initially, they dominate the sales growth of others. But we also know while it takes an increasing amount of time to develop important new products, the useful life of those new products is decreasing. Technologies are changing so rapidly that what was state of the art two years ago, we are already refining, retooling, and replacing with more advanced technology.

New products sustain our growth. We listen to the market—try to fit its needs with our ideas and business objectives: new products must meet our market size requirements and potential for growth and profitability.

Of the nearly $8 million invested in new product development in fiscal 1983, approximately 63% went to the communications segment, 27% to medical products, and the remainder to analytical instruments. These investments resulted in new or improved products in every segment of the Company. Photographs on this page show examples of new products for three of our businesses—medical diagnostics, broadcast communications and data communications.

In the next few pages of this report, we discuss in more detail two of these businesses—data and broadcast communications. We describe the size and growth potential of their markets, our business approach, and most important—why we believe our new products will keep us in leadership positions in each of those rapidly growing and changing markets.

Operating Objectives

Many companies go beyond the setting of financial goals by outlining their operating objectives.

Hewlett-Packard has set out its objectives as follows:

First Objective: PROFIT

To achieve sufficient profit to finance our company growth and to provide the resources we need to achieve our other corporate objectives.

☐ In the final analysis, profit is the ultimate source of the funds needed by any business enterprise to prosper and grow. At Hewlett-Packard it is considered the one absolutely essential measure of corporate performance over the long term—for only by meeting the profit objective can the other corporate objectives be achieved.

SECOND OBJECTIVE: CUSTOMERS

To provide products and services of the greatest possible value to our customers, thereby gaining and holding their respect and loyalty.

□ Hewlett-Packard believes that the satisfaction of customer needs is a responsibility to be shared by everyone in the company. It begins in the laboratory, where products must be designed to provide superior performance and long trouble-free service. Once in production, these products must be manufactured at a reasonable cost and with the finest workmanship. When placed on the market, each product must be supported by a wide variety of useful services, both before and after the sale.

THIRD OBJECTIVE: FIELDS OF INTEREST

To enter new fields only when the ideas we have, together with our technical, manufacturing, and marketing skills, assure that we can make a needed and profitable contribution to the field.

FOURTH OBJECTIVE: GROWTH

To let our growth be limited only by our profits and our ability to develop and produce technical products that satisfy real customer needs.

□ HP does not believe that large size is important for its own sake: however, for at least two basic reasons, continuous growth is essential for the company to achieve its other objectives. First, HP serves a rapidly growing and expanding segment of the world's technological society. If the company were to remain static it could not possibly maintain a position of strength and leadership. Second, without growth there would not be the challenges and opportunities that attract and hold good people at all levels throughout the company.

FIFTH OBJECTIVE: OUR PEOPLE

To help HP people share in the company's success, which they make possible; to provide job security based on their performance; to recognize their individual achievements: and to help them gain a sense of satisfaction and accomplishment from their work.

□ Underlying Hewlett-Packard's personnel policies is the concept of sharing—sharing the responsibilities for defining and meeting goals, sharing in profits, and sharing the opportunities for personal and professional development.

SIXTH OBJECTIVE: MANAGEMENT

To foster initiative and creativity by allowing the individual great freedom of action in attaining well-defined objectives.

Hewlett-Packard people, when asked about the company's operating policies, often refer to the concept of "management by objective" (MBO). This means that each individual at each level in the organization, insofar as possible, makes his or her own plans for achieving the company's broader objectives and goals. This management philosophy goes hand in hand with the HP policy of "home-growing" talent. MBO offers the greatest possible freedom for individual initiative and contribution, promotes creativity and enthusiasm, and helps develop people who can keep up and take on additional responsibility as the company grows.

SEVENTH OBJECTIVE: CITIZENSHIP

To honor our obligations to society by being an economic, intellectual and social asset to each nation and each community in which we operate.

□ As a corporation operating in many different communities throughout the world, Hewlett-Packard must make sure that each of these communities is better for the company's presence. This means identifying HP's interests with those of the community; it means applying the highest standards of honesty and integrity to all relationships with individuals and groups; it means enhancing and protecting the physical environment, and building attractive plants and offices of which the community can be proud; and it means contributing talent, time, and financial support to worthwhile community projects.

Consolidated Foods

Principles

We put our basic rules, our operating principles, into written form and discussed them in last year's annual report. They are central to the manner in which we conduct our business, and they warrant repeating.

1. To build our business on demonstrably better products or services than those offered by our competition.

Only through our dedication to uncompromising quality can our customers—and our employees—know that all of our products and services consistently meet the highest expectations.

2. To achieve leadership positions in each principal product or geographic area in which we compete.

To achieve leadership, we must participate selectively in large and attractive markets and be willing to make the necessary investment of both funds and effort. If we have no realistic prospect of achieving leadership in a specific business, we do not belong in it.

3. To ensure that our corporation and each of its operating companies has in place a management group superior to our competition.

The markets in which we compete are demanding. Our competitors are intelligent and aggressive. To excel, we must be better and work harder. We put major effort into identifying talent at all levels and helping individuals to develop their special skills. We evaluate our people against consistent standards of measurable performance, not simply on form or style. We judge our managers on their ability to develop and inspire management teams, on creativity, on willingness to take intelligent risks, and —most importantly—on integrity.

4. To manage ourselves as a decentralized operating company.

To be superior, management at all levels must have the right and the opportunity to make its own decisions. Corporate management is responsible for company-wide goals and strategies and for assuring adequate resources for operating companies to achieve agreed-upon goals. The operating companies themselves must be responsible for the development and execution of the programs necessary to achieve those goals.

5. To dedicate ourselves to consistent improvement in the productivity and efficiency of our business.

As managers, we are custodians of the investments of others. While we will never lose sight of the requirement for quality and value, we thoroughly understand the need to control costs and manage assets carefully.

6. To search always for better ways to manage our company.

We encourage new ideas and listen to them and try them. We have developed the capacity to anticipate changes in our environments, not merely to respond to them. We constantly seek ways to improve every aspect of our operations, and we approach all of our activities with a sense of competitive urgency.

We know the ultimate judgment of management is based upon the return it can consistently generate for its investors. If certain activities cannot offer a satisfactory return, assets must be redeployed where they can do so.

7. To deal with integrity, fairness, and responsibility toward all our constituencies.

For our stockholders, we try our best to provide fair and increasing returns on their investments.

For our employees, we provide fair compensation, equal opportunity, safe and pleasant working conditions, and the opportunity for all to develop and utilize their individual talents to the maximum.

For our trade and suppliers, we base our relationships on honesty and dependability.

And in our business communities, we fulfill our obligations to help make our society stronger.

CSC MANAGEMENT GOALS AND OBJECTIVES

Business Areas:

CSC's business goal is to be the preeminent company worldwide in solving client problems in information systems technology and, in so doing, to earn a profit return sufficient to enable us to achieve our other objectives.

We will focus our corporate capability on the following basic areas of business activity on both a national and international basis:

- ☐ The solution of individual client problems in the collection, communication, processing, presentation and evaluation of data through the application of CSC products and our computer and communications technology; and
- ☐ The solution of data processing problems through the provision of proprietary products and services offered through CSC computer centers, communications networks and a branch-office service structure.

The specific objectives that follow will enable us to attain our overall business goal, and reflect our responsibilities to our clients, employees and shareholders.

1. Profit Objective:

To achieve a profit on each client engagement or service; moreover, to attain in each business sector and organization a level of profitability that is in the top ranking as compared with its competition.

To establish overall profitability levels that provide adequate funds to meet our growth objectives, and that provide an adequate base for our acquisition and diversification program when supported by conservative levels of debt.

2. Service Objective:

To maintain CSC's commitment to excellence and dedication to customer satisfaction through the provision of high-quality products and services that fulfill customer needs.

To maintain high professional standards at all levels in both our client relations and our own internal activities in management, technical, marketing, financial, operational, administrative and support functions.

To provide accurate and professional documentation for proposals, products and brochures.

To project the high quality of the company to customers, employees and the public through our visual and oral communications, through the appearance of our facilities and through high standards of conduct and appearance of our staff.

3. Growth Objective:

To pursue internal growth in all business sectors in both domestic and international markets, at levels consistent with market potential and limited only by our commitment to quality in each client activity or marketplace.

To aggressively seek out and identify opportunities for expansion into new markets and services that meet our criteria for high growth and profit potential. Furthermore, upon the decision to engage in a new business activity, to focus sufficient resources on the program to assure its success.

To conduct a selective acquisition program under corporate auspices to supplement current products and services, and to facilitate expansion into new areas.

4. Personnel Objective:

To maintain the professionalism and motivation of our staff, who are critical to our business success as a services organization.

To provide each employee the opportunity for a satisfying career with CSC through a company environment and management attitude that encourage individual development through opportunities for growth and continued education.

To provide all employees a compensation and benefits program that is competitive with comparable industries, and to provide special recognition for individual performance and contribution to CSC.

To treat all employees fairly with respect to job opportunities, compensation and evaluation, and to assure their access to CSC management for review of individual problems.

5. Management Environment Objective:

To develop our management staff through promotion from within, providing levels of increased responsibility to those managers who exhibit the skills, commitment and leadership necessary to achieve the company's goals and objectives.

To delegate well-defined objectives for performance, business conduct and growth to individual business units, and to evaluate the performance of each unit and manager against those objectives.

6. Business Conduct Objective:

To conduct our business activities within the laws of the United States and each country and community in which we do business, and to honor the social customs of each country in which we work.

To carry out our relationships with clients on a high professional level; to commit only to that which we can accomplish, and to meet our commitments with a high degree of responsibility.

To maintain high ethical standards in the aggressive pursuit of new business and in the execution of our marketing programs.

7. Shareholder Objective:

To recognize that our most important obligations are to guard the value of our shareholders' investment and provide adequate total return on that investment.

To meet those obligations to shareholders through capital appreciation derived from the reinvestment of company profits in our business.

Operating Practices

Allegheny International employs four basic operating practices in managing its diverse businesses. The consistent application of these practices enables the management to monitor the business units at all times, while encouraging flexibility and individual initiative at the operating level.

1. AI engages in comprehensive business planning for each company on an annual and three-year cycle and measures performance against the annual plan on a monthly basis. Three-month rolling forecasts for sales, earnings, and cash flow are used to indicate short-term anticipated results. Key operating executives are compensated to a large degree based on performance against the business plan.
2. AI uses sophisticated, uniform financial measurements and controls in every business unit. All significant cost and balance sheet items are available at all levels of management at the same time.
3. Division presidents and general managers are responsible for the operations of the business units on a day-to-day basis. Division management are specialists in their own fields and run their businesses accordingly. Group presidents, who report directly to the Chief Executive Officer, have the responsibility for several business divisions. They provide direction in strategic areas for their assigned business units and are available to take charge of a particular division in a time of illness or change.
4. Strategic decisions that affect the Corporation and approval of all major expenditures of funds are reserved for the Chief Executive Officer and the Board of Directors, but all group strategies are formulated and proposed by the group executives. They must be in conformance with the corporate strategy.

The Principles That Guide Us

1. To build our business on demonstrably better products or services than those offered by our competition.
2. To achieve leadership positions in each principal product or geographic area in which we compete.
3. To ensure that our corporation and each of its operating companies have in place a management group superior to our competition.
4. To manage ourselves as a decentralized operating company.
5. To dedicate ourselves to consistent improvement in the productivity and efficiency of our business.
6. To search always for better ways to manage our company.
7. To deal with integrity, fairness and responsibility toward all our constituencies.

Several years ago, Consolidated Foods publicly committed itself to a set of standard—The Principles That Guide Us.

These Principles, seven in all, are an expression of our determination to do business the right way. To achieve success in the broadest sense. To be a leader in everything we do.

The philosophy underlying these Principles was not imposed on us by external forces. Nor did it spring from an abstract, academic consideration of the corporation's mission. As made explicit in these seven statements, it is an attitude held by the *people* of Consolidated Foods. Call it a company-wide sense of price and dedication, a sharing of the notion that rewards and satisfaction come most readily to those who aim for nothing less than excellence.

Excellence, of course, comes in many forms. As an economic force in an increasingly competitive international environment, Consolidated Foods constantly seeks to be number one in whatever markets it serves. Not just the biggest, but the best—offering superior value and service, meeting real needs with products of consistently high quality. To achieve our expressed financial goals, our people apply their skills and judgment every day, in a wide variety of situations.

In so doing, we help ensure that the company maintains and enhances its status as an innovative, productive member of the business community. But no corporation is *solely* an economic institution. Its actions affect the lives of thousands of people. Its influence extends far beyond the shop floor and the executive suite.

So Consolidated Foods' pursuit of excellence encompasses our relationships with our fellow workers, with the communities where we operate and with society as a whole. It is expressed in an unwavering commitment to equal opportunity for all employees, in all circumstances; in a consistent and thoughtful program of corporate philanthropy; in a dedication to employee safety that has resulted in a reduction in on-the -job accidents; in student loan and scholarship programs for employees and their families; and in dozens of other ways, large and small, personal and institutional.

This statement of the company's purpose and objectives is the foundation on which our seven Principles are built. We do not believe that a dedication to winning in the marketplace and a commitment to the highest standards of corporate citizenship are mutually exclusive goals. They are, in fact, complementary. They are based on an understanding that recognizing and responding to the needs of people is the surest way to guarantee our long-term survival and success.

And we intend to succeed. Consolidated Foods is a company that believes in itself—in its people and its products, its traditions and its commitments.

In the following pages, we will talk briefly about each of these seven Principles, and introduce to you some of the people who apply them in our businesses. Together, the people and the Principles of Consolidated Foods are pointing the way toward new levels of excellence.

Product Review

As we approach our 40th anniversary, we are fully committed to the field of electrical/electronic connection devices. For the first decade, our entire business consisted of a few product lines of simple electrical terminals and splices. Today, we have more than 110 product families in over 70,000 types and sizes. Over two-thirds of our sales are now of products applied by AMP machines and another one-fourth by AMP tools.

More than 90% of our sales are still concentrated in electrical/electronic connections—an area that participates in the amazing growth of electronics, offers broad product and market diversity, and contributes to the drive for greater productivity.

Key factors in our growth have been the prolific creation of new AMP products and application tooling, and their extremely long life cycles. We spend 9% of sales on research, development and engineering for the creation and application of new and improved products and processes—$104,000,000 in 1980 and over $550,000,000 in the past decade. Over 2,900 AMP people are involved in these technical efforts. Over 2,300 U.S. patents were issued or pending at year-end 1980—with over 6,800 corresponding patents in 50 other countries.

The product development opportunities presented by the emerging end market needs of the 1980's are better than ever before in our history. This report shows over a dozen relatively new product lines, over a dozen new application machines, and many extensions of existing product lines. They are recent responses to customer requirements arising from higher-speed, more miniaturized electronic circuitry devices; new types of conductors; more demanding performance and environmental criteria; and the need for more reliable, labor-saving application methods. Many new components will be needed by equipment makers in the 1980's. Thus, while maintaining our position as the world's leader in electrical and electronic connection devices, we will continue to diversify into logically related component areas such as filters, cable assemblies, flexible circuitry assemblies, switches, card readers, and heat shrink products.

New AMP products are generally becoming more complex, of higher value, and far more critical to the functioning of customer equipment. The capabilities required to develop, produce and market these products are accordingly becoming more varied and sophisticated. Our basic manufacturing skills are precision metal forming, metal plating, plastic molding, and automated assembly. AMP's marketing approach stresses our "early involvement" in our customers' design efforts, and focuses on providing lower installed costs through labor-saving application tooling.

Productivity

American industry is duly concerned over the need to improve productivity. The gains in efficiency obtained through more productive manufacturing processes and service activities will not only help offset the deleterious effects of inflation but will also strengthen our position in our various markets. Productivity is defined as a measure of output to input. The input is everything required to produce goods and services, and the output is the quantity and quality of what is produced.

In describing the ways in which your company is closing the productivity gap, consider making reference to the following:

1. Your company's philosophy on improvement of productivity.
2. Productivity goals that have been established.
3. Investments in improved production facilities.
4. Research and development.
5. The manner in which you involve your employees in finding ways for the company to become more productive.
6. The development of programs to minimize the threats of layoffs.
7. Monetary rewards for productivity suggestions from your employees.
8. Improvements in your computer technology.
9. Improvements in materials handling.
10. New energy systems installed to improve the company's self-generation capabilities.
11. Training programs for your employees.

Productivity and Product Quality

Textron Focuses on Quality and Productivity—Textron began emerging from the global recession in 1983 with a strengthened commitment to improving productivity and product quality.

Productivity gains were achieved by most Textron Divisions through improved utilization of capital and human resources.

The types of productivity improvements being emphasized by Textron are broad-ranging, while the programs themselves are tailor-made to meet the special needs of individual Textron Divisions. The mix includes automation and computerization, investments in new plants and machinery, cost reductions through plant closings and consolidations, improvements in asset management and increased emphasis on quality control.

The Human Element—Textron continued to focus on the human factors that cause people to achieve extraordinary results in the workplace. Greater emphasis was placed upon "people" programs that encourage employee participation across the entire quality improvement spectrum.

The human resource activities being employed include Quality Circles, Corrective Action, Quality of Work Life, Quality Assurance, Interaction Management and Performance Improvement Programs, Employee Suggestion Plans and Opinion Polls.

The result has been a renewed awareness at Textron of the importance of producing the best possible products at the lowest possible cost.

At textron's Fafnir Division, for example, there are currently 28 Quality Circles with more than 225 members. Volunteers meet regularly to indentify, analyze and solve quality problems in their areas. Current plans call for a total of 40 Circles with 325 members. Similar types of participatory, problem solving programs also exist or are being introduced at many other Textron Divisions.

Westinghouse Canada

One highlight was an increase in small group activities, generally known as quality circles. These are employee groups, trained in evaluation and analysis methods, whose objective is to make improvements within their work areas. More than 50 such volunteer groups exist, with a combined membership in excess of 400 people. These people, who meet regularly on company time, are making a valuable contribution to productivity improvement. They are also increasing their personal job satisfaction through greater participation in company affairs.

A second productivity technique, value analysis, was used extensively during the year in both plants and offices. It involves assessing the value and cost to the company of specified activities. Value analysis methods were applied in completing plans to transfer all corporate functions to a new central office location in downtown Hamilton during 1983.

Another highlight of the year was a team visit to Japan led by the president, to study first-hand the methods employed by the Japanese in achieving their high rate of productivity improvement. While not all Japanese techniques are applicable in Canada, some are adaptable. One such program is the Minimized Inventory Production System (M.I.P.S.) being introduced in the company's London plant. Encouraging results have been obtained in reducing inventories and in establishing a more responsive manufacturing system. Planning is underway to expand the program to other divisions.

The relationship between technological innovation and the fulfillment of corporate objectives, such as productivity improvement, has been reinforced through the establishment of an Engineering Council.

Brown & Sharpe

Internally, we took a major step to improve our productivity in the distribution of our products sold through industrial supply houses. A new and sophisticated warehouse system located at four points in the United States was developed and implemented during the year. Each center is joined to a central electronic order processing and tracking system that permits immediate answers to inquiries for inventory, price, delivery and open order information and makes it possible to enter orders and generate shipping documents from each of the warehouses.

Another major contributor to in-house productivity has been the contra-cyclical "Bridge-building" program initiated in the U.S. to minimize the threat of layoffs should an extensive downturn take place. On its part, the Company has continued level production and, in response, employees at all levels made a commitment to increase their individual productivity. Improving product availability is an integral part of this program as well, and during the fourth quarter it fostered several highly successful sales programs. The productivity improvement in excess of 5% achieved to date is a reflection of teamwork motivated by this partnership in "Bridge-building."

Whether strengthening our own productivity or building state-of-the-art electronic inspection systems for our customers, "productivity improvements *is our business;* we know it both inside and out."

Another major contributor to in-house productivity has been the contra-cyclical "Bridge-building" program initiated in the U.S. to minimize the threat of layoffs should an extensive downturn take place. On its part, the Company has continued level production and, in response, employees at all levels made a commitment to increase their individual productivity. Improving product availability is an integral part of this program as well, and during the fourth quarter it fostered several highly successful sales programs. The productivity improvement in excess of 5% achieved to date is a reflection of teamwork motivated by this partnership in "Bridge-building."

Parker

Improving productivity and profitability is an ongoing challenge. To achieve meaningful results in these interdependent areas, Parker has set up a number of programs to reduce unit costs in manufacturing, enhance skills and attitudes of employees and hone management techniques. A brief discussion of some of these programs follows.

Quality Circles—One of the most talked about new techniques for improving productivity, quality circles were initiated at selected Divisions early last year, and expansion of the program has continued. For an hour a week foremen meet with their regular work-groups in a creative, free atmosphere to discuss job-related problems. There are currently over 50 quality circles active throughout the Company. From the experience of other companies, the investment of only 2½ percent of workers time should yield a productivity gain of 5 to 10 percent in the department.

Computer-Aided Design and Manufacturing—Generally called "CAD/CAM," computer-aided design and manufacturing improves Parker's productivity by facilitating the design of complex components and development of the most effective manufacturing programs.

The system enables engineering and manufacturing personnel, working at computer display terminals, to create designs and machining programs and to monitor the graphic "operation" of moveable designs before setting up in the shop. This capability often avoids the cost and time-loss of rework or scrap.

MRP Program—MRP (manufacturing resources planning) is a management approach in which all operating elements—demand forecast, production plan, shop capacity and lead times—are combined in a master schedule to optimize inventory and customer service. The technique improves productivity by maximizing production quantities, setting shop loads consistent with capacity and achieving other efficiencies. It provides a comprehensive plan from order entry to ultimate shipment of the order.

Interaction Management Training—Five full-time instructors using behavioral modeling techniques are working with foremen throughout Parker, training them in methods to improve productivity and quality of work-life through better foreman-worker communications. The training focuses on such matters as work habits, disciplinary action, and individual performance. Skills in coaching, problem-solving and building worker self-esteem are taught in the program.

Public Offering

On July 17, 19__ the Company sold, in a public offering, 6,000 units of securities, each unit consisting of a $1,000 principal amount, 12⅞%. Convertible Participating Subordinated Depenture due in 1994, 133 shares of Common Stock, $.01 par value and warrants to purchase 67 shares of Common Stock (see Notes 11, 13 and 14). The Company received approximately $6,800,000 net cash proceeds from the sale of the units.

Public Service

Heinz companies around the world continued to demonstrate responsiveness to individual and institutional needs in their various communities.

In the U.S., Heinz met the challenge that asked the private sector to take up some of the slack in efforts formerly carried out exclusively by government agencies.

The H.J. Heinz Company Foundation boosted its outlays by more than 75%, to $3.5 million. The number of organizations receiving aid rose to 775, more than 30% above the year before.

Some outstanding grants included $500,000 to the University of Pittsburgh for a program to train future leaders of Third World nations; $150,000 to Westminster College for the McKee faculty chair in business and economics; $100,000 to Notre Dame University for a facility devoted to control of diseases in the Third World; $100,000 to the College of Idaho for its J.A. Alberston School of Business; and $50,000 to the Rehabilitation Institute of Pittsburgh for its adult head injury trauma unit.

Heinz U.S.A.'s food aid and food subsidy programs, for the 15th year, helped community service groups in the Pittsburgh area and other company locations. Further long-term aid programs included support for United Way campaigns and for drug rehabilitation programs. Special donations went to Midwest flood victims.

Donations for overseas relief included more than 7,000 cases of baby food sent to Poland and contributions to missions located in Mexico and Haiti.

Other company-assisted activities included sponsorship of the Merit Awards Program of the National Newspaper Publishers Association, which honors outstanding black journalists; support for public television broadcasting; and the annual Heinz Swim Meet.

The City of Los Angeles dedicated a park in the San Pedro harbor area to honor Martin J. Bogdanovich, founder of Star-Kist Foods, citing the many civic and economic contributions made by him and his company.

Ore-Ida played host to 1,000 young people at Les Bois Invitational Soccer Tournament, which attracted more than 55 U.S. and Canadian teams.

Foodways National enrolled in the Wethersfield (Connecticut) Advisory Committee for the Handicapped, posting all its job openings with that organization.

Gagliardi Brothers donated an auxiliary pumping station to the West Chester (Pennsylvania) Municipal Authority, which provides fire protection for both the company's factory and the surrounding community.

Weight Watchers' public service activities reflected the growing international character of its operations. In Cetraro, Calabria, the company worked with the Italian Society of Human Nutrition to cosponsor a conference that attracted a large number of nutritionists and government officials, as well as members of the press.

In the United Kingdom, Weight Watchers classroom members raised money for buses to transport handicapped children in two communities near London and donated money for guide dogs for the blind and for treatment of children suffering from leukemia.

Heinz-Canada reaffirmed its commitment to a leadership role in research and dissemination of information on nutrition. Company specialists, using data obtained in surveys of infants and preschoolers sponsored jointly with the National Research Council, have estimated consumption levels of trace elements, mycotoxin and contaminants in young children. The survey results were published by the Canadian Public Health Association.

Heinz-U.K. conducted a promotion to support the Save a Baby charity program. The company redeemed more than two million of its baby food labels and donated the sum of £40,000 to The Spastics Society.

In the Netherlands, the Central Europe Office donated a handmade glass sculpture to help celebrate the opening of a new town hall in the Heinz factory town of Elst.

Quality Chrysler Corp.

In just four years, Chrysler has improved the quality of its cars by 36 percent and its trucks by 40 percent. This has enhanced our reputation in the marketplace and, most important, helped cut our warranty costs by 45 percent over the past five years. Sustained high quality is the foundation for our unique 5-year/50,000-mile warranty, the best warranty on the market today.

Only 7,403 Chrysler Corporation vehicles were recalled for defects last year, compared to 1.6 million for Ford, 1.2 million for General Motors, and 1.2 million for Japanese imports.

Rapidly increasing use of computers and robotics is of paramount importance to the achievement of Chrysler's goals of higher quality and productivity. We had only 16 robots in 1975. Now we have 375, and the number is increasing rapidly. By 1988, we will have well over 1,000.

Our robots are doing more than 95 percent of the welding on our front-wheel-drive cars and 97 percent on our mini-wagons. They are also used increasingly for difficult and undesirable jobs, such as painting and sealer application.

New Manufacturing Technical Center

To ensure that we use robotic technology effectively, we have established a new Manufacturing Technical Center in Detroit, incorporating engineering, development labs, and tool and die making operations under one roof. The Center improves the manufacturing feasibility of engineering designs, oversees the use of CAD/CAM techniques in manufacturing, and makes certain that our new designs are compatible with robotic manufacturing technology.

Building Quality into the Car

Higher quality also comes from improving the technology and materials in the car itself. Buyers of our popular new mini-wagons, the Voyager and Caravan, get increased anti-corrosion protection because 88 percent of the body metal in these vehicles is galvanized steel. Because we use galvanized steel so extensively in our pickup trucks and sport utility vehicles, we're now able to offer the industry's first 5-year/100,000-mile rust perforation warranty.

State-of-the-Art Computer System

Computer technology is now an integral part of Chrysler's operations, from initial design through road testing to final manufacture. Our high-technology operations are supported by one of the largest integrated computer systems in the world, with 16 large computers processing 64 million instructions a second, connected to 700 terminals throughout the Corporation.

Our computer system provides a common data base for all of our design, engineering, and manufacturing operations. It is the foundation for improved products and productivity, through faster design, simulation, and testing.

We shall strive for excellence in all endeavors.

We shall set our goals to achieve total customer satisfaction, and to deliver error-free, competitive products on time, with service second to none. Burroughs Quality Policy

"First say to yourself what you would be," advised a Greek philosopher, "and then do what you have to do." Burroughs Corporation takes that piece of wisdom seriously – and acts on it vigorously. Incorporated in the Company's strategic, business and product plans is another set of standards – the values and ideals that guide it as it pursues technical excellence, develops and motivates its people, and enhances its Corporate citizenship in the community.

Burroughs is, as President Paul Stern put it at a management conference earlier this year, "preoccupied with quality"; the Company "plans for it, teaches it and breathes it into everything it does." The quality conviction begins at the highest levels of management. A key to making it a reality is the Burroughs Quality Organization, now in its second year of efforts to infuse quality into every aspect of Corporate life.

Burroughs is organizing for quality. It has established Product Assurance Organizations that are independent of the development and manufacturing groups, as well as Quality Councils that set objectives and measure results.

It is training for quality. Burroughs managers take courses in this multifunctional subject, which encompasses the development, manufacture and support of a product. Soon to come are more courses in such advanced fields as statistical process control and software engineering.

Increased attention to quality throughout the Company has proven to be an important benefit to both Burroughs and its customers. For example, Company experts say that installation times for the well-received new B 7900 large systems are running near one-third the normal times for mainframes in this range.

Improving also was the response time to field problems, thanks in part to an extensive training program for field engineers and support people. Response time to field problems improved by about 9% in 1983, while the response time to resolve application software problems improved more than 30%.

But to understand fully the meaning of the quality ideal, one must look beyond the individual product triumphs and also view its impact on the organization as a whole. As more problems are found and fixed in the earlier stages of product development, the engineering costs go down. So do the service costs once the product is in the customer's hands. Quality thus allows the Company to regenerate its internal resources. The effect on Burroughs people is just as significant: doing better work helps raise their morale, pride and job satisfaction.

Reindustrialization

It will be of interest to your stockholders to read your corporate thoughts concerning the reindustrialization of America.

General Electric

Bringing about the 'factory of the future'

The urgent challenge of U.S. reindustrialization presents General Electric with significant market opportunities for its wide range of sophisticated products and services.

Large portions of U.S. productive facilities are now obsolete. World competition is forcing American industry to replace its outdated facilities with advanced manufacturing equipment and processes.

The industrial automation market is growing at well over 20% per year. General Electric during 1981 launched major efforts to provide the advanced automation systems needed to modernize U.S. industry. Using its own factories as laboratories for the development of new concepts, the Company plans to be a leader in equipping the "factory of the future."

Such factories will use computer graphics for design and planning. Final designs will be transferred directly to controls on the machine tools that manufacture product parts.

On the factory floor, programmable controls will team with numerical controls, lasers and industrial robots to build product parts, and solid-state inspection cameras linked to computers will assure quality.

Computers will link work stations, stock rooms, marketing activities, transportation and other job functions needed to get higher-quality products to customers faster, while lowering manufacturers' inventories significantly.

An important step toward the "factory of the future" was the acquisition of Calma Company, a leading supplier of computer-aided design and manufacturing equipment (CAD/CAM) based in California. To supplement this capability, General Electric acquired a 48% interest in the Structural Dynamics Research Corporation, a computer-aided engineering company located in Ohio.

Computer-aided engineering enables engineers to simulate product performance before prototypes are built. It streamlines product development and slashes costs.

To become a full-service supplier of automation equipment, GE also entered the rapidly growing industrial robot business. It presently is assembling and selling robots under worldwide licenses, and expects to offer its own innovative robots by 1984.

Research and Development

Stockholders recognize the importance of the expenditure of funds for research and development. They want to know how your company's funds for research programs are expended toward:

1. The improvement of existing products and processes.
2. The development of new uses for existing products and processes.
3. The development of new products compatible with existing businesses.
4. The development of new products and processes for investment opportunities.

Provide the following types of information to describe your research and development (R & D) programs.

1. Policies of the company towards R & D.
2. The amount invested in R & D during the year covered by the annual report.
3. A comparison of the current year's R & D to prior years.
4. Government contracts for research.
5. Percentage of sales devoted to R & D expenses.
6. Effect of research on sales.
7. New products being developed through R & D.
8. A description of the staff involved in R & D.
9. The outlook for R & D in your company.

Research and Development: Sperry's strong research and development program is the technological base for our future direction. Our R&D expenditures were $397 million in fiscal year 1983. Contracted R&D activities provided an additional $248 million. Measured against total revenue, Sperry continues to be an industry leader in the amount of research and development spending.

A $200 million semiconductor development program, begun three years ago, will start to pay off this year with the opening of new laboratory and production facilities in Eagan, Minnesota. These are among the most advanced semiconductor facilities in the world, and will provide the high quality integrated circuits that are at the heart of electronic systems.

Applied research and advanced development programs explore new technologies for use in new products and product improvements. Research is generally aimed beyond the immediate business horizon, serving as a forerunner and a supplement to larger, more product-oriented development work. Efforts directed toward the practical use of new materials, processes or devices include Josephson-junction semiconductors for computers and millimeter-wave devices for radar systems. Although the programs are built on the ideas of our scientists and on an awareness of scientific developments, they directly address the marketing needs of the company.

Anticipating technological changes and providing user-oriented systems are the keys to top performance in our industries. Sperry has always been in the electronic systems business, and has built up a reservoir of talent and technology that is among the best in the business. We are well-equipped to provide the advanced electronic systems that the market will demand.

Masco

Research and Development

What is Masco's strategy with respect to research and development?

An integral part of our goal of building a unique growth company are our activities in the planning and development of new products.

Our financial new product objective is to develop quality value-added products with the potential to realize a 10 percent after-tax profit on sales and a 20 percent after-tax profit on investment. Strategies employed in pursuit of this objective include the following:

1) explore the long-range growth potential of appropriate market opportunities;
2) work closely with customers to ensure that we are responsive to their needs;
3) evaluate our product uniqueness compared to competing products to determine if a premium value will be accorded by the user; and
4) avoid products where frequent incidence of obsolescence adds inordinately to the risk.

Our goal is to accelerate the rate at which we develop new products. Thus, we are making an increasing commitment to recruiting professional talents, developing current staff and giving them the necessary tools and support. We are also determined to lead in those technologies associated with our manufacturing processes.

New products have been a major contributor every year to our growth, indicating our strategy for product development has been successful.

FMC

Research and development programs incorporating advanced technologies require long time horizons, high risk tolerance and sustained management support. Properly selected and nurtured, however, these programs represent a major opportunity for the company to enter new product areas which offer substantial financial rewards.

In the petroleum equipment business, for example, FMC is introducing a walking beam pump management system which controls the pump and alerts the operator to major changes in pumping conditions. The system applies advanced digital microprocessing and telecommunications techniques to reduce energy consumption and avoid costly shutdowns in the oilfield. Petroleum equipment operations have historically achieved high returns for FMC, and the pump management system promises to expand market participation in this high-return business.

In the defense equipment business, the Bradley Fighting Vehicle (BFV) was designed to fulfill changing customer requirements. Military doctrine now calls for a fighting vehicle rather than a traditional troop transporter. The Bradley Fighting Vehicle features increased fire power, enhanced troop protection and improved mobility for the infantry squad. The defense equipment business has consistently earned good returns on FMC's investment, and the BFV promises to continue that trend.

In the agricultural chemical business, the worldwide need to increase food and fiber production creates a growing market for more effective, safer, and less costly pesticides. Over the last three years, FMC has doubled the R&D spending in this business and has recently opened a new $30-million research facility. This effort includes the application of computers to the screening and synthesis of chemical compounds and the use of biotechnology in areas likely to make major contributions to crop protection science. With many high-potential products already in the laboratory, several are expected to make a sizable contribution to higher returns in the later 1980s.

FMC's most dramatic new technology undertaking is Immunorex, a two-year-old joint venture with Centocor, Inc. Immunorex seeks to develop products which will prevent and treat cancer and other diseases through regulation of the human immune system. The goal is to combine the technology of bioengineering with knowledge of the human immune system to produce human monoclonal antibodies in commercial quantities outside of the body. This is an area of rapid scientific growth and discovery, as well as intense competition. A number of the world's foremost scientists are working with Immunorex in the pioneering of this critically important research effort. If the Immunorex process is successful, these products will be of immense importance and application worldwide.

Robots

The press constantly reports the growth and impact of robots in American factories. Your stockholders will be most interested in how, if at all, robots will be utilized in your company. Photos of robots at work in your company will help describe the impact of your company's robots.

Example:

A special opportunity is presented in the field of robotic technology and manufacture. In recent years, we have become an important supplier of components to robot manufacturers in the U.S. and in various foreign nations. That exposure has provided valuable insights into the technological concept of robotics, as well as understanding and expertise in diverse manufacturing processes. For these reasons, we concluded that an entry into robotic manufacturing would be both a logical and natural extension of our operations, and would provide additional benefits in the expansion of robotic component sales as volume and demand increased in this emerging environment.

In 1982, we initiated preliminary research and development programs to design a line of small tabletop robots, popularly known as "teaching" robots, and related products. We believe that many of these potential products may have broad applications such as for light industrial transfer, inspection and assembly operations, research and feasibility studies, and of course, educational and hobby uses. We will also endeavor to develop the tabletop robots, which we refer to as TSRs, or Tabletop Specialty Robots, that can be assembled from mass-produced parts, and hope that we can market these TSRs in both fully-assembled and in kit configurations. We hope, additionally, to develop a specialized input device with memory capable of interfacing with the TSRs, creating a self-contained unit that can operate independently.

In December, 1982, development of a robot prototype commenced, and progress has been encouraging. At the beginning of 1983, we organized a new subsidiary, Techno, Inc., for the purpose of conducting research and development in microprocessor-controlled automation and robotics under exclusive agreements with two thoroughly experienced New Jersey consulting firms, subject to our option to terminate those agreements and enter into three-year employment contracts with the two engineers who are principals of the two corporations. Furthermore, a contribution was made to Columbia University to provide funding for a robotics research laboratory project at their Mechanical Engineering School, specifically concerned with the sector of our interest, and it is anticipated that we will consult with the faculty members concerning developments in this area.

Strategies

Baldor presented its various strategies in its annual report. It brought the readers into the strategies through a statement on the front cover, "Baldor Management discusses its strategies for achieving real growth in the 1980s in face of inflation." Baldor carried out its strategy theme throughout its report by discussing the following.

1. *Targets and Goals Through 19—.* In this section, Baldor provides its forecast of sales, net earnings, and earnings per share. In addition, the company reviews its past forecast by showing annual forecast versus actual results.
2. *A Strategy for Increasing Productivity.* Baldor describes its investments in machinery leading to improved productivity.
3. *A Strategy for Increasing Self-sufficiency.* Baldor describes its policy—make, rather than buy component parts when economically feasible.
4. *A Strategy for Expanding Manufacturing Capabilities.* Baldor describes its plans to expand production facilities ahead of anticipated sales increases.
5. *A Strategy for Assuring Product Quality.* Baldor describes how to zero in on four major areas to improve product quality: namely, design engineering, incoming material, production engineering, and operator skills.
6. *A Strategy for Expanding Markets.* Baldor describes its competitive pricing policy, the balancing of sales between distributors and original equipment manufacturers, support of its marketing efforts with consistent advertising programs; etc.
7. *A Strategy for Positioning Baldor Products.*
8. *A Plan for Encouraging Further Development of Individual Skills and Capabilities.* Baldor describes its employee oriented programs; its sharing corporate goals and objectives with employees; and profit sharing plans that reward Baldor people for their skills and capabilities.

9. *A Strategy for Maintaining Financial Strength.* Baldor describes its policies for the purchase of property, plant, and equipment; its maintenance of a conservative ratio of long-term obligations to total capitalization; its dividend policy; etc.

10. *A Program for Sustaining Effective Investor Relations.* Baldor describes its listing on the New York Stock Exchange; its attendance at meetings of financial analysts; etc.

Strategies for Leadership

Hewlett-Packard Company is in one of the most dynamic periods of its 44-year history. It is a time of change in the needs of customers, in the technologies available to meet those needs, and in the size and shape of HP itself.

When a company changes as rapidly as HP, there is the possibility of it growing apart, of its product lines and operations diverging. For HP, the opposite is true. Its organization and products have become better integrated to shape and support the company's purpose.

Although HP's 6,400 products serve many different markets, their common purpose is to provide customers with the information needed to solve technical and business problems. HP's strength lies not only in its wide spectrum of products, but also in its ability to merge technologies to provide comprehensive solutions to a variety of specific problems. HP products are information tools in a three-tiered business strategy.

Tier One. HP is continuing a strategy that has served it well over the years: offering products that represent state-of-the-art technology and that are useful on a stand-alone basis. Each product is a tool that provides information to help solve a problem, such as the measurement of an electronic function, the analysis of a chemical compound, the monitoring of a vital life sign, or the computation, analysis, display or transmission of data.

Tier Two. Joining individual products to create systems is the second way HP is making information an effective decision-making tool. Increasingly, HP is designing its products as modules that can interact with other HP equipment or with products of other vendors. HP's systems may consist of test and measurement instruments, data-processing equipment, instrumentation for chemical analysis or medical monitoring, or combinations of these product groups.

This ability to combine product groups is one of HP's main strengths and is manifest in many ways. Networks of computers and personal workstations help organizations create, move, store and use information effectively. Measurement systems linked to computers translate what is happening on the factory floor into information that managers can use in decision-making. In laboratories, analytical instruments and computers combine to computerize and automate the preparation and analysis of chemical compounds. In health care facilities, patient-monitoring and critical-care equipment, data management, financial and order-entry systems combine to improve care while helping control costs.

Tier Three. The third tier of HP's strategy is to provide software packages that further integrate HP equipment in order to solve customer problems. Productivity networks is the term HP uses to describe its integrated software packages. Just as a system represents linked equipment, productivity networks represent software programs that are linked to provide total business solutions.

Some of these networks are designed to meet the needs of a wide variety of customers. For example, HP's Information Productivity Network allows any organization to effectively use word processing, data base management and electronic mail. Other productivity networks serve specific kinds of organizations, such as manufacturers, retail trade and distribution industries, laboratories, hospitals and educational and financial institutions.

HP's Manufacturer's Productivity Network (MPN) illustrates the combination of products, systems and software applications. MPN's goal is to build on a manufacturer's existing base of HP hardware and software and integrate the information used in activities such as computer-aided engineering, materials management and financial accounting. Individually, these application programs already offer powerful solutions to business problems. However, the MPN concept recognizes that the effectiveness of all software applications will be greatly enhanced when they 'talk' to each other.

For example, computer-aided design products linked to automated test equipment will allow a manufacturer's engineering section to directly transmit its performance criteria to the factory. The factory, in turn, will be able to communicate its requirements and process constraints to the design team. Input from the marketing department—customer preferences and order forecasts—will be transmitted to both the engineering and manufacturing areas.

Whether in a manufacturing environment or a service organization, the possibilities for the constructive coupling of information are numerous. It is this linkage of software programs that is called for in HP's productivity network strategy.

State-of-the-art products, systems linking them together, and productivity networks to maximize their usefulness to customers—these are some of the ways HP is working to provide customers with the information they need to make their organizations more productive.

Intermark is a publicly owned company with a unique corporate concept, philosophy and strategy.

The Company was founded in 1960 as Southwestern Capital Corporation, a federally licensed S.B.I.C. In 1968 it changed its name to Intermark, Inc., and the basic nature of its business to an operating/holding company. Intermark was envisioned as a new and different kind of force on the business horizon and has lived up to that ideal. The Company's stock is listed on the American Stock Exchange.

Unlike many companies which start out by serving one industry and later struggle to diversify, Intermark did not inherit an *operating* history which would control or confine its future. Intermark chose a new concept of diversification and a unique strategy for implementing it. Since its inception, the Intermark strategy called for employing the company's assets in several different businesses — growth businesses — operating in broadly diversified industries and serving a variety of markets.

Intermark's Strategy For Diversification Is By Design, Not By Circumstance.

Each Intermark affiliated business is treated as a "Partner Company" rather than a corporate subsidiary. Additionally, no one Partner Company dominates the group. In our latest Fiscal Year, our largest Partner Company represented only 29% of Intermark's total revenues.

A model growth company built on the strategy of owning all or part of other successful growth companies — that has been the basic concept of Intermark since 1968, and that concept is proving more viable every day.

Intermark Strategy At Work.

To maintain balanced diversification, Intermark regularly reassesses the industries in which it operates and the *market position* of its Partner Company in each of those industries. We like to know that each industry is healthy and that our participating Partner Company is healthy, too. As a result of this constant re-evaluation, the number and mix of our Partner Companies is likely to vary from year to year. It is important to us to be sure at all times that Intermark's assets are deployed as productively and prudently as possible.

A Preeminent Position In Its Market Is A *Must* For Each of Our Partner Companies.

Today, Intermark owns all or part of eleven mid-sized, Sunbelt-based growth companies representing eight different industries. Six of these are wholly owned; one is majority owned; four are minority owned by Intermark. Together they represent more than $174 million in assets and $172 million in annual revenues.

Intermark has established certain basic criteria which a business must meet to be a Partner Company. Among these the company must:

have its headquarters in one of the Sunbelt States, even though it may serve worldwide markets.

be a growth company . . . capable of doubling its sales and earnings in five years or less.

have already achieved or have the potential for achieving a preeminent position in its market or industry.

have a broadly diversified customer base and not be dependent upon one or two large customers.

have a seasoned management team capable of autonomously managing its company's affairs.

Intermark has three primary strengths, which have built a solid foundation for its growth. First is its unique concept of diversification and its clear understanding of how to make that concept effective. Second is its ability to provide its Partner Companies with growth capital when needed. Third is its skill in working with Partner Company executives. These successful executives are encouraged to preserve their entrepreneurial instincts while sharpening their professional skills in the following areas:

- market positioning
- disciplined planning
- goal setting
- written commitments
- strict budgeting
- priority establishment
- tight financial controls
- delegation of authority

Strengths of Your Corporation

Your stockholders are interested in knowing what you consider to be the strengths of your company. The Kroger Co. defined its strengths as follows:

We believe these proven strengths to be:

- Retail stores that are young in age, modern in design and decor, and contemporary in their appeal to customers;
- Dedication to research in all its forms in order to determine what kind of stores to build and where to build them;
- Demonstrated excellence in the merchandising of the perishable products so influential in the customer's choice of where to shop;
- Strategically located, highly efficient manufacturing facilities providing a wide variety of quality label products uniquely available to our customers;
- Marketing strategies based on everyday low prices the customer can depend on consistently in the search for values;
- An executive team which combines youth and experience in a blend of talents pledged to the attainment of aggressive goals.

While we expect the mainstream of our business in the foreseeable future to remain as it is today (food/drug retailing and manufacturing), we will not be reluctant to examine—on a selective basis—opportunities to enter new ventures which could capitalize on our strengths.

But we will resist the temptation to reach beyond our ability to manage or to divert our attention from the primary activities of the enterprise. Our primary focus will continue to be our retail businesses and our responsibility to keep them a consistent, dependable source of corporate profitability.

Technology

3M

One of the most important outgrowths of 3M innovation has been the development of a broad and growing store of technologies. Today, 3M product lines are based on expertise in some 75 areas of science and technology.

3M technological innovation traces its roots to the 1920s. Our first proprietary product, a waterproof sandpaper, did away with dust hazards in automobile sanding. A few years later, 3M research produced the first pressure-sensitive masking tape, a breakthrough in auto painting.

Since that time, internal development of new technologies also has led to a number of other 3M firsts: reflective sheetings for highway signs; magnetic tape for audio, video and data recording; stain-resistant fabric and carpet protectors; low-dosage X-ray films; presensitized printing plates, and popular Scotch brand transparent tapes.

3M innovation has been marked not only by the development of technology after technology, but by creativity in finding wide application for any single technology. For example, products as different as garment insulating materials, surgical tapes, disposable face masks, floor maintenance pads and facial sponges are based on the technology of nonwoven fibers.

Innovation in research continues to result in problem-solving technologies and products and is helping fuel the growth of 3M businesses, old and new. Among recent developments are:

- Advanced ceramic materials which have led to coated abrasives with up to three times the life of the best commonly used abrasives, as well as to the first fibers capable of withstanding temperatures of up to 2,600 degrees Fahrenheit.
- Very High Bond adhesives, which are so strong they are doing away with the need for mechanical fasteners in demanding assembly jobs.
- The first tooth-colored dental filling durable enough to be used instead of gold and silver in posterior teeth.
- A totally new material for extended-wear contact lenses that appears to offer greater durability, comfort and safety than any lens now available.
- A surgically implantable device that offers a sense of hearing to the profoundly deaf.
- A magnetic media technology that increases by about 20 times the storage capacity of floppy disks.
- An optical disk the size of an LP phonograph record that stores as much data as up to 20 rolls of computer tape.

Contributing to technical advances such as these is a strong commitment to basic, or long-range, research and product development.

Exemplifying that commitment is a pioneering venture with the National Aeronautics and Space Administration (NASA) in which 3M will play a leadership role in exploring space for potential new products and technologies.

Initial 3M efforts will focus on materials research, where the Company already has considerable expertise, with the aim of advancing the state of the art in such fields as computer memory storage, electronics, imaging and health care.

Manufacturing

In today's competitive business environment, it is not enough for a company just to have a strong flow of innovative products. These products also must be produced efficiently.

New concepts in manufacturing are helping 3M stay competitive and maintain above-average profitability through reduced costs.

Among these concepts: alternatives to costly petroleum-based solvents in the manufacturing process.

Today, innovative techniques which eliminate use of solvents in coatings are being used to produce a variety of pressure-sensitive tapes. These solvent-free processes not only are more economical to use, but are resulting in greater environmental safety and higher performance characteristics.

3M people also are working to reduce costs by applying leading-edge manufacturing technologies and systems. Examples include:

- In the fast-growing videocassette market, automated equipment helps control the manufacturing process from start to finish. Numerous complex operations are performed in seconds at a single work station, and electronic intelligence monitors every stage of the manufacturing process to insure the highest possible quality.
- In the production of polyester base film, which is used in 3M products ranging from computer tape to photographic film, a new automated production line is among the fastest and most efficient in the world. Process settings are microprocessor-controlled, and deviations during film manufacture are compensated for automatically.
- Computer-controlled equipment automates the production of parts used in surgical cutting and drilling tools. Previously, a dozen or more separate steps were required to produce finished parts. Now, thanks in large measure to automatic tool-changing capabilities, the process has been greatly streamlined, with just a few steps required.

More consistent quality and reduced inventory levels are among the ways newer manufacturing technologies are helping increase efficiency.

Combined with the efforts of employees and raw material suppliers, automated equipment helps reduce waste, rework and other errors, which can substantially increase product costs.

The cost of carrying inventory also is being reduced because, with newer technologies, products can be produced in smaller quantities as they are needed, rather than in extended production runs. This saves both on floor space and working capital.

Managing Our Technology Resources

Our technical strength continues to increase through a twofold commitment to technology:

- Longer term research and development objectives, aimed at new product and process development and new applications for, as well as improvements in, existing products.
- Shorter term metallurgical objectives, focused on coordinating service and technical assistance to ensure the uninterrupted conduct of our daily business.

A leading strategy of our technology commitment is the creative, but practical, application of new ideas and new processes to improve the performance of our own products and, in turn, the degree they can contribute to better performance of our customers' products. Most of our research and development effort involves **product** and/or **process** research and development.

Through Product R & D, we have developed:

- New and proprietary products.
- Improved metals that help our customers raise the quality and increase the service life of the products *they* manufacture.
- Specialty metals that enable our customers to lower their own fabricating cost through easier, faster production and reduced rejects—metals that perform consistently and dependably in customers' plants, shipment after shipment.
- Products that solve specific problems and meet exclusive needs of individual, high-volume customers.
- Improved materials that fill gaps in our product line for broad-based applications in many industries.

HP

Technological advances are driving the cost of electronic functions down—those that cost a dollar today will cost only 50 cents in 1986 if the trend of the past five years persists. Hewlett-Packard believes it will well into the 1990s. To remain competitive in this dynamic environment, HP is maintaining a strong research and development effort.

In 1983, the company spent $493 million on R&D, representing 10.5 percent of sales revenues. Engineering remains central to HP's business strategy because new products fuel the company's growth. In 1983, for example, more than two-thirds of incoming orders were for products introduced during the last four years.

Improving R&D productivity throughout the company is a priority. This is because the pressure for bringing new ideas to the marketplace has never been greater. At the same time, the strong trend toward systems in all HP's product groups has brought a burst of growth in software activities. All this puts a premium on making sure that the R&D job is done smoothly and integrated effectively.

During the year, HP began offering an in-depth seminar on R&D project management for its nearly 4,000 engineers and scientists involved in R&D activities. The course helps spread HP's best practices uniformly across the company. The company also emphasized designing more and better tools for R&D engineers, such as computer-aided design and computer-aided engineering programs. It established an Engineering Productivity Division to produce a stream of software products that will be useful inside HP as well as in the marketplace. Already introduced commercial products for HP 9000 series computers include an integrated-circuit simulation program, a two-dimensional mechanical drafting program and an engineering graph system for technical drawings.

More high-quality HP products that can be manufactured at low cost also is an R&D goal. It is achieved by working closely with manufacturing throughout the development process and by designing products that are as complete, yet as uncomplicated, as possible. New HP thermal printers and digital plotters represent progress toward this objective.

During 1983, HP also gave special attention, especially within the computer groups, to dramatically reducing the time required for designing new products. The result has been more than 15 major new product programs begun and completed within one year's time.

Office of Technology

As a part of its effort to build for the future, Varian has formed an Office of Technology, under the leadership of Executive Vice President Larry L. Hansen. The Office will provide general guidance to the operating units relating to research, engineering, manufacturing, and facilities. From its corporate vantage point, the Office will stimulate technical innovation and promote methods for achieving increased effectiveness through professional development, information exchange, and plant and equipment modernization.

To facilitate its mission, the Office of Technology will be responsible for a number of areas, including Central Research Laboratory, Engineering and Manufacturing staff functions, and the Facilities and Patent Departments.

In addition to its ongoing mission of doing forward-looking research in new product areas, the Central Research organization will be more closely coupled to the needs of the marketplace and will support operating divisions through direct technical effort, program reviews, and loans of technical personnel and other resources.

The Office of Technology also plans to include a mechanism for nurturing ventures when products developed in Central Research or elsewhere do not specifically fit into the existing division or group structure.

The Corporate Engineering and Manufacturing Department is planning a number of programs to improve efficiency, including consolidating some operations to serve several divisions rather than individual units. The consolidated operations will be extensively equipped with the latest automation technologies. Some of these programs have already begun, but some will take many years to implement. These investments in automation should result in significantly reduced manufacturing costs, as well as in improved quality.

Additional savings are possible through better material management. Several materials resource development teams have been created and are working throughout the Company to strengthen the production control and purchasing functions of individual divisions by providing training and assisting in problem identification and correction.

Additionally, the Corporate Engineering and Manufacturing department has evaluated the utility of computer-aided design and manufacturing (CAD/CAM) systems. By the end of fiscal 1983, six standardized systems of this type were installed in several units of the Company, and six additional systems are expected to be installed by the end of 1984.

By means of these and other planned steps, the Office of Technology gives Varian a broader base from which innovative ideas can be introduced to many parts of the Company. This effort allows the latest materials, techniques, and equipment to be made available for use companywide both to minimize unnecessary duplication and to realize maximum cost advantages. In the aggregate, the assistance provided by the Office of Technology will result in increased efficiency and a more optimal use of engineering resources leading to better quality at lower costs.

X
REPORTING SEGMENTS OF YOUR BUSINESS ENTERPRISE

Before preparing your divisional reports, it would be well for you to analyze Standard 14 issued by the Financial Accounting Standards Board (December, 1976) so that you become familiar with the reporting requirements for the various business segments of your company.

FAS #14 requires that "the financial statements of a business enterprise (hereinafter enterprise) include information about the enterprise's operations in different industries, its foreign operations and export sales, and its major customers. This statement also requires that an enterprise operating predominantly or exclusively in a single industry identify that industry."

As pointed out in FAS #14, "The purpose of the information required to be reported by this Statement is to assist financial statement users in analyzing and understanding the enterprise's financial statements by permitting better assessment of the enterprise's past performance and future prospects."

FAS proscribes the information required, determining reportable segments, and grouping products by: industry lines; information about foreign operations and export sales; information about major customers; etc. Review FAS #14 with your accountant as you prepare your corporation's annual report.

SIXTEEN ITEMS TO BE INCLUDED IN YOUR DIVISIONAL REPORTS

In preparing your divisional reports, you will want to consider including the following:

1. A description of the business of the division.
2. Domestic sales for the current year versus prior year.
3. Domestic operating earnings for current year versus prior year.
4. Percentages of increase or decrease.
5. Same information for foreign sales.
6. A chart showing domestic sales versus foreign sales for the year.
7. A chart showing domestic operating earnings versus foreign earnings for the current year.
8. A chart showing identifiable assets employed in the division versus total assets.
9. A chart showing various margins.
10. A discussion of problems of the division, and actions taken to correct the problems.
11. Expansion programs.
12. Marketing programs.
13. Staff.
14. Impact of inflation on the profits of the division.
15. Sales and earnings projections.
16. Outlook—where sales increases will come from.

You will get greater readership of your annual report if the Executive VP—a VP of operations—describes the work and financial results of the division. A picture of the executive at work helps to hold readership.

It will be easier for the reader of your annual report to understand the operations of your various divisions if you have subheadings, and provide answers to such questions as:

- What are your division's products?
- How significant is your market position?
- What edge do you have on competition?

- What has been your overall marketing strategy?
- What major markets do you serve?
- What are the industrial applications of your product?
- How would you characterize the technological requirements of your business?
- How does your company go about product development?
- Can your leadership be extended into other markets?

I suggest you start your divisional discussions with a brief and readily understandable presentation of the financial results.

Examples:

Building and Home Improvement Products

	5-Year Growth Rate	1982	1981	1980	1979	(In Thousands) 1978
Net Sales	12%	$322,210	$305,594	$303,672	$270,946	$225,491
Operating Profits	9%	$ 76,630	$ 70,588	$ 70,472	$ 65,613	$ 54,903
Net Income*	8%	$ 37,230	$ 32,729	$ 31,817	$ 30,501	$ 25,798

**It should be noted that in this and the following product sections, net income has been determined before extraordinary income but after allocating general and other corporate expense, net (including interest) on a basis proportional to the sales of the group. Thus, acquisitions may contribute to the income of a particular group but the related interest expense would be charged proportionally to each group.*

"For those involved in the housing industry, 1981 was a year for records—most, if not all of them, bad." This quote from last year's annual report unfortunately characterized 1982 as well. Housing activity, by any measure, continued at depressed levels not experienced in almost four decades; the industry recession has spanned four years, an unprecedented period.

The reasons for the housing construction collapse and the misfortunes of most companies involved with this market are well documented. Fortunately, activity in the Do-It-Yourself market was up slightly from the prior year.

Masco's building and home improvement products business, as it has for almost 30 years, achieved record sales and earnings despite the negative housing environment. Sales and operating profits increased, albeit modestly, before inclusion of any of our recent acquisitions. Increased faucet sales, many new product additions and market share increases offset the general industry decline and continued inventory cutting by the trade.

MASCO IN PERIODS OF HOUSING RECESSION

	1982 vs. 1981	1981 vs. 1980	1980 vs. 1979	1979 vs. 1978	1975 vs. 1973	1966 vs. 1965
Masco Faucet Sales (Domestic)	+ 2.0%	+ 7.0%	+ 2.1%	+ 9.7%	+27.6%	+13.3%
Masco Building Products Sales	+ 5.4%	+ .6%	+12.1%	+20.2%	+73.1%	+40.4%
Housing Starts	− 2.7%	−16.2%	−25.4%	−13.5%	−43.1%	−20.8%
Housing Completions	−20.9%	−15.8%	−19.7%	+ .3%	−37.3%	N/A

N/A—Not Available

OUTLOOK

The dramatic decline in both the rate of inflation and interest rates during 1982 certainly portends well for the housing industry. This favorable trend began during the latter part of 1982 and sets the stage for a meaningful housing recovery. It may be prudent to temper one's optimism, however, as significant unemployment, the continuing high cost of housing, and limited availability of financing may limit near-term recovery.

We expect housing starts, which averaged 1.4 million units during the 1960's and a record 1.8 million units in the 1970's, will average 1.5 million units during this decade. We anticipate starts of at least 1.4 million this year and 1.6 million in 1984 compared with approximately 1 million units in each of the last two years.

Masco's building products divisions as a group have continued to grow and prosper during the recent difficult period. With more favorable prospects for increased construction activity, we remain confident about our future, and, including our recent acquisitions, we forecast that sales will grow at an average annual rate of 21 percent over the next five years, reaching $835 million in 1987.

SALES GROWTH–BUILDING AND HOME IMPROVEMENT PRODUCTS

(In Thousands)

	Forecast		Actual		
	5-Year Growth Rate 83-87	1987	5-Year Growth Rate 78-82	1982	1977
Faucets	16%	$400,000	7%	$189,000	$133,000
Other	27%	435,000	20%	133,000	53,000
Total	21%	$835,000	12%	$322,000	$186,000

ELECTRONIC CONTROLS AND SYSTEMS

Sales

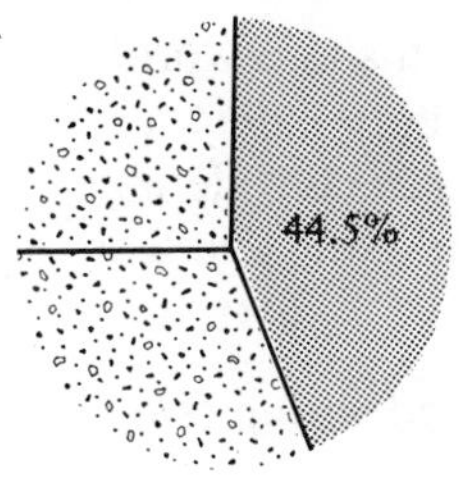

Pretax Earnings

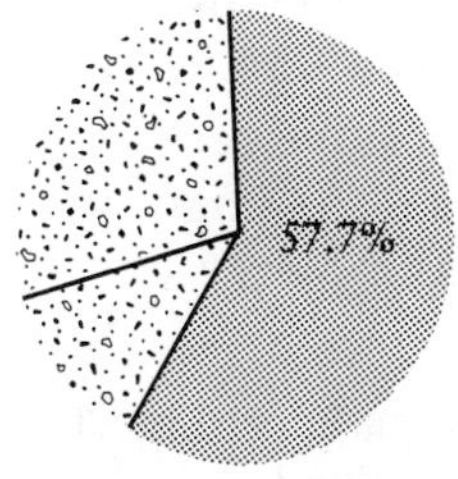

($ in millions)	1983	1982	1981	1980	1979	1978
Net sales	$701.3	$662.7	$643.9	$556.4	$483.2	$249.5
Earnings before taxes	89.3	87.9	78.2	74.0	56.8	28.2
Pretax margin	12.7%	13.3%	12.1%	13.3%	11.8%	11.3%
Capital expenditures	32.2	18.8	25.1	20.3	14.4	8.8
Assets	557.5	442.0	458.8	421.8	334.1	282.2

Sales of the electronic controls and systems sector were $701.3 million in 1983, up 5.8% from 1982's $662.7 million. Earnings before income taxes rose 1.7% to $89.3 million, from $87.9 million the year before.

Spurred by the rapid recovery of the electronics industry, sales and orders of semiconductor production equipment led the sector's growth. Demand was strongest for the equipment that allows semiconductor manufacturers to produce more advanced devices and improve their yield; but sales closely tied to capacity also showed very strong improvement over 1982.

During 1983 General Signal introduced a more advanced model of its 1:1 wafer stepper, with faster throughput and six-inch wafer processing capability. Six-inch wafers are coming into wider use among semiconductor manufacturers, both in the new facilities they are opening to meet rising demand and to improve the productivity of existing plants.

Four 1983 acquisitions advanced General Signal's strategy of offering equipment and systems that can raise semiconductor manufacturing efficiency or produce faster, smaller, and more complex devices.

Sales and orders of telecommunications test and measurement systems and instrumentation also grew rapidly in 1983. Test and monitoring equipment for optical fiber transmission showed the strongest rise, followed closely by instruments and systems for digital radio and telephone service remote monitoring and fault location. The restructuring of the U.S. communications industry is creating a larger number of customers for these products, customers whose success depends upon quality assurance and efficient operation.

The sector also achieved good growth in sales and orders for electronic controls, systems, and components for air and sea transportation, particularly for defense. Sales of rail signaling and centralized traffic control systems reached record levels in 1983, but orders failed to keep pace.

Sales of electronic instruments, controls, and systems to the process industries and electric utilities declined in 1983. Orders in this area also fell, particularly for energy management systems. The MAX-1® distributed control system, however, continued its outstanding performance.

Shipments of power conditioning equipment posted a good gain. The improvement came from sales for the protection of computers and other sensitive electronic equipment.

For 1984 this sector expects higher sales and an even stronger increase in earnings. U.S. manufacturers plan a 13% rise in overall capital spending, but many of this sector's markets should grow more rapidly. World sales of semiconductor capital equipment, for example, are expected to increase more than 35%; test and measurement systems and instruments sales for fiber optic and microwave radio telecommunications are expected to rise nearly 30% in 1984.

While electric utilities are projecting a lower level of total capital spending in 1984, spending for energy management and coal-fired generation, the areas of this market most important to General Signal, is expected to rise from 1983 levels.

The increase in capital spending has so far been concentrated on raising the productivity of existing plants. As the general business recovery progresses, industry will begin to purchase controls, instruments, and systems for new capacity, as well.

Industrial and Consumer Sector

(millions)	1983	1982
Sales	**$2,510**	$2,282
Operating Income	**574**	477

1983 was an excellent year as all major operating units in our sector achieved improved results. Double-digit unit volume gains were accompanied by strong increases in operating income.

Some of the larger increases, particularly in the second half of the year, came in product lines that had been most impacted by the U.S. recession. A number of operating divisions benefited from the rebound in the automotive, housing and consumer durable-goods markets.

Sector operating income rose 20 percent in 1983 on a 10 percent gain in worldwide sales. Increases in sales and earnings would have been even greater had it not been for the strength of the U.S. dollar.

In addition to the more favorable business environment in the U.S., each of our four product groups benefited from aggressive programs to help increase sales and control costs. Continued productivity improvements are helping us attain our goal of being the low-cost producer in major product areas.

We continue to build on our strengths as a worldwide supplier of a broad range of both industrial and consumer products, utilizing our considerable capabilities in manufacturing, marketing and technology development.

Many of our products have achieved strong brand recognition and market positions.

We made good progress during the year in implementing strategies for continued, profitable growth. These include:

- Development of unique, proprietary products for both industrial and consumer markets.
- Discovery of entirely new applications for our products. For example, customers increasingly are using our new-generation tapes instead of mechanical fasteners.
- Increased presence in overseas markets to meet global competitors on their home ground.
- A comprehensive sales effort, with strong 3M sales forces working in partnership with extensive and well-established independent distribution.
- A strong quality effort, focused on improving the quality of our products, as well as our ability to help customers improve their products.

New Products and Product Applications

New product contributions increased in 1983, and we expect an even greater contribution in 1984. Our research will continue to exploit our traditional coating, bonding, film and chemical technologies, as well as unique new technologies such as advanced ceramic materials.

Very High Bond (VHB) tapes and double-coated foam tapes made strong contributions in 1983. This technology, as well as our ceramic technology, shows long-range potential in a number of additional product applications. Our Interam mat mount for catalytic converters also showed excellent growth in 1983.

Post-it Notes and extensions of the Post-it adhesive technology again showed outstanding growth in commercial markets, both in the U.S. and abroad. Further extensions of the Post-it line of repositionable notes are planned for 1984, including custom-printed note forms as well as a market test in selected cities of Post-it Notes for home use.

The Regal abrasives line, using our ceramic technology, and microabrasives for fine finishing and polishing of components requiring critical tolerances, recorded good gains.

Our new fluorochemical treatment, which provides soil and stain resistance to carpet fibers before the finished carpet is made, has been gaining rapid acceptance in the industry.

In addition to traditional packaging markets, we also are addressing a number of primary packaging applications, such as tamper-evident packaging. We also are continuing to shift our adhesives emphasis to specialized, high-technology applications, and we are working on ways in which our products can be applied by robotic manufacturing systems.

We expanded our European technology center, designed to aid faster introduction of new products and product applications.

Sales and Marketing

Several sales and marketing developments, both in the U.S. and abroad, will help us achieve our long-term objectives. These developments include:

- Formation of a consumer strategic business center to improve the planning of consumer businesses located within all four 3M business sectors. This will help insure more efficient operations in meeting 3M's opportunities for growth in consumer markets.
- Establishment of new marketing organizations in the Consumer Products Group to serve important user markets.
- New programs to give added support to our sales effort. A new, comprehensive sales and marketing information system in one group helps provide our sales force with more accurate and timely information, such as account identification and help in sales planning.
- Sales of data recording and visual products by our office sales force, which produced strong gains in 1983.

Sales Performance

Many important product lines, in addition to those previously mentioned, experienced good demand in 1983. These include:

- Decorative films and other products, including double-coated foam tapes, for automotive applications worldwide.
- Roofing granules for both new construction and reroofing jobs.
- Products for the retail do-it-yourself markets, led by strong sales of window insulation kits and other retail energy products.
- Glass bubbles, computer-imprintable label stocks, hot melt adhesive systems and box sealing tapes.
- Scotchgard protectors for apparel and upholstery applications, and new high-performance, rubber-like fluoroelastomers with exceptional temperature and chemical resistance for demanding automotive and industrial uses.

We have the worldwide manufacturing, marketing and research strengths to enable us to continue our profitable growth record. ■

Review of Operations

New Lines of Business	During the 1983 fiscal year Consolidated Foods adopted a new format for reporting the results of our several lines of business. This format, used throughout this report, provides a meaningful description of the nature of our business and illustrates our "core business" philosophy. Simply stated, that philosophy is that our corporation will be structured around a few "core" businesses, all leaders in their respective markets and each significant to our overall corporate performance. Our five lines of business and the operating units included in each are detailed below.	
Consumer Foods	The products of the Consumer Foods segment include baked goods, fresh and processed meats, fruits and vegetables and other packaged food items marketed under many leading brand names.	Bloch & Guggenheimer, Bryan Foods, Chef Pierre, Gallo Salame, Hi-Brand Foods, Hillshire Farm, Hollywood Brands, Idaho Frozen Foods, Jonker Fris, Kahn's, Kitchens of Sara Lee, Lauderdale Farm, Popsicle, Rudy's Farm, Smoky Hollow Foods, Standard Meat, Union Sugar
Foodservice Distribution	In the Foodservice Distribution business, we distribute fresh, frozen and packaged foods and many non-food items to establishments which serve food for consumption away from home.	Booth Fisheries, PYA/Monarch
Beverages	The Beverages segment markets coffee, tea, other beverages and tobacco products, primarily in Europe, and carbonated soft drinks and fruit drinks in the United States.	Douwe Egberts, Shasta Beverages, Superior Coffee
Consumer Personal Products	The Consumer Personal Products segment manufactures and markets hosiery, intimate apparel, knitwear and other non-food consumer products.	Aris-Isotoner, Bali, Canadelle, Direct Marketing Division, Hanes Hosiery, Hanes Knitwear, Hanes Printables, Intradal, Lardenois, L'eggs Products, Sav-A-Stop/Hanes DSD, Sirena
Consumer Direct Sales	In Consumer Direct Sales, we sell a variety of products and services directly to end users. Customers are reached through sales in their homes, through retail convenience stores and through restaurants.	Electrolux, Fuller Brush, Lawsons, Lyon's Restaurants

Sherwin-Williams at a glance by segment

		Principal Products	Major Markets
Paint Stores	Stores Division	Sherwin-Williams labeled architectural coatings and industrial finishes, wallcoverings, floor coverings, window treatments, paint sundries, spray equipment.	Professional users (including painters, contractors, industrial maintenance and commercial accounts), do-it-yourself consumers, small to medium sized manufacturers of products requiring factory finish.
Drug Stores	Gray Drug Fair	Prescriptions, health and beauty aids, cosmetics, general merchandise.	General public.
Coatings	Consumer Division	Architectural finishes (under the Sherwin-Williams, Dutch Boy, Martin-Senour, Kem-Tone, Baltimore, Lucas Group and private brand labels), special purpose coatings, custom packaging of aerosol products, brushes, rollers, adhesives, labels, color cards.	Do-it-yourselfers, industrial and commercial maintenance accounts, painting contractors.
	Automotive Aftermarket Division	Automotive refinish products under Sherwin-Williams, Martin-Senour, Acme, Rogers, Aclose (factory-packed colors for Japanese cars).	Automotive body shops, fleets, body builders.
	Chemical Coatings Division	Sherwin-Williams labeled industrial finishes for original equipment manufacturers.	Business machines, general products, forest products, transportation equipment, coil products, metal furniture, farm and off-road equipment.
Chemicals	Chemicals Division	Organic intermediates, saccharin, antioxidants and corrosion inhibitors.	Plastics, rubber, food, pharmaceuticals and agricultural chemicals.
International	International Group *Sherwin-Williams Canada* *Sherwin-Williams Mexico** *Sherwin-Williams Caribbean* *Sherwin-Williams Brazil** **(unconsolidated)*	Architectural coatings, industrial and automotive repaint finishes, paint sundries and a variety of home decorative items.	Independent paint dealers, painting contractors, automotive body shops, commercial and industrial maintenance accounts, original equipment manufacturers and do-it-yourselfers.

XI
HOW TO PRESENT CHARTS AND GRAPHS

The readers of your annual report can get a better picture of your financial reports through well-designed charts. There are numerous charts that are being used by corporations, such as:

- Annual Sales
- Average Invested Capital and Return
- Average Number of Employees
- Backlog
- Book Value per Common Share
- Capital Expenditures
- Capital Requirements and Sources of Funds
- Cash Dividends
- Compound Annual Growth
- Consolidated Capitalization Ratios
- Disposition of Sales Dollar
- Dividends per Share
- Flow of Funds
- Geographical Distribution of International Orders
- Incoming Orders
- Market Diversification and Growth
- Net Fixed Investment per Employee
- Net Income
- Net Sales
- Operating Trends
- Pre-tax Earnings
- Property, Plant, Equipment
- Research and Development Investment
- Return on Average Net Worth
- Return on Average Total Assets
- Return on Net Assets Employed
- Revenues
- Sales and Income by Business Lines
- Sales/Assets/Earnings per Employee
- Shareholders' Equity
- Shareholders/Investment per Common Share Outstanding at Year End
- Shipments/Bookings
- Total Assets
- Total Debt versus Capitalization
- 25-yr Dividend Record
- Working Capital (at year end)
- Worldwide Employment

A word of caution: Oftentimes, the artist will create charts that are colorful and interesting to look at from a design standpoint, but are almost impossible to understand. I suggest you make the charts easy to read rather than complicated and difficult to understand—even though in the latter case, they may prove that you have a talented artist working on your charts. The best advice I can give in the preparation of charts is, "Keep it simple," even though your artist may want to dress up your annual report with colorful and complicated charts.

Financial Review

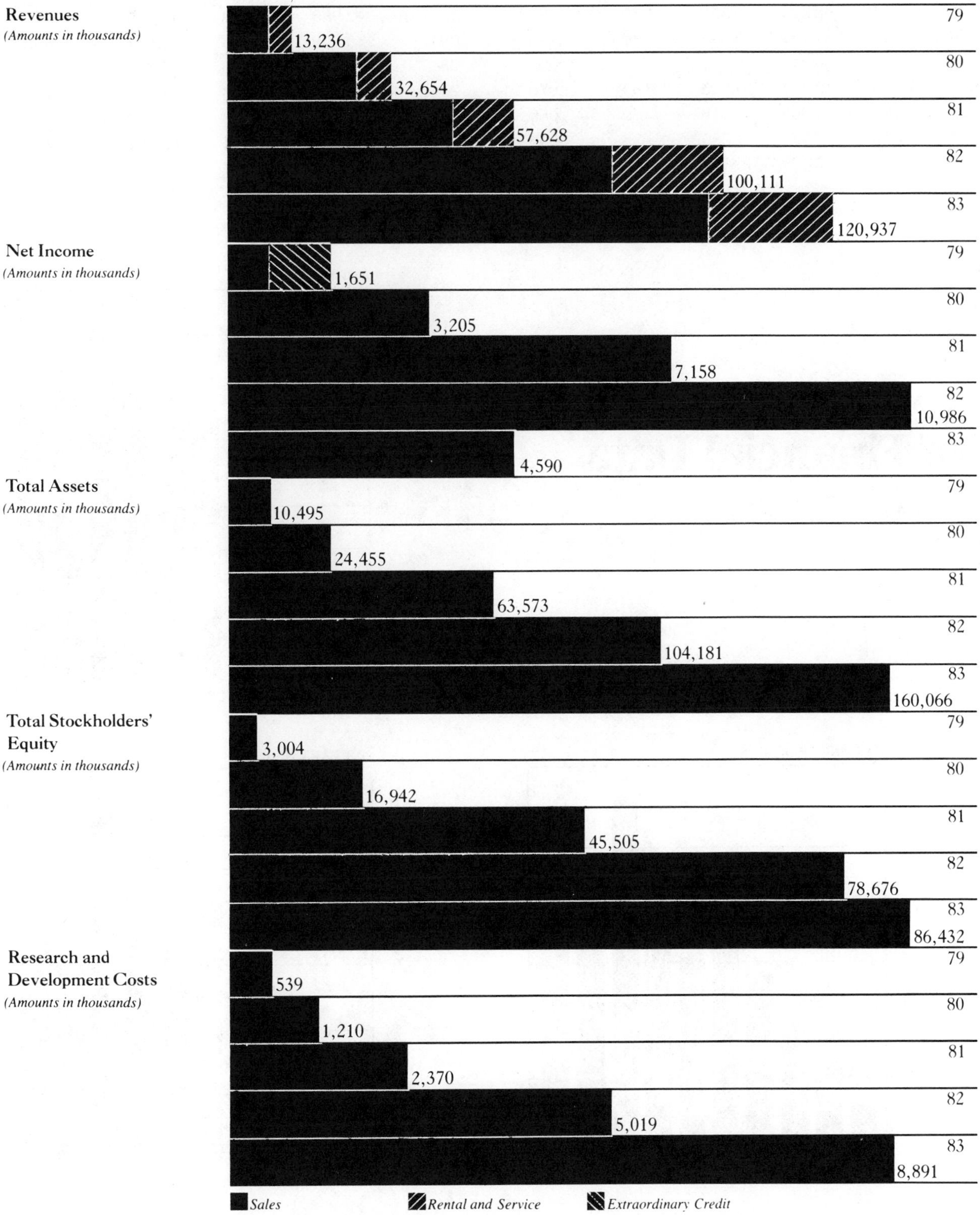

Revenues
(Amounts in thousands)

79 13,236
80 32,654
81 57,628
82 100,111
83 120,937

Net Income
(Amounts in thousands)

79 1,651
80 3,205
81 7,158
82 10,986
83 4,590

Total Assets
(Amounts in thousands)

79 10,495
80 24,455
81 63,573
82 104,181
83 160,066

Total Stockholders' Equity
(Amounts in thousands)

79 3,004
80 16,942
81 45,505
82 78,676
83 86,432

Research and Development Costs
(Amounts in thousands)

79 539
80 1,210
81 2,370
82 5,019
83 8,891

Sales *Rental and Service* *Extraordinary Credit*

In thousands, except percents and per share data	NET SALES	COST OF GOODS SOLD	NET EARNINGS	PER SHARE DATA NET EARNINGS	DIVIDENDS	PERCENT RETURN ON AVERAGE EQUITY	STOCK-HOLDERS' EQUITY	TOTAL ASSETS	LONG-TERM OBLIGATIONS	WORKING CAPITAL
1983	$148,661	$107,209	$ 7,765	$1.20	$.320	10%	$77,364	$114,742	$11,805	$54,885
1982	150,031	108,373	8,518	1.33	.320	13%	70,844	106,065	12,610	53,639
1981	160,162	110,556	11,733	1.84	.290	20%	63,470	102,276	13,497	52,217
1980	146,454	102,286	9,409	1.50	.240	20%	52,448	81,973	10,318	43,733
1979	140,018	98,304	9,331	1.50	.193	24%	42,985	74,112	11,210	36,310
1978	120,105	81,251	8,642	1.40	.140	29%	33,929	60,466	7,427	28,462
1977	94,277	66,149	5,741	.95	.093	25%	25,582	48,466	6,106	20,983
1976	70,832	49,405	4,043	.69	.070	24%	20,258	36,348	4,458	17,769
1975	56,081	41,095	2,418	.50	.050	21%	12,951	27,628	4,688	11,854
1974	51,123	39,651	1,285	.26	.033	13%	10,632	25,214	5,041	9,826
COMPOUND ANNUAL GROWTH RATE—										
10 Yr.	14%		16%	12%	26%					

Ten Year Summary of Financial Data

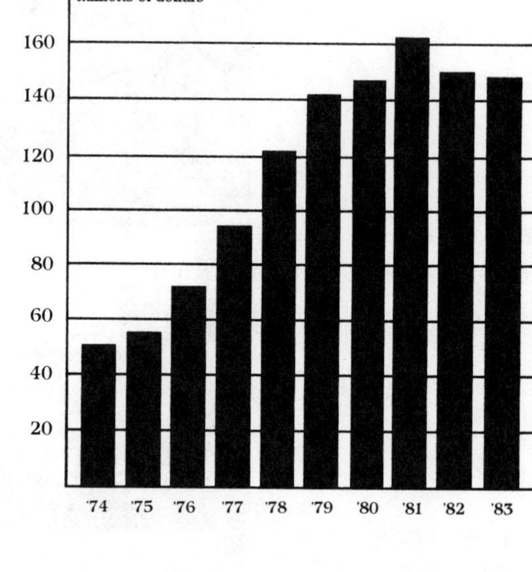

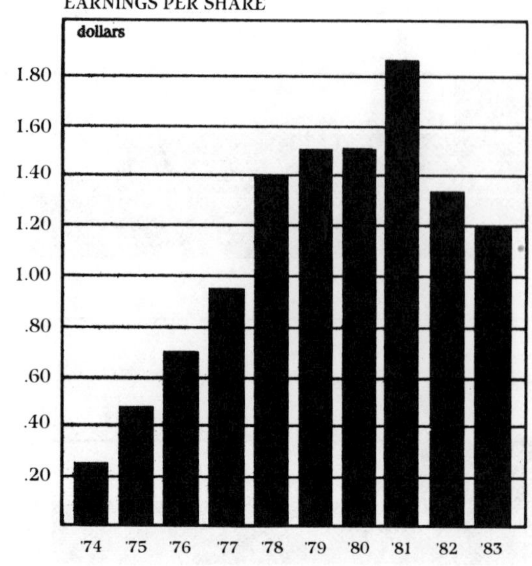

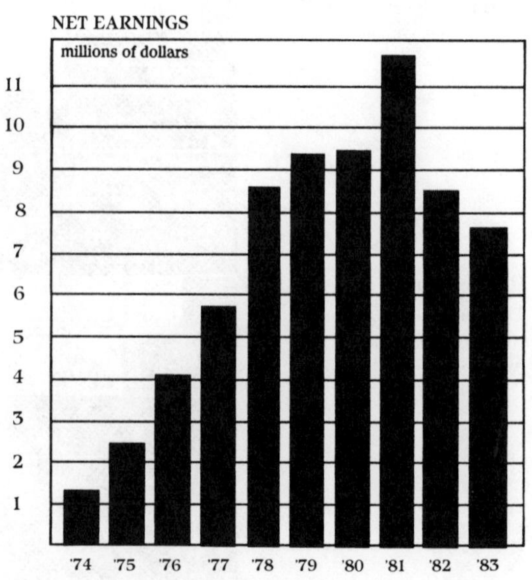

ADDITIONS TO PROPERTY, PLANT & EQUIPMENT*

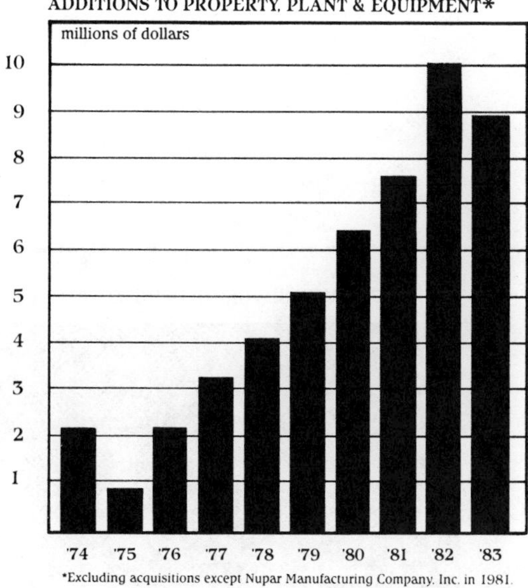

*Excluding acquisitions except Nupar Manufacturing Company, Inc. in 1981.

TOTAL ASSETS

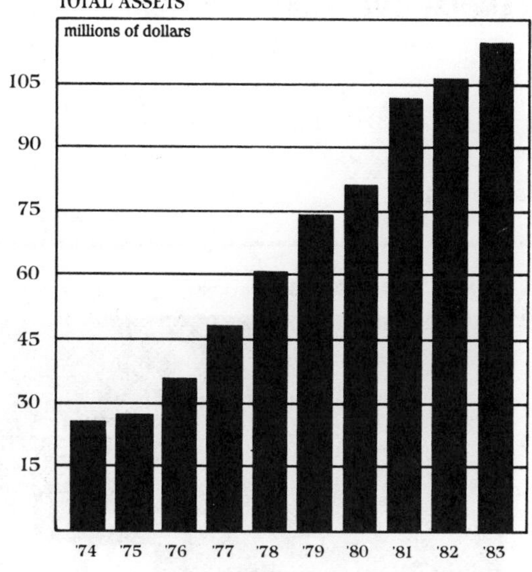

STOCKHOLDERS' EQUITY

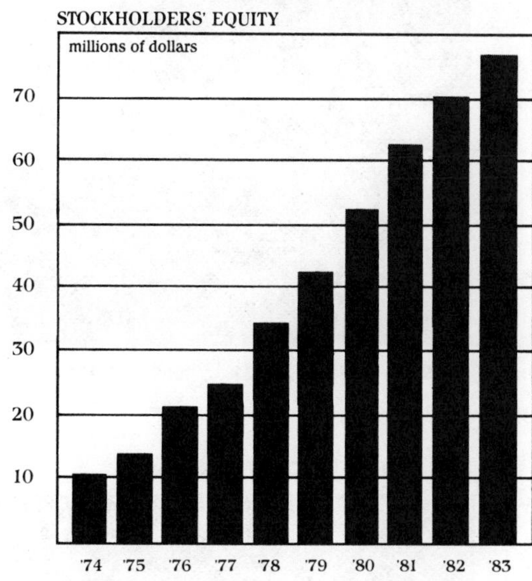

RETURN ON AVERAGE EQUITY

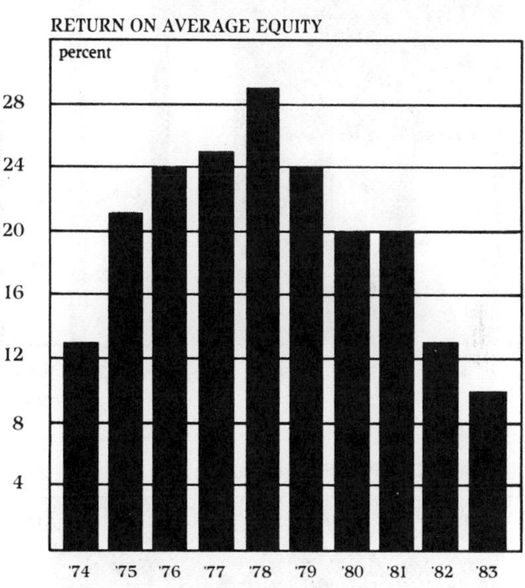

WORKING CAPITAL

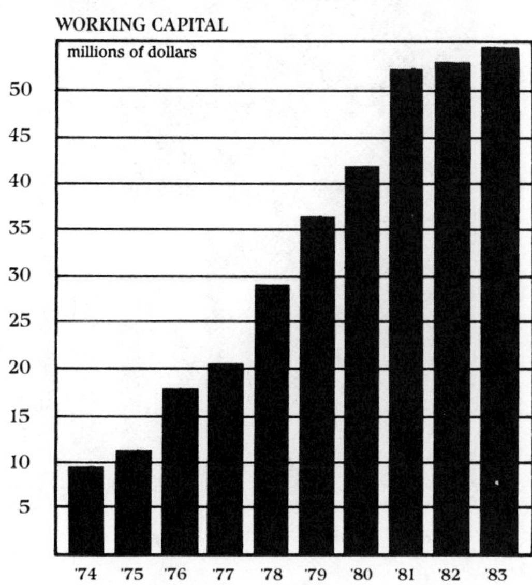

RESEARCH & DEVELOPMENT

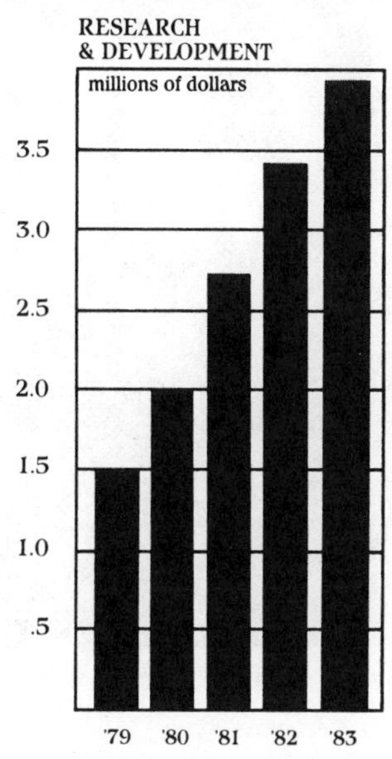

FINANCIAL OVERVIEW (1979-83)

Balance Sheets

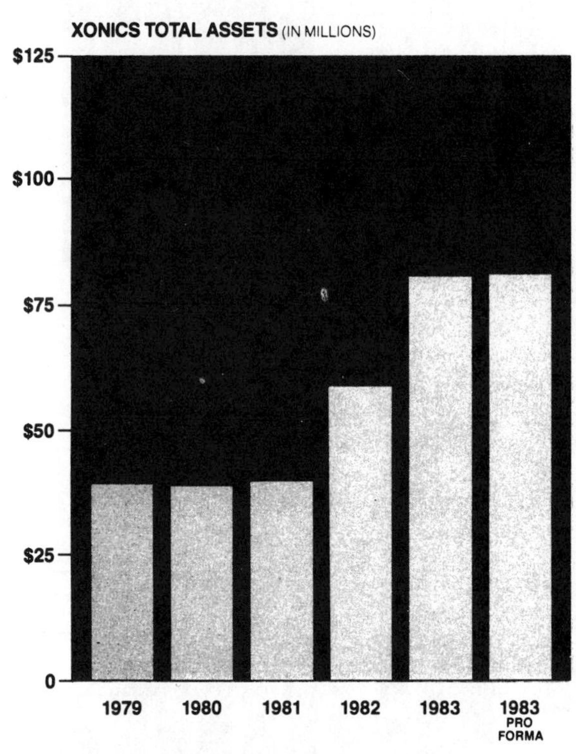

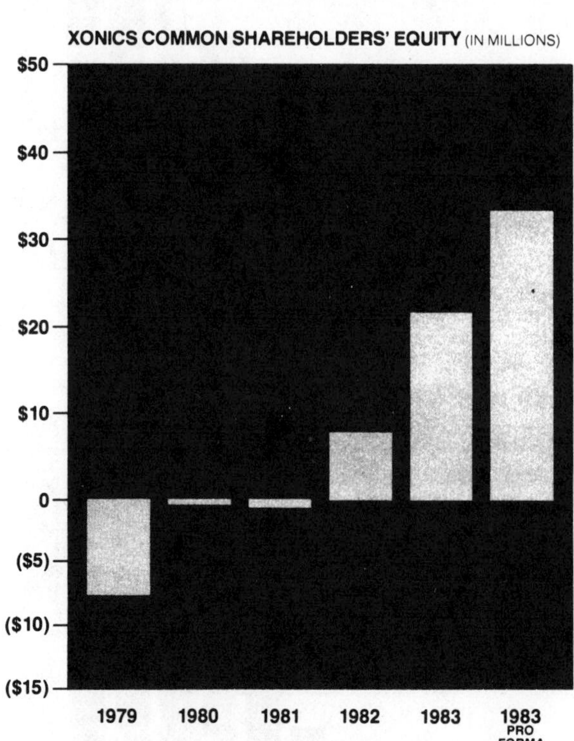

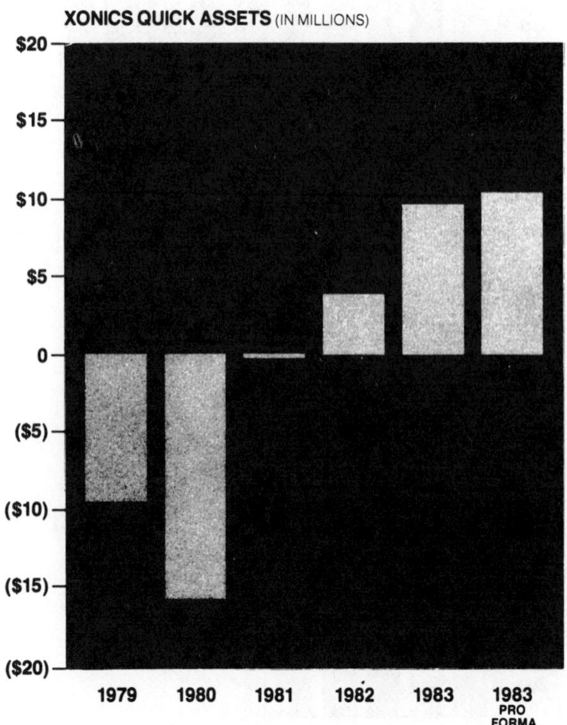

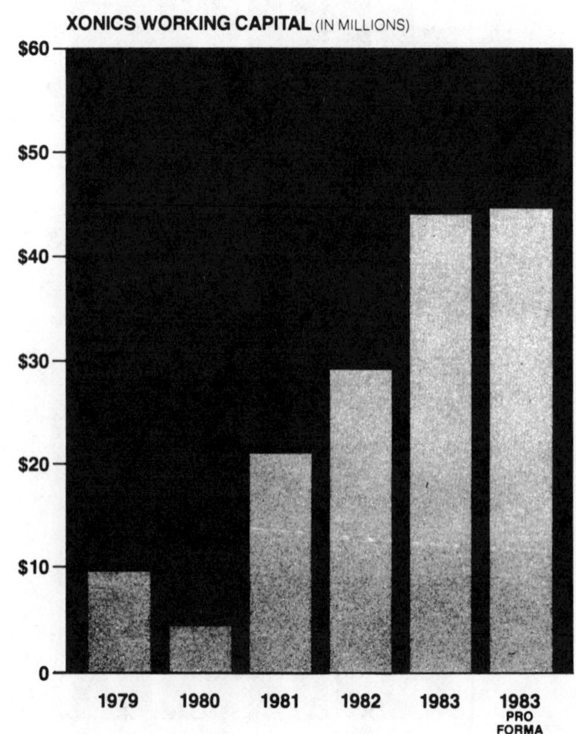

Statements of Operations

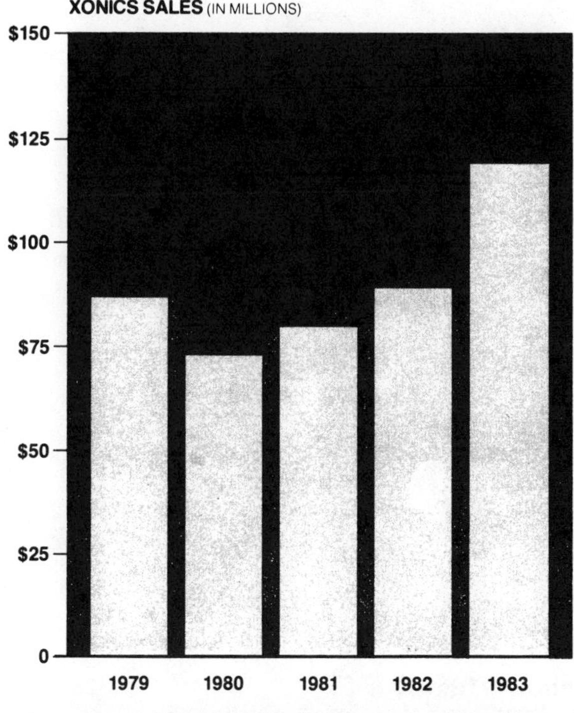

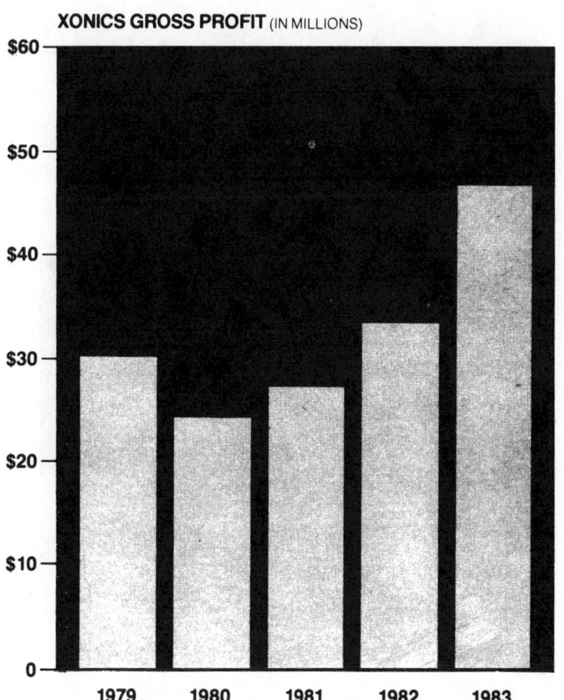

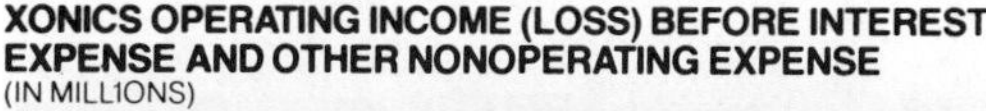

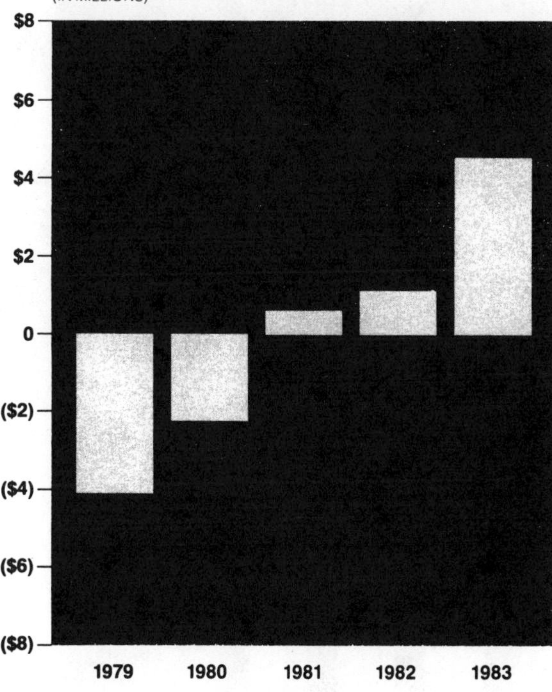

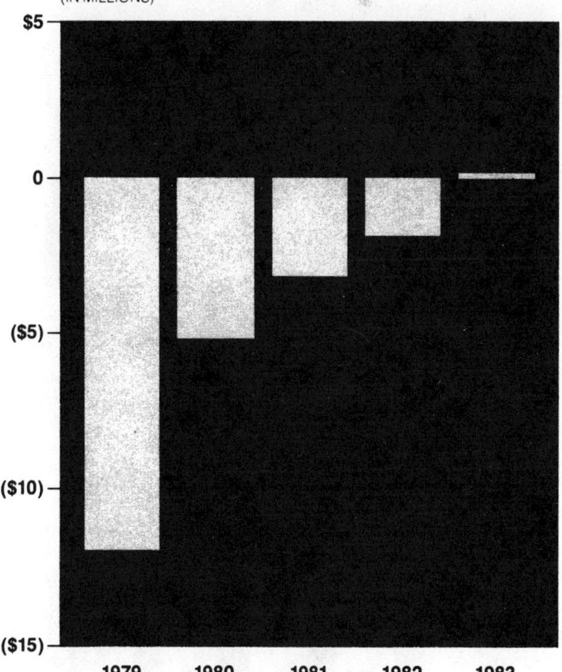

Five Year Corporate Operating and Financial Performance

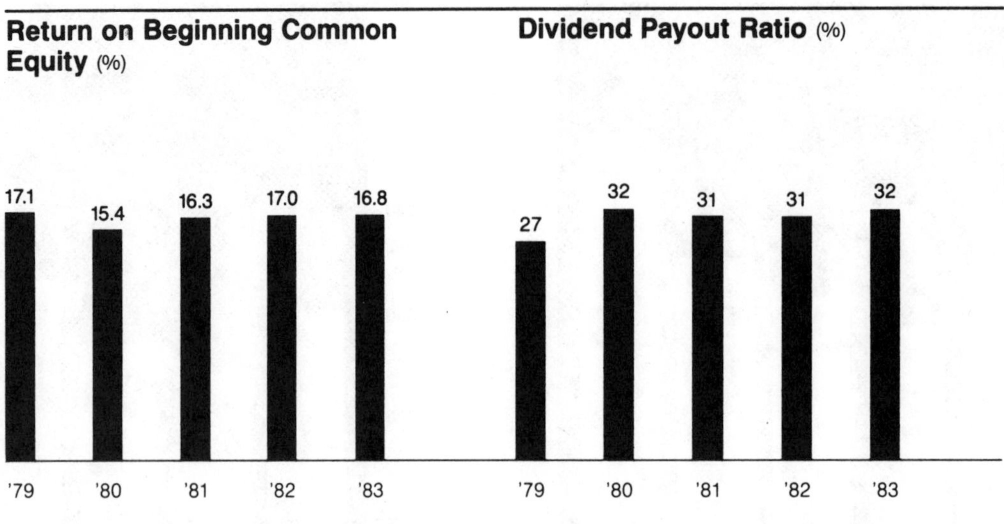

Debt-to-Total Capitalization (%)

Accounts Receivable Turnover ■
(Times/Year)

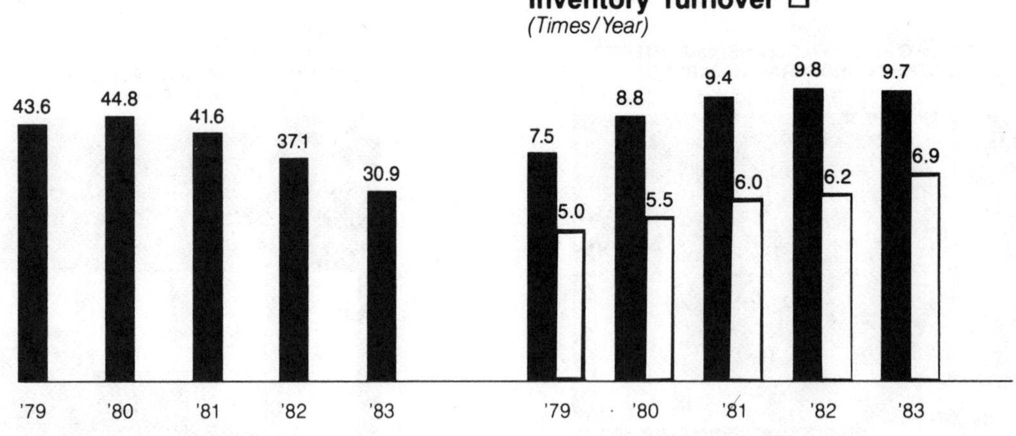

Return on Invested Capital (%)

Pretax, Preinterest Margin (%)

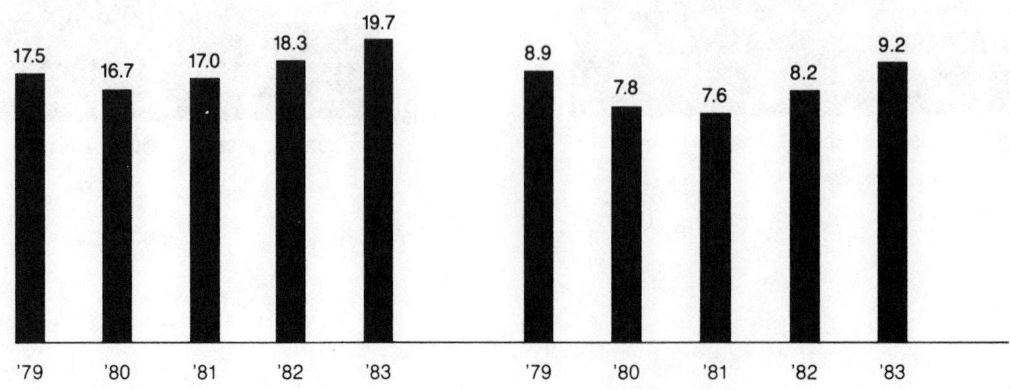

Ten Year Financial Performance

Return on Investment
($ in millions)

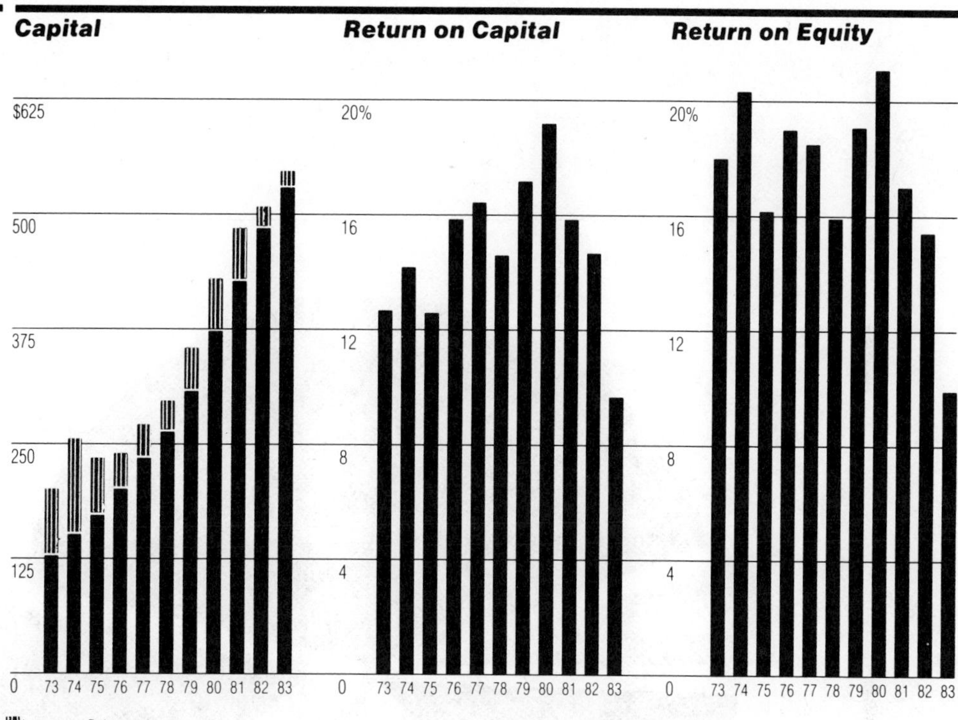

Capital

The total assets less the current liabilities is the Company's capital, represented by funds borrowed on a long-term basis plus the shareholders' equity.

During the last ten years, Avnet's shareholders' equity has grown $400 million, but long-term debt has decreased $54 million. The increase in capital of $346 million was required primarily to support the Company's sales growth.

Return on Capital

The after-tax amount earned (before interest on long-term debt) in relation to the average capital employed is the Company's "return on capital."

In a very depressed economy during 1983, the Company was still able to achieve a return on capital of 9.7%, after taxes. During the last ten years, the return on capital has averaged 15%, after taxes, well above the average for major U.S. companies.

Return on Equity

The after-tax amount earned by the Company in relation to the average shareholders' equity is the Company's "return on equity."

Like its return on capital, the Company's return on equity in 1983 of about 10%, after taxes, was achieved in a depressed economy. During the last ten years, the return on equity has averaged 17%, after taxes, well above the average for major U.S. companies.

THE SOURCES OF YOUR COMPANY'S SALES

A pie chart divided into various business segments will give the reader of your annual report a quick overall view that oftentimes makes a greater impression than a listing of figures by division. A good example of this is the following:

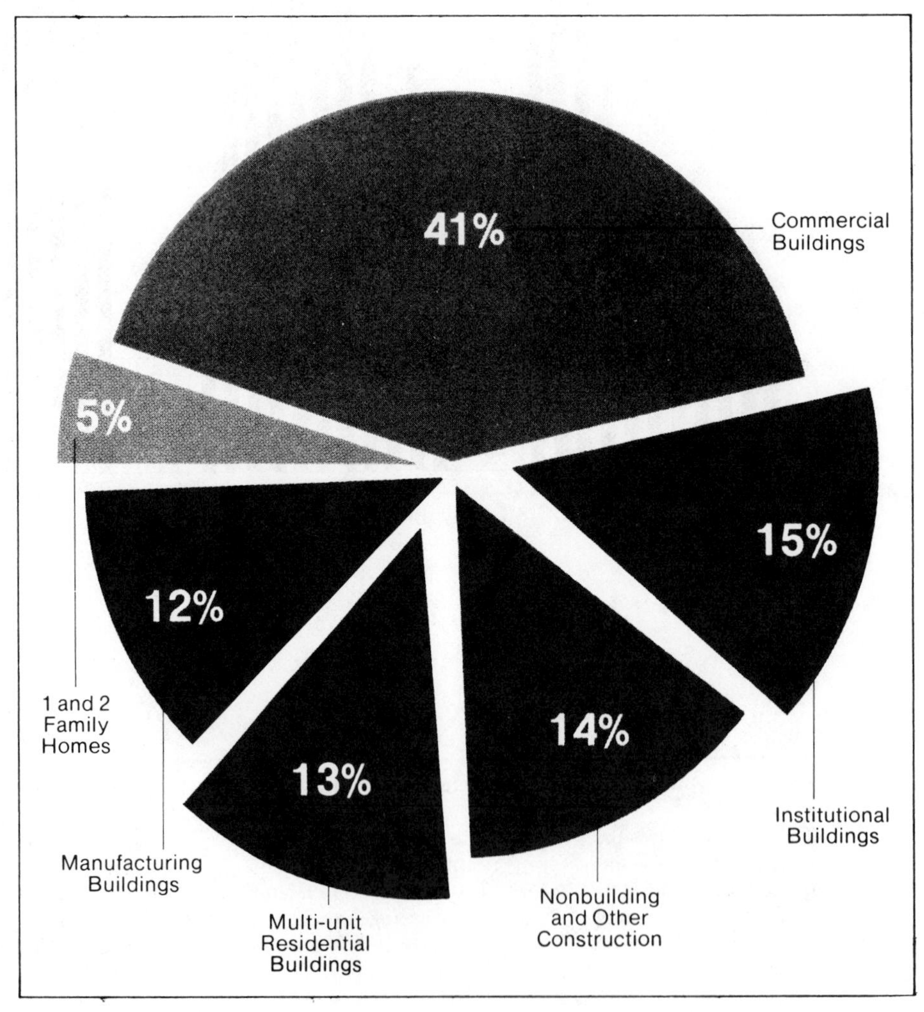

Pie Chart Showing Analysis of Operating Revenues

Molex

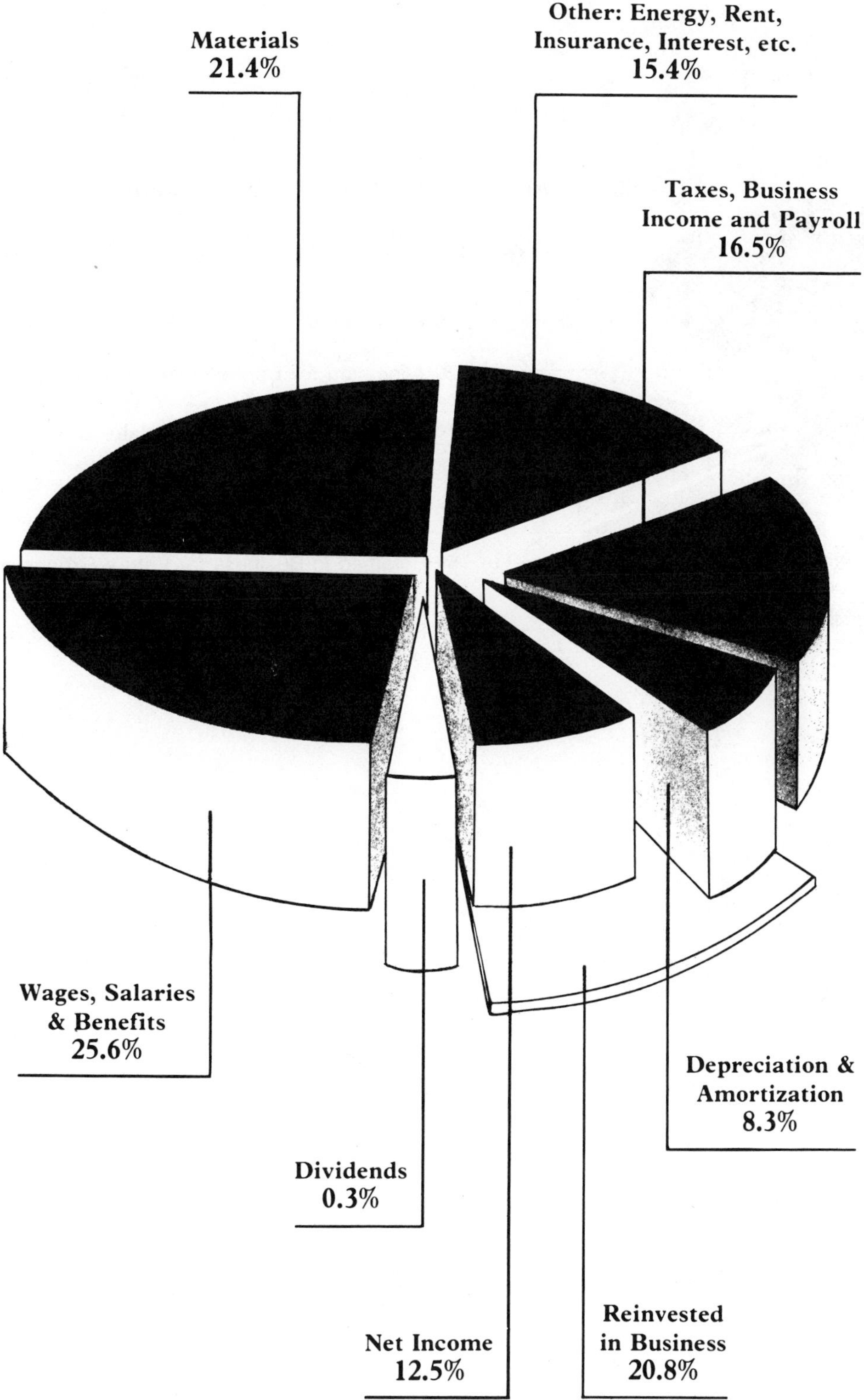

Molex Incorporated (Consolidated) Analysis of Operating Revenues for the Fiscal Year Ended June 30, 1982.

Carpenter

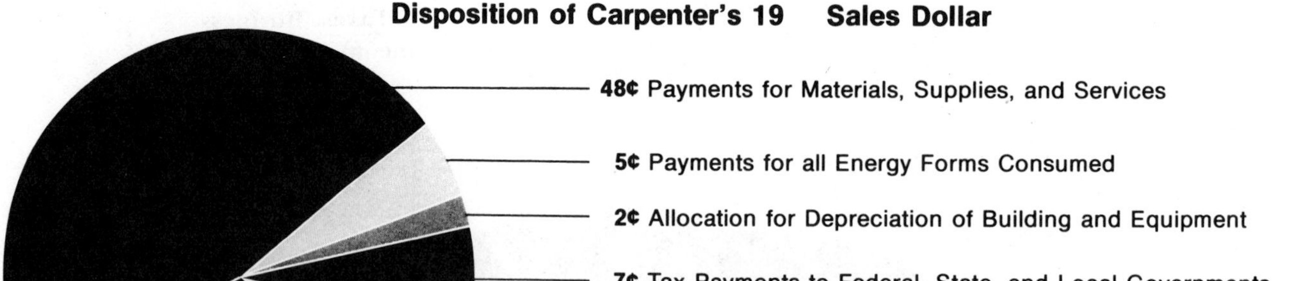
Disposition of Carpenter's 19 Sales Dollar
48¢ Payments for Materials, Supplies, and Services
5¢ Payments for all Energy Forms Consumed
2¢ Allocation for Depreciation of Building and Equipment
7¢ Tax Payments to Federal, State, and Local Governments
3¢ Dividend Payments to Shareholders
5¢ Retained in Business for Future Expansion
Net Income
30¢ Payments to Employees for Wages and Benefits

FINANCIAL SECTION

INTRODUCTION

We come now to the section where the information to be published will be provided by the CPA. Strict reporting rules must be followed. This does not preclude clarity and ease of understanding. Try to make this section interesting as well as informative to the readers of your report.

XII
TABLE OF CONTENTS

You will want to provide a Table of Contents for the financial section of your report. There is no particular order for the best presentation of the information to be contained in this section. My preference is:

1. Financial Review
2. Management's Responsibility for Financial Controls
3. Auditors' Report
4. Financial Statements
5. Notes to Consolidated Financial Statements
6. Supplementary Financial Information

Examples

Financial Statements

Table of Contents

L O C K H E E D   C O R P O R A T I O N

Consolidated Financial Information

Contents

XIII
MANAGEMENT'S DISCUSSION AND ANALYSIS OF FINANCIAL CONDITIONS AND RESULTS OF OPERATIONS

This section is generally divided into two sections:

1. Financial Position of the Company
2. Results of Operations

The Chief Financial officer in many corporations describes, in depth, the financial condition of the company.

The Financial Review section is of particular importance to security analysts, bankers, and vendors who extend credit to your company. Consider describing the following in this section of your report.

Borrowings
Capital expenditures
Convertible debentures
Days sales outstanding to accounts receivable
Debt reduction
Dividends
External financing
Generation of funds from operations
Industrial revenue bonds
Internal funds
Leverage
Mortgage financing
New facility
Public offerings
Ratio of Current Assets to Current Liabilities
Receivables
Redemption of securities
Revolving credit
Sales and lease back
Working capital

It will be helpful to the readers of your annual report if you include complete statements in subheadings.

Examples:

- Consolidated net sales for 19__ increased 18 percent over 19__.
- Dollar incoming orders declined 6 percent during 19__ levels, which had increased 37 percent from 19__ levels.
- Cost of goods sold as a percentage of sales remained at approximately 71 percent during 19__ and 19__ which was improved from 72 percent during 19__.
- Selling, general, and administrative expenses were approximately 17 percent of net sales during 19__, an improvement from approximately 18 percent during 19__ and 19__.
- Interest expense increased $768,000 (21 percent) during 19__ over 19__.
- Other income decreased $1,003,000 during 19__ as compared to 19__.
- Taxes on income in 19__, 19__ and 19__ have been provided at rates of 32.9 percent, 32.1 percent, and 29.4 percent, respectively.
- Net income for 19__ was $14,505,000 ($4.81 per share: $4.46 fully diluted) as compared with $12,688,000 ($4.55 per share: $4.13 fully diluted) for 19__, an increase of 14 percent.
- Net funds required in the business and for dividends were $34,142,000 in excess of $21,509,000 funds generated from operations in 19__, as compared with $18,800,000 in 19__.

- Brown and Sharpe had 4,373 employees worldwide at year-end 19__, about the same as year-end 19__, and up from 3,713 at year-end 19__.
- On October 24, 19__, an annuity for payment of retirement benefits to 882 retirees or their beneficiaries was purchased by the company's retirement trust.
- Our 19__ business plan assumes orders will improve from their current levels, and envisions higher dollar shipments than in 19__, but slightly lower physical volumes.

Management's Discussion and Analysis

1983 and 1982

Revenue from continuing operations increased 6.3% from $26,007,000 in 1982 to $27,635,000 in 1983. Major Systems Sales, Major Systems Rentals and Field Service revenues all increased, with only the miscellaneous parts and equipment category declining. This miscellaneous category declined due to the nonrecurrence of a large GRAFIX I system upgrade which impacted 1982, together with lower revenues from miscellaneous product lines. Major Systems Sales showed the strongest growth, up 32.8% from $7,990,000 in 1982 to $10,611,000 in 1983.

Gross profit margin from continuing operations improved from 53.0% in 1982 to 53.5% in 1983. This was due to small positive changes in revenue mix and improvement of the price/cost relationship within the miscellaneous category. The combined impact of the increase in revenue, together with the gross margin improvement, was a 7.3% growth in total gross profit dollars from continuing operations. Gross profit generated in 1983 was $14,777,000, up from $13,774,000 in 1982.

Operating expenses in support of continuing operations were up only 2.5%, increasing from $11,075,000 in 1982 to $11,353,000 in 1983 due to overall tighter spending controls. Marketing expenditures increased only 2.0% from $3,531,000 in 1982 to $3,603,000 in 1983. This increase reflected higher trade show expenditures. General and Administrative expenses decreased 6.7% from $3,058,000 in 1982 to $2,854,000 in 1983. This was primarily due to decreased profit-sharing expense in addition to lower manpower levels. Customer Support expenses increased only 3.5% from $2,053,000 in 1982 to $2,125,000 in 1983, in line with management's goal of maintaining strength in this key area. Research and Development expenses were up 13.9%, from $2,433,000 in 1982 to $2,770,000 in 1983. Much of this increase is attributable to the lower level of customer-funded R & D projects in 1983, together with additional spending in 1983 in support of future newspaper system programs. In summary, total operating expenses declined as a percent of total revenues from continuing operations—42.6% in 1982 to 41.1% in 1983.

Income from operations increased by 26.8% due to the combined effects of revenue growth, gross margin improvement and tight controls over operating expenses. Income from operations reached $3,423,000 in 1983, up from $2,699,000 in 1982.

Working capital increased by $3,327,000 or 35.8% from $9,300,000 at year-end 1982 to $12,627,000 at year-end 1983. This was primarily the result of the working capital generated by operations, together with the continued tight control over capital expenditures. The Company did not have to use its line of credit in 1983 due to its strong working capital position.

Total shareholders' equity increased by $1,987,000 from $20,003,000 at year-end 1982 to $21,990,000 at year-end 1983. Shareholders' equity per share increased from $7.96 per share to $8.43 per share.

Discontinued operations. During the third quarter of 1983, the Company discontinued its digital scene simulation activities. Computer-simulated animation has, since its inception, accounted for less than 5% of the Company's total revenues. This action was taken to allow the Company to devote its full efforts and resources to prepress publication systems.

The Company established a pretax reserve of $1,639,400 for the estimated loss on the disposition of the related equipment. The net impact on after-tax fiscal 1983 earnings was a loss of $990,700 or $.38 per share.

The income or loss associated with the discontinued activities have been shown separately for each period covered by the Consolidated Statements of Income and the Five-Year Financial History. For 1983, the profit from discontinued operations was $218,800, attributable to the revenue recognition for the special effects project associated with the motion picture "TRON."

Analysis of Financial Condition

Carpenter's historically strong, positive cash flow from operations continued through the business downturn of the past two years. Here is a summary of our cash flows and financing requirements for the past three fiscal years:

(dollars in thousands)	Years Ended June 30 1983	1982	1981
Cash from Operations	$ 51,898	$42,849	$75,771
Used for Investments	(66,778)	(64,906)	(31,992)
Dividends Paid	(18,130)	(18,084)	(17,195)
Financing Requirements	12,517	49,093	(14,747)
Increase/(Decrease) in Cash	$(20,493)	$ 8,952	$11,837

( ) indicate cash decrease.

The financing in the past two years was necessary to supplement our internally generated funds in order to finance record levels of capital investment. The discussion and analyses in this section highlight the sources and uses of cash over the past two years. In addition, we provide management's assessment of the Company's liquidity position and availability of capital.

Cash Provided from Operations

Cash provided from operations—net income plus noncash charges and changes in working capital—continued to provide strong cash inflows to meet most of our needs over the past three years.

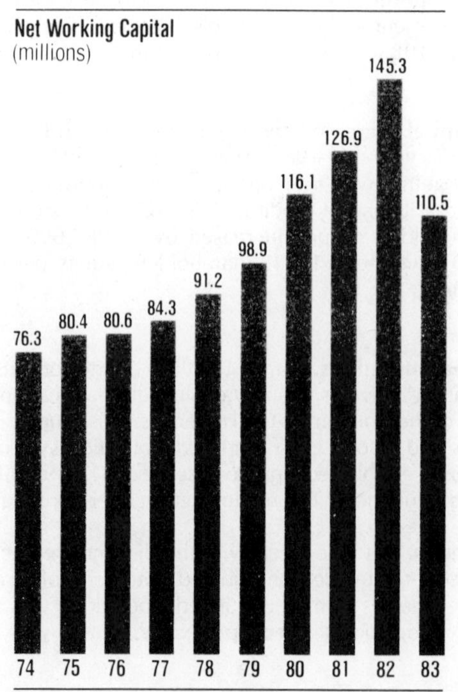

The net cash provided from operations in fiscal 1983 was $51.9 million compared to $42.8 million in fiscal 1982 and $75.8 million in fiscal 1981. The higher level of cash provided in fiscal 1981 resulted primarily from a significant reduction in working capital.

Effective management of working capital is an integral part of managing our cash position. Accounts receivable levels have fluctuated in proportion to changes in sales levels. We actively monitor these accounts in order to minimize loss exposures and to assure timely collections. This control has been particularly important over the past two years of high interest rates, economic downturn, and severe competition.

Inventories decreased $7.1 million in fiscal 1983, following a $3.5-million rise in fiscal 1982. Finished inventory levels were reduced in the past year, after increasing in fiscal 1982, reflecting our efforts to balance needs for high customer service levels with the requirement to conserve cash. Process inventories dropped substantially in each of the past two years as a result of lower production levels. Inventories of raw materials were increased toward the end of fiscal 1983 in order to take advantage of favorable prices and to position these materials for future needs.

Cash Used for Dividends
Cash dividends in fiscal 1983 were maintained at an annual rate of $2.10 per share, despite the sharp decrease in earnings for the year. The dividend rate was last raised in fiscal 1982 from the previous rate of $2.00 per share. Our policy is to pay dividends averaging 40 percent of earnings over an extended period of time. Here are the amounts paid and the ratio to net income for the past three fiscal years:

	Year Ended June 30		
	1983	1982	1981
Dividends Paid (in thousands)	$18,130	$18,084	$17,195
Dividends as a Percent of Net Income	113%	55%	38%

Cash Used for Long-Term Investments
A total of $71.9 million was spent on additions to property, plant and equipment in fiscal 1983, following expenditures of $62.1 million in 1982 and $32.1 million in 1981. The high level of spending in the past two years was a direct result of progress on our major capital investment program for added capacity, cost reduction, and modernization. A discussion of the objectives of this program and progress of the major components is provided on page 10 of this report.

Cash Provided from Financing
During fiscal 1983, long-term debt increased by $11.2 million as a result of a financing arrangement for the purchase of the rotary forge equip-

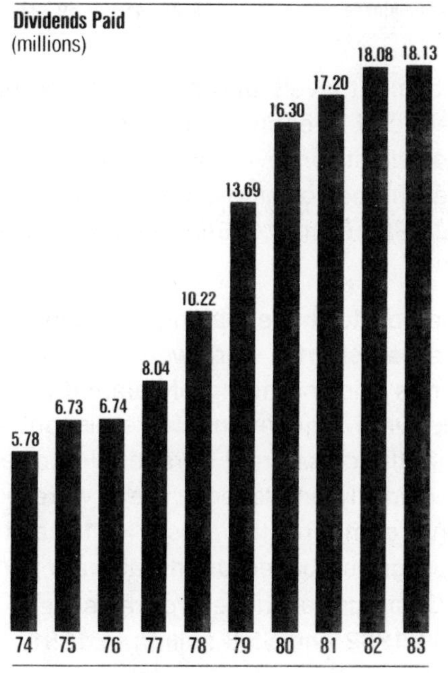

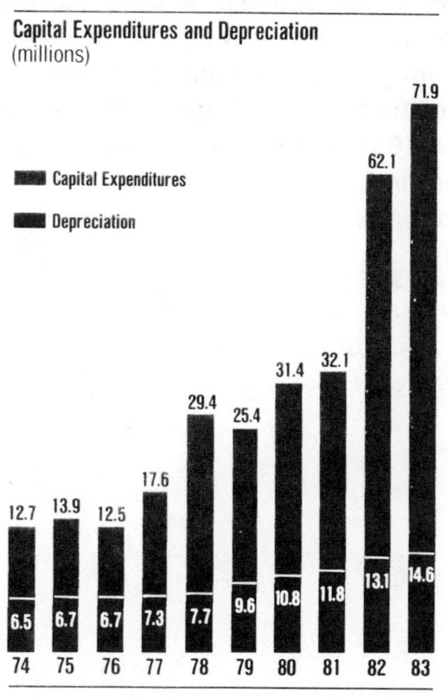

ment. There were no short-term borrowings during fiscal 1983. The new long-term debt and the use of proceeds from the $50-million long-term note issued in fiscal 1982 supplemented internally generated funds to provide the required financing for the capital spending. We anticipate that additional long-term borrowings will be required, at some future time, to meet planned capital expenditure levels.

Total debt at June 30, 1983, was $63.9 million, representing 16.4 percent of total capital employed. You will find further information regarding outstanding borrowings and financing arrangements in Note 4 to the financial statements on page 31.

Assessment of Liquidity and Capital Resources Carpenter's ability to provide adequate cash to meet its needs results from our strong cash flow from operations, our management of working capital, and our ability to use outside sources of financing to supplement internally generated funds.

We ended fiscal 1983 in a strong liquidity position, with current assets exceeding current liabilities by $110.5 million (2.6 to 1). This favorable ratio is conservatively stated because inventories are valued at $124.5 million less than current cost as a result of using the LIFO method.

Our ratio of total debt to capital employed increased to 16.4 percent at June 30, 1983. However, it is still well within our self-imposed 25-percent limit and is consistent with our plans for financing the major expansion program. At June 30, 1983, Carpenter had $120 million available under credit arrangements with a group of banks to provide future borrowing flexibility.

In summary, we believe that our present capital resources are adequate to meet our foreseeable needs.

Supplemental Financial Data

Certain Key Operating Costs

Raw Material Costs fell significantly during the past two fiscal years because of the very low level of specialty steel production worldwide. Here is a summary of the percentage changes in average purchase costs of some key raw materials for the past two fiscal years:

	Percent Change in Average Cost from Previous Year	
	1983	1982
Nickel	−28%	−12%
Chromium	−26%	+9%
Molybdenum	−30%	−31%
Cobalt	−49%	−47%
Ferrous Scrap	−21%	−13%
All Purchased Raw Materials	−27%	−16%

Employment costs over the past three years trended as follows:

Total Costs (thousands)	1983	1982	1981
Wages and Salaries	$120,167	$136,950	$136,492
Employee Benefits:			
Retirement Plans	17,543	18,824	17,659
Group Insurance	10,586	9,778	9,018
Social Security & Other Taxes	9,431	9,481	9,338
Other Benefits	4,396	7,185	5,787
Total Benefits Cost	41,956	45,268	41,802
TOTAL EMPLOYMENT COSTS	$162,123	$182,218	$178,294
Average Total Employment Costs per Employee	$ 39,141	$ 39,390	$ 36,937

Employment levels and hours worked have been reduced in each of the past two fiscal years to adjust for lower shipment levels. The average number of employees dropped to 4,142 in fiscal 1983 from 4,626 in 1982 and 4,827 in 1981.

In addition to these staffing reductions, we implemented shorter work weeks and a freeze on salaries and the hiring of salaried personnel. Cost of Living Adjustments were discontinued permanently for salaried personnel and temporarily for hourly employees. There were no additional compensation costs for fiscal 1983 under programs based upon earnings per share. Costs under these programs were $4.7 million in 1982 and $5.8 million in 1981.

Management's Discussion and Analysis of Financial Condition and Results of Operations

1983

Cash Flow

- The cash position improved primarily because of increased earnings and the disposition of a wholly-owned subsidiary.
- Net cash flow provided by operations has enabled the company to fund its capital needs without external financing, except for financing in the Sherwin-Williams Development Corporation ("SWDC"), an unconsolidated real estate subsidiary. SWDC purchases and develops properties to be leased to the Paint Stores segment and to others.

Working Capital

No Domestic Short-Term Borrowings Since 1979.

- The 1983 current ratio of 2.0 has not varied substantially since 1979.
- The LIFO method of inventory valuation results in a lower reported current ratio. On the FIFO basis, the ratio would have been 2.2 in 1983; 2.4 and 2.2 in 1982 and 1981, respectively.
- The working capital increase of $8.5 million was primarily due to the increase in Drug Stores' inventory caused by distribution inefficiencies offset to some extent by inventory reductions in the Chemicals segment. These reductions were associated with discontinued businesses.
- The disposal during November 1983 of the company's wholly-owned subsidiary, Sherwin-Williams Container Corporation, also increased working capital.
- Our current cash position and anticipated future net cash flow provided by operations should be sufficient to finance working capital needs.

Capital Expenditures/Acquisitions/Divestiture

- Capital expenditures were $31.9 million compared to $30.6 million in 1982, excluding fixed assets acquired through acquisitions of $1.7 million in 1983 and $3.0 million in 1982.
- This increase occurred primarily because of remodeling or adding to the number of paint and drug stores.
- Expenditures for manufacturing improvements in the Coatings segment were partially offset by reduced expenditures in the Chemicals segment.
- Reported capital expenditures do not include SWDC expenditures, which were $20.2 million.
- SWDC has financed its real estate activities with revolving credit borrowings that are not guaranteed by the parent company.
- The disposal of Sherwin-Williams Container Corporation reduced net fixed assets by $35.9 million.

Lines of Credit

- We have an unused line of credit totaling $150 million with a group of eleven banks. This credit agreement was entered into August 31, 1983, and expires August 31, 1988.
- SWDC has a line of credit from a group of four banks for $50 million. This agreement was entered into December 22, 1983, and expires December 22, 1989. Borrowings under this agreement were $28.5 million at December 31.

Management's Discussion And Analysis Of Financial Condition And Results Of Operations

Key Statistics

(Continuing Operations)	***April 1, 1983***	*April 2, 1982*	*March 27, 1981*
Working Capital (in thousands)	**$29,662**	$36,326	$28,701
Current assets as a % of current liabilities	**229.3%**	273.1%	265.4%
Long-term debt as a % of equity	**46.1**	54.6	37.3
Total interest bearing debt as a % of equity	**69.3**	69.7	52.1
Total interest bearing debt as a % of itself plus equity	**40.9**	41.1	34.3
Gross profit as a % of net sales	**56.0**	61.3	60.3
Research and development expenses as a % of net sales	**9.8**	7.8	7.6
Selling, general and administrative expenses as a % of net sales	**43.2**	38.3	37.1
Interest expense as a % of net sales	**3.9**	2.4	2.2
Net income as a % of net sales	**0.5**	7.6	7.6
Growth from preceding year — net sales	**3.8**	21.4	54.1
Growth from preceding year — net income	**(92.5)**	21.7	66.6

Management's Discussion and Analysis
Liquidity and Capital Resources

Working Capital

The Company continued through 1983 in strong financial condition. Working capital as of December 31, 1983 was $263,768,000, an increase of $66,402,000, or 33.6%, from December 31, 1982. The ratio of current assets to current liabilities at December 31, 1983 was 2.50 to 1, compared to 2.17 to 1 at December 31, 1982. Receivables, inventories, accounts payable and accrued expenses at December 31, 1983 increased, reflecting the Company's higher sales level.

All previously outstanding commercial paper and notes payable were retired in 1983. Liability for taxes on income was up in 1983 due to the higher level of earnings.

Cash Flow

The Statement of Cash Flows on the following page reports the cash resources generated from operations, disposition of net working capital and fixed assets, and financing activities, together with how they were used.

As a result of improved liquidity in 1983, the Company provided for working capital and capital investment requirements from internally-generated cash. The Company does not anticipate any additional short-term or long-term financing in 1984, except for a minor amount of industrial revenue bonds in connection with certain Company capital projects. The Company maintains lines of credit agreements with several banks which would provide adequate liquidity for the foreseeable future.

Long-Term Debt

The ratio of long-term debt to stockholders' equity was reduced to 15.9% from 16.8% in 1982, reflecting an increase in stockholders' equity, primarily resulting from the higher level of earnings. Debt issues of the Company continue to receive high ratings and management anticipates that additional funds could be obtained without affecting these ratings.

Capital Expenditures

Capital expenditures during 1983 totaled $61,323,000, a reduction of $20,316,000, or 24.9%, from the 1982 level. Capital expenditures were limited during the early part of 1983 as the result of the prudent capital budgeting policy of 1982. Capital expenditure commitments for the replacement, modernization and expansion of existing facilities totaled $39,403,000 at December 31, 1983, up from $26,890,000 at December 31, 1982.

The Company is identifying major business opportunities that are related by product, service or market to current Company activities. The Company plans to acquire and/or develop internally businesses within such areas. The fast-growing repair and remodel market is one such major market opportunity.

Therefore, annual capital expenditures should continue to increase and should exceed $100,000,000 by 1985. The Company's capital structure and earnings strength will support major capital spending programs and acquisitions.

Dividends

The Company's recovery during 1983 and its strong financial condition and favorable long-term outlook prompted the Board of Directors, at the November 1983 Board meeting, to increase the quarterly cash dividend rate to 65 cents per common share, from 60 cents, an 8.3% increase from the previous level that had prevailed since the third quarter of 1979.

Inflation Information

Financial information on the effects of inflation, using measurement techniques prescribed by the Financial Accounting Standards Board appears on pages 33 and 34. Those disclosures include explanatory comments on the effect of changing prices on the Company's operations.

RESULTS OF OPERATIONS

It is standard procedure to compare the revenues, costs and expenses, and earnings to the prior year in this section of the annual report. Similarly, the prior year will be compared to the year immediately preceding.

MANAGEMENT'S DISCUSSION AND ANALYSIS

RESULTS OF OPERATIONS

Chrysler posted record operating earnings of $927.4 million in 1983, up from losses of $68 million in 1982 and $537.8 million in 1981. The company also posted record net earnings of $700.9 million in 1983 despite a $223.9 million writedown of the company's Peugeot investment. In 1982, net earnings were $170.1 million, including a $239 million gain from the sale of Chrysler Defense, Inc., and in 1981 a net loss of $475.6 million was incurred.

Measuring Progress

Earnings from continuing operations were $301.9 million in 1983, compared to losses from continuing operations of $68.9 million in 1982 and $555.1 million in 1981.

Earnings from continuing operations in 1983 reflect the income tax provision that was offset by operating loss carry-forwards, while losses in 1982 and 1981 were not reduced by any income tax credits.

Chrysler's performance in 1983, 1982, and 1981 can best be made understood by comparing the operating earnings for these three years, which were not affected by provisions for income taxes, or by the writedown of the Peugeot investment in 1983, the gain from the sale of Chrysler Defense, Inc. in 1982, or the earnings of Chrysler Defense, Inc. in 1981. The following discussion should be read in conjunction with Chrysler's 1983 consolidated financial statements, including Note 17 regarding inflation accounting.

Record Operating Earnings

Operating earnings rose $995.4 million in 1983 over 1982. In 1982 the operating loss was $469.8 million less than 1981's loss. The dramatic improvement in 1983 is the result of higher sales volume coupled with cost reductions, increases in efficiency, and the marketing of new, more profitable models.

During 1980 and 1981, obsolete facilities were closed, and employment levels were cut drastically. At the same time, efficiency improved through heavy investment in new equipment and facilities. By 1981, these actions, coupled with profits from the successful new K-car compacts, brought Chrysler's breakeven volume down to 1.4 million North American units. Unfortunately, North American factory sales in the depressed 1981 market amounted to only 1,150,660 units, 17 percent below the breakeven point, resulting in a 1981 operating loss of $537.8 million previously mentioned.

In the fall of 1981, Chrysler introduced the upscale mid-size front-wheel-drive Chrysler LeBaron and Dodge 400. But 1982 domestic industry car sales–down 7 percent from the depressed 1981 market–were disappointing; the worst performance for the domestic auto industry in nearly 25 years. Although Chrysler secured 10 percent of the domestic retail car market, up from 9.9 percent in 1981, and 9.5 percent of the truck market, up from 8.2 percent from the prior year, North American factory sales dropped 5 percent, to 1,095,698 units.

Product Successes

The success of the Chrysler LeBaron and Dodge 400, and a market shift to larger cars, such as Chrysler's luxury New Yorker Fifth Avenue, helped to raise average profit per unit significantly. At the same time, Chrysler continued to reduce fixed costs and improve productivity, and interest costs declined. As a result, North American breakeven volume declined to 1.1 million units. And, in the fall of 1982, average unit profitability increased again with the introduction of the larger front-wheel-drive Chrysler E Class and Dodge 600 models. The operating loss for 1982 was $68 million, reflecting the $71 million loss from Chrysler's Mexican subsidiary.

With Chrysler's reduced breakeven point, the company was well poised to take advantage of an upturn in the automotive market, an upturn that finally took place in 1983 as the economy began to recover from the prolonged recession. Chrysler's North American car and truck sales rose 32 percent in 1983, to 1,441,922 units. Even though fixed costs increased somewhat, primarily from the launching of new sports cars and mini-wagons, Chrysler's North American breakeven volume remained at 1.1 million units as a result of the continued sales

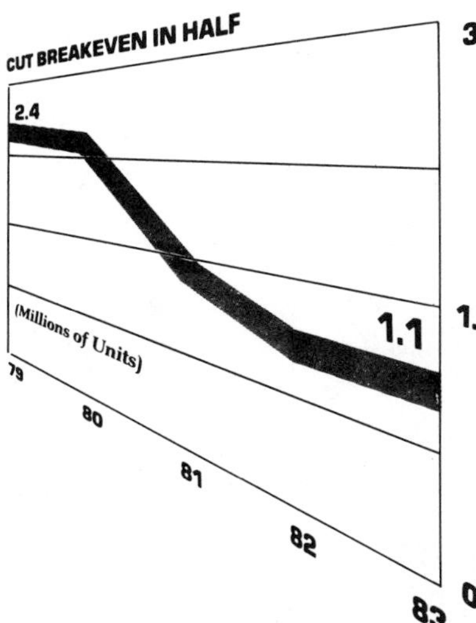

success of upscale models, another decline in interest costs, and further increases in productivity.

With North American factory sales 300,000 units above Chrysler's breakeven, operating earnings rose to $927.4 million in 1983. Chrysler gained 10.3 percent of the domestic retail car market, while its share of the truck market declined slightly to 8.7 percent.

The real measure of Chrysler's accomplishments in the past few years is indicated by the fact that in 1983 the company posted record net earnings of $700.9 million on unit sales that were 37 percent lower than the previous record year of 1976 when Chrysler earned $423 million.

The agreement signed with the U.A.W. in September 1983 will add $1 billion to wage and benefit costs by October 1985, putting further pressure on the breakeven point. However, Chrysler intends to hold the breakeven volume down by producing attractive and profitable new products within cost targets and by further gains in productivity. In addition, the early repayment in 1983 of the $1.2 billion in government-guaranteed loans will favorably affect Chrysler's performance by reducing future interest costs.

Continued significant productivity increases are essential to maintain Chrysler's breakeven point at current levels and to reduce its vulnerability to future economic downturns.

Selected Comparisons of Elements of Revenue and Costs
Net sales for 1983 increased 32 percent to $13.2 billion from the 1982 level of $10.0 billion. Worldwide unit factory sales rose 26 percent from 1982. Most of the increase in net sales reflects the increase in unit sales. Improvement in product mix and, to a lesser extent, price increases also contributed to the increase. In 1982, net sales were virtually unchanged from 1981 while worldwide unit sales declined 101,287 units or 8 percent from 1981. The impact of this decline in unit volume was offset primarily by price increases and to a lesser extent by improved product mix.

Other income includes proceeds from the sale of tax attributes ("safe harbor leases") of $19.8 million in 1983, $10.1 million in 1982 and $38.4 million in 1981. Other income in 1981 also includes a $21.7 million gain from that year's debt restructuring.

The increase in selling and administrative expenses in 1983 over 1982 resulted from increased levels of advertising and merchandising effort for Chrysler's new product offerings as well as year-to-year economic cost increases. The 1982 increase over 1981, in addition to economic cost increases, reflects actions taken in 1981 to contain cost levels compared to a return to more normal levels in 1982.

Portfolio investment interest income rose significantly in 1982 from 1981 because of improved liquidity resulting from the sale of Chrysler Defense, Inc. early in 1982. Interest expense-net was further reduced by the full year effect in 1982 of Chrysler's 1981 private debt restructuring. The level of interest expense-net was further reduced in 1983 as portfolio investment interest income remained strong and the government-guaranteed loans were repaid.

Earnings from continuing operations in 1984 will also reflect an income tax provision that is offset by operating loss carryforwards as in 1983. Chrysler's operating loss carryforwards in the U.S. and Canada totaled approximately $1.6 billion at year-end 1983 and investment tax credit carryforwards approximated $260 million. As a result, until Chrysler's future taxable earnings aggregate approximately $2.3 billion, no significant income tax liability will be incurred.

Results of Operations

1983 vs. 1982

Net Sales

Net Sales Increased 6.6 percent in 1983.

- Consolidated net sales increased primarily because of a 16.6 percent increase in the Paint Stores segment and a 6.9 percent increase in the Drug Stores segment.
- The Coatings segment's increase of 1.0 percent was adversely affected by the disposition of the wholly-owned subsidiary in November. Comparable Coatings' sales increased 2.7 percent compared to 1982.
- The Chemicals segment's sales declined 2.2 percent despite increased volume reflecting the effects of competitive pricing.
- The International segment's lower sales reflect the deconsolidation of the company's Mexican subsidiary on January 1, 1983.

Gross Profit

- Gross profit margins increased to 33.8 percent in 1983 from 31.9 percent in 1982.
- All segments, except for the Drug Stores and International segments, improved gross profit margins.
- The Paint Stores segment accounted for 54.1 percent of the increase in gross profit.
- The Drug Stores segment's margins were lower than in 1982 due to distribution inefficiencies.
- The Coatings segment gained significantly in margins because of operating efficiencies and a more favorable product mix.
- The Chemicals segment increased gross profit by curtailing unprofitable operations, realizing the associated LIFO inventory reductions, and by operating efficiencies.

Management's Discussion and Analysis Results of Operations

Net Sales

The Company achieved record net sales of $1.6 billion in 1983, surpassing the previous record of $1.5 billion in 1979. This 1983 sales record was up 21.6% over 1982, following an 11.2% decline in 1982. Net sales of $435.7 million in the fourth quarter marked an all-time high for any quarter in the Company's history. Overall unit volume increased 15% in 1983 versus an 11% decline in 1982. Realized selling prices rose 7% in 1983 while 1982 prices were unchanged from 1981. These 1983 achievements primarily reflected the strong recovery in construction activity, particularly new residential construction, resulting in higher demand for the Company's products. Housing starts were up 60% in 1983, following a decline of 3% in 1982. These gains were partially mitigated by a decline in sales to the industrial processes markets which were adversely affected by the continuing recession in basic manufacturing industries.

Cost of Products Sold

Cost of products sold in 1983 increased 13.7% from 1982, reflecting the net effect of the above-mentioned increased unit volume and a slight decline in unit costs. Cost of products sold decreased in 1982 from 1981 as a result of the decline in unit volume and a 2% increase in unit costs.

Gross Profit

Gross profit in 1983 improved 62.7% from the comparable 1982 level as a consequence of the favorable changes in overall realized selling prices, volume and unit costs. Gross profit as a percent of net sales improved to 21.5% in 1983, compared with 16.1% and 17.9% for 1982 and 1981, respectively. Gross profit in 1982 declined 20.2% from 1981, reflecting the combined effect of lower unit volume and higher unit costs.

Selling and Administrative Expenses

Selling and administrative expenses for 1983 rose 11.5%, due mainly to higher levels of compensation and related fringe benefits, and increased marketing and travel expenses. In 1983, total selling and administrative expenses as a percent of net sales were 11.5%, compared with 12.6% and 11.1% for 1982 and 1981, respectively.

Interest Expense

Interest expense declined in both 1983 and 1982 from the respective preceding year, mainly due to a lower level of external short-term borrowings by a Canadian subsidiary.

Other Income and Expense

Interest income for 1983 remained virtually unchanged from 1982 due to the net effect of lower interest rates and a higher level of short-term investments. Interest income for 1982 declined from the preceding year due primarily to a lower level of short-term investments. Included in 1983 other expense was a loss of $3,959,000 on the sale of Canadian roofing plants. This sale eliminated losses in that business and provided capital that can be employed more effectively elsewhere. Additionally, other income and expense was unfavorable in 1983 compared to 1982, reflecting the 1983 write-downs of certain facilities and an increased 1983 absorption for Mexican currency losses. Other income in 1982 was unfavorable versus 1981 due to a 1981 gain on the sale of a subsidiary company.

Taxes on Income

Taxes on income for 1983 increased from 1982 due principally to the higher level of earnings before taxes and a lower level of investment tax credits. As a result of the lower level of earnings in 1982, taxes on income declined from 1981. The effective tax rate for 1983 was 45.4% as compared to 21.9% for 1982.

Net Earnings

Net earnings for 1983 increased 83.0% and for 1982 declined 40.8%, compared with each preceding year. Although 1983 net earnings increased substantially, they did not eclipse the record 1979 level, due primarily to the continuing recession in the basic manufacturing industries. Performance in these industries, however, is expected to improve in 1984.

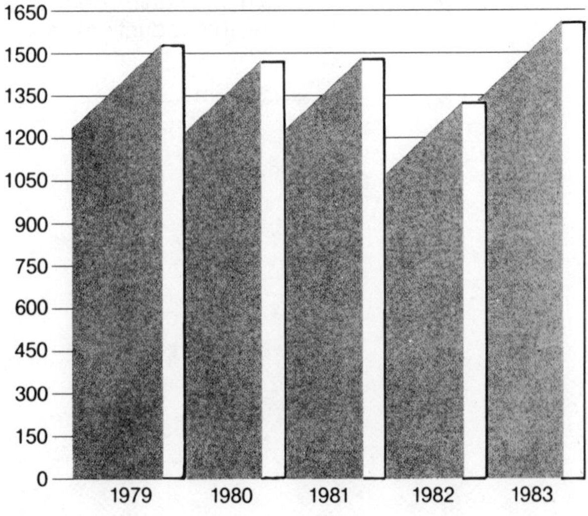

Emerson Electric

RESULTS OF OPERATIONS

Net Sales
For 1983, net sales were $3.48 billion – 0.8 per cent lower than the 1982 sales level of $3.50 billion. This modest decline in sales resulted from the weak economic climate that prevailed, throughout the world, for most of the fiscal year. For the fourth quarter of 1983, sales were $878.1 million – up $52 million or 6.4 per cent over the comparable period of 1982 – reinforcing management's belief that the prolonged recession may well have bottomed out for most of Emerson's product lines.

The balanced diversification of the Company once again provided an important assist in coping with the impact of the recession. For 1983, Government and Defense sales increased by 15.3 per cent as compared with fiscal 1982. Sales for the Consumer Products segment increased by 0.4 per cent reflecting good year-to-year performance by the appliance component businesses which offset continued softness in other product lines serving the consumer market. Commercial and Industrial sales, which normally lag economic turnaround, declined by 4.2 per cent as compared with 1982.

Gross Margins
For 1983, gross profit margin was 34.4 per cent – down from the 35.0 per cent achieved for 1982 but better than the 33.9 per cent for 1981. The fact that gross profit margin was higher in 1983 and 1982 than it was in 1981, despite lower sales levels, reflects the extent to which the Company has been successful in the major emphasis that it has given to productivity and cost reductions aimed at improving operating margins.

Selling, General and Administrative Expenses
Selling, general and administrative expenses for 1983 amounted to $661.7 million – equal to 19.0 per cent of sales. This compared with a 1982 expense level of $677.5 million or 19.3 per cent of sales. The Company's ability to reduce the actual level of selling, general and administrative expenses for 1983 by $16 million reflects a disciplined approach that held these costs below the two-year ago level despite the impact of inflation creep.

Other (Income) Deductions, Net
This net figure derives from a variety of nonoperating sources and resulted in income of $20.7 million for 1983 as compared with $7.8 million for 1982. The 1983 improvement was attributable primarily to a higher level of gains on sales of corporate investments and a lower level of foreign exchange losses offset partially by the costs of plant closings and consolidations.

Earnings Before Income Taxes
Two significant items of a nonrecurring nature affected pretax earnings for 1983. The first of these reduced 1983 pension expense by $7.8 million. Changes were made in 1983 to increase the assumed rate of return on pension fund assets from 6.5 per cent to 8.5 per cent and, recognizing the impact of projected future rates of inflation, to increase anticipated growth in compensation. As indicated in the Notes to Consolidated Financial Statements, in the aggregate plan assets continue to exceed plan liabilities by a significant amount.

In addition, as noted above, significant expenses were incurred as a result of a program involving plant closings and consolidations. This program involved plants and organizations in 17 divisions and resulted in a charge to expense for 1983 of $14.0 million.

Income Taxes
The Company's effective tax rate for 1983 was 43.7 per cent. This compared with 43.9 per cent for 1982 and 44.5 per cent for 1981. An analysis of the effective tax rate for each of these years is presented in Note 7 of the Notes to Consolidated Financial Statements.

Word of Caution: Try to structure this section so that it is relatively easy to read. Stay away from across-the-page sentences such as:

Results of Operations

Sales for the year ended April 30, 1982 reached $114,756,000 an increase of 23 percent over the 1981 level of $93,105,000 and 54 percent over the 1980 level of $74,400,000. The Company's compounded average growth rate of sales over the past three years was 37 percent, principally reflecting increased deliveries of the Company's products and the continued expansion of the Company's United States and international markets. Cost of sales for the year ended April 30, 1982, expressed as a percent of sales, was 56 percent, a 7 percent increase over the prior year and a 4 percent increase over 1980. Strong competitive pricing, particularly in the turnkey interactive graphic systems and pattern grading and marker making systems, was the primary cause of this decline in gross profit margins. While the growth of sales in some of the Company's established product lines continued to increase, expected sales volumes in the GERBERcutter and interactive graphic systems were severely impacted by the worldwide recession, high interest rates and general decline in capital goods purchases. Gerber Systems Technology, Inc. (GST), the Company's 80 percent owned subsidiary, reported net losses from operations of $3,117,000 and $1,769,000 for the years ended April 30, 1982 and 1981, respectively. These losses are included in the consolidated financial statements of the Company, 100 percent prior to April 7, 1981 and 80 percent thereafter. In the third and fourth quarters of fiscal year 1982 GST's management reduced personnel and made changes in its structure which should significantly reduce its operating costs. Net earnings in 1981 included a $2,575,000 capital gain from the sale of 370,000 shares of Boston Digital Corporation common stock. The sale reduced the Company's investment in Boston Digital from 40 to 21 percent. Net earnings in 1980 included $106,000 derived from the favorable settlement of a lawsuit and $645,000 in 1979 from the sale of technology. The Company maintained its strong emphasis on technological developments with research and development efforts continuing at approximately 7 percent of sales. Selling, general and administrative expenses increased 26 percent in 1982 and 45 percent in 1981 primarily as a result of expanded domestic and foreign marketing activities to support future sales growth and increased production volumes. The increase in interest expense in 1982 is due to increased short-term borrowings principally at foreign subsidiaries and the increase in 1981 reflects the issuance in August 1979 of $18,000,000, 12-1/8 percent Subordinated Sinking Fund Debentures Due 1994.

XIV
AUDITORS' REPORT

Your auditors will provide their written opinion of the financial statements to be contained in the annual report. Auditors must conform to all accounting rules, financial principles, and SEC regulations in the preparation of the financial reports to be included in the annual report.

The report of your auditors will describe the responsibility they have assumed. This responsibility does not go beyond the financial statements and the accompanying notes.

Jane Bryant Quinn, business commentator, suggests that the reader "Start at the back" of the report. She advises:

First, turn to the report of the certified public accountant. This third-party auditor will tell you right off the bat if Galactic's report conforms with "generally accepted accounting principles."

Watch out for the words "subject to." They mean the financial report is clean only if you take the company's word about a particular piece of business, and the accountant isn't sure you should. Doubts like this are usually settled behind closed doors. When a "subject to" makes it into the annual report, it could mean trouble.

Accountants' Report

The Board of Directors
and Shareholders
Avnet, Inc.

We have examined the consolidated balance sheets of Avnet, Inc. and Subsidiaries as of June 30, 1983 and 1982, and the related consolidated statements of income, shareholders' equity and changes in financial position for each of the three years in the period ended June 30, 1983. Our examinations were made in accordance with generally accepted auditing standards and, accordingly, included such tests of the accounting records and such other auditing procedures as we considered necessary in the circumstances.

In our opinion, the financial statements referred to above present fairly the consolidated financial position of Avnet, Inc. and Subsidiaries as of June 30, 1983 and 1982, and the consolidated results of their operations and changes in their financial position for each of the three years in the period ended June 30, 1983, in conformity with generally accepted accounting principles applied on a consistent basis.

Laventhol & Horwath

New York, NY
August 24, 1983

Auditors' Report

To the Board of Directors and Stockholders, Consolidated Foods Corporation:

We have examined the consolidated balance sheets of CONSOLIDATED FOODS CORPORATION (a Maryland corporation) AND SUBSIDIARIES as of July 2, 1983, July 3, 1982, and June 27, 1981, and the related consolidated statements of income, stockholders' equity and changes in financial position for the years then ended. Our examinations were made in accordance with generally accepted auditing standards and, accordingly, included such tests of the accounting records and such other auditing procedures as we considered necessary in the circumstances. The financial statements of Douwe Egberts, N.V., whose total assets and net sales constitute 21% and 14%, respectively, of the related consolidated totals for 1983, 22% and 17%, respectively, for 1982 and 25% and 19%, respectively, for 1981 were examined by other auditors whose reports thereon have been furnished to us.

In our opinion, based on our examinations and the reports of other auditors, the consolidated financial statements referred to above present fairly the financial position of Consolidated Foods Corporation and Subsidiaries as of July 2, 1983, July 3, 1982, and June 27, 1981, and the results of their operations and the changes in their financial position for the years then ended, in conformity with generally accepted accounting principles which, except for the change in the year ended July 3, 1982, (with which we concur) in the method of accounting for foreign currency translation as explained under "Summary of Significant Accounting Policies" on page 32, have been applied on a consistent basis.

Arthur Andersen & Co.
Chicago, Illinois,
August 16, 1983.

EXCEPTIONS IN THE AUDITORS' REPORT

Security analysts will carefully scrutinize your auditors' report for any exceptions that might be described. Your accounting firm will candidly describe these exceptions and evaluate the impact on your corporate earnings.

ACCOUNTANTS' REPORT

The Board of Directors
Eagle-Picher Industries, Inc.

We have examined the balance sheet of Eagle-Picher Industries, Inc. and subsidiaries as of November 30, 1983 and 1982 and the related statements of income, shareholders' equity, and changes in financial position for each of the years in the three-year period ended November 30, 1983. Our examinations were made in accordance with generally accepted auditing standards and, accordingly, included such tests of the accounting records and such other auditing procedures as we considered necessary in the circumstances.

As discussed in note H of the notes to financial statements, the Company's liability resulting from asbestos litigation cannot presently be reasonably estimated; and, the amounts of insurance recoveries ultimately collectible from two of the Company's carriers, estimated to be $16,000,000 at November 30, 1983, cannot be assured until agreements with them have been finalized.

In our opinion, subject to the effects on the financial statements of such adjustments, if any, as might have been required had the outcome of the uncertainties referred to in the preceding paragraph been known, the aforementioned financial statements present fairly the financial position of Eagle-Picher Industries, Inc. and subsidiaries at November 30, 1983 and 1982 and the results of their operations and the changes in their financial position for each of the years in the three-year period ended November 30, 1983, in conformity with generally accepted accounting principles applied on a consistent basis.

Peat, Marwick, Mitchell & Co.
Cincinnati, Ohio
January 13, 1984

XV
SIX ITEMS TO BE INCLUDED IN YOUR STATEMENT OF MANAGEMENT'S RESPONSIBILITY FOR FINANCIAL STATEMENTS

In this section management reports the manner in which the annual report was prepared and its responsibility for the integrity and and objectivity of the financial statements.

As you prepare your report of management, include the following:

1. A discussion outlining how management's statements have been prepared.
2. Your system of internal controls.
3. Your training and development of professional financial managers to implement corporate controls.
4. The role of your public accountants in providing an objective, independent review.
5. The role and activities of your audit committee.
6. Your company's obligation to conduct its affairs in an ethical and socially responsible manner.

Management's Responsibility for Financial Statements

Management of Kimberly-Clark is responsible for conducting all aspects of the business. Among these responsibilities is preparation of all information in this annual report, including the financial statements. We have prepared these financial statements using generally accepted accounting principles which we consider appropriate in the circumstances.

As can be expected in a complex and dynamic business environment, some financial statement amounts are based on estimates and informed judgments. Even though estimates and judgments are used, we believe that readers of Kimberly-Clark's financial information should be aware of the measures we have taken to ensure the accuracy and integrity of our financial reports. These measures include an effective control-oriented environment in which our Internal Audit Department plays an important role, independent audits and an Audit Committee of the board of directors which oversees the quality of financial reporting.

One characteristic of a control-oriented environment is a system of internal accounting controls which provides reasonable assurance that assets are safeguarded and transactions are appropriately authorized, recorded and reported. We consider this system essential for effectively managing the business. We support it with written policies and procedures and by giving the Internal Audit Department the authority to monitor the system to help ensure that it is working effectively.

The financial statements have been examined by independent auditors, Deloitte Haskins & Sells, whose report appears on page 25. Their examination included a review of our system of internal accounting controls, tests of the accounting records and other auditing procedures which they considered necessary to form an opinion as to the fairness of the financial statements.

The Audit Committee of the board of directors, composed entirely of directors who are not employees, is responsible for selecting and recommending for stockholder approval the Corporation's independent auditors as well as overseeing the internal audit program. This committee meets with management, internal auditors and independent auditors to discuss internal accounting controls, results of audits and the quality of financial reporting. Both internal auditors and independent auditors can and do meet with the committee without members of management present.

In addition, we have prepared and distributed to our employees a policy statement for conducting business affairs in a lawful and ethical manner in each country in which we do business. Specific internal accounting controls have been developed and instituted to provide assurance that these policies are followed.

THE SINGER COMPANY

The Company is responsible for the preparation and integrity of the accompanying consolidated financial statements. The statements have been prepared in conformity with consistently applied generally accepted accounting principles appropriate in the circumstances, and include amounts based upon management's best estimates and judgments. The financial statements are believed to reflect, in all material respects, the substance of events and transactions that should be included. Financial information presented elsewhere in this Annual Report is consistent with that in the financial statements.

In meeting its responsibility for preparing reliable financial statements, the Company depends on its system of internal accounting control. This system is designed to provide reasonable assurance that assets are safeguarded and transactions are executed in accordance with the appropriate corporate authorization and recorded properly to permit the preparation of financial statements in accordance with generally accepted accounting principles. The Company believes that its accounting controls provide reasonable assurance that errors or irregularities that could be material to the financial statements are prevented or would be detected within a timely period by employees in the normal course of performing their assigned functions. The concept of reasonable assurance is based on the recognition that judgments are required to assess and balance the cost and expected benefits of a system of internal accounting controls. Written internal accounting control and other operating policies and procedures supporting this system are communicated throughout the Company. Adherence to these policies and procedures is reviewed through a coordinated audit effort of the Company's internal audit staff and independent certified public accountants.

The independent certified public accountants review and test the system of internal accounting controls to the extent they consider necessary to support their opinion on the consolidated financial statements of the Company. Their report, which is included on this page, is the result of an independent and objective review of management's discharge of its responsibilities relating to the fairness of reported operating results and financial condition.

The Company's Board of Directors has an Audit Committee composed solely of outside directors. The committee meets periodically with the Company's independent certified public accountants, management, and internal auditors to review matters relating to the quality of financial reporting and internal accounting controls, the nature and extent of internal and external audit plans and results, and certain other matters. The independent certified public accountants, whose appointment is recommended by the Audit Committee to the Board of Directors, have full and free access to this committee.

A statement of business ethics policy is communicated annually to the Company's employees. The Company monitors compliance with this policy to help assure that operations are conducted in a responsible and professional manner with a commitment to the highest standard of business conduct.

J. B. Flavin
Chairman and
Chief Executive Officer

A. E. MacKay
Chief Financial Officer

UNITRODE

Unitrode Corporation has prepared the financial statements and related data contained in this Annual Report. The Company's financial statements have been prepared in conformity with generally accepted accounting principles and reflect judgments and estimates as to the expected effects of transactions and events currently being reported. Unitrode is responsible for the integrity and objectivity of the financial statements and other financial data included in this report. To meet this responsibility, the Company maintains a system of internal accounting controls to provide reasonable assurance that assets are safeguarded and that transactions are properly executed and recorded. The system includes policies and procedures, internal audits and reviews by officers of the Company.

The Audit Committee of the Board of Directors is composed solely of outside directors. The Committee meets periodically and, when appropriate, separately with representatives of the independent certified public accountants and officers of the Company to monitor the activities of each.

Coopers & Lybrand, independent certified public accountants, have been selected by the Board of Directors to examine the Company's financial statements; their report follows.

Controller	Vice President– Finance and Treasurer	President
William Sangplust	Walter B. Gates	George Berman

XVI FINANCIAL STATEMENTS

Your CPA will provide the following statements to be included in your corporate annual report:

1. 5- to 10-Year Summary of Financial Highlights
2. Consolidated Statement of Income
3. Consolidated Balance Sheet
4. Consolidated Statement of Changes in Financial Position
5. Consolidated Statement of Changes in Shareholder's Equity
6. Industry Segments
7. Geographic Data
8. Common Stock Price, Dividends, and Related Data
9. Unaudited Quarterly Financial Data
10. Ratios

FIVE TO TEN YEAR SUMMARY OF FINANCIAL HIGHLIGHTS

Cessna

Five Years in Review

(Thousands of dollars except for per share data)	1983	1982	1981	1980	1979
Operating Results					
Sales	**$ 524,395**	$ 831,528	$1,060,097	$1,000,061	$ 939,311
Earnings (loss) before income tax	**$ (37,445)**	$ 34,860	$ 118,666	$ 55,140	$ 90,107
Percent of sales	**(7.1)%**	4.2%	11.2%	5.5%	9.6%
Net earnings (loss)	**$ (18,845)**	$ 18,078	$ 60,566	$ 28,122	$ 45,955
Percent of sales	**(3.6)%**	2.2%	5.7%	2.8%	4.9%
Dividends paid	**$ 7,663**	$ 11,500	$ 11,435	$ 11,292	$ 14,163
Expressed per Share: [1]					
Net earnings (loss)[2]	**$ (.98)**	$ .94	$ 3.19	$ 1.51	$ 2.47
Dividends	**$ .40**	$ .60	$ .60	$ .59	$ .76
Balance Sheet Data					
Current Assets	**$ 391,161**	$ 329,315	$ 412,912	$ 393,676	$ 404,016
Current Liabilities	**$ 220,809**	$ 206,033	$ 262,295	$ 237,611	$ 235,552
Working Capital	**$ 170,352**	$ 123,282	$ 150,617	$ 156,065	$ 168,464
Total assets	**$ 698,787**	$ 611,858	$ 657,641	$ 583,026	$ 563,228
Fixed assets, net after provisions for depreciation and amortization	**$ 92,930**	$ 99,031	$ 90,782	$ 81,675	$ 73,902
Short-term borrowings	**$ —**	$ 14,000	$ —	$ 35,000	$ 32,000
Long-term borrowings	**$ 129,455**	$ 33,943	$ 35,700	$ 39,936	$ 42,683
Stockholders' Equity	**$ 327,782**	$ 351,966	$ 345,578	$ 290,014	$ 272,267
Equity per share [1]	**$ 17.08**	$ 18.37	$ 18.00	$ 15.53	$ 14.60
Other					
Common shares outstanding at year end [1]	**19,186,594**	19,157,081	19,202,552	18,674,482	18,654,755
Number of Stockholders (year-end)	**11,900**	13,675	13,503	14,647	13,806
Number of Employees (average)	**7,657**	11,542	15,838	18,024	18,956
Expenditures for fixed assets	**$ 6,636**	$ 19,000	$ 19,136	$ 16,947	$ 11,952
Depreciation	**$ 12,639**	$ 11,913	$ 9,900	$ 8,937	$ 8,168

(1) Shares outstanding have been adjusted to reflect the stock splits and dividends declared through September 30, 1983.
(2) Based on average common shares outstanding.

TEN YEAR COMPARISONS

(All amounts other than per share data are stated in thousands)

For the Years Ended June 30	**1983**	1982	1981
SUMMARY OF OPERATIONS			
NET SALES	**613,807**	635,666	568,986
GROSS PROFIT ON SALES (1)	**97,491**	105,295	77,533
PROVISION FOR INCOME TAXES	**27,020**	34,250	19,470
NET INCOME (1)	**31,762**	39,353	23,495
AVERAGE NUMBER OF SHARES OF COMMON STOCK OUTSTANDING (2)	**14,464**	14,464	14,464
PER SHARE OF COMMON STOCK (2):			
Net Income	**2.20**	2.72	1.62
Cash Dividends	**1.58**	1.54	1.52
Shareholders' Investment	**18.05**	17.44	16.31
OTHER DATA			
SHAREHOLDERS' INVESTMENT	**261,054**	252,240	235,923
TOTAL ASSETS	**387,780**	366,656	333,167
PLANT AND EQUIPMENT	**310,449**	283,147	265,644
PLANT AND EQUIPMENT NET OF RESERVES	**179,436**	165,689	160,872
PROVISION FOR DEPRECIATION	**15,726**	14,038	12,541
EXPENDITURES FOR PLANT AND EQUIPMENT	**32,110**	21,275	28,572
WORKING CAPITAL	**108,836**	111,008	95,476
Current Ratio	**2.1 to 1**	2.2 to 1	2.2 to 1
NUMBER OF EMPLOYEES AT YEAR-END	**9,254**	8,138	8,179
NUMBER OF SHAREHOLDERS AT YEAR-END	**10,006**	11,140	11,865
QUOTED MARKET PRICE:			
High	**37¼**	26⅝	28¼
Low	**23⅞**	22	22

(1) Years prior to 1977 reflect the first-in, first-out (FIFO) method for pricing inventory while 1977 and years after reflect the last-in, first-out (LIFO) method.

(2) Number of shares of common stock and per share data have been adjusted for the 2-for-1 stock split in 1976.

SALES (in millions)

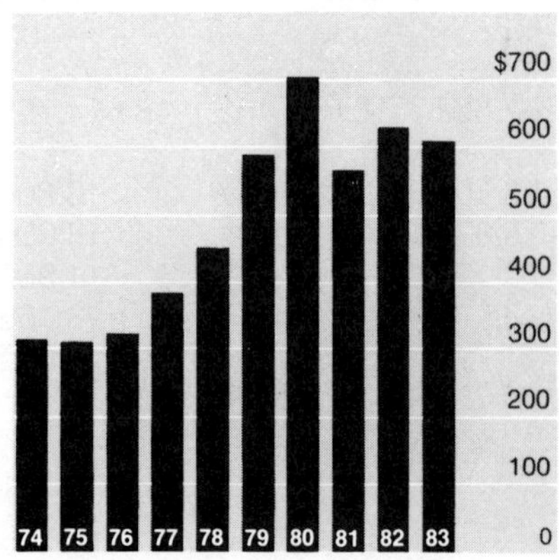

INCOME (in millions)

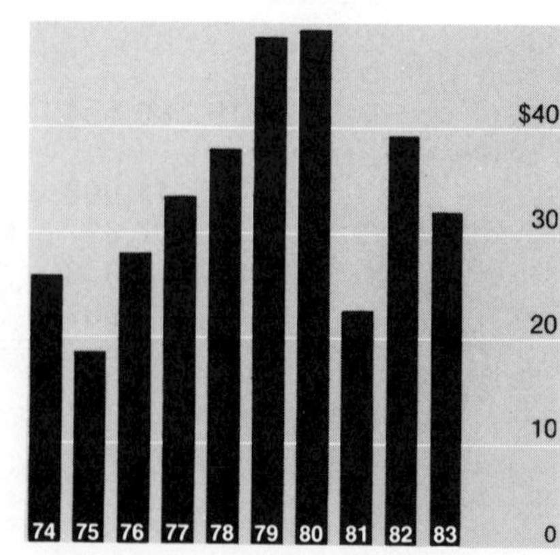

1980	1979	1978	1977	1976	1975	1974
708,562	590,964	456,960	388,852	326,959	316,286	317,852
126,771	118,838	96,501	86,389	72,024	51,439	65,801
42,370	44,770	36,570	32,140	26,690	17,050	26,630
49,098	48,455	37,466	33,360	27,572	18,269	25,873
14,464	14,464	14,464	14,464	14,464	14,464	14,464
3.39	3.35	2.59	2.31	1.91	1.26	1.79
1.46	1.35	1.22	1.12	.93	.80	.88
16.17	14.24	12.24	10.87	9.68	8.70	8.24
233,915	205,934	177,005	157,185	140,025	125,832	119,134
341,484	290,047	241,922	213,303	191,524	153,183	155,830
240,435	190,277	168,320	150,839	137,508	127,359	107,609
148,303	107,659	93,862	83,803	77,218	72,911	59,219
10,684	8,901	8,092	7,585	6,708	5,856	4,999
55,115	24,782	19,300	15,252	12,302	20,760	24,771
102,082	111,206	94,010	82,410	69,379	57,148	62,026
2.1 to 1	2.6 to 1	2.7 to 1	2.8 to 1	2.5 to 1	3.5 to 1	2.8 to 1
10,873	10,605	8,931	7,936	6,950	6,378	8,601
12,893	13,185	13,388	12,973	12,634	13,037	13,535
29⅛	31¼	30⅜	33⅜	32¾	25	31¼
20¾	25	23½	25⅛	20⅞	14¾	17½

DISPOSITION OF 1983 SALES DOLLARS

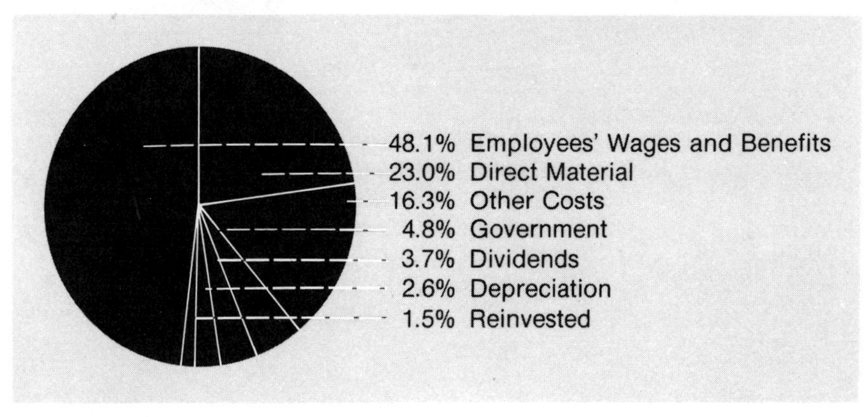

Selected Financial Data

SYKES DATATRONICS, INC. AND SUBSIDIARIES

Years ended last day of February	1983	1982	1981	1980	1979
	(thousands of dollars except per share data)				
Sales	**$42,800**	$45,408	$24,174	$12,298	$ 6,552
Cost of sales	**19,191**	18,300	10,949	5,654	3,083
Selling, general and administrative expenses	**16,614**	11,255	5,427	2,615	1,581
Engineering and development expenses	**6,067**	4,069	2,057	1,209	768
Interest (income)	**(122)**	(1,592)	(569)	—	—
Interest expense	**978**	325	149	203	159
Other (income) expenses, net	**(112)**	(28)	15	(21)	(29)
Provision for (benefit from) income taxes	**(425)**	5,232	2,792	1,146	484
Income before extraordinary item	**609**	7,847	3,354	1,492	506
Extraordinary item— reduction of income taxes arising from carryforward of net operating losses	**—**	—	—	—	208
Net income	**609**	7,847	3,354	1,492	714
Weighted average number common shares and common stock equivalents outstanding	**12,738,937**	12,736,401	11,221,503	9,149,118	8,889,282
Per share data:					
Income before extraordinary item	**$ .05**	$ .62	$ .30	$ .16	$ .06
Extraordinary item	**—**	—	—	—	.02
Net income	**.05**	.62	.30	.16	.08
Total assets	**45,621**	47,786	30,432	7,789	4,849
Long-term debt	**4,246**	6,813	798	1,405	1,392

CONSOLIDATED STATEMENT OF INCOME

There are several ways to present your Statements of Consolidated Income. There is the short form, examples of which are as follows:

Financial Statements *(in millions of dollars)* Sperry Corporation

Consolidated Statements of Income and Retained Earnings

Years ended March 31	**1983**	1982	1981
Revenue			
Net sales of products	**$3,639.9**	$4,195.0	$4,239.8
Rentals and services	**1,436.1**	1,376.4	1,187.4
Total	**5,076.0**	5,571.4	5,427.2
Other Income (Note 2)	**67.0**	54.4	42.7
	5,143.0	5,625.8	5,469.9
Costs and Expenses			
Cost of sales of products	**2,404.0**	2,687.5	2,598.9
Cost of rentals and services	**761.6**	745.2	666.5
Selling, general and administrative expenses	**1,169.4**	1,146.6	1,118.5
Research and development	**397.1**	397.6	336.5
Interest (Note 3)	**246.8**	294.1	211.6
	4,978.9	5,271.0	4,932.0
Income before Taxes on Income	**164.1**	354.8	537.9
Provision for Taxes on Income (Note 4)	**46.0**	133.0	226.7
Net Income	**118.1**	221.8	311.2
Retained Earnings, Beginning of Year	**1,954.1**	1,813.7	1,574.2
Cash Dividends Declared	**(86.1)**	(81.4)	(71.7)
Retained Earnings, End of Year	**$1,986.1**	$1,954.1	$1,813.7
Net Income per Share (Note 5)			
Fully Diluted	**$2.65**	$5.25	$7.46
Primary	**$2.65**	$5.25	$7.63
Cash Dividends Declared per Share	**$1.92**	$1.92	$1.76

See notes to financial statements.

SQUARE D COMPANY AND SUBSIDIARIES

Consolidated Statements of Net Earnings

(Dollars in thousands, except per share)

	Year Ended December 31		
	1983	1982	1981
Net Sales	**$1,144,137**	$1,056,981	$1,151,615
Cost and Expenses:			
Cost of products sold	**782,032**	744,419	762,643
Selling, administrative and general	**234,866**	182,642	186,262
Operating earnings	**127,239**	129,920	202,710
Non-operating income (Note J)	**19,853**	8,192	13,710
Interest expense	**(24,341)**	(19,315)	(18,331)
Earnings before Income Taxes	**122,751**	118,797	198,089
Provision for Income Taxes (Note I)	**59,840**	47,097	94,407
Net Earnings	**$ 62,911**	$ 71,700	$ 103,682
Net earnings per share based on weighted average number of shares outstanding during the year	**$ 2.22**	$ 2.61	$ 3.77

See accompanying notes to consolidated financial statements

1978	1979	1980	1981	1982	
$598,886	**$786,936**	**$971,306**	**$1,061,834**	**$1,195,748**	**NET SALES** and rentals to customers for products, replacement components and services
266,474	359,740	458,464	513,145	595,340	COST OF SALES—the materials, labor and facilities related to manufacturing goods and providing services
332,412	**427,196**	**512,842**	**548,689**	**600,408**	**GROSS PROFIT** remaining from sales revenue after production costs
49,832	60,561	77,797	91,147	109,086	ENGINEERING EXPENSE — for research and the development of products and components
86,850	113,461	135,405	157,105	180,631	SELLING EXPENSE—for marketing and sales programs, and the distribution system
53,063	68,044	88,343	100,715	108,977	ADMINISTRATIVE EXPENSE—for general management and supporting services
48,528	63,682	63,448	61,686	55,267	PROFIT SHARING — the incentive portion of employee compensation
94,139	**121,448**	**147,849**	**138,036**	**146,447**	**OPERATING INCOME** remaining from sales revenue after the costs and expenses of operations
4,246	6,428	15,956	25,274	29,537	INTEREST EXPENSE — the cost of borrowed funds and banking services
6,068	11,631	5,029	19,630	9,493	NON-OPERATING INCOME—investment income, joint venture earnings, currencies, and other income and expense
95,961	**126,651**	**136,922**	**132,392**	**126,403**	**INCOME BEFORE TAXES** remaining from sales revenue after operating costs and expenses and non-operating items
39,115	49,500	51,850	52,225	46,950	INCOME TAXES—provided for income related taxes levied by United States and foreign governments
56,846	**77,151**	**85,072**	**80,167**	**79,453**	**EARNINGS** remaining from sales revenue for reinvestment in the business and for dividends
256,219	302,364	370,850	441,494	505,029	REINVESTED EARNINGS—from prior years
(10,701)	(8,665)	(14,428)	(16,632)	(18,310)	DIVIDENDS—declared for payment to the shareowners
302,364	**370,850**	**441,494**	**505,029**	**566,172**	**REINVESTED EARNINGS** at year-end
17,808	18,031	18,264	18,482	18,691	COMMON SHARES—the weighted average number of shares outstanding during the year
$3.19	**$4.28**	**$4.66**	**$4.34**	**$4.25**	**EARNINGS PER SHARE**—the earnings allocated to each of the weighted average common shares outstanding
.60	.48	.79	.90	.98	DIVIDENDS DECLARED PER SHARE—accrued for payment
.48	.60	.79	.90	.98	DIVIDENDS PAID PER SHARE—received by the shareowners

The accompanying notes are an integral part of these financial statements.

The Controller of Interlake, Inc., has provided a helpful guide, "What to look for when reading the Income Statement:"

What to Look for When Reading the Income Statement

The statement of income is often referred to as the statement of profit and loss. It is a summary of revenues and related costs and expenses which indicates the profitability of the Company.

The statement focuses on the income producing activities of the Company and, therefore, reflects the results of operations for the fiscal year and provides the reader with a basis for assessing the Company's performance.

Revenue growth is usually one of the things the reader looks for. Interlake's revenues come mainly from the net sales of its various businesses and, while sales have been over the billion dollar level for the last three years, there has been slippage in the last two. As indicated in the financial comments and notes, this slippage is the result of discontinuing certain operations in 1980 and of recent turbulent economic conditions.

Other revenues include royalties, interest income and gains on sales of property and equipment. The big jump in 1981 was due to substantially higher interest income and gains on asset sales.

Operating profitability is the reader's primary concern and attention is usually concentrated in this area. On a pre-tax basis, earnings from on-going operations were $79,119,000 in 19__, $57,553,000 in 19__, and $45,177,000 in 19__. Although 19__ included benefits of $15,400,000 from liquidation of LIFO inventories, earnings from on-going operations reflect a strong pattern in light of the recent economic climate.

INTERLAKE, INC.
Statement of Consolidated Income and Retained Earnings

For the Years Ended December 27, 19__ , December 28, 19__ and December 30, 19__

	19__	19__	19__
	(In thousands except per share statistics)		
Sales and Revenues:			
Net sales	$1,016,605	$1,055,883	$1,104,588
Other revenues	16,706	7,880	7,847
	1,033,311	1,063,763	1,112,435
Costs and Expenses:			
Cost of products sold (excluding depreciation and taxes) (Note 1)	772,692	815,586	888,773
Depreciation, depletion and amortization	25,976	26,869	25,015
Taxes other than income taxes	111,442	116,523	106,871
Taxes other than income taxes	30,675	31,485	31,645
Interest expense (Note 1)	13,407	15,747	14,954
	954,192	1,006,210	1,067,258
Income Before Nonrecurring Item, Taxes on Income and Minority Interest	79,119	57,553	45,177
Shutdown/Disposal Provision (Note 6)	—	37,000	—
Income Before Taxes on Income and Minority Interest	79,119	20,553	45,177
Provision for Income Taxes (Notes 1 and 8)	30,953	5,998	3,129
	48,166	14,555	42,048
Minority Interest in Net Income of Subsidiary	1,589	737	2,313
Net Income for the Year	$ 46,577	$ 13,818	$ 39,735
Net Income Per Share of Common Stock (based on average shares of 6,134,310 in 1981, 6,038,764 in 19__ and 5,967,415 in 1979)	$7.59	$2.29	$6.66
Retained Earnings at Beginning of Year	$ 239,606	$ 239,075	$ 212,467
Net Income for the Year	46,577	13,818	39,735
	286,183	252,893	252,202
Deduct—Cash Dividends Declared or Paid ($2.40 per share in 19__ and $2.20 per share in 19__ and 19__)	(14,735)	(13,287)	(13,127)
Retained Earnings at End of Year	$ 271,448	$ 239,606	$ 239,075

(See notes to consolidated financial statements)

Consolidated Balance Sheet

Assets

June 30 (dollars in thousands)	**1983**	1982
Current assets:		
Cash and short-term investments	**$ 17,343**	$ 12,954
Accounts receivable, less allowance of $3,088 in 1983 and $1,996 in 1982	**130,949**	111,199
Inventories:		
Raw materials	**29,986**	30,659
Work in process	**34,168**	34,600
Finished goods	**50,689**	45,773
Total inventories	**114,843**	111,032
Prepaid expenses, taxes and other current assets	**42,266**	38,162
Total current assets	**305,401**	273,347
Property, plant and equipment:		
Land	**18,080**	13,387
Buildings	**116,806**	102,454
Machinery and equipment	**152,773**	131,720
Leasehold improvements	**16,878**	13,662
Total property, plant and equipment	**304,537**	261,223
Less accumulated depreciation and amortization	**117,508**	95,635
Net property, plant and equipment	**187,029**	165,588
Other assets	**6,748**	4,714
Total assets	**$499,178**	$443,649

See accompanying notes

Liabilities and Stockholders' Equity

June 30 (dollars in thousands)	**1983**	1982
Current liabilities:		
Notes payable to banks	**$ 51,785**	$ 48,873
Accounts payable	**33,799**	26,806
Income taxes	**29,178**	26,962
Accrued liabilities	**53,236**	45,645
Long-term debt due within one year	**2,222**	955
Total current liabilities	**170,220**	149,241
Long-term debt due after one year	**17,452**	14,218
Deferred income taxes	**16,472**	16,975
Other long-term liabilities	**8,083**	4,900
Commitments		
Stockholders' equity:		
Common stock: authorized 12,000,000 shares without par value; issued and outstanding, 1983 – 9,551,498, 1982 – 9,298,970	**109,786**	96,869
Retained earnings	**224,007**	197,654
Foreign currency translation	**(42,097)**	(32,227)
Notes receivable from sale of stock	**(4,745)**	(3,981)
Total stockholders' equity	**286,951**	258,315
Total liabilities and stockholders' equity	**$499,178**	$443,649

See accompanying notes

CONSOLIDATED BALANCE SHEET

Zero Corporation and Subsidiaries

Consolidated Balance Sheets

March 31, 1983 and 1982

ASSETS	**1983**	*1982*
Current Assets		
Cash	**$ 30,000**	$ 254,000
Short-term investments	**21,606,000**	15,654,000
Receivables (less allowance for doubtful accounts of $168,000 in 1983 and $172,000 in 1982)	**12,382,000**	12,592,000
Inventories		
Raw materials and supplies, etc.	**4,498,000**	4,794,000
Work in process	**4,336,000**	5,128,000
Finished goods	**3,300,000**	3,437,000
Prepaid expenses	**264,000**	309,000
Deferred income taxes	**931,000**	743,000
Total Current Assets	**47,347,000**	42,911,000
Property, Plant and Equipment	**31,197,000**	29,223,000
Less accumulated depreciation and amortization	**13,451,000**	12,112,000
Net Property	**17,746,000**	17,111,000
Investment in Ocean Technology, Inc. (at equity plus excess cost: 1983, $544,000; 1982, $567,000) (40% owned)	**3,035,000**	2,630,000
Excess Costs (costs in excess of the value of assets acquired in purchase transactions; less accumulated amortization of $346,000 in 1983 and $300,000 in 1982)	**1,889,000**	1,176,000
Notes Receivable and Other Assets	**514,000**	2,333,000
Total Assets	**$70,531,000**	$66,161,000

LIABILITIES AND SHAREHOLDERS' EQUITY		
Current Liabilities		
Current portion of long-term debt	**$ 1,138,000**	$ 1,110,000
Accounts payable	**1,752,000**	2,235,000
Income taxes payable	**863,000**	1,281,000
Accrued liabilities		
Other taxes	**1,181,000**	955,000
Interest	**245,000**	300,000
Wages, commissions, etc.	**3,209,000**	3,416,000
Workers' compensation claims	**632,000**	829,000
Other	**1,032,000**	939,000
Total Current Liabilities	**10,052,000**	11,065,000
Deferred Income Taxes	**214,000**	151,000
Obligations Under Capital Leases	**1,096,000**	502,000
Long-Term Debt	**7,577,000**	8,688,000
Subordinated Debt (net of discount of $308,000 in 1983 and $520,000 in 1982)	**2,505,000**	3,563,000
Other Non-Current Liabilities (including deferred compensation of $1,980,000 in 1983 and $1,628,000 in 1982)	**2,018,000**	1,666,000
Minority Interest in Consolidated Subsidiary	**952,000**	737,000
Shareholders' Equity		
Preferred stock—authorized 1,000,000 shares of $1 par value; none issued		
Common Stock—authorized 10,000,000 shares of $1 par value; outstanding shares, 5,060,419 in 1983 and 5,011,494 in 1982 (as adjusted for stock split)	**5,060,000**	4,009,000
Additional paid in capital	**10,381,000**	10,827,000
Retained earnings	**30,676,000**	24,953,000
Total Shareholders' Equity	**46,117,000**	39,789,000
Total Liabilities and Shareholders' Equity	**$70,531,000**	$66,161,000

The notes to financial statements are an integral part of these statements.

Interlake Inc. provides the following information in its annual report to assist stockholders to do a more intelligent job of analyzing balance sheet items:

Understanding the Balance Sheet—A Real Asset

The purpose of a balance sheet is to summarize the financial position of a business on a specific date. It is a "snapshot" of how the Company stands on the last day of its fiscal year.

The asset section of the balance sheet shows the Company's assets—everything that the Company owns. This consists of property rights, physical goods, uncollected claims, and prepayments. Those items that can be converted into cash or will be consumed within a year are called current assets. The remaining assets are referred to as long-term or fixed assets, because they generally are investments intended to produce revenues and earnings and are not intended to be sold in the ordinary course of business.

The other section of the balance sheet lists the Company's liabilities and the equity investment of the shareholders—everything that the Company owes. Liabilities which will fall due within a year are called current liabilities.

The reader can gain insight into the financial vigor of an enterprise from its balance sheet. The primary considerations usually center around the firm's ability to pay its debts as they fall due (liquidity) and to take advantage of new opportunities (flexibility).

There are three key statistics which analysts frequently use to measure financial strength:

- Current Ratio—current assets divided by current liabilities.
- Quick Ratio—cash, cash equivalents and receivables divided by current liabilities.
- Debt to Equity Ratio—the proportion of total debt, including short-term borrowings, to shareholders' equity.

A review of these statistics demonstrates Interlake's solid financial strength:

	19	19	19
Current Ratio	2.2/1	2.0/1	1.7/1
Quick Ratio	1.1/1	1.0/1	.9/1
Debt/Equity	28/72	31/69	35/65

Tektronix Consolidated Financial Position in thousands

1978	1979	1980	1981	1982	
$357,704	**$428,787**	**$540,917**	**$573,791**	**$621,981**	**CURRENT ASSETS** are cash and assets that should be converted to cash or used in operations within one year
66,208	41,788	57,145	47,862	73,331	CASH AND CASH EARNING INCOME — bank deposits and short-term investments
115,100	153,568	198,069	204,952	230,573	ACCOUNTS RECEIVABLE — due from customers after an allowance for doubtful accounts
163,523	214,533	263,563	293,705	290,268	INVENTORIES — materials, accumulated manufacturing costs and finished products awaiting sale
12,873	18,898	22,140	27,272	27,809	PREPAID EXPENSES — supplies and services that have not been used, and deposits that will be refunded
107,556	**153,135**	**193,831**	**214,527**	**233,267**	**CURRENT LIABILITIES** are obligations that are to be paid within one year
10,351	28,997	45,809	50,175	66,334	SHORT-TERM DEBT — borrowed for less than one year and that portion of long-term debt repayable within a year
33,108	42,033	49,034	60,405	63,856	ACCOUNTS PAYABLE—owed for materials, services, interest and miscellaneous taxes
18,458	20,444	27,404	28,788	23,118	INCOME TAXES PAYABLE — to United States and foreign governments
45,639	61,661	71,584	75,159	79,959	ACCRUED COMPENSATION — payable to employees, and their retirement and incentive plans
250,148	**275,652**	**347,086**	**359,264**	**388,714**	**WORKING CAPITAL** is the current assets in excess of the current liabilities
119,533	194,454	276,771	340,912	379,122	FACILITIES—the cost of land, buildings and equipment after deducting accumulated depreciation
13,893	19,666	24,005	39,050	41,184	OTHER LONG-TERM ASSETS — the equity in joint ventures, receivables not due within a year, and intangibles
37,086	62,094	136,196	146,143	132,060	LONG-TERM DEBT — funds borrowed for more than a year, less that portion due within a year
16,029	19,150	23,974	30,765	41,124	DEFERRED TAX LIABILITY — income taxes which have not become payable
3,763	5,728	4,354	4,774	5,387	OTHER LONG-TERM LIABILITIES—incentive compensation payable in future years
326,696	**402,800**	**483,338**	**557,544**	**630,449**	**SHAREOWNERS' EQUITY** is the book value owned by the shareowners
24,332	31,950	41,844	52,515	64,277	SHARE CAPITAL — the proceeds of common shares sold less the cost of any shares repurchased
302,364	370,850	441,494	505,029	566,172	REINVESTED EARNINGS — accumulated earnings that have been reinvested in the business
17,913	18,143	18,372	18,574	18,807	COMMON SHARES — the number of shares outstanding at year-end, of the forty million no par value shares authorized

The accompanying notes are an integral part of these financial statements.

STATEMENT OF CHANGES IN CONSOLIDATED FINANCIAL POSITION

This section summarizes the source of financial resources and the disbursement of the funds during the fiscal year. It is intended to give the reader of your report a better understanding of the financing and investing activities of your company.

Examples:

Statement of Changes in Financial Position

Carpenter Technology Corporation

for the years ended June 30, 1983, 1982, and 1981

(in thousands)

	1983	1982	1981
CASH PROVIDED FROM OPERATIONS			
Net income	**$16,042**	$33,162	$44,731
Depreciation	**14,571**	13,099	11,820
Deferred income taxes	**9,275**	6,056	3,131
Total from earnings	**39,888**	52,317	59,682
Changes in working capital:			
Receivables	**5,748**	15,088	(5,683)
Inventories	**7,145**	(3,527)	9,060
Other current assets	**(598)**	(4,481)	(44)
Accounts payable and other current liabilities	**(285)**	(16,548)	12,756
Net cash provided from operations	**51,898**	42,849	75,771
CASH USED FOR DIVIDENDS	**(18,130)**	(18,084)	(17,195)
CASH USED FOR LONG-TERM INVESTMENTS			
Additions to plant and equipment	**(71,853)**	(62,139)	(32,141)
Disposals of plant and equipment	**1,278**	829	228
Other	**3,797**	(3,596)	(79)
Net cash used for long-term investments	**(66,778)**	(64,906)	(31,992)
CASH PROVIDED FROM (USED FOR) FINANCING			
Additions to long-term debt	**11,236**	49,500	737
Reductions of long-term debt	**(1,457)**	(780)	(757)
Reductions of short-term debt	**—**	—	(15,222)
Issuance of common stock	**2,738**	373	495
Net cash provided from (used for) financing	**12,517**	49,093	(14,747)
INCREASE (DECREASE) IN CASH AND SHORT-TERM INVESTMENTS	**(20,493)**	8,952	11,837
Cash and short-term investments at beginning of year	**28,479**	19,527	7,690
Cash and short-term investments at end of year	**$ 7,986**	$28,479	$19,527

( ) indicate cash decrease.
See accompanying notes to financial statements.

INTERLAKE INC.

Making Sense of Cash Flows

The statement of changes in financial position summarizes where the Company acquired its financial resources during the fiscal year and where it applied or used these resources. It is intended to give the reader a better understanding of the financing and investing activities of the Company.

The statement is designed to emphasize changes in working capital from the viewpoint of cash entering and leaving the Company on a permanent or long-term basis. The circulation of cash through the working capital components is treated separately because current asset and current liability balances are variable and will roll over in fairly brief time periods.

The Company's primary source of funds over the last three years has been cash generated by operations. This is different from net income, because some of the income and expense items do not involve cash movements during the current year. When net income is adjusted for non-cash items, it indicates working capital provided from operations or cash income.

Financial resources can also be acquired by selling properties which are no longer needed in the business, borrowing, or raising equity capital. The disposal of discontinued operations generated substantial funds in 1981, no major borrowings have occurred since 1978, and the dividend reinvestment program has been an increasing source of capital.

The focus of generating cash inflows is to maintain and expand the Company's productive base, repay creditors, and reward investors. Interlake's capital expenditures and investment activities have been significant, and fully funded by current operations. Debt is being retired at a rate that exceeds minimum requirements and dividend payments have been increased.

Interlake has substantial capital resources to meet future financial requirements. In addition to the Company's basic earning power and long-term debt borrowing strength, Interlake's liquidity is enhanced by bank credit lines totaling $136,000,000 and only $10,179,000 was borrowed against these lines at year end 1981. This includes a domestic credit arrangement for $75 million. Interlake can borrow against these lines at year end 1981. This includes a domestic credit agreement for $75 million. Interlake can borrow up to the full amount during the period ending July 1, 1984 and, at its option, may convert any balance to a five-year term loan.

INTERLAKE, INC.
Statement of Changes in Consolidated Financial Position

For the Years Ended December 27, 1981, December 28, 1980 and December 30, 1979

	1981	1980* (In thousands)	1979*
Financial Resources Were Provided By:			
Net income	$ 46,577	$ 13,818	$ 39,735
Depreciation, depletion and amortization	25,976	26,869	25,015
Equity in earnings of affiliates and joint ventures, less dividends received	(1,828)	1,248	(923)
Shutdown/disposal provision—non-current portion	—	25,584	3,941
Future income taxes	7,407	(7,509)	3,941
Other long-term liabilities	(847)	1,934	1,680
Minority interest in net income of subsidiary, less dividend paid	192	(258)	715
Working capital provided from operations	77,477	61,686	70,163
Long-term borrowings	—	1,233	2,864
Disposals of property, plant and equipment	3,568	1,341	2,133
Disposal of shutdown facilities	13,860	—	—
Decrease in construction funds held by trustees	1,237	1,305	8,016
Dividend reinvestment plan	2,173	1,896	903
Other	3,197	(307)	1,166
	101,512	67,154	85,245
Financial Resources Were Used For:			
Capital expenditures	37,393	31,276	69,556
Reduction of long-term debt	6,402	3,716	3,640
Cash dividends declared	14,735	13,287	13,127
Acquisition of businesses, net of working capital acquired	9,896	—	—
Investment in tax leases, net of amortization	4,967	—	—
Change in exchange rates	9,461	—	—
	82,854	48,279	86,323
Increase (decrease) in working capital	$ 18,658	$ 18,875	$ (1.078)
Increase (Decrease) in Working Capital Comprises:			
Cash and short-term investments	$ 14,214	$ 9,944	$ (9,897)
Receivables	(22,918)	(11,528)	33,587
Inventories	7,739	(17,659)	21,694
Other current assets	3,647	5,298	(2,689)
Accounts payable and other accrued liabilities	6,914	19,469	(27,325)
Income taxes payable	928	(8,444)	8,421
Debt due within one year	8,134	21,795	(24,869)
	18,658	18,875	(1,078)
Working capital at beginning of year	181,145	162,270	163,348
Working capital at end of year	$199,803	$181,145	$162,270

*Certain amounts have been reclassified to conform to the presentation in 1981.

(See notes to consolidated financial statements)

CONSOLIDATED STATEMENT OF CHANGES IN FINANCIAL STATEMENTS

Textron Inc. Consolidated Statement of Changes in Shareholders' Equity

For each of the three years in the period ended December 31, 1983 (Dollars in millions)

	Preferred stock (1)		Common stock (1)	Capital surplus	Retained earnings	Currency translation adjustment	Cost of treasury shares (1)
	$2.08	$1.40					
Balance							
January 3, 1981	$59.4	$16.7	$8.7	$120.6	$ 983.0	$ –	$34.6
Conversion of preferred stock	(9.8)	(1.5)	.1	11.3	–	–	–
Purchase of common stock	–	–	–	–	–	–	11.9
Exercise of options and warrants (2)	–	–	–	–	–	–	(.5)
Net income	–	–	–	–	151.8	–	–
Dividends:							
Preferred stock	–	–	–	–	(5.6)	–	–
Common stock ($1.80 per share)	–	–	–	–	(61.7)	–	–
Balance							
January 2, 1982	49.6	15.2	8.8	131.9	1,067.5	–	46.0
Opening balance of currency translation adjustment	–	–	–	–	–	(1.9)	–
Conversion of preferred stock	(3.9)	(1.1)	.1	4.9	–	–	–
Purchase of common stock	–	–	–	–	–	–	22.9
Exercise of warrants (2)	–	–	–	–	(.1)	–	(.1)
Currency translation adjustment	–	–	–	–	–	(12.5)	–
Exchange of common stock for debentures	–	–	–	–	(2.6)	–	(21.9)
Net income	–	–	–	–	84.4	–	–
Dividends:							
Preferred stock	–	–	–	–	(5.1)	–	–
Common stock ($1.80 per share)	–	–	–	–	(61.0)	–	–
Balance							
January 1, 1983	45.7	14.1	8.9	136.8	1,083.1	(14.4)	46.9
Conversion of preferred stock	(3.6)	(1.3)	.1	4.8	–	–	–
Exercise of options and warrants (2)	–	–	–	–	(.1)	–	(.8)
Currency translation adjustment	–	–	–	–	–	(5.6)	–
Net income	–	–	–	–	88.7	–	–
Dividends:							
Preferred stock	–	–	–	–	(4.6)	–	–
Common stock ($1.80 per share)	–	–	–	–	(61.9)	–	–
Balance							
December 31, 1983	$42.1	$12.8	$9.0	$141.6	$1,105.2	$(20.0)	$46.1

(1) Shares issued at the end of 1980, 1981, 1982 and 1983 were as follows: $2.08 Preferred–2,516,000, 2,096,000, 1,932,000 and 1,780,000 shares, respectively; $1.40 Preferred–1,413,000, 1,283,000, 1,189,000 and 1,087,000 shares, respectively; Common–34,718,000, 35,297,000, 35,561,000 and 35,821,000 shares, respectively. Shares held in the treasury at the end of 1980, 1981, 1982 and 1983 were as follows: $2.08 Preferred–69,000 shares at all such dates; $1.40 Preferred–487,000 shares at all such dates; Common–836,000, 1,271,000, 1,371,000 and 1,337,000 shares, respectively.

(2) Exercises of options and warrants aggregated 21,000 shares in 1981, 4,000 shares in 1982 and 35,000 shares in 1983.

See notes to consolidated financial statements.

Business Segments

		Raychem	Chemelex	Bentley-Harris	Corporate	Consolidated Total
Sales to unaffiliated customers	**1983**	**$491,409**	**$73,245**	**$18,048**	**–**	**$582,702**
	1982	455,913	59,505	19,531	–	534,949
	1981	453,643	49,685	22,070	–	525,398
Operating income	**1983**	**105,984**	**4,594**	**2,347**	**–**	**112,925**
	1982	94,630	4,967	2,651	–	102,248
	1981	110,717	5,008	4,105	–	119,830
Corporate expenses	**1983**	**–**	**–**	**–**	**$58,415**	**58,415**
	1982	–	–	–	44,886	44,886
	1981	–	–	–	49,924	49,924
Interest expense, net	**1983**	**–**	**–**	**–**	**–**	**5,299**
	1982	–	–	–	–	8,364
	1981	–	–	–	–	9,960
Income before income taxes	**1983**	**–**	**–**	**–**	**–**	**49,211**
	1982	–	–	–	–	48,998
	1981	–	–	–	–	59,946
Identifiable assets	**1983**	**430,443**	**41,994**	**11,859**	**14,882**	**499,178**
	1982	383,774	30,412	12,918	16,545	443,649
	1981	369,708	23,803	13,004	18,381	424,896
Capital expenditures	**1983**	**48,328**	**3,040**	**447**	**6,382**	**58,197**
	1982	28,725	1,509	417	3,563	34,214
	1981	43,828	1,356	369	5,043	50,596
Depreciation and amortization	**1983**	**22,834**	**1,274**	**416**	**2,845**	**27,369**
	1982	20,736	1,215	418	2,010	24,379
	1981	17,410	878	504	1,460	20,252

Sales between segments are immaterial.

SEGMENT AND GEOGRAPHIC DATA

The company is engaged principally in one line of business—processed food products—which represents over 90% of consolidated sales. Information about the business of the company by geographic area is presented in the table below.

There were no material amounts of sales or transfers between geographic areas or between affiliates, and no material amounts of United States export sales.

(in thousands of U.S. dollars)	Domestic	Foreign					
		United Kingdom	Canada	Western Europe	Other	Total	Worldwide
1983							
Sales	**$2,381,054**	**$547,527**	**$216,726**	**$383,784**	**$209,354**	**$1,357,391**	**$3,738,445**
Operating income	**246,780**	**61,282**	**34,146**	**29,146**	**25,111**	**149,685**	**396,465**
Identifiable assets	**1,362,152**	**265,218**	**112,620**	**294,732**	**143,971**	**816,541**	**2,178,693**
Capital expenditures	**72,712**	**12,262**	**13,790**	**8,253**	**4,368**	**38,673**	**111,385**
Depreciation expense	**42,279**	**8,364**	**3,592**	**6,355**	**3,606**	**21,917**	**64,196**
1982							
Sales	$2,317,279	$605,645	$216,757	$327,010	$221,809	$1,371,221	$3,688,500
Operating income	235,924	60,135	26,696	19,290	20,190	126,311	362,235
Identifiable assets	1,318,848	303,356	96,547	265,698	145,121	810,722	2,129,570
Capital expenditures	87,948	24,400	7,716	12,669	7,718	52,503	140,451
Depreciation expense	37,659	10,794	2,947	4,711	3,121	21,573	59,232
1981							
Sales	$2,143,306	$711,976	$176,358	$323,344	$213,905	$1,425,583	$3,568,889
Operating income	220,256	67,619	20,460	7,078	20,198	115,355	355,611
Identifiable assets	1,245,868	354,943	84,874	203,780	150,113	793,710	2,039,578
Capital expenditures	57,394	41,139	5,736	13,781	10,554	71,210	128,604
Depreciation expense	33,540	12,405	2,722	5,153	2,542	22,822	56,362

Quarterly Results

The following table shows net sales, gross profit (net sales less cost of products sold, research and development, and depreciation), net earnings and net earnings per share for each quarter during the past three years.

Dollar Amounts in Thousands— Except Per Share Data	Continuing Operations			Discontinued Operations			
	Net Sales	Gross Profit	Earnings	Loss	Provision For Disposal	Net Earnings	Net Earnings Per Share
1983							
First	**$120,815**	**$ 51,359**	**$ 6,117**	**$ —**	**$ —**	**$ 6,117**	**$ .25**
Second	**137,785**	**59,627**	**9,867**	**—**	**—**	**9,867**	**.39**
Third	**144,907**	**65,080**	**12,804**	**—**	**—**	**12,804**	**.51**
Fourth	**164,100**	**77,649**	**13,876**	**—**	**—**	**13,876**	**.56**
Total	**$567,607**	**$253,715**	**$42,664**	**$ —**	**$ —**	**$42,664**	**$1.71**
1982							
First	$126,166	$ 57,869	$ 9,550	$ —	$ —	$ 9,550	$ .38
Second	135,711	61,991	11,765	—	—	11,765	.48
Third	130,705	58,563	8,360	—	—	8,360	.33
Fourth	122,810	46,398	102	—	—	102	.01
Total	$515,392	$224,821	$29,777	$ —	$ —	$29,777	$1.20
1981							
First	$125,226	$ 57,804	$ 8,827	$ (866)	$ (7,300)	$ 661	$ .03
Second	139,518	65,028	13,401	(72)	—	13,329	.54
Third	140,540	65,155	13,602	(1,422)	—	12,180	.49
Fourth	133,932	60,856	11,536	(1,897)	(25,800)	(16,161)	(.66)
Total	$539,216	$248,843	$47,366	$(4,257)	$(33,100)	$10,009	$ .40

Stock Market Data

Talley Industries, Inc. and Subsidiaries

Securities

Three of the Company's securities are listed on the New York Stock Exchange: Common stock (TAL), Series B $1.00 Cumulative Preferred stock (TALB) and 8⅛% Sinking Fund Debentures maturing in 1997. Series A Preferred stock is traded occasionally in the over-the-counter market. As of April 29, 1983 there were 7,141 holders of record of Talley Industries, Inc. Common stock.

The high and low sales prices of the Common and Series B Preferred stock on the New York Stock Exchange, by quarter, for fiscal 1983 and 1982 were as follows:

	Common (TAL)				Series B (TALB)			
	1983		1982		1983		1982	
Quarter Ended	High	Low	High	Low	High	Low	High	Low
June	5⅜	4⅛	6½	5⅛	8	6⅞	8¾	7¾
September	5⅜	4⅛	5⅞	3⅞	8⅛	7⅛	8¼	6⅜
December	7¼	4¾	4¼	3⅜	10¾	7¾	7½	6½
March	9⅞	6⅛	5¾	3⅝	13⅛	10⅛	8⅛	6⅝

Dividends

Quarterly dividend payments on Series A Preferred and Series B Preferred stock amounted to 27.5 cents and 25 cents per share, respectively, during each quarter of the past two fiscal years. No common stock dividends have been paid since 1980.

Selected Financial Data

(Dollars in thousands, except per share)

Common Stock Data

Square D Company's common stock is traded on the New York Stock Exchange. The high and low sales prices and the dividends per share by quarter for 1983 and 1982 were:

	Market Price		Dividends	
1983	High	Low	Paid	Declared
First Quarter	$38.250	$32.375	$.46	$.46
Second Quarter	40.000	32.500	.46	.46
Third Quarter	35.875	30.375	.46	.46
Fourth Quarter	41.250	33.500	.46	.46
1982				
First Quarter	29.375	22.875	.46	.46
Second Quarter	27.500	24.250	.46	.46
Third Quarter	28.625	21.750	.46	.46
Fourth Quarter	34.750	27.250	.46	.46

The number of shareholders of the Company's common stock as of January 31, 1984, was approximately 14,500. See Note H of Notes to Consolidated Financial Statements for information regarding dividend payment restrictions.

Selected Quarterly Financial Data (Unaudited)

Quarter Ended	Net Sales	Gross Profit	Net Earnings	Net Earnings Per Share
1983				
March 31	$262,165	$ 77,926	$12,087	$ .43
June 30	277,346	84,542	14,610	.52
September 30	302,759	100,665	18,270	.64
December 31	301,867	98,972	17,944	.63
1982				
March 31	266,218	74,395	19,314	.70
June 30	279,480	90,809	18,758	.68
September 30	271,422	81,079	18,051	.66
December 31	239,861	66,279	15,577	.57

COMMON STOCK SPLIT AND DIVIDEND HISTORY

Farm House Foods Corporation

SPLIT OR DIVIDEND	Date
Five-for-four stock split	September, 1972
Two-for-one stock split	July, 1975
Three-for-two stock split	March, 1976
Five percent stock dividend	July, 1977
Five-for-four stock split	November, 1977
Five percent stock dividend	January, 1978
Five percent stock dividend	July, 1978
Ten percent stock dividend	September, 1978
Five percent stock dividend	January, 1979
Ten percent stock dividend	March, 1979
Five percent stock dividend	July, 1979
Five percent stock dividend	January, 1980
Five percent stock dividend	July, 1980
Five percent stock dividend	November, 1980
Five-for-four stock split	January, 1981
Five percent stock dividend	August, 1981
Ten percent stock dividend	November, 1981
Five percent stock dividend	February, 1982

MARKET PRICE RANGE OF COMMON STOCK

Farm House Foods Corporation stock is traded over-the-counter (FHFC) and is quoted on NASDAQ. The Company has paid no cash dividends. The price ranges of the common stock have been retroactively adjusted to reflect stock splits and stock dividends.

	Fiscal 1982				Fiscal 1981			
	Bid		Ask		Bid		Ask	
	High	Low	High	Low	High	Low	High	Low
1st Quarter	6¾	4⅜	6⅞	4½	2⅞	2⅛	3	2½
2nd Quarter	6⅞	4⅝	7⅜	4⅞	4⅛	2¾	4¼	2⅞
3rd Quarter	8	5⅞	8¼	6	5⅜	4⅛	5½	4¼
4th Quarter	7⅜	5⅜	7⅝	5½	5¼	4½	5¼	4¾

Quarterly Financial and Stock Information 1983 and 1982
(Unaudited)

(In millions except per share amounts)	1st Quarter 1983	1st Quarter 1982	2nd Quarter 1983	2nd Quarter 1982	3rd Quarter 1983	3rd Quarter 1982	4th Quarter 1983	4th Quarter 1982
Income Statement								
Sales	$717.7	$773.8	$745.4	$775.4	$696.4	$669.3	$820.3	$717.5
Costs and expenses:								
Cost of sales	561.0	605.8	586.5	612.1	540.6	519.2	658.2	578.0
Selling and administrative	117.1	125.6	117.3	125.5	119.1	119.1	126.6	111.2
	678.1	731.4	703.8	737.6	659.7	638.3	784.8	689.2
Operating income	39.6	42.4	41.6	37.8	36.7	31.0	35.5	28.3
Equity in pre-tax income of unconsolidated finance company	5.4	3.5	4.4	3.4	3.6	4.9	3.9	5.1
Interest expense–net	(6.6)	(9.9)	(6.0)	(8.9)	(4.5)	(7.9)	(5.1)	(9.6)
Gain on exchange of common stock for debentures	–	–	–	6.0	–	4.3	–	–
Income before income taxes	38.4	36.0	40.0	38.3	35.8	32.3	34.3	23.8
Income taxes	16.1	15.2	17.3	13.6	15.0	9.9	11.4	7.3
Net income	$ 22.3	$ 20.8	$ 22.7	$ 24.7	$ 20.8	$ 22.4	$ 22.9	$ 16.5
Net income per common share	$ .60	$ .57	$ .62	$ .67	$ .56	$ .61	$ .62	$ .45
Common Stock Information								
Price Range:								
High	$28	$28⅛	$35	$24⅜	$36⅞	$24¼	$36¼	$27⅜
Low	$23½	$20¼	$26⅛	$17½	$31⅛	$17¼	$32	$23⅜
Dividend per share	$ .45	$ .45	$ .45	$ .45	$ .45	$ .45	$ .45	$ .45

QUARTERLY RESULTS

Summarized quarterly financial information is as follows:

(in thousands except earnings per share)	Sales	Gross Profit	Net Income	Earnings per Share
1983 By Quarter				
First	**$ 909,179**	**$ 340,471**	**$ 55,304**	**$1.17**
Second	**956,106**	**344,065**	**54,410**	**1.14**
Third	**866,643**	**318,428**	**46,253**	**.98**
Fourth	**1,006,517**	**379,676**	**58,283**	**1.22**
Total	**$3,738,445**	**$1,382,640**	**$214,250**	**$4.51**
1982 By Quarter				
First	$ 860,179	$ 310,613	$ 54,439	$1.16
Second	954,898	323,920	50,751	1.08
Third	876,461	301,811	39,144	.83
Fourth	996,962	367,990	48,468	1.03
Total	$3,688,500	$1,304,334	$192,802	$4.10

Net income and earnings per share for the first quarter of 1982 reflect a $7.1 million reduction of income taxes due to the permanent forgiveness of certain previously deferred United Kingdom taxes.

RATIOS

Consider presenting ratios in your company's annual report:

W. R. Grace & Co. 1982 Annual Report
Key Financial Ratios—Five Years

	1982	1981	1980	1979	1978
Income Statement					
% Pretax, pre-interest income to sales	9.9%	10.4%	10.4%	10.0%	9.4%
% Net income to sales	5.2	5.6	4.7	4.3	3.9
% Income taxes to pretax income	34.8	33.8	42.3	45.8	46.9
Balance Sheet					
Debt ratio	37.1%	39.6%	37.8%	34.1%	35.0%
% Total debt to total capital	40.1	42.9	42.5	40.4	41.5
Current assets/current liabilities	1.7x	1.6x	1.5x	1.6x	1.8x
Profitability					
% Operating income to sales	5.9%	7.1%	6.1%	5.5%	5.1%
% Return on total capital	11.7	15.3	13.9	12.4	10.4
% Return on shareholders' equity	15.6	20.2	18.1	16.3	13.9
Asset Turnover					
Sales/inventories	6.8x	7.5x	7.7x	7.1x	6.6x
Sales/receivables	8.5	8.3	8.2	7.7	7.5
Sales/total assets	1.2	1.4	1.5	1.5	1.4
Cash Flow					
% Cash flow to total debt	41.0%	40.6%	41.9%	38.6%	35.0%
% Dividends to cash flow	21.6	18.4	18.0	20.8	20.5
% Dividends to net income	40.8	32.1	35.5	38.0	41.3
Stock Market					
Average yield	7.0%	5.7%	3.9%	5.2%	6.4%
Year-end price/earnings (P/E)	5.8x	6.0x	9.7x	8.1x	6.6x
Year-end price/book value	.8	1.1	1.6	1.2	.8

XVII
FOOTNOTES

INTRODUCTION

Basically, this section is divided into two parts:

1. Summary of Significant Accounting Policies
2. Footnotes Tied into Financial Reports

Your accountants will provide the information to be included in "this section." A word of caution: Work with your accountants to use language that the average stockholder can understand—difficult as this may be. Insurance companies are rewriting policies to take out the legalese. Try to do the same in setting up your corporate "Footnotes."

Summary of Significant Accounting Policies

The Accounting Principles Board (APB) requires corporations to include a summary of significant accounting policies either just preceding the notes or as the initial note. According to the *Opinion,* the summary must encompass the accounting principles and methods that involve any of the following:

a. A selection from existing acceptable alternatives;
b. Principles and methods peculiar to the industry in which the reporting entity operates, even if such principles and methods are predominantly followed in that industry;
c. Unusual or innovative applications of generally accepted accounting principles (and, as applicable, of principles and methods peculiar to the industry in which the reporting entity operates).

Some examples of policies to be disclosed cited in the *Opinion* include those relating to basis of consolidation, depreciation method, amortization of intangibles, inventory pricing, translation of foreign currencies, recognition of profit on long-term construction contracts, and recognition of revenue from franchising and leasing operations.

Honeywell

Notes to Financial Statements

Consolidation—The consolidated financial statements and accompanying data include Honeywell Inc. and subsidiaries except finance and real estate subsidiaries, whose operations are dissimilar to the manufacturing operations of the consolidated group. All material transactions between the consolidated companies are eliminated.

Revenue—Revenue from product sales is recorded when title is passed to the customer. This usually occurs at the time of delivery or acceptance. Revenue from cost reimbursement-type contracts is recorded as costs are incurred. Revenue from long-term contracts is recorded on the percentage-of-completion basis.

Revenue from most computer lease contracts is recorded as earned over the lives of the contracts. A portion of future rental receipts under such contracts is sold to Honeywell's finance subsidiaries and classified as "obligation for rental contracts conveyed to finance subsidiaries." Long-term lease contracts that qualify as sales-type leases are recorded as sales when the equipment is installed.

Tax Credits—U.S. tax credits are included in income as a reduction of the federal income tax provision in the year the credits are realized for tax purposes.

Earnings Per Common Share—Earnings per share amounts are based on the average number of common shares outstanding during the year.

Marketable Securities—Marketable securities are carried at cost, which approximates market.

Inventories—Inventories are valued at the lower of cost or market. Cost is determined using the weighted-average method. Market is based on estimated realizable value.

The cost of manufactured products is based on standards developed for individual items from current material, labor and overhead costs at normal activity levels. Standard costs are adjusted to actual by application of manufacturing variances.

Payments received from customers on uncompleted contracts are deducted from applicable inventories.

Investments—Investments in nonconsolidated subsidiaries and companies owned 20 to 50 percent are valued at cost, adjusted for Honeywell's cumulative share of the undistributed earnings since acquisition.

Property—Property is carried at cost and depreciated over estimated useful lives using the straight-line method. Equipment for lease to others is depreciated over a five-year life.

Goodwill—Goodwill is amortized over not more than a forty-year period.

Reclassifications—Certain amounts in the 1981 and 1980 financial statements have been reclassified to conform with the presentation of similar amounts in the 1982 financial statements.

NOTES TO CONSOLIDATED FINANCIAL STATEMENTS

FOR THE YEARS ENDED JUNE 30, 1983, 1982 AND 1981

(1) Summary of Significant Accounting Policies:

The significant accounting policies followed by Briggs & Stratton Corporation and subsidiaries in the preparation of these financial statements, as summarized below, are in conformity with generally accepted accounting principles.

Principles of Consolidation: The consolidated financial statements include the accounts of the Company and its wholly-owned domestic and foreign subsidiaries after elimination of intercompany accounts and transactions.

Inventories: The last-in, first-out (LIFO) method was used for determining the cost of approximately 94% of the total inventories at June 30, 1983, 93% at June 30, 1982 and 91% at June 30, 1981. The remaining portion of the inventories was valued using the first-in, first-out (FIFO) method. If the FIFO inventory valuation method had been used, inventories would have been $36,812,000, $35,806,000 and $31,758,000 higher in the respective years. The LIFO inventory adjustment was determined on an overall basis and accordingly each class of inventory reflects an allocation based on the FIFO amounts.

Plant and Equipment and Depreciation: Plant and equipment is stated at cost, and depreciation is computed on the straight-line method at rates based upon the estimated useful lives of the assets. Expenditures for repairs and maintenance are charged to expense as incurred; expenditures for major renewals and betterments, which significantly extend the useful lives of existing plant and equipment, are capitalized and depreciated. Upon retirement or disposition of plant and equipment, the cost and related accumulated depreciation are removed from the accounts and the resulting gain or loss is recognized in income.

Investment Tax Credits: The Company follows the deferral method of accounting for the Federal investment tax credit. This tax credit is recorded as an addition to accumulated depreciation and amortized to income over the estimated useful lives of the related assets via a reduction of depreciation expense. The deferred investment tax credits arising from the purchase of depreciable assets totaled $2,118,000 in 1983, $2,149,000 in 1982 and $2,628,000 in 1981. The amounts amortized into income in each of the respective years were $1,370,000, $1,210,000 and $1,015,000. At June 30, 1983 and 1982 unamortized deferred investment tax credit aggregated $10,202,000 and $9,454,000 respectively.

Future Income Tax Benefits: Future income tax benefits, classified as a current asset, represent the tax effect of timing differences relating to current assets and current liabilities. These result in a higher taxable income than that recorded in the accounts for financial reporting purposes.

Deferred Income Taxes: Deferred income taxes, classified as a noncurrent liability, provide for the tax effects of timing differences relating to noncurrent assets and noncurrent liabilities resulting in the recognition of certain income and expense amounts in different periods for tax and financial reporting purposes. These timing differences principally result from additional tax deductions available due to the use of accelerated methods of depreciation and lives for tax purposes and are offset in part, by accrued employees benefits which are not tax deductible until paid.

Research and Development Costs: Expenditures relating to the development of new products and processes, including significant improvements and refinements to existing products are expensed as incurred. The amounts charged against income were $5,251,000 in 1983, $5,176,000 in 1982 and $4,768,000 in 1981.

Retirement Plan Costs: Current service costs are accrued and funded on a current basis. Prior service costs are being amortized and funded over 30 years.

Accrued Employee Benefits: The Company's life insurance program includes payment of a death benefit to beneficiaries of retired employees. The Company accrues for the estimated cost of these benefits over the estimated working life of the employee. Past service costs for all retired employees have been fully provided for and the Company is accruing for the prior service costs associated with active employees over thirty years. The Company also accrues for the estimated cost of supplemental retirement and death benefit agreements with certain officers.

Foreign Currency Translation: Foreign currency balance sheet accounts are translated into United States dollars at the rates of exchange in effect at fiscal year-end. Income and expenses are translated at the average rates of exchange in effect during the year. The related translation adjustments are made directly to a separate component of shareholders' investment, which contained the following changes during the two fiscal years:

	1983	1982
Balance at beginning of year	**$(262,000)**	$ 500,000
Translation adjustment for year	**(96,000)**	(762,000)
Balance at end of year	**$(358,000)**	$(262,000)

International Business Machines Corporation
and Subsidiary Companies

Notes to Consolidated Financial Statements:

Significant Accounting Policies

Principles of Consolidation: The consolidated financial statements include the accounts of International Business Machines Corporation and its U.S. and non-U.S. subsidiary companies, other than the IBM Credit Corporation, a wholly owned financing subsidiary. The equity method is used to account for the investment in IBM Credit Corporation and for investments in joint ventures and affiliated companies in which IBM has 50 percent or less ownership.

Translation of Non-U.S. Currency Amounts: For consolidation purposes, the financial statements of non-U.S. subsidiary companies are translated to U.S. dollars in accordance with the provisions of Statement of Financial Accounting Standards (SFAS) No. 52, "Foreign Currency Translation." This Statement was adopted by the company in 1982, and consolidated financial statements for the years 1981 and 1980 have been restated.

Gross Income: Gross income is recognized from sales when the product is shipped, or in certain cases upon customer acceptance, from rentals in the month in which they accrue, and from services over the contractual period or as the services are performed. Rental plans include maintenance service and contain discontinuance and purchase option provisions. Rental terms are predominantly monthly or for a two-year period, with some covering periods up to five years.

Depreciation: Rental machines, plant and other property are carried at cost and depreciated over their estimated useful lives. Depreciation of rental machines is computed using the sum-of-the-years digits method. Depreciation of plant and other property is computed using either accelerated methods or the straight-line method.

Retirement Plans: Current service costs are accrued currently. Prior service costs resulting from improvements in the plans are amortized generally over 10 years.

Selling Expenses: Selling expenses are charged against income as they are incurred.

Income Taxes: Income tax expense is based on reported earnings before income taxes. It thus includes the effects of timing differences between reported and taxable earnings that arise because certain transactions are included in taxable earnings in other years. Investment tax credits are deferred and amortized as a reduction of income tax expense over the average useful life of the applicable classes of property. Purchased tax credits and deductions are offset against the purchase cost.

Inventories: Raw materials, operating supplies, finished goods and work in process applicable to equipment sales are included in inventories at the lower of average cost or market. Work in process applicable to equipment rentals is similarly valued and included in rental machines and parts.

EXAMPLES OF FOOTNOTES

Your accountant, in preparing the financial statements, will refer to "See Footnote No. ______." The following are examples of how various companies have set up the footnotes in their annual reports. In some instances, these footnotes are included in "The Summary of Significant Accounting Practices."

Accounting Changes
Accounts Receivable
Acquisitions
Advertising Expense
Capital Stock
Cash and Short-Term Investments
Commitments and Contingencies
Common Stock
Compensated Absences
Contingent Liabilities
Contingencies
Contract Accounting
Convertible Debentures
Debt
Defense Contracts
Deferred Compensation
Discontinued Operations
Disposition of Assets
Earnings per Share
Employee Benefit Plans
Employees' Stock Option Plans
Extraordinary Items
Facilities
Fiscal Year
Foreign Currency Translation
Foreign Operations
Foreign Subsidiaries
Income Taxes
IRS Examinations
Intangible Assets
Interest
Inventories
Investment in Affiliates
Labor Agreements
Leases
Litigation
Loans to Officers
Merger, Acquisitions and Divestitures
Pension Plans
Performance Share Plan
Personnel Expenses
Plant Closing
Property, Plant and Equipment
Proposed Acquisitions
Provision for Losses on Disposition of Property and
Discontinuance of Product Lines
Purchase of Property Tax Benefits
Redeemable Preferred Stock
Related Party Transactions
Repurchase of the Corporation's Stock
Research and Development
Retirement Plans
Sale of Wholly Owned Subsidiaries
Short-Term Investments
Stock Options
Stock Splits
Third-Party Transactions
Treasury Stock
Unusual Charge
Vacation Accrued
Working Capital

Accounting Changes

During 1982, the company adopted the provisions of statements of Financial Accounting Standards No. 43, "Accounting for Compensated Absences," and No. 52, "Foreign Currency Translation." Financial statements for previous years have been restated to reflect the provisions of these statements.

The effect on net income and earnings per share as a result of the restatement is as follows:

	1981		*1980*	
(in thousands except per share data)	*Net Income*	*Primary Earnings Per Share*	*Net Income*	*Primary Earnings Per Share*
Amounts as previously reported	$167,454	$3.63	$142,887	$3.12
Net effect of accounting changes	(6,627)	(.15)	(11,390)	(.25)
Amounts as restated	$160,827	$3.48	$131,497	$2.87

Changes in the cumulative translation component of shareholders' equity which result from the application of Statement No. 52 are as follows:

(in thousands)	*1982*	*1981*	*1980*
Balance at beginning of year	$(32,175)	$(23,525)	$(31,093)
Adjustments arising from translation of foreign currency assets and liabilities	(45,077)	(8,650)	7,568
Balance at end of year	$(77,252)	$(32,175)	$(23,525)

—Accounts Receivable

The following tabulation shows the components of accounts receivable:

In millions	1983	1982
U.S. government, principally on long-term contracts	$210	$177
Commercial and foreign government		
Long-term contracts	119	72
Other	49	27
Unbilled costs and accrued profits, principally related to U.S. government and foreign government contracts	495	416
Total accounts receivable	$873	$692

Unbilled costs and accrued profits consist primarily of revenues on long-term contracts that have been recognized for accounting purposes but not yet billed to customers. Of the total at December 25, 1983, it is expected that approximately $428 million (including $22 million applicable to Saudi Arabian contracts) will be billed and collected within 90 days and $44 million, applicable to a project to install an air traffic control system in Saudi Arabia, will be collected upon completion of final contract negotiations which is expected to occur in 1984. A major portion of the remaining $23 million represents Lockheed's estimate of contract price adjustments and is expected to be billed and collected upon completion of negotiations within two years.

Accounts Receivable

	1983	1982
Trade and other	$213,054,000	$30,789,000
Allowance for uncollectible receivables	(924,000)	(1,499,000)
Federal income tax refund receivable	—	1,612,000
Long-term contracts:		
Billed	7,685,000	5,750,000
Retainage generally liquidated within one year after completion of contracts	1,044,000	463,000
	8,729,000	6,213,000
	$30,859,000	$37,115,000

ACQUISITIONS

In February, 1983, the Company acquired Topaz, Inc., a manufacturer of power conditioning equipment, for $31,890 in cash and $24,273 in shares of the Company's common stock (713,915 shares). This acquisition was accounted for as a purchase. Sales and net earnings for the periods prior to acquisition were not material.

In October, 1983, the Company acquired all of the outstanding common stock of KB-Denver, Inc., a manufacturer of snap dome switches, in exchange for 135,132 shares of the Company's common stock in a transaction accounted for as a pooling of interests. Results of KB-Denver's operations preceding the combination were not material. The consolidated financial statements have not been restated to reflect this acquisition.

In February, 1983, the Company acquired for $261 in cash an existing facility in Little Island, Irish Republic, for the production of electrodeposited copper foil, which is used in the manufacture of printed circuits for electronic and electrical applications. In March, 1983, the Company acquired Lumacell, Inc., a Canadian company that manufactures and markets a range of emergency lighting equipment, for $42 in cash. In October, 1983, the Company acquired, for $1,000 in cash, the remaining 50% interest in Gividi Glass Fabrics, a manufacturer of woven glass fabrics for electronic and industrial applications. These acquisitions were accounted for as purchases and their sales and net earnings for the periods prior to the dates of acquisition were not material.

Acquisitions:

EkoLine

In November 1981, the Company acquired the business and net assets of the medical ultrasound division of SmithKline Corporation ("SmithKline") in a transaction accounted for as a purchase. The Company formed a domestic subsidiary, EkoLine, Inc. ("EkoLine") and two foreign subsidiaries in England and in Australia, to conduct the business activities of the former SmithKline division.

The purchase agreement provided for the issuance of 16,000 shares of Series G non-voting preferred stock valued at $1.6 million, convertible into 1.6 million shares of the Company's common stock (Notes 7 and 19). SmithKline provided loans to the Company in the amount of $5.8 million. The loans bear interest at the rate of 8% per annum, with quarterly interest payments commencing June 1983 until December 1986, at which time the related notes are due and payable. The notes and related accrued interest, which were convertible into an aggregate of approximately 1,400,000 shares of the Company's Class A common stock (restricted), were subsequently retired (see Note 19).

The 1982 consolidated financial statements include the results of EkoLine since the date of acquisition. Sales of the former SmithKline ultrasound division approximated $11 million and $14 million in 1982 and 1981, respectively (unaudited). In the periods prior to the acquisition, the SmithKline ultrasound division incurred significant losses. Subsequent to the acquisition, the Company reduced or eliminated certain expenses and product lines which contributed to the aforementioned losses. Accordingly, pro forma combined information, which might be misleading, has been omitted.

The excess of the fair value of the net assets purchased over cost in this transaction approximated $3,049,000; of this amount, approximately $1.7 million was applied against noncurrent assets, $869,000 was recognized in 1982, with the remainder recognized in 1983.

Advertising Expense

Advertising expense for newspaper, television, radio and other media, including catalog preparation and distribution costs, was $199,128,000 in 1983, a 23.8% increase from the expenditures of $160,905,000 in 1982. For the first time since 1979 the percentage increase in advertising expense was greater than the sales increase. Heavy competition in the computer marketplace coupled with the difficult sales environment of a recession required an increased level of advertising expenditures during fiscal 1983 to maintain sales at acceptable levels. Fiscal 1982 sales gains of 20% were achieved with a 17% increase in advertising expenditures while fiscal 1981 and 1980 advertising expenditures increased only 11% and 9% but produced sales gains of 22% and 14%. Because sales grew faster than advertising expenses during this three year period, advertising expense as a percentage of sales declined from a high of 9.4% in 1979 to 7.9% in 1982. In 1983 advertising expense as a percentage of sales increased slightly to 8.0%. Advertising costs were $137,722,000 in 1981, $124,138,000 in 1980 and $114,238,000 in 1979. These amounts exclude salaries and other overhead expenses related to the Company's advertising departments.

CAPITAL STOCK

Following is information related to shares of stock outstanding and in treasury.

	Cumulative Preferred Stock			
	3.65% $100 Par	$1.70 First Series Third $10 Par	Common Stock $1.50 Par	Common Stock in Treasury
Balance April 30, 1980	12,864	1,710,228	45,574,312	707,502
Reacquired	(597)	—	—	—
Converted to common stock	—	(889,570)	733,686	(600,618)
Issued on exercise of stock options	—	—	194,834	(106,884)
Balance April 29, 1981	12,267	820,658	46,502,832	—
Reacquired	(2,684)	—	—	—
Converted to common stock	—	(244,060)	366,063	—
Issued on exercise of stock options	—	—	217,232	—
Balance April 28, 1982	9,583	576,598	47,086,127	—
Reacquired	(558)	—	—	111,729
Converted to common stock	—	(320,725)	481,086	—
Issued on exercise of stock options	—	—	278,620	(1,429)
Balance April 27, 1983	9,025	255,873	47,845,833	110,300
Authorized—April 27, 1983	9,025	255,873	80,000,000	—

The 3.65% cumulative preferred stock is redeemable through the sinking fund at $102.75 per share. Payments (or open market purchases of such stock) aggregating $200,000 are required to be made to the sinking fund on or before October 1 of each year.

Each share of the third cumulative preferred stock, $1.70 first series is convertible into one and one-half shares of common stock at any time or may be redeemed by the company at $30.50 per share at present and at decreasing prices until December 1, 1986, when it may be redeemed at $28.50 per share. Each share entitles the holder to one-half vote.

At April 27, 1983, there were authorized, but unissued, 2,200,000 shares of third cumulative preferred stock for which the series had not been designated.

As of April 27, 1983, there were 3,365,130 shares of common stock reserved for conversion of convertible preferred stock outstanding and in connection with the employees' stock option plans.

Cash and Short-Term Investments

Cash and short-term investments include:

	1983	1982
Cash in banks	$16,524	$10,292
Time deposits	32,642	10,330
Short-term investments	30,528	26,020
	$79,694	$46,642

Commitments and Contingencies

On August 11, 1983, a panel of arbitrators issued an award in Condec's favor in the arbitration proceeding relating to Condec's claims in connection with the termination for convenience on March 3, 1976 by Kaiser Aluminum & Chemical Sales, Inc. ("Kaiser") of a contract for the fabrication of large aluminum panels to be used for assembly into tanks for the transportation of liquefied natural gas by ship. The award of approximately $25,800,000 includes interest to June 30, 1983. Additional simple interest, which at current rates accrues at approximately $120,000 per month, is due from June 30, 1983 until the award is paid. On August 12, 1983, Condec filed a Petition to confirm the award in the U.S. District Court for the District of Columbia. On September 15, 1983, Kaiser filed a motion to partially vacate and to reduce the award. It cannot be determined at this time when and in what amount the award will be confirmed and what effect Kaiser's opposition to confirmation and the pending District court proceedings described below may have on the Company's ability to secure confirmation and collection of the award. District Court actions by Kaiser are pending against Condec in the District of Columbia seeking in excess of $8 million in damages (which Kaiser may increase to over $25 million plus interest) and, in part, to convert the termination for convenience into a termination for default. It is the Company's opinion and that of Messrs. Arnold & Porter, its special counsel, that, while the outcome of this litigation cannot be predicted, Kaiser's claims against the Company in the district court are without merit and that Kaiser's claims are precluded by various reasons including the convenience termination and the results of arbitration. The Company believes that it will ultimately have a substantial net recovery; however, since the outcome of the proceedings will depend on the resolution of disputed issues, neither the Company nor its special counsel makes any estimate at this time of their ultimate result.

In fiscal 1983, 1982 and 1981, Condec charged approximately $1.1 million, $1.2 million and $.9 million (before income tax benefits), respectively, to income due to legal and administrative costs related to the disputes concerning the LNG contract and lease costs for plant and equipment entered into in connection with this contract. Additional legal and other costs are expected in connection with these matters, which costs may be substantial.

In 1982, a judgment of $5.2 million after trebling was entered against certain of the Company's subsidiaries in the Flow Control Group. The judgment was based on a finding that the subsidiaries conspired among themselves to restrain trade. Condec has appealed the judgment; oral argument was held on May 6, 1983 and Condec has been advised by Messrs. Kaye, Scholer, Fierman, Hays & Handler, its special counsel, that although arguments can be made to the contrary, defendants have a meritorious appeal, which, if successful, would entitle them to either a judgment as a matter of law or a new trial on some or all issues. The Company does not believe that the matter will ultimately result in any material liability to it.

Certain other claims, suits and complaints arising in the ordinary course of business have been filed or are pending against the Company. In the opinion of management, all such matters are adequately covered by insurance, or if not so covered, are without merit or are of such kind, or involve such amounts, as would not have a significant effect on the financial position or results of operations of the Company.

At July 31, 1983, Condec was committed under long-term operating leases (with aggregate rentals of approximately $4,215,000) expiring on various dates through 1991. Minimum annual rentals amount to $1,473,000 for 1984 and decrease thereafter. Total rent expense amounted to $3,578,000 in 1983, $3,607,000 in 1982 and $3,338,000 in 1981.

Condec has entered into an agreement to sell the property it owns in Old Greenwich, Connecticut for $13,500,000. The sale is expected to take place in the first quarter of fiscal 1984. The book value of the property ($2,107,000) has been reclassified to current assets in anticipation of this sale. The manufacturing operations formerly located in Old Greenwich have been moved to a new facility in Waterbury, Connecticut. The Company has agreed to purchase the Waterbury facility for approximately $5,000,000 in January 1984.

Common Stock

Beatrice Foods

Common Stock. As of February 28, 1983, an aggregate of 14,231,332 shares of Beatrice common stock was reserved for issuance for:

	Shares of Beatrice Common Stock
Exercise of stock options	2,000,000
Conversion of preference stock	9,195,099
Conversion of debentures	1,975,283
Incentive deferred compensation plans	1,060,950
Total	14,231,332

In 1983, Beatrice's shareholders approved the "Beatrice Foods Co. Performance Unit Plan." This plan is directly related to Beatrice's financial performance and permits payment in cash or Beatrice Common stock at the end of the performance period. The maximum number of shares of Beatrice common stock available for payment under the performance unit plan will not exceed 200,000. During the year, shareholders also approved the "1982 Stock Option Plans" (individually the "1982 Incentive Stock Option Plan" and the "1982 Non-Qualified Stock Option Plan"). These plans permit purchase of Beatrice's common stock at prices not less than 100% of market value at the date of grant. The number of shares of common stock which may be issued under the 1982 stock option plans, in the aggregate, may not exceed 2 million. Options granted under these plans may not be exercised during the first twelve months after the date of grant and expire not later than ten years thereafter. Options may not be granted under the 1982 plans after February 29, 1992. All other stock option plans had ended by February 28, 1983.

The shares under option at the beginning and end of the year, and changes during the year, are:

	1983	1982
Beginning of year	20,337	107,998
Options granted	1,568,500	—
Options exercised	—	(14,283)
Options cancelled	(69,487)	(73,378)
End of year	1,519,350	20,337

The total option price of options exercised during 1982 was $.2 million. The total option price of options outstanding at February 28, 1983 and 1982 was $29.3 million and $.6 million, respectively. As of February 28, 1983, no stock options were currently exercisable.

Treasury Stock. During 1983, Beatrice announced plans to purchase up to 3.0 million shares of its common stock to replace stock issued for the acquisition of Coca-Cola Bottling Company of San Diego. Additionally, in 1982, Beatrice adopted a plan to acquire treasury shares for purposes of conversions, exercises of stock options, and issuances under the incentive deferred compensation plans. Total shares purchased under these plans were 2.7 million and .1 million in 1983 and 1982, respectively. Treasury shares also were acquired in 1983 and 1982 upon the forfeiture of shares previously issued under incentive deferred compensation plans.

Compensated Absences

In November 1980 the Financial Accounting Standards Board (FASB) issued Statement #43, "Accounting for Compensated Absences." Effective 1981, corporations are required to accrue vacation pay for all employees exempt and non-exempt at the time their vacation is earned.

AccuRay set forth its liabilities under FASB #43 as follows:

It has always been the Company's practice to accrue vacation pay for non-exempt employees as the vacations are earned. Compensation for exempt employees has been viewed on an annual basis and therefore, vacation pay has been expensed in the period vacation was taken. In November 1980, the Financial Accounting Standards Board issued Statement No. 43 "Accounting for Compensated Absences" which requires a company, beginning in 1981, to accrue vacation pay for all employees, exempt and non-exempt, at the time their vacation is earned. Had the Company elected to comply earlier than required by the FASB, the effect in 1980 would have been to reduce beginning retained earnings by $620,000 and net income by $130,000.

Economics Laboratory, Inc.

Effective July 1981, the company adopted, retroactively, the provisions of Financial Accounting Standard No. 43, "Accounting for Compensated Absences", which requires that a liability be accrued for employees' earned rights to receive compensation for future absences. Formerly, the company followed the common practice of recognizing these vacation benefits as they were paid. Financial statements for all prior years have been restated. The effect of this restatement was to reduce net income by $153,000, or $.01 per share in 1981 and $77,000 in 1980 with no effect on net income per share.

Contingent Liabilities

In April 1983, the Grumman Corporation filed suit against the Company in a U.S. District Court of New York for $250 million in compensatory damages plus punitive damages for an equal amount. The suit alleges that at the time of the sale by the Company of a transit bus business to Grumman Corporation in January 1978, the Company materially misrepresented and concealed material facts relative to the development and testing of the Model 870 bus. The Company has engaged counsel, filed an answer to the complaint totally denying the allegations, and has commenced pretrial, discovery proceedings. The Company intends to vigorously defend this matter. It believes that it has numerous and substantial defenses, that it will ultimately prevail in the lawsuit, and that the resolution of this matter will not have a material adverse financial impact upon the Company.

Textron

There are pending against Textron a number of lawsuits and proceedings, including some which purport to be class actions. Several of these suits and proceedings seek unspecified, treble or punitive damages and other relief. Although these suits and proceedings are being defended or contested on behalf of Textron, it is not possible at this time to predict with certainty their outcome or the ultimate effect on Textron. However, on the basis of information presently available, Textron is of the opinion that it is not likely that any such liability, to the extent not provided for through insurance or otherwise, would have a material effect on Textron's consolidated financial position or results of operations.

Fiscal Year	Buildings	Equipment
1984	$ 732,988	$108,470
1985	484,771	77,443
1986	258,919	22,461
1987	204,246	4,189
1988	151,343	—
Minimum annual rental commitments	$1,832,267	$212,563

The Company also leases certain buildings and equipment which have been capitalized in accordance with the requirements of Statement of Financial Accounting Standards No. 13. Debt related to these leases is discussed in Note 3.

Additional Example

On September 29, 19__, the Company and each of its Directors (the "defendants") were served with a class action suit filed in the United States District Court for the Western District of New York. The plaintiff, Steven Goldman, seeks to maintain a class action for alleged violations of Section 10(b) of the Securities Exchange Act of 1934 and Rule 10(b)(5) promulgated thereunder. In general, the Complaint alleges that the defendants misled purchases of the Company's securities between May 7, 1982 and August 30, 1982 by means of overly optimistic projections of the Company's sales. The plaintiff seeks to represent all such purchasers who were allegedly damaged by the claimed misrepresentations and to recover an unspecified amount of damages for the class.

The defendants have filed a Motion to Dismiss upon the grounds that the Complaint fails to state any claim or claims against the defendants upon which relief can be granted, fails to contain the circumstances constituting fraud with particularity and fails to differentiate between the defendants in its claim of fraud. The District Court has ordered a stay of all discovery and disclosure as well as the plaintiff's motion for class certification, pending a decision on the defendants' Motion to Dismiss.

Company management believes that all Company statements made during the period were proper and there is no basis for any liability.

Contract Accounting

The company recognizes income on contracts using the percentage of completion method. Accrued income is based on the percentage of estimated total income that costs incurred to date bear to estimated total costs after giving effect to the most recent estimates of cost and estimated sales price at completion. When appropriate, increased selling prices expected as a result of anticipated contract price adjustments for changes ordered by the customer are considered. Some contracts contain incentive provisions based upon performance in relation to established targets to which applicable recognition has been given in the contract revenue estimates. Since many contracts extend over a long period of time, revisions in cost and price estimates during the progress of work have the effect of adjusting earnings in the current period applicable to performance in prior periods. When the current contract estimate indicates a loss, provision is made for the total anticipated loss. In accordance with these practices, contracts in process are stated at cost plus estimated profit but not in excess of realizable value.

Convertible Debentures

The convertible subordinated debentures due 1987, bearing interest at 4¾%, amounted to $13,644,000 at both December 31, 1983 and 1982. They are convertible into Revlon common stock at $39.75 per share and are redeemable in whole or in part, at the option of Revlon, at 101% of the principal amount, decreasing ½% annually to 100% in April 1985.

The 4¾% convertible debentures due 1983 amounted to $3,591,000 at December 31, 1982 and were classified in "Current liabilities—Other." During 1983, $2,850,000 of the principal amount of such debentures was converted into 83,806 shares of Revlon common stock at $34 per share. The principal balance remaining of $741,000 was redeemed at 100% in June 1983.

Restrictive convenants relating to the convertible debentures are less restrictive than those of the long-term debt agreements.

Debt

There are numerous items to be included under the footnote "Debt."

Your stockholders and security analysts will want to be informed as to the following:

Short Term Debt

Long Term Debt

Bank Credit Agreements, Including
- Revolving Credit Loans
- Compensating Balance Agreements
- Dividend Restrictions

Industrial Development Bonds

5 SHORT-TERM DEBT AND COMPENSATING CASH BALANCES

The components of Beatrice's short-term debt and related interest rates for each fiscal year are:

(Dollars in Millions)	1983	1982	1981
Domestic borrowings, principally commercial paper	$122	$ 44	$ —
International borrowings, principally bank debt	87	94	122
Total short-term debt at year-end	$209	$138	$122
Weighted average interest rate at year-end	10.9%	15.1%	14.7%
Maximum amount outstanding during the year	$261	$316	$227
Average amount outstanding during the year	$192	$133	$119
Weighted average interest rate during the year	14.2%	16.6%	17.1%

The average amounts of short-term debt outstanding during each of the years are calculated by averaging all month-end balances for each year. The associated weighted average interest rates are exclusive of the cost of maintaining certain compensating balances. These average rates represent total short-term interest expense divided by the average balances outstanding.

Beatrice's credit lines are adjusted as needs change. As of February 28, 1983, Beatrice has $250 million committed lines of credit under revolving credit agreements, and $273 million informal lines of credit, with both foreign and domestic banks. Commitment fees for these credit lines range between ¼ and ⅜ of 1% of the unused credit. Alternatively, in some cases Beatrice has informally agreed to maintain compensating balances ranging between 3% and 10% of the unused credit. Such compensating balance requirements were approximately $1 million and $6 million as of February 28, 1983 and 1982, respectively. There are no legal restrictions on the use of such compensating balances. Borrowings under any lines of credit are at interest rates ranging between prime and 104% of prime or, at Beatrice's option, borrowings under the revolving credit agreements may instead be priced at rates based upon U.S. dollar bank certificates of deposit rates or provided in Eurodollars or other convertible currencies at rates based upon the London interbank rate. At February 28, 1983, these revolving credit agreements are available to Beatrice for periods of three and four years. Beatrice's informal lines of credit as of the last day of February, 1983 and 1982 are:

(In Millions)	1983	1982
Maximum lines of credit:		
Domestic	$161	$168
International	112	161
Borrowings under lines of credit:		
International	$ 32	$ 60

6 LONG-TERM DEBT

The balance of long-term debt is composed of:

(In Millions)	1983	1982
Sinking fund debentures:		
9% due 1983 to 1985	$ 2.0	$ 3.0
7⅞% due 1983 to 1994	21.8	22.2
8½% due 1989 to 2008	54.9	54.9
10⅞% due 1991 to 2010	150.0	150.0
Convertible subordinated debentures:		
7¼% due 1983 to 1990	2.7	3.3
6¼% due 1983 to 1991	19.1	19.9
4½% due 1983 to 1992	22.5	24.6
4⅞% due 1993	4.3	5.8
Other debt:		
9.5% notes due 1983	8.5	8.5
7¾% notes due 1983	—	100.0
8½% notes due 1983 to 1984	12.2	12.2
8.9% notes due 1983 to 1986	20.0	25.0
8¼% notes due 1983 to 1987	11.1	11.5
9⅞% notes due 1983 to 1995	48.0	52.0
Zero coupon notes, payments due: May, 1984—$114.3 Feb., 1992—$250.0 May, 2014—$114.3	176.9	64.4
Miscellaneous, due various dates through 2012 (10.5% weighted average effective rate)	146.5	122.6
Capital lease obligations (7.7% weighted average effective rate)	134.7	130.1
	835.2	810.0
Less current portion (Includes capital lease obligations of $16.1 and $15.4 for 1983 and 1982, respectively)	62.8	51.0
Total long-term debt	$772.4	$759.0

Short-Term Debt and Lines of Credit

Short-term debt includes notes payable to banks, commercial paper and foreign overdrafts.

Textron maintains lines of credit with a number of foreign and domestic banks. The aggregate of such lines was $738 million at December 31, 1983 and included both short-term as well as revolving credit facilities. The facilities are made available to Textron and its unconsolidated finance company on both a formal committed basis and an informal confirmed basis with the former requiring payment of specified fees and the latter in some cases requiring maintenance of certain balances. At December 31, 1983, approximately $467 million of the above facilities were on a fee paid committed basis with fees averaging approximately ¼ of 1% per annum on the unused portion of the facility. Where balances are required, they are normally generated by the time lag in presentation of company checks for payment.

Lines of credit not used or reserved as support for outstanding commercial paper were approximately $650 million at December 31, 1983 and approximately $612 million at January 1, 1983.

Long-Term Debt

(In millions)	December 31, 1983	January 1, 1983
8% Notes due 1984-1997	$ 70.0	$ 75.0
7¾% Subordinated Debentures due 2005	85.3	85.4
7¾% Eurodollar Sinking Fund Debentures due 1987	19.0	20.5
7½% Sinking Fund Debentures due 1997	19.2	19.2
5⅞% Sinking Fund Debentures due 1992	6.5	6.5
5% Subordinated Debentures due 1984	2.1	2.5
Other notes (average approximately 11%)	44.3	45.0
	246.4	254.1
Less current maturities	14.8	8.2
	$231.6	$245.9

The 7¾% Subordinated Debentures are exchangeable at any time prior to maturity, unless previously redeemed, for shares of common stock of Allied Corporation owned by Textron (1,446,111 shares at December 31, 1983; 1,447,085 shares at January 1, 1983) at an exchange rate of 16.949 shares per $1,000 principal amount of debentures (the equivalent of $59 per share), subject to adjustment in certain events. Textron continues to receive dividends and to exercise voting rights on the Allied shares, which are held in escrow for the benefit of debenture holders. Its investment in such shares, ($61.6 million at December 31, 1983; $61.7 million at January 1, 1983) is included in other assets in the consolidated balance sheet.

In 1982, Textron exchanged a total of 928,217 shares of its Common Stock for $12.0 million of its 7½% Debentures and $17.6 million of its 5⅞% Debentures. The gains included in net income relative to these transactions aggregated $10.3 million, or $.28 per share.

Under provisions of certain indentures and notes, retained earnings at December 31, 1983 available for payment of cash dividends and acquisition of treasury stock approximated $520 million.

Required payments on long-term debt during the next five years are as follows: $15 million in 1984; $25 million in 1985; $18 million in 1986; $12 million in 1987 and $5 million in 1988.

Long-Term Debt

Long-term debt consists of the following:

	1983	1982
Revolving term loan	$ —	$3,000
8¼%, 8¾%, 9¼% mortgages payable in monthly installments through 2009	5,416	5,499
Other borrowings	1,887	1,042
	7,303	9,541
Less amount due within one year	514	244
	$6,789	$9,297

The Company has Revolving Term Loan Agreement with four banks for an unsecured revolving $20.0 million term loan. At year end 1983, no notes payable have been reclassified to long-term debt under this agreement, and at year end 1982, $3.0 million were reclassified.

During the revolving period, the agreement provides for:

- U.S. dollar advances with interest payable at the bank's prime rate plus fees in lieu of compensating balances;

- Bankers' Acceptances with interest computed at the Prime Bankers' Acceptance rate plus commissions; and
- Multi-currency advances with interest payable at ⅝% over the London Interbank Offered Rate (LIBOR).

On February 29, 1984, all outstanding Bankers' Acceptances are to be repaid and all outstanding U.S. dollar and multi-currency advances convert to three-year term debt with twelve approximately equal quarterly payments at the following rates:

- U.S. dollar advances with interest payable at the bank's prime rate plus ½% with fees in lieu of compensating balances; and
- Multi-currency advances with interest payable at 1% over LIBOR.

This loan agreement requires the Company to maintain minimum working capital and indebtedness ratios, interest coverage and a minimum shareholders' equity.

Aggregate principal payments on long-term debt in each of the next five years and thereafter are as follows:

1984—$514	1987—$ 354
1985—$491	1988—$ 220
1986—$491	Thereafter—$5,225

Revision and expansion of the Company's bank line of credit:

In June 1983 the Company entered into an agreement pursuant to which the maximum amount that the Company could borrow under its bank line of credit was increased to $25 million from the previous $19 million maximum, the interest rate was reduced to 2½% over the prime rate (from 3% over the prime rate), and the formulae determining the amount of "eligible" accounts receivable and inventory (the level of which determines the amount that the Company may borrow) were liberalized so that a greater amount of receivables and inventories would be "eligible" under the new agreement than under the old line. The bank line continues to be secured by the Company's accounts receivable and inventory. The institutions participating in the line of credit are First Wisconsin National Bank of Milwaukee, Wells Fargo Bank, Continental Illinois National Bank and Trust Company of Chicago, and First Wisconsin Financial Corporation.

Defense Contracts

Approximately 27%, 25% and 27% of the sales and service revenues of the Company for the years ended July 31, 1982, 1981 and 1980, respectively, arose from U.S. Government contracts and subcontracts. Approximately 51% of these revenues for 1982 related to fixed-price type contracts.

As in common with U.W. Government contracts, the Company's defense contracts are unilaterally terminable by the U.S. Government at its convenience with compensation for work completed and costs incurred.

At July 31, 1982, of the total backlog of $5.3 billion, the amount of worldwide defense contract work backlog to be completed was approximately $4.4 billion of which $3.5 billion has been funded. The amount of worldwide defense contract work backlog was $3.2 billion and $3.4 billion at July 31, 1981 and 1980, respectively.

Deferred Compensation

In connection with the formation of the Company's subsidiary, Universal Antennas, Inc. (Universal), options for ownership of up to 42% of the subsidiary were granted to the three co-founders of Universal. These options would have become exercisable in October 1981 for a total price of $10,500.

In September 1980, the Company acquired the stock options held by the three co-founders of Universal. The terms of the agreement called for an initial cash payment of $260,000 in October 1980 and subsequent cash payments of 100,000 each in fiscal years 1982, 1984 and 1986. In addition 61,425 shares of the Company's stock were issued in October 1980, and put into escrow with 30,713 shares released in October 1982 and 30,712 shares to be released in fiscal year 1985.

The total cost of the transaction of $851,000 is being charged to expense over a five year period through fiscal 1985. For the years ended June 30, 1983, 1982 and 1981, $184,000, $150,000 and $150,000, respectively, were charged to expense.

Discontinued operations

On October 10, 1983, the company announced plans to discontinue the manufacture and marketing of word processing equipment. In connection with that discontinuance, the company made a special provision which reduced 1983 earnings by $22.5 million ($50 million before taxes) for the wind-up of those operations. The provision includes amounts for asset write-offs, employee severance payments, customer support and service, and other wind-up costs.

Summary results of word processing operations prior to its discontinuance, which have been classified separately in the statement of consolidated income, were as follows:

Years ended December 31	9-months 1983	1982	1981
(in thousands)			
Revenues	$ 35,935	$ 33,848	$ 23,338
(Loss) before taxes	$(15,958)	$(19,581)	$(12,181)
Tax benefit	7,733	9,010	5,272
Net (loss)	$ (8,225)	$(10,571)	$ (6,909)

In the statement of consolidated changes in financial position, results of discontinued operations have also been presented separately. These results are net of non-cash charges and credits to income which include depreciation and the special provision for discontinuance.

In 1983, the Corporation disposed of two operating divisions. The effect was to increase net earnings by $269,000 for the year.

The gain relates to the sale of those divisional assets for an amount greater than their corresponding book value.

As a result of selling one of the aforementioned operations, the Corporation has entered into an unconditional purchase obligation to purchase approximately $7,000,000 in resale inventory during 1983 and each of the next four years.

The disposition of the divisions was part of management's effort to dispose of businesses that do not fit strategic objectives of the Corporation.

Earnings Per Share

For the years ended March 31, 1983 and 1982, earnings per share are based on the weighted average number of shares outstanding. For the year ended March 31, 1981, fully diluted earnings per share assumes that outstanding convertible debentures were converted into common stock and primary earnings per share are based on the weighted average number of outstanding common shares and common share equivalents.

The number of shares used in the computations were as follows:

Years ended March 31	1983	1982	1981
Fully diluted	44,602,332	42,263,718	41,862,468
Primary	44,602,332	42,263,718	40,764,748

EMPLOYEE BENEFIT PLANS

The Company has a profit sharing plan for eligible employees, which provides for contributions of up to 10% of consolidated income before provision for income taxes and amounts payable under the plan.

The Company has a management incentive plan which provides for payments to officers and senior management employees from an annual incentive fund determined by several factors relating to the financial performance of the Company.

The Company has reserved 360,292 shares of its authorized but unissued common stock for issuance under an employee stock purchase plan. The plan covers substantially all the employees of the parent company and its domestic subsidiaries. The participant's purchase price is 85% of the closing market price on the last trading day of the quarter in which the stock is purchased by the employee. The 15% discount is treated as equivalent to the cost of issuing stock for financial reporting purposes. For tax purposes, it is treated as compensation to the employee, and the resulting tax benefit to the Company is credited to common stock. The Company has issued 139,708 shares of its stock under this plan as of November 30, 1983.

In October, 1983 the Corporation purchased $4,425,000 of its 6 percent debentures for $3,806,000 cash. As a result of this exchange the Corporation recognized an extraordinary gain of $335,000 (net of deferred taxes amounting to $284,000).

For fiscal 1981, the Corporation determined that an outside sales agent had made substantial misrepresentations in connection with orders submitted for certain export customers. This determination was made because of discrepancies discovered between orders presented by the agent and actual orders verified by the customers. As a result the Corporation determined that accounts receivable and prepaid expenses related to these orders should be written off. The non-recurring write-off of these amounts in 1981 gave rise to an extraordinary loss of $11,721,000 (net of taxes totaling $11,860,000 of which $11,412,000 were deferred taxes).

EMPLOYEES' STOCK OPTION PLANS AND MANAGEMENT INCENTIVE PLAN

The company has three employees' stock option plans. All of the company's stock option plans have been approved by the shareholders and are administered by the Management Development and Compensation Committee ("Committee"). Unless otherwise noted, each option entitles the holder to purchase one share of the company's common stock at the fair market value of the stock at the date of grant. Options granted under the plans are subject to various holding periods as established by the Committee at the time of the grant.

The 1970 Stock Option Plan authorized the granting of 900,000 shares through June 9, 1980. Currently outstanding options expire on varying dates through July 11, 1983.

The 1976 Stock Option Plan authorizes the granting of 1,500,000 shares through June 8, 1986. The 1982 Stock Option Plan authorizes the granting of 2,000,000 shares through January 12, 1992. Under both of these plans, the Committee is authorized to impose restrictions on the exercise of these stock options, in which case the option price is equal to the fair value of the option, as established by the Committee. The duration of the options may not exceed ten years.

Stock Appreciation Rights (SAR's) may be granted in conjunction with the company's stock options. SAR's enable the holder to surrender unexercised options and to receive in exchange therefor shares of common stock with aggregate market value or, at the option of the Committee, cash, equal to the excess of the fair value of shares under option surrendered over the option price. SAR's are subject to a holding period of at least six months to one year, depending on the plan under which the SAR's are granted. The amount charged to earnings with respect to SAR's was $3,119,000 in 1983, $586,000 in 1982 and $2,776,000 in 1981. This charge is associated with those SAR's which, it is presumed, will be exercised.

Data regarding options granted and exercised and shares reserved for additional grants appear in the table below.

	Shares	Range of Fair Market Value (and Option Price) at Date of Grant
Shares under option April 29, 1981	1,153,702	$13¼-28
Options granted	791,680	25¾-28⅜
Options exercised	(272,832)	13¼-21⅜
Options surrendered	(12,000)	21½-28⅜
Shares under option April 28, 1982	**1,660,550**	**$13¼-28⅜**
Options granted	**341,090**	**31 -43**
Options exercised	**(307,912)**	**13¼-32¾**
Options surrendered	**(2,000)**	**25¾**
Shares under option April 27, 1983	**1,691,728**	**$13¼-43**
Options Exercisable at:		
April 28, 1982	835,610	
April 27, 1983	817,298	
Shares Reserved for Granting of Options:		
April 28, 1982	1,628,682	
April 27, 1983	1,289,592	

The Management Incentive Plan covers certain key employees of the company and its subsidiaries. Participants in the plan may elect to be paid on a current or deferred basis. The aggregate amount of all awards may not exceed certain limits in any year. Management Incentive Plan expense was $10,792,000 in 1983 ($10,146,000 in 1982 and $8,600,000 in 1981).

Facilities and Bank Financing

The Company's corporate headquarters and factory totaling 86,000 square feet was built in 1980 with a 57,000 square foot addition completed in August 1982. The facilities are located near Dulles International Airport in Northern Virginia. The Company's subsidiaries occupy facilities in Dallas, Texas and Atlanta, Georgia.

A mortgage agreement was obtained during 1979 through the Company's bank in the form of an industrial revenue bond. The mortgage financed $2,800,000 which represents the cost of the Virginia building (exclusive of the addition) plus costs of some equipment.

Principal payments on the mortgage commenced in 1980. The mortgage is being paid in monthly principal installments plus interest (at a rate of 7%) over 20 years. Principal payments are $178,000 per year for the first 8 years and $115,000 per year thereafter for the remainder of the term.

The mortgage requires the Company to maintain minimum amounts of working capital and stockholders equity and to obtain prior approval of additional long-term borrowing. At June 30, 1983 and 1982, respectively, all of retained earnings was available for dividends.

The Company's bank credit agreement provides for short-term borrowings of up to $1,000,000 at an interest rate equal to the prime rate.

Fiscal Year

The Company's fiscal year ends on the Sunday nearest December 31.

Foreign Currency Translation

Many corporations have been troubled by the American accounting rules dealing with exchange-rate volatility. In 1976, the Financial Accounting Standards Board, (FASB) adopted a requirement that companies show all foreign-exchange gains or losses, whether realized or unrealized, in quarterly earnings reports.

In December 1981, the FASB revised its rules. Beginning with the 1981 reports, companies could post foreign-exchange gains and losses from balance sheet transactions directly in their stockholders' equity on the balance sheet rather than in the earnings statement. As of 1983, they have to do so.

FAS #52 establishes revised standards of financial accounting and reporting for foreign currency transactions in financial statements of a reporting enterprise. It also revises the standards for translating foreign currency financial statements that are incorporated in the financial statements of an enterprise by consolidation, combination, or the equity method of accounting.

Examples:

ACCOUNTING FOR FOREIGN EXCHANGE—AN EXPLANATION

How best to account for foreign exchange and currency translation has been debated by the financial community for decades. Professional accounting groups in the United States have, at various times, proposed differing solutions to the problem. The latest is Financial Accounting Standard ("FAS") No. 52, which Grace adopted for 1982, issued by the Financial Accounting Standards Board in December 1981. Our prior years' financial statements, rendered in accordance with FAS No. 8—the controversial predecessor guideline—have not been restated.

Under FAS No. 8, the book values of certain foreign assets, such as inventories and plant and equipment, were translated into U.S. dollars at exchange rates in effect when the assets were acquired. Deferred income taxes payable were also translated on this basis. Only items such as foreign money owned or owed (for example, cash or loans payable) changed in dollar value as exchange rates varied. The subsequent translation of inventory sold and depreciation using historical exchange rates produced a mismatching of costs and revenues in the income statement. Often giving an impression contrary to the economic effects of an exchange rate change, this system frequently caused radical and unpredictable fluctuations in income, dismaying management, analysts and shareholders alike. For this reason, Grace chose to present to shareholders financial data by line of business (see page 36) based on translation principles it had followed prior to the existence of FAS No. 8. To minimize confusion, Grace consistently separated the effects of FAS No. 8 in reporting results so that readers of our financial statements could evaluate earnings before and after any distortion it produced.

FAS No. 52 mandates a different, somewhat simpler alternative to the complex problem of translating foreign currency financial statements into U.S. dollars. Now, *all* assets and liabilities are translated at the rate of exchange in effect as of the balance sheet date. Under FAS No. 52, gains and losses arising from this translation are reported in a separate account in the equity section of the balance sheet and are *not* reflected in net income. Translation of all revenues and costs in the income statement are made at the average rates of exchange during the period. This new methodology should produce much smaller exchange fluctuations in income from one period to another.

However, the ''all-current'' method of FAS No. 52 cannot be used without modification when subsidiaries are located in countries with consistently high rates of inflation. At present, Argentina, Brazil and Mexico are the only nations with Grace operations that fall clearly into this ''hyperinflation'' category; in these cases, the FAS No. 8 rules continue to apply. Translation effects on Grace investments in these markets are not significant to the consolidated results.

Unchanged from FAS No. 8, net income will include the results of completed foreign exchange transactions, e.g., gains or losses realized on actual payments or collections of foreign payables and receivables. Again, such foreign exchange effects for Grace have been negligible.

In essence, changes in the equity section of the balance sheet caused by FAS No. 52 occur when the relationships of the foreign currencies of overseas businesses to the U.S. dollar change. Simply stated, when those currencies become less valuable (i.e., the dollar strengthens), an erosion of reported shareholders' equity occurs; if the dollar weakens, an improvement in shareholders' equity is reported.

Translation of Foreign Currencies

Effective October 3, 1982, the Company adopted the provisions of the Statement of Financial Accounting Standard No. 52 (SFAS 52), ''Foreign Currency Translation.'' In accordance with that standard, assets and liabilities of most international subsidiaries have been translated at current exchange rates, and related revenues and expenses have been translated at average rates of exchange prevailing during the period. Translation losses of foreign subsidiaries that operate in highly inflationary economies have been charged against income in 1983, as in prior years. The aggregate effect of all other translation gains and losses in 1983 has been reflected as a separate component of stockholders' investment. The total cumulative translation adjustment at October 1, 1983, includes a translation loss of $1,073,000 as a result of translating assets and liabilities of the Company, as of the beginning of the year, at the then-current exchange rates. Transaction gains or losses are reflected in income as they occur. The financial statements for1982 and 1981 have not been restated, as permitted by SFAS 52. The Consolidated Statement of Operations includes exchange losses of $388,000 in 1983 and $869,000 in 1982. Exchange losses in 1981 were not material.

Foreign Currency Translation and Foreign Operations

Financial statements of foreign subsidiaries are translated into U.S. dollars in accordance with FASB statement No. 52.

The Company's major foreign operations are located in West Germany, the United Kingdom and France, and their business activities are conducted principally in their local currency. The assets and liabilities of these subsidiaries are translated at the current exchange rate at the balance sheet date. Income statement items are translated at the weighted average monthly rate. The strengthening of the U.S. dollar against these foreign currencies is reflected in the negative translation adjustments included in shareholders' equity in each of the three years ended June 30, 1983. These adjustments will be included in net income only upon sale or liquidation of the underlying foreign investments, which is not contemplated at this time.

For foreign subsidiaries whose operations are situated in highly inflationary economies (Argentina, Brazil and Mexico) the financial statements are translated into U.S. dollars using: (1) current exchange rates at the balance sheet date for all liabilities and current assets except inventories; (2) exchange rates applicable at the time of acquisition for inventories and properties; and (3) weighted average monthly exchange rates for the year for income and expense amounts, except depreciation and cost of goods sold. Resulting translation gains and losses are included in income currently. Such losses amounted to $4,796, $2,731 and $987 in 1983, 1982 and 1981, respectively.

Realized gains and losses from foreign currency transactions are included in the statement of income as incurred and amounted to an after tax gain of $235 in 1983 and losses of $1,150 and $1,132 after tax in 1982 and 1981, respectively.

Net sales and net income include the following amounts from foreign operations:

	1983	1982	1981
Net sales	$211,014	$225,894	$213,512
Net income	$ 2,683	$ 7,339	$ 9,844

Net assets of foreign operations at June 30, 1983 and 1982 amounted to $128,991 and $116,193, respectively.

Accumulated undistributed earnings of foreign operations reinvested in their operations amounted to $33,850, $34,046 and $30,407 at June 30, 1983, 1982 and 1981, respectively.

It might be well for you to explain FAS #52 to your stockholders in your annual report.

Example:

Throughout this report, frequent mention is made of the new accounting standard, FAS No. 52. The following will, we think, help our shareholders better understand its impact on their company and its financial reporting.

What is FAS No. 52?
The 1981 standard established by the Financial Accounting Standards Board (FASB) directs multinational businesses to eliminate most foreign currency translation fluctuations on assets and liabilities (representing either gains or losses) from their current income statements.

What does it mean?
In essence, under the old rules, the effects of fluctuating foreign currency exchange rates on translating international balance sheets from local currencies into dollars were included in the income statement, sometimes causing wide swings in earnings that did not fairly reflect the economic performance of the company. Now, these swings—favorable or unfavorable—are incorporated in the shareholders' equity section of the balance sheet. As a result, the earnings now more clearly present a true indication of the economic operating realities of the company.

How does it work?
Let's use an example of the effects of FAS No. 52 . . .

Under the old method—
Assume that at the beginning of the year a company had 1,000,000 French Francs in assets, valued then at $.20 each. These would be translated onto the balance sheet at $200,000.

At the end of the year, during which the dollar had strengthened against the Franc, the value of the Franc had fallen to $.15 each, and the original 1,000,000 Francs would then be translated onto the balance sheet as $150,000—an unfavorable adjustment of $50,000. Historically, this had been reported on the income statement.

Under FAS No. 52—
This $50,000 adjustment would have no impact on the year's earnings, but would be reported as a part of shareholders' equity, reducing it by the amount.

Bristol Myers

Effective January 1, 1982, the company changed its method of accounting for foreign currency translation by adopting Statement No. 52 of the Financial Accounting Standards Board. The financial statements for 1981 and prior years have not been restated to reflect this change. Under the provisions of the statement, substantially all assets and liabilities of the company's foreign operations are translated at exchange rates prevailing at year end and the resulting translation adjustments are accumulated in a separate component of stockholders' equity. Operating results are translated at exchange rates prevailing during the year. Gains and losses resulting from foreign currency transactions and translation adjustments relating to foreign entities operating in highly inflationary economies, principally Argentina, Brazil, Mexico and Peru, are reflected in income.

The opening balance in the cumulative translation adjustments component of stockholders' equity is the effect of translating certain balance sheet accounts (principally inventories, property, plant and equipment and intangible assets) at January 1, 1982 at rates in effect on that date. For 1981 and prior years, these accounts were translated at historical exchange rates.

Cumulative translation adjustments at December 31, 1982 were:

(in millions of dollars)	
Balance, January 1	**$21.2**
Effect of balance sheet translations (includes income taxes of $2.6)	**57.1**
Balance, December 31	**$78.3**

The translation effects on earnings from exchange rate fluctuations were as follows:

	Year Ended December 31,		
(in millions of dollars)	**1982**	1981	1980
	Increase (Decrease)		
Effect on gross margin from charging cost of products sold with inventory at historic rates	**$(11.7)**	$(40.1)	$ (8.5)
Effect of balance sheet translations and other foreign currency transactions	**(5.8)**	(1.8)	1.2
Earnings before income taxes	**$(17.5)**	$(41.9)	$ (7.3)
Net earnings	**$(16.8)**	$(41.5)	$ (7.5)

Foreign Operations Information

The Company is engaged in the development, manufacture and sale of photocomposition equipment and the sale of related supplies, accessories, service and parts. The following schedule summarizes the Company's activities by geographic area for three years ended October 1, 1983:

(Dollars in thousands) 1983	U.S. Operations	Foreign Operations	Eliminations	Total
Sales to unaffiliated customers	$262.046	$ 44.256	$ –	$306.302
Intercompany sales	18.670	1.771	(20.441)	–
Total revenues	$280.716	$ 46.027	$ (20.441)	$306.302
Income from operations	$ 19.541	$ 5.885	$ (1.321)	$ 24.105
Profit sharing				(2.299)
Interest expense, net				(1.120)
Income before income taxes				$ 20.686
Identifiable assets	$222.665	$ 29.284	$ (29.225)	$222.724
Corporate assets (cash and marketable securities)				45.232
Total assets				$267.956

(Dollars in thousands) 1982	U.S. Operations	Foreign Operations	Eliminations	Total
Sales to unaffiliated customers	$236.774	$ 39.630	$ –	$276.404
Intercompany sales	17.977	1.093	(19.070)	–
Total revenues	$254.751	$ 40.723	$ (19.070)	$276.404
Income from operations	$ 15.699	$ 100	$ 569	$ 16.368
Interest expense, net				(4.460)
Income before income taxes				$ 11.908
Identifiable assets	$198.443	$ 26.418	$ (16.249)	$208.612
Corporate assets (cash and marketable securities)				24.741
Total assets				$233.353

(Dollars in thousands) 1981	U.S. Operations	Foreign Operations	Eliminations	Total
Sales to unaffiliated customers	$234.998	$ 42.598	$ –	$277.596
Intercompany sales	19.753	916	(20.669)	–
Total revenues	$254.751	$ 43.514	$ (20.669)	$277.596
Loss from operations	$ (2.592)	$ (315)	$ (688)	$ (3.595)
Interest expense, net				(12.063)
Loss before income taxes				$ (15.658)
Identifiable assets	$211.544	$ 25.917	$ (20.656)	$216.805
Corporate assets (cash)				5.065
Total assets				$221.870

Amounts identified as "Foreign Operations" in the above schedule are attributable to the Company's wholly owned subsidiaries in France, Germany, Canada, and Ireland. No individual subsidiary had sales to unaffiliated customers or has identifiable assets of 10 percent or more of the related consolidated amounts.

Of the U.S. operations' sales to unaffiliated customers, $42.123.000 in 1983, $40.859.000 in 1982, and $53.421.000 in 1981 were export sales to foreign distributors, principally in Europe, or to U.S. dealers exporting to foreign customers.

INFORMATION ON FOREIGN OPERATIONS

Net assets of consolidated foreign subsidiaries translated to United States dollars using current exchange rates at each year end appear below.

(in thousands)	1983	1982
Current assets	$500,946	$ 509,684
Current liabilities	(274,858)	(286,902)
Working capital	226,088	222,782
Fixed and other assets	315,595	301,038
Long-term debt and other liabilities	(132,645)	(140,029)
Net assets	$409,038	$ 383,791

Changes in the cumulative translation component of shareholders' equity that result from the translation of consolidated foreign subsidiaries' financial statements to United States dollars are as follows:

(in thousands)	1983	1982	1981
Balance at beginning of year	$ (77,252)	$(32,175)	$(23,525)
Adjustments arising from translation of foreign currency assets and liabilities	(29,541)	(45,077)	(8,650)
Balance at end of year	$(106,793)	$(77,252)	$(32,175)

Foreign Subsidiaries

At December 25, 1983 and December 26, 1982, total assets and liabilities of foreign subsidiaries, including intercompany accounts, were as follows:

Dollar Amounts in Thousands	**1983**	1982
Current assets	**$131,362**	$107,356
Property, plant and equipment, net	**12,618**	14,253
Other long-term assets	**3,767**	2,115
Total Assets	**$147,747**	$123,724
Current liabilities	**$ 50,544**	$ 43,008
Long-term liabilities	**22,697**	30,042
Shareholders' equity	**74,506**	50,674
Total Liabilities and Shareholders' Equity	**$147,747**	$123,724

Note 5 Income Taxes

The components of the provision for income taxes were as follows:

(In thousands)	***1983***	***1982***	***1981***
Currently payable:			
Federal	***$10,480***	$ 9,056	$41,696
Foreign	***17,831***	17,774	21,050
State and local	***3,186***	4,171	7,245
Total currently payable	***31,497***	31,001	69,991
Benefit from safe harbor leases	***6,079***	12,111	—
Tax effect of timing differences:			
Federal	***(564)***	2,563	(1,268)
Foreign	***760***	(976)	(2,048)
State and local	***(354)***	42	(452)
Total timing differences	***(158)***	1,629	(3,768)
	$37,418	$44,741	$66,223

Income before provision for income taxes was as follows:

(In thousands)	***1983***	***1982***	***1981***
United States	***$48,754***	$ 69,387	$106,042
Foreign	***38,906***	38,023	42,786
	$87,660	$107,410	$148,828

A reconciliation of the federal statutory rate to the Corporation's effective tax rate follows:

	% of pre-tax income		
	1983	***1982***	***1981***
Federal statutory rate	***46.0%***	46.0%	46.0%
Effect of income from operations in Puerto Rico	***(3.6)***	(5.0)	(3.0)
State income taxes	***1.7***	2.1	2.5
Investment tax credit	***(2.3)***	(1.8)	(1.1)
Miscellaneous items	***.9***	.3	.1
Effective income tax rate	***42.7%***	41.6%	44.5%

Income Taxes

The United States and foreign components of pre-tax income were:

	1983	*1982*	*1981*
United States	$210,768	$185,815	$164,317
Foreign	86,117	86,488	118,944
	$296,885	$272,303	$283,261

Current and deferred provisions were:

	1983	*1982*	*1981*
Current			
Federal	$ 12,676	$ 1,822	$ 71,427
Foreign	10,845	12,285	45,404
State	8,435	11,639	11,733
	31,956	25,746	128,564
Deferred			
Federal	57,794	62,689	108
Foreign	14,916	9,518	4,811
State	8,603	2,672	871
	81,313	74,879	5,790
	$113,269	$100,625	$134,354

Following are the components of the deferred income tax provisions, which represent the tax effects of timing differences between financial and tax reporting:

	1983	*1982*	*1981*
Tax benefits purchased	$ 64,060	$ 57,496	$ —
Excess of tax over book depreciation	8,121	12,457	5,273
Unremitted earnings of foreign subsidiaries	5,839	8,010	9,897
Inventory valuation methods	6,819	6,943	(5,677)
Installment receivables	1,642	5,990	1,593
Other, net	(5,168)	(16,017)	(5,296)
	$ 81,313	$ 74,879	$ 5,790

Reconciliations of the difference between the U.S. statutory rate and the effective tax rate follow:

	1983		*1982*		*1981*	
	Amount	*% of Pre-Tax Income*	*Amount*	*% of Pre-Tax Income*	*Amount*	*% of Pre-Tax Income*
Taxes at U.S. statutory rate	$136,567	46.0%	$125,259	46.0%	$130,300	46.0%
State income taxes, less federal income tax benefit	9,200	3.1	7,728	2.8	6,806	2.4
Tax credits	(9,362)	(3.2)	(8,120)	(3.0)	(6,815)	(2.4)
Difference between U.S. and foreign rates	(11,381)	(3.8)	(13,691)	(5.0)	(12,630)	(4.5)
Restructuring businesses	(10,479)	(3.5)	(9,837)	(3.6)	—	—
Exchange of stock for debt	—	—	(3,040)	(1.1)	—	—
Translation effects	1,222	.4	—	—	16,969	6.0
Other, net	(2,498)	(.8)	2,326	.9	(276)	(.1)
Provisions at effective tax rate	$113,269	38.2%	$100,625	37.0%	$134,354	47.4%

Income taxes The provision for income taxes is different than the amount computed by applying the federal statutory rate to pre-tax income for financial reporting purposes. The reasons for this difference are as follows:

	1983	1982	1981
		(Amounts in thousands)	
Federal tax computed at statutory rate	**$2,615**	$9,022	$6,165
Increase (reduction) resulting from:			
State taxes, net of federal tax benefit	**200**	795	473
Losses of foreign subsidiaries not recognized for tax purposes	**557**	—	—
Investment tax credit	**(1,015)**	(589)	(357)
Dividends excluded from taxation	**(283)**	—	—
Tax effects of earnings of DISC	**(51)**	(307)	(237)
Research and experimentation tax credit	**(888)**	(706)	—
Other	**(40)**	412	201
	$1,095	$8,627	$6,245

The components of income tax expense are as follows:

	1983	1982	1981
		(Amounts in thousands)	
Current:			
Federal	**$ (279)**	$5,372	$3,624
State	**162**	1,323	650
	(117)	6,695	4,274
Deferred:			
Federal	**1,003**	1,782	1,746
State	**209**	150	225
	1,212	1,932	1,971
	$1,095	$8,627	$6,245

The principal components of deferred income tax expense are as follows:

	1983	1982	1981
		(Amounts in thousands)	
Tax depreciation in excess of book depreciation	**$ (161)**	$ (163)	$ 640
Equipment sales treated as leases for tax purposes	**167**	1,723	813
Equipment leases treated as sales for tax purposes	**61**	134	38
Income of DISC not currently taxable	**(373)**	177	271
Equipment sales reported on installment method for tax purposes	**1,487**	—	—
Other	**31**	61	209
	$1,212	$1,932	$1,971

The Company has $1,186,000 foreign tax loss carryforwards, of which $760,000 may be carried forward indefinitely and $426,000 expire in 1988.

Internal Revenue Service Examinations

In September 1983, the U.S. Tax Court issued its decision on issues raised by the Internal Revenue Service (the Service) in its examination of the Company's 1973 income tax return. The Service had asserted approximately $17,000,000 in tax deficiency as a consequence of an alleged transfer of a seven-year management contract by the Company to one of its foreign subsidiaries. The Court held that the Company did not transfer the contract as alleged and the Company is not liable for the $17,000,000 in taxes for 1973. The decision stated, however, that a portion of the income earned under the contract for 1973 must be allocated to the Company and, thus, is taxable in the United States. The Court made no determination as to whether an allocation was required for later years. The liability for 1973 has been adequately reflected in the financial statements and, in the opinion of management, the ultimate resolution of this issue will not have a material effect on the Company's financial position or results of operations.

Apart from the Court decision, the Company has settled all tax issues resulting from the Service's examinations of the Company's federal income tax returns through 1978, except for an issue related to the deductibility of insurance premiums paid by the Company and its subsidiaries in 1977 and 1978. The Service has asserted that premiums paid to the Company's wholly owned insurance subsidiary for general and professional liability risks are not deductible to the extent that they exceed claims paid. The Company believes that the premiums are deductible in full. Should the Company be unable to sustain its position, additional taxes would be required to be paid. Any additional taxes required to be paid would be recognized as timing differences, recoverable in the years that claims are paid, rather than charged against operations in the period of final settlement.

The Service is presently conducting an examination of the federal income tax returns of the Company and its subsidiaries for the years 1979 and 1980.

Intangible Assets

Di Giorgio

The excess of purchase price over tangible assets of certain subsidiaries acquired prior to October 31, 1970 of $6,660,000 is not being amortized as the Company believes that these assets have an indefinite life. The excess of purchase price over tangible assets of certain subsidiaries acquired subsequent to October 31, 1970 is being amortized over periods ranging from ten to forty years.

Interest

The Company capitalizes interest costs relating to certain assets that are in the process of being constructed. Interest costs relating to continuing operations capitalized in each of the three years ended June 30, 19__, were $5,099,000, $4,464,000, and $4,184,000, respectively.

INVENTORIES

Inventories at September 30 are summarized as follows (in millions):

	1983	1982
Finished goods	$ 207.7	$ 249.1
Inventoried costs related to long-term contracts and programs principally with the United States Government	248.1	318.0
Work in process	373.8	431.3
Raw materials, parts and supplies	336.3	321.5
Total	1,165.9	1,319.9
Less allowance to adjust the carrying value of certain inventories to a last-in, first-out (LIFO) basis	140.6	163.5
Remainder	1,025.3	1,156.4
Less progress payments received on long-term contracts and programs	211.5	208.4
Inventories	$ 813.8	$ 948.0

Inventories are stated at the lower of cost (using LIFO, FIFO or average methods) or market (determined on the basis of estimated realizable values), less progress payments received. Title to all inventories related to those United States Government contracts that provide for progress payments vests in the United States Government.

There were liquidations of LIFO inventories carried at lower prior-year costs which decreased cost of sales by $29.6 million in 1983, $32.7 million in 1982 and $10.4 million in 1981, and increased net income in those years by $15 million, $16.6 million and $5 million, respectively. These liquidations occurred in the company's Automotive and General Industries businesses (see Note 21).

Inventoried costs related to United States Government fixed-price-type contracts and other long-term contracts and programs of the Aerospace and Electronics businesses are stated generally at the total of the direct costs of manufacturing, engineering and tooling, and overhead costs applicable thereto; less costs relieved based on items delivered or percentage of completion (cost-to-cost) and reductions, where applicable, to estimated realizable values. Generally, such overhead costs include general and administrative expenses (including bidding expenses and independent research and development costs) allowable in accordance with United States Government procurement practices. In accordance with industry practice, such inventoried costs include amounts which are not expected to be realized within one year.

Investment in Affiliates

EAC Industries

Summary financial information for 50% owned affiliated companies accounted for by the equity method is as follows:

	In Thousands					
	St. Paul Metalcraft			Canadian Affiliates		
	1983	1982	1981	**1983**	1982	1981
Current assets	**$3,347**	$3,163	$3,209	**$1,723**	$1,844	$1,958
Property, plant and equipment and other assets	**815**	576	620	**855**	988	1,067
Current liabilities	**289**	233	409	**800**	1,121	1,022
Long-term debt	**—**	—	5	**—**	—	435
Other long-term liabilities	**—**	—	—	**—**	129	117
Net sales	**7,110**	7,688	8,212	**5,176**	6,006	5,404
Gross profit	**1,571**	1,264	1,887	**1,395**	1,608	1,378
Operating income	**929**	526	1,173	**262**	450	215
Net income	**516**	291	645	**174**	402	134

Labor Agreements and Related Programs

In connection with the extension of collective bargaining agreements at The New York Times to March 30, 1987, the Company recorded a charge of $6,500,000 in 1983 for wage adjustments retroactive to March 31, 1983.

The Company offered early retirement/termination benefits programs to The New York Times's stereotypers in 1983 and printers in 1982. In connection therewith, the Company recorded charges of $2,500,000 in 1983 and $14,100,000 in 1982. As a result of a favorable Internal Revenue Service ruling obtained in October 1983, payment of certain benefits are being made in the form of a pension benefit payable pursuant to a tax qualified pension plan.

Leases

Property under capital leases is classified as follows:

	1983	1982
Equipment	**$192,000**	$161,000
Less accumulated depreciation	**127,000**	100,000
Net	**$ 65,000**	$ 61,000

The following is a schedule of approximate future minimum lease payment commitments for capital and operating leases:

Future Commitments	Capital Leases, Minimum Lease Payments	Operating Leases, Future Rental Commitments
1984	$ 45,000	$ 1,985,000
1985	42,000	1,660,000
1986	10,000	1,413,000
1987	10,000	1,233,000
1988	4,000	864,000
Later years	—	3,497,000
Total	111,000	10,652,000
Less amount representing interest	21,000	
Present value of net minimum lease payments	$ 90,000	$10,652,000

The Company has leases covering plant and office facilities and equipment which expire at various dates through 2003. Total rental expense was approximately $2,126,000, $1,692,000 and $1,566,000 in fiscal 1983, 1982 and 1981, respectively.

Lease information and commitments

The Company and its subsidiaries have entered into certain renewable non-cancelable leases primarily for marketing facilities. The rental payments are based on a minimum rental with certain agreements requiring payment by the Company of executory costs. These leases require minimum annual rentals as follows:

(millions)	Operating leases	Capital leases
1984	$ 68.9	$ 9.0
1985	55.3	8.8
1986	44.0	8.4
1987	34.9	7.7
1988	28.6	6.1
Later years	113.9	30.3
Total minimum lease payments	$345.6	70.3
Less – Executory costs		11.8
Net minimum lease payments		58.5
Less – Amount representing interest		22.1
Present value of net minimum lease payments		$36.4

The total minimum lease payments for operating leases have been reduced by minimum sublease rentals of $9.5 million due in the future under non-cancelable subleases.

Rental expenses for 1983, 1982, and 1981 were $94.3, $91.9, and $72.2 million, respectively.

Lease Commitments

A. C. Nielsen

The Company has certain lease arrangements which relate primarily to the use of data processing equipment and rental of office facilities. Certain of these leases contain escalation clauses whereby rental payments may increase as a result of future increases in taxes or maintenance costs. Rent expense under all operating leases amounted to $41,014,000 in 1982, $33,202,000 in 1981 and $28,638,000 in 1980.

Minimum rental commitments under leases having initial or remaining noncancellable terms in excess of one year at August 31, 1982 are:

	Operating Leases	Sublease Rentals	Net Operating Leases	Capital Leases	Total
1983	$20,623,000	$ 68,000	$20,555,000	$ 4,089,000	$24,644,000
1984	14,489,000	51,000	14,438,000	3,420,000	17,858,000
1985	9,994,000	35,000	9,959,000	2,141,000	12,100,000
1986	8,331,000	—	8,331,000	744,000	9,075,000
1987	5,974,000	—	5,974,000	210,000	6,184,000
Thereafter	4,430,000	—	4,430,000	—	4,430,000
	$63,841,000	$154,000	$63,687,000	10,604,000	$74,291,000
Less: Executory costs and future interest payments				3,689,000	
Capital lease obligations				$ 6,915,000	

Furniture and equipment in the accompanying balance sheet includes $11,223,000 and $10,394,000 of gross capital leases at August 31, 1982 and 1981, respectively. These amounts represent the present value of future rental payments at the inception of the leases. Long-term Debt includes $3,491,000 and $4,102,000 at August 31, 1982 and 1981, respectively, representing the noncurrent portion of the present value of future rental payments.

At August 31, 1982, the Company was committed to future expenditures of approximately $16,204,000 for building construction and equipment.

Litigation

The Company is among many defendants in suits claiming damages because construction products manufactured and sold by the Company which contained small amounts of asbestos were installed many years ago in buildings, allegedly creating a hazard and damaging the property to the extent that remedial action to encapsulate or remove the asbestos-containing products is required. Through December 31, 1983, the Company has been served in 23 such cases, including three wherein plaintiffs have requested certification of the lawsuits as class actions. In addition to the cost of the remedial action, claims also are made in some of the cases for attorneys' fees and punitive damages. No property damage case has yet been tried. The Company has denied the substantive allegations of each of the complaints, believes that none of the few asbestos-containing construction products it manufactured where properly used and installed will create a health hazard or damage the property, and intends to vigorously defend each of the actions.

At present, the Company also is one of numerous defendants in approximately sixteen hundred cases seeking damages for bodily injury allegedly resulting from exposure to asbestos and asbestos-containing products. Most bodily injury asbestos cases have arisen out of insulating activities in shipyards and industrial facilities, and plaintiffs' work did not involve exposure to a type of product containing asbestos manufactured and sold at any time by the Company. Therefore, the Company has been able to dispose of more than half of all such cases in which it has been served for a nominal average payment of a few hundred dollars per case.

Based upon the information presently available to the Company, including its experience in these cases, it is management's opinion that resolution of asbestos cases, and all other litigation in which the Company presently is involved, will not have a material adverse effect on the financial position of the Company.

Loans to Officers

During fiscal 19__ the Board of Directors authorized loans amounting to $200,000 to six officers primarily for the purpose of purchasing common stock of the Company in the open market. The loans bear interest at five percent but were granted with the intention that they and the interest accruing thereon be forgiven over the terms of the officers' subsequent employment careers with the Company. The loan agreements provide that, so long as the officers remain employees of the Company, the Company will annually forgive five percent of the original loan amount as well as the interest that accrued on the loan during that year. Amounts forgiven each year are accounted for as compensation expense. The loans are collateralized by the shares of common stock of the Company initially purchased under this program, reduced each year by a pro rata amount based on loan forgiveness. At September 30, 19__ , 22,888 shares (as adjusted for the July 19__ 3-for-2 stock split described in Note 7) were held as collateral.

—Merger, Acquisitions and Divestitures

On June 17, 1983, the Company acquired all of the outstanding equity securities of Micro Peripherals, Inc. (MPI), in exchange for 1,302,139 shares of the Company's common stock held in treasury and $1,884,000 in cash paid to shareholders for equity securities representing less than ten percent of the outstanding securities of MPI. MPI, founded in 1977, manufactures floppy disk drives principally for original equipment manufacturers of mini and microcomputer systems and related word processors. Major production facilities are located in Singapore with additional manufacturing operations in Mexico and in Chatsworth, California.

The merger was accounted for as a pooling of interests. Accordingly, the consolidated financial statements of the Company for all periods have been restated to include the results of operations of MPI. MPI's previously reported financial results have been recast from a fiscal year ending on or near April 30, which periods were covered by the reports of other independent accountants, to a calendar year basis and include the accounts of Micro Peripherals Singapore (Private) Limited. Net sales and net earnings of the separate companies for 1981, 1982 and the six months ended July 3, 1983 (the end of the interim period nearest the date of merger) are as follows:

	CTS, as previously reported	MPI	Combined
Net sales:			
Year ended January 3, 1982	$209,572	$21,901	$231,473
Year ended January 2, 1983	223,388	33,566	256,954
Six months ended July 3, 1983 (unaudited)	111,150	31,635	142,785
Net earnings:			
Year ended January 3, 1982	13,106	246	13,352
Year ended January 2, 1983	8,825	543	9,368
Six months ended July 3, 1983 (unaudited)	4,597	2,170	6,767
Nontax-deductible merger expenses (deduct)			(1,535)
As reported at July 3, 1983			5,232

Pension plans

Retirement income plans cover substantially all employees. The Company and its domestic subsidiaries have retirement plans under which funds are deposited with trustees. All major subsidiaries outside the U.S. provide for employees' pension plans in conformity with local requirements and practices.

Pension costs charged to operations in 1983, 1982, and 1981 amounted to $52.4, $53.9, and $48.1 million, respectively, including amortization of prior service costs over periods up to 30 years. Generally it is the Company's practice to fund pension costs as accrued.

A summary of estimated accumulated plan benefits and plan net assets for the Company's U.S. defined benefit plans is presented below:

(millions)	December 31	1983	1982
Actuarial present value of accumulated plan benefits			
Vested		$529.9	$508.4
Nonvested		30.6	26.8
Total		$560.5	$535.2
Net assets available for benefits, at market value		$646.7	$557.4

The weighted average assumed rate of return used in determining the actuarial present value of accumulated plan benefits was 8.57% for 1983 and 8.61% for 1982.

At December 31, 1983 and 1982, it is estimated that the market value of fund assets and balance sheet accruals for plans outside the U.S., in the aggregate, exceeded the actuarially computed present value of vested benefits.

Performance Share Plan

Koppers

—The Company has a Performance Share Plan for key employees that provides for an award of performance shares (up to an aggregate maximum of 500,000 shares), each equivalent to one share of the Company's common stock and cash. Distribution of the common stock plus cash equal to the fair market value of the common stock will be made at the end of designated periods if specified earnings are attained.

Currently, 73,375 performance shares are outstanding for the award period ending December 31, 1983 and 134,650 for the period ending December 31, 1984. Based on profit performance, no provision has been made for the years 1982 and 1981.

Performance Unit Plan

The Company has a Performance Unit Plan as an incentive for certain key employees of the Company and its subsidiary corporations. Within one hundred twenty (120) days after the close of the Company's fiscal year, upon the recommendation of the Compensation Committee of the Board of Directors, a number of performance units may be awarded by the Board of Directors to eligible employees. The value of a performance unit is computed by multiplying a performance factor reflecting the annual compound growth rate in earnings per share for the three fiscal years beginning with the year in which the award is made, by the earnings per share for the three-year period.

The value of the performance units will not vest to the employee until the end of the third fiscal year. Except for provisions for death or retirement, an individual who is not an employee of the Company at the end of the third fiscal year is not entitled to benefits under the plan. The plan commenced in fiscal 1977.

For the years ended August 31, 19__ and 19__ the charges to income representing the estimated value of performance units was $370,000 and $161,000, respectively. During 19__ income was credited for $415,000, representing an estimated reduction in the value of performance units.

Personnel Expenses

Personnel Costs

Personnel costs, the highest component of non-interest expenses, increased to $67,474,500 for the year 19__ from $62,289,000 for the same period in 19__. This represents an 8 per cent increase. Table E gives the breakdown of the items comprising this cost.

Salaries rose to $44,691,900 for 19__ as compared to $40,362,100 in 19__ reflecting increases in wages and other merit pay increases. Pension and other benefits increased to $11,493,700 from $10,173,700 due to the higher salaries and the increased cost of employee benefits, principally payroll taxes and hospital and life insurance. As a result of the decrease in the ratio of net operating income to the Bank's capital funds, our deferred compensation (profit sharing) contribution decreased to $11,288,900 in 19__ from $11,753,200 in 19__. Annual contributions to the deferred compensation (profit sharing) plan are based on a formula which relates net operating income to the Bank's capital funds.

Plant Closing:

In order to improve overall efficiency in the Company's production of United States household and personal care products, management decided, in 1981, to close a manufacturing facility located in Berkely, California. Closing this plant resulted in a charge in 1981 of $7,927 (net of income tax benefit of $6,752). This charge is composed principally of employee termination expense, pension costs, estimated loss on disposal of assets and other costs expected to be incurred.

3. Property, Plant and Equipment

A summary of property, plant and equipment at cost, together with depreciation methods and rates, is as follows:

	Method	Depreciation Rates	June 30, 1983	1982
Land			$ 200,604	$ 200,604
Buildings	Straight-line	4%	447,010	447,010
Building improvements	Straight-line	4%–10%	1,110,996	675,496
Machinery and equipment	Straight-line and declining-balance	8⅓%–20%	2,400,971	2,143,502
Leasehold improvements	Straight-line	Lives of leases	830	830
Furniture and fixtures	Straight-line	10%–33⅓%	250,485	187,429
Automobiles	Straight-line	20%–33⅓%	64,600	51,046
Automated data processing equipment	Straight-line	12½%–16⅔%	530,287	240,183
Construction in progress			25,283	77,694
			5,031,066	4,023,794
Less accumulated depreciation			1,905,609	1,604,325
			$3,125,457	$2,419,469

Proposed Acquisitions

Savin Corp.

Proposed Acquisition of Magnetic Laboratories, Inc. In June 19__ , the Company entered into a formal agreement to acquire Magnetic Laboratories, Inc., a manufacturer of electro-mechanical products. Final closing of the agreement is subject to a favorable tax ruling from the Internal Revenue Service and the approval of Magnetic's shareholders.

The purchase price will be approximately $13,000,000 consisting, principally, of shares of a new series of $1.50 cumulative convertible preferred stock of Savin. Each share of the preferred stock will be convertible into one share of Savin common stock.

The transaction will be accounted for as a purchase. Accordingly, Magnetic's results of operations will be included with the Company's consolidated results of operations for periods subsequent to the date of acquisition.

In connection with the proposed acquisition, the Company has guaranteed lines of credit of Magnetic up to a maximum of $2,500,000.

For the fiscal year ended May 31, 19__ Magnetic reported sales and net income of $32,996,388 and $661,739, respectively.

Provision for Losses on Disposition of Property and Discontinuance of Product Lines

The Company has made a $17,094,924 provision for losses on the sale or discontinuance of twelve product lines. Each of these charges is of relatively equal significance; no item appreciably exceeds 10% of the total. The provisions are largely due to the write-down of book values of real property to their estimated realizable values. Sales and profits of these operations are not material in relation to the Company's operations as a whole.

Purchase of Tax Benefits

PURCHASE OF TAX BENEFITS—In August, 1982, the Company entered into a tax lease of machinery and equipment in order to purchase tax benefits as permitted by the Economic Recovery Tax Act of 1981 and the Tax Equity and Fiscal Responsibility Act of 1982. The actual cost of the investment is being amortized over the life of the lease.

Redeemable Preferred Stock

Revlon has authorized 33,060,841 shares of $1.00 par value Preferred Stock.

During 1980, Revlon issued 11,435,040 shares of Series A Adjustable Rate Convertible Preferred Stock, par value $1.00 per share ("convertible preferred stock"), in connection with the acquisition of Technicon Corporation ("Technicon"). The convertible preferred stock was recorded at $20 per share which represented the estimated fair value at issuance. This amount is being periodically increased to the mandatory redemption price of $26.67 per outstanding share through a charge to retained earnings.

In July 1983, Revlon's stockholders approved an amendment to the Certificate of Designation governing the convertible preferred stock, which allowed Revlon to purchase such stock prior to 1985. During July 1983 Revlon purchased 8,580,034 shares for cash of approximately $217,200,000 and, in August 1983, purchased an additional 2,750,000 shares for cash of $1,000,000 and a 9.25% per annum note payable as to $32,500,000 in each of November 1983 and February 1984 and $3,800,000 in August 1984. The shares had been held, directly or indirectly, principally by persons from whom Revlon had purchased Technicon. The aggregate purchase price, including related expenses, exceeded the book value of the shares at the dates of purchase by approximately $47,200,000; retained earnings was reduced by such amount in 1983. The redemption premium and related expenses had no effect on earnings per share.

At December 31, 1983, after the above purchases and the conversion of 366 shares in the period from 1980 to 1983, there are 104,640 shares of convertible preferred stock outstanding. Each share receives, if declared, a cumulative dividend at the rate of $1.95 per annum, which rate is subject to increase under certain circumstances to a maximum of $3.61 per annum. Each share is convertible at any time into approximately 30/66 share of Revlon common stock, subject to anti-dilution protections. Under the terms of the convertible preferred stock, Revlon is required to purchase or to redeem all remaining shares by the year 2000.

Each share is entitled to Fifteen One Hundredths vote on all matters, voting with the Revlon common stock, and to class voting on certain matters. Each share is entitled to a liquidation preference of $26.67, plus accrued dividends.

Related Party Transactions

Related Party Transactions

Certain officers, directors and employees participated on an equal basis with outside participants in the drilling of 13 oil and gas wells in 19__ , 18 in 19__ and nine in 19__ . Such participation aggregated $481,000, $301,000 and $168,000 in 19__ , and 19__ and 19__ respectively. Three of the 1980 wells were dry holes, eight were completed as producers and two were in progress at December 31, 19__ . Of the 19__ wells, four were dry holes, 13 were completed as producers and one is in progress at December 31, 19__.

Of the 19__ wells, five were dry holes and four were completed as producers.

Southern Railway Company and subsidiaries have normal business relationships with Brown Brothers Harriman & Co., of which R. L. Ireland, III, is a Partner. These relationships include the borrowing of money from time to time, the existence of lines of credit, the maintenance of bank accounts and various other banking relationships. These relationships were entered into in the ordinary course of business on substantially the same terms as those prevailing at the time for comparable transactions with other banks.

14. Transactions with Related Parties

On February 1, 1982, Agfa-Gevaert Graphics, Inc., a wholly owned subsidiary of Agfa-Gevaert, Inc., acquired an approximately 69 percent interest in the Company by purchasing 3,082,000 shares of newly issued common stock and approximately 2,500,000 shares of common stock pursuant to a cash tender offer. During fiscal 1983, Agfa-Gevaert Graphics, Inc. purchased 833,000 shares of common stock in the open market, increasing its interest in the Company to approximately 79.3 percent as of October 1, 1983. Afga-Gevaert, Inc. is a subsidiary of Agfa-Gevaert N. V., of Belgium.

The Company engages in business transactions with subsidiaries of Agfa-Gevaert N.V. Products purchased for resale from these subsidiaries amounted to $16,713,000 in 1983 and $13,412,000 in 1982. Sales to these subsidiaries amounted to $6,567,000 in 1983 and $2,213,000 in 1982.

The accompanying Consolidated Balance Sheet includes the following related-party amounts:

Dollars in thousands	1983	1982
Accounts receivable	$2,364	$ 965
10.25% note receivable due Dec. 12, 1983	4,000	–
Accounts payable	1,472	1,277

Di Giorgio Corp.

In 19__ real estate sales in the aggregate amount of $800,000 were made to officers and employees of the Company. Terms of these sales required approximately 20 percent down payments in cash and provided that the remainder of the selling price be financed by secured promissory notes which are receivable over periods of from 5 to 12 years at interest rates ranging from 12 to 15 percent. At December 31, 19__ approximately $640,000 was due to the Company on notes received from these transactions. All of these sales were made at substantially the same prices and terms as are available to unrelated individuals.

Also during 19__ the Company purchased a parcel of land for $1,120,000 from a trust, of which a beneficiary is related to a corporate officer. The purchase price of $1,120,000 was determined by an independent appraiser's valuation. Under the terms of the sale, the company paid 20 percent down and financed the balance through the issuance of 6 percent per annum 5-year promissory notes in the face amount of $896,000. At December 31, 19__ the Company owed the face amount of the notes.

Repurchase of the Corporation's Stock

Many companies have gone into the stock market and repurchased shares of their corporate stock. Associated Hosts describes their repurchase activity as follows:

Stockholders' equity at year-end was $22,095,000, equal to $7.03 per share versus $20,423,000 or $6.49 per share a year ago. With regard to the common stock shortly before the end of the fiscal year, your board of directors authorized management to purchase from time to time in the open market up to 200,000 shares of Associated Hosts' common stock. We believe that this is an attractive investment for the Company at this time.

Research and Development

The Financial Accounting Standards Board has issued a statement that specifies how companies should account for the funding from outside sources for research and development activities.

FASB Statement 68 guides a company in determining whether to show its outside R & D funding as a liability or as a contract for the sale or performance of services.

Statement 68 states that a company should account for this arrangement as a contract for the sale or performance of services, and disclose the significant terms of the agreements under the arrangement as of the date of each balance sheet presented.

If under the terms of the funding a company obligates itself to repay outside R & D funds, Statement 68 requires the company to record a liability and to charge R & D costs to expense as incurred.

Example

Research and Development Expenditures for Company-sponsored research and development for the past three years is summarized as follows:

	1983	1982	1981
Total Costs (thousands)	$12,500	$14,400	$13,500
% of Sales	3.1	3.0	2.4
% of Pretax Income	57.9	25.7	15.9

Staley

Total research costs charged to income in 1982, 1981 and 1980 were $10,000,000, $9,000,000 and $7,000,000, respectively. Research activities include basic and applied research, product development, process development and technical service to customers.

Research and Development

Research and development costs of $220,940, $151,151 and $107,783 have been charged to expense in 1983, 1982 and 1981, respectively.

Retirement Plans

Pension and profit-sharing expense was $27,800,000 for 1983, $36,100,000 for 1982, and $35,100,000 for 1981. A comparison of the present value of accumulated plan benefits and plan net assets for the Company's domestic defined benefit plans as of the most recent actuarial valuation dates (generally January 1, 1983 and 1982, respectively), is set forth in the following table:

	Thousands of Dollars	
	1983	1982
Actuarial present value of accumulated plan benefits:		
Vested	**$140,800**	128,500
Nonvested	**21,800**	22,000
Total	**$162,600**	150,500
Net assets available for plan benefits	**$283,300**	233,000

The actuarial present value of accumulated plan benefits was calculated in accordance with Statement of Financial Accounting Standards No. 35. The assumed rates of return used to determine the present value of plan benefits were primarily the rates published by the Pension Benefit Guaranty Corporation as of the respective valuation dates. For 1983, the weighted average rate was 9.0 per cent and for 1982 it was 9.2 per cent.

Effective with the most recent plan valuations (generally as of January 1, 1983), the Company changed certain assumptions used for purposes of determining annual pension expense of defined benefit plans. An increase in the assumed rate of return on fund assets from 6½ per cent to 8½ per cent and an appropriate increase in anticipated compensation growth were the most significant changes. These changes were primarily responsible for the decrease in pension and profit-sharing expense for 1983 as compared with amounts reported for 1982 and 1981.

Retirement benefits for employees in foreign locations are funded principally through either annuity or government programs. Assets and liabilities of the Company's foreign plans are not significant.

2. Sale of Wholly Owned Subsidiaries

On February 22, 1983, the Company sold the assets, subject to existing liabilities, of Key Electro Sonic Corporation (Key) for $1,500,000 in cash and a $2,000,000 12% secured note receivable. The purchaser was a corporation formed by Harold R. Frank, Chairman of the Board, a private investor, and certain management personnel of Key. A gain of $395,243 was recorded on the sale after providing for applicable income taxes of $334,616.

Key comprised the Company's activity in the manufacture and marketing of process control equipment and systems. As a result of the sale, the operations of Key have been shown as a discontinued business in the accompanying Consolidated Statements of Income and all footnote information excludes amounts related to Key.

A summary of Key's net assets on the date of sale is as follows:

Net current assets	$ 836,831
Plant and equipment, net	1,247,826
Other assets	10,023
	$2,094,680

The operating results of Key are summarized as follows:

	For the Period Ended February 22, 1983	*For the Year Ended September 30*	
		1982	*1981*
Net sales	$1,408,800	$7,390,204	$6,300,054
Cost of sales	979,673	4,507,459	4,025,365
Research and development expenses	236,251	434,871	375,669
Selling, general and administrative expenses	614,523	1,708,068	1,355,566
Income (Loss) from operations	(421,647)	739,806	543,454
Other, net	24,879	(12)	7,285
Income tax provision (benefit)	(198,384)	369,897	275,369
Net income (loss)	$ (198,384)	$ 369,897	$ 275,370

Amounts due under the note received in connection with the sale are as follows:

1987	$ 133,333
1988	1,866,667
	$2,000,000

On February 6, 1981, the Company sold the common stock of its wholly owned subsidiary, Geo Space Corporation, which together with its subsidiaries comprised the Company's activities in the manufacture and marketing of energy exploration products and systems. Accordingly, the Consolidated Statements of Income have been restated to reflect the operations of Geo Space Corporation as a discontinued business and all footnote information excludes amounts related to Geo Space Corporation. The consideration received was $22,500,000 in cash. A gain of $9,493,089 was recorded on the sale after providing for applicable income taxes of $5,500,000.

Short-Term Investments

Short-term investments at March 31, 1983 and 1982 consisted of:

	1983	1982
Certificates of deposit	$12,500,000	$13,300,000
Municipal bonds	6,493,000	2,002,000
Commercial paper		316,000
Marketable equity securities	2,613,000	36,000
Total	$21,606,000	$15,654,000

Marketable equity securities are carried at the lower of aggregate cost (computed on a first-in, first-out basis) or market. Certificates of deposit, municipal bonds and commercial paper are carried at cost which approximates market.

D-Stock Options

The Company has granted stock options under two plans to employees at prices not less than the market value at the date of grant. Outstanding options under the plan expire five years from the date of grant. At December 31, 1983 and 1982, the Company had 650,478 and 666,628 shares, respectively, reserved for future option grants.

A summary of certain information regarding stock options follows:

	Option Price Per Share	Number of Shares
Balance at January 1, 1983	$ 9.67–$23.00	161,439
Granted	21.88– 25.25	18,438
Exercised	9.67– 20.00	(22,913)
Cancelled		(5,307)
Balance at December 31, 1983	$17.50–$25.25	151,657
Exercisable at December 31, 1983		88,051

— Stock Purchase and Stock Option Plans

Approximately 6,321 employees currently are participating through regular payroll deductions in the company's Employee Stock Purchase and Savings Plan. In this employee fund at December 31, 1983 there were 3,947,509 shares of common stock, representing approximately 17% of the total number of common shares outstanding. The company's contribution charged to operations during 1983 amounted to approximately $5,921,000.

During 1983 the company established The Sherwin-Williams Company Payroll Based Stock Ownership Plan ("PAYSOP"). Under this PAYSOP, substantially all company employees not covered by a collective bargaining agreement are eligible to participate equally in the Plan. The company's contribution to the PAYSOP of approximately $1,204,000 for 1983 resulted in a corresponding reduction of applicable income tax liabilities.

Shares of company stock credited to each member's account under these employee stock ownership plans are voted by the trustee under confidential instructions from each individual plan member.

Non-qualified and incentive stock options have been granted to certain officers and key employees under the company's stock option plan, at prices not less than fair market value of the shares at date of grant. The options generally become exercisable to the extent of one-third of the optioned shares for each full year of employment following the date of grant and expire ten years after date of grant. Options granted to certain officers in 1979 under related employment contracts carry substantially the same terms as options granted under the stock option plan.

A stock appreciation rights plan was approved by the shareholders in 1979; however, no rights have been granted under the plan.

	1983		1982		1981	
	Shares	Aggregate Price	Shares	Aggregate Price	Shares	Aggregate Price
Stock Option Plan:						
Options outstanding beginning of year	1,076,240	$9,031,000	1,103,200	$8,141,000	1,279,200	$8,618,000
Granted	217,850	4,631,000	348,000	3,518,000	176,000	1,727,000
Exercised	(220,762)	(1,645,000)	(218,160)	(1,484,000)	(227,676)	(1,407,000)
Canceled	(156,876)	(1,686,000)	(156,800)	(1,144,000)	(124,324)	(797,000)
Options outstanding end of year	916,452	$10,331,000	1,076,240	$9,031,000	1,103,200	$8,141,000
Exercisable	223,198		154,640		179,200	
Reserved for future grants	605,858		666,832		858,032	
Employee contracts:						
Options outstanding beginning of year	194,000	$1,012,000	194,000	$1,012,000	244,000	$1,270,000
Exercised	(121,500)	(632,000)	—	—	(50,000)	(258,000)
Options outstanding end of year	72,500	$380,000	194,000	$1,012,000	194,000	$1,012,000

—Stock Splits

During February, 1983 and February, 1981, the company's board of directors authorized two-for-one splits of the common stock outstanding effected in the form of 100% stock dividends. These dividends were distributed during March of each respective year. The par value of the additional shares of common stock issued in connection with these stock splits was credited to common stock and a like amount charged to other capital and retained earnings.

Third-Party Transactions

The Company has agreements with bank leasing subsidiaries under which the leasing companies may purchase Measurex systems subject to leases to Measurex customers. Generally, sales of systems under these agreements are at amounts approximating end user purchase prices.

In addition, at various times, the Company has sold portions of its domestic and foreign lease contracts receivable and the related equipment to certain unrelated third-party lessors and has discounted purchase contracts receivables with unrelated financing institutions.

These transactions have been made on both a nonrecourse and full-recourse basis. In certain instances, the Company is entitled to participate in revenues received at the conclusion of the basic lease term. In addition, in certain instances, the Company has agreed to assist, for a fee, in remarketing systems when they come off lease.

At November 30, 1983, the Company was contingently liable for approximately $10.7 million relating to these transactions.

Treasury stock

Treasury stock transactions for each year in the three-year period ended December 31, 1983 were:

Number of shares	1983	1982	1981
Beginning of year	50,231	40,758	39,370
Common stock acquired*	1,120	10,312	2,205
Common stock issued under the company's incentive compensation plan	(824)	(839)	(817)
End of year	50,527	50,231	40,758

*Consists primarily of appreciated shares exchanged for new shares issued under the company's stock option plan.

Unusual Charge

In 1982 the Company provided for costs associated with the restructuring of certain areas of the Company's business, including product line liquidations, plant closings and consolidations, and related personnel termination costs. The principal components of this charge were:

Provisions of approximately $4,800,000 relating to programs, product lines and related inventories, principally of the Automotive Accessories business.

Provision for the anticipated loss on disposal and phase-out of certain plant facilities in the amount of approximately $2,400,000.

Provision of $1,600,000 related to expected costs and losses associated with the restructuring of several operating programs.

During 1983 the Company substantially completed its aforementioned restructuring and incurred or charged against reserves provided in 1982 amounts relating to the disposal of certain product lines and inventories, termination costs and certain European restructuring costs. These included the loss and disposal costs with respect to the sale of the Company's division engaged in the manufacture of custom wheels. Net sales of this division for the years 1983, 1982 and 1981 were $11,500,000, $15,900,000 and $15,300,000, respectively. Consolidated net assets and net income of this division were not significant.

Vacation Accrued

The Corporation has retroactively adopted FAS No. 43, "Accounting for Compensated Absences." Prior to the adoption of this standard, the Corporation accounted for vacation benefits on a vested basis. All prior years have been restated to reflect this accounting change, which was not material in relation to earnings in any period presented.

Working Capital

Changes in the components of working capital for the years ended June 30, 1983, 1982 and 1981 were as follows:

	1983	1982	1981
Increase (decrease) in current assets:			
Cash and short-term investments	**$ 4,389**	$ (3,109)	$ 5,938
Accounts receivable	**19,750**	4,834	836
Inventories	**3,811**	6,678	(21,006)

	1983	1982	1981
Prepaid expenses, taxes and other current assets	**4,104**	7,344	13,468
(Increase) decrease in current liabilities:			
Notes payable to banks	**(2,912)**	11,068	23,046
Accounts payable	**(6,993)**	(5,086)	4,298
Income taxes	**(2,216)**	5,057	(6,123)
Accrued liabilities	**(7,591)**	(1,755)	(3,532)
Long-term debt due within one year	**(1,267)**	515	141
Increase in working capital	**$11,075**	$25,546	$17,066

INFLATION ACCOUNTING

This chapter will apply to your company if your company meets the following criteria:

1. Your corporate inventory, property, plant, and equipment (before deducting accumulated depreciation) amount to more than $125 million; or,
2. Your company's total assets amount to more than $1 billion after deducting accumulated depreciation.

Financial Accounting Standard #33 of the Financial Accounting Standards Board requires your company, if it meets these two standards, to disclose as supplementary information the impact of inflation on your company's business. Careful thought should be given to a review of Financial Accounting Standard #33, published by the Financial Accounting Standards Board, High Ridge Park, Stamford, CT 06905. Your accountant will advise you as to the manner in which to present this information.

Impact of Inflation on Accounting Data (Unaudited)

It would be helpful to the readers of your annual report if you were to discuss the impact of inflation on your profits before adjusting for changing prices as required in FAS #33.

Example:

Impact of Inflation on Accounting Data (Unaudited) Financial statements, which report amounts reflecting historical costs using dollars assumed to have stable purchasing power, do not measure the effects of inflation and changing prices on financial position and operating results. Two methods are currently used to develop such data. The first method, constant dollars, adjusts costs for general inflation. Under this method, historical costs are restated to dollars of current purchasing power using the average level of the Consumer Price Index for all Urban Consumers (CPI) during the year. The second method, current cost, adjusts costs to reflect specific prices of resources actually used by the company in its operations. Both methods are experimental and inherently involve the use of assumptions, approximations, and estimates. The amounts shown below should be viewed in that context and not as precise indicators of inflation's effects.

Lockheed has reached no conclusions as to the best method for recognizing inflation and changing prices in its financial statements and as to the usefulness of the information presented below.

10. EFFECTS OF INFLATION (UNAUDITED)

FASB Statement No. 33, "Financial Reporting and Changing Prices," as amended by FASB Statement No. 70, "Financial Reporting and Changing Prices: Foreign Currency Translation," represents an attempt to highlight some of the financial statement effects of inflation. In accordance with the above Statements, the following supplementary data present the effects of inflation measured in current costs.

The current-cost method uses price changes of specific assets (inventory and fixed assets) to gauge the impact of inflation. This method requires many subjective judgments, assumptions and estimates. Further, it does not consider technological or other improvements that would be made if current operating capacity were to be replaced. In addition, the inflation information may not be comparable from company to company because of variations in methodology, assumptions and companies' operating environments. These factors and the experimental nature of the information should be considered when reviewing the company's inflation-adjusted data. Also, this information should not be taken as an indication of the company's ability to maintain productive capacity or its position in the marketplace.

The company used the following techniques to compute current costs:

—Fixed assets were revalued using indices, independent appraisals and unit pricing. The current cost of fixed assets, net was $1,163,119,000 at April 27, 1983.

—Depreciation was calculated on a straight-line basis using estimated useful lives consistent with those in the historical-cost financial statements. Fiscal year 1983 current-cost depreciation was $107,208,000; it was allocated to cost of products sold and operating expenses.

—Inventories were revalued using end-of-the-year prices. Current costs for raw materials that were out of season at year end were based on anticipated contract prices for the following season. The current cost of inventory at April 27, 1983 was $627,013,000.

—Cost of products sold was adjusted to reflect current costs at the time of sale.

No adjustments have been made to income tax expense because inflation adjustments are not deductible for income tax purposes. The higher effective tax rate that results is an indication of the increased tax burden that may occur in an inflationary environment.

Five-Year Selected Financial Data in Average 1983 Dollars

(in thousands except per share data and indices)	**1983**	1982	1981	1980	1979
SALES	**$3,738,445**	$3,866,976	$4,085,714	$3,762,077	$3,583,209
CURRENT-COST INFORMATION					
Net earnings	**$ 159,607**	$ 110,129	$ 90,108	$ 82,217	
Earnings per share	**$ 3.35**	$ 2.33	$ 1.92	$ 1.75	
Net assets at year end	**$1,533,663**	$1,517,274	$1,556,230	$1,613,201	
Translation and parity adjustments	**$ (41,099)**	$ (75,098)	$ (15,360)	$ 39,644	
Increase in current costs in excess of increase in the general price level (a)(b)	**$ 14,369**	$ 46,860	$ (17,918)	$ (63,891)	
OTHER INFORMATION					
Purchasing power gain (a)	**$ 22,488**	$ 45,225	$ 69,168	$ 92,527	
Dividends per share	**$ 1.61**	$ 1.47	$ 1.37	$ 1.36	$ 1.33
Market price per common share at year end	**$ 44.35**	$ 34.47	$ 30.42	$ 23.37	$ 28.35
Average consumer price index (1967 = 100)	**292.5**	279.0	255.5	227.4	201.7

(a) This information reflects the effects of general inflation based on local currency general price level indices (restate-translate method).

(b) The increase for 1983 in current costs in excess of the increase in the general price level for inventories and property, plant and equipment was calculated as follows:

Increase in current costs	$97,582
Increase in general price level	83,213
Increase in current costs in excess of increase in the general price level	$14,369

The Consolidated Statement of Income for the year ended April 27, 1983, as reported (historical costs) and as adjusted for specific prices (current costs) is presented below.

(in thousands except tax rates)	As Reported (Historical Costs)	Adjusted for Specific Prices (Current Costs)
Sales	$3,738,445	$3,738,445
Cost of products sold	2,355,805	2,406,243
Gross profit	1,382,640	1,332,202
Operating expenses	986,175	987,968
Operating income	396,465	344,234
Other income, net	4,261	1,849
Interest expense	50,354	50,354
Income before income taxes	350,372	295,729
Provision for income taxes	136,122	136,122
Net income	$ 214,250	$ 159,607
Effective tax rate	38.9%	46.0%

Changing Prices (unaudited)

The accompanying five year summary of selected financial data and statement of earnings were prepared in accordance with the Financial Accounting Standards Board's experimental standard on inflation accounting. The reporting requirements attempt to identify and illustrate the impact of inflation on business enterprises and deal with both the effect of general inflation (constant dollar) and the effect of changes in the prices of certain specific assets (current costs).

In preparing this data, the Company followed the FASB's recommended method which is generally recognized as experimental and should not be considered a complete or precise indicator of the effects of inflation on the Company. Since the use of numerous assumptions, approximations and estimates is required in the computations, management believes that the data should be used only after cautious evaluation.

The constant dollar data attempts to measure the effect of changing prices on the purchasing power of the dollar. Historical financial information is reflected in dollars of equal value by restating such amounts into equal units of general purchasing power using the Consumer Price Index.

Current cost amounts attempt to measure the impact of price changes specific to the Company, based on estimates of the current cost to replace, in kind, inventories and properties currently in use. As a practical matter, the Company attempts to replace its assets and facilities using the best available technology. However, in determining the current cost of inventories and facilities in accordance with FASB guidelines, no adjustments were made to take into consideration product line changes or the availability of technological improvements to increase efficiency and cost effectiveness. Related cost of goods sold and depreciation expense were similarly stated at their estimated current cost.

The current cost amounts include inventories (determined on a FIFO basis), adjusted for depreciation on a current cost basis, and cost of goods sold adjusted to current costs. The current cost of property, plant and equipment was estimated using appropriate construction and equipment indices. Assets which are to be sold were recorded at their estimated net realizable values. Realty inventory was included in the constant dollar disclosures, and was included in the current cost data at historical amounts.

During inflationary periods, a corporation holding monetary assets such as temporary investments and receivables loses purchasing power because these items can purchase less at a future date. Alternatively, a corporation holding monetary liabilities such as debt and accrued liabilities gains purchasing power because the payment in the future will be made with dollars having less value. For 1983, 1982, and 1981 the Company showed a loss in general purchasing power of net monetary items of $2,775,000, $4,343,000 and $6,576,000, respectively

Rising costs of raw materials, labor, energy, interest and services all impact the Company's earning power. Although higher costs are periodically recoverable through increased product prices, this is not always possible. The Company is limited in the amount it can increase its prices by the highly competitive markets in which it sells and by contractual agreements in long-term contracts.

The net earnings adjusted for the impact of changing prices for fiscal year 1983 is reflected in the accompanying statement. For fiscal year 1982 the net loss, adjusted for the impact of general inflation (constant dollars) and adjusted for changes in specific prices (current costs), stated in average fiscal 1983 dollars, was $17,830,000 and $11,329,000, respectively. For fiscal year 1981, the net loss, adjusted for the impact of general inflation, (constant dollars), and adjusted for changes in specific prices, (current costs), stated in average fiscal year 1983 dollars, was $20,014,000 and $9,988,000, respectively. The net earnings per share and net assets at year end stated in average fiscal 1983 dollars, adjusted for the constant dollar impact and for current costs, is $.38 and $106,836,000 and $.45 and $117,094,000 for 1983, respectively. The net loss per share and net assets at year end for 1982 stated in average fiscal 1983 dollars, was $4.15 and $97,607,000 adjusted for the impact of constant dollars; and $2.80 and $107,681,000 adjusted for current costs. The net loss per share and net assets at year end for 1981 stated in average fiscal 1983 dollars, was $4.65 and $117,131,000 adjusted for the impact of constant dollars; and $2.57 and $131,205,000 adjusted for current costs.

Notes to Consolidated Financial Statements

Talley Industries, Inc. and Subsidiaries

Changing Prices (unaudited) (continued)

A statement of earnings for the year ended March 31, 1983 adjusted for the effects of changing prices, and the historical cost information reported in the primary financial statements for the same period, are shown below:

	Historical Costs	Adjusted for General Inflation (Constant Dollars)	Adjusted for Changes in Specific Prices (Current Costs)
(thousands)	(in average fiscal year 1983 dollars)		
Sales	**$264,109**	$264,109	$264,109
Cost of sales and operating expenses, excluding depreciation	**248,991**	252,339	249,826
Depreciation expense	**4,626**	6,725	8,692
Other income, net	**9,746**	9,746	9,746
Interest expense	**8,109**	8,109	8,109
Earnings before income taxes and extraordinary gain	**12,129**	6,682	7,228
Provision for income taxes	**6,701**	6,701	6,701
Earnings (loss) before extraordinary gain	**5,428**	(19)	527
Extraordinary gain	**2,762**	2,762	2,762
Net earnings	**$ 8,190**	$ 2,743	$ 3,289

The current cost decrease of inventories and property, plant and equipment held during 1983 stated in average fiscal year 1983 dollars, was $144,000 excluding general inflation increases of $4,679,000. At March 31, 1983, the current cost value of inventory and property, plant and equipment (net of accumulated depreciation), stated in fiscal year end 1983 dollars was $73,765,000 and $53,413,000, respectively.

Income taxes reflected in the supplemental statement of earnings are as reported and are not adjusted for the effects of inflation.

Selected financial data adjusted for the effects of changing prices are summarized as follows:

Years Ended March 31	1983	1982	1981	1980	1979
(sales in thousands)	(in average fiscal year 1983 dollars)				
Sales	**$264,109**	$327,495	$433,694	$513,558	$631,692
Dividends per common share	—	—	—	.97	1.46
Market price of common stock at year end	**9.07**	5.15	6.60	5.93	14.65
Average consumer price index	**291.7**	277.4	253.4	225.0	200.1

XVIII MANAGEMENT

INTRODUCTION

As you prepare your annual report, keep in mind that your stockholders and security analysts want detailed information about your management team and your Board of Directors. Go behind the scenes. Describe the experience and strengths of your management and their ability to move your company forward.

YOUR MANAGEMENT TEAM

Peculiarly enough, few annual reports describe in detail the makeup and experience of the top management team. Certainly stockholders and analysts want to have some insights into the present and future management of the company.

I would suggest that there be a section on management—background and experience. This page would have pictures of top management personnel, the role they play in the company, their background, experience, etc. Some statements from them about the future and their various departments would be of considerable interest.

Electro-Nucleonics

The complexities of a technology-based business, particularly one with as broad a scope as that of Electro-Nucleonics, demand management that is capable of controlling and integrating a wide range of activities and focusing clearly on objectives. Electro-Nucleonics' management style emphasizes planning and relies heavily on project teams to achieve intended results.

Our management approach provides the individual with maximum opportunity and flexibility to gain experience from new situations. Recognizing that good results come about through teamwork, we strive to maintain an atmosphere which encourages participation and a free exchange of ideas.

A standing committee of senior executives from key functional areas meets regularly to screen and select projects, establish priorities and monitor progress. This approach properly focuses the product development effort and successfully integrates the concern of both the R&D and marketing disciplines.

Project teams bring together people from all areas of the Company under the direction of a team leader, who may be selected from any level of management. Serving as team leader allows less seasoned people to gain management experience, and participating as team members permits specialists to gain exposure to other disciplines and other areas of the Company. Typically, a senior executive follows each project closely and provides counsel and guidance to assure that goals are attained. This philosophy permeates activities throughout the Company and is even apparent in our manufacturing operations, where teams focus on maintaining product quality.

The long tenure that many of our managers have with the Company is indicative of their maturity and an environment that stresses concern for them as people. We believe that much of our success is attributable to our managers who possess a unique blend of qualities—innovative thinking, scientific mastery and business acumen.

PLAN OF ORGANIZATION

Vulcan's organization is structured around eight operating divisions (exclusive of the International Division and Southport Exploration, Inc., referred to below), two group executive offices and a corporate office. There are six domestic construction materials divisions comprising the Construction Materials Group, and the Chemicals Division and the Metals Division comprise the Chemicals and Metals Group. Each division is operated under the direction of a division president who is responsible for the management and performance of his division and who is afforded a high degree of operating autonomy. The president of each domestic construction materials division reports to the Executive Vice President, Construction Materials, and the presidents of the Chemicals and Metals divisions report to the Executive Vice President, Chemicals and Metals. The Executive Vice Presidents responsible for the Construction Materials and Chemicals and Metals groups report to the President who is the Chief Executive Officer of the company. These Executive Vice Presidents are responsible for the overall general management and performance of the divisions in their groups.

In addition to the two Executive Vice Presidents responsible for operating groups, the Executive Vice President and Chief Administrative Officer, the Senior Vice President and General Counsel, a Senior Vice President, and the Vice President, International, report to the President and Chief Executive Officer.

The Senior Vice President, Human Resources, the Vice President and Treasurer and the Vice President and Controller report to the Executive Vice President and Chief Administrative Officer who is responsible for financial public relations.

The Senior Vice President and General Counsel heads the legal department. The Secretary and General Attorney and several other attorneys report to the Senior Vice President and General Counsel.

In 1976 the company became a participant in and the manager of a construction materials venture in Saudi Arabia. This and other Saudi Arabian business ventures are under the direction of the Vice President, International. The Vice President, International, also serves as President of the International Division.

The reporting relationships of the corporate and group officers of the company are indicated on the accompanying organization chart.

In 1975 the company entered the oil and gas exploration business by providing funds to an independent organization that carried out exploration activities for Vulcan's account. In early 1981 Vulcan purchased certain assets of that company and formed Southport Exploration, Inc., a subsidiary which now manages Vulcan's oil and gas operations. Southport Exploration, Inc. is operated under the direction of a President and Chief Executive Officer who reports to the President and Chief Executive Officer of Vulcan.

Each of the constituent parts of the company is designated as a profit center. Each profit center has an annual performance goal, primarily an earnings objective, but also has other major objectives. The performance achieved by each profit center largely determines the total compensation, including bonuses, of the center's principal executives.

Within the framework of company policy and procedures, and subject to accountability for performance, division management is given broad decision-making authority to manage its own business, subject to functional authority with respect to accounting personnel and practices. The company centrally manages its cash balances and investments in short-term marketable securities. Division management's recommendations with respect to capital spending and inventory levels are subject to the ultimate authority of the Executive Vice Presidents and the Chief Executive Officer.

The organization of each domestic division, in addition to its operating and sales executives, includes a division controller, a human resources manager and other staff executives who are responsible for such functions as industrial relations, engineering, purchasing, marketing, accounting, industrial health and safety and community relations. The size of each staff depends upon the scope, diversity and size of the division's operations. In addition to the operating and administrative functions for which they are responsible, division presidents and members of their management teams are responsible for the development of operating and capital expenditure plans and budgets that are subject to corporate review and approval. The operating plan involves the projection of sales, costs and earnings, and the capital plan involves a determination of the working capital and the property, plant and equipment needed to accommodate the operating plan, including expansion of operating capacity in existing and new markets. The operating plans are frequently reviewed by the corporate office and appropriate revisions are made to recognize changing conditions.

Corporate Organization

Shareholders

Board of Directors

Corporate Executive Officers

J. Peter Grace
Chairman and Chief Executive Officer

F. E. Larkin
Chairman of the Executive Committee

D. W. Robbins, Jr.
Vice Chairman

C. N. Graf
President and Chief Operating Officer

C. H. Erhart, Jr.
Vice Chairman and Chief Administrative Officer

H. R. Logan
Vice Chairman

Operating Group Executives

Agricultural Chemicals Group
L.L. Jaquier
Executive Vice President

General Industrial Products Group
R. A. Clabault
Executive Vice President

Industrial Chemicals Group
J. Rimmer
Executive Vice President

Natural Resources Group
H. R. Logan
Vice Chairman

Restaurant Group
A. Soliman
Executive Vice President

Retail Group
E. H. Tutun
Executive Vice President

DESCRIBING THE BACKGROUND AND EXPERIENCE OF YOUR CORPORATE EXECUTIVES

Surprisingly, most annual reports describe the background of the directors, but merely *list* the officers and major executives of the company—showing just their titles. I believe this is a mistake. Your stockholders and investment analysts want to know the background, experience, and age of the people who run the company on a day-to-day basis.

Dayco Corporation
Corporate Officers

Richard J. Jacob
Chairman of the Board and
Chief Executive Officer

Mr. Jacob, 61, joined Dayco Corporation when the Cadillac Plastic and Chemical Company was acquired by Dayco in 1957. He and his late brother, Robert B. Jacob, founded Cadillac in 1946. He was elected to the Dayco board of directors in 1961. In 1965, he moved to Dayton and joined headquarters operations as the executive vice president. He was elected president in 1968 and chairman of the board in 1971. He attended Butler University and the University of Miami.

Ernest F. Dourlet
President and Chief Operating Officer

Mr. Dourlet, 56, joined Dayco Corporation in 1957 as a manager for Cadillac Plastic and Chemical Company and was named president in 1968. He became executive vice president and a director of Dayco Corporation in 1972 and was elected president of Dayco in 1973. He is a chemical engineering graduate of West Virginia University and received his MBA from the Wharton School of Business, University of Pennsylvania.

Edwin J. Gordor
Senior Vice President, Administration
and Secretary

Mr. Gordon, 47, joined Dayco Corporation 13 years ago as vice president and secretary. He was elected senior vice president, administration in 1971 and to the board in 1974. He is a business administration graduate of the City College of New York and received his law degree from Columbia University.

Nick G. Crnkovich
Vice President and Controller

Mr. Crnkovich, 54, joined Dayco Corporation in 1951 as a general accountant. He progressed through several positions before being named chief accountant in 1965, assistant controller in 1967 and controller in 1968. He was elected vice president and controller in 1975. He is an accounting graduate of the University of Dayton.

David S. Gutridge
Vice President and Treasurer

Mr. Gutridge, 34, joined Dayco Corporation in 1976 as assistant controller, became treasurer in 1978 and was elected vice president and treasurer in 1979. He is a Certified Public Accountant and has an MBA from Wright State University.

TANDY CORPORATION OFFICERS

		Age	Years with Company*
John Roach	Chairman of the Board, Chief Executive Officer and President	44	16
John McDaniel	Senior Vice President and Controller	65	17
Charles Tindall	Senior Vice President and Treasurer	57	17
Herschel Winn	Senior Vice President and Secretary	51	14
Billy Roland	Vice President	57	29
Loyd Turner	Vice President	65	11
Donald Bock	Assistant Treasurer	41	15
Louis Neumann	Assistant Secretary	51	9
Radio Shack Officers			
Bernard Appel	Executive Vice President—Marketing	51	24
Robert Keto	Executive Vice President—Operations	42	19
David Beckerman	Vice President—Advertising	55	27
George Berger	Vice President—Director of Personnel	44	20
Robert Bourland	Divisional Vice President	42	19
Jerry Colella	Vice President—Franchise International	54	25
Timothy Diachun	Vice President—Telephone Marketing	42	8
Ray Hicks	Vice President—Distribution	61	11
Dean Lawrence	Divisional Vice President	53	28
Carroll Leu	Vice President—Tandy Data Processing	46	17
Robert Miller	Vice President—Merchandising-Consumer Products	40	4
Caroline Nemser	Vice President—Merchandising Control	69	29
Jim Nichols	Divisional Vice President	40	15
Dick Richards	Divisional Vice President	47	18
E. W. Spieckerman	Vice President—Real Estate	50	15
Ron Stegall	Vice President—Computer Marketing	36	13
Paul Wofford	President—Tandy Transportation, Inc.	61	14
Chuck Wyse	Divisional Vice President	39	15
Tandy International Electronics Officers			
David Christopher	Senior Vice President—TIE	41	16
Clifford Atfield	Vice President—Operations-TIE Europe	36	19
Marvin Cash	Vice President and Managing Director—Radio Shack Canada	50	27
Mike Murray	Vice President—Australia	34	15
Robert Owens	Vice President—Marketing and Support-TIE Europe	46	23
John Sayers	Managing Director—United Kingdom	44	9
Elaine Yamagata	President—A&A Trading Companies	61	28
Tandy Electronics Manufacturing Officers			
Sy Bogitch	Senior Vice President—TEM	57	12
John Humphreys	Vice President and General Manager—Memtek Products Division	43	13
Robert McClure	Vice President—North American Manufacturing	47	11
Jim Mortensen	Vice President—Computer Manufacturing	49	16
John Patterson	Vice President—Research and Development	42	5

* Includes prior service with companies acquired by Tandy Corporation.

Radio Shack, Tandy International Electronics and Tandy Electronics Manufacturing are divisions of Tandy Corporation.

Officers

(as of February 17, 1983)

Directors

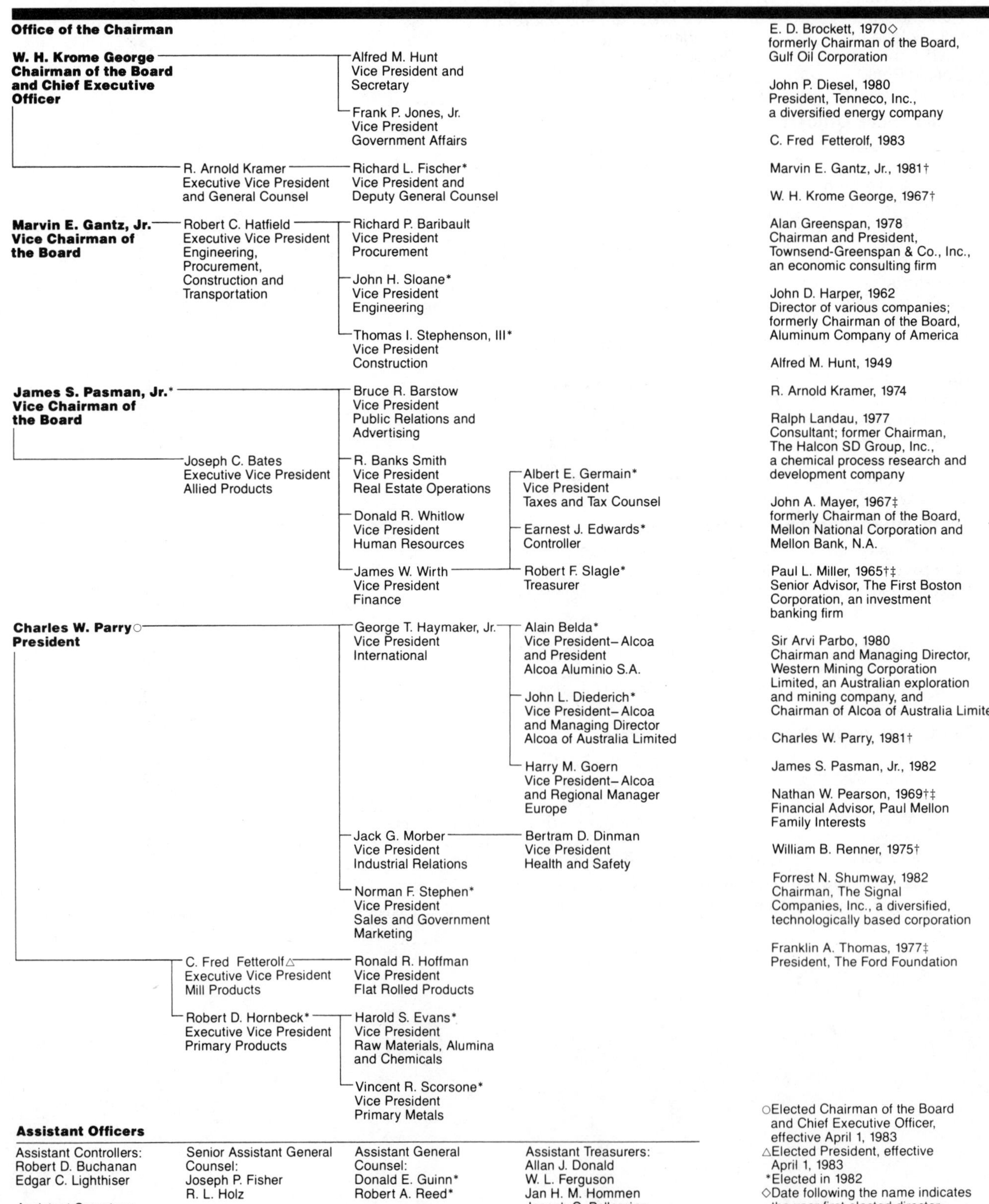

Office of the Chairman

W. H. Krome George
Chairman of the Board and Chief Executive Officer

- Alfred M. Hunt, Vice President and Secretary
- Frank P. Jones, Jr., Vice President, Government Affairs
- R. Arnold Kramer, Executive Vice President and General Counsel
  - Richard L. Fischer*, Vice President and Deputy General Counsel

Marvin E. Gantz, Jr.
Vice Chairman of the Board

- Robert C. Hatfield, Executive Vice President, Engineering, Procurement, Construction and Transportation
  - Richard P. Baribault, Vice President, Procurement
  - John H. Sloane*, Vice President, Engineering
  - Thomas I. Stephenson, III*, Vice President, Construction

James S. Pasman, Jr.*
Vice Chairman of the Board

- Bruce R. Barstow, Vice President, Public Relations and Advertising
- R. Banks Smith, Vice President, Real Estate Operations
- Donald R. Whitlow, Vice President, Human Resources
- James W. Wirth, Vice President, Finance
  - Albert E. Germain*, Vice President, Taxes and Tax Counsel
  - Earnest J. Edwards*, Controller
  - Robert F. Slagle*, Treasurer
- Joseph C. Bates, Executive Vice President, Allied Products

Charles W. Parry○
President

- George T. Haymaker, Jr., Vice President, International
  - Alain Belda*, Vice President–Alcoa and President, Alcoa Aluminio S.A.
  - John L. Diederich*, Vice President–Alcoa and Managing Director, Alcoa of Australia Limited
  - Harry M. Goern, Vice President–Alcoa and Regional Manager, Europe
- Jack G. Morber, Vice President, Industrial Relations
  - Bertram D. Dinman, Vice President, Health and Safety
- Norman F. Stephen*, Vice President, Sales and Government Marketing
- C. Fred Fetterolf△, Executive Vice President, Mill Products
  - Ronald R. Hoffman, Vice President, Flat Rolled Products
- Robert D. Hornbeck*, Executive Vice President, Primary Products
  - Harold S. Evans*, Vice President, Raw Materials, Alumina and Chemicals
  - Vincent R. Scorsone*, Vice President, Primary Metals

Assistant Officers

Assistant Controllers:
Robert D. Buchanan
Edgar C. Lighthiser

Assistant Secretary:
Harold E. Meeks

Senior Assistant General Counsel:
Joseph P. Fisher
R. L. Holz

Assistant General Counsel:
Donald E. Guinn*
Robert A. Reed*

Patent Counsel:
David W. Brownlee

Assistant Treasurers:
Allan J. Donald
W. L. Ferguson
Jan H. M. Hommen
Joseph C. Pellegrino

Directors

E. D. Brockett, 1970◇
formerly Chairman of the Board, Gulf Oil Corporation

John P. Diesel, 1980
President, Tenneco, Inc., a diversified energy company

C. Fred Fetterolf, 1983

Marvin E. Gantz, Jr., 1981†

W. H. Krome George, 1967†

Alan Greenspan, 1978
Chairman and President, Townsend-Greenspan & Co., Inc., an economic consulting firm

John D. Harper, 1962
Director of various companies; formerly Chairman of the Board, Aluminum Company of America

Alfred M. Hunt, 1949

R. Arnold Kramer, 1974

Ralph Landau, 1977
Consultant; former Chairman, The Halcon SD Group, Inc., a chemical process research and development company

John A. Mayer, 1967‡
formerly Chairman of the Board, Mellon National Corporation and Mellon Bank, N.A.

Paul L. Miller, 1965†‡
Senior Advisor, The First Boston Corporation, an investment banking firm

Sir Arvi Parbo, 1980
Chairman and Managing Director, Western Mining Corporation Limited, an Australian exploration and mining company, and Chairman of Alcoa of Australia Limited

Charles W. Parry, 1981†

James S. Pasman, Jr., 1982

Nathan W. Pearson, 1969†‡
Financial Advisor, Paul Mellon Family Interests

William B. Renner, 1975†

Forrest N. Shumway, 1982
Chairman, The Signal Companies, Inc., a diversified, technologically based corporation

Franklin A. Thomas, 1977‡
President, The Ford Foundation

○Elected Chairman of the Board and Chief Executive Officer, effective April 1, 1983
△Elected President, effective April 1, 1983
*Elected in 1982
◇Date following the name indicates the year first elected director
†Member of the Executive Committee
‡Member of the Audit Committee

It is important to list your senior executives and staff.

3M

Industrial and Consumer Sector

Abrasives, Cleaning Products and Industrial Minerals Group

Richard P. Hegrenes
Industrial Abrasives

***William H. Madden**
Industrial Mineral Products

Paul I. Roth
Building Service and Cleaning Products

Chemicals, Film and Allied Products Group

****Sidney M. Leahy**
Commercial Chemicals

Robert A. LePage
Specialty Chemical and Film

Consumer Products Group

Edward A. Dawson
Household and Hardware Products

Richard F. McGrath
Automotive Trades

Francis S. Webster
Commercial Tape

Tape, Adhesives and Decorative Products Group

David J. Brydon
Packaging Systems

Carl J. Calabrese
Industrial Specialties

Arthur E. Higinbotham
Industrial Tape

Clement A. Nelson
Decorative Products

Joseph M. Warren
Adhesives, Coatings and Sealers

Sector Staff

E. Theodore Thompson, Jr.
International

Electronic and Information Technologies Sector

Electrical Products Group

L. G. Bewick
Industrial Electrical Products

***D. Drew Davis**
TelComm Products

Russell J. McNaughton
Electronic Products

Vincent J. Ruane
Electro-Products

***John P. Ryan**
Static Control Systems

Information Systems Group

John O. Frisvold
Office Systems

***Richard A. Lidstad**
Equipment Service and Support

Calvin W. Pipal
Electronic-Mechanical Resources

Rolf E. Westgard
Business Communication Products

Memory Technologies Group

***Alfred E. Smith**
Magnetic Audio/Video Products

***Bruce A. Torp**
Data Recording Products

***John E. Povolny**
Industry Relations

Sector Staff

Ennio Fatuzzo
Research and Development

Edoardo Pieruzzi
International

Graphic Technologies Sector

****James J. Gibson**
Advertising Services

Photographic and Audio Visual Group

William L. Conroy
Dynacolor Corporation

Marshall R. Hatfield
Audio Visual

***Robert W. Keith**
Photo Color Systems

***Paul A. H. Pankow**
Imaging Systems

Graphic Arts Group

A. Guy Shelley
Transportation and Commercial Graphics

***Benjamin L. Shely**
Graphic Preparation Systems

***Donald C. Vadnais**
Printing and Reprographic Products

Sector Staff

George F. Duffin
Research and Development

***Charles M. Eldridge**
International

Life Sciences Sector

Health Care Products and Services Group

J. Marc Adam
Medical Products

***Ronald O. Baukol**
Riker Laboratories, Inc.

William E. Coyne
Surgical Products

***William J. McLellan**
Orthopedic Products

Traffic and Personal Safety Products Group

***Lawrence E. Eaton**
Traffic Control Materials

***Einar D. Horne**
Safety and Security Systems

***Robert J. Hershock**
Occupational Health and Safety Products

Sector Staff

Ronald A. Mitsch
Research and Development

Joseph E. Van Kirk
International

Staff Executives

Cruzan Alexander
Chief Patent Counsel

Bertrand Y. Auger
Program Development

Earl P. Bassett, Jr.
Federal Government Affairs

Stanley G. DeLaHunt
Associate General Counsel

Wallace R. Forman
Compensation, Benefits and Organization

Richard L. Herreid
International Distribution

John A. Hess, Jr.
Purchasing

D. L. Hitt
Assistant General Counsel

James R. Jensen
Office Administration Systems

Lorne E. Joines
Placement, Development and Services

Joseph C. Juettner
Plant Engineering Administration

Harold B. Klenk
Controller, Staff Operations

Clair R. Larson
Facilities Engineering and Real Estate

J. T. Ling
Environmental Engineering and Pollution Control

Dale A. Nelson
General Auditor

Richard D. Peters
Controller, International Operations

Audrey N. Pierce
Consumer Affairs

Julianne H. Prager
Corporate Technical Planning and Coordination

Willis C. Rech
U. S. Distribution

***R. C. Richelsen**
International Manufacturing

****Roger W. Roberts**
Controller

Thomas J. Scheuerman
Assistant General Counsel

Donald M. Sell
Deputy Chief Patent Counsel

John J. Ursu
Assistant General Counsel

C. J. Wheeler
Human Resources

International

Bent Bjorn
3M France

Peter Danos
European Government Affairs

Bo A. Ekman
3M Germany

Douglas R. Hanson
3M Italy

Paul A. Linnerooth
3M Brazil

John T. Myser
3M Canada

Klaus D. Nicolai
3M Europe S.A.

Robert C. Olney
3M United Kingdom

Donn R. Osmon
Africa-Latin America-Middle East

Wolfgang H. Strehlow
Sumitomo 3M

*Appointed in 1982
**Appointed in 1983

Management Changes

ConAgra's management team was strengthened by several moves during the past year. We gained top-notch executives and management teams through merger and acquisition activities. Many of our people were promoted to important management positions. And a number of managers joined ConAgra to fill key posts.

LEWIS A. REMELE was named president of Peavey Grain Companies. He joined Peavey in 1947 and had headed grain operations since 1975 as a group vice president.

JEROME W. TREBIL became president of Peavey Retail Companies. He has been with Peavey for 27 years and had been retail group vice president since 1973.

Peavey also named two executive vice presidents. **T. TRUXTUN MORRISON**, who came to Peavey in 1961, was named executive vice president, Peavey Grain Companies. **JOHN W. MURDOCH**, who joined Peavey in 1968, became executive vice president, Peavey Retail Companies. Both had been vice presidents in their respective companies.

RONALD R. JENSEN joined Sea-Alaska Products Company as president. He previously was senior vice president and general manager of seafoods for Castle & Cooke, Inc. and is past-president of the National Fisheries Institute.

PATRICK K. STEWART was named president of ConAgra Pet Products Company. He joined ConAgra in 1979 as vice president and general manager of pet accessories and became vice president and general manager of ConAgra Pet Products in 1981.

RONALD W. HALL was named chairman of the board of Caribbean Basic Foods Company in addition to his duties as vice president, ConAgra Europe, and managing director, Bioter-Biona, S.A.

FRANK A. MATHIAS was named president of Caribbean Basic Foods Company. He joined ConAgra in 1952, moved to Caribbean Basic Foods in 1961, and became vice president and general manager in 1979.

JOHN R. HAMMOND joined ConAgra as president of Country Skillet Catfish Company. He previously held management positions in Central Soya's food and animal feed businesses.

PAUL L. CHERRIER was named president of Northwest Fabrics, part of Peavey Retail Companies. He joined Peavey in 1967 and had been vice president and general manager of Northwest Fabrics.

ROBERT E. RENCH joined AgriBasics Company as president of the newly-acquired Southern Micro Blenders of Tennessee, Inc. He is one of the founders of Southern Micro Blenders.

Acquisitions by United Agri Products Companies included Georgia Ag Chem, Inc., where Ag Chem co-founder **RALPH R. LAWHORN** continues as president, and the newly-named United Agri Products (Hawaii), where **JOHN S. CLARK** continues as general manager.

JOHN M. CRABB was named president of International Seafood Traders, a new business unit which includes ACLI Seafood Company, acquired during the year. He continues as executive vice president, procurement for Singleton Seafood Company.

THEODORE H. SHEPARD, JR. became vice president, Louisiana operations for International Seafood Traders. He had been an ACLI executive and is president of the National Fisheries Institute.

OTTO W. SEIDENBERG was named president of Burdick Grain Company, a unit of Peavey Grain Companies. He had been a vice president of Burdick since 1979.

E. ROBERT KERN was named vice president, procurement of ConAgra Flour Milling Company. He joined Peavey Company in 1951 and had been vice president, operations for Peavey flour milling since 1978.

TOMAS G. VEGA was named vice president and operations manager of Molinos de Puerto Rico, Caribbean Basic Foods' feed and flour milling operation. He joined ConAgra in 1960 and most recently was Molinos' operations manager.

Country Skillet Poultry Company named two vice presidents. **HORACE M. SEWELL**, who joined ConAgra in 1963, became vice president and general manager of the Georgia Division. **DR. DWIGHT B. BOND**, with ConAgra since 1965, was named vice president and general manager, South Alabama Division. Both previously were division general managers.

Peavey Grain Companies named **EDWARD C. MENZEL** vice president-general manager, Barge, Southern Division, and **CHARLES O. BUIRGE**, vice president, manager, country operations for the Southern Division. Both previously held management positions with Peavey Grain.

SCOTT W. RAHN joined Banquet Foods Company as vice president, marketing. He had held key marketing positions with other food companies and previously was corporate vice president and general manager of Sunfield Foods.

GERALD B. VERNON joined Banquet Foods Company as vice president, human resources and administration. He has over 18 years of experience in human resource management and manufacturing in the food industry and previously served with The Pillsbury Company.

Peavey Retail Companies named three vice presidents: **HOWARD L. JOHNSTON**, vice president-general manager, Wheelers Stores; **HOWARD E. JONES**, vice president-general manager, Peavey Building Supplies Company; **GERALD E. SCHMIDT**, vice president-general manager, S & S Stores. The three executives previously held management posts in Peavey's specialty retailing businesses.

Three managers in the Pet Accessories Division of the Pet Products Company were named vice presidents. They are **ROBERT H. GEISLER**, vice president, sales and marketing; **RICHARD W. HOLMES**, vice president, distribution; and **MICHAEL R. LEINEN**, vice president, manufacturing operations and administration.

Photos of Executives

Corporations vary in the way in which they present photographs of their chief executives. My preference is to place candid shots of top officers throughout the narrative section with name, title, and brief description of responsibilities. Others present large-size head shots with biographies. It is refreshing to see some reports featuring informal photos of top executives in shirt sleeves.

Mead Paper points out the following words of caution:

> To avoid hard feelings, be sure you have a logical cut-off for those who don't appear. If you have too many officers to show, limit them to the executive committee, for example. If you want to show certain managers or divisional VPs, you might limit the selection to new people, or those in one or two product areas, etc. There's no question that readers of all your various 'publics' like to see what the top people in the company look like.

THE BOARD OF DIRECTORS

In preparing your annual report you should provide detailed information to your stockholders on such subjects as:

1. Name, age, background, length of service, etc. of each of your directors.
2. Number of Board meetings and average number attended.
3. The appointment of new directors and the retirement of others.
4. Committees of the Board.

Armco Inc. stated in its annual report:

> Corporate boards of directors are the elected representatives of a company's shareholders. We're proud of Armco's pioneering innovations, over the years, in responding to our owners' interests. We try hard to make sure your board's organization and activities create an atmosphere encouraging productive leadership of your company. In 19—, your board met 10 times.

Many corporations list their directors and committee assignments without describing their background and business activities. I would urge that more detailed information be provided to give the reader of the annual report a good understanding of the background and experience of the directors of your company.

BOARD OF DIRECTORS

EDWARD G. UHL, Chairman of the Board, President and Chief Executive Officer. Elected Chairman and Chief Executive Officer of Fairchild in 1976 after serving 15 years as President. Director of American Satellite Company, Fairchild Aircraft Corporation and Maryland National Bank and Trustee of Johns Hopkins and Lehigh universities. Member of Fairchild Executive Committee.

JEROLD C. HOFFBERGER, Chairman, Insurance Associates Exchange. Elected a Fairchild Director in 1961. Director of Fairchild Aircraft Corporation, Maryland National Bank and Dayco Corporation. President of Baltimore Orioles Baseball Club. Chairman of Fairchild Executive Committee.

MORTIMER M. CAPLIN, Member, Caplin & Drysdale (Attorneys). Elected Fairchild Director in 1979. United States Commissioner of Internal Revenue under President John F. Kennedy. Recipient of U.S. Treasury Department's Alexander Hamilton Award, the Tax Executives Institute's Distinguished Service Award and the Judge Learned Hand Award. Director of Prentice-Hall, Inc. and Norton Simon, Inc. and a Trustee of George Washington University. Member of Fairchild Executive Committee.

JOSEPH H. GAMACHE, Corporate Consultant. Elected Fairchild Director in 1976. Previously Senior Vice President and Director of Norton Simon, Inc. and formerly associated with public accounting firm of Touche Ross & Co., the Mohican Corporation and Litton Industries. Chairman of Fairchild Audit Committee.

ROBERT V. HANSBERGER, Chairman and Chief Executive Officer, Futura Corporation (Metal Parts Manufacturer). Named a Fairchild Director in 1982. Founder and formerly Chairman of Boise Cascade Corporation, and former Director of VSI Corporation.

CHARLES A. KUPER, Chairman of the Board, Kuper Investments, Inc. Elected a Fairchild Director in 1973. Held executive management positions in the brewing industry for 25 years and upon retirement in 1975 organized University National Bank of San Antonio, Texas. Director of Olympia Brewing Company, Fairchild Aircraft Corporation, Frost National Bank, University National Bancshares, Texas Gulf Companies and the University of Texas Development Board. Member of Fairchild Audit Committee.

DR. DEMING LEWIS, Retired President, Lehigh University. Elected a Fairchild Director in 1973. President of Lehigh from 1964 to 1982. Active in American space communications programs. A Rhodes Scholar and holder of 33 patents on devices such as microwave antennas. Director of Pennsylvania Power and Light Company, Bethlehem Steel Corporation, Zenith Radio Corporation and Fischer & Porter Company. Member of Fairchild Audit Committee.

WILLIAM T. MARX, Business Consultant. Elected a Fairchild Director in 1980. Chairman of the Board of various U.S. affiliates of Imetal, S.A., Paris, France. Director of Copperweld Corporation, New Court Partners, Prentice-Hall, Inc. and Coleman Company. Member of Fairchild Audit Committee.

THOMAS H. MOORER, Vice Chairman of the Board, Blount, Inc. (General Construction), Admiral, U.S.N. (Ret.). Elected a Fairchild Director in 1974. A 41-year veteran of the Navy. Appointed Chief of Naval Operations in 1967 by President Lyndon B. Johnson, a position held until 1970 when he became Chairman of the Joint Chiefs of Staff, serving until retirement in 1974. Director of Texaco, Inc. and Chairman of the Naval Aviation Museum Foundation Board of Directors. Member of Fairchild Executive Committee.

WILLIAM V. PLATT, Business Consultant. Became a Fairchild Director in 1964 when Republic Aviation Corporation, which he served as Director from 1956, was acquired by Fairchild. Formerly President of Marsh & McLennan International, an insurance firm. Director of National Securities and Research Corporation and President of San Katy Head Foundation. Member of Fairchild Executive Compensation and Stock Option Committee.

Conversations with Your Directors

For a change of pace, you might want to raise some questions with your directors and report their answers.

Example:

Special Perspectives:
Oakite's Outside Directors

One of corporate America's most valuable resources is its outside directors, business people who, having established successful careers within their own organizations, share their experience and knowledge by serving as members of the boards of other corporations. We recently asked Oakite's seven outside directors a number of questions about the company. Here are some of their views.

Robert H. Buckman
Chairman of the Board,
Buckman Laboratories, Inc.

Mr. Buckman, in the light of your membership on three board of directors' committees, audit, nominating and strategy, what sorts of trends do you see developing at Oakite today that will most affect the company in the future?
The primary trend that I see developing is increased planning, not of a reactive nature to conditions, but of a nature intended to create conditions favorable for the company through management action and by consistently working in a direction that will produce positive benefits in the future, i.e. expansion of research and development and definition of marketplaces in which to concentrate the company's efforts.

Oakite is primarily a strong marketing company that needs to develop its product and manufacturing positions in order to enhance its competitive ability in the marketplace over the long term. Product positions are enhanced by more and more basic research and development and the manufacturing position by increasing manufacturing complexity as basic research leads in that direction.

Gerald A. Hale
President,
Hale Resources

Mr. Hale, as the company's newest director, what are your impressions of Oakite?
Oakite is a company that fortunately has a solid track record of growth over a sustained period. It is sound financially and has experienced management. The dynamic that impresses one the most is its marketing and sales capabilities. I have always followed the philosophy that the marketplace is the incubator of all successful corporations. Occasionally this is married to technology. Given a choice of only acquiring a producing facility *or* a good market, I'll always opt for the market. One can always build a plant!

It is Oakite's ability to react to a multitude of market opportunities that will determine its future—which I view as bright.

William W. Huisking
Chairman of the Board,
Glyco, Inc.

In terms of service, Mr. Huisking, you are Oakite's senior outside director. What sorts of changes have you observed in Oakite during your 13 years as a director?
In the period many, many changes have occurred. The greatest change occurred in the makeup of the board. At one time the only outsider on the board, I am now one of seven outside directors sitting on a board comprised of 12 directors.

Growth is change and thus the increases in sales and profits experienced over the past 13 years must be regarded as a significant change. Another area that has seen change has been that of management. As Oakite grew, more and more sophisticated tools of management were adopted.

Foreign operations were subject to change during this period. Investment in foreign subsidiaries and joint ventures grew in the early years of my tenure as a director. But we learned that all markets are not alike and so in recent years we have found it necessary to divest ourselves of some overseas operations and, more lately, have been considering licensing ventures.

William S. Masland
President,
C. H. Masland & Sons

Mr. Masland, what sorts of trends do you see developing at Oakite today that will most affect the company in the future? What do you feel are the prime obligations of an outside director?
Oakite's healthy gross margins and the ability of management to exercise control over below-the-line expense categories represent a healthy situation for the future of the company. One more impressive example of control has been the ability to actively

turn over receivables in a high-interest-rate environment.

Oakite is well positioned in its present markets and has the resources to not only increase its market share but to explore new opportunities in complementary areas where profits can be enhanced.

One of the prime obligations of an outside director is to bring a broad area of experience in the resolution of matters of policy. I see the outside director's role as one of being not only supportive of management but, also, constructively critical.

If your company has redesigned its Board structure, you should consider reporting as follows:

In the mid-1970s, Diamond Shamrock's Board of Directors evaluated the corporation's future needs regarding corporate governance. As a result, in 1977, the board instituted retirement and board composition policies that would provide stockholders with a predominantly non-management group of directors, and a set of working committees in tune with the needs of a fast growing, multi-billion dollar international corporation.

At that time, five of 13 board members were, or had been, employees of Diamond Shamrock. Today, except for the corporation's chairman and its president, the members of the board are from outside Diamond Shamrock's management. These ten non-management directors represent a broad range of executive experience in industry, education, finance, government service and law.

Equally important, this breadth of experience has significantly strengthened the board's key committees.

Describe the number of regular and special meetings of your Board as follows:

General Foods

In addition to its 11 regular meetings and 22 committee meetings during fiscal 1983, the Board of Directors conducted two special meetings devoted to in-depth reviews of the corporation's strategic plan and its personnel resources and organization structure. The keen interest and involvement of the directors in the affairs of the company is further evidenced by the fact that their average attendance at Board and committee meetings during the past fiscal year was over 89 per cent.

The regular quaterly dividend was increased by the Board at its November 1982 meeting from 55 to 60 cents per share.

Of particular note during fiscal 1983 was the Board's involvement with the acquisition of Entenmann's and the long-term financing required to fund that acquisition and to provide the financial flexibility to serve the future needs of the business. Importantly the Board also continued to exercise its role in the resolution of low-return businesses.

COMMITTEES OF THE BOARD OF DIRECTORS

You might consider describing the functions & membership of the following Board Committees.

Audit Committee
Banking Committee
Board Composition and Function Committee
Compensation and Stock Option Committee
Directors' Compensation Committee
Executive Committee
Finance Committee
Headquarters Building Committee
Investment Committee
Investor Relations Committee
Long-range Planning Committee
Management Development and Compensation Committee
Nominations and Corporate Governance Committee
Operating Committee
Organization Committee
Public Issues Committee
Science and Technology Committee

Some corporations list the members of the various committees of the Board without describing the functions of the committees. It is helpful to the readers of your report if the functions of your committees are described and the names of the various committee members listed.

Audit Committee
James C. Olson, Chairman
William N. Deramus III
Thomas S. Nurnberger
H. S. Payson Rowe
Erwin A. Stuebner
Stewart Turley

The Audit Committee, consisting of outside directors only, has the responsibility of insuring that proper accounting principles are being followed, that audit coverage of the corporation and its subsidiaries is satisfactory and that a system of internal controls is being effectively administered.

This committee recommends to the Board of Directors the appointment of the corporation's independent auditors. This appointment is approved by the corporation's shareholders. It determines the scope and extent of the annual independent audit and the basis for compensation of the independent auditor.

The Audit Committee reviews the broad scope of the joint independent internal audit program with both independent and internal auditors at least once each year.

Corporate Responsibility Committee
Avis G. Tucker, Chairman
William N. Deramus III
Robert G. Fuller
James C. Olson
H. S. Payson Rowe
Stewart Turley

The Corporate Responsibility Committee monitors the corporation's performance in responding to changing social needs and in conducting its affairs in consonance with the public interest.

This committee, consisting solely of outside directors, also periodically reviews the size and composition of the Board of Directors and is responsible for recommending candidates to fill vacancies on the Board.

The Corporate Responsibility Committee reviews and evaluates the corporation's activities relating to employees' safety, health and affirmative action efforts. It also reviews the community involvement activities of the corporation, its relationships with governmental and regulatory agencies and corporate contributions.

Finance Committee
Charles E. Rice, Chairman
Raymond M. Alden
William N. Deramus III
Robert G. Fuller
Avis G. Tucker
Stewart Turley

The Finance Committee regularly reviews the financial condition of the corporation and counsels the Board of Directors on the total-financial resources, strength and capabilities of the corporation.

This committee monitors changes in the capital structure of the corporation and makes recommendations concerning debt financing and the financing of acquisitions, investments and capital expenditures of a major nature. It also reviews and recommends actions on dividends.

The Finance Committee periodically reviews the corporation's cash flow and financial plans and annually reviews the corporation's risk management program and its adequacy to safeguard the corporation against extraordinary liabilities or losses.

Executive Committee
Paul H. Henson, Chairman
Charles W. Battey
Joseph D. Brenner
Thomas S. Nurnberger
Charles E. Rice

The Executive Committee meets at the call of the chief executive officer to deal with matters of an urgent nature which arise between regularly scheduled meetings of the Board of Directors.

The other principal responsibilities of this committee include counseling and advising management on contemplated business strategies and on plans for the orderly development and succession of executive management and its effective structuring.

Pension Trust Committee
Joseph D. Brenner, Chairman
Robert G. Fuller
James C. Olson
H. S. Payson Rowe
Erwin A. Stuebner

The Pension Trust Committee establishes and determines the investment policies and objectives of the United System Employees Retirement Plan and selects qualified investment managers to direct the management of pension trust assets.

The committee provides objectives and investment guidelines for the investment managers and regularly monitors and reviews their performance.

Compensation Committee
Thomas S. Nurnberger, Chairman
Joseph D. Brenner
Charles E. Rice
Erwin A. Stuebner
Avis G. Tucker

The Compensation Committee is charged with the responsibility of establishing salaries, incentives and other compensation programs so that the officers and key management personnel of the corporation may be fairly compensated and effectively motivated. This committee consists solely of outside directors.

The Compensation Committee reviews and advises management on broad compensation policies and benefit or retirement plans which have application to significant numbers of the corporation's employees. It also approves and recommends to the Board salaries and other benefits for elected officers.

The Board Composition Committee. Established in 1977, the Board Composition Committee consists primarily of non-management directors. It establishes criteria for the selection of directors, developing procedures for locating, screening and reviewing the qualifications for board candidates. When appropriate, this committee nominates potential board members to the full Board of Directors. The committee continually analyzes the composition, structure and functioning of the Board of Directors and recommends changes when appropriate. Members are:

W.H. Bricker, Chairman
B. Charles Ames
Gene Edwards
Raymond A. Hay
Allen C. Holmes
Allan J. Tomlinson

Nominating Committee

The Nominating Committee consists of four directors, none of whom is an employee of the corporation. The committee recommends nominees for election to the board. It also makes recommendations involving board and committee fees, director-retirement policy, and policies concerning employees and directors serving on the board of other corporations.

Public Issues Committee

The Public Issues Committee consists of five directors, none of whom is an employee of American. This committee makes recommendations regarding policies, programs and issues that involve American's shareholders, employees and customers, and health-care providers and consumers. It makes recommendation's concerning compliance with rules of certain regulatory agencies and concerning policies for charitable contributions and community relations.

International Paper

Management Development and Compensation Committee[4]

Reviews Company policies and programs for the development of management personnel. Makes recommendations to the Board with respect to compensation of officer-directors. Approves senior management compensation. Administers the Incentive Compensation and Profit Improvement plans.

SPECIAL NOTE: THE AUDIT COMMITTEE

Your stockholders have an interest in the work of your Audit Committee. They want to know the names and backgrounds of the directors who serve on the Audit Committee. They want to know whether they are knowledgeable in accounting, control, and financial matters. They are interested in knowing how often the Audit Committee meets. It might be useful for you to describe the function of the Audit Committee as follows:

> The Audit Committee reviews (1) the reported financial information; (2) major changes in accounting methods proposed by management; (3) the adequacy of internal accounting controls; (4) the cost, results, and scope of the outside audit; and (5) the current state of the art in generally accepted accounting principles. In addition, the committee recommends the selection of independent accountants to the board for selection and ratification by the shareholders.

The Signal Company points out in its annual report, "Present at audit committee meetings are representatives of Signal's financial management, the outside independent accountants, internal auditors from each subsidiary, and, at least once a year, the chief executive and chief financial officers of each subsidiary. These individuals meet together with and independently with the audit committee. In addition, the outside independent accountants have free access to and communication with the audit committee and, accordingly, meet privately with the audit committee."

Advisory Members of the Board of Directors

While appointing advisory members of the Board is not a customary practice in most corporations, it is well to list the advisory directors where they are serving.

Example:

Advisory Members of the Board of Directors

J.J. Adoran
Senior Vice President-
Corporate Development

J.W. Burge, Jr.
Group Vice President

M.R. Chambers
Former Chairman
INTERCO Incorporated

C. Hansen
Senior Vice President-
Law

J.C. Rohrbaugh
Vice President-
Industrial Relations

J.C. Wilson
Vice President of
Finance & Comptroller.

The Scientific Board

The members of the Damon Biotech Scientific board have played a significant role in the Company's origins and development.

The physical proximity of Damon Biotech to Harvard University and to the Massachusetts Institute of Technology, as well as the intellectual proximity made possible by this very active Board, give Damon Biotech a closeness to the latest research directions within the academic community. In addition, the Board offers Damon Biotech access to the upcoming generations of scientists who will be responsible for future discoveries.

Twice each month, the Scientific Board meets to review the research and product development programs under way at Damon Biotech, examining the objectives and the methods of each project. Ideas for new products are frequently raised at these meetings, as are improvements in design or content of research protocols.

Overall, the Scientific Board has helped Damon Biotech build its scientific expertise, and gives the Company an important and ongoing advantage within the industry.

XIX STOCKHOLDER INFORMATION

All too often, those who prepare annual reports take too much for granted in relation to stockholder interests. This is a mistake. Your stockholders have many questions that your annual report might well address. Lowe's Companies Inc. provides meaningful answers in its annual report.

Lowe's Companies, Inc.

Dividend Declaration Dates:

Usually the middle of each quarter to shareholders of record approximately the middle of April, July, October and January.

Dividend Payment Dates:

Usually the last of April, July, October and January.

Dividend Disbursing Agent:

Wachovia Bank & Trust Co., N.A.
Box 3001
Winston-Salem, N.C. 27102

Dividend Reinvesting Agent:

Citibank, N.A.
Box 3357, Grand Central Station
New York, N.Y. 10043

Dividend Policy:

Lowe's pays a cash dividend each quarter and since becoming a public company in 1961 has paid 80 consecutive quarterly dividends. The dividend has been increased in each fiscal year since 1973. Increases in dividend payment generally have been considered at the board meeting in the first fiscal quarter.

Lowe's Telephone:

919-667-3111

Lowe's Mailing Address:

Box 1111
North Wilkesboro, N.C. 28656

Lowe's Street Address:

State Highway 268 East
(Elkin Highway)
North Wilkesboro, N.C. 28659

Questions about Lowe's, Shareholder Inquiries: Call or write:

Bill Brantley
Vice President, Investor Relations
Box 1111
North Wilkesboro, N.C. 28656
Telephone: 919-667-3111, ext. 631

Annual Meeting Date:

May 29, 1981, 2 p.m.
at the Holiday Inn,
Highway 268 West
Wilkesboro, N.C.

Stock Transfer Agents:

Wachovia Bank & Trust Co., N.A.
Box 3001
Winston-Salem, N.C. 27102
Morgan Guaranty Trust Co.
9 West 57th Street
New York, N.Y. 10019

Stock Registrar:

The Northwestern Bank
Box 85
Winston-Salem, N.C. 27102
The Chase Manhattan Plaza
New York, N.Y. 10005

Lowe's Common Stock:

Ticker symbol: LOW
Listed:
New York Stock Exchange
20 Broad Street
New York, N.Y. 10005
Pacific Stock Exchange
301 Pine Street
San Francisco, Calif. 94104

Quarterly Reports:

Mailed usually the fourth week after the end of the quarter, April 30, July 31, October 31 and January 31.

Annual Reports:

Mailed usually 90 days after fiscal year-end, January 31.

Disclosure Policy:

Lowe's Companies, Inc., for the nearly 20 years of public life, has maintained a policy of complete and free disclosure of all information needed by investors to determine whether they should buy, sell or hold Lowes' stock. The Company desires and intends not only to meet the letter but the spirit of laws, regulations and rules. Annually the Company seeks new and better ways of presenting financial and other information to itself to better inform the investor. Your comment is always welcome.

What You Should Know About Being a Lowe's Shareholder

Introduction: Whether you are a new owner of Lowe's Companies, Inc. common stock, or a shareholder of long standing, we thought you might have a few questions about stock ownership itself. For example, how can you transfer stock if you should want to change the registration on your stock certificates? What should you know about the certificate itself? What should you do if a certificate is lost or stolen? On the next two pages we will try to answer these and several other questions of concern to all of you.

Stock Transfer: Before we tell you how you can transfer your stock, it might be helpful to know a little bit about the logistics of stock transfer, and the people involved in this important behind-the-scenes function. Stock transfer is the process through which changes in the ownership of a company's stock are officially registered in the company's shareholder records, and certified through an exchange of stock certificates. All of the outstanding shares of a company's stock are represented by numbered certificates, and all of the numbered certificates are registered in the name of, and issued to, a shareholder or a designated representative of a shareholder. Since the number of shares represented by certificates must always equal the number of shares outstanding, each registered stock certificate must be accounted for and correspond to a shareholder name in the company's records. Any change in the registration of a certificate must be accompanied by a comparable change in the company's shareholder records, and by the cancellation of the old stock certificate and issuance of a new one.

The Transfer Agent has primary responsibility for the efficient transfer of a company's stock including maintenance of shareholder records and the cancellation and issuance of stock certificates. The transfer agent can also issue the company's dividends and provide shareholder mailing lists for a variety of corporate communications. A company may be its own transfer agent or, as is more often the case, a bank or trust company is designated to serve in this capacity. For greater convenience and more expeditious stock transfer service, Lowe's has appointed two transfer agents: Wachovia Bank & Trust Company, N.A., in Winston-Salem, North Carolina; and Morgan Guaranty Trust Company of New York in New York City. Wachovia is Lowe's principal transfer agent and, as such, also maintains Lowe's official shareholder records and acts as Lowe's Dividend Disbursing Agent.

The Registrar verifies that when stock is transferred, the new number of shares issued is equal to the number of shares canceled. This double checking of the debit and credit of stock transfers is extra protection for shareholders and for the company, and this service is also typically performed by a bank or trust company. Lowe's also has two registrars. The registrar for Winston-Salem transfers is the Northwestern Bank, and for New York City transfers, the Chase Manhattan Bank.

When You Can Transfer Stock: As we explained, stock transfer is required whenever the registration of a stock certificate is changed. The change in registration most often occurs when shares are sold by one stockholder and purchased by another. However, in most cases, you will need to contact a broker for the purchase or sale of stock. Stock transfer is also required when a gift of stock is made from a shareowner's personal holding, or in the event that a stockholder wishes to have his shares re-registered, with his name in a different form. The latter could include name changes resulting from marriage, or consolidation of several certificates of the same stock on which there are slight variations in the way the shareholder's name is registered. A stockholder may also wish to co-register his shares with another person and this, too, would necessitate stock transfer. In all of these instances, you may initiate transfer yourself, and now we are ready to tell you how to go about it.

How You Can Transfer Stock: If, at some point, you would like to change the registration on part or all of your share holding, you can do so directly by sending the certificates to be transferred via registered or certified mail, along with a letter of instructions, to either of Lowe's transfer agents. The certificates have to be endorsed by you as they are registered which means that you must sign your name exactly as it appears on the face of the certificate. To endorse the certificate, you may sign where indicated on the reverse side of the certificate. Your signature must be "guaranteed" in order for certificates to be accepted for transfer. For your added protection, it is recommended that you fill in all of the information requested on the reverse side of the certificate, particularly the blank space designating an "Attorney," where you may insert the name of whichever of Lowe's transfer agents is performing the transfer for you. If you would rather not send an endorsed stock certificate through the mail, you may send in a separate envelope a "stock power" which can be obtained from a bank or broker. The stock power must be filled out completely and endorsed, again, with your signature guaranteed. If you decide to use the stock power, it is still recommended that you send the unsigned stock certificate being transferred via registered or certified mail, and it would be helpful to include a note indicating that a stock power is being forwarded separately.

If you wish to make a gift of stock and your shares are registered in your name, you follow the same procedure. However, please be sure to include in your letter of instructions, the number of shares to be given, along with the full name, address, and if possible, the Social Security number of the recipient. If the number of shares being given or transferred is less than the number of shares sent to the transfer agent, new certificates for the balance will be issued and returned to you.

All transfers should be sent in care of the Stock Transfer Department to whichever of Lowe's transfer agents you choose, and you will find the addresses for both of Lowe's transfer agents on Page 76.

"Customer Name" Or "Street Name?" When you purchase stock you have a choice between having your shares registered in your name, called "Customer Name," and the certificates sent to you to keep, or leaving your shares in safekeeping with your broker, in which case the certificates are registered in the broker's name, called "Street Name." There are merits to both plans, and your choice really depends on your personal requirements or preferences in owning stock. However, you should know that if you have your shares registered in your name in Lowe's shareholder records, you will receive all regular quarterly dividends

Stockholder Information

The 1983 Annual Meeting
of stockholders will be held in the John B. Hynes Veterans Auditorium, Boston, Mass., on Monday, April 25th, at 10 a.m.

Notice of Annual Meeting, Proxy Statement and Proxy Voting Card are mailed to each stockholder in March. The Proxy Statement describes the items of business to be voted on at the Annual Meeting and provides biographies of the Board's nominees for director, their principal affiliations with other companies or organizations, as well as other information about the company.

The Report of the IBM Annual Meeting,
mailed to each stockholder in June, summarizes the activities at the Annual Meeting, including the President's report on the company, questions and answers of general interest and the results of voting on items of business.

The following information may be obtained without charge from the IBM Stockholder Relations Department, 590 Madison Avenue, New York, N.Y. 10022:

The Form 10-K Annual Report
to the Securities and Exchange Commission provides further details on IBM's business, including a list of subsidiaries, summarized in the Annual Report. Form 10-K is available in April.

The Form 10-Q Quarterly Report
to the Securities and Exchange Commission is available in May, August and November.

A Transcript of the Annual Meeting

An IBM Dividend Reinvestment Plan Booklet
explains how stockholders may automatically reinvest dividends toward the purchase of additional shares of IBM stock, as well as make optional additional investments for that purpose.

IBM Business Conduct Guidelines
is a booklet sent to IBM employees worldwide describing the ethical and business principles that the company sets for the conduct of its business.

IBM Equal Opportunity Programs
in the United States are outlined in a document that describes programs for women, minorities, handicapped persons, disabled veterans and Vietnam-era veterans, and also reviews IBM's affirmative action efforts in the community.

IBM U.S. Retirement Plan Information,
which is given to all regular U.S. employees, includes the principal provisions of the plan, options available, a list of the trustees and a summary report on the plan's financial status.

IBM Company Citizenship
booklet describes support programs for education, community service, hospitals, the arts and other areas.

IBM Operations in South Africa
are summarized in a report of the company's business in that country. This report describes the personnel principles and practices to which IBM adheres in doing business in South Africa.

IBM Annual Report Translations and Recordings
are available. The report is translated into French, German and Japanese. An audio cassette recording in English is available for the blind.

A Service for Deaf Stockholders
provided by the IBM Stockholder Relations Department enables deaf stockholders who have access to a teletypewriter to communicate with the department's New York City office. Stockholders who wish to use the service should dial (212) 407-4552 between 9 a.m. and 5 p.m., Eastern time, on any weekday.

IBM Stock Transfer
is handled by the IBM Stockholder Relations Department, 590 Madison Avenue, New York, N.Y. 10022. The department maintains stockholder records and can answer questions regarding stockholders' accounts. Stockholders wishing to transfer stock or to change the name on a stock certificate should contact the department for instructions.

Stock certificates are valuable and should be safeguarded, since replacement takes time and requires payment of a surety bond premium by the stockholder. If a stock certificate is lost, stolen or destroyed, Stockholder Relations should be notified. Registered mail should be used whenever stock is mailed.

IBM Stock is Traded
on the New York Stock Exchange, other exchanges in the United States and exchanges in Austria, Belgium, Canada, England, France, Japan, Switzerland, the Netherlands and Germany.

Stock Transfer Offices:
IBM Stockholder Relations Department
590 Madison Avenue, New York, N.Y. 10022
IBM Stockholder Relations Department
One IBM Plaza, Chicago, Ill. 60611

Co-Transfer Agents:
Trust Général du Canada
1100 University Street, Montreal, Quebec, Canada H3B 2G7
National Trust Company, Limited
21 King Street East, Toronto, Ontario, Canada M5C 1B3

Registrars:
Morgan Guaranty Trust Company of New York
30 West Broadway, New York, N.Y. 10015
The First National Bank of Chicago
One First National Plaza, Chicago, Ill. 60670
Montreal Trust Company
777 Dorchester Boulevard West, Montreal, Quebec, Canada H3B 4A5
15 King Street West, Toronto, Ontario, Canada M5H 1B4

International Business Machines Corporation
Corporate Headquarters
Armonk, N.Y. 10504

Special Investor Information:

Dividend Performance

Carpenter has paid quarterly cash dividends on its common stock for 77 consecutive years.

An interesting way to look at dividend growth is how it compares with changes in general purchasing power. Your Company's dividend increases have outpaced the rate of inflation over the past ten years, as illustrated in this chart:

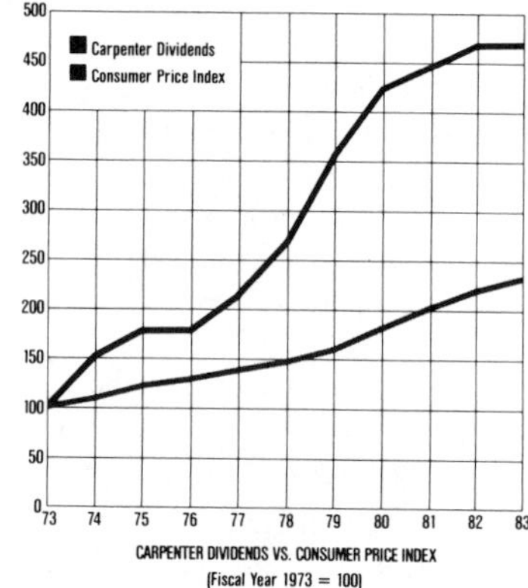

CARPENTER DIVIDENDS VS. CONSUMER PRICE INDEX
(Fiscal Year 1973 = 100)

Total Return to Carpenter Shareholders

Total return to Carpenter shareholders, assuming all dividends were reinvested, has averaged 22 percent per year over the past ten years. This return has outpaced the rate of inflation, measured by the Consumer Price Index, as illustrated in this chart:

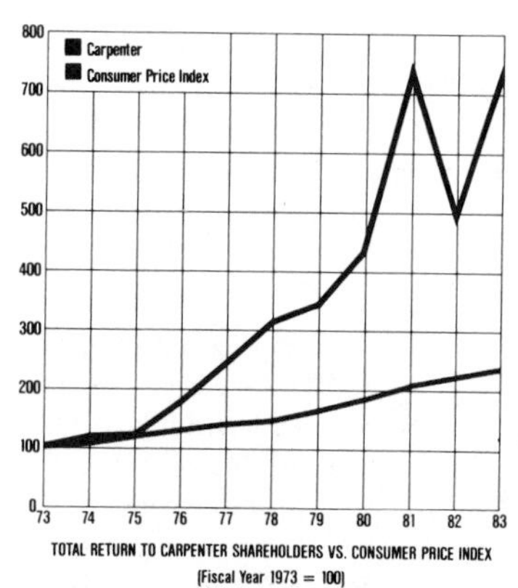

TOTAL RETURN TO CARPENTER SHAREHOLDERS VS. CONSUMER PRICE INDEX
(Fiscal Year 1973 = 100)

Stock Market Performance

Here are the high and low market prices of Carpenter stock on the New York Stock Exchange for the past two fiscal years:

	Fiscal 1983		Fiscal 1982	
Quarter Ended:	High	Low	High	Low
September 30	$35½	$28	$50	$42½
December 31	$40⅛	$29⅝	$47½	$43
March 31	$43¼	$37	$46¼	$32
June 30	$48	$37¾	$38¼	$30¼
	$48	$28	$50	$30¼

The stock outperformed the leading market indices over the past ten years, utilizing a base in which 1973 equals 100, as illustrated in this chart:

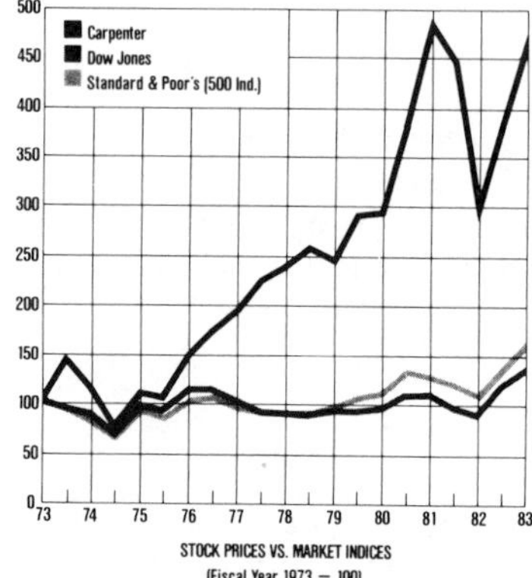

STOCK PRICES VS. MARKET INDICES
(Fiscal Year 1973 = 100)

Comparative Performance with Fortune 500 Industrials

According to the May 1983 "Fortune 500" directory, Carpenter (based on fiscal 1982 data) ranked with the nation's 500 largest industrial companies as follows:

Sales	458th
Net Income	280th
Net Income as % of Sales	88th
Net Income as % of Equity	231st
Earnings Per Share Growth Rate (1972–82)	85th
Total Return to Investors*	43rd

*dividends plus stock appreciation from 1972 to 1982

Dividend Reinvestment Plan

As a shareholder of record, you have an alternative to cash dividends—Carpenter's automatic Dividend Reinvestment Plan. Participation in this plan is voluntary and is a convenient way to increase your equity investment. You can elect to invest your quarterly cash dividends, and up to $3,000 a quarter in optional cash payments, in shares of Carpenter common stock, free of all commissions and fees.

For more information, and to find out how you can enroll, write to Carpenter Technology Corporation, Dividend Reinvestment, 101 West Bern Street, Reading, Pennsylvania 19603.

Some Things To Know About Your Armco Stock

Armco's Shareholder Publications (quarterly reports, annual report and annual proxy statement) are mailed to all shareholders of record.

For copies of our latest Form 10-K or 10-Q reports to the Securities & Exchange Commission, write to Armco Inc., Corporate Secretary, Middletown, OH 45043. This is also where you can write for our list of the organizations receiving substantial charitable, educational or cultural grants from Armco during 1983.

Dividend Reinvestment lets you invest your common stock dividends to purchase more shares—*free* of any brokerage commissions or service charges.

Our Dividend Reinvestment Plan also lets common shareholders make optional cash contributions to purchase additional common stock. You may invest from $25 to $5,000 each quarter.

If you ever want to withdraw from our plan, just write us. We'll issue your certificate(s) for the number of whole shares held in your account and send you a check for the value of any fractional shares.

You'll get your certificate(s) and check in approximately three weeks. We cannot handle withdrawals any faster because Armco has to write to Mellon Bank, the agent for our plan. Then the bank has to write to the Depository Trust Company for the certificates.

You may terminate your participation in our plan at any time. Dividends will not be reinvested in your account if we get your termination notice at least five business days prior to a dividend record date. Dividends will be invested if we get your termination notice within five business days prior to a dividend record date and before a dividend payment date.

Common Stock Dividend Checks are mailed to arrive at your address around the first Monday in March, June, September and December. The amount is declared by Armco's Board of Directors each quarter.

Class A Preferred Stock Dividend Checks are mailed to arrive at your address around the last business day in March, June, September and December. The dividend is 52½¢ a quarter—$2.10 a year.

Armco's Dividend Checks Are Dated and valid for one full year. After that, they aren't payable. You'll have to ask us to reissue your check and send us the old one.

For Your Tax Records, your dividend check reminds you of how many Armco shares you own, as well as the dividend rate. With your December dividend check or Dividend Reinvestment statement, you'll get a record showing your total dividends that year.

If You Lose Your Certificate, contact Armco's Shareholder Services as soon as you discover your loss. We'll help you get your certificates replaced.

To Transfer Stock to relatives or other people, call us. We're running into more and more grandparents who want to put some of their shares in custodial accounts for grandchildren. Write us or phone us and we'll explain the requirements. To sell your stock, call your broker.

Duplicate Mailings? Do you get more than one copy of our annual and quarterly reports? Let us know. We'll eliminate duplicates.

Changing Your Address? If you move, tell us at least three weeks before your next dividend check.

"Street Name" or Your Name? If you're not a shareholder of record, you'll experience much slower deliveries of Armco's quarterly reports.

Backup Withholding? If you open a new account in 1984, we're required by the IRS to send you a Form W-9 (Payor's Request For Taxpayer Identification Number). You're required to certify your Social Security number. You'll be subject to a 20% backup withholding on your next dividend check if you fail to furnish us with your number, if the IRS tells us you gave an incorrect number, or if you fail to tell us you are *not* subject to backup withholding.

General Information—Armco's outside auditors are Deloitte Haskins & Sells, Cincinnati. Armco's outside stock transfer agent, for common and preferred stock, is the Morgan Guaranty Trust Company of New York. (Since we also act as our own transfer agent, you might find it easier to deal with us.)

Stock registrars for common and preferred stock are: Morgan Guaranty Trust Company of New York, New York, N.Y., and Bank One of Middletown, Middletown, Ohio.

Armco's annual shareholders' meeting will be held this year at 1:30 p.m. on April 27 at The Manchester in Middletown, Ohio. You're invited.

Your Most Important Armco Phone Number: (513) 425-2517. Call collect.
If you have a question about your stock, dividend checks or dividend reinvestment and need an answer fast, simply call. Or write:

Armco Inc.
Shareholder Services
Middletown, OH 45043
Attn: Delores Judd, Transfer Officer

Toll-Free Number

Shareholders with questions about their common, preferred and preference stock, or those seeking information concerning their individual holdings, may telephone toll free.

Shareholders calling within the Hammond local calling area should dial 853-5700. Those outside this area but within the state of Indiana should call 800-552-6814. The number for calls placed outside Indiana is 800-348-6466.

Those having questions or seeking information are encouraged to call during normal business hours.

Control Data

The annual report is available on tape (cassette or open reel) to the visually or physically handicapped at no charge. Write to: The Communications Center, 1745 University Avenue, St. Paul, MN 55104. Or order by calling collect 612/296-6723.

INVESTOR COMMUNICATIONS AWARDS

It is gratifying to note that the quality of our communications with investors is recognized by professionals. For the forth consecutive year, Carpenter received one of the top awards from the Financial Analysts Federation for "Excellence in Corporate Reporting."

INFORMATION ABOUT THE STOCKHOLDERS

Your stockholders are interested in knowing about the other stockholders in your company. Information often included in the report falls into these categories:

1. Number of stockholders.
2. Geographical distribution: Number of stockholders in the various states and countries.
3. Characteristics of stockholders: Division by occupation and sex.
4. Comparison of individual and institutional holdings.
5. Nature of shareholding: Number of shareholders by size of holdings; total number of shares owned in each group; percentage of all shares owned in each group; and number of owners, average holdings, and length of time stock has been held.
6. Stock exchange transactions: Number of shares traded, at selected dates or as an average for the financial year; "highs," "lows," and "averages" of share prices; changes in yield during the financial year.

At December 31, 19__	Holders	Percent	Shares	Percent
Individuals:				
Male	65,780	35.1	11,648,065	14.7
Female	39,838	21.3	5,028,750	6.3
Joint Tenants	63,338	33.8	13,274,841	16.7
Employee Stock Programs Trustees	3	—	12,147,807	15.3
Other Trusts & Estates	16,196	8.7	1,167,693	1.5
Stock Brokers and Security Dealers	224	.1	21,707,107	27.3
Nominees	325	.2	8,072,424	10.2
Institutions and all others	1,537	.8	6,428,600	8.0
Total	187,241	100.0	79,475,287	100.0

DIVIDEND REINVESTMENT PROGRAM

Numerous plans have been adopted by corporations to interest their stockholders in automatically reinvesting dividends in additional stock. Most of these plans offer investment services free of charge to stockholders. The company generally pays all administrative and brokerage fees, thereby providing a simple and free way to put quarterly dividends to work. Many of these plans are administered by the Trust Department of a bank. When a stockholder enrolls in one of these plans, the quarterly dividend check is mailed directly to the bank. The bank then buys the stock from the company and adds it to the stockholder's account.

Examples:

Dividend Reinvestment and Common Stock Plan

The Dividend Reinvestment and Common Stock Purchase Plan is a service available to all Grace shareholders. If shares of Grace stock are registered in the name of a broker, or nominee, the beneficial shareholder may participate. Participation is entirely voluntary and withdrawal from the Plan may be requested at any time.

In addition to reinvesting dividends, participants may make optional cash payments to buy Grace common stock. Cash payments will be invested *each month* so long as sufficient funds have been received to permit an economical purchase of shares. Since interest is not paid on unused funds, it is recommended that cash payments be sent so they are received by the bank as near as possible but *prior* to the 10th day of the month. Plan improvements are expected to be made in the near future and shareholders will be advised accordingly. Among the new features to be offered is a custodial service whereby shares acquired other than through dividend reinvestment may be consolidated with shares in the Plan.

As of December 1982, there were 11,951 Plan participants (11,695 at year-end 1981) holding over 990,000 shares of Grace common stock. During 1982, Grace shareholders reinvested $2.6 million of dividends and made $1.2 million of supplementary cash payments which, combined, were used to purchase 102,927 shares of Grace common stock. Grace pays most brokerage commissions and service fees for participants. The Dividend Reinvestment and Common Stock Purchase Plan is administered by Citibank, N.A. Those interested in participating may request a Plan brochure and enrollment card by writing the Shareholder Records Department at Grace Headquarters in New York City.

Automatic Dividend Reinvestment Service

Sperry offers an automatic dividend and interest reinvestment plan to holders of common stock and eligible debt securities. Participants can purchase up to $3,000 worth of Sperry shares each quarter at the market price, and they can reinvest dividends (or interest) in Sperry common stock at 95% of the market price. There are no bank fees or brokerage charges under the plan. As of March 31, 1983, there were 13,684 participants who during fiscal year 1983:

Reinvested Dividends	$18,910,541
Reinvested Interest	$ 62,880
Made Optional Cash Payments	$ 770,302
Total Investment	$19,743,723

Number of Shares Purchased during fiscal year 1983: 748,481

To participate or to obtain additional information, write:
Sperry Corporation
Treasury Department
1290 Avenue of the Americas
New York, N.Y. 10104

Dividend Reinvestment and Cash Stock Purchase Plan

Varian is pleased to provide the stockholders a simple and inexpensive way to acquire additional shares of Varian Associates Common Stock through the Dividend Reinvestment and Cash Stock Purchase Plan administered by the First National Bank of Boston.

Advantages of the Plan

- Automatic reinvestment of dividends
- Convenient investment of other funds
- Safekeeping of your shares
- Simplified record keeping
- Low cost
- Voluntary participation

A brochure that fully describes the plan is available by writing:
The First National Bank of Boston
Dividend Reinvestment and
Cash Stock Purchase Plan
P.O. Box 1681
Boston, Massachusetts 02105

ACTIONS AFFECTING STOCKHOLDERS

Ample explanation of actions taken that affect your stockholders should be provided in your annual report.

Some examples are:

Stock Split—Cash Dividend

The Board of Directors in October declared a three-for-two split of the common stock, effected as a stock dividend, and voted to increase the cash dividend by 30 percent. This was the sixth consecutive annual increase in the cash dividend. The positive board action reflects the Company's favorable performance and strong financial condition.

On December 8, 19__ our common stock was listed on the New York Stock Exchange, with the ticker symbol ABP. This was a milestone in ABP's history, and we are pleased to join the major corporations of the nation listed on the NYSE. We believe this listing will provide increased recognition for ABP and generate broader interest in the company by the investment community.

Reacquisition of Stock

During 19__ the Company purchased 250,000 shares of AMP stock. At year-end 19__ the Treasury Stock, held for general corporate purposes, totaled 1,465,553 or 4% of the 37,440,000 shares issued. Cumulative purchases by the Company for the past three years stand at 1,162,000 shares.

STOCK OWNERSHIP

Some companies describe the stock ownership of the officers of their corporation in the annual report.

Example:

To the best of the Company's knowledge, no person or group, other than Stryker Oil Corp., 120 Broadway, New York, NY 10005, owns of record or beneficially more than 5% of the Company's outstanding common stock as of January 1, 19__ Stryker Oil owns 310,558 shares (6.5%) of the Company's common stock.

The following table sets forth, as of January 1, 19__ , the shares of common stock of the Company owned by all directors and by all officers and directors as a group.

Name of Beneficial Owner	Shares of Common Stock Beneficially Owned	Percent of Class (3)
O.F. Benecke	2,593	
William H. Clapp	352	
Charles Q. Conway	210	
Robert E. Ellis	12,111	
Mary Jane Fate	110	
Bruce R. Kennedy	94,809 (1)	2.0%
Keith J. Kennedy	37,872	.8%
Robert L. Parker, Jr.	254 (2)	
Sheldon B. Simmons	9,570	
Officers & Directors as a Group	187,961 (4)	3.9%

(1) Mr. Bruce R. Kennedy is the trustee of a voting trust covering, as of January 31, 19__, an additional 224,858 shares owned by Mr. Ronald F. Cosgrave. As Trustee, Mr. Kennedy has sole voting power over these shares.
(2) Parker Drilling Co., an oil drilling company listed on the New York Stock Exchange, is the record owner of 191, 441 shares of (4% of the issued and outstanding) common stock. Mr. Parker is not a beneficial owner of these shares. Mr. Parker also serves on the Board of Directors of Parker Drilling and the Bank of Oklahoma, N.A.
(3) Other than as noted in the table, each director owned less than .3% of the outstanding common stock as of January 1, 19__ .
(4) The officers as a group also hold stock options, entitling them to acquire an additional 103,158 shares of the Company's common stock.

Listing of Your Corporate Stock

It is important to provide information in your annual report on such subjects as to where your company's stock is traded; ticker symbol; where stock prices are quoted; what companies make a market in your stock, etc.

Example

Stock Market Information

Our common stock is traded in the "Over-the-Counter" market. Our ticker symbol is APOG. Stock price quotations can be found in major daily newspapers and in The Wall Street Journal.

During the fiscal year ended March 1, 19__ the average trading volume of our common stock, according to NASDAQ reports, was 36,887 shares a month.

As of March 31, the following securities firms were maintaining an inventory of our common stock and acting as "market makers":

Blunt Ellis and Loewi, Inc.
Dain, Bosworth, Inc.
John G. Kinnard & Company, Inc.
Moseley, Hallgarten, Estabrook
Piper, Jaffray and Hopwood, Inc.
Richardson Securities, Inc.
Rodman and Renshaw, Inc.
Troster Singer Stevens

XX
YOUR CORPORATE OFFICES

Your stockholders will welcome information concerning your new corporate offices.

Example:

General Foods

General Foods new Corporate Offices, which officially open June 25, 1983, will contribute to the company's continuing quest for productivity gains. By the early 1980s, General Foods facilities in Westchester County, New York, were spread over six separate locations, both leased and owned, and the opportunity to enhance operating efficiencies by consolidating these activities in offices updated with state-of-the art technology was apparent.

This new facility, located on 54 acres in Rye Brook, New York, continues General Foods commitment to Westchester, its corporate home now for almost 30 years. The building also permits General Foods to consolidate the activity of its Westchester employees on three sites while discontinuing operations at three other locations in the county. Our Tarrytown facility continues to house GF's Technical Research and Corporate Engineering resources while our White Plains location now will serve as headquarters for our U.S. food and beverage businesses. Headquarters for General Foods International Operations is located immediately adjacent to our new Corporate Offices in Rye Brook which in turn house our administrative systems and financial staff resources.

Our employees continuing pride, dedication and effort is essential to the achievement of our corporate mission—to be the world's premier food and beverage company through working environments such as these. General Foods ensures that its people are fully supported in their important work.

Provide the names and addresses of the following:

Auditors
Executive Offices of the Company
Transfer Agents

Corporate Data
The Annual Meeting of Shareholders will be held at 10 a.m. on Tuesday, November 9, 1982 at Harvard Club of Boston, Shawmut Bank Building, One Federal Street, Boston, Massachusetts 02110.

Shares Traded
New York Stock Exchange
(Ticker Symbol—"TYC")

Registrar of Stock, Transfer Agent and Dividend Disbursing Agent
Mellon Bank, N.A.
Mellon Square
Pittsburgh, Pennsylvania 15230

Independent Accountants
Price Waterhouse
One Federal Street
Boston, Massachusetts 02110

The Company's Form 10-K (without exhibits) may be obtained free of charge by writing to: Corporate Communications Department.

Corporate Offices
Tyco Laboratories, Inc.
Tyco Park
Exeter, New Hampshire 03833
(603) 778-7331

XXI CORPORATE FACILITIES

The readers of your corporate annual report will get a better picture of the size and scope of operations (local and foreign) if you provide a directory of facilities.

I recommend you go the route of the Nielsen Companies listing which provides information as to:

- Country
- Corporate Name
- Name of Managing Director
- Address
- Telephone
- Telex

Directory of Nielsen Companies Serving Abroad

COUNTRY		MANAGING DIRECTOR/ GENERAL MANAGER	ADDRESS	TELEPHONE	TELEX
ARGENTINA	A C Nielsen Argentina, S A[1]	C R Oller	Rivadavia 620 - 3er Piso — 1002 Buenos Aires, Argentina	1-33-0078 1-33-0079 1-30-9970	17290
AUSTRALIA	A C Nielsen Pty Ltd[1]	A.J. Kretch	50 Miller Street, North Sydney, N S W /Australia Postal Address: P.O. Box 457, North Sydney, N S W., Australia 2060 P.I. Energy Services Pty., Limited Room 1703, 111 Elizabeth St., Sydney N S W., Australia 2000	2-920-5881 2-232-3222	21763 Mamarks AA27928
AUSTRIA	A C Nielsen Company, Ges m b H[1]	D. Jauschowetz	Concordiaplatz 2 1013 Vienna 1/Austria	222-63 67 97	74469
BELGIUM/LUXEMBOURG	A C Nielsen Company (Belgium) S A[1]	J De Groote	Avenue des Arts 56, B-1040 Brussels/Belgium	2-511-22 96	21794
BRAZIL	A C Nielsen Limitada[1]	L Jancsó	Office Address: Ave. Bernardino de Campos, 98, 14° Andar (Paraiso) P.O. Box 178, CEP 01000, Sao Paulo SP, Brazil	11-284-82 60	1122306
CANADA	A C Nielsen Company of Canada Limited[1,2,3] Petroleum Information Exchange Division James A. Lewis Engineering Division	F.T. Hill/ R.W. Vipond	160 McNabb Street, Markham, Ontario, Canada L3R 4B8 100 Alexis Nihon Blvd., Suite 280, St. Laurent, P.Q. H4M 2N7 6011 Westminster Highway, Suite 211, Richmond, B.C. V7C 4V4 661 Millidge Avenue, Saint John, New Brunswick E2L 4A5 2nd Floor Pacific Build., 925 7th Ave., S.W., Calgary, Alberta, Canada T1P 1A5 Digitech Building, 635 8th Avenue S.W., Calgary, Alberta, Canada T2P 3M3	(416) 475-3344 (514) 744-5515 (604) 270-7444 (506) 642-3314 (403) 263-3822 (403) 263-6600	06966688 01447337 0582677 03822820
COLOMBIA	A.C. Nielsen de Colombia S A	A Buscaglia	Carrera 18 No. 79-25 y 79-37, P.O. Box No. 52642, Bogotá, Colombia	257 63 11 256 15 38	43137*
FRANCE	A C Nielsen Company (French Branch)[1,3]	C.Charbit	28 Boulevard de Grenelle, 75737 Paris Cedex 15 France	1-578-6120	270868
GERMANY	A C Nielsen Company, G m b H[1]	H Ruppe/W Speidel	Friedrich-Ebert-Anlage 2-14, P O Box 16580 6000 Frankfurt AM Main	611-74 08 21	412031
GREAT BRITAIN	A.C. Nielsen Company Limited[1] Petroleum Information Limited: Offshore Petroleum Exploration Service	M H Smyth	Nielsen House, Headington, Oxford OX3 9RX/England Green Dragon House, 64/70 High Street Croydon, Surrey, CRO 9XN England	865-64851 11-441-680-7031	83136 946309 OPESG
GREECE	A C Nielsen Hellas Ltd	R Kessiakoff	2 Charokopou Str 196 Sygrou Ave Kallithea Athens	1-958-8142 1-958-8771-4	219098
IRELAND	A C Nielsen of Ireland Limited[1]	A M Saunders	36 Merrion Square Dublin 2 Republic of Ireland	1-765112	25321
ITALY	A C Nielsen Company (Italian Branch)	Adolfo Pucciani	Via Dante 7 20123 Milan Italy	2-80 93 11	334059
JAPAN	A C Nielsen Company (Japanese Branch)	P A Newton	Nielsen Building 1-1-71 Nakameguro Meguro-ku Tokyo 153 Higashi-Umeda Building 9-6 Nozaki-cho Kita-ku Osaka 530/Japan	3-710-6551 6-313-0781/4	 26511
MEXICO	A C Nielsen Company (Mexican Branch)[1]	A Traslosheros	Jose Luis LaGrange 103, Col. Chapultepec Morales, 11570 Mexico, D F Postal Address: Apartado Postal M-2638, 06000 Mexico, D F	(905) 395-0399	73104
NETHERLANDS	A C Nielsen (Nederland) B V[1]	R Smit	Amsteldijk 166 1079 LH Amsterdam P O 7000 1007 MA Amsterdam	20-44 49 72	12659
NEW ZEALAND	A C Nielsen (N Z) Limited[1]	J W Scott	Molesworth House Molesworth Street Wellington 1 New Zealand Postal Address Box 2464 Wellington 1 / New Zealand	4-735-736 and 4-735-737	3778
NORWAY	Norges Markedsdata A.S.	A B Mevik	Drammensvejen 154 Postboks 1 — Skoyen, Oslo 2	2-55 42 70	72560
PORTUGAL	A C Nielsen Company (Portuguese Branch)[1]	J Alves	Rua Rosa Araujo 34 Lisbon/Portugal	19-554412	12748
SOUTH AFRICA	A C Nielsen Company (Proprietary) Limited[1]	M G Gorton	5th floor Johannesburg Stock Exchange Diagonal Street Postal Address P O Box 5637 Johannesburg 2001 Republic of South Africa	11-833-7510/19 11-833-7540-41	88425
SOUTH KOREA	A C Nielsen Company (Korean Branch)	R.B Norris	Namkyung Bldg., 10th Floor, No. 337-15, Chungdam-Dong, Kangnam-ku, Seoul, Republic of Korea — Postal Address: C.P.O. Youngdong P.O. Box 170	2-566-6548 and 2-566-8540	K26168
SPAIN	A C Nielsen Company (Spanish Branch)[1,3]	M Fuster	Luchana 23-6, P O Box 10149, Madrid 10/Spain	1-447-37-62	46278
SWEDEN	A C Nielsen Company AB[1]	L Nilsson	Storholmsgaten 11, 2nd Floor Skarholmen Sweden Postal Address P O Box 285, S-127 25 Skarholmen Sweden	8-750 5060	11277
SWITZERLAND	A C Nielsen S A[1]	M Muller	Nielsen House Buchrain/Lucerne/Switzerland Postal Address Box 516, CH 6002 Lucerne, Switzerland	41-303333	78240

PRODUCTION OFFICES ABROAD: Toronto & Saint John, Canada; Oxford, England; Abbeyfeale, Dingle, Kilmallock, Limerick, Listowel & Newscastle West, Ireland; Tokyo, Japan; Chihuahua, Juarez & Nuevo Laredo, Mexico; Lucerne, Switzerland

*Please forward this telex to A C Nielsen de Colombia, S A.

International Sales and Service Locations

(Listed by Country Headquarters)

EUROPE

Austria

Belgium
Antwerp
Brussels

Denmark
Aabyhoj
Aarhus
Copenhagen

Finland
Helsinki
Oulu
Vaasa

France
Bordeaux
Buc
Marseilles
Nantes
Paris

Germany
Berlin
Bodman/Bodensee
Bremen
Burgdorf-Sorgensen
Cologne
Düsseldorf
Essen
Flensburg
Frankfurt
Gütersloh
Halver
Hamburg
Hamm
Henningen-Westerfeld
Kaiserslautern
Kassel
Kiel
Lippstadt
Lübeck
Mannheim
Munich
Münster
Nürnberg
Remscheid
Saarbrücken
Stuttgart
Waiblingen
Würzburg

Greece
Athens
Crete[1]

Iceland
Keflavik[1]
Reykjavik

Ireland
Cork
Dublin

Italy
Ancona
Bari
Bologna
Cagliari
Cinisello Balsamo
Florence
Genoa
Milan
Naples
Padova
Rome
Turin
Venice

Luxembourg[2]

Netherlands
Amsterdam
's Hertogenbosch
Hengelo
Rotterdam

Norway
Aalesund
Bergen
Oslo
Stavanger
Troms

Portugal

Spain
Barcelona
Bilbao
Madrid
Seville
Valencia

Sweden
Gothenburg
Malmo
Stockholm

Switzerland
Aarau
Bern
Geneva
Lugano
Zurich

United Kingdom
Birmingham
Bournemouth
Bristol
Croydon[1]
Glasgow
Henley on Thames
Leicester[1]
London
Manchester[1]
Newcastle[1]
New Market
Norwich[1]
Preston[1]
Scheffield

MIDDLE EAST/ AFRICA

Bahrain
Manama

Cyprus
Nicosia

Egypt
Alexandria
Cairo

India

Iraq
Baghdad

Jordan
Amman

Kenya
Mombasa[1]
Nairobi

Kuwait
Kuwait

Lebanon
Beriut

Malawi[3]

Oman
Muscat

Qatar
Doha

Saudi Arabia
Al-Khobar
Jeddah
Jubail
Riyadh

South Africa
Bloemfontein
Cape Town
Durban
Johannesburg
Port Elizabeth
Pretoria

Syria[1]

Tunisia
Tunis

Turkey
Ankara
Istanbul
Izmir

United Arab Emirates
Abu Dhabi
Dubai
Sharjah

Zimbabwe
Salisbury

ASIA/PACIFIC

Australia
Brisbane
Canberra
Melbourne
Sydney

Guam

Hong Kong

Japan
Fukuoka
Hachinohe/ Misawa[1]
Hiroshima[1]
Kobe
Matsuyama[1]
Nagasaki/Saseho[1]
Nagoya
Narita
Niigata[1]
Okinawa City
Osaka
Tokyo
Yokohama

Korea
Seoul
Taegu

Malaysia
Kuala Lumpur
Penang

New Zealand
Auckland
Christchurch
Dunedin
Hamilton
Hastings
Lower Hutt
Nelson
Palmerston North
Wellington

Philippines
Angeles (Clark AFB)
Manila
Olongapo (Subic Bay/ Cubi Point NAS)

Singapore

Taiwan
Taipei

Thailand
Bangkok

LATIN AMERICA

Argentina
Buenos Aires

Bahamas
Freeport
Nassau

Barbados
Bridgetown

Bermuda
Hamilton

Chile
Santiago

Colombia
Bogota
Medellin

Costa Rica
San José

Ecuador
Quito

Jamaica
Kingston

Mexico
Mexico D.F.

Panama
Panama City

Peru
Lima

Trinidad
Port-of-Spain
San Fernando

Uruguay
Montevideo

Venezuela
Caracas
Valencia

Canada
Calgary
Montreal
Ottawa
Toronto
Vancouver
Victoria
Winnipeg

(1) Service only (2) Serviced from Brussels (3) Serviced from South Africa

XXII
PROVIDE A LIST OF CUSTOMERS

Consider listing your customers (with their approval, of course).

Example:

MICRO MASK, INC.

Micro Mask, Inc. is the world's largest independent manufacturer of photomasks and hard surface photoplates required in the design, engineering and production of semiconductors and integrated circuits. The Company also manufactures custom-designed electronic components for the electronics industry.

Integrated Circuit Products are manufactured by the Micro Mask and EMC Divisions in Sunnyvale and Azusa, California. Customers for these precision photomasks and photoplates comprise the leading companies in the semiconductor and related industries, including:

Advanced Micro Devices
Boeing
Collins Radio
Control Data
Data General
Digital Equipment
Eastman Kodak
Fairchild
General Electric
GTE-SEMI
Harris Semiconductor
Hewlett-Packard
Honeywell
Hughes Aircraft
IBM
Inmos
Intel
Intersil
ITT
Monolithic Memories
Mostek
Motorola
National Semiconductor
NCR
Perkin-Elmer
Plessey
Prime Computer
RCA
Reticon
Rockwell
Signetics
Standard Microsystems
Synertek
Teledyne
Teletype
Texas Instruments
Westinghouse
Xerox
Zilog

General Information

The Company

Corning Glass Works traces its origin to 1851. It is a leading worldwide manufacturer of specialized products—based mainly but not entirely on glass and glass-ceramics—for use in illumination, communications, transportation, industrial systems and equipment, food preparation and serving, health and medicine. Corning and its subsidiaries annually produce some 60,000 different products at 58 plants in 10 countries.

Competition

Corning competes with other manufacturers in most of its products. In addition, certain products are in competition with similar products manufactured of materials other than glass. Competition is especially intensive in the field of consumer products, as well as in resistors and capacitors.

Raw Materials

Corning's production of specialty glasses and related materials requires significant quantities of energy and batch materials.

Although energy in particular has been a concern in recent years—with worldwide shortages and higher prices—Corning has made important engineering changes that will allow it great flexibility should a shortage develop in a particular energy source. Specifically, the company's principal manufacturing processes can now be operated with natural gas, propane, oil or electricity—or a combination of these energy sources.

As to natural resources (ores and minerals) required in manufacturing operations, availability appears to be adequate. Corning's suppliers from time to time may experience capacity limitations in their own operations; nevertheless, the company believes it has adequate programs to ensure a reliable supply of batch chemicals and raw materials. For many products, Corning has alternative glass compositions that would allow operations to continue without interruption in the event of specific materials shortages.

Patents and Trademarks

Inventions by members of Corning's research and engineering staff have been, and continue to be, important to the company's growth. Patents have been granted on many of these inventions, in the United States and other countries. Some of these patents have been licensed to other glass manufacturers, including Corning's associated companies outside the United States. Many of the earlier patents have now expired.

Most of Corning's products are sold under one of five basic trademarks: Corning, Pyrex, Corning Ware, Corelle, Vycor. The trademark Pyroceram has been adopted for the entire family of glass-ceramic materials. Subsidiaries of Corning frequently use their own trademarks, such as Rigopal, Sovirel, Tamara.

Protection of the Environment

Corning has substantially implemented a program to bring its domestic facilities into compliance with state and federal pollution-control regulations. This program has resulted in substantial capital and operating expenditures.

Capital expenditures for pollution control were approximately $1.4 million in 1983 and are estimated to be $2.0 million in each of 1984 and 1985.

Corning's operations in 1983 were charged with approximately $7.9 million for the depreciation, maintenance, waste disposal and other operating expenses associated with pollution control. The level of these costs is not expected to change substantially in 1984 and 1985. Corning believes that its compliance program will not place it at a competitive disadvantage.

Corning is a party to two governmental actions brought under federal and state "superfund" statutes for the clean-up of waste sites, neither of which is believed to be material.

XXIII ANNUAL REPORT QUESTIONNAIRE

A number of companies include a questionnaire in their annual report. This provides feedback to you that will be helpful in the preparation of your next year's annual report.

A good example of an annual report questionnaire is the one contained in the Amhoist annual report as follows:

Thank you for reading Amhoists 19__ Annual Report. Please take a few minutes and help us make future reports more responsive by answering the questions on this questionnaire. When you are finished detach the form at the perforated line, fold it in thirds, insert the tab in the slot and drop it in the mail. No postage is necessary. Please note no signature is required.

1. Different people read annual reports for different information. Please check all the sections of the report that you read by placing a mark on the line next to the appropriate sections.

__ All of the report
__ Letter to the shareholders
__ Presidential reflections
__ Segment reviews
__ Financial report
__ Centennial review
__ Other (Please specify) ________

2. Next, please rate the quality of the sections you read. Please consider the overall quality, understandability, and readability of those sections, and circle the number which most closely represents your opinion.

	Poor									*Outstanding*
Letter to the shareholders	1	2	3	4	5	6	7	8	9	10
Presidential reflections	1	2	3	4	5	6	7	8	9	10
Segment reviews	1	2	3	4	5	6	7	8	9	10
Financial report	1	2	3	4	5	6	7	8	9	10
Graphs	1	2	3	4	5	6	7	8	9	10
Centennial review	1	2	3	4	5	6	7	8	9	10
Photographs	1	2	3	4	5	6	7	8	9	10
Other (Please specify) ________	1	2	3	4	5	6	7	8	9	10

3. The purpose of an annual report is to communicate information about where a company has been, where is is now, and where it is going. Please rate how effectively you think this report has been in accomplishing this goal.

	Poor									*Outstanding*
All of the report	1	2	3	4	5	6	7	8	9	10
Letter to the shareholders	1	2	3	4	5	6	7	8	9	10
Presidential reflections	1	2	3	4	5	6	7	8	9	10
Segment reviews	1	2	3	4	5	6	7	8	9	10
Financial report	1	2	3	4	5	6	7	8	9	10
Centennial review	1	2	3	4	5	6	7	8	9	10
Other (Please specify) ________	1	2	3	4	5	6	7	8	9	10

4. Please list below any information not provided in the Amhoist Annual Report that you would like to see included in future editions.

____

____

____

5. Please rate the overall 19__ Amhoist Annual Report by circling the number which best describes your overall impression.

	Poor	*Outstanding*
The 19__ Annual Report is	1 2 3 4 5 6 7 8 9 10	

Next, we would like some information about you. This information will enable us to more effectively respond to your information needs in the future, while helping us analyze the answers you have given us to the earlier questions.

6. Are you currently an Amhoist shareholder?

__ Yes No __ (Skip to question 8)

6a. How many shares do you currently own? _____

7. As an Amhoist shareholder, what are your primary reasons for holding Amhoist stock? Check all the answers that apply.

__ I have a long-term profit on my original investment.

__ I believe that as the economy improves. Amhoist's stock price will improve.

__ The dividends on my original investment are satisfactory.

__ I have a loss on my investment and am waiting for a recovery, at which time I will make another decision.

__ Other __________________________

____

____

____

8. As either a potential Amhoist shareholder, or a current share holder who is considering additional purchases, what will be your primary reason for buying Amhoist stock?

__ Capital appreciation

__ Dividend income

__ Both capital appreciation and dividend income

__ Other __________________________

9. How did you first become aware of Amhoist?

__ Through my stockbroker

__ Through an Amhoist employee

__ I work for Amhoist or one of its subsidiary companies

__ Through an Amhoist shareholder

__ Through previous annual reports

__ From a newspaper or magazine article

__ From a newspaper or magazine advertisement

__ From an investment publication

__ This is my first exposure to Amhoist

__ Other __________________________

10. Are you male __ or female __?

11. In what age group should you be listed?

__ Under 25	__ 35-44	__ 55-64
__ 25-34	__ 45-54	__ 65 or over

12. Please indicate which line most closely describes your current occupation.

__ Professional	__ Professional Investor
Executive	__ Homemaker
__ Skilled trade or factory worker	__ Retired Please write in previous occupation __________ ______________
__ Manager Supervisor	
__ Secretarial Clerical	
__ Accounting Finance	__ Other Please describe
__ Stockbroker	______________

ARMCO

Dear Armco Owner:

Would you please take a few minutes of your time to fill in this questionnaire and return it? We try hard to communicate with you usefully. Your answers to the questionnaire will help us. You need not give your name and address unless you want to. Thanks for your help. We'll tell you what we learn in an upcoming quarterly report.

(The small numbers are for tabulating purposes only)

Do you feel that the information you receive from Armco is:

	Yes	No
Timely	1-1 ☐	2 ☐
Informative	2-1 ☐	2 ☐
Relevant	3-1 ☐	2 ☐
Credible	4-1 ☐	2 ☐
Helpful in making an investment decision	5-1 ☐	2 ☐
Too general	6-1 ☐	2 ☐
Too infrequent	7-1 ☐	2 ☐

What would you suggest to improve it?

______________________________ 8

____

____

Please rank (1,2,3) the following types of information in the order you find most useful:

a. Annual report __ 9

b. 10-K __ 10

c. Quarterly reports __ 11

d. Your broker's report __ 12

e. Investment advisory services __ 13

f. Business magazines, Financial press (Specify) __ 14

____

____

g. Other (Specify) __ 15

____

____

How many shares of Armco stock do you own?

Common ____________________ 16-21

Preferred ____________________ 22-26

How is your Armco stock held?

28-1 ☐ In Armco Thrift Plan

2 ☐ By a bank or broker

3 ☐ In your name

On whose recommendation did you by the stock? (Check one or several)

29 ☐ Broker

30 ☐ Banker

31 ☐ Investment Counselor

32 ☐ Financial Information Service

33 ☐ Friends/Relatives

34 ☐ Own Judgment

35 ☐ Armco Employee

36 ☐ Other (Please specify) ____________________

____

____

What was your main reason for buying Armco stock? (Check one)

37-1 ☐ Long term growth

2 ☐ Short term profit

3 ☐ Income plus growth

4 ☐ Income only

5 ☐ Other (Please specify) ____________________

____

____

____

____

____

Do you rely on investments for your regular income? (Check one)

38-1 ☐ Wholly

2 ☐ Partly

3 ☐ Not at all

Approximately what percentage of the market value of your portfolio does Armco represent? __39-41

____

FOLD IN HALF

MOISTEN AND SEAL FOR MAILING

Please indicate whether each of the following statements either describes or does not describe Armco as a company:

	Yes	No
Well managed	42-1 ☐	2 ☐
Good to invest in	43-1 ☐	2 ☐
Widely diversified	44-1 ☐	2 ☐
Good outlook for the future	45-1 ☐	2 ☐
Good dividends history	46-1 ☐	2 ☐
Superior products	47-1 ☐	2 ☐
Susceptible to business cycles	48-1 ☐	2 ☐
Earnings outpace inflation	49-1 ☐	2 ☐
In the energy market	50-1 ☐	2 ☐
Too dependent on one industry	51-1 ☐	2 ☐
Recent financial performance impressive	52-1 ☐	2 ☐
A high price/earnings ratio	53-1 ☐	2 ☐

What do you see as Armco's greatest strength right now and over the next five years?

______________________________ *54*

If you were asked by a friend or associate to describe Armco in a single phrase, which of these terms would most nearly fit your description (pick just one—or supply your own).

55-1 ☐ Energy Company

2 ☐ Multi-Industry Company

3 ☐ Steel Producer

4 ☐ Insurance Company

5 ☐ (Other) ______________________________

What are the most negative recent developments at Armco?

______________________________ *56*

Do you intend to change your holdings in Armco stock over the next 12 months?

57-1 ☐ No

2 ☐ Buy

3 ☐ Sell

Why? ______________________________ *58*

What would you like to see Armco do to have a positive effect on your investment? ______________ *59*

Do you have any affiliation with Armco?

60-1 ☐ Employee

2 ☐ Retiree

3 ☐ Related to an Armco employee

4 ☐ Other

Approximate age?

61-1 ☐ Under 30	4 ☐ 45-54
2 ☐ 30-34	5 ☐ 55-64
3 ☐ 35-44	6 ☐ 65 or over

Gender?

62-1 ☐ Female

2 ☐ Male

(Optional)

Name: ____________________

Address: ____________________

____________________ 63-64

NO POSTAGE NECESSARY IF MAILED IN THE UNITED STATES

BUSINESS REPLY CARD

FIRST CLASS PERMIT NO 2 MIDDLETOWN OHIO

POSTAGE WILL BE PAID BY ADDRESSEE

Armco
Box 600
Middletown, Ohio 45042

Attn: Shareholder Relations

Are you receiving financial reports directly from Bausch & Lomb?

If your shares of Bausch & Lomb are being held by a broker, you do not appear on our list of registered shareholders. Consequently, we are unable to send our annual report and other important information directly to you. This can sometimes lead to a delay of several weeks or more between the time our reports are issued and when they are received by you.

If you would like to begin receiving financial information directly from Bausch & Lomb, and thereby stay up-to-date on our progress, all you have to do is complete and mail the postage paid card below.

Please send the company's financial reports directly to me at the following address:

Name ______________________________

Address ______________________________

City ____________________ State ____________ Zip ________

My shares are registered with ______________________________.

XXIV EMPLOYMENT INFORMATION

Some companies insert on the inside back cover information concerning job opportunities within the company. For example:

> **Openings for Engineers, Programmers & Technicians**
>
> Send resume to:
> Recruitment Director
> Simmonds Precision
> 150 White Plains Road
> Tarrytown, New York 10591
>
> An Equal
> Opportunity Employer M/F

Consider giving credit to the individuals and companies that played a role in the development of your corporate annual report—designer, photographer, and printer.

XXV TRADEMARKS

Many annual reports contain information about the trademark and service marks of the company and its subsidiaries.

Example:

ATO, INC.

Trademarks and service marks

This annual report includes trademarks and service marks owned by A-T-O Inc., its subsidiaries and affiliates. The following trademarks and service marks are registered in the U.S. Patent and Trademark Office: Adirondack, Advance, AirPax, American LaFrance, American LaFrance & cross design, American LaFrance & eagle design, AS & design, Auto-Sentry, "Automatic", Badger & flame design, Badger-Powhatan, Colonel Logan, Compact, Consolidated, CPM, "Deep Well", Essick, Essick & design, Fastback, Fire 200, Fire 311, Fred Perry & Laurel Wreath design, Heart of the Hide & steer design, HolDster, Huber, IEC & design, Kersey, Laurel Wreath design, Logan, Loomtogs, Parker, Powhatan, R, Range Guard, Rate of Rise, Rawlings, Red Label design, Safway, Safway & design, Scott, Scott AirPak, Sentinel, Sherwood, Sierra, SMG & design, Smith, Snorkel, Snorkelift, Toney Penna, Toney Penna DB, Tru-Temp, & Vanguard.

The following are common law marks: Advance & eagle design, Carcentry, IEC Security System, MAC, "The Mark of a Pro", Oliver, Omega, Pro Ring, Rusco, RXP, SAL, Scott, Waite Hill, WILX-TV, & Wing Tip & wings design.

A-T-O Inc. has rights in the United States to use the following: (1) trademarks registered in the U.S. Patent and Trademark Office: Lee Trevino; and (2) names: Earl Campbell & Tony Dorsett.

XXVI TERMINOLOGY

Financial Terminology

Capital employed	For the company: the sum of interest-bearing debt, capitalized lease obligations, deferred credits and shareholders' equity; for a segment: the net sum of the segment's assets, current liabilities and allocated corporate assets and current liabilities, exclusive of cash items and short-term debt
Cash items	The sum of cash, including certificates of deposit, and marketable securities
Common shareholders' equity	The sum of common stock (less the cost of common stock in treasury), capital in excess of par value, retained earnings and the charge or credit to the accumulated foreign currency translation adjustment account, as reported in the balance sheet, less the amount by which the minimum liquidation value of preference stock exceeds its stated value
Long-term capital	The sum of long-term debt, long-term capitalized lease obligations, deferred credits and shareholders' equity
Operating income after taxes	For the company: net earnings plus the after-tax cost of interest expense; for a segment: segment earnings less the segment's computed share of the consolidated provision for income taxes
Property additions*	Capitalized replacements of and additions to property, plant and equipment (and such assets of businesses acquired), including capitalized leases, renewals and betterments, and proved oil and gas properties, but excluding net increases in unproved oil and gas properties; each segment's property additions include allocated corporate amounts
Ratio of earnings to fixed charges	Earnings before income taxes and fixed charges divided by fixed charges (the sum of interest expense before capitalization credits, amortization of financing costs and one-third of rental expense)
Segment earnings	Earnings before interest expense and income taxes and after allocation of corporate expenses and income, other than "interest income, etc.," principally on the basis of one or a combination of the following factors: average gross investment, average equity and sales. Interest income, etc., refers principally to interest income earned on the short-term investment of funds.

Financial Terminology (*Continued*)

Short-term debt	The sum of current interest-bearing debt, including current maturities of long-term debt and capitalized lease obligations, and interest-bearing notes payable

*The company classifies its property additions into three categories based upon the predominant purpose of the project expenditures. Thus, a project is classified entirely as a replacement if that is the principal reason for making the expenditure even though the project may involve some cost saving and/or capacity improvement aspects. Likewise, a profit adding project is classified entirely as such if the principal reason for making the expenditure is to add operating facilities at new locations (which occasionally replace facilities at old locations), to add product lines, to expand the capacity of existing facilities, to reduce costs or to improve products, etc.

Property additions classified as environmental control expenditures, of course, do not reflect those expenditures for environmental control activities, including industrial health programs, which are expensed currently. Such expenditures are made on a continuing basis and at significant levels in all three of the company's principal segments. Frequently, profit adding and major replacement projects also include expenditures for environmental control purposes.

XXVII GENERAL SUBJECT INDEX

KOPPERS

To aid the annual report reader who is interested in general subject areas, the following index is an alphabetical guide with specific page references. It is based upon a judgment as to those items most often referred to and should not be considered a complete listing.

Information on Koppers Operations:

SINGER

General Subject Index

XXVIII
THE BACK COVER

Don't overlook the importance of the back cover of your annual report. Oftentimes your annual report is on a table or desk with the front cover facing down. By using photographs on the back cover, and with proper identification of your company, you get an added impression of the type of products that your company manufactures.

A Reminder . . .

All too often the back cover of the annual report does not include the name or address of the company. Make it easy for the reader of your report to find the address by including the name of your company and the address at the bottom of the back cover.

XXIX THE PREPARATION, PRINTING, AND DISTRIBUTION OF YOUR CORPORATE ANNUAL REPORT

We come now to the mechanical job of moving agreed upon concepts, written materials, facts, figures, charts, graphs, etc., into a concise printed report that will be distributed to meet your time requirements.

The following Table of Contents will serve as a checklist for you in preparing and distributing your annual report:

1. Who should be responsible for the preparation of the annual report
2. The annual report preparation team
3. The role of your company's chief executive officer in the preparation of the annual report
4. How much should you pay for an annual report
5. How to set a budget for the preparation of your corporate annual report
6. How to reduce the expenses of your corporate annual report
7. How to develop a plan and timetable for the preparation of your corporate report
8. Preliminary planning
9. Establishing the overall tone of your annual report
10. Size, number of pages, and design of your annual report
11. Use of magazine style
12. The annual report as an advertising piece
13. The use of fine art in your annual report
14. Gearing your annual report to high quality products
15. Guidelines for writing your annual report
16. Layout and headings
17. Photography
18. Overprint of figures on photographs
19. Charts and graphs
20. Making the columns of figures easier to read
21. The use of white ink
22. Preparing the rough draft of your annual report
23. Obtaining approval of the draft of the annual report
24. How to work with your printer
25. The paper
26. Size of type
27. Avoiding Snafus
28. Distribution of your annual report
29. Taking the Final Step—Having your stockholders evaluate your corporate annual report
30. Survey form

WHO SHOULD BE RESPONSIBLE FOR THE PREPARATION OF THE ANNUAL REPORT

One person should be assigned the responsibility for the preparation, printing, and distribution of the annual report. In most companies, that person would be the public relations director, or the communications director, or the treasurer. Stay away from trying to assign the responsibility to a committee; one person should be in charge.

Jules Koslow, director of publications and communications services for RCA Corporation, New York, points out:

The corporate executive responsible for producing a company's annual report should have writing and editing skills and be knowledgeable in the fields of graphics, photography, printing, finance, public relations, and management. Rarely, however, does one individual have all these attributes. In most cases, several persons—often from both inside and outside the company—form duos, troikas, quartets, quintets and divide the goodies among themselves. But heaven help the company that doesn't have one person in charge of the entire project to avoid confusion and keep dollars from pouring down a production rathole.

Ideally, too, this person should have a firm grasp of what an annual report is and what it should include. He should be able to convince top management of the report's ideological and reporting parameters. He should know that the document is reporting the corporation's performance, activities, and interests for the year. Simple? Not really. For all of us have seen reports that seem more like sales pitches for the company's products, or showoff graphics heavy on aesthetics and light on meaningful information.

It is advisable to have an annual report committee consisting of members of the legal, accounting, marketing, executive, and communications departments. However, the person who has the responsibility for getting out the report should serve as chairman, and have a sign on his or her desk, "the buck stops here."

The Annual Report Preparation Team

The preparation of your company's annual report is truly a team effort. You will want to involve all those who can and should make a contribution to the writing, preparing, presenting, and distributing of your annual report.

Your working team should consist of:

1. The captain—the person who has the responsibility to coordinate the effort.
2. The controller or treasurer—to furnish the financial information, supervise its use, and make the final check.
3. The public relations executive—who will be responsible for the presentation of the report.
4. The corporate lawyer—to check legal aspects of the report.
5. The certified public accountant—to approve the financials.
6. The industrial relations director—to supply information on labor matters.
7. The company president and/or chairman of the board—to coordinate the preparation, perhaps in cooperation with an administrative staff officer.

You will want to have the approval of each of your senior executives before your report goes to the printer. Get them to initial the final draft . . . including the placing of an "OK" by the CEO.

The role of your company's chief executive officer in the preparation of the annual report

Involve the CEO in the preparation of the annual report—the sooner the better. Set up a meeting with the CEO and find out exactly what subjects the CEO would like to cover in the report—how these items are to be presented—the willingness of the CEO to make projections for the future, etc. Determine how active the CEO will want to be in the preparation of the annual report, and at what points along the way the CEO wants to be consulted. Discuss the letter that the CEO will write for the annual report. It's best to have the CEO draft the report so that it is in his or her own words and expresses the future course for the company.

Be sure that as you proceed in the preparation of the report, the CEO is kept informed of budgets, professionals to be used, theme, overall tone of the report, etc. You will certainly want to have the CEO approve the first draft. Make certain that you and the CEO are on the same wavelength. The CEO should have the final word as to the theme to be used in the report, accomplishments to be highlighted, and the messages that are to be forthcoming from the annual report.

HOW MUCH SHOULD YOU PAY FOR AN ANNUAL REPORT

There is no one price for all annual reports. The price is determined by many factors—i.e., number of pages, art work, professional assistance, cost of paper, number of reports printed, etc.

Large corporations with enormous press runs may have a unit cost of only about 50¢ for a full-color report. Smaller companies needing only a few thousand copies may pay $2.00 or $3.00 each for just a two-color report.

Regardless of cost, it's the *value* that counts. Keep in mind that your annual report is the major vehicle of communications between your company and its various publics. You cannot afford to distribute a report that gives a poor impression of management, company policies, products, systems, future potential, etc. Any cheapening—from design through reproduction and "feel" of the paper—can be a serious mistake.

HOW TO SET A BUDGET FOR THE PREPARATION OF YOUR CORPORATE ANNUAL REPORT

Suffice it to say, the preparation and distribution of your annual report is costly—but controllable. It is imperative that you set a budget for the annual report and get the appropriate approvals. Start with the detailed costs of your prior annual report. List every item of cost and start from there. You will want to include in your budget:

Executive Time	$__________
Accountants' charge	__________
Travel	__________
Photography	__________
Graphics	__________
Typesetting	__________
Printing	__________
Binding	__________
Mailing	__________
TOTAL	$__________

HOW TO REDUCE THE EXPENSES OF YOUR CORPORATE ANNUAL REPORT

There are a number of ways to cut down on the preparation cost of your corporate annual report. Some examples are:

1. Use black and white instead of four-color.
2. Reduce the number of pages in the annual report by combining certain sections. In many reports the same financial material is covered in two or three different places.
3. Reuse photographs that you had in prior annual reports. They can be recropped so that they appear to have a freshness about them.
4. Shop around for the best prices in paper. You can downgrade the quality of the paper and still give the effect that you want.
5. Avoid changes after the text has been given to the printer, and avoid as many changes as you can in text after the type has been set by the printer.
6. Complete the printing of the report early enough so that you can mail it out third class. This will be about one-third the cost of a first class mailing.

HOW TO DEVELOP A PLAN AND TIMETABLE FOR THE PREPARATION OF YOUR CORPORATE REPORT

You will need a well-designed plan for the preparation and publication of your report. Planning should start at least six months prior to due date. Work backwards from the date you will want to put your reports in the mail.

A typical planning schedule might be as follows.

	Task	Due Date
1.	Develop the theme of your annual report.	Jan. 2
2.	Prepare tentative layout.	Feb. 1
3.	Select your designer, photographer, and printer.	Feb. 15
4.	Obtain necessary approvals of first draft of the report by senior officers.	Feb. 20
5.	Obtain from your CPA tentative financial information to be included.	Mar. 1
6.	Obtain final draft of text to be included in the annual report.	Mar. 15
7.	Shoot photos.	Mar. 20
8.	Obtain final financial reports from CPA.	Mar. 20
9.	Submit final draft of report to senior officers for approval.	Apr. 15
10.	Submit approved annual report to printer.	May 1
11.	Proofread copy and give "go ahead" to the printer.	May 10
12.	Distribute the report.	June 1

Allow for contingencies.

Estimate

Project: **Date:**

Copies to:

Design:	Rate $	x	Pages/Hours =		$
Mechanicals:	Rate $	x	Pages/Hours =		$
Art:	Bar charts	Maps	Cover	Other	$
	Illustrations	Full Page		Spot	
Photography:	Photographer	$ x	Days =		$
	Photo assistant	$ x	Days =		
	Art Director	$ x	Days =		
	Film & Processing	$ x	Days =		
	Retouching				
Travel:	Photographer	$ x	Days =		$
	Assistant	$ x	Days =		
	Art Director	$ x	Days =		
	Production supervision	$ x	Days =		
Typography:	Original setting $		Alterations $		$
Copy writing:					$
Materials:	C-prints $	B & W stats $	Color keys $	Special supplies $	$
Other:	Work prints (B & W) $		Finish prints (B & W) $		$
	Messengers $	Telephone $			
Printing:					$
Total					$

Production Estimate

The Production Estimate is a worksheet for establishing the overall budget for the annual report and recording the costs for each phase of the project. It includes such items as fees for designers and other professionals, travel expenses, printing, typography, supplies, and services.

The production estimate computed with the aid of this form provides an overview of the project's costs, and can be easily summarized and sent on to the client for purposes of establishing an annual report budget.

Estimate

Project: Multinational Corp. Annual Report **Date:** September 24

Copies to: J. Medford, V.P. Finance
S. Williams, V.P. Corp. Communications
W. Smith, Dir. Shareholder Relations
E. Jones, Ed. Shareholder Publications

Design:	Rate $ 000	x 40	Pages/Hours =			$ 00,000
Mechanicals:	Rate $ 000	x 40	Pages/Hours =			$ 00,000
Art:	Bar charts	Maps 2 x $000	Cover		Other 4 x $000	$ 0,000
	Illustrations	Full Page			Spot	
Photography:	Photographer	$0,000 x 10	Days =	$00,000		$ 00,000
	Photo assistant	$ 00 x 10	Days =	$ 000		
	Art Director	$ 000 x 10	Days =	$ 0,000		
	Film & Processing	$ 000 x 10	Days =	$ 0,000		
	Retouching			$ 000		
Travel:	Photographer	$ 000 x 10	Days =	$ 0,000		$ 0,000
	Assistant	$ 000 x 10	Days =	$ 0,000		
	Art Director	$ 000 x 10	Days =	$ 0,000		
	Production supervision	$ 000 x 3	Days =	$ 000		
Typography:	Original setting $ 0,000		Alterations $ 0,000			$ 00,000
Copy writing:		$ 000 x 7 days				$ 0,000
Materials:	C-prints $ 0,000	B&W stats $ 000	Color keys $ 000		Special supplies $ 000	$ 0,000
Other:	Work prints (B&W) $ N/A		Finish prints (B&W) $ N/A			$ 0,000
	Messengers $ 000	Telephone $ 000				
Printing:	Senefelder Lithography, Inc.					$ 00,000
Total						$ 000,000

Schedule

Project: **Date:**

Copies to:

Activity:		Date:	Comments:
Concept:	Planning meeting		
	Submit preliminary cost estimate		
	Present design concept, page distribution, and schedule		
	Select photographer/illustrator		
	Revise budget estimates and select printer and typographer		
	Submit word counts		
Photography:	Complete photography (illustration) schedule		
	Start photography (illustration)		
	Complete photography (illustration)		
	Edit photography		
	Present finished dummy with photos (illustration) in place		
	Release color (art) to printer		
	Correct first color proofs		
	Correct second color proofs		
Typesetting:	Release copy to typeset		
	First galleys		
	Second galleys		
	Third galleys		
	Repro		
	Release Financial copy for typeset		
	First galleys		
	Second galleys		
	Third galleys		
	Repro		

Mechanicals:	Start mechanicals
	Complete mechanicals
	Client sign-off on mechanicals and release to printer
Printing:	Blueline for client approval
	Final corrections approved
	Revised blueline for client approval
	Report on press
	Sample copies to client
	Start delivery
	Complete delivery

Schedule

The Schedule is a comprehensive listing of the key decisions and activities necessary to the design and production of an annual report, with space provided for the filling-in of appropriate due-dates. It is intended to be used in conjunction with the Annual Report Planning Guide Worksheet and is, in fact, a condensed summary of the deadlines established there.

Copies of the completed Schedule can be distributed to client representatives, typesetters, printers—anyone with responsibility for producing a portion of the report. In this way, each person involved gains a clearer understanding of his or her role in the overall project.

Schedule

Project: Multinational Corp. Annual Report **Date:** August 15

Copies to: J. Medford, V.P. Finance — D. Kelly, Mgr. Production
S. Williams, V.P. Corp. Communications — T. Evans, Mgr. Procurement
E. Jones, Editor Shareholder Publications — S. Chapman, Designer
S. Black, Mgr. Editorial Services

Activity:		Date:	Comments:
Concept:	Planning meeting	Sept 1-5	CEO/Exec VPs
	Submit preliminary cost estimate	Sept 24	
	Present design concept, page distribution, and schedule	Oct 5	Design Concept/Dummy
	Select photographer/illustrator	Oct 8	
	Revise budget estimates and select printer and typographer	Oct 15	
	Submit word counts	Oct 15	
Photography:	Complete photography (illustration) schedule	Nov 1	10 days - 5 locations
	Start photography (illustration)	Nov 8	
	Complete photography (illustration)	Nov 24	
	Edit photography	Dec 8-15	Review w/client 12/16
	Present finished dummy with photos (illustration) in place	Dec 22	
	Release color (art) to printer	Jan 4	At printers to review
	Correct first color proofs	Jan 24	At design office
	Correct second color proofs	Feb 14	At design office
Typesetting:	Release copy to typeset	Jan 10	To design office
	First galleys	Jan 12	Distribution (att.)
	Second galleys	Jan 20	
	Third galleys	Jan 27	
	Repro	Feb 11	
	Release Financial copy for typeset	Feb 2	To design office
	First galleys	Feb 4	
	Second galleys	Feb 7	
	Third galleys	Feb 9	
	Repro	Feb 11	
Mechanicals:	Start mechanicals	Feb 14	Windows cut Feb 12
	Complete mechanicals	Feb 16	
	Client sign-off on mechanicals and release to printer	Feb 16	8 pm messenger-NY
Printing:	Blueline for client approval	Feb 23	
	Final corrections approved	Feb 24	
	Revised blueline for client approval	Mar 2	If necessary
	Report on press	Mar 4	
	Sample copies to client	Mar 14	
	Start delivery	Mar 15	
	Complete delivery	Mar 19	

Job Sheet

Project: **Date:**

Copies to:

Client: Telephone:

Art Director: Telephone:

Designer: Telephone:

Photographer: Telephone:

Illustrator: Telephone:

Printer: Telephone:

Typographer: Telephone:

Schedule: Concept:

Photography:

Color release:

Typesetting:

Repros:

Mechanicals:

Bluelines

On press:

Deliver:

Specifications: Size: Quantity:

No. of pages:

Cover stock: No. of colors:

Text stock: No. of colors:

Financial stock: No. of colors:

Binding/Finishing:

Typeface(s):

No. of proofs:

Split delivery:

Word counts:

Job Sheet

The Job Sheet encapsulates the most important information recorded on other forms in the Annual Report Planning Guide. Its purpose is to provide a single place for the recording of a project's most pertinent data—basic specifications, dates, suppliers, and contacts.

The Job Sheet enables any member of the design or production team to answer most questions about a project by referring to one comprehensive source.

Job Sheet

Project: Multinational Corp. Annual Report **Date:** October 15

Copies to: E. Jones, Ed. Shareholder Publications
D. Kelly, Mgr. Production
T. Evans, Mgr. Procurement
S. Black, Mgr. Editorial Services

Client:	Multinational Corporation	Telephone:	218 879-2300
Art Director:	J. Hough	Telephone:	203 357-7077
Designer:	S. Chapman	Telephone:	203 357-7077
Photographer:	M. Willard	Telephone:	212 589-9855
Illustrator:	T. Jackson	Telephone:	203 666-0739
Printer:	Senefelder Lithography, Inc./D. Peters	Telephone:	212 707-6295
Typographer:	The Type House Inc./S. North	Telephone:	203 662-7510

Schedule:	Concept:	October 5
	Photography:	November 8-24
	Color release:	January 4
	Typesetting:	Text: January 10/Financials: February 2
	Repros:	February 11
	Mechanicals:	February 16
	Bluelines	First: February 23/Final: February 28
	On press:	March 4-10
	Deliver:	March 15

Specifications:	Size:	8½" x 11"	Quantity:	85,000
	No. of pages:	40 pages + cover		
	Cover stock:	Vintage gloss cover,100# basis	No. of colors:	4-c over 2-c
	Text stock:	Vintage gloss text, 100# basis	No. of colors:	5-colors
	Financial stock:	Mountie Opaque, warm white, 80# basis	No. of colors:	2-colors
	Binding Finishing:	Perfect bound, glued front + back hinge		
	Typeface(s):	Text: 10/12 Helvetica Reg./heads: 24/24 Helvetica Bold		
	No. of proofs:	3 repros + glassine		
	Split delivery:	6 sets of galleys to E. Jones/3 sets to S. Chapman		
	Word counts:	Letter to Shareholders: 1,000-1,200 words		
		Operating Review: 650-750 words per group		
		Captions: 25-40 words		

Specifications

Project: **Date:**

Copies to:

Pages: Notes/alternates:

Size:

Quantities:

Paperstocks: Cover:

Text:

Financials:

No. of colors: Cover:

Text:

Financials:

Photography: Cover:

Text:

Separations:

Bleeds:

Art: Charts/diagrams:

Maps:

Illustrations:

Solids/Tints:

Mechanicals:

Proofing: Separations/duotones:

Bluelines:

Binding:

Varnish:

Lamination:

Delivery date:

Printer's estimates: $

$

$

$

Printing Specifications

The Printing Specifications form is an item-by-item record of the production considerations which need to be included in any estimate for the printing of an annual report. The information entered here represents a thorough accounting of all production specifications and, as such, can serve as a consistent document for obtaining printers' estimates.

Certain individual reports may need to modify these categories slightly, but they should suffice for the majority of projects.

Specifications

Project: Multinational Corp. Annual Report   Date: August 15

Copies to: E. Jones, Ed. Shareholder Publications
D. Kelly, Mgr. Production
T. Evans, Mgr. Procurement
S. Black, Mgr. Editorial Services

Pages: 40 pages + cover   Notes/alternates:

Size: 8½" x 11"

Quantities: 85,000

Paperstocks:	Cover:	Vintage gloss cover, 100# basis
	Text:	Vintage gloss text, 100# basis (24 pages)
	Financials:	Mountie Opaque, warm white text, 80# basis (16 pages)
No. of colors:	Cover:	4-colors over 2-colors (process over match plus black)
	Text:	5-colors (process over match gray)
	Financials:	2-colors (black type + match color for rules, headlines)
Photography:	Cover:	(1) full bleed, 4-color photo from 35mm transp.
	Text:	(5) full page; (4) half-page; (4) quarter-page; (6) small
	Separations:	200 line scanned
	Bleeds:	Throughout
Art:	Charts diagrams:	(5) bar charts: black line + (3) 2-color bendays each
	Maps:	(1) map: half-page black line + (6) 2-color bendays
	Illustrations:	None
	Solids Tints:	70% screen of match gray on pages 1-4, full bleed
Mechanicals:		on boards in reader spreads
Proofing:	Separations duotones:	2 press proofs (float); on 4-color photos, charts, map
	Bluelines:	3 sets
	Binding:	Perfect bound w/glued front + back hinge
	Varnish:	Spot varnish 4-color subjects
	Lamination:	Liquid laminate covers 1 + 4
	Delivery date:	March 19

Printer's estimates:	Gutenberg Press, Ltd.	$ 000,000
	Senefelder Lithography	$ 000,000
	Baskerville Printing Co.	$ 000,000
		$

PRELIMINARY PLANNING

Mead Paper suggests that preliminary planning includes decisions such as:

1. Selecting main topics for brief coverage in the president's letter.
2. Whether to break out sales and earnings by division.
3. The amount of space to allot to various divisions and/or subsidiaries.
4. Specifying exactly what should be included in charts.
5. Whether to include photographs of:
   a. Directors
   b. Officers
   c. Executives of branches, divisions, and subsidiaries.
6. Retaining the status quo for items in the financial section, or revising them.
7. Including a frank discussion of company problems and solutions.
8. How lavish—or how spartan—to go in appearance (and cost).
9. Whether to distribute the report to a big or limited list.
10. Who will be delegated to do what, and with what deadlines, in putting the report together.

The Graphic Expression, Inc., suggests: "Request all outside vendors (design studios, photographers, writers, illustrators, chart-makers, paper mills, printers, binders, mailing houses) to submit a proposal guaranteeing the work to be performed and the price to be paid. Be sure the proposals are based on clear specifications. If the specs change, request revised bids. Even in the most efficient communications department, printer's overtime and author's alterations are nearly inevitable. It's best, therefore, to budget for them in advance so they won't pop up later as an ugly reminder of costs gone awry. Three to five per cent of the original typesetting estimate is a good margin for AA's."

ESTABLISHING THE OVERALL TONE OF YOUR ANNUAL REPORT

Companies differ in style. Some are quite conservative in their approach to annual reports; others are quite aggressive. Some wish to be formal; others informal. Keep in mind that your annual report reflects the image of your corporation—the image that you would like to present to your various publics.

The overall tone of the annual report is based upon the design, the artwork, the photography, color, and technique. Those that are on the conservative side will generally use the standard types of photography and typography. Companies that want to give the impression of being "on the grow" use strong and dynamic designs, bold graphics, and exciting typography. What is the overall tone that you intend to create in the annual report for your company?

Outside consultants can assist you in developing the overall tone that you will want for your corporate annual report. Explore the various alternatives before agreeing on a particular style. Submit the plan to your team and also to the chief executive officer for approval.

SIZE, NUMBER OF PAGES, AND DESIGN OF YOUR ANNUAL REPORT

I recommend the following:

1. size of report—$8\frac{1}{2} \times 11$ in.
2. number of pages—28 to 36
3. front cover—four-color
4. front cover—photos or message
5. body—four-color
6. columns of type per text page—2
7. charts—7 to 12
8. maps—to be included where appropriate
9. one gatefold
10. stock—cover: coated
11. stock—body: coated

USING MAGAZINE STYLE

Some companies are turning away from the traditional style of the annual report and turning in the direction of presenting their complete report in the form of a news magazine. A good example of this is Interlake, Inc., which has adopted the magazine style with approximately 25 percent of the pages being replicas of their product advertising. The text is popularized. Three columns are used. Headlines similar to those used in news magazines are employed.

Examples:

1. Changing Perspectives
2. Globe Metallurgical Does It Again
3. Down Under On Top in 19__
4. Imports Apply Pressure
5. Arwood Feels The Crunch
6. R&D Helps Squeeze the Btu's

The controller explains in layman's language "what to look for when reading the income statement." The treasurer describes the purpose of a balance sheet and discusses "understanding the balance sheet—a real asset."

THE ANNUAL REPORT AS AN ADVERTISING PIECE

Oftentimes it is difficult to distinguish between the corporate advertising program and the annual report. In many cases the pages of the annual report lean heavily towards portrayal of the products being sold by the company. This is particularly true of food companies. You can literally taste the Egg McMuffin of McDonald's as shown in its annual report. The Michelob on ice in the Anheuser-Busch annual report offers a tempting respite as one reviews their corporate results. The reader's mouth waters through the photographs of Kentucky Fried Chicken displayed in the Heublein report. The picture of orange juice prominently displayed by the American Agronomics Corporation in their annual report is an invitation that is very tempting.

THE USE OF FINE ART IN YOUR ANNUAL REPORT

A number of companies have turned to the use of paintings in their annual report. The paintings do not necessarily relate to the products of the company. Oftentimes, they express a philosophy of the company. Borg-Warner, in its report, had four paintings that portrayed their philosophies, i.e.:

> "Why must attitudes change? Because the way things were done in the past is rarely right for today, and almost never for tomorrow."
>
> "As modern life becomes more uncertain, the desire for physical security looms larger and larger."
>
> "In turbulent times, strength comes from mutual support, while unit autonomy provides flexibility."
>
> "For a company like this, the future is already here. The capabilities needed for 1990 must be in place now."

Borg Warner believes in encouraging the arts as a "major social responsibility, important both to the company and to the world." They have used reproductions of a number of paintings very effectively in their annual report. They describe this program as follows:

A little over a decade ago, we began a program to collect and maintain the current work of artists living and working in our own primary geographic location. In addition, through a series of grants to major museums we have been encouraging those institutions to collect and display works of local artists also.

Today, the Borg-Warner Collection of Chicago and Vicinity Artists—displayed at our corporate headquarters—is nationally known. We can show only a few representative works in this report; the collection at this time includes 406 paintings and sculptures by 302 Chicago vicinity artists, many of whom have attained international reputation.

GEARING YOUR ANNUAL REPORT TO HIGH QUALITY PRODUCTS

Lenox, Inc., manufactures high quality jewelry, china, crystal, silver-plated holloware, etc. One would expect their annual report to be of very high quality in terms of paper, photography, layout, etc. They use a rich silk background to display their products. The photograph highlights a single product in a full-page display.

GUIDELINES FOR WRITING YOUR ANNUAL REPORT

Mr. Brown, who has been a teacher, writer, account executive in financial public relations, and a partner in a graphic design firm, listed the following guidelines for writing an annual report.

1. Tell the truth, especially if it hurts.
2. Keep it short and sweet, but complete.
3. Write it in readable language.
4. Make it informative.
5. Even interesting.
6. Design it to be handsome, inviting, individual.
7. See that it has at least one core idea.
8. Don't be afraid of a new idea.
9. Let it be a solution to a clearly defined problem.
10. Produce it well.
11. Give the responsibility to one person.
12. Give him/her the authority to make decisions.
13. Retain professionals to help achieve 1–10 above.
14. Help them.
15. Trust them.

Keep in mind that many of the readers of your annual report are sophisticated investors. They are exposed to many other corporate annual reports. They want to receive from your company a well-thought out, fair, and factual report. They don't want to read an advertising piece; they want to know the facts—good or bad—presented in a fair manner. They don't want you to gloss over the negatives. If your company is in trouble in a certain division, don't sweep the results under a rug. Explain the problems and try to present what steps have been taken to bring about a change.

LAYOUT AND HEADINGS

In developing a layout for the report you will want to give thought to the following:

1. *Number of columns on each page.* There is a range of one to four columns. My preference runs to two or three columns in an $8\frac{1}{2} \times 11$ inch report.
2. *Headings.* Well-prepared headings make your report more readable. Oftentimes, your stockholders or analysts will skim a report. If you have headings—in different color ink—you will hold their attention and get your message across. You might want to consider a heading such as:

   "While our profits were somewhat disappointing, the strategy of our company developed in the decade of the '70's has put us in a strong position to take advantage of the opportunities ahead in the new decade."

PHOTOGRAPHY

A good portion of your corporate annual report will contain photos of executives, employees, customers, etc. Here's where you will want to zero in on portraying your corporation in the best possible light.

Mead Paper Company advises:

"Results of more than one readership study have proved that the majority of readers spend very little time with an annual report. After they've glanced at the highlights and checked out the president's letter, they may merely thumb through the rest of the book. (Analysts and other professionals, of course, thoroughly study the notes and financial section, but they usually are an important *minority* of the readers.)

The same readers who normally skip through the book quickly *can* be stopped by a selection of outstanding photos and carefully written captions. Some report planners use *only* photos and captions that are exciting—and significant—in telling the company story. Studies prove that photo captions—when easy to read and relatively short—enjoy a very high readership.

Unfortunately, it's not easy to have a generous supply of admirable photos available in time to meet annual report production deadlines. For this reason, two methods of photo procurement are recommended.

One is the assignment of a professional photographer (or several) to do all the shooting expressly for the annual report. He, she, or they are furnished with exact instructions—not only what, where, and when—but with detailed guidance on capturing the essence of the subjects so they will be meaningful to all readers. Considerable lead time, and careful study of all potentially good subjects, are mandatory.

The second method is to maintain a continuing search throughout the year. Every new product, application, facility, newsworthy event, etc., is automatically photographed at the opportune time; prints or transparencies are filed for consideration later at annual report time. When done properly, this method provides a surprising amount of good material that might have otherwise been missed.

Whether in black-and-white or color or both, all photos should not only be meaningful and creative. They should also be technically excellent for quality reproduction."

In photographing people, try for candid shots rather than formal portraits. Try for natural expressions rather than posed ones. Try to get the officers and directors in a relaxed mood. Having two or three together in a work environment is preferable to having so-called bust shots of smiling executives.

Trans America had pictures of its executives scattered throughout its report. Each executive was in shirt-sleeves in a work environment. This is preferable to having formal shots of executives in a studio-like atmosphere.

When it comes to photography of products being manufactured and sold by the company, there is a certain amount of material that your ad department can supply to you. Many annual reports appear to be somewhat in the nature of advertising pieces, which I do not find objectionable, unless they attempt to smother the operational facts. It is helpful to your readers to show your buyers in retail stores if that applies to you; your workers in interesting factory settings; your research department at work on new products, etc.

All too often, employees are pictured at work within the corporation, plant, warehouse, etc.—without identification. It would be helpful to the readers, and particularly to the employees of the company, if you were to identify the employees by name and department.

The E. F. Hutton Group, Inc., has effectively portrayed their executive staff, sales departments, marketing department personnel, etc., by using black and white candid shots, for the most part. Employees are shown in offices, in airplanes, on the telephone, viewing computer terminals, on the exchange floor, etc. One gets the impression of a company on the move.

OVERPRINT OF FIGURES ON PHOTOGRAPHS

I would urge you to avoid printing financial data over photographs. For the most part, this creates an unnecessary problem with the readability of your report. Black ink on white paper without a background of photographic material provides maximum readability.

CHARTS AND GRAPHS

One of the best ways to present your financial report is through the use of charts and graphs. My advice, after reviewing hundreds of charts and graphs, is "Keep it simple." Oftentimes, a designer gets carried away and tries to present charts and graphs that are impossible for the average reader to understand. It should be possible for the reader to get the message quickly and clearly.

MAKE THE COLUMNS OF FIGURES EASIER TO READ

It is oftentimes difficult to read 4–5 columns of figures. The reader's eye can't follow the figures across the page. Here are some techniques to help your reader stay with your figures.

1. If you have two columns of figures to compare, present the figures in different colors.
2. Use a bolder type for the current year.
3. Use dots or lines to connect column headings to a figure.
4. Consider the use of lines under each heading in your statement. Run the lines across the page. This facilitates the tying in of figures to the heading.

Example:

		Year ended December 31	
(dollars in thousands except per share data)	19__	19__	19__
Net Sales	**$2,342,524**	$2,038,155	$1,717,979
Cost of products sold	**1,299,405**	1,143,392	959,564
Research and development	**113,655**	97,562	85,837
Selling, general and administrative	**513,913**	458,199	391,140
Total Operating Cost and Expenses	**1,926,973**	1,699,153	1,436,541
Operating Earnings	**415,551**	339,002	281,438
Interest expense	**77,428**	51,520	41,110
Interest and dividend income	**(67,460)**	(49,150)	(36,859)
Other (income) expense, net	**13,071**	(1,027)	(5,405)
Earnings before taxes	**392,512**	337,659	282,592
Taxes on earnings	**145,229**	123,246	100,393
Net Earnings	**$ 247,283**	$ 214,413	$ 182,199
Earnings per Common Share	**$2.01**	$1.73	$1.47
Average Number of Common Shares Outstanding	**123,098,000**	123,918,000	123,838,000

THE USE OF WHITE INK

You might want to try using white ink in your financial section for your current figures while using black ink for prior years. The impact is quite startling, particularly if the paper that is used is a light buff color.

PREPARING THE ROUGH DRAFT OF YOUR ANNUAL REPORT

At the earliest possible point you will want to have a rough draft and layout you can give to an artist so that a comprehensive draft can be prepared. It would be helpful if you were to make up a dummy of the report in the size that you will want and then sit down with the artist and review what it is that you want to have in the report—with particular emphasis on what you want to stress, and the way you want the message to come through.

As you review your comprehensive draft with the artist you will want to discuss the following:

1. Headline type.
2. Text type.
3. Whether the report is to be in one color, two color, or four color.
4. The number, size, and placement of photographs.
5. The paper stock that you would like to use for the cover and the text.
6. The charts and graphs that you will want to use.
7. Gatefolds, if you plan to use them.

OBTAINING APPROVAL OF THE DRAFT OF THE ANNUAL REPORT

When you have the format of your annual report, you will want to circulate the draft and get the comments of those who are on your committee as well as those of the accountants and lawyers. It's important that the accountants and lawyers review the material from the standpoint of meeting the disclosure laws and regulations.

Set a time limit for the return of the drarft with comments from those that are on your team. It would be well to sit down with each person giving their comments and talk out their suggestions. Be sure that the chief executive officer reviews the text in its entirety so that you have an "across the desk" talk witth the CEO to get all necessary comments.

HOW TO WORK WITH YOUR PRINTER

In an article in the *Public Relations Journal* the following appeared:

Look to your printer

In the final analysis, the printer can make or break all that has gone before in the preparation of the annual report. The relationship between designer and printer is critical, and for that reason, according to Stanley Scott, owner, S.D. Scott Printing Co., the designer should be involved in the selection of the printer to do the job.

Writing on the "symbiotic" relationship between design and printing, Mr. Scott outlined the areas of support which the printer provides:

Paper. Although the designer knows the look, feel, and often, the exact quality of the paper he wants to use, the printer verifies how the selected paper will affect the final printed image. There are also additional considerations in the paper selection:

- Will the ink enhance the image on the paper (or will it reveal problems)? Can the problems be overcome?
- What paper size is the most economical? If the first preference is too costly, what are the alternatives?
- Is the weight of the paper right for the job?
- Will the paper be available or will a substitute have to be considered? Which others fill the requirements?
- Will special embossing, foil stamping, or other desired special effects work on this paper?

Printing. The printer can be important in working out specific aspects of the total plan with the designer. These include:

- Making the job fit the budget.
- Suggesting the best way to prepare art.
- Helping to plan production to get the job out on time.

THE PAPER

The Mead Paper Company advises:

"The right quality, weight, and finish of the paper specified for the annual report is indeed worthwhile insurance for the investment made in design, art, photography, preparatory, and production.

Although the body of most annual reports is printed on dull enamel, many are run on regular (gloss) enamels and on uncoated sheets. Cover stocks include cast-coated, gloss, and dull enamels; embossed texts, and other uncoated papers.

Many reports are "dressed up" by a parchment-like 4-page flyleaf insert between front and back covers. Others have short pages alternating with full size pages to carry the narrative message.

You will find precisely the right combination of cover, body, and insert grades within the popular Mead family, in a variety of prices for all budgets.

It's not your job to be familiar with all the grades of paper available for annual reports—that's up to your production people. However, it might be wise for you to provide some guidelines.

A great deal of money will be spent for such "ingredients" as design, photograph art, typesetting, color separating, plates, presswork, binding, mailing and postage. To protect the investment in the book, experienced annual report "directors" wisely insist upon the finest paper the budget will permit. To save postage, the stock can be lighter weight than usual, but it must be a grade fine enough to do justice to the photography and art being reproduced—and also to reflect the character and quality of the corporation."

SIZE OF TYPE

Make it easy for your stockholderes to read the figures in your annual report. Some of them may be wearing bifocals. Others should—but don't. An example of inadequate type size is as follows:

14. Selected Quarterly Financial Data (Unaudited):
In thousands except per share amounts)

Quarter Ended	February 28, 1982	November 29, 1981	August 30, 1981	May 31, 1981
Net Sales	$12,485	$13,523	$14,359	$14,639
Gross Margin	2,195	2,334	2,394	2,394
Net Income	388	357	374	421
Earnings Per Share	33	30	31	36
Number of Common Shares Outstanding	1,195	1,194	1,194	1,166

Quarter Ended	March 1, 1981	November 30, 1980	August 31, 1980	June 1, 1980
Net Sales	$13,775	$12,826	$11,043	$12,184
Gross Margin	2,840	2,268	1,695	2,031
Net Income	594	429	144	318
Earnings Per Share	50	36	12	27
Weighted Average Number of Common Shares Outstanding	1,195	1,191	1,183	1,181

Avoid type size for figures under 6 point.

Give your readers a break. Use large enough type size for those whose vision isn't all it should be. Type 8 point or larger for all figures is desirable.

AVOIDING SNAFUS

The article, "Watching Out for the Snafus," in *Management Review* describes some of the pesky snafus that you should look out for, such as:

1. You forget to get envelopes printed for mailing the report.

2. You check the text material, but overlook the special material, such as captions, charts, headlines, or the return address on the back. These are mistakes that crop up because they don't go through the normal proofreading channels.

3. You panic. It's a common occurrence just before press time that panic sweeps through the staff, resulting in urgent pleas for substantive changes in text and design. Keep your cool. The decisions you made in the design stage will stand up much better than the changes you make under the pressure of final deadline.

4. You let some new person enter the act. Maybe you ask a director to take a look. Or a senior vice-president who has had nothing to do with the process up to now and doesn't know the reasoning behind the plan. He feels compelled to have an opinion.

5. You don't have a style guide. Twenty-five to 50 percent of the last-minute changes are due to tinkering with capitalization and punctuation.

6. You fail to understand the high cost of late changes. A change in the typewritten manuscript costs next to nothing. At the first galley proof, it may cost $5. At the reproduction proof stage, $25. At the stage of the mechanical, $100. At the printing stage, several hundred dollars.

7. You should accept the fact that because an annual report is creative (writing and design), it is subjective in nature. What's beautiful to one is ugly to the next person. What's well written for Jack is poorly written to George. There is no absolute standard. That is why it is so important to have a strong leader heading the project, backed by the chief executive. Otherwise things can degenerate into a Tower of Babel. No one can come up with the right answer, because there is no right answer. A strong person is needed to make a decision and make it stick.

Mead Paper Company provides some good practical advice as follows:

Not enough lead time

Many annual reports are begun four to six months prior to the mailing date. Without adequate lead time—*or without adhering to scheduling deadlines*—disaster can strike. A sound basic original plan and superb design can be wiped out in the waning days as last-minute panic strikes. Costly overtime in production may be necessary to meet mailing dates.

Distribution headaches

Someone wasn't informed in time: to furnish the mailing list; to get envelopes printed and delivered; to forewarn the mailing house, etc.

Sins of omission

More than one report has been mailed before someone discovered omission of such obvious items as the corporate address; the date, place and time of the annual meeting and other "mandatory" information; the list of officers and directors, etc.

Incomplete footnotes

Surveys indicate that footnotes get higher readership today than ever before. They not only must be set in larger type (10-point minimum), but they should include every necessary explanation of the preceding financial data. Many companies use footnotes written in easily understood sentences instead of legal or "accountancy" terms.

Puffery in "Social Contributions"

Since the ecology crisis came to the fore a few years ago, some annual reports have included glowing stories of the company's accomplishments *but in general statements without documentation.* Widespread suspicion and criticism resulted.

Errors in graphics

Many responsible annual report printers have professional proofreaders to catch typographic errors. But these sharp-eyed people can't be responsible for mistakes in graphics and charts resulting from wrong figures being furnished. All graphics should be closely checked and approved by company personnel knowledgeable about the subjects being charted.

DISTRIBUTION OF YOUR ANNUAL REPORT

You will be guided by the rules of the SEC and of Exchanges, if your company is listed on an Exchange, in the distribution of your annual report. Have your attorneys give you a letter outlining the distribution requirements that have to be followed. You will, of course, mail a copy of the annual report to each shareholder. You may want to distribute copies to employees, bankers, some security analysts, customers, financial editors of newspapers and magazines, community leaders, etc. You will receive some requests from colleges and libraries. The Mead Paper Company provides the following tips on distribution:

First, be sure your print order is ample for all recipients, plus enough to distribute until next year's report is mailed. This may include requests from readers of newspapers which in many cities offer annual reports to all readers.

Made-to-order envelopes take considerable time for delivery. And, because time can be saved by addressing them prior to the arrival of the annual reports, the envelopes should be ordered four to six weeks in advance.

Consider the several methods of distribution, and decide well in advance which you will use: first class, bulk, book rate, self-mailer, or envelope.

Arrange to time the delivery of labels with the delivery of envelopes to avoid a last-minute hangup.

If you use an envelope, the proxy statement can be affixed to the outside—a method seen more and more frequently.

If you have a big mailing, and plan to give the job to a mailing house for envelope inserting, check in advance about automatic machines. Some can not handle open end envelopes.

Give the printer explicit written instructions about delivery: the quantity for shareholders to go to the registrar or mailing house, balance to go to your office, etc.

TAKE THE FINAL STEP—HAVE YOUR STOCKHOLDERS EVALUATE YOUR CORPORATE ANNUAL REPORT.

Your pride and joy—your corporate annual report—is on the way to the stockholders. You have the option of saying, "Well, that's it for this year . . . I'll forget about preparing annual reports for the next six months." Or you can say, "I would like to know how the stockholders evaluate the current report. What do they think of our total reporting effort?"

I suggest the latter course. It will help you design an even better report the next time around. You might want to send out the following type of survey:

Survey Form

Name ____________________

Title ____________________ Phone ____________

Business Affiliation ____________________

Street Address ____________________

City ____________ State ____________ Zip ____________

I am interested in receiving the following:

- ☐ 10-K Report for 1979
- ☐ 1979 Quarterly Reports
- ☐ 1980 Quarterly Reports
- ☐ Communications Industry Comparative Financial Analysis

I am:

- ☐ AMS Stockholder
- ☐ Prospective Private Investor
- ☐ Financial Analyst
- ☐ Stock Broker
- ☐ Institutional Manager

The thing I like most about AMS as a company is ____________

The thing I like least about AMS as a company is ____________

The thing I like most about this annual report is ____________

The thing I like least about this annual report is ____________

Please send a copy of this 1979 Annual Report to:

☐ **Friend** ☐ **Relative** ☐ **Broker**

Person's Name ____________________

Title ____________ Phone ____________

Business Affiliation ____________________

Street Address ____________________

City ____________ State ____________ Zip ____________

NO POSTAGE STAMP NECESSARY IF MAILED IN THE UNITED STATES

BUSINESS REPLY MAIL

FIRST CLASS PERMIT NO. 10109 CHICAGO, ILL.

POSTAGE WILL BE PAID BY ADDRESSEE

John C. Bachman, President
Automated Marketing Systems, Inc.
310 South Michigan Avenue
Chicago, Illinois 60604

Joseph Graves, Jr., management consultant and author of *Managing Investor Relations: Strategies and Techniques,* believing that "You can't be satisfied until you know the annual report did the job," reported:

You sit back relaxed with a glow of satisfaction. Your major communications project of the year, the annual report, is off press. Early reception from the president and other officers of the company strongly indicate they are very pleased with the efforts and results.

The feedback is evidence that the annual report conveyed the image and message they desired to have disseminated. But can you continue to be satisfied without knowing the desired impact of the annual report on the reader, whether the reader is a shareholder, a potential shareholder, or an investment advisor?

The question was extremely critical this year to Donald B. Romans, vice president-finance, and this writer since we recommended and executed a departure from our normal annual report approach. The difference was the creation of a two-part report. The first part contained indepth statistical information for the knowledgeable investment advisor, in addition to the standard financial information. The second part was a text and photo unit to explain the company as broadly as possible to the potential, new and/or unsophisticated investor.

We agreed that a sure-fire method of getting this feedback was the reader survey, but such a survey has its pitfalls as well as its opportunities. For a large company with a broad shareholder base, even a mail survey can be expensive in terms of costs relative to printing, postage, and evaluation of results. For a smaller company, a survey can eat up an inordinate amount of the budget. The greatest pitfall to avoid is improper structuring of the survey, which would produce useless answers.

To resolve the cost problem, and in keeping with the two-part format of the report, we decided to direct a mail survey to what we felt was a key list of individuals. On this list are financial analysts, bank trust officers and other investment advisors whom we feel are a vital link in company efforts to convey useful information about the company to potential shareholders.

We decided to seek two basic types of information:

The first was whether the Trans Union annual report fulfilled its objective of supplying sufficient information to professional investors and investment advisors. In this evaluation, participants were asked to approach the report with their own informational needs in mind.

The second was whether the annual report conveyed the essence of the company in an understandable form to new and/or unsophisticated investors. In this case, participants were asked to approach the annual report in its role of educating a new or potential investor about the company in such a way as to make the investment advisor's job of explaining the company easier.

It was our concern that "good, fair, poor", "yes or no" or "helpful or not helpful" ratings would provide helpful generalities, but would not secure specific answers, which we felt were necessary to make the survey valid. This problem was overcome by providing space for comments on each question.

The survey questionnaire was sent to 500 investment advisors in the United States and Canada. The return was 60, or 12 percent, which we felt was sufficient to at least evaluate trends in the thinking of respondents.

The wisdom of adding the comment section for each question was evidenced in the returns. For example, while 98 percent of the respondents indicated the annual report was well organized, their comments revealed they desired a one volume report instead of a financial volume and a text volume as the Trans Union annual report was structured.

In two other areas, "Overall description of the Company" and "Vital statistics," respondents gave the company 89 percent ratings on quality, yet 25 percent of the respondents added comments that will be useful in planning next year's annual report.

Our concern while preparing the report that 15 tables of information might be too much was eased by such comments as. "Excellent, wish your competition did this;" "The tables were an excellent addition to the report;" "Very useful;" and "Would like even more data."

Although the questionnaire was detailed, four pages, and the recipients were busy people, the respondents were interested enough in the company and in the annual report to contribute 208 comments to help the company with this important communication device.

Importantly, this valuable information was gathered at a cost of less than $1,500.

APPENDIX

FINANCIAL ACCOUNTING STANDARDS

The Financial Accounting Standards Board (FASB) from time to time issues various statements of accounting standards after public hearings. If the statement is approved by a majority of the members of the Board, the statement is issued.

The following are the major statements that relate to the preparation of annual reports:

No. 2—*Accounting for Research and Development Costs* (October 1974)

—Requires that research and development costs be charged to expense when incurred.

—Disclosure is required in the financial statements of the total research and development costs charged to expense in each period for which an income statement is presented.

—Additional disclosures are required of regulated enterprises that defer research and development costs for financial statement purposes in accordance with the *Addendum to APB Opinion No. 2.*

—Effective for fiscal years beginning on or after January 1, 1975. Retroactive application by prior period adjustment is required.

—Interpreted by:

- FASB Interpretation No. 4, *Applicability of FASB Statement No. 2 to Business Combinations Accounted for by the Purchase Method.*
- FASB Interpretation No. 6, *Applicability of FASB Statement No. 2 to Computer Software.*

No. 12—*Accounting for Certain Marketable Securities* (December 1975)

—Specifies that the carrying amount of a marketable equity securities portfolio shall be the lower of its aggregate cost or market value, determined at the balance sheet date.

- The amount by which aggregate cost of the portfolio exceeds market value shall be accounted for as a valuation allowance.

—All marketable equity securities classified as current in the balance sheet shall be treated as a single portfolio for the consolidated entity; likewise, all marketable equity securities classified as noncurrent shall be treated as a separate portfolio for the consolidated entity. In the case of unclassified balance sheets, marketable equity securities shall be considered as noncurrent assets. The portfolios of marketable equity securities owned by an entity accounted for by the equity method (subsidiary or investee) shall not be combined with the portfolios of the consolidated entities.

—If there is a change in the classification of marketable equity securities, the lower of cost or market at the date of change shall become the new cost basis and any difference should be treated as a realized loss.

—All realized gains and losses and all changes in the valuation for a marketable equity securities portfolio included in current assets shall be included in the determination of net income of the period in which they occur. Accumulated changes in the valuation allowance for a portfolio included in noncurrent assets or in an unclassified balance sheet shall be included in the equity section of the balance sheet.

—Disclosure is required of aggregate cost and market value (for each segregated portfolio), gross unrealized gains and gross unrealized losses (for each portfolio), and net realized gain or loss included in the determination of net income. Other disclosures are also called for.

—Special provisions are given for certain industries having specialized accounting practices.

—The Statement does not apply to not-for-profit organizations, pension funds, and mutual life insurance companies.

—Effective for fiscal periods and interim periods ending on or after December 31, 1975.

- If the initial application of the Statement requires the establishment of a valuation allowance for the current portfolio, the amount thereof shall be included in the determination of net income for that period. Similarly, in the initial establishment of a valuation allowance for the noncurrent portfolio, the amount thereof shall be reflected separately in stockholders' equity as of the end of that fiscal period.

—Interpreted by:

- FASB Interpretation No. 10, *Application of FASB Statement No. 12 to Personal Financial Statements.*
- FASB Interpretation No. 11, *Changes in Market Value After the Balance Sheet Date.*
- FASB Interpretation No. 12, *Accounting for Previously Established Allowance Accounts.*
- FASB Interpretation No. 13, *Consolidation of a Parent and Its Subsidiaries Having Different Balance Sheet Dates.*
- FASB Interpretation No. 16, *Clarification of Definitions and Accounting for Marketable Equity Securities That Become Nonmarketable.*

No. 13—*Accounting for Leases,* as amended and interpreted through May 1980 (May 1980)

—Incorporates the standards section of Statement No. 13, *Accounting for Leases* as amended and interpreted by seven Statements and six Interpretations.

Amendments:

- Statement No. 17—*Accounting for Leases—Initial Direct Costs*
- Statement No. 22—*Changes in the Provisions of Lease Agreements Resulting From Refundings of Tax-Exempt Debt*
- Statement No. 23—*Inception of the Lease*
- Statement No. 26—*Profit Recognition on Sales-Type Leases of Real Estate*
- Statement No. 27—*Classification of Renewals or Extensions of Existing Sales-Type or Direct Financing Leases*
- Statement No. 28—*Accounting for Sales With Leasebacks*
- Statement No. 29—*Determining Contingent Rentals*

Interpretations:

- Interpretation No. 19—*Lessee Guarantee of the Residual Value of Leased Property*
- Interpretation No. 21—*Accounting for Leases in a Business Combination*
- Interpretation No. 23—*Leases of Certain Property Owned by a Governmental Unit or Authority*
- Interpretation No. 24—*Leases Involving Only Part of a Building*
- Interpretation No. 26—*Accounting for Purchase of a Leased Asset by the Lessee During the Term of the Lease*
- Interpretation No. 27—*Accounting for a Loss on a Sublease*

—The Board did not vote on this document because the need for a formal vote on the integration of the components did not exist; each of the pronouncements was formally approved at the time of adoption.

—This document establishes standards of financial accounting and reporting for leases by lessees and lessors.

- A lease is defined as an agreement conveying the right to use property, plant, or equipment usually for a stated period of time.
  - Included within the definition are contracts such as a "heat supply contract" for nuclear fuel.
  - Does not include agreements that are limited to contracts for services.
  - Does not apply to lease agreements for rights to explore for or to exploit natural resources.
  - Does not apply to licensing agreements for items such as motion picture films, patents, and copyrights.
  - Applies to regulated enterprises in accordance with the provisions of the Addendum to APB

Opinion No. 2, *Accounting for the "Investment Credit"*.

- Definitions are provided for the terms used in this document such as bargain purchase option, lease term, minimum lease payments, executory costs, and the like.

—Leases are classified as follows:

- Lessee:
  - Capital leases
  - Operating leases
- Lessor:
  - Sales-type leases
  - Direct financing leases
  - Leveraged leases
  - Operating leases

—Criteria for classifying leases:

- Lessee—A lease is classified as a *capital lease* if at its inception it meets one or more of the following four criteria; otherwise, it shall be classified as an operating lease:
  - The lease transfers ownership of the property to the lessee by the end of the lease term.
  - The lease contains a bargain-purchase option.
  - The lease term is equal to 75 percent or more of the estimated economic life of the leased property. If the beginning of the lease term falls within the last 25 percent of the total estimated economic life of the leased property, including earlier use, this criterion shall not be used.
  - Present value at the beginning of the lease term of the minimum lease payments, excluding that portion representing executory costs to be paid by the lessor, including any profit thereon, equals or exceeds 90 percent of the excess of the fair value of the leased property to the lessor at the inception of the lease over any related investment tax credit retained by the lessor and expected to be realized by him.
    - This criterion is subject to the 25 percent remaining life exception referred to immediately above.
    - Lessor shall compute the present value of the minimum lease payments using the interest rate implicit in the lease.
    - Lessee shall use his incremental borrowing rate unless he can learn the implicit rate used by the lessor, and that rate is less than his incremental borrowing rate.
- Lessor—A lease is classified as a *sales-type lease* or *direct financing lease,* whichever is appropriate, if at the inception of the lease it meets any one of the preceding four criteria and in addition meets both of the following criteria; otherwise it shall be classified as an operating lease:
  - Collectibility is reasonably predictable.
    - The need to subject the receivable to an estimate of uncollectibility does not violate the collectibility criterion.
  - No important uncertainties surround the amount of unreimbursable costs yet to be incurred by the lessor.
    - The necessity to estimate executory costs to be paid by the lessor shall not constitute an important uncertainty.
    - A lease involving real estate that would otherwise be classified as a sales-type lease giving rise to a manufacturer's or dealer's profit shall be classified as an operating lease unless at the beginning of the lease term it also meets the requirements of a sale with full and immediate profit recognition under the AICPA Industry Accounting Guide, *Accounting for Profit Recognition on Sales of Real Estate.*
- A change in the provisions of a lease, other than by renewing the lease or extending its term, that would have resulted in a different classification had those terms been in effect at the inception of the lease, creates a new agreement over its remaining term for classification purposes.
  - Changes in estimates, such as economic life or residual value, or in circumstances, such as default by lessee, shall not give rise to a new classification.

—Accounting and Reporting

- Lessees
  - Lessee records a capital lease as an asset and an obligation at an amount equal to the present value, at the beginning of the lease term, of minimum lease payments during the lease term exclusive of executory costs together with any profit thereon.
  - If the amount so determined exceeds the fair value of the leased property at the inception of the lease, the amount recorded as the asset and obligation shall be the fair value.
  - The discount rate to be used in determining present value is as discussed above under criteria for classifying a lease.
  - Except for certain provisions with respect to leases involving land, the asset recorded under a capital lease shall be amortized as follows:

  - Leases capitalized under the transfer of title by the end of the lease term or existence of a bargain purchase option criterion shall be amortized over the life of the asset as if owned. Otherwise, the asset shall be amortized over the lease term.
  - If amortized over the lease term, the lease shall be amortized to its expected value to the lessee, if any.
- Special accounting provisions apply in the following cases:
  - The lease contains a residual guarantee by the lessee or a penalty for failure to renew the lease at the end of the lease term and a renewal or extension of the lease term renders the guarantee or penalty inoperative.
  - There are no guarantees or penalties and there is a change in the provisions of a lease, a renewal or extension of an existing lease, or a termination of a lease prior to the expiration of the lease term.
  - Prior to the expiration of the lease term, a change in the provisions of a lease results from a refunding by the lessor of tax-exempt debt, including an advance refunding, in which the perceived economic advantages of the refunding are passed through to the lessee and the revised agreement is classified as a capital lease by the lessee.
- Rentals on operating leases shall be charged to expense over the lease term as it becomes payable.
  - If rental payments are not made on a straight-line basis, rental expense shall, nevertheless, be recognized on a straight-line basis unless another basis is more representative of asset-use benefit.
- Disclosures with regard to capital leases in the financial statements or in footnotes include: gross assets recorded, classified by nature or function; future minimum lease payments at the balance sheet date, in the aggregate and for each of the five succeeding fiscal years, with certain deductions for executory costs and imputed interest; total of minimum sublease rentals to be received under noncancellable subleases, total contingent rentals actually incurred; and assets recorded under capital leases and the accumulated amortization thereon, and the related obligations including current and noncurrent status.
  - Disclosure for operating leases having initial or remaining noncancellable lease terms in excess of one year include future minimum rental payments in the aggregate and for each of the five succeeding years, and total minimum rentals to be received in the future under noncancellable subleases.
  - Disclosure for all operating leases includes rental expense with separate amounts for minimum rentals, contingent rentals, and subrentals.
  - A general description of the lessee's leasing arrangements is required including basis of contingent rentals, renewal terms, restrictions.
- Lessors
  - For sales-type leases, the gross investment in the lease is the minimum lease payments during the lease term, net of executory costs together with any profit thereon, plus the unguaranteed residual value accruing to the benefit of the lessor. The residual value shall not exceed the amount estimated at the inception of the lease.
    - The difference between the gross investment and the sum of the present values of the two components of the gross investment shall be recorded as unearned income.
      - The discount rate shall be the interest rate implicit in the lease.
    - The net investment in the lease is the gross investment less the unearned income.
    - The unearned income shall be amortized on an interest basis.
    - The net investment shall be classified as current or noncurrent, as appropriate.
    - The present value of the minimum lease payments, net of executory costs, discounted at the interest rate implicit in the lease shall be recorded as the sales price.
    - The cost or carrying amount, if different, of the leased property, plus any initial direct costs, less the present value of the unguaranteed residual value accruing to the benefit of the lessor shall be charged against income in the same period.
    - Special rules are provided for the following:
      - Annual review of estimated residual values.
      - Accounting where leases contain a residual guarantee or a penalty for failure to renew the lease.

    - Changes in lease provisions, renewal or extension of an existing lease, and termination of a lease prior to the expiration of its term.
    - Changes resulting from the refunding by the lessor of tax-exempt debt, including advance refunding.
- Accounting for direct financing leases is essentially similar to that described for sales-type leases except that no profit on sales is recognized.
- Accounting for operating leases requires that the leased property be included with or near property, plant, and equipment in the balance sheet. Depreciation shall follow the lessor's normal policies. Rent shall be reported over the lease term as it becomes receivable. However, if rentals vary from straight-line, the income shall be recognized on a straight-line basis unless another approach is more representative of the dimunition of use benefit. Initial direct costs shall be deferred and allocated over the lease term in proportion to the recognition of rental income. Initial direct costs may be charged to expense as incurred if the effect is not materially different from the deferral method.
- In participation by third parties, the sale or assignment of a lease, or of property subject to a lease, that was accounted for as a sales-type or direct financing lease shall not negate the original accounting treatment. The sale of property subject to an operating lease, or of property that is leased by or intended to be leased by the third party purchaser to another party, shall not be treated as a sale if the seller or any party related to the seller retains substantial risks.
- Disclosures required when leasing is a significant part of the lessor's business activities include the following:
    - For sales-type and direct financing leases:
        - The components of the net investment including future minimum lease payments to be received less executory costs, and accumulated allowance for uncollectible payments, the unguaranteed residual values accruing to the lessor, and unearned income.
        - Future minimum lease payments to be received for each of the five succeeding fiscal years.
        - Total contingent rentals included in income.
        - For direct financing leases only, the amount of unearned income included in income to offset initial direct costs charged against income.
    - For operating leases, the required disclosures include:
        - The cost and carrying amount, if different, of property on lease, or held for leasing, by major classes of property according to nature or function and the related accumulated depreciation.
        - Minimum future rentals on noncancellable leases, in the aggregate and for each of the five succeeding fiscal years.
        - Total contingent rentals included in income.
    - A general description of the lessor's leasing arrangements.

—Special topics include:
- Leases involving real estate, including land only, land and buildings, equipment as well as real estate, and leases involving only part of a building.
- Leases between related parties.
- Sale and leaseback transactions.
- Accounting and reporting for subleases and similar transactions, including accounting by the original lessor, the original lessee, and the new lessee.
- Accounting for leases in a business combination.
- Accounting and reporting for leveraged leases.

—Effective Date and Transition
- Applies to transactions and lease agreement revisions entered into on or after January 1, 1977 except where made pursuant to the terms of a written commitment made prior to that date. The disclosures called for in the Statement shall be included in financial statements for calendar years or fiscal years ending after December 31, 1976.
- If the Statement is not applied retroactively, disclosure of the effect on the balance sheet and income statement of retroactive application is required beginning with financial statements for the year ending December 31, 1977 and thereafter until years beginning after December 31, 1980.
- Financial statements for periods beginning after December 31, 1980 must include retroactive application of the Statement. Financial statements of earlier years presented for comparative pur-

poses are to be restated at least as far back as December 31, 1976.
- See each amendment or interpretation for its effective date and transition requirements.

No. 14—*Financial Reporting for Segments of a Business Enterprise* (December 1976)

—Annual financial statements and financial statements for interim periods that are expressly described as presenting financial position, results of operations, and changes in financial position in conformity with generally accepted accounting principles shall include certain information relating to:
- The enterprise's operations in different industries.
- Its foreign operations.
- Its major customers.
- Its export sales.

—Industry segments shall be established by management by:
- Identifying the individual products and services from which the enterprise derives its revenue.
- Grouping the services by industry lines into industry segments.
- Selecting the industry segments that are significant with respect to the enterprise as a whole.
    - Reference may be made to outside classification sources such as the Standard Industrial Classification, although none by itself is suitable for purposes of this Statement.
    - Profit centers are the logical starting point for establishing segments.

—Reportable segments are those that satisfy one or more of the following criteria:
- Contribute 10% or more of the combined revenue.
- Operating profit or loss is 10% or more of the greater of the:
    - Combined operating profit of all segments that did not incur an operating loss, or
    - Combined operating loss of all segments that did incur an operating loss.
- Identifiable assets are 10% or more of combined identifiable assets of all segments.

—Reportable segments shall represent at least 75% of the combined revenue from sales to unaffiliated customers of all industry segments.

—Ten segments may be a practical upper limit.

—Information to be presented by segment:
- Revenue including transfers to other segments.
- Operating profit or loss (which represents revenue less all direct and allocable operating expenses exclusive of revenue earned at the corporate level, general corporate expenses, interest expense, domestic and foreign income taxes, equity in income of investees, extraordinary items, and the like).
- Identifiable assets, including direct and jointly-used assets; assets used for general corporate purposes are excluded.

—Other disclosures include details as to depreciation, capital expenditures, equity in income of investees, and the effect of a change in accounting method.

—Foreign operations:
- In addition to information concerning industry segments, separate information shall be presented at a minimum for an enterprise's foreign operations, either in the aggregate or (if appropriate) by geographic area, if foreign operations contribute 10% or more of consolidated revenue or if the assets identifiable with the foreign operations are 10% or more of consolidated assets.
- Sales, profit, and asset data to be presented are similar to those to be presented for industry segments.

—Export sales are reportable if exports are 10% or more of total revenue from sales to unaffiliated customers.

—If 10% or more of total enterprise revenue is derived from sales to a single customer, to domestic government agencies in the aggregate, or to foreign governments in the aggregate, that fact and the amount of revenue shall be disclosed.

—Methods of presentation are specified.

—Effective for fiscal years beginning after December 15, 1976 and for interim periods within those fiscal years.

—Amended by:
- FASB Statement No. 18, *Financial Reporting for Segments of a Business Enterprise—Interim Financial Statements.*
- FASB Statement No. 21, *Suspension of the Reporting of Earnings Per Share and Segment Information by Nonpublic Enterprises.*
- FASB Statement No. 24, *Reporting Segment Information In Financial Statements That Are Presented in Another Enterprise's Financial Report.*

- FASB Statement No. 30, *Disclosure of Information About Major Customers.*

No. 17—*Accounting for Leases—Initial Direct Costs,* an amendment of FASB Statement No. 13 (November 1977) (Incorporated in the codification of FASB Statement No. 13, *Accounting for Leases,* May 1980.)

—Modifies and clarifies the definition of "initial direct costs."

—Effective for leasing transactions and lease agreement revisions entered into on or after January 1, 1978. The provisions shall be applied retroactively at the same time and in the same manner as the provisions of FASB Statement No. 13 are applied retroactively, except that enterprises that have already applied Statement No. 13 retroactively in published annual financial statements need not apply this Statement retroactively.

No. 23—*Inception of the Lease,* an amendment of FASB Statement No. 13 (August 1978) (Incorporated in the codification of FASB Statement No. 13, *Accounting for Leases,* May 1980.)

—Reconsiders the application of Statement No. 13 for a leasing transaction in which the lessor and lessee agree on lease terms prior to the construction of the asset to be leased.

—Effective for leasing transactions recorded and lease agreement revisions recorded as of December 1, 1978 or thereafter. The provisions of the Statement shall be applied retroactively at the same time and in the same manner as the provisions of Statement No. 13, except that entities that have already applied Statement No. 13 retroactively in published annual financial statements need not apply this Statement retroactively.

No. 28—*Accounting for Sales With Leasebacks,* an amendment of FASB Statement No. 13 (May 1979) (Incorporated in the codification of FASB Statement No. 13, *Accounting for Leases,* May 1980.)

—Modifies paragraph 33 of Statement No. 13 to allow for recognition of profit on a sale and leaseback under certain circumstances.

—Modifies paragraph 33 of Statement No. 13 to require that, for an operating lease where profit or loss is deferred, it be amortized over the lease term, not the period of expected use.

—Effective for leasing transactions and lease agreement revisions recorded as of September 1, 1979. Provisions of this Statement shall be applied retroactively at the same time and in the same manner as the provisions of Statement No. 13 are applied retroactively, except that enterprises that have already applied Statement No. 13 retroactively in published annual financial statements need not apply this Statement retroactively.

No. 30—*Disclosure of Information About Major Customers,* an amendment of FASB Statement No. 14 (August 1979)

—Amends the requirements of paragraph 39 of FASB Statement No. 14, *Financial Reporting for Segments of a Business Enterprise,* regarding disclosure of revenue derived from a single customer accounting for 10% or more of total sales.
- For purposes of disclosure, the federal government, a state government, a local government (for example, a county or municipality) or a foreign government shall each be considered as a single customer.
- The identity of the customer need not be disclosed, but the identity of the industry segment or segments making the sales shall be disclosed.

—Effective for fiscal years beginning after December 15, 1979. The Statement need not be applied retroactively to previously issued financial statements.

No. 33—*Financial Reporting and Changing Prices* (September 1979)

—Establishes standards for reporting the effects on business enterprises of changes in general prices (general inflation) and changes in the prices of certain specific types of assets (current costs).
- Requires that the effects of changing prices be presented as supplementary information to the primary financial statements.
  - The effects of general inflation are measured by the use of *constant dollar accounting,* a method of reporting financial statement elements in dollars each of which has the same general purchasing power.
  - The effects of changes in the prices of specific types of assets are determined through the use of *current cost accounting,* a method of re-

porting assets, and expenses associated with the use or sale of assets, at their current cost or lower recoverable amount at the balance sheet date or at the date of use or sale.
- No changes are made in the primary financial statements.

—Applicable to U.S. public enterprises, as defined in the Statement, that prepare their primary financial statements in U.S. dollars and in accordance with U.S. generally accepted accounting principles and that, at the beginning of the fiscal year for which financial statements are being presented (on a consolidatd basis, if applicable), meet either of the following two conditions:
- Inventories and property, plant, and equipment (before deducting accumulated depreciation, depletion, and amortization) amount in the aggregate to more than $125 million;
  - Inventory and property, plant, and equipment includes land, other material resources and capitalized leases, but not goodwill or other intangible assets.
- Total assets amount to more than $1 billion (after deducting accumulated depreciation).

—The information need not be presented:
- In interim financial reports,
- For segments of a business, or
- For a parent company, an investee company, or other enterprise in any financial report that includes the results for that enterprise in consolidated financial statements.

—Special problems in the forest products, mining, oil and gas, and real estate industries require further study to provide a basis for implementing the requirements of current cost disclosure.
- Pending completion of these studies, enterprises are not required to disclose information about the current costs of unprocessed natural resources and income-producing real estate properties.

—Required disclosures for the current year include the following information:
- Income from continuing operations on an historical cost/constant dollar basis and on a current cost basis.
  - Income from continuing operations excludes the results of discontinued operations, extraordinary items, and the cumulative effect of accounting changes.
- Purchasing power gain or loss on net monetary items.
- Current cost amounts of inventory and property, plant and equipment.
- Increases or decreases in the current cost amounts of inventory and property, plant and equipment held during the period net of inflation (holding gains or losses net of inflation).
- Additional information required includes disclosure of:
  - The types of information used to calculate the current cost of inventory, property, plant and equipment, cost of goods sold, and depreciation, depletion, and amortization expense.
  - Any differences from the primary statement in depreciation methods, estimates of useful lives, and salvage values used for purposes of the supplementary disclosure.
  - The fact that no adjustments were made to income tax expense as reported in the primary financial statements.

—Required disclosures for each of the five most-recent fiscal years. These disclosures include:
- Historical cost/constant dollar information:
  - Net sales and other operating revenues.
  - Income from continuing operations.
  - Income per share from continuing operations.
  - Net assets at fiscal year end.
  - Cash dividends declared per common share.
- Current cost information:
  - Income from continuing operations.
  - Income per common share from continuing operations.
  - Net assets at fiscal year end.
  - Increases or decreases in the current cost amounts of inventory and property, plant and equipment, net of inflation.
  - Purchasing power gain or loss on net monetary items.
- Other:
  - Market price per common share at fiscal year end.
  - The average level (or end-of-year-level, if used for the measurement of income from continuing operations) of the Consumer Price Index for All Urban Consumers (CPI-U) for each year included in the summary.

—The index used to compute information on a constant dollar basis is the CPI-U.
- An enterprise that presents the minimum historical cost/constant dollar information required must use, for restatement purposes, the average level over the fiscal year of the CPI-U.

- Minimum restatement covers inventory, property, plant and equipment, cost of goods sold, depreciation, depletion, and amortization expense, and any reductions of the historical cost amounts of inventory and property, plant, and equipment to lower recoverable amounts.
- Other financial statement elements need not be restated.

- An enterprise that presents *comprehensive* financial statements on an historical cost/constant dollar basis may measure the components in either average-for-the-year constant dollars or in end-of-year constant dollars.

—Items measured in units of a foreign currency shall first be translated into U.S. dollars in accordance with generally accepted accounting principles and then be restated in constant dollars.

—Guidance is provided on the classification of balance sheet items as monetary or nonmonetary.

—Details are provided for such matters as current cost measurements and sources of information about current costs.

—If the recoverable amount for a group of assets is judged to be materially and permanently lower than historical cost in constant dollars or current dollars, the recoverable amount must be used as the measure of the asset and related expense.

- Recoverable amounts may be measured by considering net realizable value or the values in use of the assets.
- Special rules apply to companies subject to rate regulation or other forms of price control.

—Effective for fiscal years ended on or after December 25, 1979.

- Information on a current cost basis for fiscal years ended before December 25, 1980 may be presented in the first annual report for a fiscal year that ends on or after December 25, 1980.
- Of the above information, only the following information need be stated in the five-year summary for fiscal years ended before December 25, 1979:
  - Net sales and other operating revenues.
  - Cash dividend declared per common share.
  - Market price per common share at fiscal year end.
- Disclosures of current cost information in the five-year summary for fiscal years ending before December 25, 1980 may be postponed to the first annual report for a fiscal year ending on or after December 25, 1980.
- An enterprise that first applies the requirements for a fiscal year ended on or after December 25, 1980 is required to state in the five-year summary for earlier years the following, in constant dollars:
  - Net sales and other operating revenues.
  - Cash dividend declared per common share.
  - Market price per common share at fiscal year end.

—Supplemented by:

- FASB Statement No. 39, *Financial Reporting and Changing Prices: Specialized Assets—Mining and Oil and Gas.*
- FASB Statement No. 40, *Financial Reporting and Changing Prices: Specialized Assets—Timberlands and Growing Timber.*
- FASB Statement No. 41, *Financial Reporting and Changing Prices: Specialized Assets—Income-Producing Real Estate.*

—*Illustrations of Financial Reporting and Changing Prices* (December, 1979)

- Issued as a supplement to FASB Statement No. 33, it contains illustrations that might be appropriate in annual reports of companies in particular industries.

—*Examples of the Use of FASB Statement No. 33, Financial Reporting and Changing Prices* (November 1980)

- Contains illustrations, drawn from 1979 annual reports of various companies, of the disclosures required by Statement No. 33.

No. 34—*Capitalization of Interest Cost* (October 1979)

—Establishes standards of financial accounting and reporting for capitalizing interest cost as a part of the historical cost of acquiring certain assets.

- Interest cost includes interest recognized on obligations having explicit interest rates, interest imputed on payables in accordance with APB Opinion No. 21, *Interest on Receivables and Payables,* and interest relating to a capital lease.
- Interest that might be imputed on owners' equity is excluded.

—Interest cost shall be capitalized as part of the historical cost of acquiring an asset if a significant period of time elapses between the initial expenditure related to development of the asset and its readiness for its intended use, and if such a period of time is required to bring the asset to the condition and location necessary for its intended use.

—Assets qualifying for interest capitalization include:
- Assets that are constructed or otherwise produced for an enterprise's own use.
- Assets intended for sale or lease that are constructed or otherwise produced as discrete projects, such as ships or real estate developments.

—Interest should *not* be capitalized for the following:
- Inventories that are routinely manufactured or otherwise produced in large quantities on a repetitive basis.
- Assets that are in use or ready for their intended use.
- Assets that are not being used in the earning activities of the enterprise.

—The amount of interest cost allocated in an accounting period shall be determined by applying an interest rate to the average amount of accumulated expenditures for the qualified asset during the period, and shall not exceed the amount of total interest cost incurred by the enterprise during that period.
- If an enterprise's financial plans associate a specific new borrowing with a qualifying asset, the enterprise may use the rate on that borrowing as the capitalization rate.
- If the average accumulated expenditures for the asset exceed the amounts of specific new borrowings associated with the asset, the capitalization rate to be allocated to the excess shall be the weighted average of the rates applicable to other borrowings.
- The relevant enterprise for interest capitalization is the enterprise for which financial statements are presented. A consolidated group of companies may be viewed as a single entity for financing purposes.

—Capitalization begins when the first development expenditure is made, and continues as long as the asset is undergoing active development that is necessary to get the asset ready for its intended use, and interest is being incurred. Interest capitalization shall end when the asset is substantially complete and ready for its intended use.

—The following disclosures are required:
- For an accounting period in which no interest cost is capitalized, the amount of interest cost incurred and charged to expense during the period.
- For an accounting period in which some interest cost is capitalized, the total amount of interest cost incurred during the period and the amount thereof that has been capitalized.

—Shall be applied prospectively in fiscal years beginning after December 15, 1979. Earlier application is permitted, but not required in financial statements for fiscal years beginning before December 19, 1979 that have not been previously issued. If early application is adopted, financial reports for any interim periods of that fiscal year that precede the period of adoption shall be restated.

—Interpreted by FASB Interpretation No. 33, *Applying FASB Statement No. 34 to Oil and Gas Producing Operations Accounted for by the Full Cost Method.*

No. 37—*Balance Sheet Classification of Deferred Income Taxes,* an amendment of APB Opinion No. 11 (July 1980)

—Clarifies the classification of deferred income tax charges and credits where no asset or liability that is related to the timing difference exists.
- Also clarifies the balance sheet classification of the tax benefits related to "stock relief" under FASB Statement No. 31, *Accounting for Tax Benefits Related to U.K. Tax Legislation Concerning Stock Relief.*

—A deferred charge or credit that is related to an asset or liability shall be classified as current or noncurrent based on the classification of the related asset or liability.
- A deferred charge or credit is related to an asset or liability of reduction of the asset or liability causes the timing difference to reverse.
  - The term "reduction" includes amortization, sale or other realization of an asset, and amortization, payment or other satisfaction of a liability.

—A deferred charge or credit that is not related to an asset or liability shall be classified based on the expected reversal date of the specific timing difference.
- A deferred charge or credit is not related to an asset or liability if:
  - There is no associated asset or liability.
    - For example, a change in accounting method for tax purposes from the cash to the reserve method of accounting for bad debts where the effect is to be amortized for tax purposes

over ten years would give rise to a deferred tax item unrelated to trade receivables or the provision for doubtful accounts. The collection or write-off of the receivables will not cause the timing difference to reverse. The timing difference will reverse over time (ten years, in this example).
- A reduction of an associated asset or liability will not cause the timing difference to reverse.
- Tax benefits related to "stock relief" that have been deferred under FASB Statement No. 31, are not timing differences, and should be classified based on the period of potential recapture.

—Effective for financial statements for periods ending after December 15, 1980.
- Reclassification in previously issued financial statements is permitted but not required.

No. 43—*Accounting for Compensated Absences* (November 1980)

—Establishes standards of accounting for employee absences such as vacations, illness, and holidays, for which it is expected that employees will be paid (referred to as compensated absences).
- The Statement does not apply to the following:
  - Severance or termination pay.
  - Post retirement benefits.
  - Deferred compensation.
  - Stock or stock options issued to employees.
  - Group insurance or long-term disability pay.
  - State and local governmental units.
- Applies to regulated enterprises in accordance with the provisions of the Addendum to APB Opinion No. 2, *Accounting for the "Investment Credit"*.

—Requires that an employer shall accrue a liability for employees' compensation for future absences if all of the following conditions are met:
- The employer's obligation is attributable to employees' services already rendered.
- The obligation relates to rights that vest or accumulate.
  - Vested rights are those for which an employer has an obligation to make payment even if an employee terminates employment.
  - Accumulated rights are those earned but unused rights to compensated absences that may be carried forward to one or more periods subsequent to that in which it is earned.
- Payment of the compensation is probable.
- The amount can be reasonably estimated.
- Disclosure is required if a liability otherwise required is not accrued solely because the amount cannot be reasonably estimated.

—An employer is not required to accrue a liability for nonvesting accumulating rights to receive sick pay benefits.
- The Statement, however, does not prohibit such an accrual providing the criteria for accrual are met.

—Effective for fiscal years beginning after December 15, 1980.
- Earlier application is encouraged.
- The provisions of the Statement shall be applied retroactively.
- In the year the Statement is first applied, disclosure shall be made of any restatement and its effect on income before extraordinary items, net income, and related per share amounts for each year restated.
- If retroactive restatement of all years presented is not practicable, the cumulative effect of applying the Statement shall be included in determining net income of the earliest year restated.
- If it is not practicable to restate any prior year, the cumulative effect shall be included in net income in the year in which the Statement is first applied.

INDEX